GEORGE RYGA
THE OTHER PLAYS

GEORGE RYGA
THE OTHER PLAYS

Edited by
James Hoffman

Talonbooks
2004

Talonbooks
P.O. Box 2076, Vancouver, British Columbia, Canada V6B 3S3
www.talonbooks.com

Typeset in Century Oldstyle and printed and bound in Canada.

First Printing: August 2004

National Library of Canada Cataloguing in Publication

Ryga, George, 1932–1987.
    The other plays / George Ryga ; edited by James Hoffman.

Contents: Indian — Nothing but a man — Just an ordinary person —
    Grass and wild strawberries — Compressions — Captives of a faceless drummer —
    Sunrise on Sarah — A portrait of Angelica — Ploughmen on the glacier —
    Seven hours to sundown — Jeremiah's place — Laddie boy — Prometheus bound —
    A letter to my son — One more for the road — Paracelsus.

ISBN 0-88922-500-1

    I. Hoffman, James II. Title.

PS8585.Y5A19 2004   C812'.54   C2004-900310-0

The publisher gratefully acknowledges the financial support of the Canada Council for the Arts; the Government of Canada through the Book Publishing Industry Development Program; and the Province of British Columbia through the British Columbia Arts Council for our publishing activities.

To Ken Smedley,
a long-time and true friend
of George Ryga

CONTENTS

INTRODUCTION

UNSETTLING COLONIAL VOICES—GEORGE RYGA'S "OTHER" PLAYS

It was at the inaugural British Columbia Theatre Conference, held at the University College of the Cariboo in 1999, that Karl Siegler, publisher of Talonbooks, first approached me with the idea of publishing George Ryga's "other" stage plays in a single volume. Since the late 1960s, Talonbooks has been both a pioneer and a leader in publishing Canadian drama. Today, under Karl and Christy Siegler's wise, tenacious guidance, Talon's drama list continues to flourish. Many of Ryga's plays, but not all, had already been published—most in single volumes, some by Talon, some by other publishers. Karl's plan was to make available in one easily accessible collection, similar to Talon's successful *Modern Canadian Plays* series edited by Jerry Wasserman, all of Ryga's plays except *The Ecstasy of Rita Joe*. He wanted to remind readers, theatre specialists, and students of literature that there is a lot more to Ryga's oeuvre than his one familiar classic.

Why a book of George Ryga's stage plays, and especially why one excluding the famous play he is best known for, *The Ecstasy of Rita Joe*? Simply put, we believe that Ryga, a generation after his death, remains one of Canada's pre-eminent playwrights; indeed, he is an enduring presence in the larger, ongoing construction of a post-colonial Canadian culture. He may be produced less than he was in his heyday in the 1960s and 1970s, but his stage work constitutes an imposing body of dramatic achievement—more so than is generally appreciated. Many readers will have read or seen one or two of his plays, but how many realize that there exist a dozen published playscripts, plus an additional five that, though unpublished before their inclusion in this volume, have enjoyed major theatrical productions? This is a considerable body of work, and the fact that most of these plays address themes of human struggle; many tackle issues of Canadian identity; some have provoked substantial controversy; and several make legitimate claims as Canadian classics are surely good reasons for the creation of an anthology that brings together the dramatic works of this seminal Canadian playwright.

Ryga's *The Ecstasy of Rita Joe* is well known of course, is widely available in two publications, and would surely appear on most people's list of a Canadian dramatic canon. It remains in print as a single edition at Talonbooks, where it is now in its twenty-third printing and remains today the best-seller it has been for over three decades. This anthology of George Ryga's "other plays," then, is a challenge, even a provocation, to re-examine George Ryga's achievement in light of the totality of his work: as more than simply the author of *The Ecstasy of Rita Joe*, or even *Indian* or *Captives of the Faceless Drummer*, his two other best known works. The fiery prophetic declarations of Paracelsus in *Paracelsus* can now be more readily measured against the self-doubts of Danny Baker in *A Portrait of Angelica*; the fate of Duke Radomsky in *Nothing but a Man* can be compared to the destiny of Ivan Lepa in *A Letter to My Son*.

There are sixteen plays in this anthology. Five are seeing their first publication here: *Nothing but a Man, Just an Ordinary Person, Compressions, Jeremiah's Place,* and *One More for the Road*. This body of work (along with *The Ecstasy of Rita Joe*), while comprehensive, is still not all the work Ryga wrote for the stage: there exist several additional plays in manuscript form in the George Ryga archive, housed at the University of Calgary, but they remain unperformed. The criteria for the inclusion of Ryga's plays in the present volume were that each play must have attained at least one important stage production and/or have been previously published. The single exception to the theatrical production criterion is his adaptation of Aeschylus's *Prometheus Bound*. Although its original commission by a theatre company fell through in the end, it has enjoyed previous publication and must certainly be considered a major theatrical work, if only because it provides the reader with the clearest dramatization of Ryga's political background and sensibilities in what, for Ryga, was to be his most classically "traditional" play.

In *George Ryga: The Other Plays* we wish to demonstrate that Ryga was much more than a one-hit wonder. In these sixteen "other" stage plays, we find not only many of the themes of *The Ecstasy of Rita Joe* which engendered such a remarkable and enduringly popular response among audiences and readers world-wide, but many other related dramatic themes and issues the world of Ryga's own time was apparently not yet ready to hear, much less engage. How many people know, for example, that he wrote a play about the opposing mythic forces that had created colonial British Columbia (*Ploughmen of the Glacier*), or a surreal adaptation of a Greek tragedy (*Prometheus Bound*), or a touching play about his own father (*A Letter to My Son*)? Probably not very many. In these works we find a surprisingly rich and visionary corpus, covering a great range of subject matter, presented in his trademark liquid dramaturgy and always, of course, framed by his outspoken radical politics. Don Rubin, founder and former editor of the *Canadian Theatre Review*, believes *A Letter to My Son* to be Ryga's "best play" (236), while Ray Conlogue, *Globe and Mail* theatre critic, hailed *Paracelsus* at the time of its production as "one of the most exotic and ambitious plays written in Canada."

These are indeed courageous, ambitious plays, marked by Ryga's soaring voice: in them, he tries to be, in his own words, "a trumpet to the gods." This voice, so sonorous, so full of import and moral concern, gives his work a sense of mission; oftentimes, when we hear his unsettling pronouncements, we feel the presence of an "elder prophet"—a term used for him in a *Maclean's* headline (16 Nov. 1981). There was, for George Ryga, much to say about what he saw as the emerging trans- or post-national global colony of the twentieth century. The result was a great variety of projects: novels, short stories, poems, radio and television plays, film scripts, and the stage plays for which he is best known. He made great demands of his protagonists, large and small—that even the greatest of them unerringly declare their fundamental participation in the world as ordinary people, as "the folk"; that they do battle with the imperialist demons of displacement and oppression; that, no matter what the struggle, they speak of the triumph of the human spirit. These, of course, are oversize themes to squeeze into any two-hour play, particularly when the author's vision, vocabulary, and empathy for the ordinary person are shunned by so many "ordinary people," duped as they are by an overwhelming propaganda machine designed to convince them that they too can become, (at least for their allotted twenty minutes), "extraordinary," simply by taking "their rightful place" in the ongoing colonial machinery of global exploitation. But, for a while at least, it worked: by the early 1970s *The Oxford Anthology of Canadian Literature* was describing Ryga as "the most successful theatre dramatist in English Canada."

At the same time, however, and for related reasons, his plays can be unwieldy, almost unplayable. They have been accused of being plot-less, too talky, too political, overwritten. Many, including the early hits that established his reputation, *Indian, The Ecstasy of Rita Joe, Grass and Wild Strawberries,* and *Captives of the Faceless Drummer*, were received with controversy, engendering puzzled responses by critics writing for the popular media so obviously out of touch with both the range of Ryga's concerns and sometimes, ironically, even with the responses of his audiences to them. Jack Richards, of the *Vancouver Sun*, found *The Ecstasy of Rita Joe* "jerky and fragmented … I don't know if it is a great play … " (24 Nov. 1967), while arguably Canada's greatest theatre critic, Nathan Cohen, of the *Toronto Star*, found it a "non-play," characterized by "weakness of the writing," "pedantic staging" and "formlessness" (25 Nov. 1967). Benson and Conolly, in *English-Canadian Theatre*, contrary to Rubin's laudatory opinion of it, call *A Letter to My Son* "deficient in theatricality and lacking in a single dominant dramatic focus" (82–83). *Time* (30 July 1973) called *Sunrise on Sarah* "laboured, hectoring." Then, witness the long period of time before any theatre tackled his monumental *Paracelsus*: even though it was published in a national journal and in book form soon after it was written, it was almost a decade and half before a theatre company staged it, and the production was, by most critical accounts, a disaster. Another ambitious work, *Prometheus Bound*, written in the late seventies and also published shortly afterward, remains unproduced.

With the *Captives of the Faceless Drummer* controversy in 1970, when his play was suddenly dropped by the Vancouver Playhouse from its season in an exercise of blatant and fearful self-censorship, he became known as the pariah of Canadian theatre, the self-proclaimed "Artist in Resistance." Of the sixteen plays in this anthology, few have had stage productions beyond the first. One of Canada's best known playwrights, canonized by critics and studied by countless students perhaps now more than ever, Ryga remains absent from Canadian stages and is the subject of few serious critical studies. Yet his plays continue to provoke us. Benson and Conolly value his plays "as additions to a literature that is [other- wise] distressingly apolitical" (83), while Rubin writes of "his primacy of place in the development of a viable and important Canadian theatre" (237). Native author Lee Maracle, discussing *The Ecstasy of Rita Joe*, believes the play "remains hauntingly true and tremendously healing for all of us, Canadians and first-nations people alike." Why is this? What is it about Ryga that endures?

As a critic of his society, Ryga participated deeply in the post-colonial re-negotiation of Canada and Canadianness. In part, his body of work is "difficult" because he lived in and dramatized the profoundly ambivalent experience of the "settler postimperial culture" (Lawson, 25) of Canada before this kind of discursive critical vocabulary of a post-imperialist and post-colonial social analysis had achieved its public currency. Ryga, therefore, could only "show" his characters in dramatic struggles with issues that, decades later, critics finally began to be able to discuss.

As a contemporary, multicultural nation of immigrants, Canada is positioned very uneasily between its historical place as a colonized society, taking its economic and cultural cues from its imperial centres in Europe (and lately from the neo-colonizing United States), and its own role as a colonizer, in turn, of its aboriginal peoples. Thus, the mythical "average Canadian" exists between shifting centres of power and culture(s), between Canada's European and its First Nations heritage, between "mother" and "other." For Ryga, as for other Canadian dramatists, the situation is a complex one, especially regarding issues of language and identity formation for all the participants involved in the ongoing construction of Canada's multicultural mosaic. In the heated debates that structure his dramaturgy, we hear the raw, contending voices of Canada's colonial and post-colonial inheritance. When the (nameless) Native protagonist of *Indian* shouts at the (equally nameless) white government agent, "I got nothing ... nothing ... no wallet, no money, no name. I got no past ... no future," to which the agent can only reply, "Let me go!" he is giving voice to the deeply distressed character of both the indigene and the settler. The issues that divide them—land, authority, language, and culture—are profound, and the Canadian dramatist, searching for an authentic Canadian narrative, faces irreducible uncertainty: a displacement and alienation from both land and history within all of his or her characters. What constitutes truthful depiction of place? Whose language most accurately describes it? Whose stories and characters are properly Canadian? What are the essential politics of such displaced, exploited, and seemingly irreconcilable identities?

In Ryga's plays we find the elements of this questioning in his stark, elemental settings, his desperate characters, their endless debates, and his authorial tone of alternating activism and negativity; in short, we witness the narratives of a society desperately fractured by its colonial past. Notice the cacophony of musical sounds—among them, Ukrainian folk dance, "O Canada," the "Marseilles," "Solidarity Forever," "Land of Hope and Glory," the Chinese "Chilai," "God Save the Queen"—that introduce the protagonists of *A Letter to My Son* and *Paracelsus*, and the "manic" choral sounds that begin *Captives of the Faceless Drummer*. Even his characters are conceived as oppositions in severe need of reconciliation: in *Captives of the Faceless Drummer*, when the cultured diplomat, Harry, calls the urban guerrilla a "hopeless, illiterate fool," (a confrontation which is a stark reprise of the confrontation between the "Indian" and the "Government Agent" alluded to earlier, merely transposed to the alternate Canadian reality of a colonized Québec) he receives the answer: "Illiterate or not, I am and you have to cope with me right now—right?" Discussing this kind of situation after the fact and in a critical vocabulary unknown to Ryga, Gilbert and Tompkins explain: "the post-colonial subject is figured as a split site defined by the remnants of a pre-contact history, the forces of the more official colonial record, and the contingencies of the current situation" (Gilbert, 109).

On the positive side, these questions offered Ryga the opportunity to explore issues of the emerging post-colonial identity of his time, especially its activist and creative elements. The fact that, for example, official imperial history, whether in the form of class, race, or economic narratives, always exists alongside competing local, often repressed narratives, and that imperial language is always challenged by colonial variants, is a productive Hegelian dialectic from which the dramatist can make powerful anti-colonial statements, create counter narratives and counter contexts, write other versions of official history, or even develop new theatrical tools for understanding both the past and the present as he moves toward creating an "other" synthesis.

All of these elements animate Ryga's plays. When we read *Captives of the Faceless Drummer*, not only are we presented with Ryga's signature polemical battle between two antagonists, one representing the colonized (Commander) and one the colonizer (Harry), but we also get a glimpse of their fundamental human commonalities. Their mutual "capture" defines the task of formulating an emerging post-colonial identity for both of them. In addition, the very real events that shadow the play, the 1970 FLQ crisis in Canada, as well as the Playhouse Theatre Company's sudden self-censoring cancellation of the play it had commissioned for its 1970–1971 season, provide a powerful counter-discourse to the traditional context of colonial play presentation, where it is assumed by both the production companies and the largely conservative audiences they serve, that plays are fictional (i.e. the narratives of Others are circumscribed by privilege) and certainly apolitical (local realities are suppressed). Ryga's achievement, through what were perceived by the popular critical media of his day as both his successes and failures, is that he adhered to such a consistent post-colonial agenda throughout his work—not an easy task when the critical vocabulary to translate his dramatic presentations into other forms of discourse was not yet readily available.

Within the interrogative frame that Ryga set for his work, he necessarily engaged in the difficult search for authenticity of both his own narrative voice and the dramatic voices of his characters. For whom and to whom does he speak? And by whose power? The solution is a complicated one as the authenticity of voice Ryga is constantly in search of in his colonial circumstance is always and necessarily derived from two authorities: the Imperial and the Native. Both of these voices are distinct and distant from him, yet both are indirect sources of his own cultural identity. Ryga's relationship with each is a deeply ambiguous one: on the one hand, as the offspring of immigrant invader-settlers, he indirectly represents the colonizing, Imperial culture which has oppressed and displaced the Native one, but, in his physical separation from Europe, his Imperial authority is reduced to mimicry, an empty simulacrum of the original. Ryga writes his plays in English within an inherited/imposed Euro-theatrical format for (largely) white audiences and even though he resists the form, he cannot entirely escape its politically-charged determining features such as, for example, its privileging of realism and textual authority over potentially disruptive performative modes such as song, dance, and spectacle. Ryga's attempt to break this frame of the conventions of the colonial stage was perhaps demonstrated most graphically when he brought the wisdom and character of the medieval physician/rebel, Paracelsus, to Vancouver audiences in 1986 through the technically impressionist means of poetry, epic staging, and historical allusion. For this he was heavily criticized: his intention of challenging modern medical (and, by extension, social, including theatrical) practice was greeted as a tiresome rant; no local commentator could find contemporary relevance in his tale of Paracelsus at the time.

There is in all of Ryga's work an ongoing attempt to "[win] freedom in form and content," as he states in his "Notes in Retrospect" that precede the published version of *Indian* (General Publishing, 1971). One of his strategies was to infuse his theatre with the common speech of ordinary people(s) as a counter to the language forms of the dominant society, although, as in *Paracelsus*, he often draws their speech from temporally and spatially distant sources. So many of his plays—*Captives of the Faceless Drummer*, *Paracelsus*, *A Portrait of Angelica*, *Grass and Wild Strawberries*—feature a parade of ordinary people from all over the world crossing the stage articulating a chorus of working-class, often politically-charged, sentiments that did not necessarily seem to have relevance to the immediate Canadian situation of his audiences.

In part because of his own inherited complicity in the Imperial voice, Ryga increasingly searched for an authenticity of voice within Native authority(s), resulting in his preference for ordinary people from all cultures, from the folk, the ethnic, in his choice of protagonists. These people, whether local (Rita Joe) or not (Paracelsus), are selected because they metonymically represent those who have traditional claims to the land. It is precisely here that Ryga finds the basis for a new synthesis of authority, a common ground in the most basic elements of the human condition, and he applies it to the process by which many of the settlers, now born on the land, are becoming indigenes themselves, beginning the long process of constructing their own distinct culture and identity. Again, this is necessarily always only partial, incomplete, a work in progress: Ryga, in his search for those born "close to the land," is as similarly reduced to mimicry, to "standing in" for the "true" Native, as he is in his search for "true" forms of "white indigeneity," particularly since, in attempting to do so, he is competing with representations of so-called "native" figures such as the woodsman or the Mountie in popular culture. In *Indian* and in *The Ecstasy of Rita Joe*, Ryga in some manner speaks "for" First Nations and is therefore open to charges of appropriation of voice; further, his demonization of many of the settler figures in these plays (the Agent, the Magistrate) reduces the true complexity and potential of the settler subject he struggles so vigorously to construct.

Agnes Grant has described how, while the presence of Chief Dan George lent "authority" to *The Ecstasy of Rita Joe*, his speeches—in their tone, emphasis, and cadence—were distinctly not authentic for the local Salish peoples: "In the play Native people were interpreted within a Western cultural paradigm, but the message of the play was so important that Dan George chose to give theatre-goers what they were looking for" (106). It is perhaps this explicit complicity between the playwright, George Ryga, attempting to speak in a Native voice and the star actor, Chief Dan George, attempting to speak in a Western voice, that accounts for the extraordinary and lasting popular success of *The Ecstasy of Rita Joe*, both in Canada and throughout the world. This play is without a doubt Ryga's most accomplished and successful attempt at creating the synthesis of Imperial and Indigenous authority so necessary as a precursor to the construction of the authentic, post-colonial identity he searched for throughout all of his work. Most interesting of all, it took a fully conscious and collaborative strategy between two credible "authoritative" representatives of both the settler and the indigenous cultures active in the creation and performance of the play to each attempt to speak in the voice of the "other," that unmistakably foregrounded the possible elements of a shared humanity and compassion so necessary for the building of an authentic bridge of solidarity between the two cultures and peoples who otherwise irreconcilably confront each other on the stage of this drama.

Ryga's work, then, exemplifies more than anything else the difficulty of cultural production within the invader-settler colony. In an essay in the first edition of the *Canadian Theatre Review*, (Winter 1974) he speaks of the "cultural disorientation of our people," due to the imperialism of, in this case within the world of Canadian theatre, corporations and the tight, class-based structure of boards of theatre companies. Ryga asserts that while "Our theatre is an accurate reflection of our economic and political reality," there is as yet "no Canadian theatre I know of. There is a lot of transplanted English and American theatre of illusion ... " which, for most people, is "a thing of no consequence" ("Viewpoint," 28). To provide an alternative theatre, Ryga first searches for authentic characters, ones that can give voices to the lives of ordinary people, the folk, those who are connected to the land and can speak knowingly of local lore, myths, and traditions. As if to make his point, Ryga has many of his characters literally rise from the earth. Note how many of his early protagonists enter directly from the land, then speak in an "earthy" vernacular: Duke Radomsky emerges from a hole in the ground in *Nothing but a Man*; the nameless Native from a pile of dust in *Indian*; Volcanic from a mine shaft in *Ploughmen of the Glacier*; and Old Lepa from a manure-drenched farmyard in *A Letter to My Son*. And when they talk, it is in the halting but energetic locutions of the emerging post-colonial Canadian. His characters are often roughhewn and argumentative, but they tell potent stories and demand attention. They do this because Ryga embodies so well the figure of the exile that haunts Canadian society. His fictional characters initiate debates of cultural identity, debates that are characteristic of a fragmented society where the position of the exile has a particular and definitive resonance. When Ryga's true voice was first heard, it rang across national television screens in 1962, with the Native farm worker in *Indian* shrieking, "I nobody. I not even live in this world ... I dead!" Exile, as in the case of the nameless Indian, involves uprooting and displacement from the land, and therewith from cultural and ethnic origin. This diasporic man must of necessity question the notion of a Canadian post-colonial "nation": is his identifying home located on the ground beneath his feet, his place of birth, now a white man's farm? Is it the place of his enforced relocation, his reservation? Or is it within the embrace of Canada as a colonizing/assimilating "nation"? The answer, of course, is that none of these work for the "Indian," with the result that he is exiled from both the foreign colonial, as well as from his own aboriginal culture.

Similarly, the non-aboriginal settlers exist in a place that is separate from their place of origin. The (equally nameless) Magistrate in *The Ecstasy of Rita Joe* coolly mouths Imperial jargon: "To understand life in a given society, one must understand the laws of that society." He becomes emotional only when he remembers a small child he once glimpsed on a highway in British Columbia's Cariboo country. When he drives back to help her, however, "She was nowhere to be seen. Yet the road land was flat for over a mile in every direction—I had to see her. But I couldn't ... " Thus the settlers too experience a fragmented home: as the offspring of expatriates, they cannot return to their distant place of origin, yet, at the same time, they continue to experience their new home as alien in which the indigenous peoples remain "invisible." Because the resettlement of the colonists, like that of the aboriginal, was all too often not of their own choosing, they also exhibit the characteristics of the true exile—they too have difficulty in constructing a notion of "home." One symptom of this is their attempt to appropriate authenticity in native culture, as in the Magistrate's desire to "capture" the lost child on the roadside, itself a constructed and imposed colonial vision of (lost) pre-contact innocence.

Given the defining characteristics of all of George Ryga's work, it is no accident that Ryga himself came to live the life of the exile in his own community of writers. For one thing, his very reputation as a dramatist is an anomaly. Widely regarded as one of Canada's pioneering playwrights, he was an outsider to the very theatre he was instrumental in creating. He had virtually no actual experience or training in the theatre: he attended no theatre classes, never worked practically in the theatre, and never played an actual role on a stage. When he began working on the stage of the Vancouver Playhouse in 1967 to prepare the performance of his greatest success, *The Ecstasy of Rita Joe*, he had to be reminded which was "stage left" and "stage right." As a playwright, he resisted what he saw as the destructive pressure of constant negotiations and internal politics with their residue of Euro-centric values and hierarchical control that are at the very heart of what he considered should be the collaborative theatrical process. Because of this, he very nearly lost *The Ecstasy of Rita Joe*. Working closely with director George Bloomfield, who had a very different vision of the play from the playwright's, Ryga drastically rewrote his play, taking it draft by draft into many new directions, coming dangerously close to abandoning it entirely. Joy Coghill, the Vancouver Playhouse's artistic director at the time, recalls: "Nobody knew this on my Board, but we lost our play just before we were to go into rehearsal."

Ryga admitted he found theatrical drama constricting. In describing it, he used the metaphor of a house and himself as a terrorist: "The play is on the top of our head like a low ceiling, you can't work with the form so you have to try to blow it up" (*Fulcrum* interview, 20 Nov. 1980). His personal preference of venues for the performing arts were not the traditional forms of Western theatre, which he saw as distancing and elitist, but places where the stories and rhythms of ordinary people, the folk, were played, such as the Ballads and Blues Club in London, England, which he frequented in the 950s and where he befriended well known folk singers Ewan McColl and Alan Lomax. In his own community of Summerland, he helped found and operate a coffee-house, Chautauqua 333. If he saw himself as a performer, it was in the tradition of the troubadours, the ancient, itinerant poet-musicians who sang of love and war and who wrote politically-charged poems. When he performed on stages in Edmonton in the mid-fifties, it was with a folk singing ensemble, Tamarack, a group that sang at festivals and union halls, with Ryga acting as both entertainer and activist, the group singing left-wing songs and participating in ban-the-bomb marches. As for the theatre, he told an interviewer with the *Ottawa Revue*, "I'm not a theatre person myself. I come from other places—music, poetry, politics" (20 Nov. 1980). His final play, *One More for the Road*, is little more than a series of reminiscences, opinions, and songs by a solo singer-performer, a modern troubadour, really a thinly disguised version of how George Ryga saw himself.

As a writer, Ryga would have preferred to be known as a novelist. When he first began to write steadily and seriously, soon after his marriage to Norma in Edmonton in 1959, he wrote novels—half a dozen or so—and short stories. These are stories of struggle, typically of people displaced in a stark prairie landscape, who exhibit increasing degrees of reaction against their colonial inheritance, much as what occurs in the first play in this anthology, *Indian*. He seemed happiest as the embattled author taking on the world, which he did in essays and in public addresses, a world clearly divided into hegemonic boundaries, between First World and Third, between the colonized and the colonizers. At the time, his political allegiance was strongly left-wing: he read Marx, befriended progressive agrarian reformer Bill Irvine, one of the founders of the CCF party, wrote poems for the socialist journal *New Frontiers*, and worked briefly for the Communist Party. Because of this political grounding, his writing anticipated a better tomorrow through the application of science and socialist cooperation among peoples. Before that day was to arrive, however, there remained an immense struggle to be fought against the demons that opposed such change: typically, his fictional characters engage overwhelming, often destructive forces, and retain only a glimmer of that vision. For the energetic, project-filled Paracelsus, who states, "I have endless things to do ... ," there awaits his eventual murder; while for Prometheus, speaking of "the ongoing struggle for perfectibility," there remains only captivity.

It can be argued that Ryga's dramatic vision inevitably evolved from the giant struggles of these heroic and mythic individuals—against the forces of nature, history, and government—a dramatic vision that was deepened by Ryga's direct participation in these struggles. Indeed, his first novel, *The Bridge*, is strongly autobiographical: in it, he recounts many of the adventures of a year spent in Europe in the mid-fifties when, with a friend from Edmonton, Michael Omelchuk, he travelled to the British Isles in search of a personal icon, Robert Burns, then to continental Europe to attend several left-wing youth rallies. Talonbooks was to eventually publish excerpts from this unpublished novel in their collection *The Athabasca Ryga* (1990). Similarly, the content of *Night Desk*, another early novel, is structured in the form of a long monologue transcribed directly from conversations he had with a colourful fight promoter who was staying at the Edmonton hotel where Ryga worked as a desk clerk. Although the narrator is portrayed as a silent listener, it is clearly Ryga doing the listening, and he retains a strong participation in the creation of the speaker's persona: clearly the fight promoter regards the "night clerk" as a potentially powerful presence, telling him that he says to his friends, "The kid on the night desk is writin' down what we do and say-about who we are an' what we might've been. The trumpet of the night. That's what you are" (16). This novel was successfully dramatized and staged several times, most lately by Ken Smedley, during the 1980s, under the title *Ringside Date with an Angel*.

As a public figure of exile, as an "artist in resistance," especially after the *Captives of the Faceless Drummer* controversy, Ryga publicly addressed issues of Canadian culture, particularly its colonized nature, in numerous instances—to the point of eventually turning on the very theatre that had earlier nourished him. He and other west coast playwrights presented a brief (Ryga was chosen to read it) to the Secretary of State in March, 1972, in which he now called his former Vancouver theatre company, the "hated symbol for local writers, the Playhouse Theatre Company, with its annual collection of jaded imports from latter day Broadway and precious antiques from London to titillate the blue rinse matrons who provide the season subscriptions" (Hoffman, 223). Soon afterwards, in another essay published in the *Canadian Theatre Review* (1977), he repeated the need for a resistant, popular theatre, one that addressed social issues and spoke with "the common voice of the people." Finding an appropriate language, however, is no easy matter he says, because: "Today's drama to a large extent concerns itself with a vanishing landscape" ("Contemporary Theatre," 9). What are the particular sources and characteristics of this "vanishing landscape" and, for that matter, of his own conflicted dramaturgy?

Ryga's dramatic oeuvre has its origins in his deeply ambivalent relationship to place. It is an unmistakable characteristic of his plays that images of the Canadian landscape are so sharply dramatized, and that his characters must contend so strongly with issues of the land: with ownership, with belonging, often with survival on, and even against, the land itself. The land is frequently characterized as an alien, unproductive place: its inhabitants are homeless and yearn to escape to a space of their own; if the land is owned, there are conflicting claims to its possession; significantly, it is frequently upset by the (reshaping) forces of turbulent weather, as in *Jeremiah's Place*. For Ryga, with his profound sense of exile, space itself is a major concern, especially the unresolved, unequal systems of power that attach to the land and the desperate need for negotiation between, as in his early plays, the settlers and the original inhabitants. To both of these contending proprietors he tries to give voice: Ryga's uniqueness, and a major reason for his controversial reputation, derives from his compelling impulse to speak for both the settler and the indigene. Speaking for both, he wants the seemingly impossible: to subvert the dominant society's authority, to initiate political action, to rewrite local histories, to reclaim land, to challenge the colonial displacement of peoples, even to recuperate indigenous cultures. Where did this enormous impulse originate?

Ryga's emotional wellspring is his Ukrainian inheritance—the romantic Ukraine of temperate climes, rich soil, music, and storytelling—as well as the troubled Ukraine of ongoing struggle against invasion and conquest. For Ryga, the memory of Cossacks, Tartars, and Mongols racing defiantly across the steppes on horseback, fiercely defending their homeland, asserting a raw sense of nation, remained strong and shaped his writing, especially in his choice of protagonists and their overwhelming adversaries: the nameless Indian against Indian Affairs; the homeless Rita Joe against Canadian Law. He traced his ancestry to the Golden Horde of the Genghis Khan, to men "fired up with that ancient sense of right and wrong" (Hoffman, 16). He claimed it was through listening as a child to the stories and poems by the great Ukrainian authors, Shevchenko, Franko, and Ukrainka, read to him by his father, that stirred his soul. In his plays, Ryga indirectly invokes these Ukrainian icons through his use of folk imagery and folk culture, used as a means of asserting identity in the face of threat and as a way of provoking political analysis. For Ryga, this was the ground of a resistant practice.

But even in this romantic reconstruction of his own roots there exists an unavoidable degree of displacement: he never saw the Ukraine until late in his life, when he visited that country in the 1980s. What he saw of life on the land in his formative years was the hard-nosed experience of the settler in western Canada during the 1930s and 1940s, which harboured its own sense of displacement. He was the son of immigrants who never believed they were "settled": for their first decade in Canada, his parents feared deportation to their native Ukraine. Born in 1932, he was raised in a northern Alberta farm environment, a place that he has described as having inhospitable land, grinding poverty, and ethnic prejudice from the dominant Angliki. His father, because he had walked away from a relief work project in protest, feared deportation and lived the hidden and haunted life of an alien. The farm meanwhile declined. Ryga claims his father was never a very effective farmer and eventually fell into sickness and a "black despair" (Hoffman, 24).

For Ryga, the place, sometimes called Deep Creek, sometimes Richmond Park, was rife with contradiction: besides being "a killer for the soul," as he once described it, the family farm was also a place of spiritual nourishment. In *Song of my hands and other poems*, his early book of verse, he initially writes fondly of life on the farm, a place "Where prairie winds and sun range free." Indeed, it was a place of recurring epiphany which he believed he could detect at an early age: "At six I reached a higher elevation of religious sensitivity and revelation than any adult human I have since spoken to ... I was a child born out of context in time and space" (Hoffman, 29). It is this combination, of a land that is both nourishing and destructive—that simultaneously brings life and meaning as well as ruin and despair to its uneasy inhabitants—that remained a benchmark of his writing. The central importance of place in the process of identity formation became the basis for his ceaseless dramatization of the elements that had formed his own conflicted character.

Because his spiritual vision was so deeply rooted in the epiphanies of his youth, Ryga wrote himself centrally (and precariously) into his plays. The nameless Native of *Indian*, the Commander in *Captives of the Faceless Drummer*, Uncle Ted in *Grass and Wild Strawberries*, are in some measure dramatized versions of the playwright himself. Few people know that only two months after the première of *The Ecstasy of Rita Joe*, another play of Ryga's opened in Vancouver, but it went almost unnoticed—staged with little fanfare by a small company in a suburban theatre. *Just an Ordinary Person* is an attempt to reconcile polar psycho-political positions, a common motif in Ryga's plays: that of the passionate, romantic visionary, aware of his huge responsibility to help "his" people who are invariably signified as the common working people; with that of the individual writer convulsing in contradiction and self-doubt as he contemplates this task. The "poet" and the "ordinary person" of this play represent warring positions within Ryga himself. Like Ryga in the mid-1960s, the Poet (who, like Ryga, is also a playwright) is newly famous (Ryga by this time has had considerable successes with *Indian* and *The Ecstasy of Rita Joe*), but he is tormented by "a personal conflict of spirit," believing that he has "no talent," that his work so far is "commonplace." *Just an Ordinary Person* reveals much about Ryga's growing dilemma as an author who had set out to speak "for the people." In it, a poet is giving a reading of his own poem about Federico Garcia Lorca, but he is interrupted by a nameless "any age man" who proceeds to question the poet's purpose. What begins as simple, genuine interest on the part of the listener/character becomes a fierce critique: "You're a mortgage holder on my spirit and theirs! (*motions with back of his hand to audience*) … lending out bits of experience for the fame we give you … when you read, your voice is thin … your pen scratches on the surface of things … " (24). He asks: "When will your poems speak so as to inspire rebellion of the spirit—here? When will your poems give wings to the soul?" (29). This "ordinary person," representing a worker, then a soldier, has lost his purpose in an indifferent contemporary world; he desperately needs the poet to act as prophet and teacher. Faced with this challenge, the poet, however, experiences increasing self-doubt, and the play ends with a weakening of his resolve (will or can the Poet be another Lorca, rather than merely celebrate, and thus in some measure merely appropriate and "import," Lorca's voice?), as the Ordinary Person retreats offstage. The Ordinary Person throughout the play considers himself the Poet's peer and equal, has a similar, immigrant European ancestry, yet feels the Poet has betrayed their solidarity by celebrating not what binds the present community they share, but a foreign, distant and Imperial community that continues to oppress and exploit them. *Just an Ordinary Person* depicts a vital debate, a kind of classic Marxist dialectic of the role of the artist in society, as it plays itself out in Ryga's own work: the poem that is read at the beginning of the play is "Federico Garcia Lorca," taken from Ryga's own self-published first book of poetry, *Song of my hands and other poems*. While *Just an Ordinary Person* was critically acclaimed, it was poorly attended. It is perhaps his simplest, most stripped-down play. In raw form it graphically presents both the strength and the weakness of all of Ryga's dramaturgy.

The fact that he staged the profoundly self-interrogating *Just an Ordinary Person* so closely on his huge success with *The Ecstasy of Rita Joe* foregrounds in very stark terms that Ryga took seriously, some might say too seriously, his self-proclaimed role as outsider and rebel—a role which always begs the question of who speaks, ethically and authentically, for whom. This internalized dilemma accounts for his often strident, lopsided protagonists, those lonely, embattled figures, physically marked as different, painfully contending with their identities, searching in vain for lost communities, for belonging, whether the nameless "ordinary people" of *Indian, The Ecstasy of Rita Joe,* or *Captives of the Faceless Drummer*, or the grandiose "heroes" with feet of clay we encounter in *Paracelsus* or *Prometheus Bound*. Even the vaunting challenges of Ryga's heroes are tempered with their strong sense of self-doubt, arising from the productively ambiguous situation of the dislocated exile. Because of this, his characters heavily engage in one central activity: they talk. Given their situation, of the ever-present likelihood of defeat in which every possible action seems compromised, they resort to long tirades, most notably and extensively in *Paracelsus*.

Essential to the drama of Ryga's plays is the struggle for the control of language as a medium of power. Because they inhabit a place where an imperial language has been imposed, resulting in a gap between the experience of place and the language available to describe it, his characters attempt to seize the language and make it their own. Whether used by the aboriginal or by the settler, English as a privileged language, with its normative, European value system, represents a site of colonial power and must be reclaimed and reconstructed by those who are colonized. One of Ryga's earliest writing projects was to reconstitute English, to develop what he called "telepathic drama," a kind of foreshortened vernacular writing marked by brevity but powerful in its ability to stir deep memories and meaning. He believed he first achieved this in his teleplay *Man Alive*, the precursor of *Nothing but a Man*. By using the vernacular in this manner, as well as frequently inserting extra-textual elements such as song and dance, Ryga employed a resistant language, thus downplaying the authority of standard English stage usage, with its hierarchical emphasis on "correct" speech and its underlying assumptions regarding (imperial) reality. His foreshortened vernacular also restores a sense of local orality, of local accent to his characters, thus allowing important (re)connections to the local topography to be made. In *Indian*, the nameless Native, found sleeping on the ground, literally rises from the dust to confront (and reclaim) his alienated topography, a scene that is replayed in so many of Ryga's plays. Volcanic, in *Ploughmen of the Glacier*, similarly emerges from a mine shaft to articulate his vision of British Columbia, while the chained Prometheus, brutally thrown to the ground, speaks of "The rightful wishes of the earth's poor / For bread, land and freedom."

In their dramaturgy, Ryga's plays are structured in an oppositional mode reminiscent of classical Greek plays built on the *agon*, the dialectical speech/reply between two protagonists. Ryga's essential strategy is to stage a lengthy, heated debate between two central characters, each of whom has claims to the land, one representing the position of the indigene, the other that of the settler. In charged yet common language, drawing from different linguistic codes and tonalities, these characters grapple with each other, often physically, as they maneuver to determine issues of identity and ownership. In this way language becomes the primary means of enacting a culturally inflected subjectivity: in *Captives of the Faceless Drummer*, the Commander stands in for the indigene, describing himself as "of the people" (in this case, the Québecois), while the diplomat, Harry (based on James Cross, the real life British Trade Commissioner held prisoner by the FLQ during Canada's "October Crisis" in 1970), represents the colonizing authority. Their debate is about control: who, finally, has rightful claim to the land—the oppressed, working-class man or the government representative? Both have a stake; both have valid claims. The implication is that they must somehow merge, must reach some sort of mutual understanding, as they seem to when Harry asks the Commander, "Have you built any bridges? ... Ploughed any fields?" to which the Commander responds, "And you?" (Both, it would seem, have appropriated their stated right to representative power). This play, like many of Ryga's, is about the potential for their characters' mutual capture: the diplomat is kidnapped by the Commander and the Commander, even before he is shot by government forces at the end, is taken by Harry's position, an unmistakable allusion to George Orwell's *1984*. In *Paracelsus*, there are multiple *agons* at work: between the characters of the historical Paracelsus and medieval authority; between the medicine of Paracelsus and modern medicine; even between the differing views of the limits of modern medicine, science and technology represented in the play by Doctors Guza and Webb.

With his plays written as giant debates, strident argument and oversize characters often seem to replace action: indeed, many of Ryga's plays seem plot-less. His characters are sketched in the outlines of local detail as much as in the larger-than-life brush strokes of national allegory. Volcanic and Lowery, in *Ploughmen of the Glacier*, are based on historical British Columbia figures, a miner and a journalist, and there are plenty of local mining references, but they also represent the mythical "two halves" (Ryga's term) of British Columbia, "the man of commitment and the exploiter" (Hoffman, 269). Since they hold and defend opposing beliefs, there appears to be little action they can take beyond lively, combative dialogue—often verging on violence. But there is nonetheless an intriguing energy in Ryga's plays, especially as he moves freely through time and space. Employing disruptive elements such as flashbacks/forwards, poetic speeches, songs, changes of setting, the weather, and sound motifs, Ryga gives his plays a sense of restless movement, even loss or disintegration of a controlling frame. His characters may be physically trapped by colonial uncertainties, but they have great capacity to envision a different tomorrow: a key moment in *Ploughmen of the Glacier* occurs when both men describe their vision of the ideal city. They may experience political stasis in their attempt to create a truly public space (to plough a glacier is, after all, fruitless in every sense of the word), never easily constructed in the invader-settler colony, but, in the intensity of their debates, they attempt to negotiate for a shared common ground and the elements of an emergent post-colonial identity.

Works Cited

Benson, Eugene, and L.W. Conolly. *English Canadian Theatre*. Toronto: Oxford UP, 1987.

Coghill, Joy. Letter to the author. 4 July 1992.

Cohen, Nathan. "A Non-Production of a Non-Play." *Toronto Star,* 25 Nov. 1967: 30.

Conlogue, Ray. "*Paracelsus'* Strength Lost in Softened Production." *Globe and Mail,* 29 September 1986: A15.

Gilbert, Helen, and Joanne Tompkins. *Post-Colonial Drama: Theory, Practice, Politics*. London: Routledge, 1996.

Grant, Agnes. "Native Drama: A Celebration of Native Culture." *Contemporary Issues in Canadian Drama*. Ed. Per Brask. Winnipeg: Blizzard, 1995. 103–115.

Hoffman, James. *The Ecstasy of Resistance: A Biography of George Ryga*. Toronto: ECW Press, 1995.

Lawson, Alan. "Postcolonial Theory and the 'Settler' Subject." *Essays on Canadian Writing* 56 (Fall 1995):20–36.

Maracle, Lee. "A Question of Voice." *Vancouver Sun,* 6 June 1992: D9.

Richards, Jack. "World Premiere Lays Bare Tragedy of Canadian Society." *Vancouver Sun,* 24 Nov. 1967: 6.

Rubin, Don. "George Ryga: The Poetics of Engagement." *On-Stage and Off-Stage: English Canadian Drama in Discourse*. Eds. Albert-Reiner Glaap with Rolf Althof. St. John's NF: Breakwater, 1996: 224–239.

Ryga, George. *Song of my hands and other poems*. Edmonton: National Publishing, 1956.

Ryga, George. "Theatre in Canada: A Viewpoint on Its Development and Future." *Canadian Theatre Review* 1 (Winter 1974): 28–32.

Ryga, George. "Contemporary Theatre and Its Language." *Canadian Theatre Review* 14 (Spring 1977): 4–9.

Ryga, George. *Night Desk*. Vancouver: Talonbooks, 1976.

Ryga, George. Interview in *The Fulcrum*, U of Ottawa, 20 Nov. 1980.

INDIAN

In the late 1950s George Ryga was a prolific but unknown writer with only a self-published book of poetry and a short story in *The Ukrainian Canadian* to his credit. But in the early sixties he was suddenly thrust into public prominence with *Indian*: this hard-hitting play was featured on CBC television, published in *Maclean's* magazine, and scheduled for an Off-Broadway theatre performance; it also established the substance and the pattern of much of his subsequent work. *Indian* is Ryga's first play, and, in many ways, his most defining work.

Ryga, at this time, was now living in Edmonton Norma and her two daughters, Leslie and Tanya. Their first son, Campbell, had just been born. For reading, he was deeply into Dostoyevsky and Gorky. With a secure home environment and part-time work at the post office, Ryga was able for the first time in his life to devote himself steadily to his writing. He produced mostly prose fiction, pounding out a handful of novels and a dozen or so short stories—many of which, typical of Ryga, were eventually reworked for publication for a variety of print media or for broadcast on radio or television.

The dominant metathemes of his work have remained the same: a romantic attraction to the land and the people who live close to it and a profound alienation from that same land—the ownership of which is often in question. In this way Ryga writes from the deeply ambivalent position of the settler culture in Western Canada, where the invader-settlers, both working-class immigrants and established middle-class citizens, exist precariously as both colonizers of the aboriginal inhabitants and are themselves colonized by external agencies, whether as an extension of Empire under Britain, the neo-colonizing U.S., or even under "home rule" by a distant urban capital, Ottawa. Ryga's self-appointed task has been to give expression to the dispossessed of all classes, those who experience desire for the land in the context of unresolved experiences and feelings of displacement from it.

He demonstrates a passion for what he called "ordinary people," a somewhat complex term that for him referred primarily to hard-working people closely connected to the land as a source of their living and their heritage; a people also necessarily involved in political struggle against oppressors who would deny them, in very literal terms, the fruits of their labour. He saw struggle firsthand: having been raised in a hardscrabble farming environment in northern Alberta, by Ukrainian immigrant parents, Ryga, in an interview, spoke of "the black despair" (Hoffman, 24) of his father, and of how "the poverty was incredible and patience an unpredictable pool of water over which a storm always threatened" (Hoffman, 22). Ryga's deep association with ordinary people, especially in their struggle to surmount colonial, racist, and classist barriers to the fruitful and productive exercise of their work, such as they continue to exist in western Canada, gives his work an explicit political underpinning. By the mid-fifties he was writing polemical pieces for the left-wing journal, *New Frontiers*, and travelling to Europe to attend rallies of the World Federation of Democratic Youth hosted by several Communist countries.

Ordinary, struggling people remained a political touchstone for Ryga; they were also a source of his poetic inspiration. The immigrant people of his childhood community north of Athabasca were racially mixed and provided a potent matrix for the young, impressionable Ryga, who since his teens had written poems and stories celebrating the vitality of people working the earth, including the local Cree native peoples. Indeed, his ticket to study writing in the wider world came with an award-winning article,

"Smoke," which memorialized the pioneer, communal ritual of clearing the land. That essay won him a scholarship to study writing at the Banff School of Fine Arts—where he worked under such notable writers as E.P. Conkle, who had also taught Tennessee Williams, and Jerome Lawrence.

He assembled ten of his short stories in a collection he called *Poor People*, (five of these were eventually published in the Talonbooks collection *The Athabasca Ryga* in 1990), declaring in a foreword his faith in ordinary people: "I write of the poor people—among which I have lived and worked here and in other places. The poor people—on whom the success or failure of all the great dreams rest." Out of this collection there emerged a story that he was to adapt for his first television play, *Indian*.

Indian began its life as "Pinetree Ghetto," one of these ten unpublished short stories. Ryga dramatized it after he had watched a CBC television program one evening: *Q for Quest*, an innovative, provocative anthology program designed as an outlet for creative dramatic talent—showcasing cutting edge work by foreign writers such as Anton Chekhov and Bertolt Brecht, and Canadian writers such as Mordecai Richler and Len Peterson. *Q for Quest* was a lively, satirical show and it was specifically a *Q for Quest* production of Edward's Albee's short stage play, *The Zoo Story,* that lead to Ryga's idea to rewrite "Pinetree Ghetto" as a dramatic work, eventually re-titling it, as part of this process of its adaptation for television, *Indian*.

In *The Zoo Story* two men meet on a bench in New York's Central Park. Both are damaged products of their society: Peter is a middle-class cipher, a man with a career, a home, a family, but who has no soul—he only wants to be left alone, especially by others less fortunate than he. Jerry is a homeless outcast, desperately in search of genuine human communication. When Jerry launches into his long monologue, "The Story of Jerry and the Dog," it turns out to be the tale of a soul pummeled to the depths of its existence. Jerry's story is so powerful and moving that Peter is shaken out of his self-satisfied complacency and momentarily embraces a wider humanity, while Jerry commits a dramatic suicide in his attempt to finally achieve a measure of contact with an other he perceives to be inaccessible.

Ryga watched this half-hour show and saw what he had been looking for. Here was a story of "Poor People," which implied, rather than explicitly thematized, a strong political context. Despite his socialist leanings, Ryga had so far written in folk forms rather than, for example, in those of a more "politically correct" Marxist social realism. He had demonstrated his signature passion and strong moral sense in his work, but had remained unsure, up to this point in his writing life, how to handle questions of "political meaning." Here, in *The Zoo Story*, were two conflicting characters set in the present and given a strong social context. Clearly, Albee's hit play inspired Ryga, who now felt he could write an equally effective piece.

He wrote the teleplay, initially calling it "Pinetree Ghetto," later, "Born of Man," and finally *Indian*, and sent it to Daryl Duke, the producer of *Q for Quest*, simply addressing it to "Daryl Duke, CBC-Quest, Toronto." Things moved quickly: Duke read it and telephoned Ryga immediately to discuss the possibility of a television production; he then sent the director, George McGowan, and the lead actor, Len Birman, out to Edmonton to meet Ryga and to conduct some of their own research on the local Native people, the subject of what had now become Ryga's television script.

Duke was so excited he showed the script to Ken Lafolii, the editor of *Maclean's*, who decided to publish the entire script in "Canada's National Magazine" before the actual CBC production. Thus, the entire script, with an introduction by Duke and numerous rehearsal photographs, appeared in *Maclean's*, where readers had access to the entire teleplay in the week before it was aired on Sunday evening, November 25, 1962. This was quite possibly the most profoundly defining week of the birth of a post-colonial Canadian theatre.

Indian, like *The Zoo Story*, pits one of society's outcasts against the smug complacency of his oppressors. Ryga's nameless Native protagonist first appears as colonial society's cliché of the "shiftless Indian": sleeping in the dust, hung over, he needs the prodding of his farmer-employer to get him to return to his work—hammering in fence posts. In his initial confrontation with the farmer, he appears to merely reinforce the assumed audience bias against the "lazy Indian"—the farmer almost seems justified in his threats of retaliation for the undone work and the squandering of borrowed money, but, in this beginning scene, Ryga has merely lured his audience into a very temporary comfort zone. Soon the Native man confronts an indifferent agent from Indian Affairs, who arrives by car and offers him the condescending, racist talk of the colonizer: "Look here, boy … don't give me any back-talk." This triggers an explosion of anger and "back-talk" that marks a turning point in the way Native peoples have been constructed in Canadian narratives. The spoken language of the nameless Native, especially the wrenching story of his brother's death, is still one of Canada's most powerful dramatic monologues and initiates Ryga's own program of resistance against all forms of cultural domination—a thematic that he was to continue to foreground in virtually all his work.

The play generated excellent critical support in the press, the *Toronto Star* saying, "CBC's *Quest* last night came up with a perceptive study of the Canadian Indian in modern life. Alberta writer George Ryga's play was simple, sound and moving" (26 Nov. 1962). Interestingly, some Alberta Native groups were less than thrilled: the Friends of the Indian Society objected to what they saw as a distortion of the public image of the Indian. Ryga responded to these charges in a letter to the *Edmonton Journal* (24 Jan. 1963), stating that he had created the play based on the "realities" he saw in the housing, health, and education of the local Native people in his own community. For him as a writer to have pretended otherwise, he asserted, would have been false: "Had I created an image of an Indian that people evidently would have wished to have seen, I would have denied the plight of the Indian race in North America today. This I could not do."

Indian has since become a milestone in Canadian drama. It was broadcast on CBC Radio on Montreal's *Late-Night Theatre* in 1963, adapted for the stage (first titled *Sementos*) for a production in Toronto in 1964 by the Finnish theatre group, the Yritys A.C. Players, and was eventually published in over a half dozen publications. Even before the play was first broadcast on CBC Television, the *Globe and Mail* announced that *Indian* "may be produced Off-Broadway" (24 Nov. 1962). Ryga had sent a copy of the play to Jerome Lawrence, his former scriptwriting instructor at Banff, who was now enjoying the success of his long-running *Inherit the Wind* on Broadway. Lawrence planned to stage the work at Greenwich Village's Theatre DeLys, but, with a protracted newspaper strike in New York City and the lack of American reviews, producers were wary and the play was not staged as planned.

Indian constitutes a watershed event not only in the development of a post-colonial indigenous Canadian drama but also in claiming a space in Canadian theatre for Native peoples: exactly five years later, in 1967, Ryga's international hit play, *The Ecstasy of Rita Joe*, premiered in Vancouver.

INDIAN

CHARACTERS

INDIAN—*transient Indian labourer. Swarthy, thin, long haired. Wears tight-fitting jeans, dirty dark shirt brightened by outlandish western designs over pockets. Also cowboy boots which are cracked and aged. A wide-brimmed black western hat.*

WATSON—*farmer and employer of Indian.*

AGENT—*comfortable civil servant. Works in the Indian Affairs Department as field worker for the service.*

SET

Stage should be flat, grey, stark non-country. Diametric lines (telephone poles and wire on one side, with a suggestion of two or three newly driven fence-posts on the other) could project vast empty expanse.

Set may have a few representative tufts of scraggy growth in distance—also far and faint horizon.

In front and stage left, one fence-post newly and not yet fully driven. Pile of dirt around post. Hammer, wooden box, and shovel alongside.

High, fierce white light offstage left to denote sun. Harsh shadows and constant sound of low wind. Back of stage is a pile of ashes, with a burnt axe handle and some pottery showing.

Curtain up on INDIAN asleep, using slight hump of earth under his neck for pillow. He is facing sun, with hat over his face. WATSON approaches from stage right, dragging his feet and raising dust. Stops over INDIAN'S head.

WATSON: (*loud and angry*) Hey! What the hell! Come on ... you aimin' to die like that?

INDIAN clutches his hat and sits up. Lifts his hat and looks up, then jerks hat down over his face.

INDIAN: Oy! Oooh! The sun she blind me, goddamn! ... Boss ... I am sick! Head, she gonna explode, sure as hell!

He tries to lie down again, but WATSON grabs his arm and yanks him to his feet.

WATSON: There's gonna be some bigger explosions if I don't get action out of you guys. What happened now? Where's the fat boy? An' the guy with the wooden leg?

INDIAN: Jus' a minute, boss. Don't shout like that. (*looks carefully around him*) They not here ... Guess they run away, boss—no? ... Roy, he's not got wooden leg. He got bone leg same's you an' me. Only it dried up and look like wood. Small, too ... (*lifts up his own right leg*) That shoe ... that was fit Roy's bad leg. The other shoe is tight. But this one, boss—she is hunder times tighter!

WATSON: (*squatting*) Is them Limpy's boots?

INDIAN: Sure, boss. I win them at poker las' night. Boss, what a time we have—everybody go haywire!

WATSON looks around impatiently.

WATSON: I can see. Where's your tent?

INDIAN: (*pointing to ashes*) There she is. Sonofabitch, but I never see anything burn like that before!

WATSON: The kid wasn't lying—you guys *did* burn the tent.

INDIAN: What kid?

WATSON: Your kid.

INDIAN: (*jumping to his feet*) Alphonse? Where is Alphonse? He run away when Sam and Roy start fight ...

WATSON: Yeh, he run away ... run all the way to the house. Told us you guys was drunk an' wild. So the missus fixed him something to eat and put him to bed.

INDIAN: He's all right? Oh, that's good, boss!

WATSON: (*smiling grimly*) Sure, he's all right. Like I said, the missus fed the kid. Then I took him and put him in the grainery, lockin' the door so he ain't gonna get out. That's for protection.

INDIAN: Protection? You don't need protection, boss. Alphonse not gonna hurt you.

WATSON: Ha! Ha! Ha! Big joke! ... Where are your pals as was gonna help you with this job? Where are they—huh?

INDIAN: I don't know. They run away when tent catch fire.

WATSON: Great! That's just great! You know what you guys done to me? Yesterday, ya nicked me for ten dollars ... I'm hungry, the fat boy says to me—my stomach roar like thunder. He's gonna roar out the other end before I'm finished with you an' him! How much you figure the fence you put up is worth?

INDIAN: (*rubbing his eyes and trying to see the fence in the distance*) I dunno, boss. You say job is worth forty dollars. Five, mebbe ten dollars done ...

WATSON: Five dollars! Look here, smart guy— ya've got twenty-nine posts in—I counted 'em. At ten cents apiece, you've done two dollars ninety cents worth of work! An' you got ten dollars off me yesterday!

INDIAN: (*pondering sadly*) Looks like you in the hole, boss.

WATSON: Well maybe I am ... an' maybe I ain't. I got your kid in the grainery, locked up so he'll keep. You try to run off after your pals, an' I'm gonna take my gun an' shoot a hole that big through the kid's head!

He makes a ring with his fingers to show exact size of injury he intends to make.

INDIAN: No!

WATSON: Oh, sure! So what ya say, Indian? ... You gonna work real hard and be a good boy?

INDIAN: Boss—you know me. I work! Them other guys is no good—but not Johnny. I make deal—I keep deal! You see yourself I stay when they run.

WATSON: Sure, ya stayed. You were too god-damned drunk to move, that's why you stayed!

What goes on in your heads ... ah, hell! You ain't worth the bother!

INDIAN: No, no, boss ... You all wrong.

WATSON: Then get to work! It's half past nine, and you ain't even begun to think about the fence.

INDIAN: Boss ... a little bit later. I sick man ... head—she hurt to burst. An' stomach—ugh! Boss, I not eat anything since piece of baloney yesterday ...

WATSON: (*turning angrily*) You go to hell—you hear me? Go to hell! I got that story yesterday. Now g'wan—I wanna see some action!

INDIAN: All right, boss. You know me. You trust me.

WATSON: Trust ya? I wouldn't trust you with the time of day, goddamn you! (*remembers something*) Hey—there's a snoop from the Indian Affairs department toolin' around today— checkin' on all you guys workin' off the reserve. I'm telling you somethin' ... you're working for me, so if you got any complaints, you better tell me now. I don't want no belly-achin' to no government guys.

INDIAN: Complaints? ... Me? I happy, boss. What you take me for?

WATSON: Sure, sure ... Now get back to work. An' remember what I told you ... you try to beat it, an' I shoot the kid. You understand?

INDIAN removes his hat and wipes his brow.

INDIAN: Sure, bossman—I understand.

INDIAN looks towards the fence in the fields. WATSON stands behind him, scratching his chin and smirking insolently. INDIAN glances back at him, then shrugging with resignation, moves unsteadily to the unfinished fence post. He pulls the box nearer to the post, picks up hammer and is about to step on the box. Changes his mind and sits for a moment on the box, hammer across his knees. Rubs his eyes and forehead.

WATSON: What the hell's the matter? Run out of gas?

INDIAN: Oh, boss ... If I be machine that need only gas, I be all right mebbe ...

WATSON: So you going to sit an' let the day go by? … Indian, I've got lots of time, an' I can grind you to dirt if you're figurin' on bustin' my ass!

INDIAN: Nobody bust you, boss. I be all right right away … Sementos! But the head she is big today. An' stomach … she is slop-bucket full of turpentine. Boss … two dollars a quart, Sam Cardinal says to me … with four dollars we get enough bad whiskey to poison every Indian from here to Lac La Biche! Sam Cardinal tell the truth that time for sure …

WATSON: What kind of rubbish did you drink?

INDIAN: Indian whiskey, boss. You know what is Indian whiskey?

WATSON: No. You tell me, an' then you get to work!

INDIAN: Sure, boss, sure. As soon as field stop to shake. Indian whiskey … you buy two quart. You get one quart wood alcohol … maybe half quart formalin, an' the rest is water from sick horse! That's the kind whiskey they make for Indian.

WATSON: An' it makes the field shake for you … Christ! *You* make me sick!

INDIAN: Oh, but what party it make!

WATSON: (*irritably*) Come on … come on! Get on with it.

INDIAN scrambles on box and starts to drive post into ground. He stops after a few seconds. He is winded.

INDIAN: Sementos! Is hard work, boss! … I tell you, Sam Cardinal sing like sick cow … an' Roy McIntosh dance on his bad leg. Funny! … Alphonse an' I laugh until stomach ache. I win Roy's boots in poker, but he dance anyhow. Then Sam get mad an' he push Roy … Roy push him back … They fight … Boy, I hungry now, boss …

WATSON: Tough! I wanna see ten bucks of work done.

INDIAN: Then you feed me? Big plate potatoes an' meat? … An' mebbe big hunk of pie?

WATSON: (*laughs sarcastically*) Feed ya? Soon's I get my ten bucks squared away, you can lie down and die! But not on my field … go on the road allowance!

INDIAN hits the post a few more times, trying to summon up strength to get on with the work. But it is all in vain. Drops hammer heavily to the box. Rubs his stomach.

INDIAN: You hard man, boss … Hard like iron. Sam is bad man … bugger up you, bugger up me. Get ten dollars for grub from you … almost like steal ten dollars from honest man. Buy whiskey … buy baloney an' two watermelon. He already eat most of baloney and I see him give hunk to friendly dog. I kick dog. Sam get mad … why you do that? Dog is nothing to you? I say, he eat my grub. He can go catch cat if he hungry. I catch an' eat cat once myself, boss … winter 1956. Not much meat an' tough like rope. I never eat cat again, that's for sure. Sementos! But the head hurt!

WATSON: One more word, Indian … just one more word an' I'm gonna clean house on you! … You wanna try me? Come on!

For a moment the INDIAN teeters between two worlds, then with a violent motion he sweeps up the hammer and begins pounding the post, mechanically with an incredible rhythm of defeat. WATSON watches for a while, his anger gone now. Scratches himself nervously, then makes a rapid exit offstage left.

Almost immediately the hammering begins to slow, ending with one stroke when the hammer head rests on the post, and INDIAN'S head droops on his outstretched arms.

INDIAN: Scared talk … world is full of scared talk. I show scare an' I get a job from Mister Watson. Scared Indian is a live Indian. My head don't get Alphonse free … but hands do.

Sound of motor car approaching. INDIAN lifts his head and peers to stage right.

INDIAN: Hullo … I am big man today! First Mister Watson an' now car come to see me. Boy, he drive! … If I not get out of his way he gonna hit me, sure as hell!

Jumps down from box and watches. Car squeals to stop offstage. Puff of dust blows in from wings. Car door slams and AGENT enters.

AGENT: Hi there, fella, how's it going?

INDIAN: Hello, misha. Everything is going one hunder fifty percent! Yessiree … one hunder fifty percent!

INDIAN rises on box and lifts hammer to drive post.

AGENT: There was talk in town your camp burned out last night … everything okay? Nobody hurt?

INDIAN: Sure, everything okay. You want complaints?

AGENT: Well, I … what do you mean, do I want complaints?

INDIAN: I just say if you want complaints, I give you lots. My tent, she is burn down last night. My partners … they run away. Leave me to do big job myself. I got no money … an' boss, he's got my Alphonse ready to shoot if I try to run. You want more complaints? (*drives down hard on hammer and groans*) Maybe you want know how my head she hurts inside?

AGENT: (*relieved*) Hey—c'mere. I'll give you a smoke to make you feel better. You're in rough shape, boy! Which would you prefer—pipe tobacco, or a cigarette? I've got both …

INDIAN drops hammer and comes down from box.

INDIAN: The way I feel, misha, I could smoke old stocking full of straw. Gimme cigarette. (*examines the cigarette AGENT gives him*) Oh, you make lotsa money from government, boss … tobacco here … and cotton there—some cigarette! Which end you light? (*laughs*)

AGENT: Light whichever end you want. You can eat it for all I care. That's some hat you got there, sport. Where'd you get it?

INDIAN: (*accepting light AGENT offers him*) Win at poker, misha.

AGENT: (*examining him closely*) Aren't those boots tight? I suppose you stole them!

INDIAN: No, boss—poker.

AGENT: And that shirt—will you look at that! Have shirt, will travel.

INDIAN: I steal that from my brother, when he is sick and dying. He never catch me!

AGENT: (*laughing*) That's good … I must tell the boys about you—what's your name?

INDIAN: You think is funny me steal shirt from my brother when he die? … You think that funny, bossman? I think you lousy bastard! … You think that funny, too?

AGENT: (*startled*) Now hold on—did I hear you say …

INDIAN: You hear good what I say.

The AGENT takes out his notebook.

AGENT: Just give me your name, and we'll settle with you later.

INDIAN: Turn around an' walk to road. If you want to see stealer in action, I steal wheels off your car. You try catch me …

AGENT: (*angrily*) Give me your name!

INDIAN: Mebbe I forget … mebbe I got no name at all.

AGENT: Look here, boy … don't give me any back-talk, or I might have to turn in a report on you, and next time Indian benefits are given out, yours might be hard to claim!

INDIAN: So—you got no name for me. How you gonna report me when you not know who I am? You want name? All right, I give you name. Write down—Joe Bush!

AGENT: I haven't got all day, fella. Are you, or are you not going to tell me your name?

INDIAN: No! I never tell you, misha! Whole world is scare. It make you scare you should know too much about me!

AGENT: (*slamming notebook shut*) That does it! You asked for it … an' by God, if I have to go after you myself, I'm gonna find out who you are!

INDIAN: Don't get mad, misha. I sorry for what I say. I got such hurting head, I don't know what I say …

AGENT: Been drinking again, eh? … What was it this time—homebrew? Or shaving lotion?

INDIAN: Maybe homebrew, maybe coffee. I don't know. Why you ask?

AGENT: You're no kid. You know as well as I do. Besides, bad liquor's going to kill you sooner than anything else.

INDIAN: (*excitedly*) Misha … you believe that? You really mean what you say?

AGENT: What—about bad liquor? Sure I do …

INDIAN: Then misha, please get me bottle of good, clean Canadian whiskey! I never drink clean whiskey in my life!

AGENT: Come on, now … you're as …

INDIAN: I give you twenty dollars for bottle! Is deal?

AGENT: Stop it! … Boy, you've got a lot more than a hangover wrong in your head!

INDIAN: (*points offstage*) That car yours?

AGENT: Yes.

INDIAN: How come all that writing on door—that's not your name? Why you not tell truth?

AGENT: Well, I work for the government, and they provide us …

INDIAN: Thirty dollars?

AGENT: Look here …

INDIAN: How come you not in big city, with office job? How come you drive around an' talk to dirty, stupid Indian? You not have much school, or mebbe something else wrong with you to have such bad job.

AGENT: Shut your lousy mouth, you …

INDIAN: Thirty-five dollars? No more! … I give you no more!

AGENT: Will you shut up?

INDIAN: (*defiantly*) No! I never shut up! You not man at all—you cheap woman who love for money! Your mother was woman pig, an' your father man dog!

AGENT: (*becoming frightened*) What … what are you saying?

INDIAN comes face to face with AGENT.

INDIAN: You wanna hit me? Come on … hit me! You kill me easy, an' they arrest you—same people who give you car. Hit me—even little bit—come on! You coward! Just hit me like this! (*slaps his palms together*) … Just like that—come on! You know what I do when you hit me?

AGENT: (*looks apprehensively around himself*) What?

INDIAN: I report you for beating Indian an' you lose job. Come on—show me you are man!

He dances provocatively around AGENT. AGENT turns in direction of his car.

AGENT: I'm getting out of here—you're crazy!

INDIAN: (*jumps in front of AGENT*) No … you not go anywhere! Maybe nobody here to see what happen, but after accident, lots of people come from everywhere. I'm gonna jump on car bumper, and when you drive, I fall off an' you drive over me. How you gonna explain that, bossman?

AGENT: (*frightened now*) I got nothing against you, boy! What's the matter with you? … What do you want with me?

INDIAN: I want nothing from you—jus' to talk to me—to know who I am. Once you go into car, I am outside again. I tell you about my brother, an' how he die …

AGENT: Go back to your work and I'll go back to mine. I don't want to hear about your brother or anyone else. (*INDIAN walks offstage to car*) Now you get off my car!

INDIAN: (*offstage*) You gonna listen, misha. You gonna listen like I tell you. (*sounds of car being bounced*) Boy, you ride like in bed! Misha, who am I?

INDIAN returns to stage.

AGENT: How in the devil do I know who you are, or what you want with me. I'm just doing a job—heard your camp got burned out and …

INDIAN: How you know who any of us are? How many of us got birth certificates to give us name an' age on reserve? … Mebbe you think I get passport an' go to France. Or marry the way bossman get married. You think that, misha?

AGENT: I don't care who you are or what you think. Just get back to your job and leave me alone …

INDIAN glances admiringly offstage to car.

INDIAN: Boy, is like pillow on wheels! If I ever have car like that, I never walk again!

AGENT: Get out of my way! I've got to get back into town.

INDIAN: No hurry. Mebbe you never go back at all.

AGENT: What ... do you mean by that?

INDIAN turns and approaches AGENT until they stand face to face.

INDIAN: You know what is like to kill someone—not with hate—not with any feelings here at all? (*places hand over heart*)

AGENT: (*stepping back*) This is ridiculous! Look, boy ... I'll give you anything I can—just get out of my hair. That whiskey you want—I'll get it for you ... won't cost you a cent, I promise!

INDIAN: Someone that mebbe you loved? Misha—I want to tell you somethin' ...

AGENT: No!

INDIAN catches hold of AGENT'S shirt front.

INDIAN: Listen—damn you! I kill like that once! You never know at Indian office—nobody tell you! Nobody ever tell you! ... I got to tell you about my brother ... he die three, four, maybe five years ago. My friend been collecting treaty payments on his name. He know how many years ago now ...

AGENT: You couldn't ...

INDIAN: I couldn't, misha?

AGENT: There are laws in this country—nobody escapes the law!

INDIAN: What law?

AGENT: The laws of the country!

INDIAN: (*threatening*) What law?

AGENT: No man ... shall kill ... another ...

INDIAN: I tell you about my brother. I tell you everything. Then you tell me if there is law for all men.

AGENT: Leave me alone! I don't want to hear about your brother!

INDIAN: (*fiercely*) You gonna listen! Look around—what you see? Field and dust ... an' some work I do. You an' me ... you fat, me hungry. I got nothin' ... and you got money, car.

Maybe you are better man than I. But I am not afraid, an' I can move faster. What happen if I get mad, an' take hammer to you?

AGENT: You ... wouldn't ...

INDIAN: You wrong, misha. Nobody see us. Mebbe you lucky—get away. But who believe you? You tell one story, I tell another. I lose nothing—but you gonna listen about my brother, that's for sure!

AGENT: (*desperately*) Look boy—let's be sensible—let's behave like two grown men. I'll drive you into town—buy you a big dinner! Then we'll go and buy that whiskey I promised. You can go then—find your friends and have another party tonight ... Nobody will care, and you'll have a good time!

INDIAN: (*spitting*) You lousy dog!

AGENT: Now don't get excited! ... I'm only saying what I think is best. If you don't want to come, that's fine. Just let me go and we'll forget all about today, and that we ever even seen one another, okay?

INDIAN releases the AGENT.

INDIAN: You think I forget I see you? I got you here like picture in my head. I try to forget you ... like I try to forget my brother, but you never leave me alone ... Misha, I never forget you!

AGENT: (*struggling to compose himself*) I'm just a simple joe doing my job, boy—remember that. I know there's a lot bothers you. Same's a lot bothers me. We've all got problems ... but take them where they belong.

AGENT pulls out cigarettes and nervously lights one for himself.

INDIAN: Gimme that!

AGENT: This is mine—I lit it for myself! Here, I'll give you another one!

INDIAN: I want that one!

AGENT: No, damn it ... have a new one!

INDIAN jumps behind AGENT and catches him with arm around throat. With other hand he reaches out and takes lit cigarette out of AGENT'S mouth. Throws AGENT to the field. The AGENT stumbles to his knees, rubbing his eyes.

AGENT: What's wrong with you? Why did you do that?

INDIAN: Now you know what is like to be me. Get up! Or I kick your brains in!

AGENT rises to his feet and sways uncertainly.

AGENT: Dear God ...

INDIAN: My brother was hungry ... an' he get job on farm of white bossman to dig a well. Pay she is one dollar for every five feet down. My brother dig twenty feet—two day hard work. He call up to bossman—give me planks, for the blue clay she is getting wet! To hell with what you see—bossman shout down the hole—just dig! Pretty soon, the clay shift, an' my brother is trapped to the shoulders. He yell—pull me out! I can't move, an' the air, she is squeezed out of me! But bossman on top—he is scared to go down in hole. He leave to go to next farm, an' after that another farm, until he find another Indian to send down hole. An' all the time from down there, my brother yell at the sky. Jesus Christ—help me! White man leave me here to die! But Jesus Christ not hear my brother, an' the water she rise to his lips. Pretty soon, he put his head back until his hair an' ears in slimy blue clay an' water. He no more hear himself shout—but he shout all the same!

AGENT: I wasn't there! I couldn't help him!

INDIAN: ... He see stars in the sky—lots of stars. A man see stars even in day when he look up from hole in earth ...

AGENT: I couldn't help him—I don't want to hear about him!

INDIAN: ... Then Sam Cardinal come. Sam is a coward. But when he see my brother there in well, an' the blue clay movin' around him like livin' thing, he go down. Sam dig with his hands until he get rope around my brother. Then he come up, an' he an' white bossman pull. My brother no longer remember, an' he not hear the angry crack of mud an' water when they pull him free ...

AGENT: (*with relief*) Then ... he lived? Thank God ...

INDIAN: Sure ... sure ... he live. You hunt?

AGENT: Hunt? ... You mean—shooting?

INDIAN: Yeh.

AGENT: Sure. I go out every year.

INDIAN: You ever shoot deer—not enough to kill, but enough to break one leg forever? Or maybe hit deer in eye, an' it run away, blind on one side for wolf to kill?

AGENT: I nicked a moose two years back—never did track it down. But I didn't shoot it in the eye.

INDIAN: How you know for sure?

AGENT: Well ... I just didn't. I never shoot that way!

INDIAN: You only shoot—where bullet hit you not know. Then what you do?

AGENT: I tried to track it, but there had been only a light snow ... an' I lost the tracks.

INDIAN: So you not follow?

AGENT: No. I walked back to camp ... My friend an' I had supper and we drove home that night ...

INDIAN: Forget all about moose you hurt?

AGENT: No. I did worry about what happened to him!

INDIAN: You dream about him that night? ... Runnin', bawling with pain?

AGENT: What the hell ... dream about a moose? There's more important things to worry about, I'm telling you.

INDIAN: Then you not worry at all. You forget as soon as you can. Moose not run away from you—you run away from moose!

AGENT: I didn't ... hey, you're crazy! (*moves towards car offstage, but INDIAN jumps forward and stops him*) Here! You leave me alone, I'm telling you ... You got a lot of wild talk in your head, but you can't push your weight around with me ... I'm getting out of here ... Hey!

INDIAN catches him by arm and rolls him to fall face down in the dust. INDIAN pounces on him.

INDIAN: What you call man who has lost his soul?

AGENT: I don't know. Let go of me!

INDIAN: We have a name for man like that! You know the name?

AGENT: No, I don't. *You're breaking my arm*!

INDIAN: We call man like that sementos. Remember that name ... for *you* are *sementos*!

AGENT: Please, fella—leave me alone! I never hurt you that I know of ...

INDIAN: Sure ...

Releases AGENT, who rises to his feet, dusty and dishevelled.

AGENT: I want to tell you something ... I want you to get this straight, because every man has to make up his mind about some things, and I've made mine up now! This has gone far enough. If this is a joke, then you've had your laughs. One way or another, I'm going to get away from you. And when I do, I'm turning you in to the police. You belong in jail!

INDIAN: (*laughs*) Mebbe you are man. We been in jail a long time now, sementos ...

AGENT: And stop calling me that name!

INDIAN: Okay, okay ... I call you bossman. You know what bossman mean to me?

AGENT: I don't want to know.

INDIAN: (*laughs again*) You wise ... you get it. I not got much to say, then you go.

AGENT: (*bewildered*) You ... you're not going to ... bother me anymore?

INDIAN: I finish my story, an' you go ... go to town, go to hell ... go anyplace. My brother—you know what kind of life he had? He was not dead, an' he was not alive.

AGENT: You said he came out of the well safely. What are you talking about?

INDIAN: No ... He was not alive. He was too near dead to live. White bossman get rid of him quick. Here, says bossman—here is three dollars pay. I dig twenty feet—I make four dollars, my brother says. Bossman laugh. I take dollar for shovel you leave in the hole, he says. My brother come back to reserve, but he not go home. He live in my tent. At night, he wake up shouting, an' in day-time, he is like man who has no mind. He walk 'round, an' many times get lost in the bush, an' other Indian find him an' bring him back. He get very sick. For one month he lie in bed. Then he

try to get up. But his legs an' arms are dried to the bone, like branches of dying tree.

AGENT: He must've had polio.

INDIAN: Is not matter ... One night, he say to me: go to other side of lake tomorrow, an' take my wife an' my son, Alphonse. Take good care of them. I won't live the night ... I reach out and touch him, for he talk like devil fire was on him. But his head and cheek is cold. You will live an' take care of your wife an' Alphonse yourself, I say to him. But my brother shake his head. He look at me and say—help me to die ...

AGENT: Why ... didn't you ... take him to hospital?

INDIAN: (*laughs bitterly*) Hospital! A dollar he took from dying man for the shovel buried in blue clay ... hospital? Burn in hell!

AGENT: No ... no! This I don't understand at all ...

INDIAN: I ... kill ... my ... brother! In my arms I hold him. He was so light, like small boy. I hold him ... rock 'im back and forward like this ... like mother rock us when we tiny kids. I rock 'im an' I cry ... I get my hands tight on his neck, an' I squeeze an' I squeeze. I know he dead, and I still squeeze an' cry, for everything is gone, and I am old man now ... only hunger an' hurt left now ...

AGENT: My God!

INDIAN: I take off his shirt an' pants—I steal everything I can wear. Then I dig under tent, where ground is soft, and I bury my brother. After that, I go to other side of lake. When I tell my brother's wife what I done, she not say anything for long time. Then she look at me with eyes that never make tears again. Take Alphonse, she say ... I go to live with every man who have me, to forget him. Then she leave her shack, an' I alone with Alphonse ... I take Alphonse an' I come back. All Indians know what happen, but nobody say anything. Not to me ... not to you. Some half-breed born outside reservation take my brother's name—and you, bossman, not know ...

AGENT: (*quietly, as though he were the authority again*) We *have* to know, you understand, don't you? You'll have to tell me your brother's name.

INDIAN: I know ... I tell you. Was Tommy Stone.

AGENT takes out his notebook again and writes.

AGENT: Stone—Tommy Stone ... good. You know what I have to do, you understand it's my duty, don't you? It's my job ... it's the way I feel. We all have to live within the law and uphold it. Ours is a civilized country ... you understand, don't you? (*turns to car offstage*) I'm going now. Don't try to run before the police come. The circumstances were extenuating, and it may not go hard for you ...

INDIAN makes no attempt to hinder AGENT who walks offstage.

INDIAN: Sure, misha ... you're right. (*hears car door open*) Wait! Misha, wait! I tell you wrong. Name is not Tommy Stone—Tommy Stone is me! Name is *Johnny* Stone!

AGENT returns, notebook in hand.

AGENT: Johnny Stone? Let's get this straight now ... your brother was Johnny Stone ... and you're *Tommy* Stone? (*INDIAN nods vigorously*) Okay, boy. I've got that. Now remember what I said, and just stay here and wait. (*turns to leave*)

INDIAN: No, misha ... you got whole business screwed up again! I am Johnny Stone, my brother, he is Tommy Stone.

AGENT pockets his notebook and turns angrily to face INDIAN.

AGENT: Look, Indian—what in hell is your name anyhow? Who are you?

INDIAN: My name? You want my name?

Suddenly catches AGENT by arm and swings him around as in a boyish game. Places AGENT down on the box he used for standing on to drive posts.

AGENT: Hey, you stop that!

INDIAN: An' yet you want my name?

AGENT: Yes, that's right ... If it's not too much trouble to give me one straight answer, what is your name?

INDIAN: Sam Cardinal is my name!

AGENT rises with disgust and straightens out his clothes.

AGENT: Now it's Sam Cardinal ... what do you take me for anyway? You waste my time ... you rough me up like I was one of your drunken Indian friends ... and now I can't get an answer to a simple question ... But what the hell—the police can find out who you are and what you've done.

INDIAN: No, sementos! You never find out!

INDIAN throws legs apart and takes the stance of a man balancing on a threshold.

INDIAN: You go to reservation with hunder policemen—you try to find Johnny Stone ... you try to find Tommy Stone ... Sam Cardinal, too. Mebbe you find everybody, mebbe you find nobody. All Indians same—nobody. Listen to me, sementos—one brother is dead—who? Tommy Stone? Johnny Stone? Joe Bush! Look—(*turns out both pockets of his pants, holding them out, showing them empty and ragged*) I got nothing ... nothing ... no wallet, no money, no name. I got no past ... no future ... nothing, sementos! I nobody. I not even live in this world ... I dead! You get it? ... I dead! (*shrugs in one great gesture of grief*) I never been anybody. *I not just dead ... I never live at all.* What is matter? ... What anything matter, sementos?

AGENT has the look of a medieval peasant meeting a leper—fear, pity, hatred.

INDIAN: What matter if I choke you till you like rag in my hands? ... Hit you mebbe with twenty-pound hammer—break in your head like watermelon ... Leave you dry in wind an' feed ants ... What matter if police come an' take me? Misha! Listen, damn you—listen! One brother kill another brother—why? (*shakes AGENT furiously by the lapels*) Why? Why? ... Why?

AGENT: (*clawing at INDIAN'S hands*) Let me go! LET ... ME ... GO!

AGENT breaks free and runs offstage for car. Sounds of motor starting and fast departure. Dust. INDIAN stands trembling with fury.

INDIAN: Where you go in such goddamn speed? World too small to run 'way? You hear me, sementos! Hi ... *sementos!* Ugh!

Spits and picks up hammer. Starts to drive post vigorously.

End

NOTHING BUT A MAN

While the biggest event for George Ryga in 1967, Canada's centennial year, was the première performance in November of his best known play, *The Ecstasy of Rita Joe*, at the Playhouse Theatre in Vancouver, earlier that same year another of his plays had premiered in Edmonton, where, on opening day, Ryga was headlined by the *Edmonton Journal* (8 March 1967) as a "Bright Patriot of Canadian Literature."

Nothing but a Man is an adaptation of a teleplay originally written in 1965 and broadcast under the title *Man Alive* on CBC's Festival anthology series in March 1966. The tale of Duke Radomsky had long pre-occupied Ryga. It was originally intended to be the first of a trilogy of plays celebrating Canada's centenary. Then, three years after writing the stage version, he altered the plot somewhat and wrote it as a novel, titled *Man Alive*, which remains unpublished.

In this play Ryga once again thematically links a series of previously drafted short stories, novels, and scripts he had been working on about ordinary people desperately struggling on the land, frequently people from broken families and thus broken lines of ownership, identity, and place. Typically, as in *Indian* and *The Ecstasy of Rita Joe*, an absent patriarch and estranged children partly reflect Ryga's period as a writer in Edmonton in the early 1960s when, newly partnered with Norma and their two adoptive daughters, he held a variety of labouring jobs, lived on the edge of poverty, and was estranged from his own family.

In 1963 he moved with his new family—soon enlarged by two sons—to Summerland, British Columbia, to a warmer, more attractive environment overlooking Lake Okanagan, where he established a long-standing home, indeed a family centre. For Ryga, already in this second play, his stories of estrangement from the land began to take a different direction: the patriarch now more energetically examines his roots and renegotiates his outdated social relationships. This figure of the patriarch also, in *Nothing but a Man*, begins to take on mythic proportions. Duke Radomsky has laboured across the country as a miner, logger, track section gang, and farm hand, making him representative of a working-class Canadian "everyman"—indeed, his name reflects the broad ethnic mix of the Canadian immigrant who "did the footwork of this country." His is figured mythically as the "iron man" who once swam Lake Ontario on his back smoking a cigarette and challenging God: "You leave us alone too much—don't be so damned sure of us, eh?"

Radomsky, not unlike Ibsen's *Peer Gynt* (a comparison Ryga himself has made), is a complex figure intended to initiate the construction of an elusive national character. He asks brashly, "What are we—pigs in a pen? Or wild hawks in the sky?" Restless, confrontational, always on the move, he is a dispossessed colonial exile yearning for identity. Motherless ("She died the hour I was born") and therefore physically separated from his forbearers' heritage, he seems to find a wife and they have a son, although his connection with them remains elusive. His role, somewhat like that of the "ordinary person" in *Just an Ordinary Person*, is to act as a touchstone, a provocateur, in depicting the long procession of workers who physically built the country and have begun to give it an "unofficial" character. The structuring dramaturgy is extremely liquid: symbolically born of the earth, emerging, literally, from a hole in the ground, Duke moves rapidly across the vast Canadian space and fifteen years of time in a quest to create his own identity, and thereby the country's, which, in an emergent post-colonial situation like Canada's, is necessarily, *sui generis*.

For Ryga, *Nothing but a Man* was an experiment, a search for form, and he believed he found it in what he termed telepathic drama, a kind of foreshortened writing in which, by means of short overlapping scenes and abbreviated dialogue, he could powerfully evoke subliminal memory and produce intense recognitions of both identity and difference in the audience. Elements of the play are close to the playwright's own experience: the character Radomsky is partly based on Mike Yartus, a larger-than-life neighbour of the Rygas in northern Alberta in the 1930s, a former member of the Imperial Guard for the Czar, then, during the Russian Revolution, a Bolshevik, who enthralled the young Ryga with extravagant tales of his part in grand events, first in Russia and later in Canada.

The creation of *Nothing but a Man* was initiated at the request of the Edmonton Theatre Associates. Under the direction of Marjorie Knowler, it opened on March 8, 1967, at the Walterdale Playhouse in Edmonton, featuring John Rivet in the lead role. It was well received by the local critics, Barry Westgate, of the *Edmonton Journal*, concluding "for things said, and even things unsaid, this is an interesting particle of Canadiana and Mrs. Knowler has a worthy production of it."

NOTHING BUT A MAN

CHARACTERS

DUKE RADOMSKY
JONATHAN
DRUMMER *and* MARCHERS
BUILDER
ANN
DRUNKARD
HENNY
BARTENDER
POTATO FARMER *and* HIS WIFE
HERMAN, *the logger*
TWO BUMS
POLICEMAN
STREET WALKER
FANATIC
INDIAN
TOBACCO FARMER, HIS SON, HIS WIFE
BERT, *the hired hand*
JUDGE
BOY

A few extras for group scenes, although many of the characters could dovetail roles and participate as crowds.

SET

Rather than formalize stage settings, I have only provided symbolic suggestions as to what each scene of the play requires. A producer and stage designer should be free to develop the most imaginative settings, bounded only by the facilities available in staging this production.

With this desire not to impose any restrictions on sets and staging, I have outlined the most elementary use of lights and scene transitions. The possibilities past this point are infinite.

I have also avoided giving a specific age to Duke for this reason. Some fifteen years pass between the opening and closing scenes. This is the only relative factor in the play.　　　　—George Ryga

ACT 1

Curtain up on dirt being thrown up out of hole on the stage. DUKE emerges, tossing out a shovel before him. He is soiled, moist, grinning.

DUKE: *(to audience)* Hullo! *(indicates hole)* After I left Toronto, or Montreal, or whatever the hell place I was at last, I came here. Some farmer ... hired me to dig a well for him ... *(looks away for a long moment as if scanning a distant horizon)* No! A mining company is starting a mine here, and this is the beginning. Or—am I digging because I had a dream last night? *(laughs)* Duke is the name—Duke, as in brother to the King! That goes well with the Empire Loyalists. *(ponders)* But the last name is Radomsky. Which wasn't always a name up here in Canada. It was a kind of badge a man won long ago, to dig holes and bash down steel with—a sort of passkey to these jobs—long ago. *(mocking)* But that was long ago! In days such as these, there are cabinet ministers with French, Ukrainian, even Chinese names. Which goes to show that walking for one hundred years even like this ... *(shuffles his feet)* ... one can come a long way! So what, you say? So nothing! I grow older every hour now. You do, too, friend! We have much in common, you and I—descendants of the hard-rock men—pick-axe swingers and the stubble-hoppers of the plains. We have much in common.

Last night, I slept on the open prairie, my arms and legs like this *(stretches his body into an X)* ... reaching over all the grass that I could touch. Thinking, if I should die in sleep, that would be my last laugh—having an undertaker sweat to bend me back into a final, humble shape for his coffin! *(laughs, then soberly)* Our jokes have ice in them—I don't want to die. I wish you long life with few tears, friend—and being a great democrat, the same for me!

Blackout and lights up on a new stage area symbolic of a street in a small city. Sounds of traffic offstage, a muffled argument in the distance. DUKE comes onto the stage, looks around himself.

DUKE: It was a street like this one—with houses such as these. Between the street and fences, I picked wild strawberries on the way to school. People, at Christmas, gave raisin bread and honey for the Holy Child. My mother? Father? Who knows? Did I bury them once among the others? Who am I? Some part of men long gone—nothing but a man ... or in my own right, a man alive? (*shouts to house offstage*) Is there anyone here who knows me?

VOICE: (*offstage*) Go away! We're having supper!

ANOTHER VOICE: (*offstage*) Stay away, Duke! Billy's got the measles!

CHILDREN SINGING: (*offstage*) ... with glowing hearts, we see thee rise, our true north strong and free. And stand on guard, O Canada, we stand on guard for thee ...

CHILD'S VOICE: (*offstage*) Where's your father from?

DUKE: I went to school from this street. (*MAN crosses in front of him. DUKE stops him*) Are you my father?

MAN: (*chuckling lewdly*) Well now, if you was to say who your mother was, I might be able to ... come on, buy you a beer!

DUKE: Forget it! (*waves MAN on. WOMAN appears, sees DUKE, stops*)

WOMAN: You're the same as ... hey! What's the Polish word for "pasture," do you know yet?

DUKE: I don't know. I've forgotten already.

Another woman approaches.

ANOTHER WOMAN: (*crisply, in the manner of a teacher*) Say to me in French, "The sky is blue today."

DUKE: I can't!

MAN'S VOICE: (*offstage, angry*) Where the hell's my wife?

Sound of a baby crying.

WOMAN: Duke—what gives with you? Do you want to be a leader?

DUKE: No.

WOMAN: Then you'd like to follow?

DUKE: No!

A MAN: (*appearing from wings, sleeves rolled up as if from work*) Then you don't fit nowhere!

DUKE: To those I like, I tell the truth. (*OLD MAN shuffles up to him and DUKE backs away to rise on a step above the group*) To the others, I say nothing.

OLD MAN: You'll have to speak up, young fella! My hearing's not what it used to be!

The sound of drums and cymbals. The group turns to what sounds like a small parade approaching.

DUKE: (*loudly, over the gathering noise*) I tell the truth, or I say nothing!

DRUMMER and small entourage march onstage, and stop abruptly before DUKE. They are dressed in rag-tag uniforms of various wars and nations.

DRUMMER: (*speaks to DUKE*) Here's another one. Well, laddie, what have you to say for yourself? (*DUKE stares down at him sullenly*) Nothing, eh? Ever seen military service in defense of country and God? (*DUKE stares at him*) Well, have you or haven't you?

DUKE: No.

DRUMMER: Well, what're you waiting for? We've done our bit, now it's your turn!

DUKE: (*softly*) Who ... are we at war with now?

DRUMMER: (*laughs, turns to his companions and to the small group*) Did you hear that? "Who are we at war with now?" (*to DUKE*) Nobody, you bastard! But we've got to be READY! What sort of question is that? We know there'll always be wars—right, men?

CHORUS BEHIND HIM: Right!

DRUMMER: So what's the argument? No argument at all! (*to DUKE*) You'll look good in a uniform!

DRUMMER strikes his drum hard. The tag of men behind him jump to attention.

DRUMMER: (*severely, as a judge at some great tribunal*) Do you believe—in a Greater Power?

Cut lights to black.

DUKE: (*in darkness*) YES!

Lights up on another area of the stage. DUKE staggers onstage with JONATHAN on his back. The stage setting is symbolic of a swamp.

DUKE: (*more softly, to JONATHAN*) Pray, Jonathan, like you've never prayed before, or we will never see the end of this!

DUKE stumbles and falls, recovers his footing, and rises slowly.

JONATHAN: "Holy Mary, Mother of God, pray for us sinners ... P ... " I don't remember the rest of it, Duke!

DUKE: Louder! God can't hear a mumbler! There's too much wind—louder, Jonathan!

JONATHAN: I don't remember the words—Duke, help me!

DUKE: What words?

JONATHAN: The prayer! I was a kid when I learned them, and now ...

DUKE: Give it to Him straight, Jonathan, exactly the way it is with us tonight! Say your leg's broken, and Duke here has carried you over a hundred miles of muskeg and has just about had it himself! Say if He doesn't help us soon, we're going to die. Give it to Him, man to man!

JONATHAN: God! I was only doing my job—building a railroad to Port Churchill. A tie flipped and broke my ankle ... supply car didn't come ... don't let me die! I was only working!

DUKE: (*bellowing angrily upwards*) It's the truth, Lord! He was only working like he says—I was there! (*fade stage light and retain only spot on his face. JONATHAN slips off his shoulders in the darkness*) Don't let him die ... he's a good working man!

Fade light, then bring up low light back of stage to silhouette DUKE, alone and turned away from the audience.

DUKE: Died ... him and the others who gave me stars, burlap, and hickory in my hands. Take all your books with police barracks and gentleman-soldier histories, and make of them a stack on which to mount a museum cannon. Cities were built where real cows ate real grass, and there was ample water for a turnip garden. (*moves slowly to the wings*) From the beginning they and I were lost among our footsteps ... looking for light in the afternoon. Looking for our fathers ... looking for our sons.

Up blaring music and lights on another area of the stage where a dance is in progress. A few girls, but mostly men are dancing, some with each other. DUKE enters and begins dancing by himself. The BUILDER (FOREMAN) pushes his way through the dancers and motions to an unseen orchestra to stop playing. The music falters and stops, but the sounds of instruments being tuned come through.

BUILDER: (*his speech wheezy, slurred*) Hey, everybody! Men ... men! Gentlemen an' ladies ... can I have your attention, please?

DRUNKARD in the audience rises and moves forward to help the man quiet the dancers.

DRUNK: (*bellowing to men onstage*) Alright, you guys! Shut up! The boss got something important to say, an' he's gonna say it now! Say it, boss!

BUILDER: Thanks there, Joey! Well, I guess you all know we've got us the big civic block project, eh? Which means jobs this winter for all of you who's willing to stick around and work. But tonight, Mister Lawry wants me to say to you just you enjoy yourselves for doing such a good job on the Devlin Building. How's about a show of thanks to Mister Lawry for throwing this shindig for us?

DRUNK: Here, here!

He applauds loudly and looks around to the audience to help. One or two feeble handclaps from the group onstage.

BUILDER: (*a little upset*) I'll say one thing—if you guys put as much into your work as you do into a show of thanks, the company would be broke long ago. (*trickle of applause from dancers onstage. Laughter*) Just one other thing—four kegs of beer have just arrived downstairs, along with a guy in a white suit to serve it out nice, so anytime you're thirsty ...

A loud cheer and group stampede to exit in the wings.

On the sound of HENNY singing, lights up on another area of the stage. HENNY is standing on top of a table. Men around her stamp their feet and pound beer glasses on the table to keep time.

HENNY: (sings "Lolly-Too-Dum")
As I went out one morning, to take the pleasant air,
Lolly-too-dum, too-dum, lolly-too-dum-day.

As I went out one morning, to take the pleasant air,
I overheard a mother, scolding her daughter dear,
Lolly-too-dum, too-dum, lolly-too-dum-day.

Oh pity my condition, just as you would your own,
Lolly-too-dum, too-dum, lolly-too-dum-day.

Oh pity my condition, just as you would your own,
For fourteen long years, mom, I've lived all alone,
Lolly-too-dum, etc.

Supposing I were willing, where would you find
your man?
Lolly-too-dum, etc.

Supposing I were willing, where would you find
your man?
Lord have mercy, mother, I'd marry me handsome
Dan,
Lolly-too-dum, etc.

Supposing he should slight you, like you done
him before,
Lolly-too-dum, etc.

Supposing he should slight you, like you done
him before,
Lord have mercy, mother, I'd find me a dozen
more,
Lolly-too-dum, etc.

There's butchers and bakers, and boys from the
plough,
Lolly-too-dum, etc.

There's butchers and bakers, and boys from the
plough,
Lord have mercy, mother, I've got that feeling
now!
Lolly-too-dum, etc.

There's doctors and lawyers, and men of high
degree,
Lolly-too-dum, etc.

There's doctors and lawyers, and men of high
degree,
Some will want to get married, some will want to
marry me,
Lolly-too-dum, etc.

Now my daughter she is married, and well for to do,
Lolly-too-dum, etc.

Now my daughter she is married, and well for to do,
Gather round you bachelors, I'm on the market,
too!
Lolly-too-dum, too-dum, lolly-too-dum-day.

DUKE has enjoyed the song more than the others.
During the earlier verses, he wanders offstage.
Lights up on him seated beside a footpath, nodding
in time to HENNY'S singing, and then himself
beginning to sing.

He fades out. The sound of a car in the background
offstage. At the end of the song, light fades on
HENNY and the crowd of men. ANN hurries onstage
just as DUKE rises. She walks into him. She freezes
with surprise and fear. DUKE smiles and reaches
out to touch her face. She retreats.

DUKE: Duke's the name. Like brother to the
King!

ANN: I'm sorry ... I'm looking for my father. I
came to bring him home. He doesn't drive. I'm
Ann ...

DUKE: Ann—yes! Come with me. We'll find him.

In the background the laughter of men, and HENNY
begins singing again. The light fades on DUKE and
ANN, and up on HENNY, now sitting at a table.
Only two men remain in the area, with the BAR-
TENDER in the background.

HENNY: (sings)
A lobster boiling in the pot,
A blue fish on the hook,
They are suffering long, but it's nothing like
The ache I bear for you, my dear, Mary Ann;
The ache I bear for you, my dear, Mary Ann.

Oh, had I but a flask of gin
With sugar here for two,
And a great big bowl for to mix it in,
I'd pour a drink for you, my dear, Mary Ann;
I'd pour a drink for you, my dear, Mary Ann.

Over singing of the song, the following actions and
dialogue occur: DUKE and ANN come onstage.
DUKE holds her by the shoulder.

DUKE: Listen!

ANN: (hesitant, fearful of DUKE and the atmosphere in the room) But ... my father ...

DUKE: (smiling) Listen—listen!

Two MEN in the background begin arguing drunkenly.

FIRST MAN: Give 'er a beer and she starts singing like a sparrow.

SECOND MAN: You mean like a swallow? Sparrows don't sing!

FIRST MAN: How in hell do you know they don't? Besides, swallows are them little things that mess up barns, right, Dukie?

DUKE nods but remains with ANN.

SECOND MAN: Don't know where you came from to hear sparrows sing! Saskatchewan, or something. Boy, you should read a book sometimes …

FIRST MAN: Well, she's a cow anyhow—tell her to shut up all this singing. I've had enough of it for one party. Get 'er out of here!

SECOND MAN: She came with me! (*loudly*) You keep singin', Henny, honey!

BARTENDER: Break it up—break it up! If you want to argue, go outside. I'm closing.

DUKE: Keep singing, Henny! Damn, but nobody will live an hour less for a good song.

ANN: (*agitated*) I want to get out of here!

DUKE does not release her shoulder.

DUKE: It's good to wake and sing. Listen—hear every song!

ANN looks around the room as if for help. DUKE is aware of her distress and has great compassion for her.

DUKE: You sing, Ann. (*sudden and complete silence in the room. The others turn to look at her*) Can't you sing, Ann? Sad song, happy. Anything?

She is humiliated. The others laugh.

FIRST MAN: That bird ain't gonna sing nothin'.

HENNY: Sing? Her sing? She's too nice to make a big sound!

Big laugh from everyone except DUKE.

DUKE: (*pounds his fist hard on the table with fury*) Yes, she can sing! If these walls were covered with cloth, with pictures of mountains, horses and the sea. And if we had better things to do with our time than drink and argue when the sun goes down—we would listen! She would sing! The wild question has a timid answer. The grass cries out to the wind that pleads with it to sing, and sing … and sing!

While he is talking, the others file offstage. ANN remains, staring at DUKE. In the long silence after, he stares at her as at a stranger.

DUKE: (*wearily*) It's cold—man, but it's cold.

ANN remains silent, but continues to stare at him.

DUKE: So you're my Ann? (*she nods*) Are there stars in the sky, Ann?

She looks at him with a deep understanding of who he is, and what he means to her.

DUKE: The smell of summer—is it still with us?

ANN smiles timidly and shrugs.

DUKE: (*very gently*) Walk with me.

They go offstage together. Dim out lights and illuminate another area of the stage to represent a field or bank of a river. ANN is now carrying her coat in her hands as she follows DUKE onstage.

ANN: In April and October we all got raises at the office … I must go home.

DUKE: (*simply*) Where? There are only nights linked by highways. Walk faster!

ANN: (*moves at his command, then falters*) You can't order me.

DUKE: Yes, I can. I'm your husband.

ANN: (*faltering*) When … did we marry?

DUKE: Back there (*points*) beside the alder. Have you forgotten so soon, and yet you remember your office so well? Walk faster!

ANN: My father will wait and worry. And then he'll try walking home. He couldn't find the car.

DUKE: The car was sold seven years ago, soon after he died. Walk faster, woman!

ANN: (*now running, stumbling up to him*) No, Duke! Where are we going? What are we coming to?

DUKE: (*turns and embraces her*) Sing me the song I taught you! Once more before morning.

She whimpers and lowers her head.

DUKE: I taught you a song—sing it for me! Annie, a woman with imagination is made of gold. Do you understand?

ANN: I don't know how to sing. (*plaintively*) I thought I did before ... but it's gone.

DUKE: Try hard to remember, Ann. Our moments together ... try!

ANN: No. It's silly! Duke, listen! I wanted to be a teacher, but I couldn't go to another city. So I stayed home and learned to type, file, take short-hand dictation. Some girls had boyfriends. I didn't.

DUKE: Yes. You've told me all this many times now.

ANN: I read twenty-nine books one winter, and you never asked for the name of one book.

DUKE: Because you don't remember. Or do you remember now?

ANN: No, Duke.

DUKE: But when we were together, the grass spoke to you, and you wanted to make up a song to sing back to tell how you felt ...

ANN: No, Duke. No! I lied to you!

DUKE: (*releasing her*) Ho, God!

He turns and moves away. She follows and takes hold of him to stop.

ANN: Duke, where are we going now?

DUKE: (*with pain*) Somewhere to live ...

ANN: Which way is home?

DUKE: (*wearily, pointing*) That way! (*starts to turn in a circle, pointing in all directions, laughing wildly now, then sobbing*) That way! That way! That way! That way!

ANN stares at him, wide-eyed and unmoving.

ACT 2

Curtain rises on DUKE and ANN picking potatoes in a field. They have aged visibly and are both dressed in coarse work clothing. ANN is untidy. A short distance in front of them, an OLD MAN and his WIFE, owners of the potato farm, are also bent over, picking.

DUKE: (*to ANN*) Does your back still ache?

ANN: I can't feel it anymore.

DUKE: (*straightens and stares after the couple in front of them*) Look at them, Annie, bent over so long they wouldn't know any other way to move across this sweet earth.

ANN: How long before we get that way ...

DUKE: Never!

ANN: I believed you last year. More the year before.

DUKE: He's deaf as a tree.

DUKE cups his hands over his mouth and shouts to the MAN in front of him. MAN'S WIFE looks up and stares with no expression at DUKE as he shouts.

DUKE: (*shouting*) Hey! Mister Potato-Boss man! You hear me, sir? Your wife is dead! Your house fell down! There's a hole with no bottom where you're standing! There's a saddle on your back, and the devil's mounted and riding you hard! Mister! Those aren't potatoes you're picking—they're round stones! (*MAN'S WIFE hurriedly examines the potatoes in the bucket she is carrying and shakes her head at DUKE that it isn't so*) You've gone crazy—that's why your fields seem like heaven at last!

The WOMAN now takes a hoe in her hand and prods her husband with it. He turns and she points to DUKE, who faces them with a strange and terrible smile on his lips. ANN looks up at him and becomes startled.

ANN: (*in soft voice*) I do love you, Duke!

Light dims and comes up on a new stage area to symbolize a street of a town or city. DUKE comes onstage, storming. ANN hurries behind him, hand-bag in hand. DUKE stops and turns to her with exasperation.

DUKE: You're slow. The street is dead. Why the hell is it so?

ANN: When you're angry, I have to run to keep up.

DUKE: Who's angry? I'm not angry!

ANN: You are so!

DUKE: What do you know about angry? Four months out of work ... even these clothes are from wages off your library job. I didn't earn tonight's movie. A man has to earn life. Man has to earn death. Annie, I want to live forever! Look! (*holds up his hands*) Two passkeys to the land of new frontiers and old habits. You walk too slow on a cold night and the price of butter rose two cents a pound. Four BC mills shut down last week and men can train to weld for jobs that have too many welders ... Once again we cannot vote they registered before we came my employment book has three stamps short to claim benefits so I'm a bum I washed the breakfast dishes like you said but went without lunch again the top of my head hurts like death was a cap half-a-size too small ... a fourteen ounce can of peaches is better than two small tins on special men make fortunes with a price-punch while the bums who built the city eat toast of week-old bread why the hell is it so?

ANN: I ... don't know ...

DUKE: (*compassionately takes her in his arms and draws her to him*) It's not you, my dearest Annie. It's not you! (*looks up*) Look—clouds! What have they done with the rain? Gave the grass a drink, I think!

ANN: (*breathless, almost pleading with him now*) It could work out, Duke ...

DUKE: Do you think wild geese get heart disease?

ANN: I don't want you to go!

DUKE: Maybe hail up there—who knows ...

ANN: What do you want, Duke? Where have I failed?

DUKE: Not you—it's me. I haven't done anything for you. I don't think I ever could.

ANN: That's a lie! I am you, Duke! You are my life—my all! (*long pause*) I know you, Duke.

DUKE: (*torn, compulsive, moves away from her*) In the morning I'm following a threshing crew or a bulldozer down the highway. If I can't make it with my own feet, then nobody can help me. Not even God Himself can help me then!

ANN: I can, Duke! I will! (*terrible and desperate*) Don't go, Duke!

Lights dim. Uproar in another stage area and light up on bush workers crowded around the closed office of a lumber mill company.

LOGGER: A lockout, that's what it is! I know he's in there. He hasn't left the camp. I say smash the damned door down and have him explain!

HERMAN: I'll buy that! (*to DUKE, who hurries up to the group of men*) You going to speak for us, Duke?

HERMAN flexes his shoulders and prepares to rush the door.

DUKE: (*with resignation*) We'd be wasting our breath.

LOGGER: Hey, you're not chickening out now, are you, Duke?

DUKE: I don't want to talk to no company manager. He's a cow ... a stump ... an old shoe. Don't stand around waiting for him—you can't argue with a stump, and an old shoe won't answer. (*louder, as if to justify himself*) Let's go! We're on wheels, everyone of us. We've got to keep chasing the next job, and the big jackpot after that! To some it'll be a nice old age—to the others, death. You and I got to keep moving, friend, or the grass starts growing up between our toes, and we become gravestones over our souls!

ANOTHER LOGGER: To hell with that noise! I spent seventy dollars coming up here!

DUKE walks offstage.

HERMAN: So when you find a giant to kill, you tell me. I don't know nothin' from nothin'. I'm dumb. Watch!

HERMAN picks up a stone, spits on it deliberately, and heaves it at the office, smashing a window. The men cheer and HERMAN bends down to pick another stone.

Lights dim and out. Up on another stage area.
DUKE is sitting at a table full of beer. TWO BUMS sit
at the table with him. DUKE is singing.

DUKE: (*sings "Lots of Fish in Bonavist Harbour"—*
Edith Fowke collection)
Oh, Sally goes to church every Sunday,
Not for to sing, nor for to hear,
But to see the feller from Fortune,
What was down here fishing the year.

Oh, catch a-hold this one, catch a-hold that one.
Sing around this one, dance around she,
Catch a-hold this one, catch a-hold that one,
Diddle-dum this one, diddle-dum-dee.

FIRST BUM: (*touching DUKE'S arm*) Man alive,
this guy! Bet nobody pushes you around, hey,
boy?

DUKE: (*continues singing*)
Lots of fish in Bonavist Harbour,
Lots of fishing round about here.
Boys and girls are fishing together …

SECOND BUM: (*giggling*) I wouldn't tangle with
you no frosty Friday, that's for sure, Mac! Mind I
call you Mac? Call my friends that …

DUKE stops singing and stares blankly first at one
then at the other BUM. The SECOND BUM reaches
out and takes one of the numerous glasses on the
table. He drinks it down quickly, his eyes foxily on
DUKE. He reaches for another glass, but DUKE
pushes his hand away.

DUKE: Listen! I hear children! You hear any
children?

FIRST BUM: I hear bells in me head—you hear
bells in your head?

DUKE picks up a full glass of beer and coldly throws
it in the face of the FIRST BUM, who wipes himself
without anger or protest.

DUKE: You going to sit there and say nothing to
me for that, you bastard?

FIRST BUM: I've got nothing to tell you. Nothing
happened, friend.

DUKE: I threw beer in your face. I spat on you,
you scum! Get mad—tell me what you think for
doing it to you!

FIRST BUM: I never scrap with a guy bigger than
me.

SECOND BUM: He never does, that's for sure.

DUKE: (*to SECOND BUM*) And who are you? I
ever see you before?

SECOND BUM: I'm his friend. We're always
together, Eddy an' me.

DUKE: You ever work? Do anything for a living?

FIRST BUM: Oh yes—I took some pictures of him
(*nods to SECOND BUM, who covers his mouth to*
suppress a wicked giggle) … and sold them here.
He was younger then, an' a bit of a devil! (*both of*
them laugh like naughty children now)

SECOND BUM: And selling cabbage to
Chinatown—remember? (*both of them chortle*
over this) They … wouldn't buy our cabbage at
ten cents a pound, so we framed this guy with
drugs, an' another with illegal entry to Canada for
his wife, an' boy—they started buying our
cabbages …

FIRST BUM: At ten bucks a head!

DUKE roars with anger, but they are now delighted
with an audience and continue eagerly.

SECOND BUM: Which was chicken-feed after
what the railway did to the yellow-men in the
Rockies … we know all about that! (*both nod*
gravely)

FIRST BUM: (*casually pulling a glass of beer his*
way) I was married once. Ran out on her twenty
years ago last June.

DUKE: (*with sudden scowl*) Drink as fast as you
can and beat it!

SECOND BUM also grabs a beer and they drink
greedily. FIRST BUM gasps for breath.

FIRST BUM: I'm telling you she loved me so
much she took in washing at nights to keep me
going in the style I was used to. So I leave her.
But I've got my foot on her neck. She's still my
wife. If she goes before me, I get the house and
furniture. Some party that'll make, eh?

SECOND BUM: (*raising his glass*) To your wife
dying!

They both begin to drink. DUKE knocks the glass out
of SECOND BUM'S hand.

DUKE: (*wild with anger, but hazed by drink*) I've
seen you before—sure! I know you!

SECOND BUM: No, you don't.

DUKE: Yes, yes I do! You came begging to our door when I was a kid, and you've come begging to every door since. You were dressed better and you smelled of talcum—and you weren't begging for raw booze like now. You were begging on behalf of stray dogs, weak hearts, and the mentally sick. God! Was there ever a civilization so dependent for survival on beggary as this one?

FIRST BUM: Now you watch your language, boy! We've got our rights …

DUKE: To everything belonging to me! (*pulls off his cap and holds it out to the FIRST BUM*) Here! Take it and give it to … what do you call it now? Charity? Or hawk it for a dime and buy yourself a glass of this slop! (*pushes a glass of beer off the table*) Will you take it?

FIRST BUM: Sure, boy. If you're giving. Deduct it from your tax. The poor got to live, too …

DUKE: (*laughs bitterly*) And this is for you. (*removes his windbreaker jacket and hands it to the SECOND BUM*) Take it!

SECOND BUM *takes the coat, pauses to swallow the remains of the beer he holds, then hurries offstage, head bent low. The FIRST BUM remains, now silent and greedy, waiting to be repelled, or for any further contributions DUKE may have to make.*

DUKE: (*staring hard at FIRST BUM*) No shame at all anymore? (*BUM shakes his head*)

DUKE *digs into his pocket and brings out a dollar bill. He brandishes it in front of the BUM'S face, which lights up with greed.*

DUKE: Smell it. What's it smell like?

FIRST BUM: Heaven!

DUKE: (*sniffs it himself*) Transmission oil … hog's blood … barley chaff and copper! You want it?

FIRST BUM: Yes!

DUKE: Then earn it like a man, you damned weasel!

FIRST BUM *smiles obscenely. DUKE turns in his chair and, raising his foot, pushes over the FIRST BUM'S chair, knocking him over. BUM rises to his feet and, replacing the chair, sits down. DUKE lifts his foot and pushes him over again. The BUM moves his chair to the other side of the table and sits down again.*

DUKE: (*putting his head in his arms sadly on slow dimming of light on the scene*) Get Out!

Lights out to black. Music and lights up on new stage area. A table at which HERMAN sits. Back of the table, a small area where a few couples dance to the fast, repetitive strains of the quick Slavic dance, the Hopak. A buxom girl comes quickly onstage, and other dancers make room for her. She begins to dance by herself.

DUKE *enters, surveys the group, then stomping a rapid double-step, arms extended to the sides, moves to her. Other dancers cheer. Girl turns. Moves to DUKE. They lock arms and do a fast turn around the floor. Music falters and stops. The group cheers and applauds for more.*

DUKE: (*startled, shouts to musicians offstage or up at the ceiling of the auditorium*) Play!

MUSICIAN: (*offstage*) We're tired, Duke.

DUKE: You play and never mind the tired! See if you can earn this—play!

He whips out a twenty-dollar bill and drops it to the floor at his feet. The music starts up again.

DUKE: (*glances at the girl, himself now darkly elated. He shouts to the musicians as he begins to beat out a faster rhythm with his foot*) Faster! Faster, Godamnit! Come on—this is a good-time dance, not a funeral. Faster!

Music breaks into double-tempo. DUKE comes to life. Girl on his arm shrieks with delight. They spin around the floor again.

Passing HERMAN'S table, DUKE collides with it and falls to the front of the stage. The buxom girl comes to lean over him. DUKE stares at HERMAN, laughing powerfully as he stares. The girl fusses over him.

DUKE: (*studies HERMAN for a long while, still laughing provocatively*) God must paint some of us with a broom. Look at you! A broken down bum with hair growing out of your ears and hardly a tooth left in your mouth—and you're only what? Seventeen years of age?

HERMAN: Cut it out, Duke! (*looks around the group uneasily, as some are pushing nearer and grinning*)

DUKE: (*playing with the buxom girl's throat as she leans low over him stroking his head*) But women love us no matter how ugly or bad we get! That's the miracle of it. They'll make of themselves steps on a ladder that takes us to heaven. You step on them and wonder why they cry out like children. Some never look at you, for fear you may drain all the love from their eyes. We hurt them and we hurt them, then go begging to be forgiven, if we are men enough to beg. Even you, Herman ...

HERMAN flies into a rage. He rises and pushes the buxom girl roughly away. Then he stands half-crouched over DUKE, ready to attack.

HERMAN: I never beg! I'll take you, bull! ... I'll take you! Come on—get up!

DUKE laughs and rises to his feet. HERMAN starts at him, but DUKE reaches out quickly and grabs Herman by the hand.

DUKE: Hey, moose! Five bucks says I can twist you! I'll make that five to your one! How about it?

HERMAN is suspicious, but after a moment nods and sits down. DUKE sits opposite him and they lock wrists. HERMAN exerts all his strength to win. DUKE twists him down easily. The group drifts in closer to watch.

DUKE: Aha! The same five bucks says I can do it again, and you can use both your hands against my one if you like!

A slight laughter from the men and giggle of proud delight from the girl inflames HERMAN who locks both his hands together and half-rises. DUKE again twists him down with a triumphant grunt and roar of laughter. HERMAN frees himself. Laughter and jeers from the men, and HERMAN jumps back from the table.

DUKE: You did use both hands! I didn't think you were the kind of guy who would.

HERMAN: (*ashamed*) You asked me to. You said so yourself! (*turns to the people around the table*) Didn't he? You all heard him! (*digs into his pocket for money*) Here—you won this!

DUKE: For God's sake, I was only having you on, man.

HERMAN: (*flaring again*) Like hell you were! You said, "Use both your hands!" I'm not deaf!

VOICE FROM THE BACK: The guy's right—I heard Duke say it!

DUKE: I didn't think you'd ... but since you did, hey! (*now challenging and imitating all he hates*) I'll pay you fifty bucks to go kill that punk of a cook for me. Fifty bucks, Herman! (*laughs fiendishly*) I'll leave you the pickaxe outside my bunkhouse to do it with. Come at him from behind when he's not looking. That'll teach him to ride rough over the meek who only come to eat!

HERMAN: (*in final attempt at redeeming his self-respect, grabs DUKE by the shoulder*) You're going to apologize—I'm asking you to apologize right now, bull!

Without warning, DUKE swings and hits HERMAN, who falls. Outcries from the group. DUKE stands and faces about four men who push in from the background. He provokes them by kicking the table against them, then laughing.

FIRST MAN: Alright, Duke—so that's the way you want it ... to have the cops come and smash a nice party?

SECOND MAN: Get out, Duke, or you'll get carried out!

DUKE laughs.

FIRST MAN: We mean it, Duke. You better go!

He throws a chair at their feet and laughs. They attack. DUKE makes no serious attempt to defend himself. He pushes away one man who comes for his throat, but continues laughing even when he is struck over the head with a chair. The attack becomes more concerted and DUKE, still laughing, begins to fall to the floor, first bending at the knees and slipping down, then toppling forward. The group leaves the stage, the buxom girl last. DUKE twists and turns in agony.

DUKE: (*through gasps*) Why didn't you kill me? Why didn't you?

He continues to contort and moan as the lights dim. Even into darkness, the voices of memory in the following dialogue come in casually and strongly.

ANN: (*pleading*) In April and October we all got raises at the office. I must go home. When did we marry?

DUKE: (*voice over*) Back there, beside the alder. Have you forgotten so soon?

ANN: My father will wait and worry ...

DUKE: (*voice over*) The car was sold seven years ago, soon after he died ...

Lights are out on DUKE now lying on the stage. The following dialogue in darkness.

DUKE: (*shouting*) Your wife is dead! Your house fell down! There's a hole with no bottom where you're standing! There's a saddle on your back, and the devil's mounted and riding you hard, Mister!

ANN: Don't go. Don't go, Duke!

Light onstage. DUKE is sitting with his back to a rock. He has a beaten and bruised appearance from the previous scene. The FANATIC approaches, carrying a placard on a pole. The placard reads "ALL HOPE IS FADING."

DUKE: (*looking up at FANATIC*) That bad, eh, brother?

FANATIC: Yes. Terrible.

DUKE: Here? In this place? (*grins and points to the blank countryside beyond*) Land of hope and glory!

FANATIC: Asia is angry. Europe is failing her past ... Our crime rate is rising ... There is a loss of faith ... Men are losing their courage.

DUKE: (*puts his hand into his mouth and traces the outline of his teeth inside his cheeks*) That's not all we have lost, brother. (*removes a broken tooth and tosses it away*) That one won't grow or chew anymore. (*rises painfully. Stretches. Looks at FANATIC closely*) You're in great shape, sport— when did you eat last?

FANATIC: Who can eat?

DUKE: Food is hope ... (*looks up at placard FANATIC carries and shrugs*) ... Yeh ...

FANATIC: Follow and I'll lead you from pain.

DUKE: What's the hurry? Pain is pain, but a thousand mornings still to be born ...

FANATIC: You are a sinner?

DUKE begins staggering away, but the FANATIC grips him firmly by the arm and drags him to a stop.

FANATIC: How many sins can you stain your soul with and still go unpunished?

DUKE: (*smiling through an aching face*) A sin is round, like a ball, man! Roll it, and not even you can tell which side is up when it stops ... (*to excite the FANATIC*) I stole once, too, but that sin came to rest on its head!

FANATIC: (*going into his own trance*) We have to destroy—quickly!

FANATIC urges DUKE to come with him. DUKE lingers.

DUKE: (*laughing as he recalls*) I stole coal in Drumheller to keep my mother and me warm in our shack. (*becomes transported into another time, another place*) Yes! It's morning. In the few hours I was away, Spring has come. Birds sing and a dog barks ... morning ... over the hill.

FANATIC: No mornings—no afternoons. The truth is a gray light that never changes!

DUKE: I'm at our gate when the Mountie drives up. "Hey, punk!" he hollers. That's the way cops talked to kids in our part of town ... in Kenora, Smoky Lake, Prince George ... "Hey, punk! Where you taking all that coal?" I've got to think quick. Turn in at my gate and he knows I stole it. So I've got to give it to charity. (*to FANATIC, who is totally lost in his own trance*) This giving to charity is a big thing on the earth you've left. (*indicates with his arm to direction behind them*) A thief gives to the poor, and he becomes a pillar in his town. "It's for the widow Delaney," I says to the cop. He pats my head and lets me go. (*climbs to the pinnacle of the rock. Speaks up to God*) Come on down and give me a hand! There's things happening down here you wouldn't believe to see!

DUKE listens, as if expecting a reply to come. There is silence. He looks down at the placard of the FANATIC. The FANATIC is now horrified at DUKE'S directness. DUKE enjoys this and looks back to the sky.

DUKE: (*speaking upwards, but nodding in the direction of the FANATIC*) He did what you wanted—no food, only water! He did what you want—but he seems to be growing weaker. Don't always understand you! Oh yes, they still say I laugh too loud! You leave us alone too much—don't be so damned sure of us, eh! (*now humbly*) If you don't mind my saying so. (*DUKE jumps down from pinnacle*) Give me that!

The FANATIC hands him his placard. DUKE is staggered as he takes it.

DUKE: (*struggling to hold it up*) I didn't know ... it was this heavy. (*his surprise turns to worry*)

Lights down and out as they move across the stage. Up lights on another area, suggesting a crest of a high mountain. Both of them pause wearily here.

DUKE: My stomach isn't the only thing that's hollow ... I didn't sleep last night ... I always slept good after a fight before. Maybe tonight it'll be different ... When is tonight coming, brother? I'm so tired I can't see my feet.

FANATIC: Wait—just a bit longer and we'll be there!

DUKE: I can't wait! I must win or lose now ... today! Don't you understand?

FANATIC: You're not ready—a little longer yet.

DUKE: I'm cold, numb. If I have to lose a hand to reach God, I want to feel it go. Because if I don't, I won't be able to tell what happens to the heart in me when I cross from my side of the mountain into yours!

FANATIC: Time—only a bit longer.

DUKE: (*this anecdote becomes progressively funnier to DUKE as he tells it*) I worked with a guy once who had trouble with time. He had trouble waking up for work mornings. One day he bought an alarm clock in a junk shop. It was a hundred years old and big as a man's head. It rang for him at two o'clock the first night ... then at three-fifteen ... and at four-thirty ... it rang twice around five o'clock, and by then the man next to him threw it out the window. At seven, our guy was too tired from waking to get up and work. He slept through his breakfast.

The FANATIC has been staring at DUKE with wide-mouthed amazement. Now he laughs, but because he has seldom laughed before, the laughter comes out as a high whinny. The FANATIC covers his mouth in shame. DUKE hears the laughter and

turns to the FANATIC, a light beginning to glow in his face.

DUKE: So you didn't make it all the way! Hey! Let me lead for a while, brother!

FANATIC: No ... no! (*his hand over his mouth, but his shoulders quivering with suppressed laughter*)

DUKE: (*pushing against him with his foot*) Let it go ... man, it's music! You'll be a long time dead—let it go!

FANATIC: (*his suppressed laughter bordering on crying*) No!

DUKE: Man rushes to the street where I walked once. He's waving his arms like this—stops me. "My wife's having a baby and I can't reach a doctor or ambulance! Can you help me?" he asks. I went with him up to his place. It was easy ... that kid came in like Superman to supper. I washed it and wrapped it like a Christmas present in a red blanket. Then I took it to the man, and when he saw it, he swallowed the gum he was chewing he was that glad!

The FANATIC starts to let go of his laugh. DUKE is excited now and laughs joyfully with him. Finally, the FANATIC is exhausted and tense.

FANATIC: No ... please leave me alone! (*looks up at DUKE, his face pleading for solitude*)

DUKE: Why leave you? What in hell gives you that right?

FANATIC: (*almost weeping*) You can't feed children ... young babies wrapped like presents ... to the bomb!

DUKE: (*after a long, searching pause*) I'll take that chance. The bomb will have to blow to beat me! (*laughs provocatively now*) Men will still dig their gardens and puppies wag their tails even at the gates of hell! (*points downward to the valley*) Listen now! Five hundred whistles in a thousand factories are blowing for lunch! (*suddenly spouting the only solution he knows*) We'll take a job—buddies! Piece-work ... by the hour ... anything ... Buddies! (*the incongruity of it all thrills him*) Buddies—you and me!

FANATIC: (*shaking his head, his mind and heart in flames*) Not where I go!

DUKE: What are you talking about?

He starts to walk away, as if certain the FANATIC will follow him now. The FANATIC hasn't moved. DUKE turns and shouts at him.

DUKE: We shared a puff of wind with no voice once ... a protest written in water! I love you, man!

FANATIC: (*turns quickly to follow DUKE. A spasm shakes his body. His hands fly to his throat, dropping the placard he has held. He topples forward*) Ooh ...

DUKE moves rapidly to him, turns the FANATIC on his back and, tearing open his shirt, puts his ear to the FANATIC'S heart. He lifts his head and closes the shirtfront of the FANATIC.

DUKE: (*to the air around him*) Annie ... he never said his name.

Scene to black. Lights up on another area of the stage. Outline of a small city in the back of the stage area. Laughter from the wings, and DUKE and an old INDIAN, arms around each other's shoulders, come dancing out onstage. DUKE is teaching the INDIAN the steps and music of the "Hopak" dance. When the INDIAN learns the basic step patterns, DUKE diddles the melody and they dance a flawless round or two. Exhausted, they break apart and DUKE lies down. The INDIAN squats near him. Both are laughing.

INDIAN: What place is this, Duke?

DUKE: You don't know?

INDIAN: You lost me twenty cities back.

DUKE: Saskatoon, Winnipeg ... maybe Dryden ... what difference? They're all windy towns, all dry as shingles in the wind. The same darkness, the same light. It's a very dry, very holy country, friend!

INDIAN: You never find her, I tell you that now.

DUKE: And how would you know that when you don't even know where you are?

INDIAN: Looking like this keeps a man from remembering he's not here forever. (*painfully*) Duke, I been married myself once. I know. I made my wife pull nets from the lake at five o'clock in the morning ... water becoming ice on our clothes and boat. She made me wear the only mitts we had between us. She got up nights to make fire to keep us warm. I swear at her at work,

sometimes even beat her up a little when work is slow and there is no money to be had. Forgetting she was with baby ... After she dies, I know then what kind of woman she was. An' I never once told her when she was alive. Is the same with you?

DUKE rises and walks offstage, his head down. The INDIAN stares after him, nodding sadly.

ACT 3

Curtain up on a picnic table in suggestion of an outdoor, farm setting. Seated at the table are DUKE, FARMER'S SON, and BERT the hired hand. FARMER comes onstage and sits at the head of the table. FARMER'S WIFE arrives with a platter of fresh pastry which she places on the table. She retreats to stand beside a smaller table backstage. The smaller table has on it an additional coffee pot. DUKE is older now, grayed and slightly hunched.

DUKE: (*gaily reaching to the platter for a fistful of doughnuts. He feels trapped by not being able to touch the people he is with*) Still more doughnuts? (*to FARMER'S WIFE*) God bless you and may you live a thousand years, missus! (*to BERT*) Eat, Bert—good food is a miracle every time it happens.

He lifts the platter off the table and holds it out to BERT. BERT declines.

BERT: No for me, thank you. Too much starch. (*touches his stomach under his ribs*) Give me gas right here.

DUKE: (*throws his head back with laughter*) Gas! The only pain I ever got was hunger pain. Some pain that is, I'll tell you. Plays tricks with your brain and makes a joke of all the nice things one learns on Sunday. When the pain was in me, I'd look at my neighbour and what I saw was no longer a plumber, clerk, janitor, or salesman. I see him then as a hundred and seventy pounds of meat. What time is it?

FARMER'S SON: (*checking his watch quickly*) Nearly three o'clock.

DUKE: (*to FARMER'S SON*) Some uncle you have in this Bert of ours ... a million-dollar heap of doughnuts, and they give him gas!

FARMER'S SON: We're a close family!

DUKE: (*trying to burst through*) So are chickens in a coop, and men on a ship. (*gently*) What time is it now, friend?

FARMER'S SON: Nearly three o'clock—I told you already!

DUKE: Couldn't be—you've already lost a minute of awareness ... soon it'll be weeks, and then years ...

FARMER: (*foolishly, but trying to say the right thing*) That's alright.

DUKE: (*ignoring the FARMER, still to the FARMER'S SON*) When your mother makes a doughnut, she makes a doughnut.

FARMER'S SON: (*reacting to DUKE'S strangeness*) That's good you can eat it.

FARMER: So the man wants to know the time—nothing to get sore about! We're a close family—all pulling our weight together. If crops are good, we do good, if not ...

DUKE: (*turning to the FARMER'S WIFE*) And no one has left since all of you were thrown together on this piece of land?

FARMER: (*proudly, but not wanting to boast*) Me an' Tracy been married twenty-four years. Bert's been living with us the past fifteen—since his stint at mining. We've got respect for each other!

BERT: You said it!

DUKE: (*raising his coffee cup*) Then long life to respect! Why is everyone so happy? Crops worse than usual? (*smiling*) Or am I eating too much?

DUKE'S persistence is getting to them. FARMER'S SON is embarrassed by a direct and amused glance from DUKE.

FARMER'S SON: Hell, no. There's lots to eat around here ... (*DUKE laughs*)

FARMER: (*turning away*) I'm going into town right away, Duke. If you want to come ...

DUKE: No. There's too much to do around here. (*holds out cup to FARMER'S WIFE*) Everywhere a man turns, there's work to be done ... Hey, missus! Have you got more of that wonderful coffee?

She has not heard him, her mind someplace else. She fills his cup. DUKE'S words grow progressively emptier and gayer as his hostility to the situation deepens.

DUKE: Thank you! (*louder, to her*) It's been years—many years, since a woman made coffee for me this good. I'm happy to work for people like you ... (*those at the table look at each other*) Is something wrong, missus?

She smiles to indicate no, nothing is wrong.

DUKE: (*to FARMER'S SON*) To have a mother at your age, friend, that is something. I had no mother. She died the hour I was born. Hell, no! She ate and wore out clothes with moving around for twenty years after I was born, but her job as a mother had been to bring me into the world, no more. A hundred uncles told me to love her, for she grew fine tomatoes in her garden! (*sadly now*) And that, in itself, is something.

FARMER'S SON: (*after a long pause. To his father*) You were going to ask him first thing this morning.

FARMER: (*to DUKE*) Yeh … We've been talking this morning, Duke …

DUKE is now watching the FARMER'S WIFE, looking for some contact. She collects dishes. He feels a new blow about to befall him. He rallies with love, joy, strength.

DUKE: (*more to the woman than the men*) She's had no easy time of it … Her face tells the story of this farm—hard work and sacrifice …

BERT nods vigorous agreement.

FARMER: (*in almost a mutter*) Yeh … a lot of hard work for very little.

DUKE: (*to FARMER'S SON*) For her birthday, I'll go halves on a present for her. When's her birthday?

FARMER'S SON: April … sometime.

DUKE: April! Spring! What a time to be born! What day in April?

FARMER'S SON: Huh?

DUKE: What day is your mother's birthday?

FARMER'S SON: Eighteenth … nineteenth April, I think. I'm not sure. (*to FARMER*) When is it, Pop?

FARMER: May the third … (*rises to his feet*) … go check the tractor for oil and fuel, son. (*nudges DUKE*) He respects his mother. I wanted to …

DUKE: Respect? The damned word falls like frozen gravel off a heap. (*takes sudden hold of the tray and swings it wide to BERT, who leans back quickly to avoid being hit*) Bert, have another doughnut, gas or no gas!

BERT: No, no! It'll hurt me!

DUKE: (*swinging the tray to the FARMER'S SON*) You have one, then!

FARMER'S SON stares back dumbly.

DUKE: (*rising to his feet and dropping the tray on the table, spilling its contents*) Again I ate well, and I ate alone …

FARMER stares at his WIFE, then speaks to DUKE.

FARMER: Don't always understand you, Duke. (*DUKE is slightly dumbfounded. Long pause as he looks at the FARMER*) My missus figures you must be married. You married, Duke? (*silence*) You don't have to say.

DUKE: (*with mounting sense of futility, kicks the bench back from behind him, thinking he now understands them*) Go to hell—the pack of you! I'm through here? Is that it?

FARMER: (*totally surprised, then big and generous*) No, no, nothing of the sort! You're the best worker I've ever had … (*turns to his WIFE for help*) You tell him, Tracy!

FARMER'S WIFE comes forward now, all benign smiles and very sure of her role.

FARMER'S WIFE: The offer we give Bert could go for you … we're a close family. There's food here and a place to sleep—no need for a man to wander the world without a home … we're all God's children!

FARMER: (*quickly*) We can't pay you for every month of the year, but when there's work like now, you'll get going wages, Duke!

DUKE: (*to the WIFE, with a sad smile, his voice dull with disappointment*) Missus! The best doughnuts I've ever eaten. (*she smiles and approaches another step*) Don't do anything else— just make doughnuts and the world won't thank you enough! Do you understand what I say to you, missus? Doughnuts and nothing else!

His words leave her confused. She retreats clumsily.

BERT: (*sidling away from the table*) That was sure a good lunch. Wish I could eat more.

DUKE: (*clear now*) The best. Now there's hay to bring in, fences to fix in the pasture … spraying to do among the tobacco rows while the weather's hot … lots of work for a million hands … what makes you think I'm married?

FARMER: (*nervous now*) We were thinking only of the best for you, Duke.

DUKE: Yes, yes, you're a nice, gentle sort of guy ...

BERT: Yeh—the best!

DUKE: You heard something about my wife?

FARMER: (*nods*) A little better than four years back ... she was workin' here. Kept looking for a Duke and just last night Tracy remembered—thought maybe it was you. Nothing to it—just meant to ask to be sure ...

DUKE: (*quietly and simply*) How was she?

FARMER: Okay, fine! She looked good. I remember she showed this bit of a limp from some accident, I guess.

FARMER'S WIFE: She say she was taking night school and goin' on to be a teacher. Jimmy sure looked good, too. Looked like he'd be smart in school.

DUKE: Who's Jimmy?

FARMER is dismayed now.

FARMER: Her boy! Didn't you ... oh, hell!

Shakes his head and starts walking away. DUKE grabs him and pulls him up short.

DUKE: (*shouting*) What boy?

FARMER: Let go of me, Duke!

DUKE: (*grimly, shaking him*) Tell me what you know, tell me! What boy?

FARMER: (*shouting*) Hers! Yours! Hell, man, I've got my own family! Let me be!

DUKE releases him. FARMER walks offstage, followed by the others, leaving DUKE standing alone. DUKE goes into deep thought and stares blankly at the countryside around him.

DUKE: (*reflectively and slowly, as if projecting his words into the mind of an imagined son*) Three thousand miles of country before you! All yours to work or play on. You'll be better off away from the concrete and glass that has no face an' no colour. All life to begin all over again.

Lights out and up on a new area of the stage. Sounds of a train departing. The setting is of a railway section gang, filling and packing gravel between railway ties.

DUKE comes onstage, big shovel in hand.

DUKE: (*to himself*) Doughnuts, and nothing else ...

FOREMAN: (*good-naturedly*) Talking to yourself again, Duke?

DUKE: (*forcing himself to be cheerful*) Beside my bunk I've got a duffle-bag with two blankets ... two changes of work clothes and a suit for stepping out in. Does any man alive carry more with him from job to job?

FOREMAN: I'd say you've got it made, Duke!

DUKE: How long have I lived? Fifty—a hundred years already? Where was I born? Where will I die? Can you tell me that?

FOREMAN: (*sobering*) Come on now, Duke. I thought you were joking ...

DUKE: I want to know! Somebody's got to be able to tell me! I did the footwork for this country—I was there at the beginning of everything! I threw away my life and unborn family doing it! Now who am I? What do I want? What's in it all for me?

A WORKMAN: You're Duke, the iron man, that's who you are! Hey, buddy, tell us again how you once swam Lake Ontario on your back, smoking a cigarette!

ANOTHER MAN: Yeh, tell us, Duke!

THIRD MAN: Or how you beat the guy with a chain saw in bringing down a Douglas Fir ... and you with only an axe in your hands!

FOURTH MAN: Tell us, Duke!

DUKE: Hey! (*with burst of forced joy*) Look at the way iron Duke lives! And the way he works! There's more gray in my hair than in the scalps of the rest of you put together, and just look at me—all you guys have small shovels, but the Duke gets a scoop shovel for moving his gravel! And you know, it's for the same wages you get! Not a cent more per hour. Sit down—have yourselves a smoke! Duke will do this job himself!

The MEN step back. DUKE takes over with the enthusiasm of a demon. Some of the MEN light cigarettes. One goes for the water jug. He returns and the jug is passed from mouth to mouth. DUKE suddenly stops and straightens with a long, soul-wrenching sigh.

FOREMAN: (*holding out the jug to DUKE*) Have a drink of water, Duke. Too hot to work like that.

DUKE takes the jug and has a long drink. He stares at the MEN around him.

DUKE: (*loudly, as if talking beyond the circle of workers*) One day I'll say to my son—these are men, kid. They've all come from Cape Breton mines, black flies of north Ontario, the muskegs of Alberta. They've all come through hard times—some ice chips in their blood never had a chance to melt. But they sure can laugh, eh, fellows?

MEN nod and agree nervously. Some begin to move away. DUKE puts down the water jug and his shovel, and moves from them.

FOREMAN: Hey, Duke … where you going? It's only three o'clock!

DUKE: Only three o'clock you say? No, it's later … the sun's going down now … over there … (*points in direction away from the work site*) … over there only a few blackbirds are watching us from the scrub willows. But they'll fly away for the night, and then there'll only be us and all the lonely, lonely country. (*sudden great elation*) To hell with death and dying, I say! I want to live! Sing! Dance! Fight! I'm bursting inside!

Quick dim of lights. Up on another area of the stage to suggest a deserted street at night. Sounds of DUKE shouting. He appears from the wings as if from around a building.

DUKE: (*shouting*) Annie! Where in hell are you?

His voice echoes back tauntingly from the walls of vacant buildings.

DUKE: (*shouting again*) I've thrown hog's blood and copper to the wind all my life! Annie! Show me my son!

A POLICEMAN approaches from backstage. DUKE is aware of him and explodes in laughter.

POLICEMAN: Hey, keep it quiet! It's two in the morning!

DUKE: I don't care if it's dawn of the day of damnation! I had a wife once, and I had money. Look at me now!

DUKE takes out a dollar bill from his pocket.

DUKE: This is all between me and starvation. Tell me, buddy, why are we such wasters?

POLICEMAN: Move along, fellow … and spend your dollar on a cab to take you home. Move along!

DUKE: Why? Because I killed my father?

POLICEMAN: (*startled*) What?

DUKE: We each had to kill a father—that's what fathers are for, to kill! You're a cop, and I'm a waster. We both had to kill our fathers to get that way!

POLICEMAN: You're drunk! (*takes DUKE by the shoulder and shoves him*)

DUKE: (*staggering back as if drunk. The POLICEMAN comes at him and continues pushing as DUKE talks*) I'm sober. Listen to me—I'm running here and there like I'm trying to find summer. There are claws going into my flesh when I stop, so I have to keep running. Your claws are breaking through my skin now, friend. Another place, another time, claws hold me a foot off the ground—woman claws … the mother holding up her eternal baby. The thieves claw for my blood …

POLICEMAN: I'm taking you in, punk!

DUKE: Drop dead! I could fly!

POLICEMAN: What are you—some junkie? Come on!

POLICEMAN grips DUKE'S shoulder with one hand while with the other he withdraws his night-stick. DUKE strikes him with the back of his arm and the POLICEMAN falls, losing his hat. He rises and charges at DUKE, happy for the chance to fight. Again DUKE hits him, knocking him down. The POLICEMAN fumbles for the whistle in his pocket, but DUKE lifts him and hits him again. POLICEMAN falls and remains lying. DUKE crouches over him.

DUKE: (*exhausted*) You big, dumb, flat-footed farmer! What kind of life is this for you? Why interfere with another man's freedom so late at night? Hey? (*pause*) Throw you in the sewer and open the river on you! You're a bum like all the bums!

POLICEMAN, winded, rises to his elbows but says nothing.

DUKE: You arrest me—that will bring it back into proper focus again, eh? Forget it, kid. There are no heroes in this city tonight.

POLICEMAN: It's my job, Mac.

DUKE: (*lies down beside POLICEMAN, his head on his arm*) No more than a butcher carving up a quarter of beef. So the knife slips, and he ends up with five pounds more for mincemeat. Two guys meet in the night ... both so lonely they have to fight to keep from crying ...

DUKE laughs and starts to tickle the POLICEMAN at the ribs.

POLICEMAN: (*twisting to move away from DUKE*) Don't bug me! You're nuts!

DUKE: (*turning away from POLICEMAN and giggling as he says*) I'm talking to the sidewalk, not you! Yesterday I was a baby, and tomorrow they will drive me away in a holy wagon. What am I today? I had a wife. I ate food she made and slept with her, and now ...

DUKE looks around himself, bewildered, suddenly quiet. Long pause.

POLICEMAN: (*hoarsely*) You ... alright, Mac?

POLICEMAN tries to rise to his feet, but slumps down weakly, coughing.

DUKE: Yeh, alright. (*rises to help him*) Can you walk now?

POLICEMAN: Never you mind—I'll manage. (*on his feet with great effort*) And keep your hands off me. You're under arrest!

DUKE: You can't move alone, you goddamned fool! I won't leave you like this. Come on—I'll help you!

DUKE half supports the hatless POLICEMAN down the street. POLICEMAN stops.

POLICEMAN: Stop shoving me around, will you! I'm fine.

DUKE: I'll take you—to my room. You can sleep in a soft bed there.

They move again. At the back of the stage, a STREET WALKER rushes around the corner and stops when she sees them. She stands undecided whether to turn back or walk past the two men.

DUKE: (*seeing her, turns the POLICEMAN aside*) Hey, policeman! You want a woman?

POLICEMAN: (*coughing again*) You're nuts.

DUKE: (*intensely*) Lift up your head—be a man. Look at her, will you? Have you a wife?

POLICEMAN: No.

DUKE: Then talk to her. She knows the same people ... the same ...

POLICEMAN: She's just a common ...

DUKE: Aye—a queen! Tomorrow she will give a princess to the world, and the day after, a white prince with blue eyes! (*laughs*) Oh, man!

POLICEMAN: Shut up!

DUKE: (*more laughter*) What are we—pigs in a pen? Or wild hawks in the sky? What are we, eh?

The POLICEMAN averts his face from DUKE, but DUKE makes him look into his eyes by taking his chin and turning his face back. The STREET WALKER decides to walk past them. She moves towards them quickly, her handbag swinging with exaggerated unconcern. DUKE reaches out and takes her wrist. He is smiling.

STREET WALKER: (*staring at POLICEMAN*) Nothin' doing? I don't want any trouble with cops.

DUKE: Come on. (*pulls at her hand*)

STREET WALKER: You let go of me! What's with you anyhow?

DUKE: (*nodding to POLICEMAN*) We had a fight.

STREET WALKER: Oh, that's just great!

POLICEMAN: Leave her alone.

DUKE: Let her decide!

Lights dim and out. Raucous, neurotic music of an all-night radio station in the darkness. Establish music well and lights up on a new stage area suggesting DUKE'S bedroom. The POLICEMAN is lying on a bed, arm over his face. DUKE and the STREET WALKER are in a single chair near a window, she on his lap chewing gum in time to the music from the radio.

DUKE: (*gruffly to POLICEMAN*) You feeling any better now?

POLICEMAN: (*painfully rising to a sitting position on the bed*) Fine. I feel good.

DUKE: They've built a few stone men on cement horses in some parks of the city, but these are for pigeons to sit on and admire—not for men. (*pause*) I was drunk and sad when I met you.

POLICEMAN: (*rubbing his head*) Forget it. (*gets up to leave*) Where's my hat? You pick it up when I fell?

The STREET WALKER suddenly lets out a shrill laugh, as if the situation was wildly humourous to her. DUKE lets her off his knee and rises to pace the room.

DUKE: I don't know. It's a hat. (*turns to the WOMAN*) You can stay here until morning. I'm leaving.

DUKE goes to the window and throws it wide open. Sounds of early morning traffic. Faint light of morning in his face. The STREET WALKER exchanges a long look with the POLICEMAN and nods some secret agreement, then leaves. The POLICEMAN rises from the bed, buckles and smoothes out his tunic and also leaves for work.

DUKE: (*still at the window, staring out*) Look out there! They started from the sea and built Vancouver backwards. If I'd been first man here, I'd of done it the other way. I'd have gone on top of the mountain and started building my city from there downward. A golden city ... for men to look up to! (*chuckles and cranes out the window with rising excitement*) Yes, sir! I'd have started right up there on the mountain!

He is still smiling happily as he turns from the window and finds himself alone in the room. The smile fades slowly and is replaced by a look of profound sadness. Dim lights and out. Up on another playing area to suggest a small courtroom. The JUDGE is seated and strikes a gavel. A drowsy CLERK snaps awake below him. DUKE is led onstage by a POLICEMAN. There is a weakness in DUKE'S walk and bearing now.

DUKE: (*talking to the JUDGE as he approaches the bench*) The clouds are coming, heavy and black, Mister Judge. Yesterday, two men I knew from twenty years back got put on half-time at the rolling-mill. Automation, they call it! Tomorrow, it'll be thirty other men—which thirty? Men like me, or the young?

JUDGE: (*severely studying his notes*) Your concern has little to do with the charge against you ...

DUKE: It has ... for I want long life so I won't spend my days totally as a fool.

JUDGE: (*amused slightly now*) You've been brought here because of the offence of carrying a loaded rifle down a city street on a busy after ...

DUKE: That's only one charge—there are other offences to living—you know that. (*he is regaining his vitality*) I've lost my name, and my home is everywhere. I stood, or sat, or fell asleep before the home of a man who owned this small plot of earth. I was silent, but he saw me, and he heard whimperings of his children—but his children are never supposed to whimper. He heard shouts from the rooftops and laughter in the graveyard! He wanted immortality, but all I could tell him was of the sound a pencil made in the post office as it stroked out his name with his death!

JUDGE: Our docket is a busy one this morning. Would you prefer to appear in court another day?

DUKE: I'm leaving in an hour. Whatever it is, if I should be guilty by the law books, then I'm guilty—it's the same to me. (*shivers*) Why is it so cold here? Did you understand what I said to you, Mister Judge? (*JUDGE looks up and shakes his head very slowly*) You didn't?

JUDGE: No. There are only the charges against you ...

DUKE: Is it ... because ... you're here? And I'm from over there where highways are nailed into white dust, and men hold back rivers with their knees and elbows so there may be light and peony gardens in the new homes of their children? (*shivers again*) It's June outside this courthouse. Why should a man with two shirts on be cold in June? Can you tell me that, Mister Judge?

JUDGE: (*with a sigh and benevolent smile*) I'm dismissing the charges against you. You are free to go!

DUKE is led away. On his way out, he passes a young BOY being brought in by another POLICEMAN. DUKE stops. He stares at the BOY as he is led before the JUDGE. Lights out on this scene. Up lights on another stage area suggesting a long and endless road leading to the far horizon. DUKE and the BOY come onstage. The BOY is lost, morose. DUKE sits down and begins to shake the dust from his boots.

DUKE: Boots of real leather ... always get the good boots for the long road. Do you want to eat?

BOY: No! (*swats at flies on his neck. Scratches at bites flies have given him*) Mosquitoes ever stop biting here?

DUKE: No. But after a while you won't notice them. Look! (*points to the horizon. Reflectively*) Three thousand miles of country before you! All yours to work or play on ... you'll be better off away from the concrete and glass that has no face and no colour. All life to begin all over again. (*almost casually*) Where's your father?

BOY: He ran off with some woman, or something like that ... I don't know.

DUKE: And your name's Jimmy?

BOY: I told you yes! You've asked me ten times already!

DUKE: But tell me again, and I won't ask no more ... your mother ... she picked tobacco once, and then taught school?

BOY: (*chuckles cynically*) My mother? She couldn't read a word that long—and she's never been out of Toronto.

DUKE: (*with despair*) No, that's not true!

BOY: Listen, Mister—I think you bailed out the wrong kid or something. Who are you?

DUKE: You're lying to me, Jimmy! You know who I am, and you keep on lying!

BOY: I never seen you before today, so help me. I'm going home!

BOY starts walking away. DUKE slips on his boot and hurries after him.

DUKE: Jimmy—wait!

BOY: Leave me alone! I've got friends could help me pay my fine. I didn't ask you to!

BOY springs away as if to run, but DUKE grabs him and holds him. BOY starts to whimper. DUKE stands over him, breathing heavily. BOY crumples to the road. DUKE kneels beside him and now tenderly strokes his hair.

DUKE: Never mind, kid. You've got your foot on the first morning star and all I can give you is this fifty cents. A mile back is the garage where we had coffee. The bus will stop there on the way to the city. You go back, and try to forgive her for not giving you a father. I'll be him, if you'd like.

BOY: What?

DUKE: Yes! (*holds out both his hands before the BOY. Turns left hand palm up*) This is the angel that brings home candy! (*turns right hand palm up*) And this is the devil that throws dishes!

BOY: You? My father? (*laughs caustically*) I remember my father good. He was a small, sawed-off guy with one eye that was crossed. A real sawed-off sort of guy.

DUKE: How long since you last saw him?

BOY: Six, seven years, maybe.

DUKE: He grew since then, and God give him two new eyes!

BOY: He was younger than you, Mister!

DUKE: How young? Young enough to sing? Dance? Like this?

DUKE slaps his hands together and springs to his feet. Humming a fast dance tune, he does a wild dance on the road, his cap in his hand and his white hair dancing in the breeze. BOY smiles, then laughs.

BOY: He only sang at Christmas. He got himself gassed up then, and he sang one song in Norwegian, over and over, until he fell asleep. Then when he woke, he didn't sing again until next Christmas.

DUKE: Listen! I hear the bus ... forty miles down the road, but I hear it plain as I hear you. You better go now. Good luck to you, Jimmy. And I love you, boy!

BOY: (*struggling with great effort and fear at betraying himself*) You know where you're going?

DUKE is watching him, an intense smile on his face. With gestures of his hands, he is coaxing the next words of compassion out of the BOY.

DUKE: Yes?

BOY: It'll be night in a couple of hours ... you can't go anywheres now. I'm sure she wouldn't mind ... if you wanted to stay, that is ... over 'til morning!

DUKE claps his hands together joyfully.

DUKE: Tell her when you see her ...

BOY: Tell her what?

DUKE: Tell her nothing ... Jimmy! Grow big quickly! And when low clouds come down on you, full of rain and thunder, run from them, holding the hand tight that loves yours! Into the wind, or the mouth of a blast-furnace oven. But together with whoever wants you ... for love is everything once the long, hard day is over!

BOY: You sure you'll be ...

Again DUKE coaxes concern and pity out of the BOY, and claps his hands with excitement when he finds it.

DUKE: Fine—yes! Now run back!

BOY: Duke, where can I write if I feel like it sometimes?

DUKE: (*a smile of fulfillment breaking out on his face*) I am you—inside out—a mile under the sea—in the sky! I give you lightning and stars ... white stones and hurt rabbits ... shining tool-kits and carnations ... the last prayer of Riel ... exploding winter rivers ... apricots and ice-worms ... white glaciers and a new pink baby born to a copper-skinned mother ... cowboy songs in the cockpit of a new jet airplane. Go! Jimmy, go! For the bus is now thirty-nine miles away!

BOY: Goodbye! (*turns off*)

DUKE: (*shouting after the BOY*) I never found God or the devil ... but a lot of heaven and hell!

Lights up on another area of the stage, revealing the shovel and dirt from the hole of the opening scene of the play. DUKE crosses the stage as the light of the previous scene dims out.

DUKE: (*picking up the shovel and facing the audience*) A lot of heaven and hell ... the truth made of hailstones and dandelion ... no monument will yet withstand the snow ... no school book tells the legend of the man who dug your sewers. Be sure of one thing, friends, shyness is our natural virtue, and sorrow the darkness in our eyes!

He lowers himself into the hole from which he emerged in the opening scene. A long pause on the silent, lifeless set that remains. Slow curtain.

End

JUST AN ORDINARY PERSON

After the considerable popular impact of the Vancouver première of *The Ecstasy of Rita Joe* in November of 1967, it is surprising that when another play of Ryga's ran in that same city only two months later, the event passed almost unnoticed. *Just an Ordinary Person* opened on January 22, 1968, at the Metro Theatre, to good reviews but poor audiences. There were many reasons for this: perhaps strongest among them is that the production contained little in the way of character or plot development; rather, it presented a thinly disguised Ryga himself in a state of wrenching, personal anguish. For those just getting to know him, it must have been a painful evening, like watching a powerful acquaintance suddenly break down in a torturous confession of self-doubt.

The work began as a half-hour television drama that Ryga had completed in February, 1967, well before the première of *The Ecstasy of Rita Joe*. On the title page of the typescript he notes that the story was "inspired by an M. Gorky short story" ("The Poet, a Sketch"). It was well and professionally produced by the CBC and broadcast on the Studio Pacific series on April 10: the director, Don Eccleston, would later direct the hit stage production of Ryga's *Grass and Wild Strawberries*; the actor playing the Poet was John Juliani, director of his own Savage God production company (who also worked in subsequent stagings of Ryga's plays, most notably *Paracelsus* at the Vancouver Playhouse Theatre); while John Stark, director the Canadian Art Theatre, played the Ordinary Person. The Vancouver stage version of *Just an Ordinary Person* was produced by Stark's company (Stark also directed) and was paired with Eugene O'Neill's *Hughie*. Edward Brooks played the Poet, while Karl Wylie played the Ordinary Person in the live theatre production.

This play, one of Ryga's shortest, is also his most soul-searching, especially as so much of conventional theatricality is stripped away from it and the playwright locates himself so directly in the work. It begins simply enough with the Poet playing a guitar on a bare stage. It is an image Ryga dearly loved: that of the simple, travelling troubadours, the ancient singers who gave voice to the poetry, politics, and truth of the people, clearly a version of how Ryga saw himself and his mission as a writer. The Poet on the stage reads a poem about Federico Garcia Lorca, the Spanish poet/playwright who died for his beliefs during the Spanish Civil War. The Lorca poem is Ryga's own, from his first book of verse, *Song of my hands and other poems*, published in 1956. But the Poet is soon interrupted by the Ordinary Person who has been planted by the playwright, not onstage with the Poet, but in the audience—in the front row—from where he harshly questions the Poet's purpose: " ... for what reason do you write?"

The Ordinary Person is Ryga's alter ego, the plain, honest working man who seeks genuine spiritual satisfaction from his labour. Like Ryga, he has an immigrant background; he also has a passion for helping humanity deal with oppression in its various forms, seen as a struggle against dark forces of authority, including all forms of control over language and its "appropriate" or "legitimate" usage, and he has an unlimited appetite for knowing "the truth." For Ryga, it is the accomplishments of a people's poets by which their success is measured: if it can be shown that the lives of ordinary people are actually uplifted and improved by their poets' works, then that becomes the measure of social progress. For the "true poet," particularly in a Marxist context, this is an incredibly onerous task because it involves, as Ryga had done by making the main characters of both *Indian* and *The Ecstasy of Rita Joe* Native people, the risk of the charge of "appropriation of voice." While with his Native characters, the risk of this potential charge was grounded in culture, in *Just an Ordinary Person* Ryga shifts this risk to the ground of class.

While Gorky may have romanticized the potential for the poet to become "the voice of the people," and certainly Ryga himself had penned an homage to Lorca as speaking for the "ordinary people" of Spain against the fascist ambitions of Franco's forces, many of Ryga's contemporary left-wing writers questioned their craft as a potential bourgeois-individualist indulgence, which either exploited, appropriated, or failed to contribute meaningfully to "the people's" (working class) struggle for legitimacy, ownership, and liberation. This ambivalent critique of the role of the poet in revolutionary Marxist contexts was most elaborately developed by the exiled Russian author Boris Pasternak in his epic novel, *Doctor Zhivago*.

In the ongoing critical and cultural debate of the question of appropriation of voice, *The Ecstasy of Rita Joe* in particular has at times been cited as a negative example of this issue. It is important to recognize, in this context, that while the current outlines of this critical debate were framed well after Ryga's creation of both *Indian* and *The Ecstasy of Rita Joe*, it was George Ryga himself who was one of the very first to not only raise this issue, but to effectively put himself on public trial over it. In *Just an Ordinary Person* we witness the desperation of Ryga interrogating the social and cultural significance of his work from its very first beginnings in such terms and finding himself wanting. As he would continue to do throughout his writing life, Ryga had dramatized a public issue that his potential critics did not yet, at the time, even have the vocabulary to address in a discursive, analytical context.

JUST AN ORDINARY PERSON

CHARACTERS

POET, *a young man*
PERSON, *any age man*

SET

Curtain up on nondescript staging to suggest a coffee-house background. Faint light from front apron of the stage illuminates the POET sitting on a small bench, playing a guitar softly.

After an interlude of music, during which the theatre quietens, the POET rises, props his guitar against the bench and moves to forward centre stage where a light floods him. He takes out a sheaf of papers from the inside pocket of his coat.

POET: Good evening. To begin my reading tonight, I have selected a poem which I wrote a few years ago, but which I feel still has relevance today. (*unfolds papers and begins reading*) Federico Garcia Lorca ... Spanish poet and patriot ... playwright and folklorist ... was shot to death in Granada thirty-two years ago by executioners who didn't know what they were doing ... who didn't even know the name of the man they killed:

With fire in his wild eyes
He turned to go ...
Then paused,
And defiantly replied the taunting chant:

"You're mad! ... You're mad!"
"Mad?" he cried. "Yes, mad
As the flowers in the sunwhite field,
Or stars in our Spanish night
Who weep with me at what
Has come to pass."

"If ... I am mad, then mad
Is our sobbing earth that whispers
'Free me, so I may dream with you
My glorious children!'"

"Mad?
Then mad were the souls
Of our fathers
Whose lovely books you
Burned in the village square;
Mad as my poems, whose verse
Froze on your lips in fear
When they hushed with sword
And flame
The songs of free men!"

"I go
But let my madness live
In the hungry hills
And not in the sunless dungeons."

Proudly then
Lorca walked the dusty road
And through the silent, shamed mob
Passed a sob
As of a frightened child.

The POET lowers his sheaf of papers and nods to the audience to indicate the poem has ended. Sound of one loud, rhythmic applause from the audience.

PERSON: (*in the front row of the theatre, still applauding*) Hear! Hear! That's very good! I like that poem!

POET: Thank you ... thank you.

The PERSON continues applauding, his applause becoming suspiciously that of a heckler. He rises and moves to the apron of the stage. The POET is ill at ease.

PERSON: It's a good poem. You read it good!

POET: Thank you. I'm glad you like it.

PERSON: Where you from? Lethbridge? Winnipeg? I thought I knew the accent!

POET: I'm from here, now.

PERSON: Is that so? I thought ... it doesn't matter ... that was a good poem!

POET: Thank you.

PERSON: It takes a good man to write a good poem! I want to shake your hand!

PERSON approaches with a certain bravado and extends his hand which the POET accepts in a self-conscious handshake.

PERSON: (*laughing softly*) It's good to know somebody who writes and says poems in front of people …

POET: There are others who do it.

PERSON: But not like you … none like you. To me, you're something special.

POET: You haven't heard the others …

PERSON: My father … long ago owned five hectares of land in Poland. He carried a small bag of soil from this land wherever he went in Canada. He used to say he was carrying the dust of his ancestors in his pocket. I buried it with him. That five hectares of land was nothing to me, so why the hell should I carry it? I left it in his pocket. (*ponders, then laughs*) But you know what that means! I bet you'd be able to write a poem about that, eh?

POET: You flatter me.

PERSON: I don't flatter. I never flatter. (*pause*) I seen your name in the doorway, so I came in to see and hear you. I'm glad I came now!

POET: Do you often … come here?

PERSON: I never come … no sir, this place isn't for me! But I felt it's the same for you, so when I seen your name, I came in. My kind of people stay away from a place like this … at least, at a time like this!

The POET motions to him to stop, but the PERSON continues with a swaggering swing of his shoulders as he half-turns to the audience.

PERSON: You and I know where we're not wanted, don't we? (*laughs*) When a general takes down his pants he looks the same as Joe Holobitsky of Grande Forks—we know that, don't we?

POET: (*now very ill at ease*) I wonder if possibly you're confusing me with …

PERSON: (*smiles and turns quickly to POET*) It's you alright! I've talked to some men about you and we've had some good arguments. (*laughs softly*) It flatters you, doesn't it? That you are known in this city by a stranger. That your poems are remembered and discussed by people you've never even met!

The POET nervously shuffles through papers in his hands.

POET: If I may, I'd like to continue with my readings!

PERSON: Now that's a lie if I ever heard one! You want me to continue talking like this … saying more … what the men said when they argued about you, how long they spoke, where? It is good to feel you are exceptional, isn't it?

POET: Yes, but …

He realizes he has been tricked by his own vanity. He shakes his head and turns away from the PERSON, who laughs again.

PERSON: Isn't it?

POET: Could we talk later, in the lobby?

PERSON: You're not wasting my time …

POET: (*angrily*) It's their time!

Points to the audience in the theatre.

PERSON: (*directly to the POET, earnestly*) There's nobody here but us … just the two of us … any two people in a hurry. I'm happy to have found you and been able to strike up a conversation. Meeting you like this means a lot to me …

POET: They've paid for my services. I owe them something in … (*the PERSON laughs and the POET becomes annoyed*) You amuse easily! I don't think this is funny at all!

PERSON: But it is funny! I am amused. Curious, too. I want to know everything. There must be nothing too sacred to explore for me. I want to know everything … how long I slept last night, the colour of sky, stones, the other side of the moon. How an atom is split and why leaves fall in the autumn of the year. Because I want to know, I live, and have some chance at happiness. But tell me … this poem you just read … what did it cost you to make a poem such as that?

POET: Cost me? What do you mean?

PERSON: Did you suffer much for it? What happened to you as a person in creating the poem?

POET: (*still annoyed*) Look … I really don't think it's any of your business!

The PERSON becomes impetuous and expansive.

PERSON: It's nothing you should hide out of pride or shame … don't be a little girl. The way I see it—a plumber makes out his bill to a contractor. A boy shovels snow from a sidewalk and asks for wages. So a poet might ask society for a timesheet on his labour. Did it cost you much of your life? Or your work time?

POET: You can't place value on a poem in that way!

PERSON: Why not? Is it really that sacred?

POET: (*with resignation*) It took me a week to perfect that poem.

There is a long pause between them. The PERSON chuckles. The POET turns away from him, upset. He is shamed at having made an admission that he would not ordinarily confide to a stranger.

POET: (*in a dull voice*) I enjoyed meeting you …

PERSON: No, you didn't.

POET: I've more work to do tonight … it's late.

He turns and extends his hand to the PERSON for a handshake.

POET: It was good meeting you, but I've more work to do, and then I've an early appointment in the morning.

The PERSON ignores the extended hand. Instead, he turns away from the POET and indicates the audience in a sweeping gesture.

PERSON: Only a week's work, and already two hundred people in this building are listening and thinking your thoughts! Soon it will be a thousand at some other theatre … and then perhaps as many as ten thousand across the country!

POET: (*moving forward resolutely to intercept the PERSON*) You've no right to … .

PERSON: (*laughing now*) And perhaps after you die … like that young kid-actor Dean, or twist your neck in a motorbike caper like this Bob Dylan, then … oh, but not so fast! Not so fast!

Time is forever, and we are here only a little while.

POET: I said you've no right to interfere with a performance!

PERSON: For your immortality you must be prepared to work harder and give us more … far, far more!

POET: I put as much effort as any man into my work!

PERSON: (*laughs*) A great deal more than one poem! Lorca, he had to work longer hours than you! There were no weekend clubs, no advertising agencies for him.

POET: I'm not apologizing to you!

The PERSON turns to him. They stare at each other in silence for a long moment.

POET: Who said … Lorca was very unusual in what he did?

PERSON: You said so … in your damned poem! You know how well he wrote all the thoughts that came to him. You know what it takes to write a good poem.

POET: I've sung songs and written poems about many things. (*hesitates*) Who are you? Why are you here like this?

PERSON: They who shot Lorca didn't even know his name … what does a name mean to them? To you?

PERSON turns to the audience. Light on the apron of the stage dies down and soft rear-stage lights come up to throw POET and PERSON into silhouette.

PERSON: To anyone? These are good people here, but what concern is one person to any of them? I would say very little.

POET: You know me, yet we've not met before this evening … that happens …

PERSON begins pacing in front of the stage, looking for a way to step up onto the stage.

POET: (*following him. Sarcastically*) Who knows—you might even be one of those men who calls people on the telephone late at night to frighten them by coughing and breathing hard, but not saying a word … who in hell are you?

The PERSON laughs and loosens the buttons of his coat as if to make himself more comfortable. He continues pacing, followed on the stage above him by the POET.

PERSON: Can't you guess? Why should I tell you everything? Or is my name more important than what I have to say? Don't be a child!

POET stops following the PERSON and stares down at him with hostility and confidence.

POET: I'll go anywhere, talk to anyone ...

PERSON: (*laughs*) Like President Johnson!

POET: Life's like that ... but ... I wasn't expecting a disturbance in a theatre where I am engaged to perform!

PERSON laughs again. The POET continues as if not hearing him.

POET: I live simply in a small apartment ...

PERSON: Two blocks north of the river! Yes, I know the place!

POET: (*shaken*) But ... how could you when ...

PERSON: That is not important ... what is important is that you not be afraid to go beyond the limits of the ordinary and the safely commonplace once in a while.

POET: I don't understand.

PERSON: Let us say that you are a poet that's become pretty famous, and I, just an ordinary person ... who asks you now ... (*begins removing his coat as he talks*) ... who asks you ... for what reason do you write a book? But be honest with me, for that is not a light question with me.

POET: (*compelled, unable to resist the PERSON*) There is no need to phrase your questions as threats ... I am honest.

PERSON: I am not threatening you!

POET: I'm honest. I've always been honest ...

The PERSON springs lightly onto the stage. The light in back of the stage dies and warm orange light floods over the POET and the PERSON. The PERSON drops the coat he has removed to the floor. He is now dressed in a check work-shirt. He confronts the POET jovially.

PERSON: A dog or a kangaroo can't read or write ... so let's you and I speak about the aims of literature, for this makes us men above animals!

The POET is nervous and tries to avoid the open candour of the PERSON.

POET: I find it easier to write than speak.

PERSON: Nothing to worry about ... but a poet, like a housepainter, has to stand back at times to see where he is and how far he has to go, don't you agree?

POET: I'd like to stay and talk, but I've a play to rewrite, and a reading to prepare for the university ... and I must sleep sometime to be fresh for the performance here tomorrow night. It's late.

PERSON: (*prophetically*) For you, it's not yet too late!

The POET turns sharply to him, his face expressing fear and concern.

POET: What do you mean when you say that? ... I came to read to a theatre full of people. I didn't ask to see you! You are taking up everyone's time, do you not see this?

PERSON: Why do we mince words like two lawyers at a cocktail party? We are men of blood and flesh, you and I! Let us speak to each other as men speak and to hell with the "may I please" and "thank you kindly" crap! Life is a high wind that dries us out until we become skeletons. There is no time to waste on nonsense!

POET: I speak and sing to people for two hours each night, and then I go my way and they go theirs. My relationship with all things has been simple and of my choosing. (*shakes his head slowly*) What is happening between us now ...

PERSON: Has its reasons! Everything in this world has its reasons! (*smiles poignantly at the POET*) Let us run ... down, into the depths, just you and I.

POET: Why the depths? When I see pain, I naturally feel compassion. But I'm a poet, not a martyr. I am not out to make history, merely to record it ...

PERSON: (*thoughtful for a moment*) The way I see it ... and I am not as wise as some. I have not been to schools that would make me wise and content. The way I see it, the purpose of all this is to help man to know himself. To support his push after truth ... to find the good in people and tear out the ugliness. To kindle shame, anger, courage in people's hearts. Perhaps even to make their lives holy with the spirit of beauty. But that will not come easily. Do you agree?

POET: (*nodding, but not facing the PERSON*) Yes. We can agree the purpose of literature, art, theatre, songs ... is to make men better.

PERSON: (*enthusiastically*) Then see for yourself what a great cause you serve! Aren't you happy?

POET speaks to himself, as if asking the question of thin air.

POET: Happy?

Light changes to icy blue. Sounds of a departing train and high wind. The POET shudders and moves away from the PERSON. He peers into the theatre auditorium, as if searching for an exit he cannot see.

POET: What do you want with me? What time is it now?

PERSON: (*smiling. Softly*) Maybe you think I'm insane.

POET: I missed my train for the third time this morning and I'll never see my publisher today as I had arranged.

PERSON: Sometimes one man thinks another is insane when there is an argument.

POET: I don't think you're insane.

PERSON: I have heard it said out there in the streets that it is bad form to argue about anything anymore. Our schools manufacture children who are alike, even to the cut of hair and length of skirt and pant leg. They turn out equipment for industry, not human beings ...

POET: Who can say what the schools today will produce?

PERSON: What the children think or dream matters for nothing. They must be agreeable and obedient. They must all be alike, travel at the same speed now and later ... eat food and make love at a given hour ... live by watches synchronized from one end of the earth to the other. What a hell of a way to live! Gods don't live like that ... so why must men be so regimented?

POET: (*intending humour, but his words are dull and heavy*) My watch stopped at two o'clock last night. Perhaps that's why I missed my train again.

PERSON: (*laughs provocatively*) You've been late before ... you'll be late again.

POET: I haven't been able to sleep or work.

PERSON: Lorca threw one helluva long shadow across the earth. A man can easily hide in it. There is safety in this, don't you think, my friend from the prairies?

POET: If we have to talk, then let's talk. There is no need to be insulting!

PERSON: Sure, we can talk like grown men.

POET: I'm glad we've come to that understanding!

PERSON: (*smiles, looks at the POET as if understanding his inner thoughts*) We can talk any way you want.

POET: (*almost apologetically*) I'm sorry. My mind wanders at times ... I work under pressure and I'm not sure what I do. Time passes ... a schoolmate of mine died a week ago and he was a year younger that I ... I have so much to do and time passes ...

PERSON: I'm also sorry. But time must be made to listen to earth and lumber and grey cement over land that many never again feel sun.

POET: I have so much to do ...

PERSON: Cities grow larger by the hour. A man grows cattle and lettuce heads but he no longer touches that which he cultivates. Electricity and steel feed the hungry. Man's love of man is lost in the steamy atmosphere. The waters are polluted ...

Light changes to white. Harsh and strong. The PERSON moves away from the POET.

PERSON: ... so we turn cold and hard, with eyes of stone. Life, we once were set on changing, has broken us. What are we to do? Tell me!

POET: I don't know. I'm trying to find the answer, if there is an answer!

PERSON: Imagination, my boy … can help man rise above this world, if only for a little while. For a man such as I has lost his place on earth, hasn't he?

POET: (*nodding*) And he will lose the stars next if he is not careful.

PERSON: (*loudly, fretting against unseen restraints*) He is no longer lord of his earth, but a slave to it and machines … and trying to recover his dignity, he takes drugs that further delude him with assurance of beauty that is no longer there! He makes new religions from a psychedelic pill, and then elevates to godhood the ordinary pimp, bootlegger, and pusher of dope. He worships his feeble facts and publishes them as eternal laws. And these laws keep enslaving him until he can no longer struggle … and why should he struggle?

POET: Yes, why should he?

PERSON: Why should he, indeed! War is a god-damned good sport … on somebody else's soil. The food he eats is ample and fortified beyond reason with vitamins. The lights and clatter of his civilization numb his sense of feeling and compassion. Where are the beliefs for which he will perform feats of heroism? Or work through a night without counting his overtime or chances of promotion?

POET: I've asked that question a thousand times and have gone to sleep a thousand nights without an answer. Do you know?

PERSON: (*savagely*) No, I don't know! I'm asking you to tell me!

POET: (*startled, defensive*) I haven't found the answer!

The PERSON walks away. Becoming less agitated, he looks over his shoulder almost playfully at the POET. He laughs and speaks gently, but with a touch of irony.

PERSON: Let all those bastards who wander off the road die—let them. To hell with them … don't waste your pity on them! There are others in the world. The important thing is the longing to find God. So long as there are men longing for God, He will show Himself and stand beside them, don't worry. For God is what makes man reach up for perfection from the moment he first stood on two feet. Do you agree?

POET: Yes, God is alive in all men. But only alive.

PERSON: (*now taunting*) Why don't you speak up? Are you afraid? Don't agree … argue with me, damn you!

The POET is agitated, torn by a personal conflict of spirit. The PERSON goes to him and places his arm over the POET'S shoulder.

PERSON: It's difficult to speak when you can't … I know. You are a writer and thousands hear you. One night, I came to hear you. What do you preach? What right have you to teach others?

POET: There are days when I am so afraid I can't move! I'm afraid of man's power to destroy. Man can destroy himself and all life on this planet now!

PERSON: Aha! Then maybe Lorca has to be left behind in his Gypsy camp, for he doesn't know this!

POET: (*with feeling*) But I do! I live! There is a great deal of hate in my heart, and at times it breaks into bright flames of wrath. There is doubt, and for days I live out an empty existence, believing in nothing … lying on my bed like a corpse, feeling that only some bizarre oversight has kept me from being buried.

PERSON: (*releasing his arm from the POET'S shoulder and moving away*) There was a time when on this earth there lived great masters of the written word … students of life and the human heart, men inspired by burning desires to improve the world, as well as mountainous faith in human nature! They wrote books to outlast Armageddon, they gave birth to characters so inspired they still live and will continue to live. There is courage in these books, my friend … flaming anger and love that is free and sincere as a summer day!

POET: I know. This is not news to me!

PERSON: (*considering the POET thoughtfully for a moment*) It's easy to see you've had a good meal on these books. But your soul has badly digested what you've read, for your own words are forced out of you like sausage meat, and your truth and love are as thin as the paper on which you write them!

POET: You mean nothing to me. I've listened to you and I'll think about what you said, even if there is little consequence to your ideas. I'll think, and perhaps I can at some future time explain something to myself and to you. We'll see.

POET moves as if to step down from the stage, but the PERSON blocks his escape.

PERSON: (*sadly*) My child … you are like the moon now, reflecting other men's light … throwing many shadows but giving little illumination of your own and no warmth at all.

Light onstage turns green. Faint sounds of birds and falling water.

POET: What time is it? How long have we been …

PERSON: You're too poor a man to offer anything of value. I'm just an ordinary person … a worker and a wanderer … but when you recite words to me now I feel you're not enriching life by adding to its beauty … but rather, playing with your own ego.

POET: (*dryly, conscious of being restrained from leaving*) You don't know me. I've grown and changed. You've no right to speak to me in that way. I'm not the same man you spoke to before … you don't know me now!

PERSON: (*pushes the POET roughly back*) Sure, I know you! You're a mortgage holder on my spirit and on theirs! (*motions with the back of his hand to the audience*) Lending out bits of experience in return for the fame we give you … when you read, your voice is thin … your pen scratches on the surface of things. You reach into the grave for the rags and crown of a dead Spanish poet … and it is as ridiculous as planting a palm tree on the blue-black landscape of a prairie field in early autumn. It means nothing. It might even seem like an absurd ridicule of a man who was a giant alongside of you! Have you stopped to consider this?

As the argument rises, the sounds of birds and water are amplified. The POET is frustrated. He recovers slowly.

POET: You waste my time … cloud my judgment. But my confidence is still left, and I won't let you damage my ability to write as I think!

PERSON: You can't escape from me … this is the springtime of your optimism and you are trapped by it! (*laughs cruelly*) How often have you spent time describing stupid feelings of stupid people when you worked on your most original ideas?

POET: People are not stupid! All my work is important! I've created to the best of my capabilities!

PERSON: Can you then write in a way to give wings to the human spirit?

POET: (*sharply, thinly*) Yes! Some people have thought so.

PERSON: No, not you! (*laughs bitterly*) You rake through the crumbs, looking for truth that says man is evil and without hope or honour. That he is weak and forever alone. Why tell him this? Why? He is already convinced by others who have dulled his mind and spirit and commonsense with the garbage of bad television and low-grade films … by dashes of colour that would dazzle an ox … by hypnotic music and empty-worded songs that strike with the volume of thunder … by drugs and poverty and death-fear … by senseless violence that makes entertainment out of war and its sufferings … by glibness without talent and books without purpose to cloud the judgment of people who otherwise have the genius for putting life on the soil of the moon. (*pauses*) Man continues to see his own ugliness and failure with no possibility of improvement, no possibility of betterment. Can you show this possibility to me? Do you know how?

The POET is groping, moving away from the PERSON. But on the PERSON'S last words, he becomes still and brooding.

PERSON: (*smiling*) At last, you are listening! That is good. An honest teacher has to be a damned good student!

Light becomes golden and dim onstage. Guitar music faintly in the background.

PERSON: (*demanding*) Who are you really?

POET: If I must, I'll listen …

PERSON: You and I are the most important people in this hour of history! (*takes out a book from inside his shirt and waves it to the POET*) See this! Here is the old history … the memories of kings and bandits who did nothing with their time except keep blacksmiths busy making armour for them and chastity belts for their women.

The POET laughs softly, covering his mouth with his hand.

PERSON: Why do you laugh? I look to you for hope, yet you take more from people than you give them ... and you laugh. Is it funny to see human virtue chewed up in a prison or at a dog race?

POET: That was not the reason for my laughter.

PERSON: Then what was? Me? Or yourself? In what damned way are you different than the grey, colourless people you write of so harshly? You come as a self-styled prophet turning out dime magazines four pages long for other poets like yourself to read ... exposing vice so virtue might triumph, as they say, yet vice and virtue are only words to you. I doubt that God sent you down as His prophet. He'd have chosen a stronger man than you if He had!

POET: What do you expect of me? I was molded by the times into which I was born. If the times created weakness in me, then I am like others ... (*hesitantly*) but ... I will be stronger ...

PERSON: When? A pacifist burned himself to death before the UN building while you ate your cornflakes and homogenized milk. When will you be strong? When will you come to full life?

POET: Soon ...

PERSON: God didn't appoint you! At best you smoke like a spark out of hell and the smoke seeps into the hearts and minds of men like me, filling them with lack of faith in you ... in themselves.

POET: I, too, am searching for truth and reason!

PERSON: (*sardonically*) Of course ... and you come to tell me the ghost of Lorca has entered and begun to burn in you?

POET: Not only a ghost—he is still a poet capable of speaking to me in terms I understand. When he came to New York, he understood the sounds and solitudes of man in the super-state ...

PERSON: And when he went back home he told the Spanish scholars and Spanish peasants and Spanish gypsies about it, and they thought he was mad. But he became immortal, even if they shot him, not knowing his name or the white-hot music within him!

POET: It was only a stupid accident. Death is stupid when it happens that way.

PERSON: (*smiling*) There, there ... let Lorca sleep. It is you I want!

POET: (*wary*) What do you want with me?

PERSON: Every thought, character, place, incident you create is commonplace. When will your poems speak so as to inspire rebellion of the spirit—here? (*slaps his breast*) When will your poems give wings to the soul?

POET: (*quietly and earnestly*) Soon ... very soon. A little more time and I will become wise and without confusion ...

A loud crackling noise and the stage becomes alive with a projection of harsh, rapid impressions of lights and colours that flicker and fade. The crackling continues below the dialogue, becoming the music of a jazz combo faintly heard.

PERSON: For God's sakes ... you are not an eternal child! It has to happen before I, too, give up hope. I'm not important. I can rise above life and fear of the times as well ... so give me the real world and real people in your stories and songs so I may want to create a new form of existence for myself—free of intolerance, evil and pain.

The POET collects his guitar and handful of papers and holds them up to the PERSON.

POET: This is my hammer and my anvil! Here is an instrument capable of surrounding the sun! At the moment it is all silence for me ... but in an hour ... perhaps I can write and sing better than ever before!

Crackle and music of the jazz combo rises in the background.

PERSON: (*loudly, over sounds*) It's a mighty gift! Use it to make laughter to purify the air! People have forgotten how to laugh ... they laugh with anger ... they laugh maliciously ... they laugh through tears. Give me the laugh that can shake a house and make a tree in a garden shiver! Give me a healthy man's laugh—right from the balls! No more laughter at what is pathetic! Give me sentiments that are like sledge hammers, knocking down dusty walls to make room for statues of God in the garden of my life! Give me anger, hatred, courage, shame, disgust ... and in the end, enraged despair ... so that anything less than worthy of me can be destroyed today! Give me hatred for human shortcomings, but give me also love for the common man ... a love from knowing his suffering and the needless drudgery of his work. If you cannot provide me with these things ... then consider whether you should ever write another word to use up my precious time in reading.

During the latter part of the above dialogue, the PERSON sheds his outer clothing, revealing a tattered military uniform. He jumps off the stage into the auditorium where he is handed a rifle with fixed bayonet.

The background music and lights from the projection die out. The stage is lit by a faint glow from backstage.

As the PERSON comes back onto the stage with the gun in hand, a black light on him illuminates invisible wounds on his face and hands and blood in his clothing.

A rumble of war in the background. The faint stage light in back begins to pulsate in time to the sounds of explosions suggesting a battle nearby.

The POET fearfully moves to the PERSON, then steps back in horror.

POET: My God ... I didn't know ... this might happen! Why didn't you tell me? Why did you wait so long to tell me?

PERSON: (*beckoning to the POET*) Come to me ... come nearer ... I can't hurt you ... Look! (*holds out rifle to POET, who steps back*) Look! See how the nations with their boundaries and political systems have clipped my wings, child! And enslaved my thoughts and heart with this! (*holds rifle over his head*)

The POET retreats another step, his face still registering horror

PERSON: They consider this man no longer wants to live decently, but will live with no more ambitions than those of a pig, (*sharply, an outcry*) Don't let them do it! (*in firm, normal voice*) Corrupted into a sack of bones covered by flesh, thick skin and cloth cut and sewn to tell all who see him of his servitude to damned weapons of lust and death. (*again an outcry*) Help me to fight back! (*in normal voice, beckons to POET*) Come to me ... this man needs your attention in one helluva bad way ... hurry! Teach him to live while he still resembles a human being! Come on! The stink of decay hangs over the earth ... our hearts are those of cowards ... fat laziness has snared our minds in a steel trap. Go to him—hurry! Ech! How shallow, how insignificant you are! And how many others there are like you—self-indulgent, weak, hopeless ...

POET: (*trying to reach the PERSON, but stumbling*) Wait! I'm coming!

POET can come no closer. He stands and shakes his head sadly and with futility as he looks at the PERSON.

PERSON: So far, and no further?

POET: (*with self-contempt*) I, too, need help!

PERSON: (*sadly*) Is that all you have to say to me?

POET: I've nothing to say. I'm ashamed to have been born without talent!

PERSON: How will you go on living?

POET: (*dismally*) I don't know.

The PERSON moves to the POET, but he is limping and stooped now.

PERSON: And what will you write now, child?

The POET does not reply but stares without flinching into the face of the PERSON.

PERSON: (*nodding*) I understand. And you would teach others to live? You know who I am now, eh? (*POET nods*) Don't be afraid. All the rest of the youth who are born old men would be as frightened and humiliated if they had to deal with me ... so don't be afraid. Only the man who's already sold his soul to the devil would not wince to hear the judgment passed on him by his conscience. Don't be afraid. (*loudly*) But look at me!

The PERSON suddenly turns to the audience. The flame behind him leaps higher to renewed sounds of explosion.

PERSON: Look at me, will you? Since the first sun rose in my eyes I have wandered through sorrow. Speak one word to me. Only one word in your defence. Deny what I have said. Be strong, if only for a moment and I will take back all I have said! Every damned word! I will bow low before you ... even before that child back there ... (*points into the theatre*) ... I will give you a crown of gold for your head. (*long pause. He turns to the POET*)

Teacher! I need to be taught! For I am but a man. I have become lost in this dark atmosphere of life and I am searching for a highway to the light ... to truth ... to beauty and wisdom that will liberate me and set me free forever! I am but a man! (*humbly*) So hate me, beat me down, kick filth into my face when I fall, but for God's sake rescue me from your indifference! I wish to be better than I am, but how can I be? Teach me how!

POET: (*slowly, with intensity*) I saw ... two birds fly overhead. One was rich in plume and crest, the other torn with wings blood-red ...

PERSON: (*joyfully, to the POET*) The love I have for you—without end! How many people this planet has given birth to, and how few monuments there are to great men! Why is this so?

He laughs and pats the POET over the shoulders and face, then steps away, checking his rifle.

PERSON: Never mind ... just don't be afraid.

POET: (*haltingly, intensely*) An arrow ... dangling from ... its breast ... I watched ... and soon began ... to feel ... my own heart ... borne on wings of steel!

POET turns to the PERSON, happily, as if he had just delivered a valuable prize. But the PERSON is turned away from him, fingering his rifle.

PERSON: Man is sleeping and there is nobody to wake him. Your Lorca has returned to earth and the new poets are jetting through the heavens as if the soil below them was no longer of any consequence, yet we grow potatoes, peaches, and marigolds here. So man sleeps, growing fur and fangs on his soul, reverting slowly to the beast again. He needs the lash, and after the lash, the caress of love. (*turns to the POET, but speaking with gravity*) Hurt him ... don't be afraid to hurt him if you love him, for he will understand he deserves pain for his complacency. And when he has suffered and is ashamed, resurrect Man with your caresses and kisses. Are you capable of loving people?

POET: (*dubiously*) Loving people? ... I don't know if I love people or not. A deep, dark gulf separates me with silence from my neighbour ...

PERSON: It makes no difference. I'm going now. (*waves with his rifle and moves away from the POET to the back of the stage*) Long life to you!

POET: (*quietly, as if to himself*) So soon? ... must you go so soon?

The PERSON continues retreating, walking backwards, buckling his tunic and helmet straps, the gun in the crook of his arm. Explosions and flashes of light increase.

PERSON: Lorca is dead ... will there ever be another? Never mind ... the name doesn't matter. The heart in flames will be seen around the world the next time it catches fire ... don't be afraid! Wait for me. Live wisely and work as if God Himself was driving you headlong down an endless hill!

The PERSON turns and suddenly rushes headlong into the light that flares and dies to darkness at the back of the stage. The explosions end. The lights on the apron of the stage illuminate the POET, who stands for a long moment in deep thought. Then slowly he picks up his guitar and collects his sheaf of poetry.

POET: (*softly*) I never considered ... it might end this ... way. Life ... demands everything ... all at once ...

He leaves the stage and the curtain comes down.

End

GRASS AND WILD STRAWBERRIES

Ryga was extremely busy after the successful première production of *The Ecstasy of Rita Joe* in late 1967: just two months later *Just an Ordinary Person* played at the Metro theatre in Vancouver, and there were plans for a remount and a tour of *The Ecstasy of Rita Joe*, along with a request that his hit play be rewritten for publication (Talonbooks published the first of its many printings of *The Ecstasy of Rita Joe* in 1970). At the same time, Joy Coghill, artistic director of the Playhouse Theatre, wrote to Ryga: "I am fascinated with the idea for the new play and think we should pursue it as soon as possible." Thus the commission, as well as a major theme of *Grass and Wild Strawberries* originated with Coghill, who had been invaluable to Ryga in nurturing *The Ecstasy of Rita Joe* through its many rewrites during the intense collaboration between the playwright and its first director, George Bloomfield.

Coghill was fascinated by the phenomenon of the "counterculture revolution" of the rock/hippie generation, now in full bloom. 1967 was the "Summer of Love," with one of the populist leaders of the movement, Abbie Hoffman, declaring, "We are here to make a better world." The next two years would see John Lennon and Yoko Ono's famous Bed-In for Peace in Montreal, then the generation-defining "Music and Art Fair" at Woodstock, New York. Balmy Vancouver was becoming a magnet for "Hippies," who eventually came into increasingly violent conflict with the city's mayor, Thomas "Tom Terrific" Campbell, known for his tough law-and-order plans to "clean up" city streets (which he finally and notoriously attempted to do four years later in 1971 on a grand and apocalyptic scale during a huge public demonstration in the city's heritage district known as "Gastown"). The Ryga home in Summerland at the time was a hotbed of strident debate as visitors, some of them Americans fleeing military service in the Viet Nam war, outlined grandiose plans to escape to the seemingly remote wilderness of Canada and live a life of imagined freedom. For his part, Ryga questioned the politics of the counterculture revolution: to him they sounded dangerously fascist, especially as they relentlessly criticized the older generation; increasingly stressed modes of behaviour the "movement" considered to be "politically correct"; and demonstrated only the slightest understanding and regard for of any of the world's previous, often historically effective, protest movements.

Grass and Wild Strawberries didn't come easily for Ryga—neither in the writing nor in the staging. Indeed, while he mulled over writing this play, he wrote another that revealed his preoccupation with the darker side of the late 1960s. The teleplay, *Long Morning of a Short Day* (never produced), created an apocalyptic vision of Vancouver under a totalitarian regime, with deserted streets, empty buildings, and roving bands of storm troopers: clearly Ryga had developed a disturbing image of urban culture gone badly wrong, and this play, like *Grass and Wild Strawberries*, was meant to be a forewarning.

Coghill's idea for the play was a musical work to be done in collaboration with The Collectors, one of the city's most popular and enduring rock bands (later known as Chilliwack). Ryga had produced a set of lyrics for them and unbeknownst to him, the band recorded an album, under the same title, which excited Ryga when he heard it and he now began serious work on the play. His "outline for new play" that he sent to Coghill in February 1968 begins—and ends, "A boy and girl, opt-outs from school and from their homes, determined that innocence and fine intention will triumph over comfort and indifference, form the focus of this play ... must come to grips with the enemy of youth—the ordinary man and woman they have all become." The play was clearly meant to warn of the dangerous excesses and questionable politics of rebellious young people without either a socio-economic or a political agenda to propose as an alternative to the "outdated social forms" of their elders they had dedicated themselves to undermine and reject.

Grass and Wild Strawberries opened on April 10, 1969, at the Vancouver Playhouse Theatre, directed by Don Eccleston and starring recent National Theatre School students Thomas Hauff as Allan and Nicola Lipman as Susan. The production was full of glitter, with film clips, slides, dance, recorded sounds and voices, and of course the live music of The Collectors. It easily attracted the largest mainstage audience of the Playhouse's 1968–1969 season. Critical responses in the media ranged from the ecstatic to the epic: the *Province* (11 April, 1969) found the production "a beautiful experience," while Christopher Dafoe of the *Sun* (11 April, 1969) perceptively noted that Ryga "appears to be a sort of human sacrifice for the switched-on crowd."

Indeed he was. For Ryga, the production had gone seriously astray. The director, Don Eccleston, had worked with Ryga previously in television, and was keen on a production utilizing the more psychedelic, media-driven aspects of "rock culture," even travelling to San Francisco's Haight-Ashbury district to tape and film images of youth for projection during the show. It was his suggestion to include the character Captain Nevada and his group, a latter addition to the play, no doubt in an attempt to reflect the popular "tribe" of the hit rock musical *Hair* in this spectacle. Captain Nevada, originally intended by Ryga to represent the more irresponsible elements of youth culture, in Eccleston's hands became instead a celebration of the Hippie ethos, and, with complaints flowing in from season ticket holders about the inclusion of loud music and pot-smoking, the play became controversial in ways the playwright had never intended. In an interview, Ryga admitted, "[audiences] were getting a reconfirmation of the smell, colour, form of their own lives. I'm not under any illusion that they were getting many of the significances of the Allan-Ted grind." A play originally meant by Ryga to warn had finally come, in the hands of his collaborators, merely to dazzle—and annoy.

GRASS AND WILD STRAWBERRIES

CHARACTERS

ALLAN
SUSAN
ALLAN'S FATHER
ALLAN'S MOTHER
UNCLE TED
THE GROUP: CAPTAIN NEVADA
            MICHELE
            NESTOR
            JOAN
WHITE RABBIT
POLICEMAN
BARRACK'S OFFICER
SUSAN'S FATHER
OLD MAN
SOCIAL WORKER

ACT 1

SCENE 1

Play opens on dark house. In darkness, members of the GROUP, including SUSAN and ALLAN, approach the stage through aisles of theatre.

Film collage of impressions of the current world flicker onto projection screen design onstage—impressions of the generation confrontation, crisis of peace, religion, campus revolutions, etc. These impressions grow in pace and intensity with the rising barrage of vocal and mechanical sounds—impressions which build layer on layer as orchestrated composition. Some voices and sounds are recorded and come from various speakers in the theatre. Other voices are live voices of performers as they move toward stage. This dialogue can be staccato, running into itself.

VOICE: (*recorded*) GROMITCH!

VOICE: (*recorded*) Someday you'll settle down, because you'll look around and see you are hurting others beside yourself ...

MEMBER OF THE GROUP: I couldn't get the word *goodbye* out of my throat ...

VOICE: (*recorded*) Dead, dead ... you'll be dead in ten years ...

MICHELE: What's a street for, if you can't stand on a corner waiting for no one?

VOICE: (*recorded*) Dead ... dead ...

MEMBER OF THE GROUP: ... I smiled sadly and told her I wanted to marry a partridge ...

MICHELE: I have a friend who goes to jail just to test reality ...

VOICES: (*recorded*) One, two, three, four—we don't want your filthy war!

VOICE: (*recorded*) ... Good afternoon, ladies and gentlemen—we are now entering the Haight-Ashbury district of San Francisco ... For those of you wishing to take photographs we shall make a ten-minute stop at the end of the block. To the right you will see ... (*trailing off*) ... a *mirror?* ...

VOICES: (*recorded*) (*louder*) One, two, three, four ... we don't want your filthy war!

MEMBER OF THE GROUP: May the baby Jesus shut your mouth and open your mind!

VOICES: (*recorded*) One, two, three ...

POLICE RADIO: Attention ... All cars in the vicinity of 23rd and Westbend report immediately! Attention ... will all cars in the vicinity ...

MEMBER OF THE GROUP: Man has more than the capacity to be a flower-picking primate!

VOICE: (*recorded*) What the hell kind of shit is this?

MICHELE: Mother!

Sounds of rioting and shouting.

POLICE RADIO: Attention! Will all cars report ...

MEMBER OF THE GROUP: I think I'll hitch-hike down and see the straight world ...

VOICE: (recorded) It's organized by communists and homosexuals ...

MEMBER OF THE GROUP: ... What a weird trip ... wish I could tell how this lettuce tastes ...

MICHELE: ... Is there anybody ... anybody ... I would want to make a baby for me? ... I cannot see your faces ... there is no face for my baby ...

MEMBER OF THE GROUP: Man has more capability than to barbecue other men!

MICHELE: Somebody here is scratching his wrist ... It's tickling my eardrums ... Who's doing it? ... I want mother ... I need a goddamned mother!

VOICE: (recorded) I'm just going for some cigarettes and milk ... What the hell's happening?

MEMBER OF THE GROUP: I see the sun! ... Help me watch the sun!

Sound of shots.

MEMBER OF THE GROUP: It isn't true ... we have blood ... we are not computers or dead packing crates!

MEMBER OF THE GROUP: Will this place ... ever ... be God-fingered?

VOICE: (recorded) No! Oh, no!

Rising tumult and screams of riot.

MICHELE: Look at the cucumber! ... Whoever sliced it up is a murderer. I'm going to be one, too ... I'm going to tear it up and see what it's made of!

VOICE: (recorded) Get that bastard in the brown hat!

VOICE: (recorded) Hey—he's got a camera! Smash the camera!

MICHELE: I don't know what to eat—the cucumber, the sandwich ... or the plate ...

VOICE: (recorded) ... Society may well become depersonalized and desexualized within 50 years, two New York scientists said yesterday. Anyone who tries to be an individual will be looked upon as odd, reactionary and anti-group ...

VOICE: (recorded) Freedom is a privilege that has to be earned ... those who don't earn it should be denied freedom!

MEMBER OF THE GROUP: We must liberate ourselves, or we will be liberated by outsiders!

VOICE: (recorded) Vote for me if you value your property—that is the issue ... the *only* issue in this election!

MEMBER OF THE GROUP: Man has the capacity ... TO BE ONE WITH GOD!

ALL VOICES: (*over tumult*) Amen! ... Amen! ... Ommmm ...

VOICE: (recorded) (*frantically*) Bring out the goddamn dogs!

VOICE: (recorded) ... The weather for the Vancouver area is for more rain becoming intermittent showers in the late afternoon ...

VOICE: (recorded) There are a lot of children around ... the women in the community are very, very female ... weaving and cooking ... cooking and weaving ...

GIRL: (recorded) (*screaming*) Her eye! ... Jesus, they knocked out her eye!

MEMBER OF THE GROUP: Man has the capacity ... TO BE GOD!

ALL VOICES: Amen! ... Amen! ... OMMM ...

The sounds of battle, violence, turbulence of voices become one sound of high-pitched madness, ending abruptly.

House goes to darkness.

Sound of "OMMM" continues.

Sound of music, profound and deeply religious, rises.

Light on CAPTAIN NEVADA. He raises his arms to members of the GROUP who approach and stand in front of him. On his speech they posture down before him in a gesture of primordial religious homage.

CAPTAIN NEVADA: Groups! Forces! Give your attention to the fly which appears where your eyes are closed, for it is a spiritual light that is the manifestation of your own concentration. We are all one God! As you see the fly—become one with the fly! As you see the light, become one with that light ... flow with it ... So I will ask you to be silent for the long moment ahead ... Understand me well when I say we must have this planet ... And it's ours, if anybody's going to have it!

Music rises and soars into "Things I Remember."

CAPTAIN NEVADA leads GROUP onto stage through a dance of time, like rising and falling of waves. THE GROUP goes into dissolve of themselves on screen image.

On Screen: Street scene of GROUP in wild, joyous antics among busy population of city. They dance, leapfrog, turn harassed shoppers in their tracks, surrounding and dancing past amazed people at bus stops, etc. All in tempo and within mood shadings of song.

SONG: Things I remember
Things I have seen
Through the smoke of the willow
Through the waters of the city

Things I remember
Things I have seen
Things I remember ...
    The copper-dandy morning
    Astride a black horse
    Things I remember
    Things I have seen ...
Things I remember ...
The faces of tomorrow
Polished like stone
Things I remember
Things I have seen
    A tree in the river
    Twisted by thirst
    Things I remember
    Things I have seen ...
Things I remember ...
    A queen with no heart
    Her mind blown apart
    Things I remember
    Things I have seen ...
    A sun-flower face
    In a garden of rain
Things I remember
Things I have seen ...
    Two weeks of love
    And a night of regret
Things I remember
Things I have seen ...
    My love lie easy
    Life is forever ...

GROUP dances out of the screen image.

SCENE 2

ALLAN and SUSAN enter stage. SUSAN is laughing.

ALLAN'S FATHER enters and is isolated by light. He is disembodied, out of another life.

FATHER: Who's here?

ALLAN and SUSAN embrace and dance tenderly. On FATHER'S words, ALLAN breaks free. He is thoughtful.

ALLAN: (*gently*) Father ...

SUSAN: Today ... I prayed ... among the trees ... I lifted my arms to the sun ... and I prayed by dancing ...

She dances away and past FATHER, but with no awareness of him.

FATHER: You all right, kid? ... Life treating you good?

ALLAN: I'm here. I didn't know you might still be with me ... so long after ... I tried to forget ... You came down off a scaffold ... such a long way down ...

GROUP enters and hovers in background. SUSAN dances to GROUP and dissolves into it.

FATHER: Can't see you ... (*testily*) I can't see you, I said! You wanted to talk ...

ALLAN: It's too late ...

FATHER: ... Come on and talk! We never did much talkin' ... I'm listening.

ALLAN: (*smiling*) I was thinking I'd like to steal a car and drive to Mexico!

FATHER: (*plaintively*) Can't see you ... can't hear you! What the hell's wrong, do you know? ... Maybe wax forming in the ears ... that happens to some men at my age ... prostate trouble, too ... been peeing something awful ...

ALLAN: I'm going to become a fascist on a motor-cycle and run down all the social democrats and pinkos like you and Uncle Ted!

FATHER shakes his head, listening for unheard voices.

SCENE 3

UNCLE TED enters. He is aged and on rough times, his clothes outsized and seedy.

UNCLE: (*scolding, peevish*) So you've dropped your courses at the school and taken off? ... Just like that?

ALLAN: I wasn't learning anything, Uncle Ted. The instructor was old and out of touch ...

UNCLE: Why did you drop your studies? Have you nothing to say?

ALLAN: I've explained why ...

UNCLE: I didn't hear you ...

ALLAN: As I said before ...

UNCLE: Hey! A bastard thing happened ... an agent from a publishing house came today offering me five hundred bucks ... He wanted me to write a history of the labour struggle during and after the war years ... I couldn't do it, and I told him so.

ALLAN: Why not?

UNCLE: I could never do it ...

FATHER: Ech! Who's going to thank a man for putting his head on the block? I ask you—eh?

UNCLE: It would've been a betrayal to sell the story of what happened to us here to a commercial book house. I couldn't do it! ... Five hundred measly bucks would've been the price of my betrayal!

FATHER: When was the last time you seen a paycheck?

UNCLE: (*with pathetic pride*) Something will come along, boy ... I've put my name in a few places as night watchman. They can always use a steady man in places like that!

FATHER: No, sir ... I wouldn't thank a man for being stubborn like that ... not a chance I'd thank him.

UNCLE: You know something, Allan? ... Some men learn to compromise even when there's no compromise left for them ...

UNCLE TED retreats offstage. FATHER shakes his head in anger.

FATHER: Damned fool man will end up in jail ... or even worse, on welfare!

SCENE 4

ALLAN moves towards FATHER, but the move is blind and groping.

ALLAN: Please, Dad ... stop letting me have the car!

FATHER: Workers are a bugger lot ... They won't thank a man for going in fists swinging on their behalf!

ALLAN: Dad?

FATHER: ... Some of them act like there's no working class left ... they've all become some kind of middle-class ... two cars ... shares in companies ... what the hell! Middle-class my ass!

ALLAN: Don't be afraid for me ... don't be afraid for yourself!

FATHER: Men are men ... no need to be ashamed of that ... They laid off a guy at the shop because he was late for work a couple of times. I said to the others maybe we should say something about that ... threaten to walk out to get Jerry rehired, because he has a couple of kids to raise. But the men weren't keen on trouble, so the idea was kind of dropped ... (*with a snort*) That's middle-class for you!

ALLAN: Stop giving me an allowance even when I'm working! ... Tell me to pay for food and the telephone calls I make! I would have done it if you told me to ...

FATHER: I'm tired ... I'm real tired ... I've been working a long time without a break, darned near twenty-four years. Think I'll take a trip to California ...

ALLAN: Dad! Listen to me! ... It was a long way down that time!

FATHER: Always wanted to see California before I got too old ... Never been that far south in my life ...

ALLAN: ... I have to hate you if you don't start seeing me as I am! You can't accommodate me all your life!

FATHER laughs softly to himself. Moves thoughtfully away.

FATHER: And why not? ... A man has to give himself a break sometimes ... Family almost grown up ... so what the hell's holding me back now?

ALLAN tries to follow his FATHER'S memory, but loses it. FATHER leaves.

SCENE 5

SUSAN: *(languidly moving away from GROUP)* I like to pray ... among the trees ... my arms to the sun!

ALLAN: *(anxiously)* If he was to drive in that condition ... Suppose he was to run off the road with the car ... Or have a bad spell of dizziness like he gets sometimes after eating? ...

SUSAN: Allan—what has happened has happened. He didn't know he would fall off a scaffold and kill himself a week before he was to go on holidays ... it can't be helped. I love you.

ALLAN: Did he really? ... How sad life gets all of a sudden ...

SCENE 6

Light on screen—large blowup of Group leader (CAPTAIN NEVADA) with his name printed over picture.

CAPTAIN NEVADA sweeps onto stage with flourish, his cape flying, clapping his hands—the eternal jester.

CAPTAIN NEVADA: Hullo! ... We are the people our parents warned us about! *(SUSAN and ALLAN pick up his handclapping)* Kiwanians, Elks, Moose, Bears, rowdy-dowdy girl guides of whatever age, J.C.'s and all other disciples of manufactured possessions ... I introduce to you ... the White Rabbit!

Screen photo of youth, who enters stage, joining in hand clap rhythm.

CAPTAIN NEVADA: And Michele—your daughter of abundance!

MICHELE blowup on screen.

CAPTAIN NEVADA: Joan!

JOAN on screen and entering onto stage.

CAPTAIN NEVADA: Here's Nestor!

NESTOR enters with blowup. Handclapping increases in tempo. SUSAN sways and dances to the beat.

CAPTAIN NEVADA: Hey—mama Sue! ... Lightning is a crack in the window of heaven!

MICHELE steps forward, swaying to the rhythms but her face anxious.

MICHELE: I could see it ∴ ... they were hurting all over to have me break down again and say I was sorry and not have things end this way ...

SUSAN: *(dancing)* Today ... I prayed ... among the trees ... I lifted my arms to the sun ... and I prayed by dancing rain and summer ... with my dolls in the garden!

WHITE RABBIT: *(angry)* If I catch him, he's going to burn ... I'm going to pack his own stuff down his throat until he screams ... He'll be put in the hospital, and not just for one afternoon ... it'll take nine months patching him together!

NESTOR: *(mocking)* It's all regression, I tell you. Just look at us—smoking pot, flying kites, chasing rainbows in a muddy ditch ... Regression!

CAPTAIN NEVADA: Nonsense! We are partisans of chaos ... makers of discontent ... Pied Pipers for children of IBM and the nuclear silence! ... Grave-diggers for dead totality! ... Killing pigs with laughter ... Building monuments of air on the sludge of the river!

NESTOR: Wow, you mad bastard!

ALLAN breaks away from the laughter and antics of GROUP.

SUSAN: *(calling)* Allan ... papa Al ...

CAPTAIN NEVADA: Come on, papa Al ... I give you a rainbow—take it and be free!

SUSAN: Allan ...

SCENE 7

Screen film—ALLAN leaving home.

FATHER and MOTHER enter stage, screen impression playing over scene.

FATHER: Allan, use your head! At what age do you change from ... this ... to becoming a bum?

MOTHER: Where are you going to sleep tonight?

FATHER: Stick with it, kid. Get your school behind you ... then you can play around for a while. But you'll be ready to come back and dig in!

ALLAN: Dig into what?

FATHER: What do you mean?

ALLAN: Dead ... I'll be dead in ten years ...

MOTHER: (*uncomprehending*) You wanted a painting kit ... we bought you a nice kit for your birthday.

ALLAN laughs without mirth.

FATHER: (*after long moment*) I've ... never pleaded for anything, but I'm gonna do it now ... please stay away from that sort of thing. I'll give you anything you want—okay?

ALLAN: (*shaken*) I don't *want* anything you can buy to give me ... I want to be a person—to love you for what you are!

FATHER: I'm your father ... you're all ... listen! If you want to work at the shop with me ...

ALLAN: No!

MOTHER is first to understand they have lost him.

MOTHER: I'll send you money ... and you phone home if you get into trouble ...

Screen image fades away. FATHER and MOTHER leave.

SUSAN: Allan ...

Handclaps change to breath chant at low level of sound.

ALLAN: I think I helped to kill him ...

Music up.

ALLAN: You never knew him, Sue. He was a poor, petty bastard ... He was a good man, my father ... I wish it had been different between us ...

THE GROUP dance out of scene on song.

Film on screen—high scaffold. A man falling.

ALLAN stares at the screen. SUSAN stands apart from him, immersed in her own memories.

SONG: A sliver of glass in a busted house
And Mother stands there cryin'
They say a dead man touched my eyes
But I know they're lyin'
Son I wish that I may go
Down where the deep still waters flow,
Down where the deep still waters flow
Down where the deep still waters flow ...
Holy child they did say of him
Where will you be
When the long rain
Starts to fall?
    I dreamed last night
    Went in search of him
    Cotton-candy man showed me the way
    Standing over him
    I called his name
    Said hello to him
    He didn't hear—
    They paved the graves
    Of men like him
    ... Father of the child
Holy child they did say of him
Where will you be
When the long rain
Starts to fall?
    I dreamed last night
    Of him seated there
    Glowing fading lights
    Like nights and days
    Washing over him
    He didn't hear
    When I spoke to him
    He didn't hear—
    So I touched him
    And he fell over
    And I awoke ...
Holy child they did say of him
Where will you be
When the long rain
Starts to fall?

SCENE 8

SUSAN and ALLAN hold each other at arms' length.

SUSAN: There was wind and dust when I was a child ... I wonder if I will live like that again?

ALLAN: The tide came in at five. I heard it strike the rocks along the beach and for no reason at all I remembered being on a train one winter in northern Ontario ... so groovy ... moonlight on snow-covered rocks and dying into darkness behind me ...

ALLAN begins collecting and assembling painting gear.

SUSAN: (*still in her own world*) ... I wouldn't want to live like that. I used to think once I could always go home if I became lonely or desperate ... I don't want to go back ... never!

ALLAN: So big daddy's coming here instead ... the gothic man in a Pepsi-Cola land.

SUSAN: Oh yes ... my daddy's gonna love you, Allan baby!

She teases him, mocks him, then takes a gruff stance in imitation of her father.

SUSAN: Harrump! ... What's this? You're rather a scruffy specimen for my daughter, aren't you?

ALLAN: (*in a piping voice*) I'm not a specimen, sir. I'm really a man underneath!

SUSAN: Underneath? ... How far underneath? ... Don't believe it ... Still—if you *are* a man down there, I don't want any screwing around with my daughter!

ALLAN: It's all right, sir ... isn't the first time ...

SUSAN: What?

ALLAN: I know her first name now ... so ... we can do our thing as friends ...

SUSAN: Well, you just understand I'm not having any screwing around!

ALLAN: Screwing *around*? Oh, sir—that would be horrid!

They break up in laughter and embrace. SUSAN touches his lips.

SUSAN: You will always love me—promise again?

ALLAN: Sure, baby—always. Did you get the linseed?

SUSAN: One man and one woman—how lucky I am!

ALLAN: Did you get the linseed?

SUSAN: It's in my handbag ... (*with mock annoyance*) You talked in your sleep last night and you said bad things ...

ALLAN: What'd I say?

SUSAN: If I told you I'd have to leave you and that would never do ... so how can I tell you?

ALLAN prepares to paint. She sits before him.

SUSAN: Paint me a dog with a kinky tail!

ALLAN: Get lost ...

SUSAN: The doctor said I needed calcium. Rice and shellfish off the beach won't do, he said ... I would suffer damage to my teeth ...

ALLAN: What does he know ...

SUSAN: Milk ... My God, will we ever buy milk for a quarter again?

ALLAN: I'll look around for a milkhouse tomorrow ...

SUSAN: We might keep a goat on the beach ... Strawberries grow right beside the sea ... the grass must be good for a goat.

ALLAN: Why not? I could cut its hair for brushes while you milked its milk ... and if we got desperate for meat ... (*turns and winks knowingly at her, then runs forefinger across his throat*) ... Where will we put big daddy when he comes?

SUSAN: (*deflated*) He won't stay. No ... he'll just come and go. (*frightened*) Don't let him take me back!

ALLAN: (*flatly*) He can't do that.

They are both uneasy. She tries to cheer herself and him.

SUSAN: If I went home I'd have lots to eat and a new ski jacket ...

ALLAN nods but looks away from her.

SUSAN: The doctor asked me how old I was. I said I was eighteen. He thought *that* was too young ... (*laughs*) What would he say if I told him the truth?

ALLAN: The days before a storm are longer than other days, aren't they?

SUSAN: I'll do it ... I'll tell him next time!

ALLAN: Don't worry about it—it's not important.

SUSAN: I'm not worried.

She huddles in fear. He moves away and she becomes alarmed.

SUSAN: Allan ... I read yesterday that a tree howls when it's cut down and begins to fall. But we don't hear it because the sound is different than a baby crying ...

ALLAN: Don't worry, I said ...

SUSAN: There was a dead magpie on the road ... A car drove over him ... Do you think we will ever put dead magpies together so they fly again?

ALLAN: Susan, honey ... please ...

SUSAN: I'm asking so I know what to believe!

ALLAN: I walked to the beach when you were gone. The wind stopped blowing. Everything was still except for the waves telling me what they were doing in Singapore ... And I thought of you on their white table with linoleum and white walls ... I saw you leave their table, but it wasn't white any more. There were two dust marks where your shoes had dirtied their white table ...

SUSAN goes to him.

SUSAN: Sometimes the baby moves and I'm both so happy and so scared I want to cry!

Music up softly.

SONG: Grass and wild strawberries
Incense and wine
A crow on the cradle
Will never be mine ...

She is cheerful now. Tries to help him with his painting. As he strokes the canvas with his brush, flashes of colour scan the stage in abstract designs.

SUSAN: I could never live to be thirty. That would be a disaster ...

ALLAN: There is always a third person watching ... waiting ...

SUSAN: Yes! ... I feel his presence ... everywhere, and I feel good then! There was light, coming out of the leaves and trees ... A green light ... I couldn't walk home ... I had to run! An' I was thinking of you like you were the last person on earth!

ALLAN: (*grinning*) You're a depraved young chick!

SUSAN: (*childish, defensive*) I'm not ashamed of my age ... Doctor didn't have to say that.

ALLAN: He was talking off the top of his head ... Lots of things gather on tops of heads—birds and crowns and straw hats ...

SUSAN: Mushrooms and snow ...

ALLAN: (*boyishly*) My grandfather wore a cloth cap on top of his ... I've been an' seen, he used to say, and he'd scratch his head through his cloth cap!

SUSAN: (*worried*) I wonder if he'll know right away when he comes?

ALLAN: Poor Grandpop ... we took a camping trip north one summer with him. He took me walking in a circle around the tent—never more than fifty feet from the tent. We saw a tired cow, a lot of bush an' we heard a truck go by on the highway. "What a country, eh, boy? Now *you've* been an' *you've* seen!" he said to me.

They both laugh. Music lingers in background.

SUSAN: My mother was thirty-five when I left. I remember that good ... I ran away on her birthday.

ALLAN: Why on her birthday?

SUSAN: I don't know ... just to hurt her, I suppose. She'd baked a cake with candles, an' she was in the bedroom putting on a new dress ... she ... wanted to look nice for when Daddy came home ...

ALLAN: Why talk about it?

SUSAN: I was looking at the cake ... an' it was there for a celebration—for what? For all the times I saw her sitting, combing her hair, when it was already combed too much? ... I thought ... if I went now ... maybe she'd be free then. And the next birthday she could celebrate something real ...

ALLAN: But she didn't.

SUSAN: No ... I couldn't tell her why I did it ... because I knew all she would remember after was my leaving ... on her birthday. (*earnestly*) How do you put a magpie together, Allan? Does anybody know?

Music out. ALLAN is despondent and distant.

ALLAN: The paintings aren't drying in this humid air ... the canvas will rot before it dries ... I'm gonna have to write and ask her for a loan!

SUSAN: But only yesterday you said ... you said we'd never do it again.

ALLAN: There are days—weeks, when I can't work. I sit and think of lightning and bells ... hot rain and cold smiles ... I question why and there's no answer ... What the hell do I do?

SUSAN: No sense in worrying. There are days like that ...

ALLAN: What do you know about such days?

SUSAN: I know some things ...

ALLAN: *(with impatience)* You've stopped me from doing ... At first, I thought there'd be pure freedom to feel, express, explore. But the light goes out ... and there are shadows through which I cannot see!

SUSAN moves away. He follows her.

ALLAN: Hey, Sue! Where you going?

SUSAN: Dishes have to be washed ... the bed made.

ALLAN: Don't go—it's not important.

SUSAN: I don't want to talk when you're like this ...

ALLAN: Susan ... I'm sorry, baby ... I'm sorry.

ALLAN steps behind her and embraces her, his hands over her breasts. She pulls at his hands.

SUSAN: Don't press me so hard ... it hurts me now.

ALLAN: I didn't know ...

He releases her. She drops her head backwards on his shoulder and laughs happily.

SUSAN: I don't want you to worry. There's nothing to worry about. I never liked my father, but maybe you will.

ALLAN: I wish I didn't have to see him.

SUSAN: He worried a lot about my teeth ...

ALLAN: It was different for me ...

SUSAN leaves.

ALLAN: Yep ... it was different for me. I was doing a long-distance run against time ... I inherited a revolution that couldn't succeed without me. There were supposed to be workers and farmers going to take over the big place at the end of the road. So when I was five I started running to catch up. Only ... when I got there, the big man had already invited the revolution in to dinner. He fed them steak and two servings of dessert ... they got fat overnight ... and I saw them behind the gate with stones and bricks in their hands, ready to smash me if I spoke or took a step through the gate ... Behind them were the cats with guns and plastic helmets, but they were grinning, holding their guns like iron cocks between their knees ... And up on the roof was the big man himself, laughing and holding his guts with his hands to keep his pants from splitting ...

SCENE 9

Screen projection of a kitchen setting. UNCLE TED enters. He is shy, awkward, dressed in work clothes and younger than in earlier scene.

UNCLE: Good morning, boy. Did you sleep well?

ALLAN: I did, Uncle Ted ... and you?

UNCLE: I slept very well. But I had some thinking to do so I had me a walk. Is your mother up yet?

ALLAN: I heard her leave ... *(long, awkward pause)* ... She said you had some luck with a job.

UNCLE: Not so ... not so. They changed their minds at the tool and die shop ... I went clear across town to be told ... the time of working men has no value. The bosses don't care if a telephone call saves you half a day riding buses for nothing ...

ALLAN: Did you give them shit for it?

UNCLE: They know what they do—they deliberately attack their commodities—the working man. For we're only commodities, boy, that eat and recreate to produce other commodities ... some get driven to work by a chauffeur, some walk four miles ... I have no illusions about my worth, neither should you. But if we struggle without compromise for a change in the social and economic system, we can win— and we cease being commodities then. We become full personalities!

ALLAN: That is only half the road, man ... even socialism has its aristocrats. The fight doesn't end there.

UNCLE: Oh, people are people ... They will make kings out of horses' arses. Or stand hypnotized by television like cattle in a field watching a motorcycle go by on a road that was once their meadow. Brainless, mindless behaviour that has kept us back from progress ... has given rise to religion, confusion, pettiness ... but people are people, and there is always hope.

ALLAN: In Czechoslovakia ... young communists died defending their right to live away from mother!

UNCLE: Allan ... worse things have happened. Don't take a narrowed view of history because of this ... the struggle is yours now. There is no escaping your commitment to history!

ALLAN: I have no commitment. I want to be left alone!

UNCLE: Heaven forbid ... but who knows? ... Perhaps that *will* be your commitment in the end ...

ALLAN: To hell with your commitments! There's nothing in it for me to be a joiner ... Where are the men now you talk about from fifteen years back? They've gone for the piece of the action— that's where they're at!

UNCLE: Now you just hold on ...

ALLAN: I'm not interested in gradualism! ... I must take this and all systems that threaten me apart ... I grew up on marbles, hopscotch and plastic junk. I want an end to it, not more of the same!

UNCLE: (*orating now*) Allan ... your father and I lived and worked with real men—and after we stop living we may very well be forgotten ...

ALLAN: You're forgotten already!

UNCLE: (*ignoring him*) History is all that lives on. Never neglect your history or traditions, particularly the revolutionary side of it. For it rages on like a firestorm, devouring its wastes and creating new life ... new social systems on the graves of the old!

ALLAN: I'm not a meeting. You don't have to politic with me.

UNCLE: (*amused suddenly*) Yes ... even the language we speak is different now. Is it because you were brought up by mothers and bachelors?

ALLAN: I have a father.

UNCLE: The fathers were away working so life might be easier for you. What will become of you, cut off so from reality? ... Suspended to necessities whose significance you do not understand ...

ALLAN: I understand more than you give me credit for ...

UNCLE: You understand nothing! The historical class struggle has passed you by ... you've even had your survival instinct removed from you!

ALLAN: (*angry*) I'd like to live a life that is free, so I begin living that way ... I don't do it to teach or convert ... I WANT TO LIVE! Is that so complicated? Is it wrong?

UNCLE: (*moved*) It isn't wrong ... I believe in you, boy ... And I want to hear something of what I believe in because ... because. I, too, am sometimes thinking if I've done enough ... or if what I did matters now. I am what I am because I, also, want to live ... can *you* understand that?

ALLAN: I'm not sure ...

UNCLE: That's because you're young ... So let's you and I clean up the kitchen for your mother. She works hard and comes home tired.

UNCLE slaps ALLAN playfully over shoulder and leaves. Light on screen setting kitchen dies.

SCENE 10

Film on screen: four pall-bearers around an open grave, lowering a casket with excruciating slowness. ALLAN, in silhouette, watches the burial. Funeral music.

SUSAN enters but remains away from ALLAN.

CAPTAIN NEVADA enters, carrying an enormous book from which he reads his oration.

CAPTAIN NEVADA: O nobly-born, your present body is not a body of gross matter. You have now the power to pass through hills, earth, houses and mountains—straight forward, backwards, or from side to side ... You are endowed with the power of miraculous action, not as the fruit of discipline and ecstasy, but naturally, freely ... You can instantaneously reach what place you will. Yet you do not desire these powers of illusion and shape-shifting ... Pray to the Teacher.

SUSAN: My father bought an acreage and we moved there when I was a baby ... the house was big and always cold ... During the winter my mother wore a heavy sweater even when she cooked our meals ...

ALLAN: (*facing funeral*) I hardly saw my father ... Uncle Ted was around a lot, but not my father. And then he died ...

SUSAN: She left him twice ... she went to town and worked as a waitress. But she came back. She always came back ... Once she said she came back because she was afraid of the Manitoba winter ... I don't know what she meant ... she combed her hair a lot ...

ALLAN: ... He'd wanted to be a machinist, but there wasn't a school for his trade, so he took carpentry, he said. He worked a lot on construction outside the city ...

SUSAN: ... She sang in the church choir ... when she was down she talked of God and suffering ... Reading the Bible and cryin' ... an' I was afraid of what it was made her cry like that ...

ALLAN: Six years ago he and I went on a camping trip ... It was my birthday ... There was a boat tied up beside the river. We took it out for a row. But the bottom was rotten and broke open ... Almost drowned the two of us because he was no better a swimmer than I. He asked me not to tell about it, and I said I wouldn't ...

Screen funeral fades out.

SUSAN: There is something wrong when a woman cries like that in times of peace.

ALLAN: (*turning to her*) He died ... I was thirteen and he died ... At the graveside it was very quiet while they lowered him down, down ... I heard a meadowlark singing ...

SCENE 11

Screen projection of kitchen. MOTHER and UNCLE appear before it.

UNCLE: (*angry*) Stop obstructing the union, Helen! The investigation shows there were only two nails in the scaffold which broke under him!

MOTHER: Leave me alone! I don't want to talk about it ... I don't want to think about it!

UNCLE: It was an avoidable accident ... You've got a boy to raise and put through school!

MOTHER: It's grubbing off the dead ... the man doesn't deserve this! (*shouts*) I DON'T WANT THEIR GODDAMN COMPENSATION—he didn't have to die!

UNCLE: (*comforting her*) Helen ... Helen ...

MOTHER: Ted, I'm so tired of it all. Please let me be ...

UNCLE: Sure, Helen. I'll stay in town and help out. You go and rest.

Film dies. MOTHER and UNCLE leave.

SCENE 12

SUSAN: (*starting to laugh*) Wow! What a bad trip that was!

ALLAN goes to her—laughing, for they must either laugh or weep. They hold each other. Music up.

SONG: Boom, boom, all around
Go the wheels of the town
And the teletype ... goes click
    Look up, stay still
    Said the man on the hill
    To the child by the edge of the creek
And she looks down
On the meadows and town
While her toes turn to pebbles and dust
Boom, boom, all around
Go the wheels of the town
And the teletype ... goes click
    Don't hurry—wait
    Cries the man at the gate
    To the child by the edge of the creek

And she looks ahead
Not a word was said
But her eyes became sorrowing dreams

Boom, boom, all around
Go the wheels of the town
And the teletype ... goes click
        Too late now—run
        Shouts the man in the sun
        To the girl by the edge of the creek
She turns in surprise
And the mist in her eyes
Has cleared, and the child is gone

ALLAN throws a new canvas on his easel and begins to paint. Bold lines of colour appear on screen and throughout theatre.

ALLAN: In the beginning, there was only the god-damned firmament!

SUSAN dances joyously, punctuating his moods with body movements of equal vitality.

SUSAN: Only the firmament!

ALLAN: Then there was thunder and lightning!

SUSAN: Thunder and lightning!

ALLAN: The rocks split and waves rose a mile high!

SUSAN: Wow!

ALLAN: Mountains and pools of oil for British America!

SUSAN: Yeh—I dig!

ALLAN: Then came Adam and Eve ...

SUSAN stops and stares whimsically at him.

SUSAN: Why bugger up a good thing?

ALLAN: Let's go back then ... way back before all that ... Yes! ... Stars were thrown past the sun ... Stones lived and the cosmic winds howled and sang!

SUSAN: Where was God then?

ALLAN: He was up there ... But He was lonely as hell! ... He looked out from the middle of the biggest department store in the universe, gassed out of his head ... First He tried to put some colour into the heavens ... (*brush stroke*) ... But He only had blues and greens and it made Him cold ... So He gave that up as a bum trip!

SUSAN: He should've danced to keep Himself warm ...

ALLAN: Couldn't ... no place to stand ... He tried singing, but nobody to hear Him. It was like a jail for Him up there ... Poor God, busted and put away for doing nothing and the jailer gone ...

She leans over him. He dabs paint on her nose. They laugh.

SUSAN: So what's He to do?

ALLAN: Zap! He built an earth ... He put trees and mountains, wild grass and rain on it ...

SUSAN: An' cops and hippies ...

ALLAN: And a lot of square people running around building cities and writing books on investments and returns, prison psychology and etiquette ... yet!

ALLAN crosses out error on his canvas.

ALLAN: Nope ... First came Adam and Eve and a treeful of goodies they weren't supposed to touch. Then came the stoneheads and horse-breeders, clerks and mechanics.

CAPTAIN NEVADA has been dancing as an alter-ego to SUSAN in the shadows. He continues hand-clapping softly, with SUSAN responding to rhythms he makes. ALLAN rises and moves away, disturbed.

ALLAN: Then came the master-minds ... the grey men one never sees but who influence everything you do, say or feel ... the disc-jockeys of persuasion.

SUSAN: What is it, Allan?

ALLAN: I can't go the road, Sue ... it's not that easy ... I sometimes think we've been led into a great big, warm trap ... that acid was invented by the establishment as a grotesque joke against life ...

CAPTAIN NEVADA: Wow ... out of sight!

ALLAN: Somebody is laughing quietly behind boardroom doors while we scream and twist with revelations which are only chemicals in conflict with our bodies! Maybe ... it's a weapon to defeat the very thing we feel most ...

CAPTAIN NEVADA: Take it, man!

SUSAN: I don't understand what you're saying ...

ALLAN: Have you ever thought—we are so harmless when we dream. We are children then ...

SUSAN: Are we dreaming then? Is nothing real?

ALLAN: I love you more than I can ever tell ...

Music up.

They embrace. Members of GROUP enter during song. They lead SUSAN and ALLAN through an erotic dance. At end of song members of GROUP leave.

SUSAN collects ALLAN'S painting gear and also leaves. ALLAN is left, lying exhausted onstage.

SONG: In her seventeenth summer
She had found fulfilment
She was soon to be a mother
Her love gave her warmth
As anyone could see
But her ties with the earth
Would never let her go free ...
            Sing hey! By the seashore
            Where freedom is sweet
            But hunger bites deep in the sinews.
In her seventeenth summer
The black afternoons
Turned to white-pebbled days
Of barefooted laughter
To free her heart
From its nest of marigolds
Bitter wishes and drowsy perfumes
            Sing hey! By the seashore
            Where freedom is sweet
            But hunger bites deep in the sinews.
Remember to love her
She has no malice
Her lips are a blossom
Of trust and devotion
The Tide of her truth
Would fill a wide ocean
Of stones, salt and strange fishes ...
            Sing hey! By the seashore
            Where freedom is sweet
            But hunger bites deep in the sinews.
In her seventeenth summer
She had found fulfilment
She was soon to be a mother
Her love gave her warmth
As anyone could see
But her ties with the earth
Would never let her go free ...

Sing hey! By the seashore
Where freedom is sweet
But hunger bites deep in the sinews.

SCENE 13

Film on screen: living room. UNCLE enters and stands over ALLAN.

UNCLE: Allan, boy ... I read your report ... your social studies assignment ... You write well, your mind is large.

ALLAN: Thank you.

UNCLE: You have a large mind ... But you are too cynical for one your age. That ... disappoints me.

ALLAN: I didn't mean you to read it that way. I'm not cynical ...

UNCLE: I read it the only way I know how ... I couldn't help it. Life is positive, boy. Revolutions enrich history ... It is not true that for youth of this time all social organizations they have not made and movements they have not struggled in, are oppressive and out of touch ... That is not true.

ALLAN: I was expressing an opinion ... I have a right to this, have I not?

UNCLE: Yes, you do ...

ALLAN: The brotherhood of man is a hollow phrase when spoken by the dead who have no brotherhood ... There is so little love in your beliefs. I cannot accept this.

UNCLE: Why do you feel there is no love?

ALLAN: Is there a social system that will stop building tanks out of concern for the grass over which they roll? Must all life be so violent?

UNCLE: When you were born, the world was already there to receive you; we had no choice. But love makes us understand the reasons for this state of affairs.

ALLAN: History is a record of wars and lies and hatred. If this is all civilized men are capable of, then the cities don't deserve to stand!

UNCLE: What of the *men* ... who dug the water-holes and built roads and towns? ... They are history, too. For what reason did they get born and labour? For you to come along to squat and crap over them before you are twenty because their design was not to your liking? How can you be so stern?

ALLAN: (*angry*) There is nothing surrounding you or me here, Uncle Ted. No music, no love ... nothing except the expense and time spent at work which never has and never will give pleasure or satisfaction!

A moment of silence between them, neither wishing to hurt the other.

UNCLE: I'm sick of drudgery ... I have no education except what I forced myself to learn nights at the public library ... There is no future for me except death ... no hope except socialism! I am already three times your age. I can say this ...

ALLAN: Death on those terms is ugly.

UNCLE: You'll live and accept it as I do.

ALLAN: Why a revolution whose cost you already know? What have we gained, when a successful revolution becomes establishment the moment it succeeds?

UNCLE: The seeds of still another revolution! (*sadly and tenderly*) You're so young. It is both cruel and beautiful to speak with someone so young ... That is the love I have for you!

Film projection behind UNCLE dies and he disappears.

SCENE 14

CAPTAIN NEVADA sweeps onto stage, bells jingling and castanets rattling. Following him are other members of GROUP and SUSAN.

Film projection—street scene, crinkly and out of focus. ALLAN watches GROUP, but remains detached from them.

CAPTAIN NEVADA: (*embracing SUSAN*) Mama Sue ... We don't need anybody! We have everything! Love ... Brotherhood ... soon we'll have a farm and grow our own food. Then we shall build a temple for me and I shall heal the sick ... cure the stupid ...

NESTOR: (*embracing MICHELE*) See how she kisses me back? I'm young ... I'm forever! I love

her and I'm not afraid to say it ... I love her! (*kisses MICHELE and she returns his kiss, but as a baby kissing her father*) I want to ball her ... now! In front of everybody! I want to lift her to the sky ... I'll do anything for her ... She's closer to me than my own family. And I found it out seven minutes ago!

A POLICEMAN on beat enters. CAPTAIN NEVADA bows to him, the others fall back. ALLAN does not move. The POLICEMAN notices this.

POLICEMAN: All right, kid ... either home you go or I'm taking you in to help fight fires!

ALLAN: There are no fires in this vicinity.

POLICEMAN: How do you know? Are you an authority on fires? Suppose I called the forestry people and told them I found a guy looking for a forest fire to fight?

ALLAN: Man, you do whatever you think is best for the common good ...

POLICEMAN: Never mind the lip ... A gang of smart asses with long hair can complicate my life ... So keep moving and go give another constable a headache!

The GROUP giggles. The POLICEMAN has difficulty controlling his own laughter. He saunters away.

NESTOR: Hey, that cat has soul!

SCENE 15

SUSAN'S FATHER: (*offstage*) Susan!

They turn in direction of his voice. SUSAN'S FATHER appears from opposite side of stage to where POLICEMAN left. He is loud, healthy, blustering.

SUSAN: Daddy? ...

SUSAN'S FATHER: Hey, lovey! ... Susan, darling ... come to me ... Hey, you're such a big girl now! ... Don't cry, what's the matter? I had a helluva time finding you. Police in five cities were on the lookout for you ... Let's have a kiss and hug-up, eh?

SUSAN: (*running to him, embracing him, sobbing*) Daddy ...

NESTOR mimics the father-daughter relationship with MICHELE.

NESTOR: Hey, lovey ... come to me! ... You're such a big girl now ...

CAPTAIN NEVADA: (*to MICHELE and NESTOR*) It is a foolish thing to laugh at angels.

NESTOR and MICHELE wave him away and continue giggling.

SUSAN'S FATHER: There, there ... don't cry. It's all right now, lovey ... we'll go home and everything will be just fine.

SUSAN: I couldn't write, Daddy ...

SUSAN'S FATHER: I understand. You're young ...

SUSAN: I wanted to write ... about Allan and me ...

SUSAN'S FATHER: Allan? ... Who's Allan?

SUSAN: That's Allan ... back there ... me and him are good friends.

SUSAN'S FATHER: (*with surprise as he peers into the room*) Them? ... He's not one of them, is he? ... Susan, what the hell's going on?

She shrugs noncommittally.

SUSAN'S FATHER: Well, never mind—you're all right now.

SUSAN: Allan's a painter, Daddy—he's a good artist!

SUSAN'S FATHER: (*trying to plumb the depth of their relationship*) Is he? ... I wasn't one for art, so I can't tell ... Does he make any money at it?

SUSAN: Oh yes ... yes! He does ...

SUSAN'S FATHER: Listen, girl ... you're all right, eh? I mean, nothing's wrong?

SUSAN: (*blurting*) Daddy—we're married ... me an' Allan are married!

CAPTAIN NEVADA rattles his castanets and moves forward with GROUP following to take up position before SUSAN and her FATHER. SUSAN'S FATHER is dismayed. ALLAN stands apart from all of them.

SUSAN'S FATHER: But—when? How could this be? ... What the hell's wrong with you, child?

SUSAN: Allan, honey—tell him!

ALLAN: You tell him yourself, baby. He wouldn't believe me.

CAPTAIN NEVADA: (*bowing to the FATHER*) We wish you a rainbow, sir!

SUSAN'S FATHER: What the hell's all this about? Where in the hell are the cops?

He tries to pull SUSAN away. She resists. He turns to the GROUP, ready to fight.

SUSAN'S FATHER: All right! One at a time or all of you together—I can still take you! Come on—who's first?

CAPTAIN NEVADA: Peace—we wish you a rainbow, sir.

SUSAN: We cut our wrists, Daddy ... an' ... we rubbed them together in the park. We were alone ... it was beautiful, Daddy!

SUSAN'S FATHER: (*horrified*) And that ... is your marriage? You're out of your mind—come on!

Attempts to drag her away, but she will not go.

SUSAN: (*desperately*) We're going to have a baby!

SUSAN'S FATHER: (*freezes, looks down at her*) That's a goddamn lie!

CAPTAIN NEVADA: It's the holy truth, sir.

GROUP: (*in unison*) ... The holy truth ...

FATHER unashamedly runs his hands down over SUSAN'S abdomen. Pushes her away.

SUSAN'S FATHER: It's a goddamn lie!

ALLAN: It's the truth, sir.

SUSAN'S FATHER: (*to SUSAN*) What are you doing to me? ... Why? ... What have I done?

SUSAN: (*touches him*) Daddy ... I'm happy ... I want you to know it!

SUSAN'S FATHER: (*unresponsive, staring at GROUP*) Why? ... Look at you ... what is becoming of all I worked for? ... The things *I* wanted? ... The things I couldn't have because ... Around you stands a city—cars, airplanes ... When I was your age, this was all a dream for the future ...

CAPTAIN NEVADA: And you have paid for it with no place to stand ... It is nothing without love. Peace, brother ...

SUSAN'S FATHER: Oh, no ... I'm calling the cops! This girl's under-age ...

SUSAN: (*appealing*) Daddy ... please ... I want to love you!

CAPTAIN NEVADA: Peace, brother. Laws are laws ... but people are sacred!

SUSAN'S FATHER: Grubby, dirty, hungry bastards! ... I feel sorry for you!

CAPTAIN NEVADA: Thank you. Now tell me, what is sorrow?

MICHELE: Sorrow is a golden bird perched on my head!

WHITE RABBIT: Sorrow is the baby-Jesus, wiser than its mother!

NESTOR: Sorrow is Colonel Borman behind the moon remembering the seagull's cry!

JOAN: Sorrow is the song I sing, when I walk alone ...

SUSAN'S FATHER retreats. SUSAN runs to ALLAN.

SUSAN: Hold me, baby ... hold me tight!

SCENE 16

POLICEMAN enters. He sees SUSAN'S FATHER and goes to him.

POLICEMAN: These kids bothering you, sir?

SUSAN'S FATHER adjusts his tie slowly and regains his poise.

SUSAN'S FATHER: No ... it's all right, officer ... I was only ... talking to them.

Music up softly.

POLICEMAN turns to ALLAN and SUSAN.

POLICEMAN: Come on, kids ... no necking in public. Haven't you got digs to go to?

ALLAN: (*smiling*) I'm sorry, sir ... I was keeping the street in place so you wouldn't have to walk uphill!

Castanets rattle. Laughter. The POLICEMAN shakes his head good-naturedly. Film projection of street scene fades out.

SCENE 17

ALLAN: You're trembling ... take my coat.

He removes his flimsy jacket and drapes it over SUSAN'S shoulders.

SUSAN: He's gone. It was like talking down a grave.

ALLAN: We're safe here. The walls are crumbling to dust ... the lights are out in the city hall building ... but the trees keep growing. What birds are left will sing in the morning.

SUSAN: You said once ... that God lived at the edge of the sea ... God had left the hassle behind and sat waiting at the edge of the sea. We could find Him if we went there!

ALLAN: Where are we safe? We hallucinate love, peace, understanding ... Are we alone in this? ... When I was a kid she took me to church, leading me by the hand ...

SUSAN: Who?

CAPTAIN NEVADA lights a joint which he passes to SUSAN and ALLAN. They draw on it and pass it to others.

ALLAN: My mother ... they were Catholics, my father and mother. Uncle Ted never came with us ...

CAPTAIN NEVADA: The sand lives and tells us of the first snail that left the water behind ...

ALLAN: He said the church was an instrument for exploitation of the poor and ignorant ... He said only those who owned everything and those who owned nothing were afraid of changes.

SUSAN: We were Lutherans.

ALLAN: There was warmth and security there ...

SUSAN: The pews were of pinewood ... they were white and waxed ... When the sun touched them, the grain in the wood quivered as if the wood was still living and growing inside of trees ... or remembering something ...

ALLAN: The incense and the sound of prayers ...

CAPTAIN NEVADA: The snail climbed the mountain and saw freedom!

SUSAN: We're at the edge of the sea now ... and in the beginning ...

She and ALLAN posture and laugh. ALLAN paints imaginary canvas.

ALLAN: In the beginning, there was only the firmament!

SUSAN leaves him to begin dance of creation. The music dies abruptly. She turns to ALLAN with adoration and wonder.

CAPTAIN NEVADA: And the wind blew over the snail ... it was a cold wind up there on the mountain peak ... the snail twisted and grew afraid ...

ALLAN goes to SUSAN and holds her.

ALLAN: In the beginning, only the firmament ...

She nods agreement in a bitter-sweet gesture.

SUSAN: I get very hungry now ...

ACT 2

SCENE 1

Music-prelude and into song. Film Projection— Helicopter moving shot of a city.

SONG: Grass and wild strawberries
Incense and wine
A crow on a cradle
Will never be mine
I've a purse of good leather
And sandals of mist
A halo of morning
That my lips have kissed.
    ... My God, what a generous morning!

Music out.

CAPTAIN NEVADA: (*recorded recitation*)
Living on the outskirts
Of the holy city ...
Eating prayers and sunsets
Beside the unknown river
Bleeding tears and water
Like some sacred fountain
Climbing shafts of sunlight
To touch the rim of heaven—
Don't you turn away from me ...

SONG: Grass and wild strawberries
Incense and wine
A crow on the cradle
Will never be mine
Last Sunday by moonlight
I lay at her side
Convinced that our being
Would not be denied
    ... My God, what a night of forgiveness!

Music softly in background.

ALLAN and SUSAN—apart from each other. He is withdrawn.

ALLAN: Go away ... the sky is falling ...

SUSAN: Tell me what's wrong. You won't talk ... you won't look at me ... I feel so alone.

ALLAN: I'm so goddamned mixed up ... she sent me money again.

SUSAN: Your mother?

ALLAN: My mother sent me money again! ... There was a money order in the mail for fifty dollars yesterday. I knew I had to send it back for our sakes ... but I didn't.

SUSAN: When you sell a painting, we'll return it.

ALLAN: A flat field with no roads ... only bushes. And behind every bush stands a lie—the enemy! Lies betray us, and betrayal kills—that is the enemy. There is no other ...

SUSAN: I made some fresh coffee if you'd like to ...

ALLAN: I cashed the money—for the baby! That's the reason I gave myself. You know what I bought with the money?

SUSAN knows and looks away from him.

SUSAN: Don't lay that trip on me ... If you get busted, what will happen to us?

ALLAN: With the money in my hand I was burning up ... I couldn't come to you ... I went alone, to curl up in a cave. But the enemy was laughing out of the pores of my skin ... so I ran to the beach ... I ran to the beach, into the water ... For seven hours I was king of the seven great waves ... I was out there waiting for Godot to come out of the sea and explain everything ... But Godot doesn't know we're waiting ... then ... then the gold left my eyes and I was still staring out to sea, but now I was crying like a baby!

Music up.

SONG: Grass and wild strawberries
Incense and wine
A crow on the cradle
Will never be mine
If my baby is happy
And his joy never varies
I'll bless him with moonlove
And wild strawberries
   ... My God, what a wealth of abundance!

SUSAN runs away from ALLAN.

SCENE 2

Music down into a sustained, menacing tone.

ALLAN moves with animal anxiety.

ALLAN: (*recorded*) Who's there? ... Why am I so afraid? ... I need a goddamned father!

He stiffens.

From gloom of wings a BARRACK'S OFFICER, who resembles his father, approaches woodenly until his face is practically touching the back of Allan's head.

ALLAN: (*recorded*) The memory of the cave and the first fire is with us still ... Can I ever escape?

OFFICER: (*sharply*) Attention!

ALLAN springs to military rigidity.

ALLAN: Yes, sir!

The OFFICER stands for a long moment, his face in ALLAN'S hair. His breathing is amplified on speakers—it has animal ferocity.

ALLAN: (*recorded*) If I die and return as a leaf ... who will eat me? A worm?... Or a dinosaur?

OFFICER: (*belching, then shouting*) You lousy crud!

ALLAN: Yes, sir!

OFFICER: Yes, sir what?

ALLAN: I'm a lousy crud, sir!

OFFICER: That's right—you're a lump of god-damned shit!

ALLAN breaks into fearful laughter which OFFICER does not hear.

OFFICER: I'm gonna take your goddamned head an' wrap it around your goddamned arse ... How'd you like that for a trick? ... Before I'm done with you you'll show respect, you lousy crud!

ALLAN'S laughter ends in a gasp.

OFFICER: Do you think I can hear good, boy?

ALLAN: Yes, sir.

OFFICER: You bet your pea-pickin' life I hear good! I hear you thinkin' ... I can hear what you're thinkin' about me! How's that grab you? ... I know what you're thinkin' in your goddamned woolly head ... You stop thinkin' them thoughts or I'm gonna bust you wide open down the middle ending up at your ars-h-o-o-o-l-e!

ALLAN: No, sir!

OFFICER: No, sir ... yes, sir ... no, sir—what?

ALLAN: I'll stop thinkin', sir!

OFFICER: That's right—that's a good boy ...

ALLAN: (*recorded*) I must be ashamed ... I *must* be afraid ... I must be afraid enough to fight!

OFFICER: Turn around, boy ... Turn around ... it's all right now ... Let me be your father—please ...

ALLAN: Oh, Christ, no!

Stage lights out.

Film Projection—Helicopter moving shot of city.

Music up sharply.

SONG: Grass and wild strawberries
Incense and wine
A crow on the cradle
Will never be mine
     If my love should leave me
     And turn love to pain
     I'll cry and love no one
     No, never again
     ... My God, what a bitter transgression!

Projection of film fades out.

SCENE 3

POLICEMAN and ALLAN. The POLICEMAN, moving in half-time, but conversing normally, is friendly and reassuring. ALLAN is shaken, confused.

POLICEMAN: You're next, kid ... They want you in next. Pull yourself together—it's Spring!

ALLAN: What'll I get, man?

POLICEMAN: Six months ... maybe a year. Maybe even a suspension ... all depends on how the old man feels today. You look clean ... don't stand cocky an' don't slouch, either ... just ... be yourself. I think he'll go easy if you do.

ALLAN starts to move away.

POLICEMAN: What the hell—where do you think you're going?

ALLAN: Outside ... to get some fresh air ...

POLICEMAN: There's enough air here, so you just stay put.

ALLAN: (*bewildered*) I was giving away love I never thought I had ... do you understand that?

POLICEMAN: No, I don't. I'm what is called a pretty simple guy ... do you know what *that* means?

ALLAN: ... If a man digs a well, will he always get water? ...

ALLAN turns to the POLICEMAN suddenly.

ALLAN: It's insane what's being done! ... I was talking to this kid from Windsor ... fourteen years old ... left home because they gave him nothing to do at home. He talked of jumping off the bridge if nobody listened now. I listened ... he had so little to tell me ... but it was important enough that somebody should listen ...

POLICEMAN: Yeh ... I listen too ... I hear stories on my beat every night. Life is hard. So's the street ... by morning, my feet hurt ...

ALLAN: (*long pause*) I don't know anything ...

POLICEMAN: That makes two of us ... Lawyers have the answers, but I think they're full of bull-shit, too ... It's a big hockey game in a wheelchair ... You ready?

ALLAN: I don't know who I am or why I am!

POLICEMAN: Let's go.

They move, but ALLAN lingers.

ALLAN: Hey, man! My feet carry my body, an' that's attached to the head where all the action is! ...

POLICEMAN: My head holds my hat up ... (*smiles*) An' when I get old, it'll hold spare teeth, glasses and a hearing aid ... let's go.

ALLAN: I'm an artist ... a good artist! My work was in the civic gallery last winter and it got written up in the papers!

POLICEMAN: That's good ... a guy's got to do something with his time. I've worked hard all my life. I'm not ashamed ...

ALLAN: Nothing to be ashamed of there ...

POLICEMAN: Let's go then.

ALLAN: I'm not ashamed of being born ... of living ... you know that?

POLICEMAN: (worried about being late for court) No reason you should be. We've got to go, kid.

ALLAN: (laughs) No reason I should be …

POLICEMAN: What's so funny? I don't see anything, funny.

He takes ALLAN by the arm and leads him.

Music up another tone.

ALLAN: Your face … was tickling my eyes …

POLICEMAN leads ALLAN on.

POLICEMAN: You poor bugger … everything's going to be all right … don't slouch when you go in, an' don't get sore. The old man doesn't like it when a kid gets sore!

They leave.

SCENE 4

SUSAN and CAPTAIN NEVADA, now SOCIAL WORKER, enter stage from opposite wings. She moves towards him, but he restrains her with a motion of his hand.

SUSAN: Captain Nevada! … I'm so glad it's … ooh … I thought you were … that I knew you …

Mockingly, he bows with a flourish to her.

SOCIAL WORKER: I am … and you do, mama Sue …

SUSAN: But … you couldn't be doing this … if you really …

SOCIAL WORKER: It's the only way. The revolution is lost … the head fires are dead, so I do social work to save the children of disaster … Otherwise, I would have to become disenchanted with the world, and that would never do!

He takes out a report book and examines it, then makes some notes.

SOCIAL WORKER: Susan … can you not go home to your parents? Is there any reason why you can't?

SUSAN: (touching her abdomen) In this condition?

SOCIAL WORKER: Yours is an imaginary pregnancy in an imaginary world … Open your eyes wide, mama Sue.

SUSAN: My baby will come on the 22nd of July!

SOCIAL WORKER: (recorded) As you can understand, our agency concerns itself with the crisis of generations. But too often that is an undertaking outside the capabilities of an office this size …

CAPTAIN NEVADA takes notes, gesticulating to SUSAN. SUSAN moves towards audience.

SUSAN: Please help me … my baby is coming!

SOCIAL WORKER: (recorded) So you think you are pregnant and you are without money or employment at this time?

SUSAN: I am pregnant!

SOCIAL WORKER: You're on a bum trip, mama Sue. Come back to earth … it's air-conditioned here!

She turns to him.

SOCIAL WORKER: (recorded) Why?

SUSAN: Why what?

SOCIAL WORKER: Why did you leave home with so little reason?

SUSAN is becoming confused, moving from audience to him.

SUSAN: You dug it yourself, man—what the hell can I say?

SOCIAL WORKER: (recorded) Most girls your age can tolerate an adolescence that is not exciting and entertaining at all times …

SOCIAL WORKER: This applies to me as well, baby … for I was your age once and lived the whole scene …

SOCIAL WORKER: (recorded) Isn't it possible that some of us were placed on this earth by God to somehow or other be usefully employed and assure ourselves of grandchildren before we pass on?

SUSAN grows more confused.

SUSAN: ALLAN! … Talk to Allan!

SOCIAL WORKER: He's been busted. He's no help to you now …

SOCIAL WORKER: (recorded) What do you intend to do?

SUSAN: Do? ... I don't know ...

SOCIAL WORKER: This baby ... this baby ... this baby ...

SOCIAL WORKER: (*recorded*) Surely you're not planning to keep your baby after birth?

SUSAN: Yes! Oh, yes ... please, God—yes!

Sudden silence. CAPTAIN NEVADA looks sternly at her.

SOCIAL WORKER: (*recorded*) (*tenderly*) We spoke to him ... we know all about you now ... you were never married to each other. It was all a dream ... a fantasy.

SUSAN: Yes ... we are ... I mean ... no ... we're not ...

SOCIAL WORKER: (*notebook poised*) Yes? ... No? Which is it then?

Music pitch rises sharply.

SUSAN: We promised to care for each other forever, Captain Nevada.

SOCIAL WORKER: (*recorded*) What kind of care is this? He's in custody ... you're here. Your shack on the beach is two months in arrears on rent. Life is a helluva lot more complex than a promise to care, Susan!

SUSAN: Mama! ... Where's my goddamn mama?

SOCIAL WORKER: (*recorded*) You're a child—a little girl with pigtails and ankle socks ... you should be in school now ... You should be able to sleep late on Saturday morning ... write letters you don't have to mail ... go on dates in a group ... put Noxzema on the acne spots ... and here you are, six months pregnant you say.

SOCIAL WORKER: When did you eat last, mama Sue?

Music dropping in pitch.

SUSAN: I had breakfast ... yesterday.

SOCIAL WORKER: It's four o'clock in the afternoon. Let me treat you to a good meal!

SUSAN hesitates, then accepts.

SUSAN: Oh, yes—thank you, man!

She takes his arm and presses her face against his sleeve. They leave.

SONG: In her seventeenth summer
She had found fulfilment
She was soon to be a mother
Her love gave her warmth
As anyone could see
But her ties with the earth
Would never let her go free
      Sing hey! By the seashore
      Where freedom is sweet
      But hunger bites deep in the sinews!

SCENE 5

On song, ALLAN, UNCLE and POLICEMAN enter. POLICEMAN remains in shadows. UNCLE is nervous at circumstances of this meeting.

UNCLE: Your lawyer called me to come see you. How are you, boy?

ALLAN: I'm fine, Uncle Ted. It'll be all right, I think.

UNCLE: I don't approve of what happened, you know.

ALLAN: Will Mom come to see me?

UNCLE: She will. But it's a shock for her. She didn't expect this ...

UNCLE trails off, not willing to say more.

ALLAN: I didn't sleep much last night ... I was thinking about all you ever said to me. You cared—you always cared.

UNCLE: I'm happy you think so.

ALLAN: I mean ... like it's all a betrayal, isn't it? The way things happen, the way and distance you fall when you first stumble.

UNCLE: Yes, I suppose ...

UNCLE is aware of POLICEMAN in background and is inhibited by his presence.

UNCLE: Whatever's happened ... don't let your feelings lead you into becoming an adventurer. There is the revolutionary, and there is also the bandit.

ALLAN: Maybe each of us has ... to find out where it's all at and then go. I mean, like last night I was thinking ... you can do a lot of thinking in here ... (*motions to POLICEMAN, who returns the salute)* … Just when it matters—first it was that cat Lumumba. Then Kennedy and Che … Now it's Luther King and another Kennedy … the Black Panthers … students in universities …

UNCLE: How in hell do you see all those people in the same …

ALLAN: Wait—let me explain. If they'd ever met … at some other time … all together, they'd be worlds apart on everything.

UNCLE: That's what I'm saying!

ALLAN: Yet me—sitting it out on a dope rap … I suddenly see they had *everything* in common … they *had to die!* The guys who killed them live on, and the dates and names go into school texts, but still not the *truth* of why. What are we prepared to *do* about it now?

UNCLE: Allan—it takes discipline to win the struggle for your own mind.

ALLAN: *(searchingly)* And you think I haven't got that discipline?

UNCLE: No.

ALLAN: I'm looking … *we're* looking to you for leadership! To opt out is not enough. They'll find us if they think we get dangerous … and then we have to fight the buildings, the streets, the machinery … we have to destroy! That would be losing what we have … Uncle Ted, *others* will become leaders if you don't, and I'm afraid of others!

UNCLE: *(the demand too great for him)* I was in jail twice in my lifetime … Once for leading an illegal strike on company grounds and the second time for political activity that was not permitted. I'm proud of those days in prison! … Can you ever say the same thing for yourself? Can you ever?

Long silence. ALLAN is deeply hurt.

ALLAN: I … asked you to come. Last night, I wanted to be like you … to have you come and tell us what to do.

UNCLE: How confused you've become! Your situation and your life-style is abnormal and anti-social. You are like the Gypsy, cut free from the smoke and soot and the Saturday good-time bottle of beer!

ALLAN: I'm afraid, Uncle Ted!

UNCLE: *(helpless, overcome)* I'll do what I can, but I'm not young. A man becomes demoralized a bit when he's worked and been involved all his life and is suddenly isolated … out of work with few prospects …

ALLAN: I'm sorry … I didn't know. *(realizing his UNCLE will never be more than he is now)* What will you do?

UNCLE: We do what we do …

ALLAN: *(trying to cheer his UNCLE)* I feel when I come out of this, I'll paint something that will be … better than I've ever painted before!

UNCLE: No doubt you will …

Music up. UNCLE turns and leaves abruptly.

SCENE 6

On recitation, SUSAN enters on arm of CAPTAIN NEVADA as SOCIAL WORKER. She and ALLAN do not communicate. POLICEMAN steps out of gloom. SOCIAL WORKER frees himself of SUSAN.

SUSAN'S FATHER, ALLAN'S FATHER, enter. The final assault on ALLAN and SUSAN is carried out by all of them.

RECITATION:
The moon is hot as the breath of hell
But the garden stones are cold
So cold …
Where the day has gone no one can tell
For I dreamed it away I'm told
I'm told …

SOCIAL WORKER: *(to SUSAN)* But you knew he was purchasing and using it … *(to ALLAN)* … And that it was illegal, man!

SUSAN: Yes …

ALLAN: Yes …

SUSAN'S FATHER: *(to SUSAN)* Lovey … if you knew it was illegal and wrong …

POLICEMAN: *(to SUSAN)* Then why didn't you …

SUSAN: This place has no doors opening out … I came for social assistance …

POLICEMAN: I'm not a policeman …

VOICE: (*recorded*) ... But I want to know where Allan bought the supply he was carrying on him at the time of arrest?

VOICES: (*recorded*) Where? ... Where?

SUSAN: I don't know!

ALLAN: Screw you! I'm not going to fink!

SOCIAL WORKER: It was Lennie Bayliss ... (*touches his head*) I've got everything in this skull, man. But Lennie's on bad times, same's everybody in the group. He was here before you ... barefoot, hungry, broke—no place to sleep ... ready and anxious to talk.

VOICES: (*recorded*) Lennie ... Lennie Bayliss!

POLICEMAN: (*to SUSAN*) When I searched him, I found your letter in his pockets. It helped us apprehend the others.

SUSAN: (*sickened*) Oh, God!

SOCIAL WORKER: (*to ALLAN*) Look, man—your mail is opened and read by the police ... an' her mail to you ... Get with it—you can't beat the system!

ALLAN: I'm not going to fink!

VOICES: (*recorded*) Fink! ... Fink! ... Fink! ... Fink! ... Fink!

RECITATION: You sang of a girl on a horse of grey
With stars on her naked skin
Her skin ...
I cried out loud when she galloped away
And left me broken within
Within ...

SUSAN: This isn't a police state yet!

ALLAN: Get off my back—I'm not talking!

SUSAN'S FATHER: (*to SUSAN, but going to ALLAN*) The drugs I will never accept ... That's why she left—what other reason did she have? Her mother cried—Jesus, she cried ...

POLICEMAN: It's bigger than that. The question as I see it ...

SOCIAL WORKER: Is civil disobedience and anarchy!

VOICES: (*recorded*) Anarchy ... anarchy ... anarchy ...

ALLAN'S FATHER: That's the choice ... it's a bad choice, son ... it doesn't help progress one bit.

ALLAN: (*shouting*) Your airplanes tear big holes in the sky ... for a profit! For death to fall in!

VOICES: (*recorded and echoed by others*) Shut your mouth! ... Shut your mouth!

ALLAN: The computers ... factories ... policeman's boots ... serve the controlled and regimented society. Fascism is consumer research—to sell more and more of what we never needed in the first place!

SOCIAL WORKER: Cool it, man ...

SUSAN'S FATHER: I will live longer than my father, but my child will die before me—why? Can anybody tell me why?

VOICES: (*recorded*) Why? ... Why? ... Why? ... Why? ... Why?

ALLAN'S FATHER: Could it be ... because of you?

VOICES: (*recorded*) Because of you ... because of you ... because of you ... you ... you ... you ...

SUSAN: I didn't do anything wrong!

SOCIAL WORKER: Like man, we're losing so much ...

VOICE: (*recorded*) Permissiveness for the few has brought restrictions of personal freedom for the rest.

SUSAN'S FATHER: Investors will shy away from our country ... we'll be set back thirty years ...

POLICEMAN: Telephone calls are monitored ... mail is intercepted ...

VOICES: (*recorded*) Intercepted ... intercepted ...

ALLAN'S FATHER: Meetings are bugged ... they bugged the meetings of our local ...

RECITATION: She offers hyacinths to the stars
I give her my shawl and ring
My ring ...
She kisses my eyes through the prison bars
To the dusk of her voice I cling
I cling ...

Dialogue is now shouted at ALLAN and SUSAN, who are alarmed under the attack.

POLICEMAN: Show me a kid who can blush! Show me a kid ...

SUSAN'S FATHER: ... who can blush? ...

POLICEMAN: Put them to work ... put them to work if what's going for them's so rotten bad!

VOICES: Put them to work!

SUSAN'S FATHER: I'm paying tax on my house and earnings ...

POLICEMAN: ...To maintain a big university in this city ...

ALLAN'S FATHER: I never had it for education like that ... nothing after grade ten ...

SUSAN'S FATHER: ... And all we get back from this university ... is a population that won't work at just any job during the summer!

VOICES: Hit the bastards before it's too late ... or they'll hit you first!

VOICES: (recorded) Bastards ... bastards ... bastards ...

POLICEMAN: (to ALLAN) Let's hear your poems ... if you think I'm so stupid then start making me smarter—I'm listening!

VOICES: (recorded) He's listening ... he's listening ...

ALLAN: (thickly) Mars is far ... from the hot ... fire-tears ... of a child ... in the desert ... of nothingness ...

A moment of silence, then derisive laughter from everyone.

POLICEMAN: Read me a poem that *means something*! I'm not as educated as you. I have to listen to somebody other than myself ... I want to *learn* something new, so give me a poem I can understand!

A roar of disapproval directed at ALLAN.

ALLAN: (in a shout) I can't live like this, baby! I'm suffocating! There's no air nor light here! ... A nightmare howl of hate by those who will achieve nothing ... Don't grow older than we are ... If we stop, the spinning earth will explode! We may hang to one stone of it and sail forever through the universe in search of another planet!

Music up.

SONG: The moon is hot as the breath of hell
But the garden stones are cold
So cold ...

Where the day has gone no one can tell
For I dreamed it away I'm told
I'm told ...
    I wander as in sleep
    Though my eyes are wide open
    You speak to me
    I hear only the wind
You sang of a girl on a horse of grey
With stars on her naked skin
I cried out loud when she galloped away
And left me broken within
Left me broken within
    I wander as in sleep
    Though my eyes are wide open
    You speak to me
    I hear only the wind
She offers me hyacinths to the stars
I give her my shawl and ring
She kisses my eyes through the prison bars
To the dusk of her voice I cling
To her voice I cling ...
    I wander as in sleep
    Though my eyes are wide open
    You speak to me
    I hear only the wind
Each distant face is a rumble of light
That dazzles my eyes with pain
I grope for her warmth through the icy night
But I cannot find her again
I can't find her again ...
    I wander as in sleep
    Though my eyes are wide open
    You speak to me
    I hear only the wind ...

On song members of GROUP enter. Strobe light on dance of appeal and rejection by GROUP as they approach and cling to their elders, who break free of the youth and leave.

ALLAN and SUSAN follow GROUP and CAPTAIN NEVADA in ritualistic dance which ends with all of them lying prostrate on the floor. At the end of song ALLAN and SUSAN half-rise and face each other. ALLAN begins dialing an imaginary telephone. She responds to the game, to the amusement of the rest of the GROUP, who rise to a sitting position to watch them.

SUSAN: Your number, sir?

ALLAN: Give me God ... I want to speak to the big man Himself!

SUSAN: I'm sorry, but that number rings busy, sir. Would you care to place your call later?

ALLAN: No, ma'm ... He's been busy a long time now. Taking all kinds of complaints, I guess. Nobody can reach Him anymore.

SUSAN: If it's an emergency ...

ALLAN: It is! ... It's always an emergency when a man calls for God!

SUSAN: Oh?

ALLAN: Yes ... I've just found myself work selling gravestones to living men and women ... They're buying them out by the gross ... I wish to report an indecency.

SUSAN: I see ... Perhaps we'll try your call again later ...

ALLAN: It's no use. God is dead ... He won't answer your trying! His phone is off the receiver and lying on His chest and everyone's frightened to go in and hang it up ...

WHITE RABBIT: Go, man—go!

SUSAN: You can't be sure, sir.

ALLAN: But I am ... God is dead! There are no cars on the highway this morning. They're parked bumper to bumper off the road ... their headlights down like eyes that are weeping with mourning for the dead ... be they God, or man ...

SUSAN laughs and both rise to embrace each other. Sound of castanets. CAPTAIN NEVADA puts on a flowing cape and leads them through a dance of love and reconciliation.

SONG: All I want is a pillow
To lay under my head
And a rainbow of fire
To cover my bed
To cover my bed ...
    The cold night of trouble
    Is such a long night of pain
    It will be tomorrow
    Before I see you again
    Before I see you again
My heart sinks inside me
To think that before
Before the long summer passes
I may not see you anymore
I may see you no more

    There are ships on the mountain
    I see black fish on the lawn
    And I watch the long highway
    Down which you have gone
    Down which you have gone
All I want is a pillow
To lay under my head
And a rainbow of fire
To cover my bed
To cover my bed

SUSAN: (*accusingly*) Why, Captain Nevada—why did you do it?

CAPTAIN NEVADA: Like it's a madcap world, baby ... the starling flies chased by a cloud ... Doggie balls hang on the willow ... the gurgle of the sewer is the death hymn of the spider in the tunnel ...

ALLAN: Level with yourself and us ... We are young for one hour of a short day.

CAPTAIN NEVADA: We is you ... the air is me ... Catch the sound of water being born and you have caught eternity ... I am seventy thousand years old this morning!

ALLAN stares at him with disbelief.

ALLAN: Then you're ...

CAPTAIN NEVADA: Yeh, man ... you dig ... but keep it to yourself!

ALLAN cannot take his eyes off CAPTAIN NEVADA.

SUSAN: I was so scared ... never been that scared before ... It was after midnight a year ago ... when Susan Mortimer made a telephone call to say she thought she had failed her exams and she had no idea what to do with herself.

CAPTAIN NEVADA: How'd it go, baby?

SUSAN: She wanted someone to come over ... talk to her ... but they all had headaches or dates ... at five-thirty that afternoon, Susan took an overdose of sleeping pills ...

CAPTAIN NEVADA: (*mocking, knowing her reply*) Did she die?

SUSAN: Yes ... that Susan Mortimer died ... sometimes when I'm afraid she comes back to see me ... to whisper in my ears and kiss my face when I sleep ... I open my eyes and tell her to stay dead ... there is no home for her now!

Music up.

ALLAN: (*loudly*) On days when the sun comes out ... all will go outside to worship, for the days of pure sun are few!

SUSAN leads entire GROUP in a spirited dance.

SONG: Wild strawberries grow
At the foot of the mountain
Hey-nonny-nonny-nonny, hey nonny-day
Sweet as the lips
Of the first child who found them
Hey-nonny-nonny-nonny, hey-nonny-day
> Man in a cradle
> Lies on his back
> Grins at the moon
> But it won't laugh back
> No it won't laugh back
> And it's hey-nonny-nonny-nonny, hey-nonny-day.

My love delights me
As winds of the summer
Hey-nonny-nonny-nonny, hey-nonny-day
Raindrops and tears
Wash the cheeks of my lover
Hey-nonny-nonny-nonny, hey-nonny-day
> Man in a cradle
> A crown on his head
> Caressing his guts
> In a warm soft bed
> In a warm soft bed
> And it's hey-nonny-nonny-nonny, hey-nonny-day.

A white dog sleeps on the
Blue hills of morning
Hey-nonny-nonny-nonny, hey-nonny-day
When he awakes
The wild geese will be flying
And it's hey-nonny-nonny-nonny, hey-nonny day
> Man in a cradle
> All painted in black
> Goes down to the earth
> And there's no coming back
> No, there's no turning back
> And it's hey-nonny-nonny-nonny, hey-nonny-day

Stage to darkness.

ACT 3

SCENE 1

Music and song up.

Film on screen: ALLAN, SUSAN and GROUP returning home, hitch-hiking, crossing bridges, boarding a bus, walking, observing the city behind them. They board a boat and sail across water. They disembark from the boat and walk on.

SONG: In the early morning
When the day is yours and mine
Take my hand and sound a warning
For love and living must be fine
My father kissed me gently
At the parting hour of three
I gave him beads and flowers
And a kiss he gave to me
> Oh a kiss he gave to me
> But his eyes were of a stranger
> A man beyond the desert
> Other side of thirst and danger
> And on this highway to tomorrow
> Looking back the way is dim
> Give me back my right to freedom
> Was all I asked of him

These roads are made for transports
Barefoot children cannot pass
Without bleeding through these cities
Paved with fear and broken glass
Paved with fear and broken glass
And bordered by the dandelion
A ring of sun around my shoulders
And pressures on my mind
> Oh a kiss he gave to me
> His eyes were of a stranger
> A man beyond the desert
> Other side of thirst and danger
> And on this highway to tomorrow
> Looking back the way is dim
> Give me back my right to freedom
> Was all I asked of him

In the early morning
When the day is yours and mine
Take my hand and sound a warning
For love and living must be fine
My father kissed me gently
There is no forgetting this

He shall keep my beads and flowers
And I'm branded with his kiss
> Oh a kiss he gave to me
> But his eyes were of a stranger
> A man beyond the desert
> Other side of thirst and danger
> And on this highway to tomorrow
> Looking back the way is dim
> Give me back my right to freedom
> Was all I asked of him

Film and music die.

Light on ALLAN and SUSAN in a serene, lonely atmosphere.

ALLAN: What'd they say?

SUSAN: They said there were no funds for a part-time art teacher. They were over budget already … they felt art would be a frill at this school …

ALLAN: Art is a frill now … drama, too … a pot-hole in the road gets repaired, but a kid with a broken wing waits for tomorrow afternoon … Only the essential grunts matter—all the rest is frill.

SUSAN: Things will work out. If we only stay out of the city. We're safe here.

ALLAN: We'll be safe, but we won't be winners from here.

SUSAN: There are no winners. But you're not a loser.

ALLAN: Nobody beats the system without battle … the act of retreat is an act of war, if we only knew it …

SUSAN: You're not a loser, papa Allan …

She takes his hand and kisses his fingers.

ALLAN: (*shuddering*) My skin howls on some mornings … I can't touch my face for the pain. I run out and look at my paintings in the shed and they seem to be wrapped in flames … but they don't burn. A moment later they are as they were, for this is the time of ice!

SUSAN: We are safe. We have each other.

ALLAN abruptly pulls his hand free, trying to escape the enormity of her love. A few paces from her he reconsiders and begins another telephone game.

ALLAN: (*his back to her*) Hello, missus …

SUSAN: (*down on her knees, answering a mock telephone*) Hello … Listen—how do you know I'm missus? Please tell me … Could be I'm a miss still.

ALLAN: Miss Still? … Oh, I'm sorry. I thought it was Missus Still! I got a card here says maybe you want to buy a bulldozer with a reconditioned motor!

SUSAN: Bulldozer? … You watch I don't give you a bulldozer to your mouth, you smart-assed-punk-hippy-kind-of-boy!

Music rises.

ALLAN: Hey! … What is the life span of a mouse?

SUSAN: It depends on the cat!

They run to each other, embrace. SUSAN dances away from him.

ALLAN: I've got things to do …

SUSAN: (*dancing*) It will rain! I feel rain in the wind!

ALLAN: (*in hollow tones*) The city I paint is a cannibal, devouring its parents … its children.

SUSAN: Think of happy things … please, Allan.

ALLAN: I am happy. But I'm older than yesterday.

SUSAN dances to him and stops.

SUSAN: To love is most important!

Music up faintly.

ALLAN kisses her tenderly. Then he grins and runs from her. She pursues him in a childish chase.

ALLAN: I won't work … I can't tell colours apart … I can't see the canvas I'm painting. I don't know anything. I even forgot my name! Is it like that for you?

SUSAN: It is now—I can't get you out of my mind or eyes!

ALLAN: Why should it be like that for me, then? … I don't think of me?

SUSAN overtakes and holds him.

SUSAN: When you're happy like this, I love you more than life!

He plays with her, to her delight.

ALLAN: There are people working in super-markets who believe in God ... I saw and spoke to a chick like that when I came out of jail. I was cold ... she said, "I believe in God, not only on Sunday, but everyday." I paid for the popsicle and I felt ashamed for asking.

Music fades out.

SUSAN: Don't talk about jail, baby. Yesterday, it was sunny all day ... the day before ...

ALLAN: (*thoughtfully*) But while I was talking to this chick, an old man came up carrying a package of oatmeal that shook in his hands. He stood watching me ... his eyes soft and full of water. He knew where I'd been. Then I asked the girl ...

SUSAN: The day was warm ... overcast! Warm and overcast ... There was a smell of soft, wet things. Like leaves ...

ALLAN: I asked if she agreed we were losing our sanity.

SUSAN: Like leaves starting to rot ...

ALLAN: ... And I knew as I asked that she wasn't going to say anything to me ...

SUSAN: Please—listen to me!

ALLAN: ... I was really asking the old man ...

SUSAN: ... I remember as a dream now ... crawling along the back lawn at home ...

ALLAN: ... Because the chick looked at him, and I looked at him ...

SUSAN: ... The blades of grass ...

ALLAN: The old man took a long time ... and when he spoke, he asked me in a thin voice what the hell was sanity?

SUSAN: ... Cutting my eyes and cheeks ...

ALLAN: I'm ten years older than I was a week ago ...

SUSAN: ... Like nails driven up from the ground! ...

ALLAN: ... Coming back, I find myself ten years older!

SUSAN: (*touches her face and winces*) It hurts me ...

ALLAN turns to her impatiently, searching for some sign of understanding in what he has been telling her. SUSAN is preoccupied.

ALLAN: Soon I will be an old man myself, either established or destroyed. I tried to explain to him what it meant to make one's choices without interference or fear ... Of two brothers vying for one available job and becoming less than brothers for it ... Of having confidence that things get born fresh from time to time and are capable of goodness ... That wars are made by sober people who have lost their sense of destiny ... The old man asked me ... if ... (*laughs incredulously*) ... He asked me if ... I'd ever gone hungry for a week with no idea where the next meal was coming from? What a helluva question to ask! ... I ate better in jail than we eat as free people! What a strange time to ask me! (*laughs*)

SUSAN: (*quietly*) When I lay on my back, and looked up at the sky ...

ALLAN: What a helluva funny question to ask me!

SUSAN: ... Clouds blew over me like mountains of snow. There was no wind ... only clouds ... over the roofs, over the fence ... I heard Mama calling, and soon there were no more clouds ...

ALLAN: ... An old man, and he didn't ask for my name, or what I thought in my head ... only if I'd ever been hungry ... Fifty thousand years of civilization didn't change the caveman's question! What revolution will help him?

SUSAN: ... Only the sun, into my eyes ... and Daddy standing over me, bigger than the sky ...

ALLAN: (*loudly*) The chick didn't speak! Only the old man, giggling away and holding his oatmeal box to me.

Music under. Film projection: fractured scenes of conflict—troops and police fighting youth, violence on campuses and on demonstration routes. ALLAN goes to screen and stands in silhouette, staring at it.

VOICE: (*recorded*) ... How much do we tolerate? They want control of universities in Vancouver, San Francisco, New York ... They want control of factories in France and Germany ... Governor Reagan recognizes an international conspiracy of great danger in this and has suggested opening classrooms at bayonet point ... (*cheers and applause*)

ALLAN: (*loudly*) The forests are green ... the threat to the earth is from those who profess to protect it from threat!

Film projection: desolate barracks grounds with ominous tanks and guns under wraps.

MILITARY MAN: (*recorded*) ... I laughed on the parade ground ... laughed out loud. The new commanding officer heard and comin' over asked why in hell I laughed like a hyena. I said I didn't know. Something had struck me funny, I guess ... Quick as a wink I'm put in detention. This new officer ... they say he had university ... leads me to the coal shed. He brings me a gallon of white paint and a four-inch brush. "Paint the lumps of coal white and mind you don't splash any goddamn paint on the floor, corporal," he says and he left me there. I laughed at first, and then I couldn't laugh no more, 'cause it wasn't goddamn funny anymore ...

ALLAN: (*to the screen*) The assassins ... they look like architects and athletes by day ... There is a sad red cloud over the moon tonight ...

Music up sharply.

Film Projection: war footage of air and ground assault, fires, etc.

SONG: The sheep on the hillside
Have left me alone
But the crow at my bedside
Sits gaunt as a stone
The lambs on the hillside
They have grown one by one
Some have climbed the far hills
Some fell to the gun
The warbird keeps gliding
Like a storm in the sky
And my children of pity
Are destined to die ...
    I'll throw shards at the moon
    I'll throw spears at the sun
    And perhaps he will leave me
    Take wings and be gone!
Had I hands of the gods
I'd comb through the mountains
Through the fleece of the earth
Sprouting temples and fountains
The lies of destruction
Are scorched in his eyes
A god I shall be
On the day that he dies

    I'll throw shards at the moon
    I'll throw spears at the sun
    And perhaps he will leave me
    Take wings and be gone ...
... A god I shall be
On the day that he dies ...
Now the sheep on the hillside
Have left me alone
But the crow at my bedside
Sits gaunt as a stone
The crow in my shadow
I shall lose him someday
No seed of my body
His homage will pay
    I'll throw shards at the moon
    I'll throw spears at the sun
    And perhaps he'll leave me
    Take wings and be gone
... A God I shall be
On the day ... that he dies!

Film projection and music dies suddenly.

ALLAN turns to SUSAN. He is weeping. She goes to him.

ALLAN: Is the only sanity then ... in death?

SUSAN: No, papa Al ... no! Our baby is coming!

ALLAN: Jesus Christ—that could've been me!

SUSAN: Perhaps it was ...

SCENE 3

OLD MAN enters. He is bent, deep in thought. In his hands he carries a small suitcase. ALLAN is aware of the OLD MAN, but will not turn to look at him. SUSAN makes a dancing motion with her hands.

SUSAN: Today ... I prayed ... among the trees ... I lifted my arms to the sun ... and I prayed by dancing ...

ALLAN: (*troubled*) Who is he?

SUSAN: When I was little ... on a cold morning I woke feeling strange ...

ALLAN: He wasn't on the boat ... he didn't come with us ... Tell him to go away!

SUSAN: ... I wanted to sleep ... to keep from waking ...

ALLAN: Susan—tell him to go away. I'm afraid of him!

SUSAN: (*as in trance*) I had a dream I was on a beach ... the water was grey and still ...

Thin shrill note of music sustained in background.

OLD MAN: (*talking to no one*) The fish in the river are grey ... I used to fish from a rowboat, towing a net, in the old days. Took the fish to town in a wagonbox full of ice ... On a hot day the water used to slush an' drip in time to the horses' hooves on the gravel road ...

SUSAN: I saw a man rise out of the water and walk towards me. He was dressed in jeans and a corduroy jacket that shone with water ...

OLD MAN: I was a farm boy ... spent most of my time on the farm across the road ... It was the farm across the road I wanted to work at, where the machinery was new. My father didn't like that, but I was young. No use to talk to me ...

SUSAN: He walked towards me ...

OLD MAN: When I was a boy ... (*looks at suitcase in his hand*) ... Why do you think I will have to move again? In the rest home ... playing checkers with others who are old like I ... talking about the long morning and short afternoon of our lives ...

ALLAN: (*with horror*) I know what you're going to say!

OLD MAN: ... I wanted to see the blossoms at Oliver ... I went around, asking for company ... did anybody want to come for a drive with me?... To see the pear trees blossom at Oliver? ...

SUSAN: (*alarmed*) ... He walked past me. A man I didn't know ... I followed him and when I touched his hand, it was cold and dead ...

OLD MAN: Two men came with me ... One was eighty-two, the other eighty-six years old. We saw the flowers that day ... the pear flowers at Oliver ... the wind blew warm and spicy down from the mountains ... On the way home, I followed a road that curved beside the lake ...

ALLAN: No!

OLD MAN: I got lookin' at the lake and thinkin' ... this was the truth ... the only truth ... the flowers in spring and the short day becoming dark in a

hurry ... We sat in the car as it went down to the bottom of the lake ... None of us said a word to the others, even when the water came in, for it felt warm as a bath after such a beautiful day.

SUSAN: (*slowly*) Cold ... and dead ... like wet stones ...

The OLD MAN shuffles away and leaves. ALLAN and SUSAN rush for each other and embrace. Music up.

SONG: (*improvised in a mood of sadness*)
Sing of good times now
For I come down the hill
Wiser than I was
At this hour yesterday.

SCENE 4

ALLAN places his hands on her abdomen. She puts her hands on his cheeks. They kneel, facing each other. Film projection: CAPTAIN NEVADA and others of the GROUP approach, offering gifts.

ALLAN: (*to CAPTAIN NEVADA on screen, but facing SUSAN*) You're too late man ... I'm not giving up the earth! I'm going to fight for it! (*to SUSAN*) The second little Jesus ... or another Che?

SUSAN: (*laughs*) I wouldn't be able to stand it!

ALLAN: No common name for this one! He will have an eye in the middle of his forehead from which joy will radiate! He will not step into the shadows of the animal!

SUSAN: (*still laughing*) And if it's a girl ... she will be called Parasa, after a Russian great-aunt of mine who was a ballerina!

ALLAN: It's a boy! I feel him call my name!

SONG: (*improvised*)
Sing of tomorrow
I am the earth
Searching the rainbow sky
For the likes of you ...

Screen projection dies. SUSAN and ALLAN rise.

SCENE 5

ALLAN and SUSAN remain pensive, close to each other. UNCLE and MOTHER enter another stage area. UNCLE TED has aged and his mannerisms are those of a lonely, neglected man.

UNCLE: ... Once, I was offered five hundred dollars for writing the story of the movements to which I belonged and in which I struggled ... Many men were hurt ... it was a good struggle ... the struggle goes on. It would have been a betrayal to accept Judas money like that ... to profit when others fell and I remained to remember ...

MOTHER: I'm selling the house ... A buyer left an option payment today.

UNCLE: (*understanding, groping for words*) That's good ... it's as well ... the house is too big now ...

MOTHER: The price is a good one. Better than I'd expected to get for the house.

UNCLE: It was a good fight ...

MOTHER: I will be moving into a small apartment ... what will you do?

UNCLE: Do? ... (*pulls himself up physically*) ... I'll ... I'll visit some of the unions again where men I know are still active ... (*hopelessly*) I can still organize ...

MOTHER: With the down payment I'll look for a partner to open a beauty salon with me ...

UNCLE: You? ... Going into business ... as a shopkeeper?

MOTHER: (*sadly*) What's to become of you?

UNCLE TED turns away, upset with her choice of a living. She touches him.

ALLAN: I sold a big painting today ... A cheque from the gallery came ... A cheque for the big painting came this morning.

SUSAN: That's groovy!

ALLAN: It was the big painting I'd painted for you to keep ... I didn't cash the cheque. I couldn't do it, baby ...

SUSAN smiles at him to assure him it's all right. MOTHER kisses UNCLE TED quickly and moves away to vanish in darkness. He peers after her.

ALLAN: I want to live with integrity.

SUSAN: I want to go to bed. I want to sleep.

ALLAN holds her in his arms. She is limp and subdued.

UNCLE: (*speaking after MOTHER*) A man should dance when he's young ... otherwise ... what is life? An existence isn't enough ...

Faint sound of tolling bell. Music up softly. UNCLE TED stiffens. He speaks with measured, careful words. Film projection: a religious hostel entrance.

UNCLE: Father? ... Listen ... I was a Catholic in my boyhood ... I think you know all about me since then ... only ... Well, I'm out of work and my chances of finding employment are ... well ...

He pauses for a long moment, listening to the voice only he can hear in reply. He slumps in spirit as he listens.

UNCLE: ... That's not true! ... Not at all! ... I've worked hard and put my earnings into what I believed in—still believe was the noblest cause man ever had ... I've not come to beg! When work is available again, I'll repay this ... this temporary arrangement! ... But for God's sake, I've not come to beg! I'd have gone on welfare first!

SCENE 6

Bell continues to toll. UNCLE goes down on one knee. MOTHER appears behind him. She is dressed in a business suit, a headpiece over her hair. Her manner is crisp and assured. He rises quickly to his feet when she speaks.

MOTHER: Ted? ... I wasn't sure I'd find you here. Are you all right?

UNCLE: Oh, I'm fine ...

MOTHER: The children were in town today. They asked about you.

UNCLE: How are they?

MOTHER: They're happy ... said to say hullo to you.

UNCLE: Poor kids ... poor homeless, beautiful kids ...

MOTHER: But for you ... in this place ...

UNCLE attempts to be reassuring without success.

UNCLE: It's nothing, Helen. Just a temporary arrangement I've made with the hostel here. I'll be back at work soon … They're preparing something for me through the research and education office … a speaking tour of the interior, I'd say … How's the business doing? Fine, I hope!

MOTHER: Fine. Thank you for asking.

SUSAN leaves. MOTHER leaves in opposite direction from SUSAN. Music fades but bell continues tolling. UNCLE moves into silhouette against screen film projection. He remains there, his head lowered.

SCENE 7

SUSAN returns with basket of food. ALLAN and she squat and begin eating.

SUSAN: Michele stopped by while you were out sketching … She spent Thursday and Friday in the city.

ALLAN: Has the city survived, then?

SUSAN: (*smiles*) Yes, but with difficulty …

ALLAN: Tough.

SUSAN: She said the gallery sold another two paintings, and they said to ask you to replace them with new ones!

ALLAN: Michele told you this?

SUSAN: Yes.

ALLAN: Tell her I don't need an agent.

SUSAN: And there was a money order for twenty dollars from your mother.

ALLAN: Send it back!

SUSAN: What will you do, then?

ALLAN: About what?

SUSAN: About replacing the paintings they sold?

ALLAN: (*shrugs*) Nothing.

SUSAN: Nothing?

ALLAN: Nothing!

SUSAN: But you said … that paint an' canvas and your imagination … was a moment remembered on the long road to freedom … that you could exchange that moment for cheese and milk and beans … if you had to … you said that!

ALLAN: Art has to be more than memory … it has to be a weapon now … the blast of cold and hot wind on the air-conditioned cheek … (*she looks at him blankly*) … no, you wouldn't understand …

SUSAN: I'm trying to! … Allan, baby—what is happening?

ALLAN: (*smiling gently*) Nothing's happening … we're just growing older.

SUSAN: Will you work today?

ALLAN: (*lightly*) Oh yes! Today I'll paint for myself … I'm painting heaven out there on the beach! I'm painting God … his digs … the green grass and wild strawberries in His garden!

SCENE 8

Members of the GROUP enter and squat around ALLAN and SUSAN. They take food from the basket. ALLAN rises and brandishes his sandwich at CAPTAIN NEVADA.

ALLAN: It's too late, Ageless Magnificence! I'm painting the backyards of paradise now, where the slums are … and the missiles and nuclear bombers … and my poor uncle eating food from his enemies, like a prisoner of war … Of meanness and stupidity … Of wings and the groping into the cosmos where loneliness is infinite and man is finally capable of shedding the skin and outlook of the beast … I have to do that today, because my child is God Himself, laughing with us and we must not disappoint Him again!

GROUP: Amen!

SUSAN: Allan, my beautiful Allan!

She rises and begins dancing, food in both hands.

ALLAN: (*enthusiastically*) When I am king, men will not live in ridicule!

CAPTAIN NEVADA: When *we* are kings!

GROUP: Amen!

Music up.

ALLAN: When *I* am king, for every *I* must be liberated before he joins other kings as equals!

GROUP: Amen!

ALLAN: When *we* are kings, the good health nurses shall be rewarded with organically grown apples and cherries, and the bad ones shall have a hot room with no door!

CAPTAIN NEVADA: Friends who are talkers and no listeners!

GROUP: Amen!

ALLAN: All policemen and no prisoners!

GROUP: Amen!

CAPTAIN NEVADA: All givers and no takers!

ALLAN: Eyes for the dying souls!

SUSAN: Ears with nothing to hear!

ALLAN: All masks and no faces!

SUSAN: Roads and no traffic!

GROUP: Amen ... Amen!

ALLAN: Bells ringing frost and morning!

CAPTAIN NEVADA: High places and no bottoms!

ALLAN: Flat rivers and no mountains!

SUSAN: Bees humming in the skull all day!

CAPTAIN NEVADA: Bees humming sunlight in the brain of sadness ...

ALLAN: Angels with quilted wings ...

GROUP: Amen! ... Amen!

SUSAN: A sky full of flowers! ... A sky full of love!

She dances away.

CAPTAIN NEVADA: A dead child laughing ...

GROUP: Amen! ... Amen! ... Amen!

Music up.

All members of the GROUP begin to dance. UNCLE TED stands alone, broken and withered. Film projection: over GROUP dancing onstage, a counter filmed dance of GROUP—dancing away into a non-landscape of water, sky and earth. They dance into infinity, except for ALLAN, who returns, his face towering on the screen. His face shows his determi-

nation for a reckoning with society for making him an outcast.

Onstage, GROUP dance through song, engaging the audience to come up and join them.

SONG: Don't turn away from me
I am what I am
And I shall be what I must be
Don't turn away from me
For we each must do
The thing we do
For we each must do
The thing we do
       Living on the outskirts
       Of the holy city
       Eating prayers and sunsets
       Beside the unknown river
       Bleeding tears and water
       Like some sacred fountain
Don't turn away from me ...
       Climbing shafts of sunlight
       To touch the rim of heaven
       Shouting to my mother
       Through a muddy window
       Opening the blossoms
       Of forgotten virtue
       Splitting stones and starlight
       With a baby's laughter ...
Don't turn away from me ...
       Sacraments of water
       To the life hereafter
       Kissing grass that whispers
       Secrets of the thunder
       Fondling a mountain
       Like morning of creation
       Wrestling the ego
       Of self-crucifixion
       Shivering in the glower
       Of unhappy cities
Don't turn away ... don't you turn away from me ...
       Lying face to face
       Transferring beaded children
       With their souls impaled
       By the silver ribbon of our love!
Don't turn away from me
I am what I am
And I shall be what I must be
Don't turn away from me
For we each must do
The thing we do ...

Film Projection: ALLAN'S face in still. Previous song may be recorded for double-play to give the final dance scene extra time to develop for participation of audience. Music—back to religious origins. GROUP stop their dance and remain still. House lights up.

End

COMPRESSIONS

Fresh from the provocative Vancouver Playhouse Company production of *Grass and Wild Strawberries*, which played—with some controversy—to youthful, overflow audiences in the spring of 1969, Ryga was asked to write another play looking at issues facing youth. *Compressions* was commissioned by Playhouse Holiday, the Company's performance group for young people, for its 1969–1970 tour of secondary schools. Founded as Holiday Theatre in 1953, this was Canada's first professional theatre for young people; it was one of the first to present issue-oriented plays at a time when school touring companies typically presented fairy tales or works from the canon of Shaw, Molière, or Shakespeare. *Compressions*, with its topical narratives and in-your-face debate, must be seen as a fairly radical departure for its day.

The play is a sustained, passionate debate about broad societal questions then current at the height of the counterculture revolution (the famous Woodstock festival took place that August); in addition, it is one of Ryga's most experimental productions—not unlike *Grass and Wild Strawberries*, which also explores similar themes. This morality play directly asks its student audiences to ponder the larger questions of identity and purpose in their lives. He invites them to live life fully, to become more aware of their own human potential: "We are capable of incredible goodness ... we are godlike!" says the character of the Teacher. Pointedly, Ryga suggests that the "world's problems" are also to be found in their own backyards, and that therefore students have no alternative but to take responsibility for them. The theatre troupe itself is made to proclaim an idealistic goal in common with its audience: "our pursuit is truth beyond the facts." To actualize these very large theatrical ambitions, Ryga uses a simple but powerful *mise en scène*.

As he did in a number of his early plays, the playwright begins with a strong *leitmotif*, in this case the physical presence of time as a marker of human progress: the play is accompanied by a "continuous soundtrack," beginning with the daily rhythms of a train whistle, footsteps, and a clock. These evoke the unfolding drama of the world; they also serve, along with "the luxuriant time-piece of history," the beating of the human heart (the "compressions" of the title), as ominous reminders of individual moral responsibility in an increasingly amoral world, a world now badly distorted by "the myth of the eternal middle-class."

Since they are invited to participate, the student audiences sit closely around three sides of a thrust stage, a six-sided platform surrounded on five sides with platforms at three levels, each painted a strikingly different colour, all intended to represent, in the playwright's words, "the form of a mind mulling over seemingly unrelated incidents." In this way Ryga attempts to force a political dialogue, mainly by foregrounding opposition to the neo-colonizing forces becoming increasingly visible throughout the world by the 1960s and 1970s—whether they be those of the military-industrial complex, organized religion, consumer society, or corrupt politicians. To stage this effectively, Ryga disrupts theatrical convention by means of direct address, overlapping dialogue, rock music, mime, dance, and a threadbare narrative.

As he had done in *Grass and Wild Strawberries*, Ryga utilizes aspects of pop/rock culture in order to claim a place for the underprivileged, symbolized by Chittigan, a homeless prospector, as well as to develop the potential for local political action by the audience/public against specific instances of this growing neo-colonialism like, for example, the production of napalm in nearby Alberta for American military use in Viet Nam. He attempts to establish an authentic voice, in this case the "real" voices of familiar people: teachers, parents, and students speaking to local as well as world issues, in a kind of agit-prop Brechtian manner of fierce rhetorical flourishes intended to galvanize the audience into action.

Compressions was performed in the Playhouse Holiday secondary school touring program of 1969–1970, directed by Ray Michal. Actors in the company included Alex Diakun, Paddy Kabatoff, Linda Kupecek, John Lazarus, and Glenn MacDonald. The stage manager was Richard Sutherland. The original song, "Chittigan," was written by George Ryga, with music by Dennis Cooper. Although it was generally regarded as a success, there exist, unfortunately, no records of the reaction of student audiences to the performances of this play.

COMPRESSIONS

CHARACTERS

TEACHER, *a man*
LINDA, *a teenaged girl*
DENISE, *another teenaged girl*
LARRY, *a young man*
SHEFFIELD, *a middle-aged man, Larry's father*

Voices on continuous soundtrack.

SET

The stage is an irregular thrust with indeterminate outline suggesting something of the form of a mind mulling over seemingly unrelated incidents.

The stage has three levels. The top elevation is for the TEACHER battling SHEFFIELD. The centre elevation is transitional. The lowest elevation is LARRY'S hideaway or spiritual retreat. The elevations are painted in solid colours: white for the top elevation, red for the middle one, and green for the lowest.

In the TEACHER'S playing area (top) there is a table and a chair.

SOUNDTRACK: *Rock music bridging into hoot and roar of a railway locomotive; bridging into clatter of an alarm clock; bridging into loudly amplified footsteps.*

In time to the footsteps, TEACHER enters carrying books under his arm. He hesitates briefly at the lip of the stage. Footsteps cease with him stopping. He is preoccupied. He looks around the auditorium, smiles, and goes onto the top stage level.

TEACHER: Good morning, or good afternoon. Does anybody know the hour of the month of the day of the week? (*no reply*) Never mind—it doesn't matter. If we knew ourselves as we know time, there would be no need for churches, psychiatric priests, magicians ... or this. (*He indicates the stage behind him*)

SOUNDTRACK: *Amplified ticking of clock.*

TEACHER: The clock above the bank ticks the time of poverty and wealth ... the clocks within this building mark your star-scattered footsteps out of childhood.

SOUNDTRACK: *"Chittigan" music softly in the background. Ticking of clock continues.*

MIME DANCE: *A brightly COSTUMED GIRL enters dancing the "Dance of Time." She enters on the lowest elevation, doing a children's game dance. Then she moves onto the second elevation and into growing maturity. When she goes to the top level, her motions are set and stiffening, all attitudes in-turned. Over her dance:*

TEACHER: And in your breast and mine, the dark, luxuriant timepiece of history, pumping out the scream of birth ... and the old man's worry, about stairs and the price of cornmeal ... pumping out the time of burning forests, stars in collision ... the first man to count the fingers on his hands. Omar Khayam in his Persian garden, scented with regret ... the time of wars and darkness brightened only by a thirst for God. Pumping out the slime of oceans and the raw-meat hunger of the jungle until ourselves, like gods, we leave the earth to kiss the moon. But we are people still ... the black-skinned miner in Rhodesia ... the Chinese student walking to his classrooms over roads built three thousand years ago. We sweat through the same pores ... thirst after truth and water ... we dream and love and fear in the same way. And there is still a remnant of the English king who killed his brother's children in our Canadian democratic blood. At Suffield, in Alberta, napalm was perfected to burn the homes and skins of children of Vietnam. The work of death-for-sale goes on in Suffield at this very moment ... the soil on which this building stands was taken from Indians who were here six thousand years or more before us ... and if you were a student of French extraction in Quebec today, you would find it easier to be taught Latin and Greek than electronics or drafting.

SOUNDTRACK: *Song and ticking stop. Electronic music faintly in the background. Mime dance ends.*

TEACHER: Then who are we and why are we? We are wandering players going here and there, working at a labourer's wages off a bus with a defective clutch. Our stock-in-trade is illusion ... our baggage is the heritage of other players across the centuries ... our pursuit is truth beyond the facts. We entertain, we howl ... we please ... we torment.

> We show why men can crucify,
> by sweep of arm, by glance of eye.

(*playfully*) I am now a teacher, you, my students. The roles can be reversed at once, had you the courage to reverse them!

SOUNDTRACK: *Crash of steel, tinkling of falling glass.*

VOICE: (*recorded*) Sir, may I then be excused from ...

TEACHER: You may be excused from all things, if that is your choice ... but you will turn your back on nothing.

VOICE: (*recorded*) In watts, the coloured people turned legitimate frustration into illegal ...

TEACHER: Let us worry about the colourless people—they are the most frustrated and dangerous of all!

VOICE: (*recorded*) Are we playing with clichés, sir? Or setting the stage for ...

TEACHER: We are setting the stage, student, with paving stones that have sharp edges, so take care where you step!

VOICE: (*recorded*) Then can you explain ...

TEACHER: I can explain nothing ... let the play begin, and perhaps you can explain to each other what you see.

VOICE: (*recorded*) Wait! If you're a teacher then let us see you teach.

SOUNDTRACK: *Hard drone sound that rises and lowers in ominous pitch almost imperceptibly.*

TEACHER: (*moves to desk. Places his books down and sits, facing the audience*) What can I teach you—how to live?

VOICE: (*recorded*) We know how to live.

TEACHER: Then perhaps you should learn how people die. What do you know of war?

VOICE: (*recorded*) We reviewed the major wars in November ...

TEACHER: We reviewed nothing except what is in here. (*indicates books with a sweep of his hand*) The conditions for war, pillage, love exist in this room. The plumber down the street can be a general ... the pound-keeper runs a concentration camp ... the SS-men of wartime Germany grew up in towns as quiet, attended schools as orderly as this one.

VOICE: (*recorded*) Sir?

TEACHER: You disagree? I know what I am saying. I am the bridge between you and society. You are under my care for longer hours than you are cared for by your home environment. It is beyond me to change society to accept you, but I must mould you to be acceptable to society. Sometimes I am timid in this role, aware of mortgages, obligations, and I slide into being an educational technician, but I cannot escape the truth of who I am and what my functions are.

VOICE: (*recorded*) (*more urgent*) Sir?

TEACHER: Listen to me! I must talk quickly, because it is late and I have left many things unsaid. Some of you are older than your years ... you speak out of habit rather than conviction ... you grasp for simple solutions to complex problems ... you accept too readily, and condemn out of boredom ... you challenge the world for the hurtful things it does, then deny any obligation to improve it all. You presume to understand the plight of the hungry and deprived two continents away, yet you know nothing of the welfare recipients in your community, of the Hank Chittigans breaking stone for grub money in the mountains around you ... of Indians and Canada Council poets whose clothes are shabby and whose teeth decay, for it is cheaper to extract a tooth than to repair it. In short, yours are the anxieties of a myth as shallow as a TV commercial!

VOICE: (*recorded*) What myth are you talking about? There is nothing in our lesson material about ...

TEACHER: The myth of the feather-bed ... the myth of consuming more than you or your parents have legitimately created ... the myth of the eternal middle-class that regards its being and welfare as the sole reason for all creation!

VOICE: (*recorded*) That's not true! I worry about the poor, sir!

TEACHER: The way a farmer worries about dandelions ... he appreciates their flower, but they are inconvenient and they cut into his profits. If the poor threatened to overwhelm you, disinherit you, compel you to walk and run on mud roads, work for wages which make a pound of good fresh meat an unthinkable luxury, then, and only then, would you worry about the poor!

VOICE: (*recorded*) You have no right to say that!

TEACHER: That is true ... you know my responsibilities better than you know your own.

VOICE: (*recorded*) We are not brainless children of technology. We are capable of greater things ... if only you would teach us.

TEACHER: Do you realize what an awesome thing you are asking me to do? The conditions for love exist in this room—yes! Your warm hands, your moist, clear eyes still reminiscent of the night—they speak of love, they invite love! Not the shoddy love of deodorant ads in your teen magazines nor the grim sexuality whose trade-in value is a marriage license, but the love of gods that makes the hills greener and the heart of an old man rejoice! You were born where and when you were born, that is not your fault, so you live with the faults and possibilities of today—and because you were born, you are entitled to the room you need to live, be it a closet apartment or the space between Earth and Jupiter. This is your right, and you must expand your love according to your God-given appetites.

SOUNDTRACK: *Sustained pitch of sound becoming opening strains of Beethoven's Ninth Symphony.*

VOICE: (*recorded*) Are you proposing a dangerous invitation to immorality?

TEACHER: No, I am not. Your heartbeats are compressions and explosions of life; they are the beats of freedom. Live as if every stroke of your heart was its last!

VOICE: (*recorded*) We are free! We are free!

TEACHER: Listen to me! There are bands stronger than steel closing around your skulls, around your eyes and mouths, reducing your vision, silencing your songs: there is no greater obscenity than this! Its fruits are religious fervour, ignorance, poverty, obscenities which turn murder into virtue and the making of a baby into sin.

VOICE: (*recorded*) (*shocked*) Good God, what are you saying? What right have you?

SOUNDTRACK: *Beethoven melts into hard, driving rock music.*

TEACHER: (*recorded*) There are bands stronger than steel closing around your skulls.

The CAST dances onto the second elevation of the stage, each dancer delivering his or her lines of dialogue in frozen stance, then continuing into contemporary dance. TEACHER laughs as he moves down to join the cast.

SOUNDTRACK: *Music softens so players are heard.*

BOY: All the world's a school ...

GIRL: And all the players are unwitting students ...

TEACHER: Each in his time plays many parts ...

GIRL: There's nothing here but a mortgage on my time. I could be a doctor in two months if they'd let me study!

TEACHER: All reluctant students ...

BOY: I could be an architect before next Christmas!

GIRL: Yesterday, at noon, I was in love ... with a marigold!

TEACHER: They have their exits and their entrance exams ...

GIRL: Through the doors of IBM ... fragmented into stainless steel savings bonds, insurance, mortgages and bonds ...

BOY: People die, but corporations live forever. We should become corporations in this galactic dream of dying meadows and growing cities! We will live!

GIRL: And who cares? Does anybody care?

BOY: My father said to keep my sleeves rolled up so he could see my veins at breakfast!

ANOTHER BOY: So we close the books and schools—what then?

TEACHER: Study our fathers and our mothers, our sisters and our pimply brothers ...

SOUNDTRACK: *Singer sings*:
>Chittigan is coming
>Has anybody seen him
>Does anyone here know Chittigan?
>Rock axe in his hand
>Plastic cups a-hanging on his belt
>And his eyes are full of water
>And his head ... still full of rainbows ...

Song goes into background music.

The MEN drift onto the top level, the WOMEN onto the lowest level. Each person now dons a wig and suggestive costuming to age them into older people. But the aging is mocking, provocative.

FIRST WOMAN: My psychiatrist accused me of being threatened. I'm not threatened ... what in heck did he say that for?

SECOND WOMAN: (*in her own world, not relating to others*) I was lonely and kind of bored when I started working on the heart campaign. I felt good after that. Then I made up Christmas hampers for the poor, but we had a lot left over because some of those never-do-wells wouldn't accept them—imagine!

FIRST WOMAN: The truth is as plain as the nose on my face. I've raised three of them myself. I know what it's all about.

SECOND WOMAN: A person has to do something ... there are people out there suffering with defective hearts, diseased lungs. I had no choice but to try and help.

FIRST WOMAN: Every child has a chance in a God-fearing society, every child, be they Indian, black, or blue, so I took her into my nice home, gave her a nice room of her own ... but she slept on the floor next to the window. It made me wonder if she really deserved the break she was getting.

SECOND WOMAN: It was simple once. My father was a judge ... he prayed to God for wisdom before he sentenced a man to jail. People were afraid of him, but they respected him, and there was order then.

FIRST WOMAN: To sleep on the floor when there is a bed standing empty ...

MAN: We did it for them ... what else do they want from us?

SECOND WOMAN: These kids stare at you, or walk by like you weren't there. I've got a right to live and think like I please. What kind of teachers teach them this nonsense in their heads?

SOUNDTRACK: *Singer sings*:
>Nobody here knows his name
>Chittigan is coming
>Has anybody seen him
>Does anyone know where he's goin'?

During the song, the SECOND WOMAN exits. The FIRST WOMAN removes her wig and becomes LINDA. TEACHER and SHEFFIELD change into roles of TEACHER and middle-aged professional businessman. All others leave the stage.

SHEFFIELD turns away from the TEACHER.

TEACHER: Sheffield, I had to come and see you. We meet on committees and we talk, but nothing changes. I want it like it used to be between us ... or have you forgotten?

LINDA: I slept on the floor because I was afraid of messing her bed with the picture-book bedspread imported from Switzerland, where all good bedspreads come from.

SHEFFIELD: I'm late for a meeting, Hal ... is it trouble at the school again?

TEACHER: The trouble isn't at the school ... it's with us ... we live and think as if we were the last people on earth.

SOUNDTRACK: *Drumming sound of heartbeat, accented with touches of music.*

SHEFFIELD: You're doing a good job—don't worry.

LINDA: My mother was fourteen when she went out to work, she said ...

TEACHER: What is a "good job"? How can a grown man live year after year with only one definition of what is good or bad? We're not fossils, Sheffield, the trees grow taller every day, the mountains smaller—nothing remains constant!

SHEFFIELD: (*turning to him*) Don't lecture me, Hal. I don't need it. I said you did a good job as a teacher—what happened is not your fault ...

TEACHER: I didn't come to talk about Larry!

SHEFFIELD: Good. I'm tired of the subject.

TEACHER: Why is it good?

SHEFFIELD: You're leaning on me again, Hal!

TEACHER: I want definitions I can relate to the students! I want five minutes of your honest opinions—the kind of thoughts that are not processed by political considerations. I'm not a newspaper reporter—my job is to teach your child about our environment and the people who shape it. It's not enough to talk about "a bad dinner—a good war"!

SHEFFIELD: You just follow the curriculum of the department and we'll all be happier!

TEACHER: I've done that for fifteen years, and it's not enough anymore! The last Remembrance Day service at the cenotaph ... there wasn't a person under thirty there. Is it possible they know something we don't?

SHEFFIELD: (*annoyed*) You could have brought your classes out!

TEACHER: And face the humiliation of nobody showing up? You can't force thinking youth to respect stupidity!

SHEFFIELD: That's your opinion!

TEACHER: It's the opinion of 60% of all people alive today. I was a good soldier, the kind of scruff good wars are made of. When you pulled the unit back, I went in alone to take out the enemy pillbox. You remember that, don't you? (*SHEFFIELD nods*) Five men showed their faces as I lopped the grenade in. I still see those faces ... staring at me with disbelief and fright. I watched long enough to see them explode and die before I went down. It's something to live with, Sheffield.

LINDA begins miming a waitress waiting on tables.

TEACHER: At first I was proud of what I had done. It was a gesture for king and country—the ultimate act of heroism. I was decorated for Dieppe. Prime Minister Mackenzie King was at the railway station to meet me and shake my hand when I returned ... and two years later I was on relief.

LINDA: Yes, I'm new. I started working here last Monday. (*smiles fixedly*) We have apple, cherry, mince, and raisin pie, or ice-cream in a dish.

TEACHER: Last Remembrance Day, I couldn't join you at the cenotaph with the others. I watched from a distance and you know what I did?

SHEFFIELD: No. What did you do?

TEACHER: I cried for the five Germans I had killed because they were victims of the same madmen on their side as had victimized me on this side. I broke down and cried ...

LINDA: Apple, cherry, mince, and ...

TEACHER: I want you to remember something you did and said in those days ... that night, in a jeep, driving in from Hatfield to London ... I saw your eyes as you lit your cigarette ... do you remember what you asked me?

SHEFFIELD: No. I don't recall ...

TEACHER: You asked me—what are we doing here? Is this what a man has to do just to live? You asked me that, and I got mad at you.

SHEFFIELD: (*disturbed*) I don't remember ...

LINDA: (*now miming at waiting at a table where there is a girl who is a close friend of hers*) Me an' Larry went to the movie last night. We saw Zeffirelli's *Romeo and Juliet*. I bawled through most of it, but Larry said it was a drag.

TEACHER: I was only sixteen, but I lied and they took me in.

LINDA: He wanted help with his math homework, but I didn't want to talk to him then, not after I saw the picture and he felt that way.

TEACHER: I was the same age as your son when I went to war. There is a difference between us and him. He wouldn't do what we did without first asking a lot of serious questions!

LINDA: He's always bored. I can't rap with him. I don't know what he wants.

TEACHER: Sixteen years old, and he's run off on you twice, Sheffield. What in hell do you make of that? Would you have run off with me that night in the jeep ... even if it meant time in the brig? (*laughs*) Not you, old buddy ... not even then! I cried over war last November, but what's special about that? Women have been crying since the beginning of history. To be a man-hero takes something more ... but what?

LINDA: I don't like this job. I think I'll quit.

SHEFFIELD: I'm finding your opinions increasingly more distasteful. I've got a meeting to address.

LINDA moves off. DENISE enters where LINDA had been. She carries an imaginary tray on her arm. Her manner and bearing are crisp, assured. She speaks in the direction of SHEFFIELD.

DENISE: I agree, sir. Society must progress along logical, orderly patterns. If the strong are to survive, they must take positive control.

TEACHER: (*to SHEFFIELD*) What are you thinking then? Tell me what you really think.

DENISE: If arguments undermine the fabric of society, then put an end to arguments.

SHEFFIELD: No!

TEACHER: No what?

SHEFFIELD: I fought against that sort of thing ...

DENISE: A man can be forgiven for poor judgment.

TEACHER: Say it—tell me what you feel!

SHEFFIELD: It is immoral!

TEACHER: What is immoral?

DENISE: Then make it a moral issue ... if they call it fascism, then point to your military record, throw the label back at your accusers. It is easy—Daley of Chicago is a Democrat. Duplessis in Quebec always proclaimed himself a man of the people. There are fascist student leaders who have paved their roads with Marxist slogans, and only a silent few are aware of what is happening but they're afraid to speak up for they would be isolated into a living hell of loneliness!

TEACHER: What is immoral, I ask you?

SHEFFIELD: (*shaken*) Nothing. Nothing, I guess.

DENISE: Think of the benefits. The machinery is all prepared. It takes a man like you to step in and become the leader of the hour. Stand firm! Move where opportunity directs you! In twenty years' time a new civilization will be ready to move in ... children of the test-tubes ... strong, obedient, beautiful children with no melancholy anxieties. Don't listen to him—he is a hunched

troublemaker. I will be your mother of tomorrow. Stand firm!

TEACHER sits himself at the table, holds his face in his hands.

TEACHER: It always ends this way. You've never told me why you're going into public office. You're not suited for the job, Sheffield.

DENISE: Men like you are meant to be kings. You were destined for greater things than a law office or a hardware merchant.

She laughs and marches off. LINDA enters, pensive, girlish.

SOUNDTRACK: *Song, over heartbeat sounds:*
Saw him this morning
By the edge of the highway
In the shade of a poplar
Chittigan ...

TEACHER: Birds sing. Winter comes despite us. Did I ever tell you I'm tired of teaching?

SHEFFIELD: No, you didn't ...

TEACHER: I am. (*looks up*) I think our priorities are wrong.

SHEFFIELD: I don't understand.

TEACHER: So much effort and money is spent on fulfilling today. As for tomorrow ... (*shrugs*) Did you know that Socrates could see where we were going—thousands of years ago he saw men failing and reaching upward, growing stronger. Much later, the French Revolution was fought by older men and women—they held the children behind and went forward to die for a future for them. It was the same with the Russian Revolution, but today ...

SHEFFIELD turns away from him, impatiently.

TEACHER: (*smiling*) Today, the young idealists have to confront their own fathers and mothers before they can reconstruct the social order they inherited.

LINDA: (*smiling*) In our neighbourhood an old man left his home one morning in June. He was wearing a dressing gown. They couldn't find him ... nobody had seen him go. In August, his son-in-law placed a classified ad in the paper offering a reward of ten dollars for information in locating his missing father-in-law (*laughs*). Poor Grandpa

Saunders ... ten dollars ... the dressing gown he wore was worth more than half of that!

SOUNDTRACK: *Music: "Lady in Blue" into background for:*

TEACHER: The birds are singing but winter's coming for both of us, whether we like it or not.

SHEFFIELD: I have a meeting to go to. If there's nothing else you want ...

TEACHER: You have the unfortunate habits of a bookkeeper, Sheffield. You follow lines others have drawn. Why are you going into politics?

LINDA: (*still smiling*) Me an' Larry found the place together on a class hike. We wandered away from the others ...

TEACHER: Surely you have a reason. I'm a constituent of yours. I want to know!

LINDA: A level spot of meadow.

TEACHER: Come on, man, we don't have to posture with each other. I never made much of a school-teacher and you were a poor excuse for a lawyer, even in this town.

LINDA: We could hear the creek running nearby. Larry said there'd be fish in there for sure.

SHEFFIELD: (*coldly*) Get out of my house!

TEACHER looks at him silently, not at all responding to the demand.

TEACHER: That's your court of last resort again. (*glances at his watch*) And you're early tonight ... usually you don't throw in the towel until nine!

LINDA: When he split from school I knew he'd gone there. His dad came, sore as anything. He threatened Mister Stevenson and the principal with a lawsuit. He was going to take the incident to the school board, all that kind of thing. Which wasn't cool because we all knew how Larry felt.

TEACHER: Surely you can't feel confident all truth is on your side. Your own son couldn't take it, and that's a public indication of something being wrong. It's been years since you could look me directly in the eye, did you know that?

SHEFFIELD: I can throw you out, if that's what I have to do.

TEACHER: That's just what you'll have to do. Either I get through to you, or I've failed myself, and I can't take that without a fight, so ...

SHEFFIELD slowly sits at the table, but not facing TEACHER directly.

SHEFFIELD: (*wearily*) You've read my campaign speech, what is there to say? The incumbent mayor is a capable man and all that, but I think it's time for a change in administration.

TEACHER: Don't play games with me, say it out loud: the incumbent mayor is a rotter with no more capabilities than a garbage collector, and so I'm willing to run as an alternative candidate— say it!

LINDA: He'd put up a pup tent ... he was cold when I saw him ... he hadn't eaten all day. The fish in the creek didn't bite ... he tried to light a fire, but the wood was soggy.

TEACHER: Well?

SHEFFIELD: I have nothing against the man personally!

LINDA: I brought him a sandwich and a Coke.

TEACHER: Then why run against him? You must have reasons. You're not a man who gets inspired by causes.

SHEFFIELD: How little you know me!

LINDA: We sat for a long time and talked ... it was getting dark.

SOUNDTRACK: *Music out. Fast heartbeat faintly in background.*

LARRY appears onstage. He moves slowly on the lowest level, passing by LINDA before he stops.

TEACHER: (*to LARRY, but facing SHEFFIELD*) So you don't feel a popular opinion can now change the course of government policies?

LARRY: (*firmly*) No, sir! Two thirds of the people demonstrated to say "no," but the other third had all the guns, so nothing changed.

TEACHER: Is it not possible to vote the guns out?

LARRY: No!

LINDA: *Romeo and Juliet* said it the way it is ... some things just happen and there is nothing to do about it.

LARRY: "Nothing" is a dead word. I hate it!

TEACHER: (*to SHEFFIELD, laughing*) When I die, who will bury me? You? The school board? I haven't a single relative living, did you know that?

SHEFFIELD: Yes, you've told me!

TEACHER: So I can't afford to die, can I? I'm supposed to interpret you and your interests to the school-children, and I have nothing to tell them. If you ask me, we're in one helluva mess, old buddy!

He takes out a deck of cards and begins to deal a hand to SHEFFIELD. LINDA and LARRY draw closer.

SOUNDTRACK: *Musical drone, interrupted by metallic or electronic tones.*

LINDA: Why did you do it? You could have stuck out the few months …

LARRY: I could have … but the compromise was too great.

LINDA: (*shaking her head*) It doesn't make sense to me.

LARRY: It would if you were in my place … every step being laid out … all the way into oblivion.

LINDA: You did it to hurt him, didn't you? My mom was saying last night what kind of man would a mayor be who can't keep his own son in line?

LARRY: That's just it—don't you see?

LINDA: No, I don't see. I couldn't do it.

LARRY: Then why did you come? I didn't ask you to come.

LINDA: (*shrugs*) I … wanted to see you.

LARRY: What did they say in school?

LINDA: Nothing.

LARRY: Nothing? They must've noticed, they must've said something!

LINDA: I didn't hear …

TEACHER: (*playing his hand in cards*) Sometimes I listen to footsteps outside my house … overhear bits of conversation.

SHEFFIELD: What sort of conversation?

TEACHER: Just people talking. And at times like those I wish I'd married.

LINDA: If I asked you … would you make a baby for me?

LARRY: (*startled*) Why? There's too many people already.

LINDA struggles to tell him.

SOUNDTRACK: *Violent music rises.*

LINDA: Because … I love you.

LARRY: I'm not listening to you!

LINDA: What are you fighting against?

LARRY: All the things he stands for … the chairman of everything! Everyone in this town belongs to something, and he's in charge. No service club, fund-raising, or civic committee meeting gets started until he arrives to chair. Well, I don't belong to anything, and he's not chairing my life.

LINDA: He saw Mister Stevenson, said he'd call the police unless the school got you back into the classroom.

LARRY: He wouldn't do that … he's too much of a small town politician to expose himself that much. He'll leave me alone, as long as I stay out of his way.

LINDA: I don't see what a person can do without school. Jeff Miller hasn't had work for ten months now.

LARRY: I asked Mister Stevenson point-blank one day if it wasn't true we were being kept in school just to keep us off the labour market, and he admitted it was true.

TEACHER: Industry dictates the quality of education … half the students I'm teaching in the graduating class are incapable of reading a serious book, yet I have no choice but to pass them with honours.

SHEFFIELD: If it keeps a country growing, I see no fault in that.

TEACHER: Learning is the development of curiosity … even a draft horse gets bored with following the same path day after day.

LARRY: I was rapping with Jeff last week, and he said he doesn't want to be an architect because his old man was one and all his life he's designed buildings any carpenter could have built without his help.

LINDA: You're not going home then?

LARRY: No.

LINDA: If you're staying here, can I stay with you?

LARRY: I don't know.

LINDA: (*annoyed*) Why not?

LARRY: Because it's not your bag. You've no reason.

LINDA: I've told you why … you really feel you're different than me?

LARRY: I didn't say that.

LINDA: You feel that because you're the son of Bert Sheffield you've got some …

LARRY: I didn't say that!

LINDA reaches out to him. He draws away from her and sits down. She stands over him, playing with his hair.

SHEFFIELD: (*with exasperation*) I'm missing an important committee meeting, Hal. Can't we finish this game another evening?

TEACHER: We've never yet finished a game we started …

LARRY: I was the first kid in school to wear the kind of trousers that never needed pressing … spared my mom the trouble of worrying about me right to the end of her life. (*looks up at her, laughs*) You've no reason to stay, Lin, you're not being hassled.

LINDA: But you are …

LARRY: Yes. My father's more ambitious than yours. I'm supposed to run for the starting gate now.

SHEFFIELD: (*suspiciously*) You knew I had this meeting tonight. That's why you came, isn't it?

TEACHER: Yes.

SHEFFIELD: So you're determined to block me in every way possible.

TEACHER: Until I get a commitment from you that you'll involve yourself with things that matter.

SHEFFIELD: Who's setting you up for this?

TEACHER: Concern for the work I do, Bert. You served on the school board under false pretences. You never had the interest of education on your mind when you took that office: you withheld budgets, fought every useful, progressive recommendation, lost half a dozen excellent teachers from staff, until finally you turned the school plant into a meek, gray baby-sitting service. I've been repairing the personal damage you've done to yourself and last week I failed. I think you owe me something.

LARRY: You know how I got those trousers, Lin?

LINDA: No.

LARRY: From the estates of the dead he probated, through rake-offs, phony probates, litigations with no end in sight. His personal fortune in the past ten years was taken from widows and children who ended up on welfare. But I was the first kid in school with those kind of trousers. Then he had the gall to suggest I go into law!

LINDA: My father said he was a good man on the school board … he saved a lot of money … that he'll make a good mayor.

LARRY: I don't know anything about that. Maybe he will. But I'm not proud of the way he used his law practice, and I don't want to be like him!

LINDA: I can talk to my father and mom.

LARRY: Yeh, but do you hear each other talking?

LINDA: If we talk enough, we're bound to hear something, Larry.

LARRY: Like I asked him the morning I decided to throw it all in. I asked him if it was true what I heard about the dirty deals he pulled on the widows whose estates he probated. You know what he did?

TEACHER: Your move …

LINDA: No.

LARRY: Without warning, without saying a word, he stood up and hit me, right across the face. A hate blow—karate—pow! And down I went. That's when I decided I wanted none of it.

TEACHER: Why did Larry leave school, did he tell you?

SHEFFIELD: (*stiffening*) I'm sure I don't know. Why don't you find him and ask him—you're getting paid to do it.

TEACHER: I get paid to educate him—if and when he appears in class.

LINDA: What are you going to do?

LARRY: (*surprised at her question*) What?

LINDA: I said, what are you going to do about your father now?

LARRY: Destroy him—what else?

SOUNDTRACK: *Sharp, harsh, driving music.*

LINDA goes to raise LARRY to his feet. They dance together, their movements languid in counterpoint to the music which rises, then diminishes. Their dance turns into a mimic of themselves and people they know. LINDA takes the role of a confused youth trying to cross a busy street, and LARRY a policeman for whom regulations are regulations. This dance mime becomes a mock of a school physical education lesson, which then becomes a school dance where two people without dates meet. Over the music and dance, the TEACHER and SHEFFIELD rise and move away from each other, as if wanting to separate, but unable to do so.

SHEFFIELD: We're not going to agree on anything, but I do want a favour from you, Hal.

TEACHER: What is it?

SHEFFIELD: I can't reach him. I did something foolish ... lost my temper. And it ended in silence, which is the worst way for things to end. I do care for him—I want to understand him—can you tell him that for me?

TEACHER: I'll try ... but why did you fight?

SHEFFIELD: Just a father and son disagreement.

TEACHER: It had to be quite a disagreement to make him leave town.

SHEFFIELD: He ... accused me of being corrupt.

TEACHER: Was he ... correct in this accusation?

SHEFFIELD: (*angrily*) It's none of your damned business how I run my affairs. I should know what the laws governing my profession are—do you think I would jeopardize my career by doing something illegal?

TEACHER: The terms "legal" and "illegal" don't mean the same things to me as it does for you. If I'm going to speak to Larry, I'll have to communicate something more than your arguments!

SHEFFIELD: What am I supposed to do? Take my clothes off in public—get down on my knees and beg?

TEACHER: Open your eyes and see, enjoy the air you breathe and the food you eat. Larry didn't kill God—you and I did it for him! We bulldozed him under, packed him in cement, darkened his eyes with smoke and soot, replaced prayers with the howl of jet engines and the scream of machinery. If you destroy God, you destroy yourself, don't you understand?

SHEFFIELD: (*amazed*) What are you saying?

TEACHER: When I killed five men in an act of war at Dieppe, I relinquished my claim to innocence. A few years later I began to realize if I was to live out my life as a man, I would have to make some small repayment for what I did.

SHEFFIELD: You obeyed an order ... you were not responsible. I don't see what ...

TEACHER: We're all responsible for what we do ... we're responsible for carrying out the orders and we're responsible for the orders having been given in the first place.

SHEFFIELD: Don't be ridiculous!

TEACHER: I've never been more serious. We are capable of incredible goodness—we have that capacity. In this capacity we are God-like! This is what our children want to see in us ... so they can genuinely believe we are real and warm and concerned. I didn't have to kill. I could have retreated. I could have dropped my gun. I could have spent all my energies in my own country, begging to be heard, explaining that war was madness, that each of us was responsible for it happening!

SHEFFIELD: And you want me to share that responsibility?

TEACHER: Yes!

SHEFFIELD: You do your penitence by teaching, if that's your choice. But leave the running of business affairs to me.

TEACHER: And what about Larry? Is he to be wiped off as an undesirable alien on this earth at this particular time? Why did you create children if you had to take so much and give so little back to them in return?

SHEFFIELD: They are the best-fed, best-housed, best cared-for generation in history!

TEACHER: They are also the most despairing.

SHEFFIELD: Why?

TEACHER: Because they see the possibilities of fulfillment which our civilization cannot help but destroy.

SHEFFIELD: You've been leaning on us for years, blocking us, interfering.

TEACHER: I'm afraid of the forces that drive you, Sheffield. I've known you a long time and I know you better than I know myself …

SHEFFIELD: So?

TEACHER: You are capable of evil and you lack the sense to recognize and control it.

SHEFFIELD returns to the table and sits down heavily. He fingers the cards in front of him, but his mind is troubled.

SOUNDTRACK: *Sharp sound of castanets stops LINDA'S and LARRY'S dance. They break apart, placed into another time.*

LINDA: You're mean …

LARRY: Says who?

LINDA: I told you I loved you when we saw the first stars overhead. I told you I loved you then. But you didn't tell me you loved me until it was morning. You made me very sad doing that …

LARRY: My mind is full of other things …

LINDA: It's sordid to worry about other things when you're in love.

LARRY: How can we talk about love? The world is breaking apart … the river has changed course overnight … the stars are falling …

LINDA: Only if you're looking for it to happen, Larry!

LARRY: I was a child of convenience, not of love! I want my revenge for that!

TEACHER: The birds are singing, Sheffield, but the preparations for winter have begun. Who will bury me when I die?

SOUNDTRACK: *Singer sings:*
  Left his son in Toronto
  His son never writes him,
  Seems like no one knows where he's gone.
  Chittigan is coming—has anybody seen him?
  No one on the highway knows his name,
  But his eyes are filled with water
  And his head still full of rainbows.

LINDA: The sound I make is as loud as I feel it should be! It has to be as big as I think I am, otherwise …

LARRY: Otherwise?

LINDA: Otherwise, I will not be heard. That's all I ask, to be heard, by them—by you!

LARRY: It is better to be silent and deadly.

TEACHER: Have you still nothing to say to me?

SHEFFIELD: Our summer fair was a success this year. A lot of people, young and old, came and had a good time. I function as best I know how. I don't have to explain myself or apologize to you …

TEACHER: (*laughs bitterly*) You pulled in NATO to save your skin on the summer fair. Six phantom fighter jets fresh from plowing up Vietnam were brought in by your committee to do an aerial show over our town to save your stinking summer fair! What sort of price do you put on a "good time"? Canadians who believe you would believe anything.

LINDA: *Romeo and Juliet* is playing at the theatre in town. Can I take you to see it tonight?

LARRY: (*nervously*) I don't know …

SOUNDTRACK: *Ominous, sustained tone.*

TEACHER: For a few measly thousand gallons of aviation fuel they got a million bucks worth of goodwill to wipe off the obscenity of their real business in Asia—I saw your picture with the squadron leader in our paper. It also made the rat papers in Saigon a few days later. What else have you done for this town?

SHEFFIELD: It was a success—it saved our summer!

TEACHER: And what about next summer, and the next after that? I don't doubt you'll make it as mayor. Which will guarantee American fighter jet displays for a few summer fairs to come. But what happens if one of those jets goes out of control and wipes out the town? For whose sake will you be mayor then? Mine? The merchants on main street? The kids in the school? Sheffield, you're not fit to run for office. I died once so this might not happen again—have you forgotten in only twenty-five years?

LINDA: When will you know? Will you ever know?

LARRY: Leave me alone. I don't know what to think.

LINDA: What troubles you so much?

LARRY: Living without purpose!

He takes out a Che Guevara cap from behind his shirt and places it firmly on his head, then walks away from the stage. LINDA watches him go, shaking her head sadly. DENISE enters. She is dressed in off-beat but fashionable clothing. There is an exaggerated forcefulness and certainty about the way she moves.

SOUNDTRACK: *Upbeat music on DENISE'S entrance, then abrupt silence.*

DENISE: It's cool the way Larry handled the situation ... when he came in, the Lit teacher smiled and asked him how the weather had been, because you don't dress down the son of our next mayor publicly and still keep your job in our town!

LARRY: (*recorded*) The mist came in at ten o'clock ... then the wind stirred, cold and crisp ... by morning the beetles were out ... the wind still ... and the air warming with the rising sun.

DENISE: The kids laughed. Mister Stevenson got uptight. He asked what Larry planned to do with his life.

LARRY: (*recorded*) Count the starlings ... love the earthworms.

DENISE: (*giggles loudly*) By now, nobody was doing any work. Mister Stevenson was red in the face. Do you think your father will have reason to be proud of you, he snapped.

LARRY: (*recorded*) I'm not proud of my father. I am only proud of people I can bleed for.

DENISE saunters past LINDA, glancing at her provocatively.

DENISE: Get hip, kid. Get yourself a guy who'll survive ... you can't eat or raise babies on dreams. The rules are spelled out clear as day. Go get what's coming to you!

LINDA: I'd rather go hungry ...

DENISE: You will, don't worry. Guys like Larry and Stevenson will kill each other trying to save the world. In the meantime, Aristotle Onassis is out taking all the action! I like what money buys. I'm for old Ari!

She exits.

SOUNDTRACK: *Singer sings:*
Rock axe in his hand.
Plastic cups a-hanging on his belt
And his eyes are full of water
And his head still full of rainbows ...

TEACHER: While you were in law school, I was driving a truck. I carried a sign in my window saying "No Riders," company policy to prevent us picking up hitch-hikers who might get hurt in an accident, and for whom there was no coverage in the insurance the firm carried on the trucks.

LINDA: I'd rather go hungry. It doesn't have to be like this. Men can be friends, even when they fight. But women are bitches!

SHEFFIELD: While I was in law school ...

TEACHER: I drove a truck. This may be hard for you to understand, but I want to tell you ... I stopped my truck for a girl ... it was almost dark and she was very tired ...

LINDA: The loveliest thing in the world is to become aware you are a woman.

TEACHER: When she got into the truck, I was surprised to see she was only a kid, no more than fifteen. A kid—less than half my age at the time. A couple of miles from where I found her, I slowed the truck and made a pass at her ...

LINDA: Foolish, proud, scared, running, waiting ...

TEACHER: She didn't do anything. Didn't say a word to me. She just sat there, looking straight ahead … no protest at all …

LINDA: Listening for footsteps following …

SHEFFIELD: (*with surprise*) You?

TEACHER: Don't be a fool, I was telling myself, but inside of me, I knew I couldn't stop what I was doing to her.

LINDA: Younger than me, older than I was.

TEACHER: I couldn't stop myself …

LINDA: There are no secrets … all women know they are responsible for all things that happen.

TEACHER: I wanted to pull off the road and hold this … child … in my arms … because I had to hold a woman … listen to her breathing … her fear sounds … nothing more than this. And maybe in the silence she'd understand how it was with me …

SHEFFIELD: So you're also a phony … unfit for what you're doing.

TEACHER: (*smiles*) You're the worst student in the world. How did you ever make it through law school?

SHEFFIELD: Through inertia … just being there was adequate for graduation!

TEACHER: (*laughs, then becomes silent and pensive*) The birds sing, but winter is close at hand. Who'll bury us when we die?

SHEFFIELD: Why keep bringing it up?

TEACHER: It's on my mind. Dying is nothing to me. I'm afraid of not dying when I end my work, and I'm less than half the teacher I should be already. I'm afraid of ending up in some dirty side-street rooming house, counting the change in my pockets and worrying if tobacco money will last out the month, eating pork and beans and dog food from a tin, watching girls and boys hand in hand as they walk, not having a name or face of my own, trying to sift important memories out of the jumble of recollections.

SHEFFIELD: That's my answer to you! I don't intend to have those anxieties, so I'm taking care of me right here and now!

TEACHER: I'm older than you and I'm younger than you've ever been … how sad that is …

LINDA: Next Tuesday, I'll be sixteen years old.

SHEFFIELD: You can rot in hell … you won't get any sympathy from me. And I'm booting you out of my house the next time you come here digging into my motives or affairs! You tell that to my son, if all else fails.

TEACHER: I wouldn't smile like that, old buddy. I'd cry if I was you.

The TEACHER moves away from SHEFFIELD. SHEFFIELD remains at the table, staring stonily out at the audience. LARRY enters on the top level, approaches his father.

LARRY: Mister Stevenson came to see me today. We talked for three hours.

SHEFFIELD: Never mind that. What have you decided to do?

LARRY: I can't come back unless you accept me for the person I am, Dad.

SHEFFIELD: (*in a dead voice*) Then nothing has changed … we have nothing to say to each other.

SOUNDTRACK: *Hard rock music—suppressed in the background.*

LARRY moves to the second level of the stage, above LINDA, who is facing the audience.

LINDA: I never cried for Shakespeare, but I feel like crying now. I feel inside of me what happened in the movie.

LARRY: (*yawns*) It's a medieval story of museum pretensions. I dug some parts of it, but what practical value is there in the theme?

LINDA: They believed in what they felt. You could sense it so strongly you had to believe it yourself!

LARRY: The insights of an amateur, romantic sociologist. An old lady behind me started to cry, and that did it for me!

LINDA: I cried in some places …

LARRY: An old lady cried behind us: you've got to learn from that, or you'll become an old lady like her!

LINDA: Larry—the truth of being a woman is different than that!

LARRY: If my old man digs what I feel inside of me, I've got to change at once, or I'll become the same kind of reactionary he is.

LINDA: Sit with me, Larry, talk to me. Your father isn't here now ...

LARRY: He's everywhere, like the CIA. We're walking his highway, mowing his lawns, wearing his clothes, balling through his cities, reading his books in his schools, taking lessons from his servants. The stars aren't his—not yet! He's got the rivers, the air, he's killing them with a missionary conviction he's creating a better life for somebody who doesn't exist, never will exist! He's always with us, honey, like the skin on our faces!

SHEFFIELD: (*woodenly*) Herbert Elvin Sheffield, barrister, notary public, administrator. (*long pause*) Mayor, MP, cabinet minister, SENATOR Herbert Elvin Sheffield.

LARRY: It is embarrassing and stupid to be affected by *Romeo and Juliet*. Eldridge Cleaver writes the literature of NOW. I will take you only to entertainment that will strengthen your resolve as a revolutionary from now on.

LINDA: I want to grow into a real person, that's all.

LARRY: You'll grow.

TEACHER: (*not facing SHEFFIELD*) You see, tears come cheaply for me, Sheffield. It's living between two worlds that is unbearably difficult.

SHEFFIELD: That's your choice, not mine. I can still use you on my campaign committee, if you're interested.

LARRY: The talkers are nothing. They pour out their guts and then go home to a warm house and a heavy supper. There is no room for talkers now.

TEACHER: I killed to defend the system. And I killed men for nothing, nothing at all.

LARRY: They had the freedom to refuse, but that would have been a more courageous decision to make. There is no room for cowards and weaklings now!

TEACHER: You are doing what he does, Larry ... you will become like him through fighting him on grounds of his choice.

LARRY: That's a lie! And who are you to preach to me when you've been silent and a go-between for so long?

TEACHER: I was a faceless man off the roadside. I was fed with slogans. I placed my life for the disposal of king and country for the careers of a few retarded generals, a prime minister who was governed by a fortune teller, crotchety old senators unfit to sweep the building where they deliberated, aviation designers, speculators, the CN and CPR. My recognition of myself came through tragedy. And it is a tragedy somebody so ill-equipped as I should have to influence you at a time when you cried out for giants, heroes ...

LARRY: The real enemy of man was never defeated at the Brandenburg gates. We will have to fight him in the streets of this town ... on the mountains ... on the playgrounds ... beside the river.

LINDA: Juliet died for her Romeo in the tomb. She might have lived. Will I live?

LARRY: The truth would have saved her, but there was no truth!

The TEACHER turns to SHEFFIELD, pleads with him.

TEACHER: Don't do it, for God's sakes, stop now! You can still avoid the confrontation! You're not big enough, not fit for the job. Nobody can reach you, and that makes you dangerous when you achieve power! Sheffield, I beg of you ...

SHEFFIELD sits in stony silence. He rises slowly as his recorded voice booms out.

SHEFFIELD: (*recorded*) I've lived and worked in this community the better part of my life, ladies and gentlemen. My decision to seek office in public life comes at the insistence of colleagues and friends, to direct those policies which will provide you and your children with continued prosperity, social order, and a good life.

LARRY: I told you he is unreachable now!

LINDA: We must try, Larry, our futures depend on it!

LARRY: You can't talk to him. They are louder than we!

SHEFFIELD: (*recorded*) I view it as my responsibility, my duty as a concerned citizen to enter into this mayoralty race with the purpose of representing the broadest section of the community that is becoming alarmed at the disintegration of morality and responsibility!

LINDA: Women washing clothes on rocks beside the stream must be happier than we ...

SHEFFIELD: (*recorded*) I pledge myself to be receptive and alert to all your needs, and to balance these needs with the practicalities and budget limitations of a community the size of ours.

LARRY: I caught four trout this morning. I ate the two largest ones and threw the remaining two back into the creek.

LINDA: For graduation, I will wear a satin dress my mom designed and helped me sew.

TEACHER: The birds sing, but the clouds are darker than a year ago this time. There must be no wars—violence in the streets is the beginning of the worst war of all. There must be no violence. There is still time to talk and argue!

SHEFFIELD: (*recorded*) I want to be a representative for all of you ... the labour people, the businessmen and professionals. I pledge myself to a forceful pursuit of objectives to safeguard our growth and prosperity as a city!

TEACHER: (*softly*) There is still time ... to talk.

SOUNDTRACK: *Strong roll of music. Then silence.*

A long pause. Suddenly, LARRY takes off his Guevara cap and moves down to LINDA'S side. He is grinning.

LARRY: Guess they can't find me up there! At least, they've stopped looking. Mister Stevenson was the last person to see me ... and then nothing!

LINDA: Listen! I've never heard such silence!

LARRY: Isn't that funny? They've stopped looking for me. They don't want me back on the treadmill! I feel like a barefoot guerrilla moving through the trees ... only ... nobody seems to care ... what I do!

He looks at LINDA, fear beginning to register on his face as he realizes the significance of his conclusions. LINDA understands and touches his cheek.

LINDA: That's because we've never left their house. We've only shut ourselves up in ... a room that's vacant anyway!

All performers break out of character and move together to the lip of the lower elevation of the stage.

TEACHER: And that concludes our moment with you ... the insights-outsights of the players' acts, of the search for reason in an age of facts.

End

CAPTIVES OF THE FACELESS DRUMMER

In the summer of 1970, David Gardner, then artistic director of Vancouver's Playhouse Theatre Company, visited Ryga at his home in Summerland to discuss another commission. The Playhouse was in trouble. The previous season, Gardner's first with the Company, had been a financial disaster, producing a "catastrophic" budget deficit which had even introduced "the gloomy prospect of suspending operations" (as a Playhouse Company press release stated). In addition, there had been adverse criticism of the Company itself for several of its productions: her choice of William Roberts's *The Filthy Piranesi*, a play about homosexuals, had gotten its previous artistic director Joy Coghill into trouble (a city alderman publicly describing his "complete disgust" with it); and when the newly arrived director David Gardner announced his plans to stage *Hair*, he was bluntly told not to do so.

Indeed, it was a nervous time in the world generally. The escalating, increasingly violent protests over the war in Viet Nam, then the murder at the Altamont rock festival in late 1969, had graphically exposed the destructive side of what had, up to that point, been considered by most (though with the significant and prophetic exception of some, like George Ryga) the counterculture revolution's youthful idealism. Many felt that the 1960s "summer of love" had abruptly ended. In Vancouver, mayor Tom Campbell, strong on both big development and the imposition of strict law-and-order, continued to come to blows with urban reformers, street people, and, of course, the many hippies flooding his city which were to culminate in the "Gastown riots" of August, 1971. The Playhouse, in the meantime, managed to stay alive by steering away from controversy: it secured a number of emergency grants, one of them from the provincial government, said to have been given on the condition that the company avoid "experimental, vulgar, or controversial productions." The Company had also engaged in cost cutting measures—one of which would haunt them: the termination of their dramaturge, Peter Hay, and his replacement with a "production committee" whose job, somewhat vaguely defined, was to advise the director on the Company's play selections.

Three times Ryga had provided the Company with popular, even profitable works: the original production of *The Ecstasy of Rita Joe* in late 1967, *Grass and Wild Strawberries* in early 1969, and a successful remount and tour of *The Ecstasy of Rita Joe* that played Vancouver in mid-1969, then went on to Ottawa to open at the National Arts Centre. The hope was he could do it again. When Gardner talked to Ryga that summer no firm concept for a new work emerged from their discussion—only what Ryga regarded as a "soft theme," the "duplicity of a certain bureaucratic class." From his perspective, Gardner, who was new to Vancouver, was struck by how the city had become "a battleground between establishment figures and the so-called lunatic fringe … there was war." When Ryga did prepare an outline, it was for a play called *The Lovers*: "A 45-year-old man, married, reasonably well established and with a family, falls in love with a girl less than half his age … " His intention was to explore issues of inter-generational morality within a changing society increasingly characterized by what had become popularly known as "the generation gap."

Then the "October Crisis" intervened: heavily-armed members of the Front de Libération du Québec (FLQ) kidnapped the senior British Trade Commissioner, James Cross, and held him hostage while they negotiated the release from jail of several of their members. Shortly afterwards, they also abducted the

Québec Labour minister, Pierre Laporte, whom they subsequently murdered. Suddenly, with Prime Minister Trudeau availing himself of the War Measures Act, there was war on Canadian streets, and the nation was in shock. Troops began to patrol the streets of Montreal and Ottawa, and "dissidents" were arrested and held without bail or recourse to legal aid from coast to coast, including a surprisingly large number of them in British Columbia.

For Ryga, "suddenly the play was there." By November he had a rough draft, titled *Summer of the Deadly Drummers*. It featured a diplomat, Harry, held captive by a motley group of terrorists and their leader, known only as the Commander. Although not directly taken from the headlines, the play is clearly set in Canada and there is reference to the historical kidnapping and murder. With a nod to Thoreau, Ryga changed the name of the play to *Captives of the Faceless Drummer*, and sent a first draft of twenty-some pages to Gardner, who, "in all innocence," as he later recalled, gave copies to the production committee to read.

Unexpectedly, the committee reacted strongly: they said the script was incomplete, was not ready for production, required too many actors, and was too expensive to stage. They asked Gardner to withdraw plans for its production—slated for a February 1971 opening. By late December the affair had become a full-blown public controversy, with Ryga and a group called the Ad Hoc Committee for a Living Playhouse, led by Peter Hay, vociferously critical of the Playhouse decision, while the Playhouse Board issued public statements defending its position.

The première of *Captives of the Faceless Drummer* finally took place not at the Playhouse but at the Vancouver Art Gallery, on April 16, 1971. A group of actors, working with the co-operation of Equity Showcase, staged the work under the direction of Hagan Beggs. J.B. Douglas played Harry with Norman Browning as the Commander. What the audience saw was simple, hard-hitting theatre: in a fairly bare room, there was a small stage with a pipe frame suggesting temporary quarters; to the sides, there were two life-size Bert Hilckman sculptures, one of a man peering into a coffin, the other of an old man simply sitting and watching. At the back was a large panel of a Kenojuak Eskimo snowgoose, the "grey goose" the chorus sings about. At the end of the production, blood trickled from the goose. James Barber, reviewer at the *Province*, felt the work to be "a heavy and difficult play, which should be seen by anybody seriously interested in the theatre, in alternatives to the expensive structures of traditional theatre, and in the anatomy of violence" (April 17, 1971).

After the Vancouver première, there were further productions in Toronto (1972), Lennoxville, Québec (1972), an adaptation for CBC Radio (1972), and a new production in British Columbia (1976).

CAPTIVES OF THE FACELESS DRUMMER

CHARACTERS

HARRY
COMMANDER
MARCEL
JOHN
FRITZ
ADRIENNE
JENNY
CHORUS

SET

A claustrophobic playing area, centre stage front. There is a door backstage left. A table, three chairs and a cot are arranged to give the definition of a small room. Some items of clothing are hung on the backs of chairs. A Scrabble game, magazines, paper and empty paper cups and food containers are strewn about the table and floor.

Tomorrow.

ACT 1

SCENE 1

HARRY is seated at the table, writing. He has slept in his clothes. His hair is tousled, his posture hunched, there is a darkening growth of beard on his face. He is troubled. He writes slowly and thoughtfully.

MARCEL sits on the cot, rifle in his hands. He is strong, muscular, bored. He watches HARRY with disinterest. HARRY'S legs are chained at the ankles.

The CHORUS appears in the gloom stage right. They are dressed in black, only their faces showing, glowing deathly white. They clatter staccatically on wood percussion blocks to intersperse their recitivo.

CHORUS: (*voices interchanged, sing-song*)
When we came ... the people fled ...

Let it be known we've won ... the oil in Cambodia is now secured for the forces of freedom ...

Dogs cowered in the lanes. ... magpies and parakeets ... flew into the highest trees ...

... We've lost our cities ...

Laughter.

When we came ... young men fled into the hills ... women stared through windows ... faces frozen ...

... Premier Moishe Dayan has imposed an unpopular government on the heroic state of Israel ...

... He's asked for withdrawal of our fleet from the Mediterranean.....

Laughter.

... Seated in expensive seats ... comprehending what once was ... we've lost our youth ...

When we came ... the babies cried as with universal colic ... and old men retched with fear ...

We've lost our intellectuals ...

We've lost our innocence.....

But *we're* not *them* ... we are ...

The Republic of Canada?

Why not?

Printing government stationery ...

Manufacturing republican mailboxes ...

Repainting military troop carriers!

Linked to our great neighbour ...

... Through a continental resources policy ...

... Our waters ...

... Our forests ...

... Our soil ...

... Our children ...

CHORUS: When we came ... dogs cowered in the lanes ... magpies and parakeets ...

Are theirs! But that's cool ... we've strengthened our freedom ... and resolve ...

... To resist the handful of urban guerrillas ...

... Who would dare ...

... To impose through terror, kidnapping and murder ...

... A government with policies ...

... Not of our choosing!

Laughter.

CHORUS: (*singing, triumphant*)
Never seen a day like this
Grey goose on the prowl
Don't know what I'm gonna miss
Grey goose on the prowl
    Ohay!
      Break the grey goose' wings
      I'd give almost anything
      To hear that grey goose howl!

See me running at break of day
Grey goose on the prowl
Just keep runnin' but I can't get away
Grey goose on the prowl
    Ohay!
      Break the grey goose' wings
      I'd give almost anything
      To hear that grey goose howl!

Manic laughter is heard from the CHORUS.

SCENE 2

HARRY finishes writing, lifts the letter, ponders over it and reads it silently.

ADRIENNE stands in front of him, staring forward, expressionless. In this tableau, HARRY reads his letter.

HARRY: I've written and signed a letter to my wife ... as your commander requested I should do ...

MARCEL: Read it!

HARRY: I hardly think you have the authority to pass judgement on what is written or not written by me in ...

MARCEL: (*sharply*) Read it!

HARRY: ... My darling ... As I write this, I am aware of two realities ... that it is now twenty-eight days since I was abducted ... and that my abduction ... the dangers to which I am exposed ... the uncertainties of my existence from hour to hour ... is virtually forgotten by most people. I do not despair ... I am confident wisdom will prevail ... I love you ... and wish to assure you I am in good health ... My thoughts are constantly with you ...

The light dies on ADRIENNE.

SCENE 3

MARCEL rises and approaches the table. He pokes the end of his rifle through the empty food containers.

MARCEL: Okay ... okay! (*pause*) I'm hungry ... Aren't you hungry?

HARRY: No.

MARCEL: (*singing with the tuneless, aimless manner of a solitary man*)
There was a man in Saskatoon
Who shaved his head on Friday noon
On Sunday morning he had to go
For the snow it fell an' the winds did blow ...

You don't eat much, do you? ... Is it your stomach? ... Must be your stomach.

HARRY: Partly.

He lifts his legs that are chained to each other.

And with these on, I'm not exactly in training for the NHL ...

MARCEL: (*singing*)
On Sunday morning he had to go
For the snow it fell an' the winds did blow ...

He doesn't quite understand the words.

It's your stomach ... I'm damned sure of it. I had what you got once ... If I ate anything fried, or fresh bread ... it'd hurt like a bastard right here.

He touches a spot to the left of his abdomen just above his belt.

Does it hurt you there?

HARRY: (*smiling*) No, Marcel.

MARCEL: Then it wasn't what I had.

He turns away.

HARRY: No, it wasn't. Have you a family, Marcel?

MARCEL: Yes ... no. Had a wife, but we didn't get along too good. She bought a lot of things ... two of us working couldn't pay for it, so I left her a couple of years ago ... I've got two sisters.

HARRY: Do you see them now? Do they live in this city?

MARCEL: They live in ... (*suddenly testy*) The only information I'm allowed to volunteer to you is the name I use ... That's all! Do you under-stand? That's all ... The commander's late—what the hell's keeping him?

HARRY: (*indulgently*) He might have been captured by the army or police.

MARCEL: Not him—not a damned chance!

HARRY: He informed me last night the government had negotiated the release of the Soviet cultural attaché ... which leaves only me ...

MARCEL: Them stupid, clumsy bootlicking fascists did that—not us! (*he laughs and raises his rifle in anger*) One day ... One day we'll settle matters with them—the stupid fascists!

HARRY: Before you do that, you'll have to take on the 74th Armoured Regiment who're closing in on my behalf.

MARCEL: How do you know so much?

HARRY: (*irritably handing him a newspaper*) For God's sakes, man—read! It's in yesterday's paper, front page.

MARCEL reads critically, from a distance, distrust-ful of the paper HARRY holds for him.

MARCEL: So what? He won't be captured. The commander's a smart man.

HARRY: You're right, Marcel. He's clever ... so are you ... so am I, but I got captured ...

MARCEL: You don't know much ...

HARRY: (*amused*) The story you told me the other day. Did you actually *see* the man who grew claws from eating too many lobsters?

MARCEL becomes argumentative.

MARCEL: I didn't say I actually *saw* him myself, but I had a good friend who did ... two lobsters a day ... that big ... he pulled them out of the sea, boiled them and ate them!

HARRY: I don't believe it.

MARCEL: Well, *I* do! There's a lot you don't know would surprise you ... when I was in jail, the guy in my cell pulled out his own tooth with a wire snare and a chisel ... we hated the prison dentist ... fat-assed pig who'd break your jaw because you were in the can and he wasn't ...

HARRY: Suppose ... you win ... this ... this revolution. What's in it for you, Marcel?

MARCEL studies HARRY with suspicion, then grins.

MARCEL: A printing shop ... the best printing shop in the province. My old man had a printery and he lost it to a finance company. I'm getting it back—for the people!

HARRY: For the people?

MARCEL: For the people ...

A police bullhorn offstage is heard issuing indis-tinct orders. MARCEL turns in the direction of the noise and raises his rifle defiantly.

MARCEL: Up your ass, buddy! The next time *we'll* be giving the orders!

HARRY stares at the letter before him. Unthinking, he suddenly rises to his feet. MARCEL turns swiftly on him with the rifle.

Sit down! You move like that again and your god-damned head gets blown off!

HARRY freezes and slowly settles down again.

HARRY: I wasn't thinking ... I need to stretch ...

MARCEL: You ask for permission to stand up! ... I don't know you, man ... to me you're just another face of the oppressor. You remember that ... sit down ... slowly!

HARRY obeys, aware the edge he moves on with MARCEL is very thin at the moment.

Let me tell you something ... They drowned my cousin, Phil ... stuck his head into a bucket of water, trying to make him confess to handing out guns to the unemployed at Thunder Bay. He wasn't confessing to nothing, so they held him down until he drowned ...

HARRY: I'd nothing to do with that. I don't know your cousin Phil from Adam ... Would you point that thing away from me? ... I'm not that brave or foolhardy ... I need to stretch ...

MARCEL: You'll stretch when he comes ... Phil was a better guy than I'll ever be ... I'm nothing ... I was in jail seven times for a total of sixteen years ... a hood, mugger. That's all I was until the federation took me in, got my head screwed back on again and gave me this ... (*he holds up his rifle*) ... I'm free now and you're under my control! ... And that makes all the difference in the world to me! I'd kill you for that, so don't you make any mistakes with me!

SCENE 4

The CHORUS enters as three soldiers dragging a girl who is dishevelled, her head bowed. They pass through the gloom outside the playing area of the stage.

FIRST SOLDIER: Piss on it ... take her in ...

SECOND SOLDIER: Why?

THIRD SOLDIER: She's a sympathizer ...

SECOND SOLDIER: How can you tell?

FIRST SOLDIER: I can tell ... I wasn't born yesterday!

THIRD SOLDIER: She don't take orders ... she *looks* like a sympathizer ...

SECOND SOLDIER: Come on—what the hell you talkin' about?

FIRST SOLDIER: Look at her ... you can see it in 'er ... French eyes ... hunkie tits ... poems of the Jew-boy Leonard Cohen in her pockets ... Take her in!

THIRD SOLDIER: Yeh ... move it, goddamn you!

They march her off. HARRY nods to MARCEL, his confidence shaken. The sound of footsteps is heard.

MARCEL is instantly alert. Moving towards the door, he raises his rifle at HARRY'S head.

MARCEL: That's him now! Sit down ... keep still!

HARRY settles back, his eyes on the door, his face revealing his nervousness. MARCEL stands to one side of the door and trips the safety catch on his gun. There are three measured taps on the door. MARCEL relaxes. He closes his rifle safety catch and taking some keys out of his pocket, unlocks and unchains the door.

SCENE 5

The COMMANDER enters. He smiles at HARRY as MARCEL quickly relocks the door. The COMMANDER is youthful, dynamic, bullish. His hair is long, his clothes casual and nondescript. He is carrying a paper box of fried chicken and two paper cups of coffee.

COMMANDER: (*cheerfully*) The streets stink of tear-gas and gasoline ... there's a rotten stink in here ... What's been going on?

MARCEL: (*nervously*) Nothing, sir ... we had a slight argument ... it was nothing.

COMMANDER: (*glancing from MARCEL to HARRY*) Umm ... you're getting bitchy, Marcel. (*to HARRY*) Was he bitchy?

HARRY: Don't involve me in your games, for God's sake ...

COMMANDER: Are you tired, Marcel?

MARCEL: No, sir.

COMMANDER: Then I want a written report on whatever happened!

MARCEL: (*bewildered*) A written re ... but ... I haven't got any paper!

COMMANDER: (*posturing with absurd show of authority*) Never mind the excuses ... give me a report! I'm an officer now!

MARCEL: I ... don't know how to ...

COMMANDER: (*silencing him with a gesture, then nodding at HARRY*) Did he complain of his stomach this afternoon?

HARRY: (*amused by the scene*) My digestion has been excellent today, thank you.

COMMANDER: You took the pills I left for you?

HARRY takes a small vial of pills off table and tosses them to COMMANDER.

HARRY: Eat them yourself ... I need exercise and sunlight.

The COMMANDER laughs and places the food on the table.

COMMANDER: Our revolutionary budget doesn't allow for an exercise yard. But it's Sunday, fried chicken day ... like in a hotel, eh? ... Can you eat fried chicken?

HARRY: I'll pass it up tonight. I'm not hungry.

COMMANDER: Bullshit ... If I'm hungry, everybody's hungry, right Marcel? (*MARCEL nods*) Go ahead an' eat ... it puts fuzz on your luger and a new outlook on the current political situation.

HARRY: I'm not hungry.

The COMMANDER opens the food and seating himself at the table, begins to eat. MARCEL hesitates in the background, not certain what to do. He is hungry. The COMMANDER does not offer him any food.

The CHORUS hovers in the gloom. They sing.

CHORUS: (*singing*)
Never seen good times like these
Grey goose on the prowl
There's not a thing we're gonna miss
Grey goose on the prowl
      Ohay!
      Break the grey goose' wings
      I'd give almost anything
      To hear that grey goose howl ...

COMMANDER: At a time like this, Harry, it's wise to forget ...

HARRY: Forget what?

COMMANDER: (*pushes food carton to HARRY*) That the cook forgot the salt! (*laughs*)

HARRY: Good God, here I am involved in your ridiculous adventure against my will and at considerable danger to myself and all you can do is make jokes.

COMMANDER: Tch! Tch! Tch! I felt happy when I woke up ... you're going to ruin it for me, aren't

you? If you don't eat, your ulcer will start eating you up!

MARCEL: (*to COMMANDER*) If he doesn't want it, maybe I could ... He had soup for lunch!

The COMMANDER silences MARCEL with a glance. MARCEL retreats.

HARRY: If I don't want to eat, I don't want to eat— it's a simple choice. Give it to Marcel.

COMMANDER: And I was thinking when I woke up, we had no choices anymore ...

HARRY: What do you mean?

COMMANDER: What if your government of the people, for the people, forgot they meant to find you in all this looking for you?

HARRY: (*with disgust*) I can see you've slept well last night.

COMMANDER: As a matter of fact, I didn't ... but tell me ... have you ever considered yourself so ... insignificant ... Living what? Forty-five, fifty years ... To be forgotten in twenty-eight days?

HARRY: All things are possible ... I've met people I forgot in one afternoon.

COMMANDER: Ah ... yes! When they dressed like me, eh?

HARRY: Oh, is that what I said? Give my food to Marcel, Commander.

COMMANDER: (*grinning*) Nope—the chicken's for the prisoner! How famous we would all be if you were to die ... You *should* die an' make us famous!

HARRY: (*sardonically*) I take it this is one of your lighter dinner jokes?

COMMANDER: I amuse easily ... when I see five thousand people out on the streets confronting the cops, I laugh at the shape of my toenails! ... You should die ... I should kill you.

HARRY: (*nods at MARCEL*) Let Marcel do it ... He expressed that desire first.

COMMANDER: No, I'm in charge here ... I could shoot you and leave your body on the steps outside ... no ... pack it in a furniture box and ship it collect to the Prime Minister's residence! That's assassination with class! Think of it—you would be famous forever ... governments are more generous to the dead than the living ... streets and bridges would be named for you ... statues built in the parks ... and because you'd be famous, so would I! Because an assassin and his victim are like a bride and bridegroom ... you and me! Me the man, you the woman ...

HARRY is depressed by the COMMANDER'S humour. Tries to divert the discussion.

HARRY: I wrote another letter to my wife. (*he pushes the letter to the COMMANDER*)

COMMANDER: ... But when the revolution succeeds, your name would come down and mine would take its place. Only ... I still wouldn't be free ... your shadow would stand between the sun and me ... Have a piece of chicken and let's be happy.

HARRY: You're a one-man cocktail party.

COMMANDER: Good. I'm happy to hear that ...

The COMMANDER wipes his fingers and picks up the letter HARRY has written. Reads it.

SCENE 6

The CHORUS appears in the peripheral gloom of the stage, strutting confidence that all goes well with HARRY. One member of the CHORUS sings.

CHORUS MEMBER: (*singing*)
Oh, Sally my dear, I wish I could wed you
Oh, Sally my dear, I wish I could bed you
She smiled and replied, you'd say I misled you ...

The CHORUS hums a repeat of the last line and dances away into shadows.

COMMANDER: Very good ... despite your background you can be honest when it hurts you in the gut ... Soon you might even understand why everything happened the way it did.

HARRY: Never mind your amateur dialectics! Will Adrienne receive the letter tonight?

The COMMANDER hands the letter to MARCEL, who folds it and places it inside his tunic.

COMMANDER: (*with authority*) Dispatch it according to code Thursday.

MARCEL: Yes, sir.

COMMANDER: After the dispatch, get yourself some food and relieve John on station four!

MARCEL: I ... haven't got any money to buy supper!

COMMANDER: (*ignoring him*) In case of emergency, relay an alert directly to me as per present standing orders ... Marcel, the town is crawling with troops ... be prepared to evacuate to second-guard positions. They're searching house to house—keep out of their way ... Run if you have to, but keep out of their way!

MARCEL: But if we retreat, what about ... (*he nods at HARRY*)

The COMMANDER takes out a revolver from behind his jacket.

COMMANDER: (*laughs*) I'll kill him and run ... It's a dangerous night. You be careful, Marcel.

MARCEL glances at HARRY, then looks soulfully at the chicken dinner. Unbolts the door and slips out. The COMMANDER closes and chain-locks the door.

SCENE 7

The CHORUS enters, arguing, moving in a mime of disagreement. They wear the hats of a student, a workman and a businessman. HARRY is worried. They represent the causes of HARRY'S concern.

HARRY: How bad is it out there?

COMMANDER: You know how bad it is ... why in the hell ask?

COMMANDER unlocks the leg cuff and releases HARRY, who rises and stretches sensually, then faces COMMANDER.

STUDENT: (*to WORKER and BUSINESSMAN*) When we marched against martial law, you bastards stayed away! Thirty of our best people are held without charge!

WORKER: To hell with your academic liberty shit! ... The issue is unemployment and inflation ... Milk is up to fifty-two cents a quart in Winnipeg now!

BUSINESSMAN: Gentlemen ... we need less disruption and expenditure ... The cost of unrest is high to the consumer and the businessman ...

Taxation is increasing seven percent this coming winter ...

STUDENT: You bastards stayed away—we got slaughtered ... the stench of kerosene and sulphur hangs like a shroud over the city tonight ...

The CHORUS exits, shouting and cursing, exchanging mock punches and kicks.

HARRY: The government may accept your terms for release of your friends from prison ... It's not too late yet.

COMMANDER: Our demands are a fart in the wind now, unless the discontent of the people finds leadership. There's no leadership ... There are mobs with special interests, but no leadership ... I'm sick of people!

HARRY: Then why complicate things?

COMMANDER: I complicate nothing! The issues are as clear as ice for me ... the war is between you who have everything and us who have nothing ... between you with words and me who thinks with my hands ... between the drivers and the guys who own the trucks ... between the bakers and the bankers ... All my life I've been humped by someone without a name ... without a face ...

HARRY: It's as simple as that, is it?

COMMANDER: (*staring coldly at him*) It's so simple it scares me!

HARRY: Alright—let me tell you in a few words about how I became a nationalist through a series of simple observations ...

COMMANDER: Screw your nationalism! Those guns out there were put into action against us by corporations ... Yankee, British, French, Japanese, Canadian ... to protect your nationalism!

HARRY: The paranoia of governing of people with arms is self-perpetuating. Your surrender now would help this country and its people. Don't you realize that?

COMMANDER: If I had men I could trust, I would answer you this way!

The COMMANDER makes an obscene gesture with his fingers at HARRY. The CHORUS, in the background, repeats the gesture, realize they have profaned their hands and withdraw fearfully.

HARRY: I'm worried; why don't you trust them?

COMMANDER: Because one's a criminal, the other a mystic who thinks I'm God. I would've been happier if they had both been mechanics.

HARRY: Oh, if you're so concerned about people, consider what you're doing to them.

COMMANDER: I did what I did, and the government did the same, an' neither of us can back down without hurting ...

HARRY: The federal government has stronger forces.

COMMANDER: Sure, and they know it ... they also have time on their side ... but we have you!

HARRY: And ... if somebody in the justice department has put a pencil line through my name?

COMMANDER: Then you're dead ... But don't worry, so am I. Did you have a good sleep last night?

HARRY stares at him with disbelief.

Don't tell me, then ... I wish I could feel sorry for you, but I don't. (*laughs*) I slept on my left side, my good side ... the side that keeps my heart from walloping ... but it got going like an old diesel engine anyway. I tried to find the lightswitch ... trying to choke down the vomit in my guts ... I was out in the hallway before it passed and I woke enough to get the hell back into my room.

HARRY: (*smiling*) You ate too much fried chicken, and it made you dream the government had accepted your ultimatum and you had no other course left but to free me!

The COMMANDER grins and taps his revolver.

COMMANDER: Like hell I did! ... I dreamed I was loaded down by the federation with nineteen prisoners of war ... moving them five hundred miles on foot across the muskegs of northern Manitoba ... eighteen of them fled ... but you ... you wouldn't run away ... you kept following me ... telling me how to vote and pay taxes ... buy a motorcycle and see the world ... my mind was going ... the wolves were howling ... my feet were cold ... (*suddenly intimate, leaning towards HARRY*) Do you want to tell me more about Jenny?

HARRY: (*irritable*) I'm sick to the stomach with that question!

COMMANDER: Do you really have a stomach ache, or is that another coat of black paint over this paper house you wear?

HARRY: You're half my age, Commander ... the foolhardy half!

COMMANDER: Where I come from, the road doesn't start at birth and it doesn't end with death! Fifty generations of my family have walked it ... And I'm joining a long line of dead men in my family, none of whom died of old age! If your green monkeys come through that door, you'll go down like an empty sack.

HARRY: (*puzzling, subdued*) I don't understand ... the Algerian Embassy has agreed to give you asylum ... our government has committed itself to respecting safe conduct out of the country to you and two others ... *I'm* not that important ...

COMMANDER: You're important enough ... and you were easy to kidnap.

HARRY: Then where *do* you stand politically? Just what is your position on the riots and political violence in the socialist countries?

CHORUS enters as dancers, moving through combative motions by cartwheeling of flags—red banners, swastikas, peace flags—to the rhythm of staccatic, machine-gun-like percussion instruments, such as small drums. They dance in background.

COMMANDER: Whatever kills me is asking for a beating ... I don't know my next door neighbour ... I don't know what the Poles or Swedes are doing ... I don't worry for the world no more ... I worry for me now and everybody who is like me!

HARRY: We should be getting a reply to my first letter soon ...

COMMANDER: Don't live in dreams, old man ...

HARRY: Surely if you go to the danger of delivering my letters you are hoping for a positive response?

COMMANDER: I did ... ten days ago.

HARRY: I can smell smoke today ...

COMMANDER: The smell of smoke and war goes thirty miles outside the city now ...

The CHORUS freezes, terrified, their flags drooping. Their dialogue bounces from member to member.

CHORUS: Moscow, Cairo, Los Angeles, Seattle, Tokyo, Vancouver, Atlanta and Montreal ...

... have been proclaimed cities of minimal activity this morning. High temperatures and low atmospheric dispersal have reduced visibility to less than half a mile in downtown areas.

All schools will remain closed until further notice ...

The elderly and citizens suffering with bronchial ailments are urgently requested to remain indoors and limit their physical activity so as to avoid any stress or exertion ...

The World Health Organization has reported widespread epidemics of deadly new viral diseases affecting human and animal lung, intestinal and skin tissue.

A special U.N. study of world food production concluded this spring has reported that desert regions of the earth are now spreading at seventy miles per year ...

The disease was first detected in low protein equatorial areas of the world. The W.H.O. has appealed to all nations to consider restriction of air travel to prevent rapid spread of epidemics to the temperate nations of the globe.

Conclusive evidence is now available linking increased solar activity and high density atmospheric dust and debris with a chilling of the global temperature ...

Widespread incidents of massive bird suicides against windows and walls of urban skyscrapers ...

Social unrest ... pillage and violence increasing ...

Insanity now ranks second to the common cold as an industrially debilitating disease ...

Three types of shade trees in downtown Toronto ...

Budded but did not leaf ... suspect an unknown interruption in the growth cycle ... Trees are otherwise healthy and may reactivate next year ...

CHORUS: Of all of Canada's lakes and streams, only two are fit for recreation and water sports this summer ...

A recent directive from the department of labour confirms the government agencies will no longer accept job placement applications from anyone under the age of twenty-seven ...

The CHORUS vanishes in a swirl of flags.

HARRY: If I was to plead with you ...

COMMANDER: (*coldly*) No deals, Harry. There was a time weeks ago, but it's too late now ...

HARRY: I'm not asking for a deal. All I ask is to put me through on the telephone to the Minister of External Affairs! I know the man, the way his mind functions ... the emergency public order legislation was proclaimed over his objections!

COMMANDER: You've worked in the top levels of that madhouse ... and you expect him to reverse what's been done? That telephone call would seal your death, Harry—no deal.

HARRY: Look, you fool ... for nine years I've served as foreign ambassador for this country ... the country I know and love!

COMMANDER: Like fuck you do!

HARRY begins a jogging, hand-slapping routine of exercise.

HARRY: And what in hell have you done with your time except train yourself for terror and insurrection? Have you built any bridges? ... Ploughed any fields?

The COMMANDER turns quickly in his chair to face HARRY.

COMMANDER: Have you?

Both men face each other, ready to pounce. HARRY shakes his head and turns away. The COMMANDER also cannot face him.

HARRY: Then you're not a revolutionary on the side of the people. You're a small-town hoodlum ... an inconsequential, twisted Nazi.

COMMANDER: (*quietly, icily*) We kidnapped you outside the theatre on opening night of some new play. All it took was a phoney press card to get you through the door ... you followed the bait of publicity like a dog follows a bitch in heat ... out the door and into this ... That play has run for twenty-eight days now, and you'll never see it. It will close tomorrow night. I went to see it last night.

HARRY: Why?

COMMANDER: Why not? To prove to myself what I suspected ... that you didn't even risk your life for something good ... that it was a stupid play, written by some smart-assed, empty-headed hack!

HARRY: Since when have you become a drama critic?

COMMANDER: I learned something about everything the day I felt the touch of pistol steel in my fingers! It has the truth and purity of flowers and fire. Have you ever held a gun for your country?

HARRY: I was eighteen when the Second World War ended.

COMMANDER: Try it one day if you live that long and you will understand what love of country means ...

HARRY: I am not a violent man.

COMMANDER: There's no court in the world that will try you for the violence you make ... You're the drummer, beating time for those who've never had a voice. Where you've sent us, you don't know ... you don't care to know ... Have some coffee with me, before it gets cold ...

HARRY: Yes.

As HARRY approaches the table, the COMMANDER places his revolver into its holster inside of his jacket.

COMMANDER: What has happened has happened. Neither of us can change it now, that's for sure ...

HARRY: You made it happen.

COMMANDER: Bullshit! Would it have been different if I'd been a clerk scratching my crotch with a ballpoint pen? Would that have made you happier with me?

HARRY: That is not the only choice a man has.

COMMANDER: For you—yes. For me—no. I laugh and spit on everything stupid and dishonest.

HARRY: So do I ... so do I ...

COMMANDER: But I can spit farther than you! I spit like a camel ... you spit around your feet and then stand in it!

HARRY smiles.

The COMMANDER rises, lifts himself to his tallest possibility.

COMMANDER: My grandfather died in the Riel rebellion. Last summer I found the place where he was buried. I put my foot down on where his chest would be. I'd brought a bottle of gin. I drank a swig, then I leaned forward and poured the rest over his head-mound. Then I hollered down at him, "Hey, old man under six feet of Saskatchewan gumbo, what have you got to say to me now?" And up came his voice, clear as a bell, "If you don't get your foot off me, I'll sprout a willow twig up your ass, you black bastard ... I don't know you!"

To HARRY.

You know a lot about me—where I've been and what I've seen. You are a man with two women, and that's something else ...

HARRY: It's not important. I told you I don't want to talk about it.

COMMANDER: It's important to me—come on, what about Jenny?

HARRY: There is an infinite variety of experiences a man may live through ...

COMMANDER: I've been in a lot of fights, screwed a lot of women ... but I didn't become a man until I joined the federation. Everything changed ... the world became my house ... I knew where the windows were and the doors ... everything in the house meant something. I had to study how to live, not how to work, but how to live! I learned there was mud on me that had never washed off from the beginning of time ... so I had to scrub myself clean ... I had to scrub the streets and shit-houses ... the whole sky clean!

He laughs, then shudders.

To be of the people is to be alone. The wind is icy ... the mountain is glacial ... a man fights without fear, and without hope ... it is frightening to think about your own death ... to see your blood freeze on the snow ...

HARRY: Then live—dammit, man—look at me!

COMMANDER: What for? It makes me mad to look at you!

HARRY: I don't want to die either, but I'm not cowardly about it. It's more important to save life than destroy it ... I believe in the inherent goodness of man. But we must be alive to force the changes and appreciate them!

COMMANDER: Then I will give my life and stand up like a man rather than stumble and rot as a non-person, tied by his toes and cock to a non-life!

HARRY: So would I!

COMMANDER: Then why are we enemies, you bastard?

HARRY: Because the freedom you promise yourself is slavery. The gun you raise at a post office or at the head of an elected civil official will not be lowered according to any timetable you set down. Every day there will be new targets to shoot down ...

COMMANDER: (*smiles coldly*) You should know. Your kind has been doing it for ten years now.

HARRY resumes a brisk, spaceless exercising of his arms and legs.

HARRY: Yes, that's true, but a man was brutally murdered in Quebec ... There was a lot of uncertainty as to how the government might cope ... So we had to take ...

COMMANDER: *One* man was killed ... *one* man ... he was French. The Englishman was let go ... he was worth more by the inch and pound ... he was always worth more.

HARRY: Think what you will, in those days the government was willing to withdraw a state of emergency when the situation stabilized itself, as it did for a while. But activists ... terrorists like you were not content to let events resolve themselves. By provocations, bombings, terror, you succeeded in creating conditions whereby military power had to be recalled to restore order time and time again!

COMMANDER: Hah! What about the violence of defeat? Province after province, city after city ... starting with the smaller prairie towns and then into major cities ... fell to right wing fanatics, each elected with the protection of riot sticks ...

If my dream is hollow, yours is an ice castle ...
Tell me how Jenny came into your house.

HARRY stares for a long moment at the COMMAN-DER, uncertain of himself. Staccato rhythm—the CHORUS appears, moving sinuously, but reflecting the uncertainty of HARRY'S.

HARRY: Why?

CHORUS: (*in relay*)
Why?

Why?

Why?

COMMANDER: It is a surprise about you. You told me you were a married man—happy ... doing what you wanted to do ... Then what happened?

SCENE 8

JENNY enters, singing softly. She is young, beautiful, ethereal, dressed in flowing, loose clothing.

The CHORUS hover about her.

JENNY: (*singing*)
If all the young men, were hares on the mountain
If all the young men, were hares on the mountain
I'd climb to the top, and sit down beside them ...

CHORUS: (*in unison*) She'd have climbed to the top, and sat down beside them

They handclap to conclusion of musical bridge.

HARRY: Her parents were close friends to Adrienne and me ... they were divorcing ... she was upset ... left college ... travelled across the country once, the experience was unpleasant ...

COMMANDER: Were the mosquitoes bad that summer?

Laughs softly.

As JENNY talks, HARRY rises and moves towards her, but stopping at the invisible barrier of memory. The CHORUS reflects his mind.

JENNY: The trees were drying in the sun ... prairie highways were broken ... rivers were thick and brown, with long white grass choking the banks ... In Calgary I asked a man carrying an attaché case for directions to the public

library. He said he didn't know but he asked me to share his motel room for the night ...

HARRY: Why did you refuse?

JENNY: I was afraid.

HARRY: What were you afraid of, Jenny?

COMMANDER: What, oh what, were you afraid of, Jenny?

Laughs softly.

JENNY: Because he asked me, and I had to consent or refuse. It is easier to submit to seduction than to say, "Yes, I will sleep with you ... "

COMMANDER: Bullshit! How did it really happen ... what did she say?

HARRY: (*to COMMANDER*) Why, would you laugh at her?

COMMANDER: Yes, she's funny ... she's not real!

JENNY: (*to HARRY*) Harry, you know my father concerns himself only with big things. I cannot talk to him about ... music ... or the solitude of the mountains in the evening ...

HARRY: He's set in his ways, Jenny. A reactionary in his relationships with nature ... a man of pipelines and high-tension transmission towers.

COMMANDER: What did she really say to you?

JENNY: (*sings softly*)
Oh Sally my dear, I wish I could wed you
Oh Sally my dear, I wish I could bed you
She smiled and replied, you'd say I misled you ...

HARRY turns to the COMMANDER. The CHORUS surrounds JENNY, so when she sings again, her song is louder, lustier.

JENNY: (*sings*)
Oh Sally my dear, I wish I could wed you
Oh Sally my dear, I wish I could bed you
She smiled and replied, you'd say I misled you ...

CHORUS: (*singing*)
She smiled and replied, he'd say I misled you ...

They handclap to the conclusion of musical bridge.

HARRY: (*to COMMANDER, threatening now*) Don't laugh at her! Don't stamp your big boots over her face!

COMMANDER: (*embarrassed*) I'm in another space, man ... on another planet different than yours! ... The girl is not real ... you're not telling me the truth about her ... was your wife home that night?

The CHORUS goes out.

HARRY: (*subdued, confused*) There's a way out ... I don't recall ... I mustn't lose what I've got.....

COMMANDER: *You* can't lose what you've got? Man ... Algeria is hot and dry ... I am a man of the snow and wilderness!

HARRY: Alright goddamn you! ... You wanted to know and I'm trying to tell you!

HARRY turns to JENNY, the CHORUS retreats.

JENNY: Why are you afraid, Harry? You're big and strong ... like my dad ...

HARRY: (*gently*) I'm not afraid ... there's nothing to fear now except fear.

JENNY: (*she reaches out as if to touch his hands, but her reach is beyond contact with him*) You're trembling ... you should wear your ear-muffs.

The COMMANDER laughs.

HARRY: Sometimes ... a man climbing a mountain gets trapped ... between two heights ... the cliff above him and the safe levels below which he has left ... a man can be suspended like that for a lifetime ... can you understand that?

COMMANDER: No!

JENNY retreats slowly, thoughtfully, humming her song.

Percussion clatter and panic shrieks of the CHORUS. Against their will, two members lock themselves in a lascivious embrace, from which they break fearfully.

The COMMANDER laughs and rises from his seat to pace leisurely.

Over above action, one member of the CHORUS sings brazenly.

CHORUS MEMBER: (*singing*)
Blow you winds from the piney hills
Your wild bite's no concern of mine
As I drink and think of that gal of mine
With kisses bitter as turpentine ...

The CHORUS leaves into the background.

SCENE 9

COMMANDER: Your friend ... Doctor Felton ... he knew?

HARRY: Yes, Fritz knew ...

The CHORUS brings FRITZ into playing area with great propriety.

FRITZ: Twenty minutes, Harry ... that's all the time I can spare—twenty minutes! Are you capable of playing a game of Scrabble in twenty minutes?

HARRY: (*smiling*) Yes ... but it would hardly be a game of skill.

FRITZ: Skill, my foot ... when I was a lad I played baseball, just for the hell of it ... why can't we do things for the hell of it now? ... It's all skills here, specialists there ... do you know things have become so bad a doctor has no time for a healthy man?

HARRY: (*still smiling*) I seem to remember we play slow games when you're on a winning streak!

FRITZ: Don't accuse me of your cunning, Harry.

HARRY: Very well, a fast, clean game then Fritz. And no medical abbreviations or colloquial obscenities—agreed?

FRITZ moves as if to seat himself down at the table—the CHORUS urges him to the edge of memory line. He cannot go beyond.

FRITZ: Your rhetoric bores me today ... I've tried to change, to dress and speak like the younger colleagues in my profession, but I'm a conservative at heart ...

HARRY opens Scrabble board on the table.

... It's like having faith in motherhood or boat building ...

COMMANDER: (*to HARRY, sharply*) You're hedging with me! What did he say? ... What did he say about it?

HARRY: (*to COMMANDER*) Wait—I'll tell you!

FRITZ: (*surprised*) Tell me what?

HARRY: Nothing ... I was just thinking ...

COMMANDER: (*to HARRY*) I want to know ... You asked me once what it felt like to be beaten down during interrogation—I told you. It was the only time I broke down and bawled ... I'm not proud of that, but I told you! Now you tell me!

FRITZ: What are you thinking, Harry?

HARRY: (*head lowered*) It's a problem I have ... I don't know how to begin telling you.

FRITZ: I've made a comfortable living by isolating business from pleasure. Do you want me to treat this visit as a house call?

HARRY: (*laughing*) It's not a medical problem, Fritz.

FRITZ: The way you worry over Scrabble, I'm inclined to consider every problem you have as either dietary or as a bad case of nerves ... What's on your mind?

HARRY hesitates

COMMANDER: Tell him!

HARRY: I ... I can't ... Let me pose it as a hypothetical question ...

FRITZ: You're the diplomat, I'm the realist. I live with causes and effects, not abstractions!

HARRY: Why would a man—a contented, sane man ... a highly responsible man ... commit an indiscretion ... No! That's not it! Why do we use such filthy words for beautiful experiences? ... To describe acts of compassion ... Restlessness?

The laughter of the COMMANDER and the CHORUS dies.

FRITZ: (*coldly*) So, it's a woman?

HARRY: Yes ... but that's not what disturbs me ... it's my motive for doing it.

FRITZ: Motives? What motives does a cod-piece have?

HARRY: It's not as simple as that ...

FRITZ: It's simple enough for me!

HARRY: I've always understood life by deflection ... seeing it mirrored through experiences of others, through books, theatre, music. Our great Canadian word 'nice' described what I saw ... *nice* morning ... our economy is advancing *nicely*

... visitors to this country are such *nice* people ... The Soviets have a word like ours—their word is 'normal'. Adrienne always took the world on with two hands ... I didn't. I lived by regulations, tactics, acceptability. I never exposed myself to direct fear or harm. Did somebody have to assume my share of pain and danger so I could live comfortably in a world of alternative choices?

FRITZ: No!

COMMANDER: Yes!

HARRY: I involved myself in gentler ways ... through art galleries, drama ... experiencing vicariously other men's convictions. I began to realize that under the layers of ice and chill of tundra winds we were pliable and erotic as people ... that we desired happiness and the liberty to pursue our own experience with destiny.

COMMANDER: But a woman drew you into the filthy, hot darkness, eh?

FRITZ: Don't you dare fall in love again ... It will devour you! ... If you can't leave her alone, then pay her for her services, buy her things ... lie to her if you have to!

HARRY: Like a whore?

FRITZ: Yes, like a whore! The other thing is too much and too late for you now, Harry.

FRITZ rises and leaves.

CHORUS sings a refrain as they leave with him. They return to their antics of eroticism.

SCENE 10

CHORUS: (*singing*)
Keep on runnin' as the black crow flies
Grey goose on the prowl
Can't see the sun for tears in my eyes
Grey goose on the prowl
> Ohay!
> Break the grey goose' wings
> I'd give almost anything
> To hear that grey goose howl!

HARRY: (*exhausted*) Well, are you pleased now?

COMMANDER: Nothing ... all that's nothing. Show me real things ... Something I can touch—like you!

HARRY: I haven't seen the sun for twenty-eight days now ...

COMMANDER: It's out there ... some place ...

HARRY: I know everything that surrounded me is collapsing ... the environment ... the sense of security ...

COMMANDER: What are you prepared to do then?

HARRY: What *can* I do?

COMMANDER: You can play out your dreams like a drug addict ... You can die like a fossil ... under my revolver ... having outlived your usefulness. Like a sheep going baaaa for the last time ... its wool stripped, its cunt dried up, its flesh too tough for a timber wolf to chew.

HARRY: You filthy bastard!

COMMANDER: Be a man then—spit in the face of death! I dare you! ... My friends have been put into your prisons as common criminals—to protect foreign investments ... sentenced into cement walls by dwarfs not fit to polish their shoes!

HARRY: I've written two letters to the authorities, I've referred to your complaints, I've requested an inquiry into the possible abuses of the law courts ...

The COMMANDER rises to threaten HARRY, his voice is a shout.

COMMANDER: Wake up, you sonofabitch, or you'll sleep through the few hours you've left of your life.

HARRY: Don't shout at me—I'm not deaf ... I was taught the difference between right and wrong ...

COMMANDER: Hurray for you! There were no stars over Bethlehem when I was born ... no flags going up—nothing. My father had been boiled in a steam generator explosion six months earlier ... my mother was on welfare when she had me ... another useless mouth to feed, my father's name spelled wrong on the birth certificate. Mom, I asked her once, what was the first thing you heard when I was born?

CHORUS: (*in unison—in high-pitched reply*) A tomcat mewing for a piece of ass!

HARRY: Is this your reply to being born—dynamite, murder, kidnapping? You've frightened and disrupted people ... forced confrontations ... left the field open for neo-fascism!

CHORUS: (*in unison—plaintively, frightened of the implication of what they say*) A tomcat ... mewing for a piece of ass?

The COMMANDER paces angrily.

COMMANDER: You're full of shit, you know that?

HARRY exercises his legs, rubs his stomach.

HARRY: (*sardonically*) I will be if I don't get some opportunity to exercise ... what gives you people the right to inflict such a heavy penalty on people you'll never even know?

COMMANDER: To hell with them ... I wasn't born a poodle!

HARRY: I don't like poodles. They were put together by man out of boredom ...

COMMANDER: Men should put men together—eh? Isn't that right?

HARRY: I don't know ...

COMMANDER: You don't know nothing ... Listen—you made me do what I do ... I'm not blowing people apart ... only their illusions. But you have to listen to me when I've caught you ... you can't jump for the window or door or my throat ... I'll kill you if you try. The illusions, man ... we must cut away the illusions, everything, until only our eyes are alive.

HARRY: What illusions?

COMMANDER: That we are happy! Two Prime Ministers in the past five years ... young bright men, have said—it's full speed ahead, people ... we know what you want and we will look after it right now ... go back and work without fear of being betrayed ever again, or walked over, or dumped on the garbage pile.

HARRY: (*impassioned*) I know both men well ... they meant what they said!

COMMANDER: They spoke like they shaved—in front of a mirror!

HARRY: You fool! You hopeless, illiterate fool!

COMMANDER: Illiterate or not, I *am* and you have to cope with me right now—right?

HARRY: Yes, I can well appreciate that ...

COMMANDER: Okay, I'll tell you the way I see it, the illusion of government for everybody could've gone on for twenty years—maybe. Instead of building a new house, people began cleaning up the old one ... population control, women's lib, youth ... unemployment—Then the air started leaking out of the balloon ... unemployment rose ... Special deals were made to kill culture, and no more money for education. The fields began dying with poisons and chemicals ... the best-fed people in the world were round and puffy—dying of malnutrition ... crime increased like tooth decay ... the differences between rich and poor, men and women ... French and English, deepened ...

HARRY claps his hands in mock applause.

... Parents attacked their children—beating them, putting them in prison ... the children attacked their schools ...

HARRY: And then—coming out to save everything—is the urban guerrilla—with no education or understanding—just brute force!

COMMANDER: I wouldn't laugh ... this is not a beer parlour.

HARRY: (*bows mockingly*) I almost forgot!

The CHORUS reflects HARRY'S irony in their gestures and reaction. HARRY moves about, pacing tightly. The COMMANDER becomes reflective.

COMMANDER: From the first hours of the first kidnappings, those of us who could think knew we blew it ... For a while, our ranks held, but the support we expected didn't come.

HARRY: When you start killing people what did you expect—a civic reception?

COMMANDER: I killed no one! I don't know who kidnapped the four others this year. And don't confuse the panic of three or four fools with the stuff revolutions are made of. (*wearily*) All revolutionaries are naive ... like priests and doctors ... if we could see into the future, the risks would be too high ... I want to know about Jenny, and your wife ... why such things happen ...

HARRY: Knowing the personal details of my life is of no consequence in what you are doing ...

COMMANDER: You've told me nothing about yourself ... nothing ... Only what pleases you ... (*ponders*) We didn't fail ... we had no illusions except one.....

HARRY: Then who in hell do you think is losing?

COMMANDER: *You* are! It was your dream which came apart. When each kidnap victim is released you cheer—Wheee! The parts are still in our hands! The society of sell-out is safe ... you hitch up your pants and go back to drilling, mining and paving the universe and screw the consequences! Except the rules have changed ... there's no leader ... and there's no return to dreamland. Anybody can ride to power on fear ... anywhere in the country ... by piggy-backing a bombing. And it don't have to be political ... a bomb planted by a revolutionary has the same size and explosive power as a bomb planted by a hired criminal ... Thugs which even you were afraid of can now manipulate whatever laws they want to protect their investments, and you have no way of roping that tiger!

HARRY: (*sadly*) You're right there, my friend.

Both men are silent, absorbed in their thoughts. The COMMANDER fidgets restlessly.

The CHORUS enters and hovers over the gloomy scene, and then moves as if they were running from something.

CHORUS: Ha—scat!
(*singing*)
White dog sleeping in my backyard
Waterpipe's frozen and the ground is hard
White dog, white dog go home
Just keep moving and leave me alone ...

The CHORUS dances over the following dialogue— a dance of trapped people striving to break invisible bonds which hold them in captivity.

After the dance, CHORUS exits.

COMMANDER: (*quietly*) What did your wife say ... when she found out?

HARRY: I'm tired. I don't want to talk about it.

COMMANDER: Two years ago I was in London, at an international seminar on liberation front struggles around the world. I met Mara there ... she was from Jordan ... we fell in love ... (*laughs happily*) Yeh ... It was autumn in London ... At night we walked through the fog in the city … We never discussed guerrilla activity … Mara had been wounded … In the night when we walked, smelling the streets through our skins … seeing night on the wet cobbles with our fingers … I forgot how badly she limped … When we said goodbye … she giggled … like a little girl, her eyes bright as a monkey's. And then she looks up at the sky and screams like her heart was being cut out of her … "God, how long must we suffer?" … Two weeks later she was killed in a border skirmish … I was in Jordan last year. The place where she was buried is now a Mediterranean Command air landing field. This revolver belonged to her … It was given to me by her brother. There is nothing else left in this god-damned world of my Mara …

HARRY: That's very sad … I'm sorry … I really am sorry.

COMMANDER: No need for that … no need at all. One woman lies down, another stands up … that's the way the world goes … One woman keeps us from going crazy … that's the way it should be … Come on, what did your wife say?

HARRY lowers his face into his hands. The CHORUS MEMBER enters, wearing a life mask of a younger, more debonair HARRY.

HARRY: She wasn't angry … she wasn't even surprised.

COMMANDER: She wasn't … surprised?

SCENE 11

The CHORUS comes on. ADRIENNE enters carrying a small platter of sandwiches and coffee. She holds these out to the CHORUS MEMBERS.

ADRIENNE: The ambassador to Poland returned to Ottawa this morning, darling. He called while you were busy on the other phone. I said you'd return his call later …

HARRY: Adrienne …

ADRIENNE: There was nothing of consequence in the mail … Fritz was by. He will return in the afternoon.

HARRY: Adrienne … my head hurts …

ADRIENNE: Eat your lunch, Harry. I had some leftover tuna. I hope it's fresh … I can't tell … I've suddenly developed a cold.

HARRY: I've told you everything, but for days now you behave as if … nothing had changed.

ADRIENNE watches him poignantly for a long moment.

COMMANDER: (*impatiently*) Come on … come on! The woman must've said something more than that!

ADRIENNE: Then *you* tell me what has changed … the car runs well, the mortgage on the house continues to get paid … the flowers along the driveway are blooming as they've bloomed for twenty-two summers … our health is robust …

HARRY: But Jenny *lives* here!

ADRIENNE: (*with ill-disguised anguish*) What in hell do you expect me to do, Harry? What do you expect? … That I initiate legal action? Leak the story to the press? … Appeal to the senior admin-istration of your department? … I'm not made of stone, Harry, I'm a realist.

HARRY: I may have been … too busy to notice …

ADRIENNE: Nothing quite meets our expecta-tions, does it? She's a beautiful, sensitive girl … if you can live with this, so can I.

HARRY: My head hurts … as if a band was clasped around my skull.

ADRIENNE bends towards HARRY to kiss him. Both she and he retreat in opposite directions.

Drumbeats in time to their footsteps.

SCENE 12

CHORUS: (*singing as they enter*)
Let the fellow down, down
Let the fellow down
His mother said the boy was nice
But there'll be whores in paradise
So let the fellow down …

HARRY rises to his feet, shakes his head, laughs softly. He paces woodenly in a tight circle over song.

HARRY: Goddamnit! The things we do … the things we accept!

COMMANDER: I never go to the zoo ... I can't stand watching tigers in cages ... They get tame after a few years, you know that? ... Living for the handout of meat they never killed ...

HARRY: I was a firebrand ... she knew me then and she was such a warm, concerned but angry young lady too ...

COMMANDER: I like cold nights and stars ... that's the way to live! ... The nights are hot in Algeria.

HARRY: You know ... the first time I went skiing with her we fell together ... wrestled in the snow. In the evening I massaged her toes in front of the fire at the lodge. They always turned cold when she became excited or alarmed, even when I was posted to the tropics for a year ... they were cold when I told her ...

The COMMANDER turns on HARRY and bellows at him.

COMMANDER: Who? ... The girl ... or your wife?

HARRY: My wife. There are differences between women, too!

COMMANDER: Two women and no kids ... why no kids? Is there something wrong for you in ...

Points casually down at HARRY'S crotch. The CHORUS feigns horror at the direct gesture.

HARRY: (*stiffly*) We made a decision ... a philosophical decision ... the world was over-populated ...

Staccatic percussion sounds. The CHORUS beats drums that are suddenly soundless.

People can love deeply without procreating!

Percussion on drums.

COMMANDER: (*loudly*) Bullshit! They gotta screw!

Drums go into silence. The CHORUS drifts away.

COMMANDER: Listen to the shooting! People are getting killed! Who will replace those who die?

HARRY: I don't know ... (*thoughtfully*) I don't know ... something she once said ... it slipped my mind until this moment ...

COMMANDER: Who? ... What?

HARRY: My wife ... when the pulp mills in the northern Okanagan defied parliament and dumped raw sewage into lakes and streams ... she said ...

SCENE 13

ADRIENNE enters briskly, her face hard with anger. The CHORUS follows her in.

ADRIENNE: Somebody should take it on themselves, Harry ... somebody should take it on themselves to blow a series of those plants sky-high! They are an outrage against nature!

ADRIENNE storms off. The CHORUS realizes what she has said, backs away from the scene in bewilderment.

The COMMANDER flares with anger at HARRY.

COMMANDER: Words! Words! ... Subtle, nice words! Where was she when it came time for action? Words! Filthy, useless words, that's all! Forests have been cut to make paper on which apologists and gradualists write their puny words!

HARRY: Why in hell are you shouting? I'm not deaf!

The COMMANDER turns away in fury, ripping open the collar of his shirt in a defiant gesture.

COMMANDER: I'm choking on your good intentions! You *knew* ... your woman brought you to the brink of awareness and you just stood there, looking! ... Looking at tigers in cages, when they asked you to be bull-stud to the earth, driving your cock like a pile hammer ... pumping the wet stuff where the ground had gone dry ... making things ... kids ... wild oats ... bush rabbits ...

HARRY is startled for a moment, stares at the COMMANDER with dismay, then begins to laugh.

COMMANDER: Alright—what's the joke? ... Tell me so I can be happy too!

HARRY: Yes ... you're right ... it doesn't rest easily with me, but you're right! ... We were home that night ... during the first wave of widespread demonstrations ... I could see the opportunists, the lesser people ... juggling for power and authority ... Because of this, I felt one had to make a gesture—anything ... to defuse the situation.

COMMANDER: What in hell did you do?

HARRY: I requested that police protection be removed from my home ... Fritz was there that night.

SCENE 14

FRITZ: (*to HARRY, across stage*) You fool! This isn't the land or time of Ghandi ... those bastards have gasoline and weapons! Have you a gun in the house?

HARRY: (*talking to the COMMANDER, but addressing his memory of the scene*) It will pass, Fritz ... we don't need arms ... That's no way to live ... it will pass.

FRITZ: I don't understand what's happening to you ... A man has to fight to survive, and damned if he has to believe in what he fights for when he's in danger! ... There's a mob moving down in the street ... where they encounter police or troops, they shout their obscenities and move on. But where there's no protection, they're breaking fences and windows ... the other day my car tires were slashed and the windshield broken ...

ADRIENNE: Fritz is right, darling.

HARRY: The Prime Minister requested restraint ... it will pass. Let's not lose our nerve now.

Sounds of rioting, hooting, breaking glass. The COMMANDER laughs. Light on FRITZ, ADRIENNE and JENNY. The women are close together, alarmed.

ADRIENNE: (*afraid*) They're coming here, Harry.

FRITZ glances around, searching.

Sound of pounding on a door. Then silence.

FRITZ: Nothing ... not even a poker in the house! Even our homes are designed like prisons ... I certainly hope you know something I don't know, or we're in trouble.

SCENE 15

The CHORUS as three youths, enter as if coming through a window. One is armed with a knife.

YOUTH: Have you made your peace with God? ... You're blood-sucking pigs! ... The world is ending ... God will judge you!

HARRY: (*firmly*) Get out of here. You've no right entering my home!

YOUTH laughs sarcastically.

YOUTH: *Your* home ... What's *your* home to me?

HARRY: Get out!

YOUTH: Up your ass, daddy ...

YOUTH examines JENNY while his companions move about, searching the invisible room. YOUTH reaches out and pinches JENNY'S breast nipple. She moans and withdraws close to ADRIENNE.

YOUTH: Aren't you one strung-out chick ... Trust in God and come with us. We'll save you from yourself. We've saved twelve souls this summer and the flock's growing!

HARRY: If you're after money, there are a few dollars grocery money in the kitchen ...

ADRIENNE: ... Second drawer from your left as you enter ...

HARRY: Take it and go!

YOUTH: Man, we're above money ...

FRITZ: Then what in hell are you after? What are you thinking?

YOUTH takes JENNY'S chin in his hand. Presses it painfully and forces her face up. Stares at her, sneers.

YOUTH: Hey—don't tell me ... I can see it in your eyes ... rolled up from beggin' with the devils ... being humped by them—slimy degenerates! What was your price, whore? A summer cottage ... a sports car ... eh?

JENNY: Go away and leave us alone!

YOUTH: You degenerate fuck-pig!

YOUTH slaps her face, then stabs at her with the knife. JENNY turns to protect herself. She suffers an arm wound.

FRITZ throws himself at the attacker with the knife and wrests it away. The YOUTHS are thrown off-balance. Seeing that FRITZ now has their knife, they leave as they came.

YOUTH: (*offstage*) We'll burn your house down, you degenerate sonofabitch!

SCENE 16

HARRY moves to the two women, but is arrested by unseen walls short of them. They move closer to each other, hold each other. FRITZ lifts JENNY'S arm and examines it quickly.

FRITZ: She could have been killed, you fool! ... You fight violence with violence; otherwise you die ... Call an ambulance ... I'll go with her to the hospital and see she receives tetanus injections and some stitches to the cut.

HARRY: (*to JENNY*) Are you hurt?

JENNY: I don't know ...

FRITZ: Of course, she's hurt—call an ambulance!

ADRIENNE: There's tape and gauze in the medicine cabinet, Fritz.

JENNY whimpers with pain and tension.

FRITZ: Have you all gone mad? You're paralyzed—helpless ... what's happened to you? Have you ever felt pain or shock before?

FRITZ touches JENNY, urging her to go with him.

Come on, Jenny ... let me get you to the hospital.

JENNY: No. There's tape in the medicine cabinet.

ADRIENNE comforts her. FRITZ moves away angrily.

FRITZ: Now just what is it you all think you're doing? Have you all lost your senses?

HARRY: It's not important, Fritz ... it's only a superficial cut.

FRITZ: She's injured—is there something more important than that?

HARRY: I feel as if I were only half awake, seeing those faces filled with hatred and violence in the name of love ... And they're only youngsters ...

FRITZ: Criminal gangsters—punks! I'm going to phone the hospital.

He leaves, followed by JENNY and ADRIENNE.

SCENE 17

The COMMANDER stares at HARRY, shakes his head with disbelief.

COMMANDER: What is it about you? ... You look like a man ... you walk like a man ... you're even beginning to smell like one!

HARRY: (*smiling*) I'm becoming aware of that ...

COMMANDER: (*rising with anger*) I'm becoming aware of that! You're a mask ... a shell ... filled with words as soft and spongy as perfumed cotton ... I ask you questions and you tell me lies ... Where are you at, man?

He approaches HARRY threateningly. HARRY cringes back on his cot. The COMMANDER takes him to his feet roughly.

There are lies on your face ... beautiful, deadly lies!

The COMMANDER lifts up HARRY'S hair with his other hand.

Your hair—look at your hair ... it's grey on the sides and dark on the top! How can that be on a man's head? Why should it be? When I get as old as you I want to be grey all over ... who wants to be a walking contradiction—like something put together by a crazy kid with plasticine?

HARRY half smiles, struggling to regain his composure—trying to remove the COMMANDER'S arms off himself.

HARRY: Let go of my hair, you idiot! It's all grey ... I tint it on top ... for professional reasons.

The COMMANDER slowly releases him, his face a mask of incredulity.

COMMANDER: No ... Jesus, no! (*he begins to laugh*)

HARRY adjusts his clothing, brushes his hair back with his hands. He quickly recovers his decorum.

HARRY: (*soberly*) It's the way I am ... I see nothing macabre or extraordinary in being what I am!

COMMANDER: (*laughing, moving about in a frenzy of disbelief*) Mother of God ... where am I on this earth? Who are these people? ... What am I doing here?

ACT 2

SCENE 1

The COMMANDER is at the desk, seated, staring drowsily at HARRY. He is nodding off to sleep, waking violently.

HARRY, much more wasted and seedy than in the previous act, is lying on the cot, his hands over his eyes.

Light area is tight on the two of them.

The CHORUS, as three ordinary people in a state of apprehension, appear from the gloom offstage. They move to front of stage, their actions fearful.

CHORUS: Prometheus was chained to eternity for giving ...

(*sharply*) FIRE!

(*sharply*) FREEDOM!

... to the people for all time!

The moonbeam of our hope, skin-nailed to the asphalt of a silent street ... cries for ...

(*shout*) SILENCE!

(*shout*) PEACE!

... And all who hear him ... are the stone deaf snails ...

This is the time brothers, when the earth has aged a grey-whiskered hour or two ...

... And the green mother of all things removes the plastic piddle panties from our bums ...

Removes the chatter of inconsequence ...

And leads us naked to the sun ...

Where we stand ...

Silent and bewildered ...

Not knowing who we are ... or where!

Abruptly, the CHORUS fans out and leaves the stage.

SCENE 2

The COMMANDER suddenly perks up, withdraws a rifle from under the table, throws the safety release and moves to the door.

HARRY sits up. He is old-looking, harrassed, wasted.

HARRY: What's wrong? … What happened? … What time is it?

COMMANDER: Ssh! It's been quiet the past hour … too quiet!

They listen. Sounds of approaching footsteps, running. A rap on the door. HARRY shudders, moves to rise. The COMMANDER motions him down with rifle.

COMMANDER: *(in a hiss)* Don't move …

Second knock on door. The COMMANDER is uncertain, hesitates, then motions HARRY to approach quickly. Indicates HARRY is to stop directly in front of door. With rifle pointed at HARRY'S head, the COMMANDER deftly and silently unlocks and opens the door, moving with it to be out of sight.

JOHN, the second guard, enters. He has no weapons. He is wounded.

The COMMANDER closes and locks the door and directs HARRY and JOHN into the table area. He removes bolt out of rifle and puts it in his pocket, then stares at JOHN.

COMMANDER: *(to JOHN)* What's happened? … Where's your gun?

JOHN: *(frightened and pained)* They got Marcel!

COMMANDER: How? … Where?

JOHN: Crazy bastard!

The COMMANDER shakes JOHN roughly.

COMMANDER: You tell me what happened!

JOHN: He must've got confused or something like that … from the window … I could see him … he was carrying the letter to the same place as on Sunday … *(begging)* There was no way I could yell to warn him!

COMMANDER: What? … What? … Warn him of what?

JOHN: The drop-box was under surveillance!

The COMMANDER roughly pushes JOHN away.

COMMANDER: You goddamned fools!

HARRY: How did you get hurt?

JOHN: I could see the entire thing from where I was … everything … I opened the window. *(to the COMMANDER)* Marcel is weak—he can't and won't take pain … he'd talk!

COMMANDER: *(furious)* Damned—damned fools!

HARRY: *(fearful)* What did you do?

JOHN: There were so many of them … everywhere … they began coming out of the windows … doors … from behind parked cars!

HARRY: Yes—yes! Go on! What happened?

JOHN: *(desperately)* I got two shots before they returned fire! … I missed the first time, second shot hit low, in his hip … he's still *alive!*

The COMMANDER is suddenly aware of what has been said.

COMMANDER: Who?

JOHN: Marcel! … I didn't kill him! They hit me before I could shoot a third time!

HARRY turns away to sit on cot.

HARRY: My God!

COMMANDER: Do they know you're here, John? Were you followed?

JOHN: I don't think so … I came through the underground garage and out the service ramp … then back down again by way of the laundry kiosk … There was nobody there. Shit! … I'm sorry!

The COMMANDER touches JOHN, rubs his head gently to reassure him.

COMMANDER: You did the right thing … you did the right thing …

The COMMANDER moves away, pondering, pacing.

JOHN: What'll we do now? He'll talk … he can't take pain like you an' I … he knows everything!

HARRY: Yes … what *will* you do?

COMMANDER: I'm thinking ... I'm thinking! ... I'm not that bright ... it takes time for me to think!

HARRY laughs with incredulity. The COMMANDER turns on him.

COMMANDER: One more whinny out of you and I'll blow your head off! How'll that be for laughs?

HARRY: (*smiles sardonically*) Far be it for me to suggest this, but don't you think I should be moved to another location?

The COMMANDER stares at him with disbelief, then laughs mirthlessly.

COMMANDER: Hey—that's a brilliant idea ... top-level government thinking there! The rent for this is twenty days overdue ... you know of a rental agency for kidnappers that will give us credit?

The smile fades from HARRY'S face.

HARRY: Surely you don't mean that ...

COMMANDER: (*bowing mockingly*) That's right, mister ambassador ... exactly, mister ambassador! This is it, mister ambassador—there's no place else.

JOHN: If I could get a small revolver ... go down to the police station and say I was his brother ...

COMMANDER: Your fighting's finished, John ... Do you have friends? Someplace you can go until you get better?

Pathetically JOHN attempts to bandage his arm with his shirt sleeve. Shakes his head.

JOHN: I can try ... I think it's alright, but I' not ...

COMMANDER: You'll *have* to go, John! That's an order!

JOHN: (*fearful, defiant*) No, I won't leave you!

The COMMANDER moves on him quickly and slaps him hard across the face.

COMMANDER: I'm still giving the orders in this unit ... is that understood?

JOHN wipes tears of pain from his eyes and rises painfully to his feet.

JOHN: You had no right doing that ... I would've gone through hell for you.

Head lowered, he stumbles towards the door. The COMMANDER unlocks the door, but before he opens it he turns to JOHN and taking his face into his hands, kisses him on the mouth openly, unabashedly. Then he pushes JOHN roughly out the door.

COMMANDER: You gotta live, fella, go out there and live!

JOHN grins pathetically on leaving.

SCENE 3

The COMMANDER slowly relocks the door. Turns to HARRY and stares at him. HARRY returns his gaze.

Sound of JENNY offstage.

JENNY: (*sings*) Oh Sally my dear, it's you I've been missing ...

HARRY: Tell me the truth ... tell me why you're doing this? Is it out of hatred?

COMMANDER: To hell with you!

HARRY: Look me in the face and admit it's hatred that drives you!

COMMANDER: (*reeling, bellowing*) To hell with you!

HARRY: You poor, lonely ... isolated bastard ...

The COMMANDER takes out his revolver and examines it.

And to remind me that you need me ... and I need you ... we get ... *this*? How did we become this way?

COMMANDER: (*laughs*) Don't you try that with me! You haven't got the balls to pull it off ... not anymore!

HARRY: (*strangely exulted*) Alright ... who runs the revolutionary federation—you? It doesn't matter anymore whether you tell me or not, does it?

COMMANDER: Hell, no—it doesn't matter. I don't know who runs the federation—why should it worry me?

HARRY: Suppose they are traitors? ... Supposing the top command is infiltrated by criminals ... or foreign operatives ... or even police agents out to create larger budgets and influence for their departments by instigating civil disorder?

COMMANDER: Don't lay bullshit on me, Harry!

HARRY: I suppose it doesn't matter ... but you have a right to know ... you should know ... you're entitled to know ... your life wasn't entirely a waste!

COMMANDER: And how important are *you* alive to the government?

HARRY: I don't know ... I really don't know.

COMMANDER: Well, it's big game season out there ... those armoured troop carriers don't run on no forty miles to the gallon of gas ... Could you be an embarrassment? Like ... do they know you did something without asking the man above ... especially in your love life?

HARRY: Only Fritz knew ... but dossiers do exist ... Why do you ask?

COMMANDER: I was just wondering what's more important to them ... you alive, or both of us dead ... ?

HARRY: (*smiles*) That's a sober question, isn't it?

HARRY looks up at COMMANDER, realizes the question was not an idle one. HARRY'S smile fades.

COMMANDER: (*laughs*) Don't let it make you nervous ... I was only thinking aloud. (*he moves to the table, revolver still in hand, and sits down heavily*) What was it like living for you before we got you?

HARRY: (*moving away, troubled*) Life was just splendid ... the heating system in the house needed repairs ... I was developing an ulcer and Adrienne was having some problems with her legs ... but otherwise ...

COMMANDER: How different we are ...

HARRY: Yes, I think we have some basic differences ...

COMMANDER: When you were a boy did you box, sing ... fish ... ?

HARRY: I fished in the summer just for the sport and skiied in the winter ...

COMMANDER: How different we are ... He was an organizer of the bush workers in northern Quebec when everything was up for grabs and men were worth less than the clothes they wore ...

HARRY: Who?

COMMANDER: My uncle Steve.

HARRY: Who is he?

COMMANDER: It's not in your history books and no police record can be found anywhere ... I've searched for some evidence ... but there's none ... He was found when the snow melted ... shot twelve times through the body—not one of the bullets having hit a vital organ. He died slow, his legs and arms broken by the company hoods. I've dreamed of how he died ... how he felt ... and it gives me a pain hard-on ... even Christ was crucified with more mercy ... and He died to save the whole world ... My uncle Steve died trying to get twelve cents an hour more wages for the bush workers. You were honeymooning about the time he died ... did you hear him holler? Or did you ... make more noise than he did?

SCENE 4

HARRY is about to move, but becomes transfixed.

The CHORUS enter in a flutter of percussion rhythm, their arms extended to draw ADRIENNE into HARRY'S mind.

ADRIENNE enters, radiant, beautiful, dressed as a young bride. She is laughing.

ADRIENNE: It *will* be beautiful, my darling! I feel it in my face ... right to the tips of my fingers!

The CHORUS retreats from her. She tries to reach them.

... if your first posting was to be an under-developed country ... or better still, some relevant work among the poor here ... perhaps the Indians or Metis ... or a farming community with an eastern European population ... community development is as important as foreign diplomacy, don't you agree?

COMMANDER: He died ... staring at the snow diamonds in the trees ... listening to the rupture shots of poplars at twenty below zero ... listening to the men who'd killed him leave ... walking quickly through the snow ... listening to his pulse filling up his stomach ... then his bladder, then his lungs ...

ADRIENNE: (*shrugging*) As you wish, darling ... but I think you owe it to yourself to visit China ...

for background experience ... in say two years' time. I would so wish to see that experience beginning to bear its fruit ... Rewi Alley wrote me from Peking last week ... He said the summer was warm and beautiful ... naked children at the river while he wrote ... they are not afraid, he said ... the first generation of children born into a country racing for the future ... freed of its past ...

COMMANDER: There is a God, Harry. He gives us kids who have to learn everything all over again. That's merciful as hell ...

ADRIENNE hardens, removes part of her bridal attire to reveal a sombre dress beneath.

SCENE 5

FRITZ enters, staring vacantly ahead of himself.

ADRIENNE: It's a damned shame ... it's wrong, Harry! The children are ragged and hungry ... these aren't children from the lower income population ... these are middle class, well educated children ... children *we* might have raised being clubbed and chased out of the cities! Darling, they're clubbing and shoving children in every city now ... it's televised nightly like a ritual! What are they trying to do? ... Is there no better way to live? ... When a society beats and maims its own there is something terribly wrong, Harry! For God's sake, write a report about it ... we mustn't be allowed to stop thinking!

COMMANDER: What are you thinking?

HARRY: Our responsibilities are spread beyond view.

FRITZ: A man's responsibility is for this day only. Let tomorrow be looked after by tomorrow's people ...

COMMANDER: Who do you mean?

HARRY: My wife ... my family ...

FRITZ: Those who desire violence should serve their country in violent ways, by assimilation into the armed forces and police. It has worked in the past and until the nature of man changes, it will have to continue being that way ...

FRITZ leaves. ADRIENNE stares coldly at HARRY.

SCENE 6

HARRY: I waited ... I've waited a lifetime for the opportune moment. But it never came ...

ADRIENNE moves as near as she can to HARRY. She kisses her fingers and reaches out to him. He flinches from her near touch. She leaves.

The CHORUS attempts to will her back, to bridge the space between her and HARRY.

SCENE 7

COMMANDER: There's no opportune moment for anything, you old fool ... there's only now.

HARRY: How important do *you* think I am to them?

COMMANDER: How important am I? How important are *any* of us? ... A man's a piss-poor investment to educate, put clothes on ... build a house for ... feed ... and then give him nothing useful to do. You could do better investing in soap flakes.

They both laugh.

HARRY: I wish I had a drink. I wish we both had a drink.

COMMANDER: (*anxiously*) What will become of Jenny? She's very young—you're an old man. And in a few minutes ... (*he raises his revolver*)

HARRY: I'm younger today than I was at twelve. (*he thinks about it, smiles sadly*) No, that isn't true ... what I meant was if I was to be a youth again, I would live differently.

The CHORUS closes in, reflecting the growing mellowness and withdrawal of HARRY.

CHORUS: I wish I had a drink ...

Younger than at twelve ...

Who will care for Jenny?

SCENE 8

JENNY enters. She draws an imaginary curtain aside and calls in the gloom offstage.

JENNY: Harry—wake up! I brought the bicycles up front ... your breakfast is waiting ...

HARRY: (*to the COMMANDER*) I would change my name ... Harry is a stiff, grey name ...

JENNY: It's a sunny morning ... cool and sunny ...

COMMANDER: (*harshly*) Son of a bitch ... stop dreaming! Don't you leave me now!

HARRY: (*to the COMMANDER, in a rapture of internal triumph against death*) I would open my heart to every living thing ... when I entered a room or a field, it would be as a lover returning after an absence during which he was missed ... during which the universe went slightly out of balance because he hadn't been there to hold it in place! ...

COMMANDER: Harry—wake up!

CHORUS: Wake up!

Wake up!

Wake up!

JENNY: (*soft, languid*) ... You're the only man there will ever be ...

HARRY: I would not cringe from any battle ... no matter how dangerous ... I would reach beyond my capabilities ... I would split the asphalt of my home so the first blade of grass might live again ... I would beg that all things removed from mother earth be replaced ... I would place my blood, mind and body on the side of reason and compassion!

COMMANDER: (*shouting*) Stop it!

JENNY: ... I've never loved before and I will never love this way again. I am no bother ... I ask for nothing ...

COMMANDER: Be honest with yourself! Christ, for once only, be honest!

HARRY: (*still possessed*) I would move ... close ... painfully ... to the Lord Jesus Himself ... conquering fear ... violence ... the temptations of nothingness ... even death!

COMMANDER: Goddamn you!

SCENE 9

ADRIENNE enters and moves between JENNY and HARRY.

The CHORUS affirms the understanding she reveals.

ADRIENNE: That which killed men and women a generation ago now frees them ... our sexuality is music and colour ... the sparkle of brains in our eyes ... the touch of finger on finger in a darkened hallway.

CHORUS: ... We are not ashamed ...

... We are not defiant ...

ADRIENNE: ... That which liberates and provides love for one of us, liberates and gives love to us all.

ADRIENNE crosses to JENNY and FRITZ who has entered and stands watching the scene from the other end of the stage.

ADRIENNE: (*exploding*) It hurts me, Harry! ... I can rationalize and understand ... at a distance ... but I'm still a woman ... it's my home ... my life ... I'm married to you! I feel guilty ... dirtied ... I am what I am and I can't help it!

JENNY: (*to FRITZ, head lowered*) When I came back ... he would ask me to walk with him after dinner ... we talked about music, philosophy, sometimes I would take his arm and tell him how I wished my father could laugh ... and we'd laugh together about it ... he had stories about Istanbul and Warsaw ...

COMMANDER: What about the first time?

JENNY: (*to FRITZ*) I was scared then ... I had been reading in bed ... he came to say goodnight ... but he didn't leave ... we talked about my travelling ... then he said why don't I stay with them and continue with my studies ... then he touched my hair ... my face ... I was somewhat scared— I'd never been with a man before ... I couldn't think of what to do!

FRITZ: That sonofabitch! He never told me about that ...

ADRIENNE: (*to JENNY, bitterly*) Would you have submitted if you knew he might not be able to care for you? ... If he was somebody of less importance and influence?

JENNY begins to sob. ADRIENNE places her arm over JENNY'S shoulder and leads her away.

FRITZ: That sonofabitch ... imagine that!

ADRIENNE: Never mind—we're only women!

FRITZ takes one long, searching look at HARRY. FRITZ and the women leave.

SCENE 10

The COMMANDER takes out his revolver, pulls back the safety catch and bending down, slides it across the floor, where it comes to a stop nearer to HARRY than the COMMANDER.

The CHORUS MEMBERS begin to beat drums they do not hold.

The COMMANDER and HARRY face each other for one long, charged, moment. HARRY takes a deep breath.

COMMANDER: Now ... the truth!

They stand for a long moment. HARRY galvanizes internally, retreats into himself.

The COMMANDER makes a sharp gesture as if to retrieve the gun. HARRY lunges for it in a frantic animal scramble. Takes hold of it and aims it at the COMMANDER, who has not moved.

HARRY: You've held me prisoner ... you've tormented me ... you've killed, robbed, terrified ...

COMMANDER: (*in a dead voice*) Have I?

HARRY: I'm not perfect ... we'll never be, but we try for harmony of sorts. If it wasn't for you we would have a claw-hold on the stars now ... touching the unreachable, the eternal. You've reduced it to tanks and guns and narrow-mindedness once more! This gun is burning the palm of my hand, but I've got to hold it!

COMMANDER: None of us has the devil by the balls, have we, Harry?

The COMMANDER approaches HARRY, who retreats slightly, then sets himself firmly to resist the COMMANDER.

HARRY: Don't come any closer!

COMMANDER: What are you going to do?

HARRY: We're going out that door. There's no other choice now!

COMMANDER: We're not going anywhere ... give the gun back to me. It belongs to a woman I loved ...

COMMANDER takes another step towards HARRY. HARRY raises the revolver to COMMANDER'S face.

HARRY: Stand back! ... If I have to kill you to get out, I will!

The COMMANDER approaches, reaching out for the gun with his other hand. HARRY'S face reveals his terror as he pulls the trigger. The gun clicks.

COMMANDER: Did you think I'm that much of a fool? (*he takes the gun from HARRY'S hands*) To give you a loaded gun? This is Mara's gun ... it's more than a weapon ... it's my pendant ... my decoration ... for touching and loving a queen one wet week in London!

HARRY: (*sickened*) Don't do that to me anymore! Please ...

COMMANDER: (*loading the revolver*) Smile, man ... I'm not afraid ... don't you be! I have a gun and you're my prisoner ... but for an accident of birth ... you could be me and I you ... think of it and rejoice!

HARRY: (*furiously*) Fuck off!

The COMMANDER hoots with joy. Shadow dances around HARRY as he continues loading the revolver.

The CHORUS breaks from the scene in panic as the COMMANDER turns and chases them off.

Light widens to open the stage totally.

COMMANDER: I'm not going to leave you for Algeria, don't worry! You'll die first and then I! We'll have forever to straighten it out in heaven ... lots of time ... don't worry!

HARRY: (*mocking, furious*) Ha! Ha! ... I'll be buried on the hill, where they cut the grass and plant flowers ... You'll be in some corner full of weeds, if you're lucky ... or floating down some river like a bloated frog!

COMMANDER: We'll both rot the same way ... bit by bit ...

HARRY: Yeah ... we'll both rot the same way ... that's right ...

COMMANDER: We rot as we live ... I went to California with a buddy ... driving a three-ton truck to pick up honey bees in Sacramento ... weather was lousy ... the truck kept breaking down ... eating our money away ... we stopped in a motel ... took a room together, but Joey's feet were rotten ... when he unlaced his boots, I went out and got another motel ... In the Oregon wasteland Joey had to crap ... asked a garageman where he could find the john ... there was none at the garage, but he told Joey there was an out-house four miles down the highway ... I kept watching for it and saw it first ... Joey's eyes were bad ... I told him to run ... there was no roof on the crapper ... I watched him run to it, and then looked up and there against the sky was a vulture coming straight down after Joey ... down, down ... on the edge of the roof ... the head lookin' down ... I hollered at Joey, but I didn't have to ... he was already running for the truck, his belt open, pants falling down ...

HARRY: I can well imagine ...

COMMANDER: We went to Sacramento ... then to Los Angeles for a few days ... On Sunset Boulevard, we parked and changed our clothes in the cab. Joey's suitcase had been rained on, and when he took out his good sports jacket, it was growing mushrooms on the shoulders ... I couldn't go with him any further ... I said good-bye, Joey ... I'll see you around ... and the last I seen of him, Joey was going out in search of tail, mushrooms growing on his shoulders, walking down Sunset Boulevard with one foot on the side-walk, the other on the street ... limping happy like an old country cripple ...

HARRY: You were well rid of him ...

COMMANDER: You had good women ... my women were goddesses and sluts ... nothing in between, nothing a man could hold and call his own. I had a landlady who I goosed for rent ... once a week ... the rent was forty bucks so it came out to ten dollars a throw!

HARRY smiles.

It was a job I approached with a hard hat and boots ... she never remembered to wash or comb ... I was on a city bus with her once and she opened her blouse and started to sew up a tear in her brassiere ... the driver kicked us off!

HARRY laughs.

Another time she got mad ... I mean *mad* ... pushed a bowl of soup at me, like a dog ... spilled soup all over the table, all over my shirt. I swore at her and said that as soon as I got a job, I was moving out ... pigsties were cleaner than her place. She picked up the cat and wiped the table and my shirt front with the ass-end of the cat ... I still can't stand soup!

Both of them laugh uncontrollably. HARRY is the first to recover his composure.

HARRY: When I was a boy, I fell off a tree across a picket fence, opening a four-inch gash in my leg. I came into the house bawling, all covered in blood. My mother was all dressed for some party or other ... She took one look at me and started raising shit—"You did it on purpose ... on the day of the week when I have a chance to get out!"

They continue laughing, the laughter dies out slowly.

COMMANDER: We'd destroy the world if it wasn't for the women ... they keep us down by being with us ... by giving us kids to clean up and dress ... you and I have no kids ... that's sad ...

HARRY: The world being what it is, I don't think it's right to ...

COMMANDER: (*angry, grasping HARRY by shirt lapels*) Your balls were taken out by your grand-father and you can't live without reaching for mine ... that's why you kill the kids of the other men, isn't it?

HARRY: No!

COMMANDER: You lie ...

HARRY: We're all the same!

COMMANDER: Your kind has killed little girls for witchcraft ... hung blacks by their heels in the trees ... shot and starved Indians ...

HARRY: We're all the same!

COMMANDER: No, we're not ... you've replaced kids with poodles, and two cars ... sacked the rivers and the mountains ... sweet-powdered the smell of shit ...

HARRY: We share the same contradictions!

COMMANDER: No, we don't! All the time you were losing your minds, because you needed blood, real blood, to keep you from aging. You've punched the poor around … taken away their languages and then their pride with welfarism … still you can't win, can you?

HARRY: We've all shared the same experience at some stage in history!

COMMANDER: No, we haven't! … The cleverest laws … the best logic … won't stop some twisted bit of human garbage from thinking … from reaching for a stick of dynamite or a rifle when he no longer knows the words to talk to you!

HARRY: (*breaking free*) Alright! I can and will do something … but not now … not under threat … not in my lifetime, perhaps. But I will open doors. Talk to me and I'll listen! I won't interrupt you again.

COMMANDER: (*distantly*) Don't look at me … I'm dead … I've been dead from the moment I first saw you face to face.

The COMMANDER pulls out his gun and looks at it.

HARRY: (*to the COMMANDER, who has moved away to extreme range of stage*) Hey … wait! You've still got Algeria if …

COMMANDER: I'm not going to Algeria … I was born here … my people worked and laughed and fucked here … What can you do about that?

The COMMANDER laughs bitterly, his back to HARRY.

The CHORUS enters as soldiers or militia, guns held at the ready.

HARRY mimes the action of trying to hold back the armed men from entering, from killing. Two of them push their way by him. The third shakes HARRY'S hand and begins to escort him out.

HARRY instantly straightens his clothes and hair as he marches on the way out.

When the two CHORUS MEMBERS reach the front of the stage, the COMMANDER begins a slow mime of death by shooting, his revolver dropping, his limbs distorted with pain, his mouth opened wide in a death howl as he falls to the floor.

The howl the COMMANDER does not make is voiced by HARRY as he is led out.

JENNY: (*singing offstage*)
Oh Sally my dear, I wish I could wed you
Oh Sally my dear, I wish I could bed you
I smiled and replied, you'd say I misled you …

CHORUS: (*in unison*) Something in us … that is naked in the black … moose-bellowing wind … keeps laughing at God … laughs at the devil.

End

SUNRISE ON SARAH

By the early seventies Ryga had become the most political of Canadian playwrights, positioning himself as a fierce critic of the Canadian theatre, stating in the first issue of the *Canadian Theatre Review* (1974), that with the *Captives of the Faceless Drummer* confrontation at the Vancouver Playhouse Theatre, "the gloves were off for the first time" in the struggle to forge an authentic Canadian theatre. He wanted a true theatre of the people, one liberated from elitist audiences with their fondness for Euro-American plays, from funding agencies with a preference for theatre management over creative artists, and from boards of directors seen as having narrow, economically-driven agendas. Calling much of what he saw in Canadian theatre circles as "a private club," he went on the attack, dismissing major operations like the Stratford Festival as "a dinosaur" and the Shaw Festival as "self-indulgent." Later, he would describe himself as an "artist-in-resistance," his task to further awaken public concern—now over such issues as Canada's persistent and pervasive racism, its class system, and its participation in the economic exploitation of the Third World.

At the same time, however, Ryga had always been interested in the personal, private world of the individual as it confronts both its public and its social contexts. In the early drafts of *The Ecstasy of Rita Joe*, for example, a deeply disoriented Rita Joe suffers the phantasms of her inner demons in nightmarish scenes redolent of the expressionist drama of the early 1920s. While his original plan at the time had been to write a play that depicts a married, middle-aged man's affair, exploring personal, changing relationships in contemporary society, when the October Crisis occurred in 1970, Ryga re-focused the play on a political kidnapping—although vestiges of the original outline remain in the Harry-Adrienne-Jenny ménage in *Captives of the Faceless Drummer*. A full-fledged play about private obsession would have to wait until late 1971, when he began work on *Sunrise on Sarah*.

That fall Ryga was invited to teach a writing seminar at the University of British Columbia in Vancouver. He lived near the centre of the city's counter-culture area, in an old building managed by a friend. Among the people living in the building were a number of acquaintances from his rural home area in Summerland. Ryga became intrigued by the rapidly shifting personal relationships in the building. A distraught woman from Summerland, the wife of a good friend who had drowned the previous year, arrived with a woman friend and began an affair with the building manager, who in turn left his former partner, the two moving into a new suite in the same building. Ryga, as an old friend, found himself consoling a number of distressed women, especially the manager's ex-partner—a professional woman in her late thirties who became the chief model for Sarah. Then another of Ryga's old friends, Dick Clements, arrived on the scene with a new partner, a woman half his age.

George Ryga set *Sunrise on Sarah* in the interior of a woman's psyche, "set in the corners of her mind" as the original program states, an increasingly difficult presumption for any man, as Ryga himself would acknowledge. Clearly, his intent was to explore the stresses of a woman in white, middle-class urban society, her problems arising from a naturalist, determinist ethos, and not from an explicitly political one. *Sunrise on Sarah* presents us with a title character of a woman the exact opposite of the title character Ryga had created in *The Ecstasy of Rita Joe*: a well-paid, privileged, white, educated and seemingly liberated person who is seen to be destroyed by the fact that there is no place for liberated women in her kind of society. Liberation, Ryga seems to be saying, is too costly if achieved through a loss of sexual purpose and identity—an issue still current in the feminist movement today.

In place of the ideological conflict that is otherwise so characteristic of his work, Ryga has, in this play, set up a psychological dialectic between the central character, a woman, and her projected opposite, known only as the Man. Beneath what the character of her mother calls her "average" life, Sarah is profoundly disturbed by feelings of inadequacy: having had relationships with a number of men, she cannot release them emotionally and form a stable new relationship; forgetful and confused, she is in danger of losing her teaching career; and even in middle age she remains haunted by the violent death of her brutish father when she was three. Sexually confused, she is alternately interrogating and being interrogated by this protean figure of the Man, a composite character constructed of fragments of both everything she has experienced and everything her society has presented her with that is male. Gigolo, lover, friend, psychiatrist, homosexual, abuser, the Man voices and represents the inner turmoil of her attempts at sexual identity formation in the face of the other. She hallucinates, imagining a man, Lee, whom she casually meets in a supermarket, as a mythical figure, a composite of her projected sexual desires, fears, and frustrations. There are suggestions of a growing despair and madness in her inability to define her own sexuality in the limited and fragmented other of male stereotypes her white, urban, Euro-American culture has constructed and made available to her. In this sense, *Sunrise on Sarah* addresses, in a psychological context, the same metathematic of rootlessness and exile from an effectively constructed self that haunts all of Ryga's work.

The play was commissioned by the School of Fine Arts at the Banff Centre and opened at the Eric Harvie Theatre on July 29, 1972. It was directed by Thomas Peacocke and featured a student cast. Music and lyrics were by Ryga, with the music for "Lady in Blue" by Dennis Cooper.

A surprise on opening night was the appearance of Prime Minister Pierre Elliot Trudeau and his wife Margaret, who attended the show, then spent an hour afterwards discussing it with Ryga and Peacocke. A French translation of *Sunrise on Sarah* subsequently played on the French network, Radio-Canada, on *Les Beaux Dimanches* in November, 1973.

SUNRISE ON SARAH

CHARACTERS

SARAH
LEE
MAN
PETER
FATHER
MOTHER
CHARLIE
MICHAEL
EMMA
MAY
JUDY
SCHOOL BOARD CHAIRMAN
PRINCIPAL
TEACHERS' ASSOCIATION REPRESENTATIVE

SET

A bedroom which forms the core of a setting that has great flexibility in elevations, lighting potential, etc. The bedroom is a private cell with soft light, a bedside telephone, headboard with neatly arranged toiletries, books, etc.

ACT 1

SARAH, dressed in an evening dressing gown and soft slippers, is dialing her telephone with great concentration. The dialing is clumsy. She hangs up, lights a cigarette, then with even greater intensity than before dials the telephone again. She listens for the ring. The telephone is answered. In a wide spectrum of moods, she talks (soundlessly) to the person she has called. She laughs, broods, becomes agitated, shakes her head as if denying something the person talking to her has said.

Over her action, LEE sings offstage, accompanied by an oboe.

LEE: Lady in blue
In a garden of rain

Seen her last week
And this morning again
First time she
Watched a child at play
This morning I saw
Her smiling my way

Faint light now reveals LEE, singing in a deep gloom of another elevation.

Marigold stars
In her tulip rain
Weeping willow
Bends in the wind
Lovin' sun over ten thousand mountains
Will not promise
I'll see her tomorrow

Lady in blue
In a garden of rain
Seen her last week
And this morning again
First time she
Watched a child at play
This morning I saw
Her smiling my way

SARAH completes her telephone call and hangs up. She rises to her feet, examines her clothes uncertainly, then busies herself brushing her hair, adjusting her face.

A faint flow of light begins to pulse over all other cast members, in varying depths of shadow and in different elevations of the setting.

SARAH becomes fearful, physically conscious of change around her.

MAN approaches and stands in silence in entrance to bedroom. He is looking down at SARAH, smiling. He is dressed stylishly, in an expensive suit that effectively makes it possible for him to be both warm and distant, as his body is always well sheathed. SARAH is aware of his presence, but does not look up at him.

LEE: High rider am I
In chase of sunlight
Sweepin' silence
From sleepin' towns

Tiger-lily shift-stick countin' the miles
Pulse of the hills
My companions

*The light dies out on LEE and others in gloom of set-
ting, under last lines of song. But the light does not
die totally.*

SARAH: You see, it is no good leaving me alone. I
told you it would never work.

*MAN nods, smiles, but remains standing where he
is.*

I move from mood to mood like lightning ... from
depression to the passions of a dragon in heat ...
what can you do about me, doctor?

MAN: I am not a doctor.

SARAH is startled. Turns to him.

SARAH: But you are! ... Why do you lie to me?

MAN shakes his head again.

Not Charlie? ... Herbert then? ... Peter?

MAN: (*smiling*) No.

SARAH: (*confused*) There have been many men
... all different ... yet their faces are one face
tonight ... How did you get in? Who allowed you
in the building?

MAN: You invited me to dinner.

SARAH: When? ... I had dinner out tonight ... I
ate alone. At Nancy's Bar and Grille ... two
poached eggs ... a salad and some lightly but-
tered toast ...

MAN: (*entering room*) That was yesterday.
Tonight you invited me to dinner. We ate steak
sandwiches with beer!

*SARAH shakes her head, becomes agitated. Watches
the approach of the MAN with trepidation, as if
wondering how to, but powerless to stop him.*

SARAH: I don't know you! ... I want my doctor! ...
My prescription has run out—see how my hands
tremble! See that!

MAN ignores her outstretched hands.

MAN: (*petulantly*) You're lying to me again ... I
told you never lie to me! Never pretend you are
worse or better than you are for I am a very busy
man.

*Music—strains of "Lady in Blue" whistled by LEE.
It rouses SARAH.*

SARAH: Now don't start on that again ... the first
time I saw you, you said I might have to be committed for treatment. I didn't know my name ...
couldn't speak ... I would read words in a book or
newspaper, but they made no sense.

MAN: They were words you knew, but in a sentence they became a crowd of strangers, babbling
in some foreign language!

SARAH: (*impetuously*) Yes, yes ... I know! I love
you, doctor ... dance with me, for you have made
me well again!

*The whistling increases in pitch. SARAH moves
stiffly, awkwardly to the sound of LEE'S voice, as the
whistle changes into song.*

SONG: Lady in blue
In a garden of rain
Seen her last week
And this morning again
First time she
Watched a child at play
This morning I saw
Her smiling my way

The song dies abruptly.

*Lights tighten on SARAH, who stands alone in bed-
room, the MAN now in dim outline in shadows of
room.*

SARAH: Where was I? ...

MAN: You were eating salad and poached eggs ...

SARAH: No, no ... before that? ...

MAN laughs.

 ... Don't laugh at me! I don't pay you to laugh at
me!

*MAN takes out a notebook from his breast pocket
and refers to it.*

MAN: You were married once to a man who
called you by another name when he made love
to you!

SARAH: Ah, yes ... what was the name he called
me?

MAN: He called you Dolly ... in memory of a
whore he knew once in Prince George ...

SARAH: Yes … Dolly …

PETER, dressed in denim workshirt, boots and jeans, approaches and grins at SARAH.

PETER: Got paid today, lady … (*pats his breast pocket*) Seven hundred an' thirty-eight smackeroos right there … next to the tit!

SARAH turns to him cheerfully.

SARAH: That is more than last month. Did you get a raise then?

PETER: Raise, my ass … there was thirty hours overtime on that cheque! How've you been, kid?

SARAH gives him kiss on cheek. PETER responds amorously. SARAH withdraws. PETER is dismayed, and although he tries to cover his discomfort and inadequacy, he is clumsy at disguising a deeper feeling of frustration.

Hey! … that's no way to treat a man who's just cashed in his pay cheque!

SARAH: … I'll … make some food, Peter. Then we'll go to a show. There's a new Bergman film playing downtown …

PETER: Come on, Sarah … I've been three weeks from home … Got to leave again first thing in the morning …

SARAH subconsciously pulls her hair into a more severe shape. Her manners and physical bearing become more rigid. PETER reaches out to her, then drops his hands helplessly. Then he grins.

SARAH: One of the teachers saw it, and thought it was Bergman's best …

PETER: Hey! I woke up this morning with a devil in my hand and red veins popping in my eyes … you know what that means, eh Sarah?

SARAH becomes agitated.

SARAH: Let's go to a show … now! I don't like it when you come in like this and start talking dirty!

PETER, out of frustration and sheer devilry, begins to stalk her in a cat-like motion. As he does so, he sings. SARAH retreats from him.

PETER: (*singing raucously*)
Hey, Dolly—you be sweet to me!
Hey, Dolly—you be sweet to me!
(*roguishly*) There's money in me pocket
And a fire in my crotch

If I don't get what I'm after
I won't love you very much!

He slaps his knee with glee, amused by her fear and outraged propriety. Then suddenly he sighs wearily and stops his pursuit. His face has become grim. He stares at her reproachfully.

You go see your goddamned Burgerman—alone! … What the hell kind of life is this, anyway—can you tell me? Go ahead—tell me! You're smarter than me! … I'm not smart, but I've never been on welfare either, sister! … If you don't like it, then leave. Everything I've had from you, I can buy for half the price anyway—so pack up and get out. I don't care! … But if you're staying, then I'm still the goddamned boss here an' don't you forget it!

PETER exits angrily.

Light changes to include SARAH and MAN.

SARAH laughs sadly, shakes her head. Her hair falls freely around her face.

SARAH: Poor Peter … he tried in the only way he knew … he paid me for standing up, and he paid me for lying down … When that didn't work, he used his fists. Once he threw me through the plate glass window of the living room. I flew out into the garden, not a scratch on me. But when he looked out the window to see if he'd killed me, a shard of glass came down across his wrist! (*shouts joyfully*) The bastard stood there swearing, while the blood spurted over his hands with his heartbeats! I thumbed my nose at him … I spat at him … I wanted him to stand there long enough to die!

The wild triumph passes from her face. She stares at the MAN, moves to him, plays with the lapels of his coat.

(*wearily*) Will someone take me where there are flowers! In May, the alyssum blooms like music in the Okanagan valley!

The MAN examines her throat, moves his hands down her breasts to her hips. But matter-of-factly, clinically, with no eroticism. Then moving away from her as abruptly as he had advanced, the MAN begins writing in his notebook.

MAN: Even a beautiful woman's lips shrink and wither Sarah …

SARAH: (*softly*) No! …

MAN: ... The breasts become pouches of hanging skin ... the thighs crease and stiffen ...

SARAH: No, please! Don't tease me like that!

The MAN turns to her, stares at her briefly, then taps his pen over her lower abdomen.

MAN: I'm warning the child ... should there ever be a child ... which I doubt.

SARAH: No—you mustn't do that to me!

MAN smiles, puts away his notebook, takes SARAH by the shoulders and turns her from side to side, his gaze fixed on her face, her falling hair.

MAN: You, my darling, are beyond aging! ... Your hair glows like fire in the night ... your thighs are firm and smooth as those of a teenaged cyclist in the rain ... Your eyes ... are knowing, yet hot and moist ...

SARAH: (*ecstatic*) The eyes of a poet! Say it!

MAN takes his hands off her and turns away. He stretches with boredom, and yawns.

MAN: The eyes of a poet ...

SARAH: (*still ecstatic*) With men like you, a woman lives forever! ... Thank God you've come ... I feel alive again!

MAN: I would like some coffee and a doughnut.

SARAH: ... To be free of drugs and the sleep of fear ... How splendid that would be! It's the other doctors who have done this to me! They attack the womb first, and when they've destroyed that, they go for the mind ... I have had two years of neither sleep nor wakefulness ... isn't that a crime?

She sees the MAN settling into a chair and writing notes again. A note of betrayal comes into her voice.

SARAH: You agree it is a crime, don't you?

MAN: ... At dinner tonight, do you remember what we ate?

SARAH: (*confused*) We ate ... curried rice and salmon!

MAN begins to laugh.

(*upset*) Now you're cruel ... I didn't ask you in to hurt me like this!

MAN: (*waving her objections aside*) When your father died ... you were how old?

SARAH: Three. I was three years old ...

MAN: And how did he die?

SARAH stares absent-mindedly at him, then begins to laugh.

SARAH: He died of pain. How does anybody die?

MAN puts away his notebook and pen, and rising to his feet, begins to mime throughout his next dialogue.

MAN: He was a cross-eyed fool on a one-way trip to hell, Sarah! ... He lassoed a seagull ... but the seagull was bigger than he thought ...

SARAH: Now you leave my father alone, do you hear!

MAN: It was the size of a St. Bernard dog ... bigger than a Welsh pony ... more powerful than a freighter! When it flew up, he wouldn't let go ... for he was a big man with small comprehension ... The seagull carried him into the sky and smashed his brains out against the side of a mountain!

The MAN stops miming. Faces SARAH with a grin on his face. SARAH is afraid.

SARAH: No! ... He didn't die that way at all ... He fell off his tractor and was ground up by the rototiller on our ten-acre berry farm in Steveston ... I was three years old then. When they took him away, they forgot to wash the rototiller blades. The blood on the blades blackened in the sun and flaked ... I went into the field every day ... to look at the blades ... wondering ... wondering if he thought of me at the moment of his death ...

MAN: Nonsense! He had other things in mind!

SARAH: He *had* to remember me ... his only daughter ... there would never be another child ...

MAN: He was thinking of dandelion marmalade and dusty days at sea!

SARAH now pleads urgently.

SARAH: I want to know ... did he think of me?

MAN: He thought of amber eyes and blue, scented lips ... and the pillows of a sailor's whore!

SARAH slumps with defeat. Her voice quavers.

SARAH: The last time I went into the field ... I tore a loose flake of blood off the rototiller blade that killed him ... I held it to the sun ... and then ... and then ... I ate it!

MAN: And it was delicious ... as the ears and lips and skin of man!

SARAH shakes her head dismally.

SARAH: It tasted strange and frightening ... like a sliver of dried fish ... After I swallowed father's blood ... my throat burned ... I ran home, retching and sweating ... calling for help ... but nobody would help me ... the field was gray and barren as the moon!

Music in: LEE humming.

Memory of SARAH'S FATHER enters, dressed in rough work clothing, his head lowered. MAN drifts into background.

SARAH: I was only three years old! I didn't know what I was doing!

FATHER: (*slowly, struggling for every thought*) ... Men with arms reaching to their ankles will do all the work after this ...

SARAH: I don't know what you're saying, Daddy!

FATHER: Her mother ... Jesus Lord, I've never said it ... her mother never loved me ... not at all ...

SARAH: Did you remember *me* that moment? Tell me! ... I wore a green dress that day, and white shoes with black laces ...

FATHER: Lady I always called her ... lady wanted to go out workin' ... I says, nothing doing, lady ... there's work enough around the place helping me take care of things ... don't look good against a man to have his wife out workin' ... but she wanted to go work for someone else ... We had a fight that mornin' ... Jesus Lord, it was a rough one ...

SARAH: That's your half of the story, Daddy! ... No, you had to know what happened after ...

FATHER: ... So I says to her, I've given you board and bed, lady ... more'n many men I know give their women ... I've been good to you, lady ... So if you want you go, but once you go, don't ever come back again ... you hear? ... I says to her ...

SARAH: My God, Daddy ... but we lived in many houses after that ... many different towns ...

FATHER: ... And then she left, just like that ...

SARAH: ... Nothing is that simple, Daddy ...

FATHER: ... Packed up an' left me an' the kid ...

SARAH: ... But you did love *me*, even as you died?

FATHER twists his hands with anguish of another time, another memory.

Light on him begins to die.

FATHER: I wanted a son! What use is a girl to me? I've got machinery an' land for a boy an' me! You feed a girl ... dress her ... teach her things ... for what? For some other man who had a son, that's what for!

He laughs bitterly, but quickly bites back his laughter.

My life was no bed of roses ... (*reaches out to touch somebody who is invisible*) But it wasn't all your fault, lady ... Jesus, Lord, I'd never say that ... not even after you done what you done to me ...

Hurt he cannot touch the person he seeks, FATHER moves heavily away, the light dying out on him.

(*on exit*) Men with arms reaching down to their ankles will do all the work after this ...

SARAH'S anger evaporates into sorrow as she faces departing image of her father.

SARAH: Animal! ... Stupid, bad, lovely animal. How long I've worshipped your ignorance ... caressed your echoing curses like a scarf of silk ... Inhaled the vinegar scent of chairs where you sat silently, waiting for the night to put an end to your anxieties ... You to whom Beethoven might have been a river's name ... who never felt the spice warmth of tropic winds ... who showed more tenderness to farm dogs than to us ... Blind in one eye, deaf in one ear ... more at home in pigsties than in libraries ... What power you had over a mother and her daughter! ... What power you still have! You are as corrosive as rust, even in death! You are as eternal as sorrow in your smallness ... goddamn you for that!

MAN is laughing now. SARAH turns on him, her face a cold, smiling mask.

SARAH: What the hell's so funny?

MAN touches her gently.

MAN: If I had known you when you were three, I might have taken you when they left you by yourself ...

SARAH: You've come too late ... that was long ago ... I remember nothing now.

MAN: No—you recall his touch ... the sour odor of his breath!

MAN now brings his face close to SARAH'S.

Music up softly—"Lady in Blue."

SARAH stiffens, turns on him. MAN begins dancing away from her.

SARAH: Stop it! ... What in hell are you anyway— a gigolo? ... Or some teacher in a dance salon?

MAN continues dancing, erotically, provocatively.

MAN: Sarah, my darling ... I model men's wear in a fashionable discotheque!

SARAH: I'll bet you do!

MAN: ... Sometimes I beach-comb for young boys ... at other times I amuse women who have given up hope!

He bows mockingly to her, then becomes business-like.

Music continues in background.

What is your favourite food? ... And where do you buy your shoes, Sarah?

SARAH advances towards him, her gestures expansive, dominant.

SARAH: You have come to the wrong address—I am not at home!

MAN: (*writing*) And what is your favourite food, then?

SARAH: I once wanted to be a call-girl, doctor ... not just a common street walker, but the most outrageous whore in town!

MAN: With good shoes? Why?

SARAH: To get even ... to free myself.

MAN: Why?

SARAH: To prove to my mother I was alive ... to learn how to conquer the worst things in myself. Isn't that what our superman, Jesus Christ did?

MAN: He wasn't a whore, Sarah.

SARAH: He wasn't a woman, either ...

The MAN is amused, thoughtful now.

MAN: But you couldn't do it!

SARAH stands tall over him, her face setting hard.

SARAH: Listen, you nameless little wonder who milks me of my brain and juices ... if I had the will to match the strength I sometimes feel, I could move a mountain!

Sound of LEE humming "Lady in Blue" offstage.

Light up quickly on CHARLIE, his hands outstretched to SARAH.

CHARLIE is well-dressed but somehow incomplete as a man.

CHARLIE: I've parked your car ... and swept the steps clean of snow, Sarah!

She turns to him, beckons him urgently to her. He approaches and goes down on his knees before her, kisses her hand, then her thigh, and then her stomach.

SARAH: (*coarsely*) Charlie! ...

CHARLIE: Tomorrow morning, I will cut your hair and shape it ...

SARAH: ... You could never argue—never look me in the eye when you were sad ... You left too soon, you know.

CHARLIE: When I spoke to the meeting ... they applauded me ... longer than the chairman of the board ...

SARAH: Another year, and I might have taught you how to kill ... then everything you wanted would be yours!

She lovingly reaches down to caress his hair.

I've wept for you ... for what you might have been. You could've been a general ... or a statesman ... or a technologist, with power over rivers, forests, migratory birds ... people ... the grids of energy and politics that mesh water, land and sky! But I did not excite that in you. All I did ... (*smiles sadly*) ... was introduce you to domestic wines and made you change the colour of the scarves you wore ... Blue was such an unbecoming colour for your eyes!

She pushes CHARLIE away brusquely. He spins away from her into gloom.

The sound of LEE'S humming changes into sharper key.

Light up on MICHAEL in another area of stage. MICHAEL is neat, gentle, but shy and predictable.

SARAH rushes into MICHAEL'S arms.

MICHAEL: (*concerned*) Sarah, darling ... you should dress more warmly for the night! It's raining now, and a wind is starting from the north ...

SARAH: Michael ... Michael ... If I had said to you ... if I had said to you I lied ... that I wasn't SARAH YOUNG ... that I didn't have a name ...

MICHAEL: Nonsense. Let me get you a drink.

SARAH: ... You would have had to make one up for me ... you, Michael Tomaschuk ... and I ... a nameless whore from ... from Saskatoon!

MICHAEL is embarrassed by her.

MICHAEL: Shh!

SARAH laughs bawdily, ruffles his hair, then baring her teeth, moves on him as if to bite his cheek. He recoils from her, his composure upset.

MICHAEL: Not now, darling ... I have a headache ... I had problems on the job today ...

SARAH: (*expansively*) When you're righteous, you're so beautiful it hurts me to think of you ... Long after my divorce, for twelve hundred and forty nights ... I gave to you, on a proper schedule ... twice a week and once on Sunday morning ... the incomplete body of an Anglo-Saxon girl half my age. You never complained, Michael ...

He is discomfited, angry now.

MICHAEL: I will get cross with you if you don't stop! May I get a drink for you?

SARAH: No ... your reproach was in your voice, when you called me "darling" once too often as we walked hand in dry hand ... I knew your feelings, Michael ... and they iced me with regret ... I could've ruined you for the civil service ... I

should have ruined you ... by giving you the dark, hot things you craved ...

MICHAEL: No, Sarah! Not again! ... These walls are paper-thin ... there might be people listen ...

SARAH laughs bawdily.

SARAH: ... Eh ... grunts of pain and lust in the bathtub ... Fellatio, sweet as ancient music of the church, over midnight cocoa in the kitchen ... Red denyings and black, thick-lipped givings in mangers of deserted barns which line the freeways of our madness!

In anger, MICHAEL leaps for her, trying to stifle her words. Unable to do so, he grabs her around the throat with his hands. With cold precision, SARAH strikes him a judo-chop to the side of the head. MICHAEL is thrown violently away from her by the blow. SARAH comes after him, preparing to attack him with her feet. He scrambles away in a panic, sliding deeper to disappear in the shadows.

She is breathless now with anger and excitement.

SARAH: ... I betrayed you ... I'm sorry as hell I deprived you of the forbidden, soft things that attracted me to you in the beginning ... Three years later, you left me for another woman ... Woman? A pale, thin, flat-chested, arthritic accident of life ... your last self-condemnation. For I had frustrated you with walls of grey daffodils in season, and a petulantly wired womb you could not breach for your cruel chivalry and fear ... Michael! ... Had you been a conqueror but once, I would have proudly led you, naked through the streets of your ancestral Tartar village for the men to cheer and deck that thing of yours with horsehair lace and lilies of the river. But I am Sarah Young, choked with fear and madness ... and you are Michael Joseph Tomaschuk ... anglicized beyond redemption ... rehabilitated nigger of the north!

LEE'S humming dies out.

MAN claps his hands in slow rhythm. SARAH comes sharply out of her reverie and blinks at the MAN.

MAN: Bravo! Excellent! ... The heated mare is now in gallop!

SARAH: Don't make that noise! It bothers me!

MAN continues clapping, smiles provocatively at her.

MAN: Yip yip and away ... Over hill, over dale ... running hard in search of tail!

SARAH glares at him, tosses her head back defiantly. Her voice turns hard.

SARAH: I never told you this, but I took a course in unarmed combat once ... I was very good—the best in class.

MAN: So? ...

SARAH: I could kill you—quickly. You'd hardly feel the pain ...

MAN stops clapping now. Eyes her curiously.

MAN: No, you couldn't!

SARAH: Your most vital organ can be reached by hand, or knee ... (*she moves into karate stance*) Try me—I'm ready for you!

MAN: (*laughs*) No ... My defence is helplessness ... attack me if you can—I wouldn't raise a hand to stop you!

For a moment, SARAH teeters between advance and retreat. Then she moves towards him, dangerously, but with confidence, for she has him trapped. He has nowhere to go.

Faint spots isolate the face of MOTHER, JUDY and EMMA, who sway in unison to SARAH'S advance on the MAN, as a chorus line of death.

SARAH: That alone would make it fascinating! ... I would push your body out this window ... three floors to the lane below. When they found you, who could say for certain what had killed you—the fall? A blow? ... An accident with a car?

The MAN is retreating. His smile has frozen into a desperate grin. He whimpers as he retreats.

MAN: Sit down, Sarah! ... Sit down, please!

SARAH'S movements now become cat-like, moving in for the final lunge. He is now cornered in a narrow space.

SARAH: Nobody would see at this time of night, and in the morning ... the police might come from apartment to apartment in the building ... and I would honestly say, no, I didn't know you ... I don't think I had ever seen you before!

MAN: (*very alarmed now*) But that's not true! ... You ...

SARAH: Whatever I believe must be true ... You told me that yourself, doctor ... Have you forgotten?

MAN: I am not a doctor, then! ... Stay away from me!

SARAH smiles knowingly. The isolated women in faint lights in background also smile knowingly at each other.

SARAH: Only doctors and the caretaker come here now ... And you are not the caretaker. His name is Willie, and he tells me of his grandchildren ...

MAN: I am Willie's grandchild! ... The one who barks and chases cars when he is frightened!

The MAN snarls at her, dog-like, and barks sharply.

The lights on MOTHER, EMMA and JUDY die abruptly.

SARAH'S concentration is broken. She stops, becomes wooden. The MAN advances smartly to her and steering her to a bedside chair, seats her down. She shakes her head, confused.

MAN: (*crisply*) We'll have no more of that ... not ever again, Sarah! (*takes out notebook*) Tell me ... were there ... other men besides Michael and Charlie?

SARAH: Huh?

MAN: Were there other men?

SARAH: (*thoughtfully*) Yes ... there were others ... many others ...

MAN: Were they short? Dark? Pale? ... Tall?

SARAH: ... A blind girl once told me ... there is no shape or colour to people, only spirit and voice ...

MAN: If she was blind, what the hell else could she say?

SARAH: She was right! If Michael or Charlie, Dan or Jake ... were to call me on the telephone, I would only know them by their voices. I would know if they were sad or happy ... concerned ... anxious or afraid ... But I wouldn't know if they had a skin disease of the face or body ... or if they had been maimed or lost an arm or leg in an accident a year ago ... unless I asked them!

She smiles. "The Willow Branches" rises in background.

I never ask a man who phones me if his shirt is opened ... or what he is doing with his left hand while he talks to me! ... Yes there were other men.

Light on LEE in separate area of stage.

He is laughing softly, indulgently—the laugh of a total man. SARAH does not turn to him, but she senses him. Her expression turns to one of joy, surprise, uncertainty. The MAN looks at her, sees the changes in her mood.

MAN: What is it now, Sarah?

SARAH: Another man I once knew ...

MAN: Can you hear him? What is he saying to you?

SARAH: Nothing ... I did what he wanted me to do ... Because ... I loved him ... I was afraid of him ...

MAN: *(gently)* What is he saying then?

SARAH: Nothing ... He only laughs ... the way he always laughed ... the way a summer wind laughs through the trees!

MAN: *(with irritation)* You're withdrawing Sarah! You're dishonest now ... What is he saying?

SARAH listens with open-mouthed wonder. Shakes her head.

SARAH: No, Lee ... that was years ago ... three years ago now. I was somebody then ... now I'm nobody. *(pitifully)* I don't know what day of the week this is, or what month. I can't remember where I parked my car, Lee ... or what the sun was like. This morning, I forgot which classroom I was teaching in ... or who my students were ...

MAN: Yet you woke on time ... had breakfast ...

SARAH: Yes ...

MAN: What breakfast?

SARAH: I don't know. Your words hurt my ears ...

MAN: What did you have for breakfast, Sarah?

LEE laughs louder.

Music rises.

SARAH strains to remember.

SARAH: One orange ... a slice of whole-wheat toast ... black coffee ...

MAN: Why do you eat so little? ... You're a growing girl, Sarah! If you eat so little you will grow up thin and pale ... Do you want to grow up thin and pale?

SARAH turns away from him, her mind working to lock itself into a fixed time in her life—to hold her dream of LEE.

Light on LEE, standing directly in front of her, his manner expansive, his face a broad smile.

LEE: Sarah-lolly ... lolly-Sarah ... your mother made a mess of you!

SARAH looks defensively from LEE to MAN.

SARAH: No, No! ... That's not true! ... I'm trying to keep my weight down ... my mother said to stay at one hundred and thirty pounds ... that was *her* best weight!

LEE: Sarah-lolly ... I'll build a house for you of bricks and feathers!

SARAH is confused. LEE laughs boisterously.

LEE: I'll roof your house with Mamas' tears and chocolate syrup!

SARAH: *(pleading)* Lee!

LEE: She wove your hair in braids ... had your feet in high-heeled shoes at twelve ... a girdle and some lipstick were the final touch—do you remember why?

MOTHER appears in separate light on another elevation of stage. She is a frail, severe woman, somehow reminiscent of a part of SARAH'S character.

MOTHER: Sarah was an average girl ... It was right, don't you think, that she should resemble other girls her age?

LEE: Was it such a problem at the age of twelve?

MAN: *(strongly)* Yes!

LEE: No!

MOTHER: Yes! She had no father, don't you see?

Music—"The Willow Branches" softly up in background as hum or instrumental.

LEE: *(with strong feeling)* No woman has the right to raise a daughter—men should raise their daughters, like themselves, or they shall grope like helpless creatures in a night of madness! Do you understand me, Sarah?

SARAH: (*nodding*) Yes, Lee …

LEE: (*roughly*) What use are daughters to us, unless they gleam like Israeli sabrahs … competent with guns, pickaxes or a baby's tantrums! … Strong men must raise strong daughters, who must learn to fight before they vote! Only then will they be loved—do you understand me Sarah?

SARAH: Yes …

MOTHER: Your father was a brutish man in anger, Sarah … A loud woman, like a loud man, is obscene somehow …

SARAH: I know. I'm afraid of noises, mama …

LEE: Sarah-lolly … be afraid of silence, too …

MOTHER: Let them talk … you never have to listen, child. A true woman wins more with dignity and poise than with arguments. When I dressed well and combed my hair into a tidy bun like this, the postman never knew how poor we were …

SARAH: But the grocer and the landlord knew … (*shakes her head sadly*) I'm sorry, Mama …

MAN begins to pace irritably.

MAN: Enough! All I hear are riddles from you now … cute riddles, nice riddles … stupid riddles! I have no time for games like these!

SARAH: (*stares at him, confused*) Will somebody tell me where I am? Where I've come to? How many years I've lived? Who among my friends is real and who is not?

MOTHER: You are an average girl from an average home doing an average job of work … that is all that is important in the end. So why do you phone me in the dead of night?

LEE: You are below average, helpless and deprived …

Music dies out.

SARAH rubs her hands across her face, and suddenly laughs as she turns to the MAN. The laughter is that of a shaken, disarmed person.

SARAH: God … my head is going this way and that … I don't know what to think!

The MAN shrugs and sits on the bed. He rummages in the headboard of the bed, takes out a compact and hand mirror. Begins to apply makeup. His actions become feminine.

MAN: Think of roller skates and dandruff …

SARAH: What?

MAN: I've missed my last bus and I'm not walking back at night. Drive me home!

SARAH: (*disconcerted by his actions*) I … don't know where my car is parked … or how I'll find my way outside tomorrow …

MAN completes touching lipstick to his lips. Rises and begins pacing nervously.

MAN: If I had roller skates or a bicycle, I could still make it!

SARAH: There's a sleeping bag in the closet … you can sleep in the living room.

MAN: On the floor?

SARAH: Yes.

MAN: I can't sleep on the floor. I get a headache when I sleep on a hard floor …

MOTHER: For your own protection, never let a stranger spend a night in your apartment. You work hard for your shelter … they can do the same!

SARAH: (*uncertainly*) But he … *she* … isn't a …

LEE: Milkcow! Where I come from, a woman had less value than a milkcow! Are you a milkcow, lolly-Sarah?

Music up—a hum or oboe sound.

SARAH: Don't hurt me, Lee … I trust you!

LEE springs away from her to another elevation.

A new light, full of fire and shadow, plays on him.

LEE: I was born … on the outskirts of a smoky city … in a country you will never know! (*smiles spitefully*) Don't talk to me … of charge accounts and hobble-knobbled clerks with perfumed underarms … I came to life on glaciers and rivers mightier than men! When fire was as fearful as the threat of hunger … when war was still a hand to hand encounter, and heaven help the man who hesitates!

MAN: Nonsense!

LEE: ... When defective babies could be left to freeze in snow, and the doctor and the parson would neither bless nor blame the mother ... when the aged worked to the last days of their lives, then died with great pain and dignity. A woman wailed once and beat her head against my step-father's garden gate with the pangs of menopause, while in the garden my mother poured tea for two visiting neighbours ... and they talked of Copenhagen cabbage and the curse of drink among the poor ... (*laughs loudly*) Hey—that was thirty-two years and seven months ago my Sarah with the faint mascara!

SARAH: (*roused*) Let me near you, Lee! For God's sake, I need you near me! I'll be good to you ... I'll never interrupt or criticize you! I'll work and see there is always money and a place for us to live!

MAN: Easy now, Sarah ...

MOTHER: (*gently, almost cooing*) Ooh ... you worry too much, child—you've always worried. Never give more than you take ... life is a bargain a wise woman makes with God. Nothing less, and nothing more than that.

Music becomes jagged and electronic.

SARAH: Why, Mama?

MOTHER: To keep the race alive for better times.

SARAH: But I live now—I can't wait for better times, or I'll die! Lee—tell her!

LEE: I never knew your mother, Sarah. No man ever knew your mother ...

MAN: (*bitchy now*) I can't find my way home in the dark, I tell you!

MOTHER: Living with a man ... any man ... is a sacrifice of soul for a woman. I know ...

SARAH: Oh, no ... what are you saying?

LEE: (*laughing*) I have nothing to say ... I'm a black-hatted cowboy trading milkcows in a muskeg village!

SARAH: (*begging*) Lee, it hurts to hear you say that!

MAN: Nobody hurts you the way you're hurting me!

SARAH: Lee ...

MAN: What would you do if I was to cry? Do you want to see me cry?

SARAH turns sharply on him.

SARAH: Get out of here!

The MAN grins harshly.

MAN: You can't make me go—you'd die if I went!

Music fades down.

SARAH is visibly shaken. Draws her gown closely around her.

SARAH: (*more calmly to MAN*) You've no right doing this. You took advantage of me.

LEE: My mother took advantage of me. She brought me in her womb from Europe to escape the wars ...

MAN responds to the fantasy of LEE by countering him. He deepens the femininity of his character to an exaggeration.

MAN: My father paid two men to drive me around, Sarah ... entertain me ... feed me ...

MOTHER: Men are only older boys, my child ... they boast, strut, spit on us after they have had their way!

LEE: ... She was a whore for German troops in Bratislava ... somewhere in that fascist horde that rode her like a sweaty mare each night ... I had a father ... the Slovak Mary Magdalene, and I, the conquering seed inside her ... never knew his name ...

SARAH gropes to move away from LEE and MAN, both of whom are laughing now.

MAN: ... When I told my mother ... how I was, she ... made an appointment with a doctor for me. What could the doctor do? Give me a pre-scription for my problem?

LEE: It is all a lie! Your tidy bedroom is a tomb!

MAN: My father took a different tack. He hired two men ... one a former prize fighter, the other a retired lumberjack ... they were supposed to change me ... at higher wages than they'd earned as pugilist or logger ...

LEE: Lolly-Sarah, with your bone-china girlhood and the scent of talcum in your secret woman places ... the world is a filthy place for sons of whores and cripples!

SARAH: I try to understand, Lee ...

LEE snarls and dismisses her with a gesture that hurts her.

MAN: ... They drove me from the house through town, into the hills, the two of them in front, and me in back like a senator ...

LEE: The midnight hour of the soul is nothing to the twilight of an entire life, Sarah!

SARAH: Tell me—I've asked you many times ... what am I to do?

MAN: Do? Why in the hills we'd leave the car and walk. When we were hidden from the road, they'd both turn to me, hold out their hands, and say—"Louie, give us twenty dollars for showing us your cock." I did ... (*giggles obscenely*)

LEE: I want you to die, Sarah! Everything you know is wasted on you!

LEE spits and turns away.

Light dies out instantly on him and MOTHER.

Music ends.

SARAH: (*after him*) I'm sorry ...

MAN: Why?

SARAH is startled, turns to MAN, speaking quietly, thoughtfully now.

SARAH: Because somebody has to be ... I'm sorry for not knowing more ... I'm sorry people hurt ... that some are more fortunate than others ... that I am a woman and you are not ... that you try in your own ways to understand and help me ... and that I cannot help you in return. I could never tell my mother ... that I wished she'd leave ...

MAN: (*happily*) The same with my mother. I wish the two of them would go together and run a charity for dwarfs with eczema!

They both laugh, happily, playfully. The MAN stops laughing first, withdraws his notebook and opens it.

Have you any food in the house?

SARAH: I ... I can't remember. I've been here a long time now. Everything I bought is now paid for ... this summer I'll go someplace for holidays.

MAN: Have you decided where you'll go?

SARAH: Go? (*confused*) Why do I have to go?

MAN goes towards her.

You stay away from me! I'm warning you!

She forms her hands into claws, prepares to attack if he approaches nearer. MAN stops and frowns.

MAN: What the hell's the matter with you?

SARAH peers at him suspiciously, then relaxes.

SARAH: Then you're not ... Oh, God ... I'm sorry.

MAN: My time is very expensive, and I cannot tolerate any more nonsense! You will remain seated when asked to sit ... and you will be on time for appointments—is that understood?

SARAH is disbelieving now. Points to him as she advances on him.

SARAH: I know you! You're Louie Webster—the man who services equipment in the school board offices each month!

MAN: I did—five years ago.

SARAH: Oh, no—you were in the school offices this morning ... I saw you!

MAN: I was golfing until noon ... and then I had a conference over lunch ...

SARAH: I saw you this morning in the school board office!

MAN: This morning I was tracing comets over Neptune on a sheet of Kleenex in my car ...

SARAH draws a deep breath and settles on her bed, watching the MAN darkly.

SARAH: Go away ... I'm tired ...

The MAN puts his notebook away and begins to flit about her, using her bed and the area around it for a display of calisthenics.

MAN: And I am an entertainer ... some call me a sexual magician!

SARAH: Go away, you bastard! No, you're not Louie Webster ... you're my doctor ... ripping off my medical insurance for a hundred dollars a month!

MAN: A menstrual cycle of accountancy! I'm the lamplighter of the moon!

SARAH: What have you done for me with all that money?

MAN: Alarmed the wild geese by buying feathers for the wind!

SARAH: ... You've tranquilized me, hurt me ... taken my memory ... convinced me all the bad things were good ... and all good feelings which I knew and trusted were corruptions! (*shouts helplessly*) I hate you!

MAN: I am an architect of forests ... a ploughman of the cosmos!

SARAH: You're a witch-doctor ... a personality-changer! I would be criminally charged for doing to myself the things you've done to me!

Music up—a thin electronic shriek.

MAN: Nobody will defend you now, Sarah! You're alone now and dead ... stinking, rotten dead!

SARAH half rises in an attempt to expel him, then wearily slouches back into bed and draws the collar of her gown over the lower portion of her face.

MAN: I knew a man once ... who gave up in the hills with two animals sent to protect him. You are like him now, Sarah—with nobody except your memories—four walls of a room and a night that may never end ...

The MAN settles into a chair, gazes at her for a long moment.

You went to work yesterday and then you had dinner. Try and remember what you ate, Sarah.

SARAH: No ... I ... I don't remember.

MAN: It's important to remember now ... think ... concentrate.

SARAH: (*haltingly*) At work ... I had to make out a report on absenteeism from classes during April. I checked the names of students in my files. There were names of boys and names of girls ... nothing else made sense.

MAN: And you began to fantasize?

SARAH: (*nervously*) No, no ... not this time!

MAN: Yes ... this time as at other times. You drew connecting lines from names of boys to names of girls, fancying yourself a mating goddess! You obscene, filthy-minded bitch!

SARAH: Not this time, I tell you! It only happened once ... and never since that time.

MAN: How can I be sure? You've learned to lie ... You lie about the places that you visit ... who you saw ... what you ate ... what you do!

SARAH: (*a moan*) No!

MAN: Yes, you do!

SARAH: (*rising to her feet*) I don't lie! I did everything you told me, doctor. I don't argue with the school administration anymore ... I've left the peace movement ... You were right—if a woman cannot fight, she has no right to interfere with those who struggle for survival. I don't touch or fondle myself, even when I am dark with desire for all that belongs to a man ... as you told me once ...

MAN touches her briefly, gently, on the shoulder, then turns away from her.

MAN: Good. You are responding well to treatment now, Sarah. I am pleased.

SARAH: (*hopefully*) I will be looked after then? Everything I've lost will be returned to me now?

MAN: No, no. Be careful ... you try to move too quickly.

SARAH: But you said ... I heard you say ...

MAN: I said nothing. I am only the sound of your voice, dear lady. I am more than that—I am a sponge ... a confessor ... a reflector of your fears ... an amplifier of your pain! If you could forgive yourself for murder, there would be no need for me. But if you fear a butterfly, call me for an appointment, and we shall turn your dreams over this way and that ...

He laughs. SARAH stares helplessly at him.

SARAH: I'm afraid of moths ... broken glass on hot pavement ... men who shout for no reason ... the edges of high buildings ... a man called Lee ...

MAN takes her arm and seats her in the chair.

MAN: Let us begin with Lee again ... tell me what it is about him that disturbs you so.

Electronic music up on old English nursery song. Sound of LEE'S laughter, followed by the sound of him singing loudly offstage.

LEE: Hushabye my bunting
Your daddy's gone a-hunting
He'll bring back a cougar skin
To wrap your little mommy in

SARAH: There is nothing more to tell.

MAN: You are not helping me. You are not helping yourself, Sarah!

LEE laughs, then into song.

LEE: Hushabye my bunting
Your daddy's gone a-hunting
He'll bring back a baby skin
To wrap your rings and necklace in

SARAH: (*rising, peering around for invisible LEE*) Lee ... don't ... stop!

LEE appears in isolated area of stage in hard light. He is dishevelled and unruly.

LEE: Celebrate with me, Sarah! I am free! This afternoon I left the law firm, and I'm free!

SARAH: (*with surprise*) You resigned?

LEE weighs her words a moment, then laughs ironically.

LEE: I severed connections, as they say in better circles! A good pull disconnected my telephone ... which I fired across the office. My two senior partners were behind the door when it came through the frosted glass panel to meet them in their gray deliberations ...

SARAH: Did you hurt anyone?

LEE: Who cares? Men like that don't bleed ...

MAN: (*impatiently*) What did he do?

LEE: Four filing cabinets of transcripts and litigations went out the window next ... There was a good wind from the south, Sarah! My legal work is now spread across the main streets of the city ... But I'm free!

SARAH: What ... are you going to do?

LEE: Do?

SARAH: Yes ... now that you've ruined your career with your impetuous behaviour, what are you going to do?

LEE becomes sober. He chews on the knuckles of his hand.

Music becomes sustained note.

LEE: I need your help, Sarah-lolly. This shirt chaffs my skin like armour plate ... I've taken breath in tiny gasps for seven years now ... If you believe me ... if you love me ... then do what I have done and leave with me!

SARAH: I ... don't understand.

LEE: Destroy and run! Burn your house down. Run your car against a power pole ... break the icy claws reaching through your eyes into your heart!

SARAH shudders.

SARAH: I can't ... I ... have security ... my apartment ... books, records, clothes ... payments to make on my car and pension plan!

LEE: (*with rising despair*) There is no security! For every acquisition, there's a receiver in the shadows ... lurking, waiting ... preparing for an error ... a weakness of resolve. I will take my chances in the trees with the wild animals! I can and have killed with my hands ... I once strangled a dog that attacked me. As he died, the froth and blood drooling on his fangs, I inherited his wisdom through the wounds he tore into my legs and chest. Even though I'd killed him, I stepped on his back and took him by the nose and teeth, snapping his neck! And as I did, I was able to shout in a voice that was strange to me ... that frightened me ... for it was clear and loud, stronger than any legal argument I made ... braver than the bellow of an angry moose ... echoing down the dark streets ... striking walls and windows like a hammer on white steel!

They stare at each other. LEE is breathing noisily. SARAH moves a step towards him.

The music dies out.

(*quietly*) Well, Sarah?

SARAH: You're a man ... not an animal hunting other animals for food and safety! I couldn't follow you ... even if I wished to do so ...

LEE: Why not?

SARAH: I couldn't!

LEE: (*loudly*) Why not? What is your love to me otherwise?

SARAH: I provide a service ... teaching children ... a car and home are built for me ... clothes are woven, dishes made, my health and the shape of my hair are serviced in return ... food is processed ... roads are kept in order for me ...

LEE: I don't want it! How can you want it then?

SARAH: Lee, darling ... I've never seen a radish grow ... I've never learned to walk in underbrush or dig a well for water.

LEE: You'll be a slave until you learn!

SARAH: I don't want to learn ... I love you, but I am what I am ... all my life I've searched for independence on my terms ... I've wanted to erase the memory of my parents, my childhood, all the memories of being second-rate. Then came the men ... and they assured me through their smallness ... Without being a mother, I could mother men. Except for you, who muddied it ... bringing strange shadows in the middle of a day ... buildings bending in the wind ... distraught cries ... the sound of thunder in my ears ...

MAN: Is this Lee, or yet another man?

SARAH turns to the MAN.

SARAH: I loved him for his laughter ... the taper of his electric fingers... the way his hair taunted stormy weather ... the sureness of his footsteps ... the red rage and blue serenity of his nature. I loved him for the animal he evoked in me ... the passions which he fevered in me ... he made me laugh and cry in a voice that was not my own. He taught me obscenities and poetry until I could not distinguish them apart.

LEE and MAN both turn away from her, in opposite directions.

(*more excited*) I loved him for his insolence and kindness ... for the storms that flashed within his eyes ... for the way his spirit draped my bedside lamp. But as he taught me things about myself I had not known, he threatened me with howling darkness. Demanding gestures which I could not bring myself to ...

Electronic music up.

LEE: (*sharply*) Sarah, come here!

SARAH moves to him obediently, but with an argument that is like a plea.

SARAH: What began with the innocence of rain was not a bargain for my womanhood, Lee!

LEE: I will hurt you if you argue ... you know that.

SARAH moves backwards towards LEE, but now speaks to the MAN.

SARAH: I had to learn to argue ... to shout ... to fight. What could I do? He always won. He knew he'd win ...

LEE: (*shouting*) Sarah!

SARAH: What he wanted ... was some primeval slave with spirit!

LEE: Come here, goddamn you!

SARAH turns to LEE and stares defiantly at him.

MAN: (*quietly*) ... No Sarah ...

LEE: Hear me, bitch! You are not to complain to other women or that fancy faggot of a doctor again! Is that understood?

Music rises to a crescendo.

SARAH moves into LEE'S light area. She continues staring up at him, her face grimacing with pain. She suddenly spits at him. In a rapid reflex, he hits her across the face (in mime). Still in mime, she falls. As she is falling, he lashes out with a kick at her body that twists her into a grotesque shape on her fall.

LEE leaves.

Music to crescendo.

Blackout

ACT 2

Setting: as in Act 1.

Music up. "Lady in Blue" sung by LEE offstage to oboe accompaniment.

Backlight on set over song, becoming light on MAN lying on SARAH'S bed, examining his notes. SARAH stands off to one side of room, brooding over her memories.

Light slowly washes over other areas of stage to illuminate a party—with EMMA, MAY and JUDY. EMMA and MAY are older women. JUDY is younger than SARAH.

Off to one side of the women are two men— MICHAEL and the SCHOOL BOARD CHAIRMAN. But MICHAEL is not the MICHAEL of Act 1; he is only reminiscent of the earlier character. He is the PRINCIPAL of SARAH'S school.

The scene is played as a jagged, surrealistic dream.

LEE: Lady in blue
In a garden of rain
Seen her last week
And this morning again
First time she
Watched a child at play
This morning I saw
Her smiling my way

Marigold stars
In her tulip rain
Weeping willow
Bends in the wind
Lovin' sun over ten thousand mountains
Will not promise
I'll see her tomorrow

The people at the party mime discussion, laughter. At the end of the song they come into full voice.

The CHAIRMAN laughs raucously and pats the shoulder of the PRINCIPAL.

CHAIRMAN: Come on now, Mike ... You know what I think? You know what I really think? I think the system's full of crap! But you tell anyone the chairman of the school board said that, and I'll deny it! I've been in business too long to get trapped by you intellectuals!

He laughs again at his cunning. PRINCIPAL nods in polite, noncommittal agreement.

PRINCIPAL: You are a shrewd fellow, Mister Baldwin ...

PRINCIPAL moves slowly towards the women. CHAIRMAN follows him, glass in hand.

CHAIRMAN: Life is a lollipop for you people now, and you know why?

The women's conversation is now interrupted. They turn to him. SARAH slowly moves out of bedroom into scene.

MAY: That wouldn't be a biased judgment, would it, Mister Baldwin?

She smiles sweetly at him.

CHAIRMAN: Biased judgment, hell! I want students turned out capable of *doing* things ... not shaggy rebels who want the world, but can't give anything in return! As principal of the school don't you agree?

PRINCIPAL: If you examine the question carefully ...

EMMA: I'm not a teacher, so may I have another drink just to stay out of this one?

SARAH hands her a drink she had picked up for herself.

CHAIRMAN: But you're part of the *system*, lady, whether you answer the phone or teach—so what's the difference between you say ... and Miss Young?

EMMA: (*coldly*) Something like six thousand a year in take-home pay!

CHAIRMAN: Aww come on ... you women are getting as bitchy as the students who're crowding the bars instead of getting their hands into jobs!

MAY: I think what Emma is trying to say is ...

SARAH: Can Emma not speak for herself?

CHAIRMAN glares at SARAH. PRINCIPAL quickly steps towards SARAH, isolating her from the other man.

PRINCIPAL: So good of you to come, Miss Young! May mentioned you had been ill last week ...

Another fantasy of the PRINCIPAL affects SARAH. She does not wish to upset the man.

SARAH: Yes ... Everything could be better than it is, I guess ...

CHAIRMAN: I'll drink to that!

EMMA: (*icily*) You'd drink to a seven-titted cow, if it's someone else's booze, wouldn't you, Mister Baldwin?

JUDY giggles. The atmosphere stiffens.

JUDY: I'm sorry ... this is getting ... so irrational! Can we put a record on? I'd like to dance ...

CHAIRMAN: (*to EMMA*) What did you mean by that?

PRINCIPAL: She means we're all tired and on edge with the Easter workload.

MAY: Yes—we are now averaging twenty-eight students per teacher ...

CHAIRMAN: I think you ladies are adequately paid for the work you do, thank you! It took me a long time to earn the kind of money you're making as ... as civil servants!

JUDY: (*giddily*) Our principal is not a lady, Mister Baldwin!

CHAIRMAN: And damned lucky for the system that he's not ... I don't know what sort of tomfoolery we'd be into if gals like you actually started to *run* the system!

MAY: I really think this is getting out of hand ... don't you agree, Sarah?

SARAH: (*troubled*) What?

JUDY: Where are the rights of women in all this?

EMMA: (*laughing*) The rights of women? Don't be a child, for Christsake! He's only starting ... he hasn't yet gotten to the two-month per summer holiday bit ... the screwing of the taxpayer on increasing wages ... the morals of the single girl who owns her own car and doesn't go to church!

MAY: Some of us are involved in church and community affairs, Emma.

CHAIRMAN: How many, eh? How many of you in this room are?

MAY: I am ... but I didn't think that was important ...

PRINCIPAL: Ladies, I don't think we have cause to attack Mister Baldwin ... it was good of him to take the time to join us for a drink!

EMMA: He's drinking booze I helped to pay for! It wasn't important once, but it is now ... You see, I have nowhere to go ... I'm strapped down with two kids and a low-paying job. I'm a woman like Sarah, Judy ... you, May. I spend my evenings patching clothes for my children ... we use powdered milk ... I'm a woman, but I earn twenty dollars a month less than I need to live on ... I'll never earn enough and my children are my responsibility ... would it surprise you ... not you, Mister Baldwin ... but the rest of you ... that I almost agree with this pompous windbag who got elected through some democratic error to supervise you ...

SARAH: You agree to what? I don't understand, Emma ...

EMMA: (*savagely*) That I hate women, because I *suffer* being born a woman!

CHAIRMAN: Where in hell's your man, then?

EMMA: He left me.

CHAIRMAN: No goddamned wonder!

JUDY: That's terrible ... you should sue for alimony.

EMMA: I did ... two years ago. The court granted me support ... I found this job, and I was laughing. A week later, he *quit* his job and left the province. Goodbye alimony!

SARAH: Would you laugh at me ... if I was to say ...

PRINCIPAL: I think enough has been said already ... (*turns to CHAIRMAN*) I'm sorry for all this. We're under strain ... and nothing was said that wouldn't be withdrawn, I'm sure ...

SARAH: (*protesting*) Michael ... that's not true!

PRINCIPAL turns severely towards her.

PRINCIPAL: It is true, Miss Young! We will discuss this tomorrow, if you wish!

SARAH: He doesn't know ... he doesn't want to know!

PRINCIPAL: What?

SARAH: About loneliness ... the cold things that we do to others, and are done to us ...

They all look at her questioningly.

JUDY: A behavioural instructor told me once … every good party ends with an argument about politics or religion … and as I'm not interested if God lives on inside me, I'll say goodnight.

She leaves abruptly.

EMMA: I'm going, too … (*to SARAH*) I know … the fear is written in your eyes. (*smiles sadly*) As for me … even though you live on the edge of hell now … I would trade places with you anytime of the day or night … that's how bad it really is … to starve in two different ways …

She leaves. CHAIRMAN sighs with relief. SARAH moves towards the MAN.

SARAH: (*now more joyful*) Oh for some flowers! In May the alyssum blooms like music in the Okanagan valley!

SARAH and MAN begin to dance.

MAN: So you end where you began … Let's dance on the graves and shout in the tunnels! Life is a sad and weary joke!

SARAH: No—there is more … I have more to tell you.

SARAH dances away from MAN and into the arms of PRINCIPAL.

Michael! Had I known once what I know now …

CHAIRMAN cuts into dance and she is in his arms.

Father! You *did* love me, even though …

MAY cuts into her dances. SARAH freezes before the smiling MAY.

Mother!

PRINCIPAL: Are you feeling well, Miss Young?

CHAIRMAN: Somebody else?

PRINCIPAL: How could I be somebody else if I'm me?

CHAIRMAN: … Come, come now, Miss Young …

MAY now assumes the role of a TEACHERS' ASSO-CIATION REPRESENTATIVE. Together with the PRINCIPAL and the CHAIRMAN she approaches SARAH who is troubled now.

ASSOCIATION REP: Would you say your class load has been heavy or difficult, my dear?

SARAH: Heavier? More difficult? I'm sorry, but I don't understand …

CHAIRMAN: Hell, it's the strain of living all alone … nothing more than that. My lady was thirty when I married her … A bit of loving was all the medicine she needed …

ASSOCIATION REP: Come now, Mister Baldwin … I hardly see you in the role of high-priced doctor.

The PRINCIPAL laughs politely. CHAIRMAN grunts, aware he sounded more boorish than he intended.

PRINCIPAL: The three of us met earlier this morning, and our feeling is that possibly this term has been a strain on you … so I recommended …

SARAH: A strain? Are you saying my work has not been adequate?

ASSOCIATION REP: Adequate, but slow, my dear. Your Christmas reports are still outstanding …

PRINCIPAL: I had your classes monitored, and you are now two weeks late on study schedules …

CHAIRMAN: Don't worry … we're not here to fire you … yet …

PRINCIPAL: (*quickly covering*) I recommended having Mister Turner take your history classes for the time being. I spoke to Ted already, and he has no objections …

SARAH: But I'm on time with assignments … surely there is some error here!

ASSOCIATION REP: There is no error … I personally examined details of complaint. The board and administration is in the right. But don't worry, dear. We'll try a little harder when we can …

SARAH is trapped by them. They extend their hands for handshakes. Their faces are all smiles and good-will.

CHAIRMAN: It was a pleasure, young lady … always good to come in and see the tax dollars in action. You be good now, you hear!

SARAH: Yes … yes, sir … thank you.

PRINCIPAL: Let me know if you run into further problems. And sometime later this week, I'd like to see your record book on student absenteeism.

SARAH: I'll stay in this evening and prepare it for you.

Both men turn away and disappear into shadows.

ASSOCIATION REP remains a moment longer, smiling.

ASSOCIATION REP: You're not upset, are you, dear?

SARAH: A little ... I've been a good teacher, with an excellent record!

SARAH retreats into her room to sit in chair in conclusion of dream.

ASSOCIATION REP: I don't think there is any grievance here we can legitimately complain about ... I've taught in many schools before I came here, and the friendship and ease I've found here is remarkable. As the years go by, I appreciate that more and more ...

SARAH stares at the other woman and shakes her head in bewilderment. The other woman backs away slowly and vanishes.

SARAH: (*with sudden anger*) Bullshit to you, lady! You've sold me out!

The MAN laughs. Through his laughter, the distant sound of children laughing on a playground. SARAH struggles to find her reality in the growing fantasy of sound and feeling.

Electronic music up. The sound of LEE'S laughter and voice in song offstage.

LEE: First time she
Watched a child at play
This morning I saw
Her smiling my way

Sound of children's laughter dies. Music becomes a sustained note.

LEE appears from shadows. He is aged, tense.

SARAH moves to him, but is held in her own pool of light. She speaks rapidly to him.

SARAH: ... I missed you on Thursday ... waited until three in the morning, Lee. If you knocked softly, I couldn't hear you because I had gone to sleep in the chair with the music on ... And on Sunday again I waited ... it snowed on Sunday afternoon and I worried if you wore a warm jacket ... Lee, your health is such a precious thing ... you must wear heavier coats and rubber boots when it snows like that again ...

MAN: That is nonsense! You're tuning out on me! Have you a watch? What time is it now?

SARAH ignores him. MAN becomes petulant.

SARAH: Lee, darling ... you hurt me when you do that, did you know? I dreamed you had a headache ... and then you paced with pain ... kicking at the walls ... you grabbed a chair and threw it, the chair broke ... When I woke, the chair was lying broken near the door ... it lay where you threw it, Lee ... there was no other explanation!

MAN: I never got the things I wanted, Sarah ... Take me in your lap and rock me. I will sing for you ...

SARAH: The silences on Thursday, Lee, are hell to live with! I want to talk ... be held ... made love to! The hum of apartment machinery is such a lonely substitute for life ...

LEE: On Thursday night, I screwed a black woman, Sarah ...

SARAH is stricken, disbelieving.

She spoke no English ... Her moans were the sighs of warm oceans and fields of tamarisk and oleanders ...

MAN moves quickly towards SARAH. He is alarmed by what he sees in her face.

MAN: Destroy his memory while you can, Sarah! Now!

LEE: On Sunday afternoon, I went to her again ...

MAN: This is the only chance you'll have!

SARAH: (*whimpering*) Lee ... You stop saying things like that! You know what happens when I become afraid!

LEE: (*singing softly to himself*)
Marigold stars
In her tulip rain

MAN: Kill him while you can, or he'll reduce you to a vegetable!

SARAH: I will permit and forgive many things ... you know that, Lee ...

LEE: While I did it, I tried so hard to remember you ...

MAN: Sarah, wake up!

SARAH: If you have to tell me, I'll try to understand ...

LEE: ... But all that came to mind ... were visions of the Queen at Ascot ... Maiden-Form and Kotex ... and the confused imperialism of a thousand clerks confronted by ten laughing, healthy men ... who refused to work or pay attention to forms made out in triplicate ... (*smiles*) But all that was like a passing shadow ... for mounted on me was the heaving, twisting, groaning triumph of a loose-limbed, lesser woman than yourself, planting purple flowers in my brain!

SARAH: You ungrateful bastard! Is there more left for you to vomit at my feet?

LEE lowers his head and sings softly.

LEE: Weeping willow
Bends in the wind
Lovin' sun over ten thousand mountains

MAN: There never was a man called Lee! Admit it!

Music dies out.

SARAH, in towering outrage, claps her hands together. All characters in play begin to emerge from shadows, or are lit in special, isolated places. As SARAH sweeps them with a glance, they freeze.

SARAH: (*with authority*) The class will come to order! This morning, we will begin with a lesson in responsibility. Because contemporary values drift and alter, I have been liberal and tolerant of many things. To shelter you in your enquiries, I have had to lie and distract the administration of the school ... something one does in life as well!

LEE begins to hum softly to himself.

Don't stand facing me! I am not your equal—not in this place! Get down ... *ON YOUR KNEES!*

LEE gets down on his knees first. The others follow.

A pool of light isolates LEE, as the light on the others dim, except for SARAH.

She watches them kneel and smiles triumphantly for a moment.

... I lied and degraded the dignity of my person and profession in an effort to protect you. Soon this took the form of personal sacrifices deeper than I had anticipated or intended ...

MAN: No, Sarah!

SARAH: ... I began to sacrifice my life ... my dreams ... my personal ambitions ... to create responsible social animals out of each of you. My own fulfillment took the form of fantasies. Oh, how many meals I ate in the company of exotic gentlemen from around the world ... How severe and majestic I was with them in games of mysterious indignation ... How lascivious a bitch in sexual heat! It was *I* who arrived last at their parties ... and swept their nights into ashes on my pillow ... It was I who roared through their suburbs in my car at ninety miles an hour, panicking their wives ... scattering devastation in their skulls ... unsettling the foundations of their industry and politics! Although I come to you to classes in trim, sombre-blue cardigan and skirt ... the landscape and the cities tremble at my feet, if you but knew it!

MAN: That is the route of greater danger than you've ever known ... Sit down—talk to me ... I will not upset you again!

SARAH: ... When I shut my eyes in class and cover them this way, it is not to rest them from the light ... it is to keep the flames burning behind them from igniting all of you ... for sometimes the part of me that waits becomes impatient and claws at the windows like an insane cat ... (*slowly, coldly*) Because of my dedication to you, as friends ... family ... children learning to be people in an electronic age ... I expected love, tolerance and understanding for the parts of me that hurt ... ached with sorrow ... or cried with baby voices in the night ... A man called Lee has betrayed me ... I want revenge!

LEE hums a bar of song.

MOTHER: I think, my dear ... you have shown perfectly sound reasons to ...

MAN: *Kill* him!

EMMA: *Death* would be too merciful ... He reached her through the womb and then attacked her brain ... poor Miss Young ...

MICHAEL: A *nasty* bit of goods, if you'll pardon my saying so ...

LEE: (*sings softly*)
Lady in blue
In a garden of ...

JUDY: Philosophically speaking, *sin* is one road to redemption ...

LEE: ... I screwed a black woman on Thursday, and again on Sunday ...

MAN: Sarah—you're lost unless you banish this obsession from your mind!

LEE: ... She *promised* me ... things I never dreamed the world could give a man ...

EMMA: *Death* would be too kind! Take from him that which leaves him neither as a man nor woman!

MAN: *Leave* no trace of him about! You threw the chair he broke ... there is nothing of him ... never was!

LEE: (*sings softly*)
Seen her last week
And this morning again

SARAH: (*angry*) This is not helping me! I want revenge ... for I am a white woman in a darkening world ... creating goods and services with a lightning frenzy ... moulding special children for this culture, and yet ... I lose my mind at laughter in a darkened car ... at the sight of two brainless dogs humping in an alley!

MOTHER: I never speak of all the *filth* I've seen ... I raised my daughter ... with purity of heart and mind.

PETER: (*grinning*) I'll *kill* him for you, Dolly. But leave a guy like me around as an example of how rotten bad a thing can get!

Cacophony of one-word statements begins to build under dialogue, rising to a chant.

MICHAEL: Nasty!

JUDY: Sin!

FATHER laughs.

EMMA: Death!

MAN: Kill!

SARAH: Somebody ... please help me ... I don't know where I parked my car ... or what day this is.

Chant ends.

MAN: The only thing to do ... is to start at the beginning, as we've done before!

SARAH: (*with pain*) No ... no more of that! Something red and grim as death is eating at me ... the walls and floors of my room are moving, like music played by mad musicians ... Someplace, I forgot my handbag ... in it was my name ... the address of my home ... a record of possessions and the debts I owe ... soft cosmetics in my private war against the sun and wind. A satchel of my womanhood. A flower-scented holder of the tubes and cards and pastes of aging ... Something red and grim ... (*alarmed*) Lights float before my eyes ... silver fish within the skull ... cartwheels of fire in a lashing rain ... Something red and grim as death is eating at me!

MAN: I cannot treat you then! Without cooperation, it is a hollow exercise!

SARAH: ... I can't remember where I parked my car ... when I washed or changed my clothes ... (*looks closely at herself*) Yet, there is no trace of dirt, even on my lounging clothes ... (*desperately*) Help me, please ... to find the key that opens darkness!

She swallows hard, takes control of herself.

(*suddenly composed*) A younger girl terrifies me now ... (*spasm*) Something red and grim as death crawls inside me, eating ... (*composed*) Why am I like this? Resentments hard as wire in the throat ... the growing pain of small neglects of me, magnified by night and winter ... (*spasm*) Something red and grim is scratching at my window!

She stumbles awkwardly, but prevents herself from falling.

(*subdued, weary now*) Why do I fear another woman's victory that is as blind as my own defeat? The passage of the hours and years that rots the greyness of my skin? The flashing incompleteness of my brain ... moralities that stitch my body tighter than a shroud ... Why do I ... the minority earth animal ... howl in a storm of motor sounds—for immortality? Yet kill my sisters and their sons for plastic arguments of who should spend this momentary time of light near whom ... and where ...

She smiles sadly and draws her gown tightly around herself as if against cold.

I am too small for hatred ... too clean and scrubbed for jealousy. I've eaten green and orange things ... never purple ... I was afraid of purple ... shade of agony and passion ... Yet I crave passion as an oriole craves the summer ... not knowing why, or where it leads me ... (*with agony*) Working to release me from myself ... and the pain ... is driving me insane at times!

In a small girl gesture, she wipes tears from her eyes, and huddles from the sound of LEE'S voice.

MAN: ... Somewhere in the night ... one asks the wind for answers ... for the music of a haunting song lost forever on the water ...

SARAH: (*almost a whisper*) No, Lee ... it isn't necessary now ...

LEE: I never knew your name, but I remembered you for the best part of a year ... We met only once ... I cycling to college ... and you driving to your work ... We stopped side by side ... waiting for a light to change. You smiled at me ... and I smiled back at you ... and then I was embarrassed, for it was a warm morning, and I was cycling with my shirt off and tied around my waist ...

SARAH: I came down that street a thousand mornings ... remembering a shy young man resting on the handlebars of his cycle, waiting for the light to change ...

LEE: I wished ... to be an engineer ... but my father lost his job, and I had to help ... raise my two younger brothers and a sister ... (*smiles, then with profound sadness*) She graduates this year ... as an architect! She had a good brain ...

LEE lowers his head.

Light fades low on him.

He is chuckling—or weeping—quietly.

SARAH: I saw him again ... yesterday evening ... I saw him in the supermarket on Boulevard and

Regent ... struggling with two cans of discount orange juice ... in workman's coveralls ... a ... a mulatto child on his arm ... I ... fled before he saw me ... hiding like a thief behind stacks of canned spaghetti ... running around counters ... back-tracking ... dodging here and there, trying to avoid him ... feeling with my fingers the spreading crowsfeet wrinkles around my eyes ... the parched looseness of the skin around my throat ... growing like a winter scarf. I wanted air! I wanted life and flowers! I prayed for release from the gathering fear of men with tablets and stethoscopes ... and the cold expanders that made a mockery of my sex.

She moves towards the bedroom and the MAN.

Light dies out on LEE.

I will find my car ... the restaurant where I left my handbag ... the children who might have been, but are not, mine ... but this violation of my womanhood must end, doctor!

MAN: The age of gods and goddesses is past. There are no miracles. I've explained to you many times now the characteristics of a stable personality, yet something in you has constantly resisted ...

SARAH: I don't know what hell I walk through from here on, but I won't need you anymore. The frightening thing is not my sickness, but your cure ...

MAN shrugs. Smiles politely, but coldly.

MAN: Will you drive me home, then?

SARAH: No.

MAN: Perhaps dinner tomorrow, and a discussion of your progress.

SARAH: (*sharply*) Get out!

MAN: I see ... as you wish ...

MAN leaves. SARAH takes out a hairbrush from the headboard of her bed, and begins to brush her hair in preparation for bed. She smiles to herself.

SARAH: What will you be, my mother asked me once, when you grow up? It was of paramount importance, somehow ... that I *be* somebody. She never asked, how will you live? Will you be happy? Will you carry rainbows in your hands to dark and hungry places? Will you remember me

... and the short dreams in long afternoons of your early years, when there were answers in the magic we forgot?

She turns quickly, her face clouding, then breaking into joy.

... Or will you go to war? Your woman's breasts encased in steel like those of an ancient warrior? Your feet and hair crippled by demands of caste? Your brain, a propaganda mill against your body ... attacking shape of nose, pitch of voice ... scent of skin ... the tender whispers of the heart and womb?

Sound of LEE'S voice singing offstage.

LEE: The willow branches
Droop and cry
Who knows why
They bend and sigh?

SARAH: ... You whom I never knew ... to whom I once gave the name of Lee ... bicycle rider of a remembered morning ... Apollo of the super-market ... breeder of dark children in a grey con-crete wasteland ... I wish I had met you when I had no work to do! (*laughs*) I am like the things I do ... honest, efficient ... virtuous as a scream. I will not be free ... no, not I. My deepening mad-ness saves me, though. I touch myself ... kiss the pillow helmet of my dreams ... and for a moment now and then in the dark, sleepless ... suffocat-ing night ... I am whole and free! I turn, my body and my mind, to watch the sunrise ... hoping for a third being to join us ... hoping for a miracle some morning on some other road ... When other fragments such as I ... stop in our separa-tions for some other traffic light ...

Total silence.

SARAH completes her hairbrushing, puts away the brush, tidies up the chair, then on dying light, removes her gown, folds it neatly.

The light continues to die gently on her near-nakedness that is somehow mysteriously beautiful and distant, as well as painfully predictable.

Blackout

End

A PORTRAIT OF ANGELICA

When it was first staged, *A Portrait of Angelica* was subtitled in the program, *Sketches of a Sunshine Town in Mexico, 1973*. At first glance the work seems a lightweight effort for Ryga, with a meandering, episodic plot and a languid Canadian tourist as the central character. Jamie Portman, in the *Calgary Herald* (August 10, 1973), wasn't even sure it was a play, just "a series of snippets, impressions, Latinized vaudeville turns." It should be remembered, however, that Ryga originally wrote *A Portrait of Angelica* as a revue, his intention being to capture the energy and colour of a community similar to Dylan Thomas's *Under Milk Wood* (which Ryga had in mind as he wrote). By his use of numerous slides of local people and places (many taken by Norma Ryga), authentic songs, music, and poetry—some of it co-authored by the Aztek Kings who lived nearby (Ryga obtained some of their lyrics), in the staging of the play, Ryga hoped to create a giant holistic snapshot of an ancient, enduring people in the village of Ajijic, Mexico, plagued by none of the dislocations, displacements, estrangements and other forms of exile so redolently present in his other work. The final scene, typically, was to have "the effect of a three-dimensional holiday photograph in colour" (from the stage directions).

Ryga, at the invitation of friends, had moved to Ajijic in October 1972. He had just returned from Switzerland where he had been conducting research on a historical figure that had long fascinated him, the sixteenth-century physician and mystic, Paracelsus. There, he had been obsessively writing a long, rambling play, full of passion and poetry, late into the evenings, about this strange, troubled genius who raged against the medical, political, and scientific establishment of his day. In addition to the spiritual and mental anguish brought on by his writing of *Paracelsus* in Switzerland, Ryga was not well physically, suffering a gall bladder condition that was becoming increasingly painful. Finally, in March the Rygas had to suddenly pack up and return to Canada for his operation. *A Portrait of Angelica* was written during this time of return and recuperation; it was another commission from the Banff Centre and was a welcome antidote to his medical broodings—as was Ajijic, the town he had gone to for his period of healing and that became the model for his "portrait" of "Santa Angelica."

Ajijic is a small village on the north shore of Lake Chapala. Known for its perfect climate, it has become a haven for foreign retirees and artists, especially Americans and Canadians. At the same time it retains much of its old Mexican customs and appearance with its ancient colonial cobblestone streets and buildings such as the San Andres Church dating from the 1500s. The Ryga family lived in a single-storey adobe house a few blocks from the lake, making friends and enjoying the village life of the community. Ryga, as is evident in his alter-ego character of Danny Baker, became an observer of events around the village square. In a time of his own dark broodings, he welcomed the zest for life so unmistakably present in a culture that was older, seemingly wiser, and more authentic than his "native," unheroic Canada ("We are taught to endure in silence ... "). He was struck by local characters such as a vivacious girl who strutted about wearing Che Guevara and Bob Dylan slogans on her shirt: he transformed into a character in the play, the free-spirited Elena.

A Portrait of Angelica is Ryga's nostalgic love letter not to a person, but to a whole community of the ordinary people he so often wrote about. His touchstone amid the distancing and sterilizing effects of a ceaselessly growing global imperial culture was always the folk people, those who live, work, and love close to the earth, are vitally connected to their heritage, and have an unabashed zest for living—in the manner of his own idealized and romanticized imaginary Ukrainian background. The play is warm and colourful because, for once, Ryga was writing among what he so dearly wanted to be his own kind of people. Even in their foibles and hesitations, the folks of "Santa Angelica" offer his character Danny a chance to reflect and re-energize. At the same time the play is consciously troubled by its inability to offer its audience any real participatory connection to or identification with the people of this village, because Danny Baker, a white, holidaying (exiled) Canadian, remains only a foreign observer of this idealized culture, with limited, even often and obviously misapplied sympathies. In the end he learns "nothing from the songs" and vacillates, tearing up his writing and losing his will to action—a "tourist," not ultimately a participant among the folk who remain inaccessible to him behind the frame of their culture: a "three-dimensional portrait," like a terrarium.

In a very real way, *A Portrait of Angelica* became a reprise of what Ryga had done with the questions of appropriation of voice and idealization of community in *Just an Ordinary Person*, though this time these questions are framed in dramatic terms far less personal and accusatory, and far more universal and nostalgic. While the Poet in *Just an Ordinary Person* is cast exclusively a "poet," with no other existence outside of his public persona, the Danny Baker of *A Portrait of Angelica* is first and foremost cast as a tourist, who, almost incidentally, also happens to be a writer.

A Portrait of Angelica was commissioned by the Banff Centre School of Fine Arts and opened on August 9, 1973 at the Margaret Greenham Theatre. It was directed by Thomas Peacocke and featured a student cast.

A PORTRAIT OF ANGELICA

CHARACTERS

DANNY BAKER, *a young Canadian*
JOSE, *a town policeman*
ELENA, *a town girl*
YOUNG AMERICAN TOURIST, *male*
DANCER
TWO MEXICAN GIRLS, *chorus*
MRS SIMPSON
JENNIFER, *her daughter*
PADRE EDWARDO
LISA
OLD WOMAN
JANET
MRS STEFANIK
GABRIEL, *a gigolo*
MERCHANT
MERCHANT'S WIFE
TWO ROAD-BUILDERS, *two officials*
AMERICAN MAN, *cat lover*
TWO CHILDREN
AMERICAN GIRL
DRUNK

SET

Square of a small Mexican town. Set is designed in such a way that by isolating playing areas with light, various possibilities would exist for losing the set entirely and moving the players into abstract regions which are more emotional than physical. Also, parts of the set should adapt to becoming screens for slide projections.

In darkness, unaccompanied voice of a singer singing to tune of "Piedra De La Cama":

SONG: I ask you, if I should perish
I ask you, if death overtakes me
Would you return my poor body,
Return my earth-coloured body
To the arms
Of my village and mother? ...

Go tell him—the peasant who's ploughing,
Go tell him—president of the country
That I fell in the service of people,
I died for my country and brothers
To the last
I didn't flinch or surrender ...

I ask for a grave on the hillside,
I ask for a cross of mesquite
And with my machine-gun engrave
My name in a burst of hot bullets
So I sleep
Beloved and sadly remembered.

Subia la sala del crimen,
Le pregunte al presidente
Que sios delite el correrto
Que me sentencio la muerto
Ah ah,
Corazon porque no amas ...

ACT 1

Over song, a series of slides of fishermen, farmers and builders. At end of song, light on square.

Recorded rock music.

JOSE, the policeman, is leaning against a pillar at back of stage. He is protecting the municipal building entrance. His expression is bored. A bandolier of shells is buckled over one shoulder. Over the other, a weathered carbine.

Across from him at stage front, DANNY BAKER, the young Canadian, sits under a table umbrella, writing a letter.

TWO OFFICIALS emerge from the municipal hall. They are in animated, but wordless, conversation. Their business suits are badly fitted. One of them lights a cigarette as they stop momentarily to squint into the light. The other checks a sheet of paper he has been carrying, crumbles it and throws it at JOSE'S feet. JOSE salutes the back of the man and, picking the wad of paper up, flicks it with an imperceptible motion of his wrist away from the entrance of the municipal hall.

In a walk that is a caricature of busy officials hurrying nowhere, the TWO OFFICIALS cross the stage and exit.

MRS STEFANIK enters, carrying a bruised, wilted head of lettuce.

The music dies momentarily on her line.

MRS STEFANIK: For two days now, I've tried to buy some lettuce ... Everything has set like glue inside my stomach!

Music up.

Members of cast, Mexican, move onto stage and cross in contrasting patterns on their exits. They typify artisans, washerwomen, merchants, etc.

When all have left, ELENA remains, hovering in background, swaying languidly to the music. The music dies into background.

DANNY: Welcome to the town where I live this year! Welcome to my life!

The music dies out.

JOSE: When the cocks no longer crow the passing of the night, the bells of Angelica ring for mass ...

Sound of bell, ringing an incessant rhythm.

DANNY: The singers of the night are weary now ... in Santa Angelica ...

ELENA: *(languid, still swaying to remembered music)* For seven thousand years we've known mornings such as this ... The sun is love ... dew upon the grass ... baptism for the early day ...

Sound of bell goes gentler, slower now.

DANNY: The singers of the night are weary now ... they depart in various directions ...

Sound of woman's song in Spanish in distance. Recorded.

ELENA moves first to DANNY, then to JOSE, kissing each delicately on the cheek.

Enter some WHITE PEOPLE, looking about aimlessly, as tourists will in a strange culture. ELENA moves into background and, covering her face in her shawl, watches them.

JOSE: The singers of the night leave ... down alleys heavy with the smell of fish ... guitars and trumpets carried over shoulders like shovels of the swarthy campesinos ...

DANNY: Jose ... guards the morning square ... with his carbine and bandolier of rusty bullets ...

An intense young TOURIST, remnant of the radical student abroad, salutes JOSE with feeling.

TOURIST: Buenos dias, protector of the republic and the revolutionary gains of 1910!

JOSE picks his nose in an elaborate show of indifference to the young foreign radical.

JOSE: Buenos dias, norteamericanos ...

ELENA laughs. The young TOURIST is discomfited, as are the others. Some leave. Others move away.

Enter OLD WOMAN and MERCHANT'S WIFE.

ELENA dances past JOSE, swinging her hip at him seductively. JOSE grins at her and touches his hat.

Woman's song up in distance. Recorded.

ELENA: He dreams each morning in the sun ... of driving the official police truck ... a rusty Chevrolet half-ton.

DANNY: Down the highway, seven kilometres to the neighbouring town.

JOSE: Someone has to! ... Collect refuse off the roadside ... dead dogs killed by speeding gringos ... spillage of the garbage drivers who think, like their yankee counterparts ... that Mexico is only good ... for another twenty years at most!

DANNY: *(grinning)* And always Jose scans with a keen policeman's eye ... the fields and mountainsides for poachers and the whereabouts of his Elena!

JOSE giggles with embarrassment, and makes a dismissive gesture of his hand at DANNY.

ELENA: He aches for me! ... They all do! ... Politicians ... carpenters ... the mayor's clerk, dressed like death on Sunday.

MERCHANT'S WIFE: *(sarcastically)* Enrico, the tender of the horses!

OLD WOMAN: Cowherds, plumbers, two doctors and the lame Piedro, who mends chairs for widows!

ELENA laughs and dances a few paces, wiggling her hips in direction of her tormentors. The OLD WOMAN threatens her with a wagging forefinger. JOSE frowns his disapproval.

JOSE & DANNY: *(scolding)* Elena!

ELENA waves her head haughtily at them, then, taking her shawl in her hands, whips it first at JOSE, then at DANNY.

ELENA: They lust for me ... dreaming through the night of mangoes, lemon blossoms ... cobbles washed by moonlight ... wet warm things that slither like the eels of Mazatlan ... *(turns to DANNY)* Tell them it is so! They don't believe me ten kilometres from town!

Woman's song dies out.

DANNY laughs and rises to his feet.

DANNY: *(reading from his letter)* On Sunday afternoons, she rides a speckled horse down the boulevard ... two horses to the right of her ... two horses to the left, and one behind ... ridden by her current suitors!

ELENA: *(laughs)* Who fight like mountain dogs to attend to me ... should I fall and roll upon my back ... my legs spread out ... to the east and western borders of Jalisco state!

JOSE: *(angrily)* Elena! This is not a tavern!

DANNY: Monday noon to Thursday, she cuts fresh meat for tacos at Martino's window stall just off the square.

ELENA: When the customers are gone, the nightingale sings. Marti takes my hand and tells me he can feed the largest brood of children in Angelica. His eyes grow soft and gentle as a girl's ... but I turn away from him and smile at my feet ... for his breath would stun a burro ...

She turns away sharply and throws her shawl at JOSE'S feet. He bends quickly to pick it up and bring it to her.

ELENA: Jose ... Jose! You are such a specimen of man ... in braids and uniform ... your shoes well shined ... by a better class of boy ... than others of your kind!

JOSE eagerly holds her shawl out to her.

JOSE: Tomorrow, I will drive the truck at four. If you wish a ride ...

ELENA: *(laughs)* Seven kilometres, in pursuit of garbagemen and poachers?

JOSE: Si!

ELENA: *(still laughing)* I want to go to Vera Cruz, my hero ... for a month of wild fun!

Others laugh. JOSE is hurt and embarrassed. ELENA reaches out to pet his cheeks with both her hands.

ELENA: You are boyish and so beautiful, Jose. One day, when I am tired of my horses and my dogs ... when the sun of Angelica drives me to the shelter of a home ... when I have tamed the fires eating at my feet and scorching in my throat ... when I cry 'Enough! I have had enough of laughter and of dancing,' I will come to you, Jose. But until that day ... you stay just as you are ... guard our revolution and the shops of men who stare like fish!

MERCHANT'S WIFE steps between ELENA and JOSE. MERCHANT enters, but remains in background.

MERCHANT'S WIFE: *(to ELENA)* If they are fish, then we ... you and I ... are fisherwomen?

ELENA: Perhaps ...

MERCHANT'S WIFE: You have pulled your net across my waters once too often, Elena ... so beware!

ELENA smiles sweetly at the MERCHANT, who turns his face away from her.

ELENA: *(to MERCHANT'S WIFE)* You fish for sardines ... while I ... use them as my bait for sharks!

ELENA exits, laughing cheerfully. MERCHANT'S WIFE turns on the MERCHANT.

MERCHANT'S WIFE: Why were you so smug and silent, eh? Or do I have to tell them why? You stayed with her last night ... sleeping with her dogs after she had used you!

The MERCHANT puts his finger elegantly to his lips, gesturing for her to keep her voice down.

MERCHANT: Ssh! The priest will hear! You will wake the children from their morning nap!

MERCHANT'S WIFE: Don't worry about other people's children … you fat, slouching son-of-a-whore!

OLD WOMAN: (*delighted*) That's the way to tell it, Margarita! Give it to him!

MERCHANT'S WIFE: The shop-girl showed me records that you keep. Elena has three thousand pesos owing to you. Food for dogs, good wine, oil of avocado for her salads, while I, your wife, exist on garbanzos and grey lard! How, I ask you, will she pay for what she owes you at the shop?

Catcalls, whistles and cheers from others listening to the argument. The MERCHANT is trapped. He turns and leaves to the verbal assault of his wife.

MERCHANT'S WIFE: Never marry a man from Guadalajara, my mother told me! They are nothing but whore-mongers there! She was right … oh, she was right!

JOSE moves to comfort the woman, who obligingly moves close against him.

JOSE: There now, Margarita … we are not like that here. It takes one beast from the city to make a good woman bitter to all men.

MERCHANT'S WIFE: I am so pleased to hear you say that, Jose. Hold me closer if you will, for I feel faint.

JOSE embraces her and leads her clumsily to his post, where she continues clinging to him. DANNY grins and returns to sit at his table. The young TOURIST joins him, pouring coffee for himself from an earthen pot.

TOURIST: Poor Manuel … he'll avoid the square for weeks to come … but look at that chick of his, eh? (*thumbs towards JOSE and MERCHANT'S WIFE*) She's got the mean reds on her now.

DANNY: Elena's not the only one. Every pretty girl in town has an arrangement at that shop of Manuel's, if she but knew it. Christmas of the previous year, Manuel was pale and thin, as if suffering with tapeworms, or the American disease.

JOSE detaches himself from MERCHANT'S WIFE and moves toward the table, setting his hat firmly on his head.

JOSE: We advised a doctor that we knew, who, for twenty pesos added to his bill, would keep his secrets in the face of death!

DANNY: (*smiling*) But Manuel waved us all away … and pedalled off upon his bicycle … delivering … forever delivering … groceries and meat to the wise-smiling, sun-scented maidens of the town!

Woman's song up in background. Recorded.

OLD WOMAN: (*to MERCHANTS WIFE*) Let's go, Margarita … your children are awake!

MERCHANT'S WIFE moves away reluctantly, eager to catch every word of the men's discussion.

JOSE: (*feigning outrage*) I knew what went on! You knew! Each man with one eye open knew he was screwing every girl in town who owed him money from the previous year. Otherwise, word would get around that Manuel, the billygoat, was too old and weak (*grins through his outrage*) … to collect his debts!

JOSE and the TOURIST break into laughter. JOSE takes the TOURIST by the arm to his post, where he mimes further details of MERCHANT'S exploits. OLD WOMAN leads MERCHANT'S WIFE, now genuinely upset, offstage. The people also exit in various directions.

MRS STEFANIK enters, a worried expression on her face. She approaches JOSE.

MRS STEFANIK: Is the water from the filtration plant really fit for drinking, senor? I went there yesterday … I couldn't see a filter … a man was filling jugs from a garden hose. When I asked him … he said … the filter is buried underground where nobody can see it.

JOSE: The water from the filter plant … is as pure as tears, senora!

MRS STEFANIK is assured, and leaves more happily. Woman's song continues for another verse.

DANNY sits, deep in thought. JOSE and TOURIST are in animated but silent discussion. Song ends.

DANNY: Danny Baker is my name, lista de correos my address. The postmaster is a fascist with a trace of Spanish blood. He treats me as an equal of the master race. It is a self-deluding wish … for, in this country, Cortes is a bandit. Brown is the colour of the people's skin … the rest is an outrage which biology and climate will in time erase.

Roar of laughter from JOSE at something the TOURIST has said.

JOSE: Ay, muchacho ... you are learning fast ... for a gringo!

DANNY stirs uncomfortably. TOURIST and JOSE have turned towards him and are discussing him in undertones.

DANNY: My white face glows like a swollen lantern in the sun-washed streets of Angelica. I call myself a Canadian of Irish-French descent ... born in Sudbury and raised in Edmonton. Here, they call me ...

JOSE: (*loudly*) El tomàte!

DANNY winces.

TOURIST: (*questioning*) The tomato?

JOSE: Si! You are learning fast indeed! Soon you will speak Spanish like my father ... Caramba! Estupido burraco! Vete el diablo!

JOSE roars with laughter at the cunning way he is snowing the intense young TOURIST.

DANNY smiles, takes out notepaper and begins writing, then hesitates and considers.

DANNY: How absurd it is to dream big dreams of nationhood and racial pride ... when I am seen in Santa Angelica as ... a tomato that has learned to drive a car!

TWO OFFICIALS enter and march quickly to the door to the municipal office. JOSE quickly dismisses the TOURIST, who leaves, then JOSE salutes the OFFICIALS as they pass him. THE OFFICIALS ignore JOSE'S salute. As they exit, he is angered by their neglect and directs his fury off in direction of the TOURIST.

JOSE: Americanos—ech! They come here to die or write a book, even the young ones! Every norteamericanos has something eating at him when he comes to Angelica for the weather!

DANNY: (*writing*) They have sayings here, dear Mother, that are beautiful and startling. 'Farewell, my friend—stay good and honest. But if you cannot, then leave a message where you'll be, so I may join you!'

JOSE struts back and forth, still disturbed by the official neglect of him.

JOSE: I am not a piece of rag that salutes and takes orders! It's the gringos that are doing this to us! I observe them from my vantage point with a policeman's careful eye ... and see the same cloudy things in their faces. The younger women look for men ... and the men stand in the shadows, looking through the town for their madre's titty!

JOSE spits with contempt, then rubs the spittle into the dirt with the toe of his boot.

DANNY: They say, too ... foreigners own everything except Mexican vanilla ... leaving us to flavour what someone else has made!

JOSE: I am not like the bureaucrats—I am an honest man, with the interests of the republic on my mind! (*glances at DANNY and grins*) You can quote that if you wish ... such sentiments keep an honest man from being poor!

DANNY: Without your uniform and carbine you would pass for a merchant or corrupt politician, Jose.

JOSE: (*angry now*) Don't underestimate me, friend! The people know me, and I know my people here. I am prepared to stand beside them, even to the death!

DANNY laughs.

DANNY: That is too severe, Jose. The same television shows made in American heaven are screwing up the people of your country and of mine. We will not hear the miners' marching in the streets for the sound of *I Love Lucy* re-runs.

JOSE: (*with an obscene gesture at DANNY*) Chinga tu madre! My uncle was the first Marxist mayor of this town. A market stall and two culverts on the road are named for him to this day! (*glares at DANNY, who is grinning back at him*) Talk to you? Talk to a brickpile. Half-gringos are more stupid than a willing woman.

The TWO OFFICIALS enter through municipal office door. JOSE snaps to attention. In a brief pause, one of them scratches his ass, the other reties his shoelace.

JOSE: Como esta, senors?

They ignore him as they exchange some paperwork, then separate to depart in two different directions.

JOSE: (*softly*) Como esta, senors ...

Sound of bell, tolling slowly.

DANNY: (*writing*) The dogs of Mexico, dear Mother ... are possessed of human souls and intelligence!

JOSE: They didn't even see me! If I had been a sack of corn with a carbine, they would not have known the difference!

DANNY: They are lean and often homeless, but are gifted with incredible perception.

JOSE: Because I am of the country, I am nothing ...

DANNY: They visit kitchens of the restaurants ... pharmacias ... in backroom clinics, they knowingly observe medical examinations and minor surgery ... You may leave a grocery basket in an open doorway for hours, Mother. No dog of Mexico will pee into it, as would ours. I salute the dogs on my morning walks as I salute the people whom I meet.

Bell out. Up rock music in the square. Recorded.

TWO GIRLS enter, dancing, then stop. One turns to face JOSE, the other faces DANNY. They chant in time to the music.

FIRST GIRL: On the feast of Lupe
I will stand in the darkness
Of my father's doorway, waiting
For Manuel to whistle from the meadow ...

SECOND GIRL: Four sisters do I have:
Carmen is the brightest
And Estella the most beautiful ...
Julia can clean the house
Angelica sews our clothes
   What chance have I for marriage
   In this town?

FIRST GIRL: On the feast of Lupe
I will call into the shadows
With a voice as soft
As nightingales in the Spring ...

SECOND GIRL: Caballeros with your hair like night
We are maidens of the mountains ...
Waiting by our father's door
For the songs we hear no more ...

The music softens in the background. The TWO GIRLS giggle and preen before the men, but JOSE and DANNY pay no attention to them. Pouting, they leave. The music dies out.

Woman's song softly, in distance. Recorded.

DANNY: (*writing*) There are two hotels in town, Mother ... an American-style supermarket, selling supermarket rubbish to Americans who are unnerved by narrow streets and peeling plaster ... a brick kiln ... two leather shops ... and a whorehouse where men urinate into a trough of trickling water ...

JOSE: (*pacing angrily*) The ladies of the north object, amigo. They say the brothel is a tourist service, to trap their men for money. A burro's fart to that, muchacho ... Their good men turned the house into a tavern, where they drink and fight on Friday night!

DANNY shrugs away JOSE'S intrusion into his soliloquy.

DANNY: Angelica is a dream in the mornings, Mother.

JOSE: There's nothing to it ... it's a small town for people of small spirit ... When I retire, I will move to Tepic.

DANNY: Ladies, bent and grey, walk slowly from the lake in the grey bent light ... carrying baskets of moist laundry on their bent grey heads.

JOSE: (*shuddering*) It would be a graveyard except for the lovely girls of Santa Angelica!

The TWO GIRLS return, carrying woven baskets of produce on their heads.

FIRST GIRL: I cannot sleep for thinking of the wars ... and men who suffered so ...

JOSE: Those lovely, lovely girls ... a thousand years of sunlight burned into the copper glitter of their slender legs! Giggling in the doorways, their eyes soft with sleep and innocence.

DANNY: Giggling in the lanes and open gardens ... too young to know ... that in time they will carry baskets of moist laundry on their bent grey copper glowing heads.

Music up strongly. The TWO GIRLS sway to it as they move to exit.

FIRST GIRL: On the feast of Lupe
I will give Manuel
A mango from my father's garden ...

SECOND GIRL: The first man who is kind to me
Shall have dreams on mountains

Covered in hibiscus ...

They exit. Music dies out.

Light separates JOSE and DANNY in two isolated areas, which could be their homes. JOSE adjusts his clothes, dusts his hat, checks out his carbine.

DANNY scans his notes and lights a cigarette. He slowly pours himself coffee.

DANNY: I came to write a book ... but all morning, every morning, I write letters to my mother. I came to write a book in a town the new arrivals from Texas, Alabama and New York call Se Vende for a week or so. There are no markers on the highway to announce the entrance to Angelica, only "Se Vende" signs on fields, sheds, houses, shops and even refuse heaps now overgrown with banana palms sheltering scorpions who know nothing of inter-American economics ... or the meaning of "For Sale" signs.

JOSE: What have they learned? They who now come to buy what they could not take with war? My uncle was mayor of this town. I am content that I, too ... can serve the people ... That which is real never changes!

DANNY: I write letters to my mother which I'll never mail through the fascist postman. These are conversations with myself ... my state of life is altered ... and so is my awareness.

JOSE: They come to die, or write a book ... so let them! It doesn't interfere with the avocado harvest ... so why do I wake at night, staring into darkness, my teeth bared like those of an angry dog?

Sound of cock crowing. Recorded.

Projected slides of open countryside, ruins, evening mountains in the desert.

DANNY: Yet I cannot forget my place or time ... the whole world is for sale now. A great "Se Vende" sign hangs in seven languages across the land ... from Alaska to Buenos Aires. It haunts me as the scent of death. So I write letters to my mother ... describing dew and winter roses in the tropics.

JOSE: Nothing changes, friend. The earth is constant, even in a storm, my uncle told me once.

DANNY: The scent of women ... freshly baking bread in hidden courtyards ... oranges with skins of flame ... the rasping happy sound of mariachis in the barroom of a rich hotel.

JOSE: Should Elena want me, should Elena care ...

DANNY: Saddened that my country has so few heroic men, I sit in the early sun on the balcony of my apartment ... in a country that abounds with heroes ... and watch two thieves in purple shirts remove four wheels, muffler and headlamps of a yellow car with license plates from Arizona.

JOSE: I would bring her scarlet sashes for the holy days.

DANNY: In twenty minutes, the car sits like a yellow turtle on the cobbles of Calle de Revolucion.

JOSE: A bearded man with short pants spoke to me this morning.

Projected slides end. Sound of cock crowing dies out.

Light on another area of stage, where local Americans in residence amble through, led by the man in shorts, who mimes a conversation with JOSE. Following him are MRS SIMPSON and JENNIFER. MRS SIMPSON is reading her mail. JENNIFER nags from a few paces behind.

JOSE: He pointed to Calle de Revolucion and mewled like a cat. He spoke no Spanish ... so how in hell could I tell if he wanted coffee, a whorehouse ... or an address of a friend? I was polite to him, but thought of all the unlocked doors in Angelica. These yankee youth ... would screw and rob their mothers, so I'm told.

DANNY: The thieves in purple shirts depart ... the obscene car remains. The morning sun brings Missus Simpson past my balcony, followed by her daughter. Both need a daddy ... and a place to stay.

JENNIFER: (*nagging*) Mommy ... did Daddy write a letter?

MRS SIMPSON: Shut up, darling ... Mommy's busy now ...

JENNIFER: Mommy! Did Daddy write? You said he'd write.

MRS SIMPSON ignores JENNIFER. She moves ahead, then stops to read a postcard. As if on cue, JENNIFER follows, then stops when her mother stops.

JENNIFER: Mommy! You said you'd tell me!

MRS SIMPSON: I told you already, dear ... that sonofabitch never writes! So stop bugging my ass, will you?

MRS SIMPSON resumes her slow walk, still reading. JENNIFER follows.

JENNIFER: I want a chocolate malteada ... you promised me if I was good and didn't bug your ass you'd buy me a chocolate malteada ...

MRS SIMPSON ignores her. They exit.

Light on full stage.

Sound of bell. Sound of dog barking. Recorded.

PADRE EDWARDO enters, followed by a few village locals: a shoeshine boy, tinker, etc. The PADRE greets JOSE with respect, and merely nods in DANNY'S direction.

DANNY: *(to JOSE)* The rusty bells of Angelica are like penance, Jose! Their tones die of death by hanging in the steeple!

JOSE glowers at DANNY.

JOSE: You be careful now ... the church is still a power here!

DANNY: Your bells, Jose, were inspired by the sound of half-filled Esso drums struck by a garden spade!

JOSE: It's not the bells, but the ringers!

DANNY: You can't play a symphony on a pig's bladder!

JOSE: It's the ringers, I tell you! Padre Edwardo hires village idiots as ringers of the bells ... fools who can neither count nor read the time of day or night on the steeple clock!

DANNY: The bells of Angelica ring to some pattern of their own ... twenty times in the dead of night ... one solitary ping to announce a wedding.

JOSE: Some weddings I have known should have settled for a ping!

DANNY: Padre Edwardo, like the government of Canada, helps the helpless by providing them with work for which there is no need!

JOSE: Don't confuse an honest man like the padre with a presidente. But write that in your book, amigo, and I'll arrest you for defamation of a public office!

Both JOSE and DANNY break into laughter.

PADRE EDWARDO, dressed in robes of a priest, speaks first to one of them, then the other. But neither JOSE nor DANNY pay much attention, for the old man's words are as familiar as myth to them.

Sound of dog barking dies out, but bell continues chiming erratically.

PADRE EDWARDO: On fiesta evenings, the children line up like bright dolls in the courtyard of the church. The women bring lemonade and cake and as the sun sets, they are fed like chirping birds.

DANNY: *(writing)* In the morning, Padre Edwardo walks the town on visitations to the sick ... the aged ... houses where weddings are in preparation ... or where births have taken place. He describes flowering trees and birds to the blind. Men who beat their burros with a stick get scolded by him ... for to the padre, man and beast are brothers in this land.

PADRE EDWARDO: I am a Spaniard by birth and breeding, and the burden of this handicap rests as a rock upon my heart.

DANNY: If God were to visit Santa Angelica, he would look and walk like our padre.

PADRE EDWARDO: This pale skin I wear is a curse of the conquistadores. The people come to church and worship in the Spanish tongue, but a distance separates me from them that neither life nor death can bridge.

DANNY: So he walks the streets of Angelica, urging men to be like brothers to the burros ... praying over drunkards sleeping in the sun near buildings with peeling plaster and ragged window holes.

MRS SIMPSON and JENNIFER return, hand in hand, and pass through a group of people.

MRS SIMPSON: Would you like a taco for your breakfast, dear?

JENNIFER turns up her nose.

JENNIFER: Andy Whalen says tacos here are made of dog-meat, Mommy!

MRS SIMPSON: (*muttering, on exit*) That little bastard will get us all in trouble yet!

PADRE EDWARDO looks around him at the remnants of his congregation, and throws up his hands in a great sigh of resignation.

PADRE EDWARDO: The visitors only complicate my work with their shameless clothes and music that invites fornication in the white light of God's day!

JOSE: We are Christians here, but we are not fanatics ... like the women of San Carlos ... who crawl on their knees across the cobbled streets to church on the sacred days.

DANNY: Confessions are such energetic incidents ...

PADRE EDWARDO: One man killed his brother with an axe in a dispute over twenty bricks. I forgave him, as would God himself, for he had seven children.

MAN IN CROWD: And I'd do it all again, Padre, for I was in the right! That burraco tried to cheat me!

PADRE EDWARDO winces and motions to the man for silence.

PADRE EDWARDO: Another man stole tobacco through his neighbour's window. He was remorseful and terrified of hell ... and gave me thirty pesos for the poor.

JOSE: The sins of women are a priest's reward!

DANNY: He has no interest in the sins of women.

JOSE: Nonsense! Something burns even in a holy man!

WOMAN IN CROWD: He yawned when I confessed adultery for the seventh time this year ... God would have shown some interest. Everybody else did.

LISA and MRS STEFANIK enter. LISA is dressed in a mini-skirt and see-through blouse. MRS STEFANIK is severe in her clothes. They have been arguing.

MRS STEFANIK: Well, young lady ... take my advice and just don't sit on park benches dressed like that!

LISA: Why?

MRS STEFANIK: You know why! Don't play the fool with me!

MRS STEFANIK bows to the priest and, after closely examining a cup, pours herself coffee at DANNY'S table, which she sips standing up.

LISA approaches DANNY and embraces him.

DANNY: Buenos dias, Lisa. Has Maria had her baby?

LISA: Ted split for California on Wednesday ... I don't know what she'll do now. You should see her soon.

JOSE: (*to PRIEST*) Only married couples have babies in this country!

LISA glances at JOSE and grins warmly.

LISA: Don't you believe it, Jose. One hears the strangest rumours in this town!

She moves away from DANNY and waves to the PADRE. MRS STEFANIK nervously places her cup down on the table and exits in a different direction from the one LISA takes.

LISA: Hasta luego, Danny. (*to PRIEST*) Say a prayer for us, and in return ...

DANNY: (*annoyed*) Don't, Lisa!

She arches her brows at DANNY.

LISA: And in return ... I was about to say ... we'll wish good things for you! What's wrong with that?

She exits. DANNY faces the PRIEST, who is shaken.

DANNY: Before you say it ... let me assure you they are people like your villagers, except they are on holidays and you are not.

PADRE EDWARDO: No, no! Some different culture breeds these people with impunity, for money falls like water from the skies for them!

DANNY: There are more beggars for the population in New York than in ...

PADRE EDWARDO: Forgive me, friend, but we are meek and that has always been our weakness!

The meek shall inherit nothing but dry winds from the hills for our submissiveness!

JOSE: This culture has withstood a thousand hurricanes!

PADRE EDWARDO: You are both young ... it is easy to impress you! You know nothing of this culture! Two thousand years of heritage sells for twenty pesos a square metre this very hour on the edge of town. I have a dream the people sold my church from underneath my feet for a parking lot ... and I was reduced in my old age to herding goats upon the mountain for the milk and cheese consortium! When the price of land is high, history and culture is a dying calf with three legs!

He dismisses them all with an angry gesture of his hand and exits quickly.

Sound of rock music.

A MAN in the crowd pushes his way forward, singing raucously.

MAN: (*singing*) Santa Angelica
Sold her favours for a peso
To a soldier and two peddlers
When the padre wasn't looking!
  In the morning she was lying
  In the garden, softly crying
  On her shoulder sat a locust
  On her lap a cucaracha ...

JOSE moves threateningly towards the MAN, who retreats behind a woman for protection.

JOSE: (*shouting*) Silence! In the name of decency!

Music dies abruptly as does sound of bell.

The MAN who sang picks up a sack of corn and his hat, which he places on his head, sack first, and hat on top of the sack. He leaves, followed by the majority of the group. Only two people remain, busying themselves with handicraft displays and cutlery for sale off the cobbles of the street.

DANNY stares at JOSE, who paces angrily.

DANNY: The village is a mother to her children, Jose. No government can regulate her love. The children age and go their way, as children must.

JOSE: You go to hell! You mix up my thoughts like wind across a dusty field!

TWO GIRLS, one Mexican, the other American, enter from opposite sides of stage. They eye each other coldly.

Woman's song in background.

MEXICAN GIRL: I shall be an operator
Writing numbers on a paper!

AMERICAN GIRL: I shall be a fighting sister
To some future draft resister!

DANNY sighs and returns to his writing. JOSE continues pacing, his hat pulled low over his eyes.

DANNY: From December to May, no clouds crease the sunny rooftops or the open faces of the people, dear Mother ...

JOSE: From May to November, the rain pisses away good land into the gullies!

MEXICAN GIRL: We would not be poor and meek If we had schools five days a week!

AMERICAN GIRL: I'll fight against society To remain both sane and free!

They make a gesture of repulsion against each other, turn and exit from where they had entered. JOSE stops to watch them leave, then shrugs wearily.

Woman's song dies out.

JOSE: Tell me, white man from the north, will the men after us all wear short pants ... and their women, skirts cut off at the ass? Is that what has to come with electricity and clinics for the sick?

DANNY ignores him. Continues writing.

DANNY: The northern ice in my blood melts in Angelica in the morning sun ...

JOSE: (*shouting at DANNY*) They've all come here to die, or write a book! The taverns overflow with rotting poets and biographers who waste empty paper on their empty lives! Climb a mountain, or screw up a storm, amigo! ... It will be better for your system than sitting at a table all day long!

Light dies out abruptly on JOSE and the TWO OTHER PEOPLE. A pool of light isolates DANNY, still writing.

Sound of incessant birds. Recorded.

DANNY: It was in Angelica that I first found love ...

JOSE: (*shouting, from darkness*) Learn not to ignore me if you prize your health, amigo ... for we are still masters in our land!

DANNY: In my second month ... I had to move to new quarters. I met Elena ... old as wisdom in her knowing eyes ... fresh and young as hope in the manner of her walk, the sad Aztec smile on her lips ...

Light on ELENA, approaching DANNY, who hurriedly rises and goes to embrace her. She pushes him away playfully.

ELENA: Hey, americano! Do you think that what you want is simply there for the taking?

DANNY: I will write and dedicate a book to you!

ELENA: A kilo of fresh pork for me and a bundle of green corn for my horses would be more to my liking!

DANNY laughs as he moves around her.

DANNY: I will dedicate *two* books to you!

ELENA: I want no arguments from you with my other suitors ... or with my son of nineteen fathers!

DANNY is discomfited. She laughs at his show of prudishness.

DANNY: I brought few things with me ... I am used to indifferent meals and washing in cold water now ... I will be no bother to you.

ELENA: Besides getting what you want, you will be a keeper of my dogs ... and walk my horses four kilometres each day, even when it rains, or a fiesta takes me to the town!

He turns away from her, musing gently.

Sound of woman's song in distant background. Recorded.

DANNY: Out of pain known only to a lonely man in a distant country, I promised her I would ... as well as fifty dollars monthly for my bed ... and hers. Buying groceries and sweeping out her hallways to the street at nine o'clock each night, when no other men were near to see my degradation ...

ELENA: Four dinners weekly in the town, and two dances in between ... for I crave music to excite my feet as the poor crave heaven. New shirt and trousers for my son each winter ... spring and autumn ...

DANNY: Out of pain known only to a lonely man, I promised her I would, even when she told me ...

ELENA: This is no novice that you get! But a lusty woman from fingertips to toes, knocked over by every second man in Angelica ... twice by some ... on beds, sand, hay, on burro's backs, roof-tops, seats of cars, kitchen tables, once on a baker's heap of fresh-baked bread ... (*laughs lustily*) It took me half an hour to clean my ass of flour!

Woman's song dies abruptly.

Separate pool of light on JOSE, down on his hands and knees, blowing into the open door of a portable iron stove, over which OLD WOMAN stands, stirring a vat of soup.

JOSE: Enough?

OLD WOMAN: No. It needs a little more ...

Woman's song up.

ELENA: I demand you do what my whim desires. You will walk, run ... bark like a dog ... sweep the streets before my house ... brush my horses ... comb my hair ...

DANNY: Yes, Elena.

Woman's song dies.

JOSE: (*to OLD WOMAN*) Not enough?

Woman's song up.

ELENA: Massage my back ... play with my little cousins ... husk corn ... pound the meat!

DANNY: Yes, Elena!

ELENA: In short, you will play the fool I have never had. I was born a woman, and this town will remember it, when other things are long forgotten!

DANNY nods and advances to her, reaching out. ELENA laughs, sidesteps him and exits into darkness.

Woman's song dies out.

JOSE: (*complaining*) When do I stop blowing, woman? I am dizzy now!

OLD WOMAN: It's not enough.

JOSE continues blowing and fanning with his hat.

DANNY: Elena's son was four. He ate potato chips by the bushel ... drank more Pepsis in a day than her horse drank water ... threw rocks at Jennifer and other gringo children ... cursed with the purple language of a docker ... demanded that he drive my car ... and at night, came to sleep between us in our bed.

JOSE rises to his feet and slaps his hat over his head.

JOSE: (*to OLD WOMAN*) Ask a younger man to help you! I have more important duties to attend to.

OLD WOMAN kneels and blows into the open stove.

DANNY: One night, I gave him money to go out and buy ice cream and Pepsi. But, when he left, the dogs came in, all four of them.

ELENA enters with a stack of woven hats. She approaches JOSE at his post and holds a hat for him to buy. He indicates he does not want it.

ELENA: What's the matter? Are you shy?

DANNY: (*raising his voice to ELENA, who is facing JOSE*) I want to do it, Elena, my beloved. But do the dogs have to stand over us, watching?

ELENA: (*to JOSE*) Think how lovely it would look!

DANNY: (*loudly, with exasperation*) Then why don't we bring the goddamned horses in as well?

ELENA shrugs at JOSE and walks away, flaunting her body at him, which flusters him. He fingers the stock of his rifle nervously.

ELENA: (*to JOSE*) If you wish, I'll bring a German helmet for you later. They were designed for sleeping on your side, I'm told.

She exits.

OLD WOMAN struggles with her stove. JOSE and DANNY go to help her move it out of sight. But they glare at each other as they lift and carry the stove.

DANNY: It wasn't on account of her, Jose ... it's your attitude!

JOSE: One more insult to my manhood, amigo, and boom! I shoot your head off!

DANNY: In my homeland, we struggle six months of the year to keep ourselves from freezing during winter. Our children are well fed ...

the old have a living pension. You are as wealthy in resource as we, yet to boil soup takes a woman and two men!

JOSE: But the soup gets made, even though we had to lose Texas, New Mexico, Arizona, Nevada and California to get to this! Come on, amigo with the sunburned face, lift!

DANNY struggles with the stove.

DANNY: That is not the point I'm making!

JOSE: Screw your points and what they make— just lift!

DANNY: You don't want to hear the truth, do you? Dumb peasant with a rifle on your back!

JOSE: In this town, the truth is an old woman with an iron stove, whose husband died a young man, fighting Spanish gentry who kept us all in slavery. Now that is progress, friend ... Come on, help me lift!

They place the stove in one corner of the square. JOSE grins at DANNY, who is shaken and breathless.

JOSE: What else can you not do? ... Rope a cow? ... Cut sugar-cane twelve hours a day? ... Carry forty bricks upon your head?

DANNY: (*staring at JOSE, then at OLD WOMAN*) I will always love this place. What hope is there for me if I am looked upon as enemy?

OLD WOMAN: Who are you then—a lover, or a murderer?

JOSE: It is *your* problem. We have no obligation to you.

OLD WOMAN: We are people ... we will endure ...

JOSE: Even when we fail to live up to your expectations. (*sarcastically*) Can you forgive us for that?

DANNY: There are such differences ... it takes time to understand ...

OLD WOMAN pats DANNY'S arm and smiles at him.

OLD WOMAN: Trust us, then ... we will not betray you!

Enter MRS SIMPSON. She carries a magazine, which she opens when she sits at DANNY'S table. She senses tension, and looks up questioningly.

JOSE stares at DANNY, then breaks the tension with a laugh, as he moves to sit beside MRS SIMPSON. DANNY follows him to the table. They pour coffee.

MRS SIMPSON: I've put the brat to bed ... nobody gets hurt today!

JOSE: It is a strange and gloomy town ... Senor Baker knows!

MRS SIMPSON glances from JOSE to DANNY.

MRS SIMPSON: Is something wrong, Jose? What in hell is going on?

JOSE: (*mischievously*) Nothing ... I was going to suggest ... you should tell my friend how the avocados bloom!

MRS SIMPSON: Don't lay into me now, Jose. I pay my bills and stay out of trouble!

JOSE: No, no. It's for my Danny friend I need your help. He loves Angelica and he can't tell why. That and diarrhea are common problems here.

MRS SIMPSON rises.

MRS SIMPSON: I'll go then. I'm sorry ...

JOSE reaches out and takes her by the arm, pulling her back into her chair.

JOSE: No ... please stay. I need a friend who knows me.

DANNY: Forget it all, Jose ... this does not concern her.

JOSE: (*to DANNY*) But it does ... the first year she came, her husband left her and the girl ... a well-educated man ... went back and left her with no money.

OLD WOMAN: She has a child—you are not to hurt her, Jose!

JOSE glances at OLD WOMAN briefly.

JOSE: They are not to hurt us, either, then! (*turns to DANNY*) The old woman from the taco market found a place for her and Jennifer to live ... fed them ... took their clothes to wash and press. No one, amigo, not a fool nor enemy of our people, will be allowed to starve or die forgotten in this country!

DANNY: I understand that.

JOSE: But do you understand that once you've taken of feeling that we have ... you must accept us and our country as your equals ... and not curiosities in your winter travels?

DANNY turns away, hurt and upset. JOSE grins at him and MRS SIMPSON, who sits woodenly, staring ahead of herself.

JOSE: That's what the old women say ... who am I to argue?

He rises, holds out his arm to MRS SIMPSON.

JOSE: Jennifer's in bed ... nobody gets hurt today ... So may I take you to the restaurant, senora, for coffee, beans and tacos?

MRS SIMPSON nods and, mechanically collecting her magazine, rises and takes his arm. She and JOSE exit.

DANNY waves to them, and to the OLD WOMAN, who follows them with her pot of soup. DANNY suddenly breaks into hearty laughter.

Up rock music in background. Recorded.

Enter FOUR GIGGLING GIRLS, led by GABRIEL, the town dandy. They hang on his arms and around his neck. He is bedecked with jewellry and rings. Following him a few paces, glowering with disapproval, is JANET, a blonde American woman in her late thirties.

JANET: Gabriel! I want a word with you when you've a moment!

GABRIEL half-turns and laughs mockingly.

DANNY: I am not a hero or a man of strong convictions ... arguments unsettle me ... I am more like Gabriel ... the male whore of Angelica. Eleven in the morning ... escorting ladies of his choosing in the square. Mid-afternoon, he will need to earn his dinner ... but at eleven in the morning ...

JANET: (*sharply*) Gabriel!

DANNY: Ah, Janet ... it is too early in the day for Gabriel to be your servant!

JANET: I am missing two hundred pesos and my purple shoes, Gabriel! There will be trouble if I don't have a word with you about them!

DANNY: Gabriel sold them to Pepe, the fence of San Juan, at six this morning ... the hour Pepe comes down from the mountains for theft and business ...

JANET: Gabriel!

DANNY: In volcanic peaks above the town, there is a community of outlaws ... men who long ago abandoned families and friends because of crimes ... careless driving on the highways ... madness ... or difference of political opinion with the government of Mexico ...

GABRIEL disengages himself from the GIRLS and goes to shake DANNY'S hand.

Sound of rock music rises.

GABRIEL: Danny ... buenos dias, amigo! How goes the search for truth with you?

DANNY: Bueno ... bueno, Gabriel.

The handshake breaks apart. DANNY moves away, swaying to the music, his voice rising.

DANNY: In time, Gabriel will follow Pepe to the mountains, where he will eat wild corn and beans, drink cactus juice, grow a beard and gaze with longing on the pale town below ... where men and women bed ... and laugh ... and suffer in their quiet ways.

GABRIEL: I eat well, my friend! (*strikes his stomach*) Yesterday, I ate a taco of boiled coyote in my cousin Pancho's house. Today, I have three hundred pesos to my name!

JANET: I want two hundred pesos and my purple shoes returned! They were a present from my sister, from her trip to Venice, Gabriel!

GABRIEL laughs mockingly again, and, taking hold of the TWO GIRLS nearest him, lifts them and swings them in a wide arc.

GABRIEL: Whee!

DANNY: He laughs for reasons I will never understand. The Indian of Mexico ... a smile masks his hatred, and when he has dazzled and disarmed you with his teeth, he will through a gesture show you his contempt for your stupidity and helplessness.

GABRIEL: Hola, Danny ... amigo! If you are a Canadiense, as you say, why do you look so much like an Americanos? I wish the frost of Canada had changed your face so I could see the difference without asking.

DANNY: Gabriel, Gabriel ...

GABRIEL: If your nose was frozen flat, I would know you better!

GABRIEL and THE GIRLS laugh. DANNY moves away from them.

DANNY: I saw him one morning early, through a window of the Grand Hotel, on the beach chasing Santayana, the one-eyed dog of the peddler Lupe. The dog had caught a fish and Gabriel was trying to seduce the dog, to rob him of the fish, for it had been a gaunt week for lonely women in the town.

GABRIEL and the GIRLS begin to move to the sound of the music on their exit.

GABRIEL: It is my business to be ready. It is God's business to bring me luck, amigo. Stay home when there's a hurricane coming. Your feet are useless in a storm, my friend!

He waves nonchalantly and exits.

JANET: Gabriel—wait! Where in hell do you think you're going?

GABRIEL: (*on exit*) To kiss a hummingbird! You can follow, if you wish!

JANET hesitates, then, slouching with resignation, moves towards DANNY but not relating to him, trapped in her own frustrations.

Rock music dies out.

DANNY: In the morning, Gabriel dances out of reach of her. At night ... he waits, hands in empty pockets, head propped against a street lamp standard ... his face an Aztec mask.

JANET: Asking how much money I had brought, cursing ·if the sums are small, for my Gabriel loves food and drink, and after that—the dance! I am a puritan. I never learned to dance at all.

Woman's song up in background. Recorded.

DANNY: She follows him to where the music plays ... her shoulders hunched and tears of humility streaming down her cheeks.

JANET: My mother beat me once around the head with a teapot until it smashed when I asked if I could go dancing with the sailors.

DANNY: The last time my mother sent me money, Gabriel took me to a brothel in

Guadalajara where the men drank and pissed into an open trough that circled round the bar.

JANET: In Iowa in June, the corn grows green and righteous as a field of saints.

DANNY: One afternoon with Gabriel and whores and piss troughs that carried hope and sperm back into the earth was enough for me. But Gabriel was like a demon ... dancing, singing, celebrating. He asked for all the money I had brought and stayed two weeks in the brothel with the tiled trough.

JANET: On his return from Viet Nam, my husband was an addict and an amputee. I deserved better things. (*as an outcry*) Don't you think I deserved better things than that?

DANNY: In Angelica ... in the morning ... the sun is hot as liquid gold ...

JANET: You pass me in the street, looking through me ... We made love many times in your car when first you came. Now, you look through me as if I wasn't there, Danny!

DANNY: I know your body, but the rest of you is a terrifying secret. I fear honesty as I fear the winter now, Janet.

JANET moves past him and exits.

Woman's song dies out.

DANNY cartwheels across the stage. Spotlight on him as light onstage dies out. He is grinning.

DANNY: At noon, the late sleepers rise ... and rub the scum of rum from inflamed eyes!

Spotlight on another area of stage, on TWO MEXICAN ROAD-BUILDERS entering, carrying a basket of round stones and a hammer. MRS STEFANIK is crossing through spotlight, but stops on the sound of DANNY'S voice.

DANNY: Missus Grace Stefanik ...

MRS STEFANIK: From Saskatoon, Saskatchewan, which is in Canada!

DANNY: Rents a house for three hundred and eighty dollars monthly rent ...

MRS STEFANIK: Equipped with deep freezer, two maids and a gardener with a wart upon his nose ...

DANNY: Covers her toilet seat with three thicknesses of tissue before she settles down ...

MRS STEFANIK: Boil my drinking water ...

DANNY: Already purified and filtred at the agua plant ... dips her meat in a jar of alcohol ...

MRS STEFANIK: Dab mercurochrome three times a day ...

DANNY: On real and imagined scratches on her skin. Sees a doctor with her husband twice a month for examination of all orifices and their secretions ... because ...

MRS STEFANIK: You can't trust anyone nowadays, can you? I mean, it's so hot here ... and they're too poor to buy disinfectant. I mean, I think the people are just wonderful ... but ... I'm sure their houses smell of pig-shit ... don't you think?

FIRST ROAD-BUILDER: No, senora ... it's the natural air!

MRS STEFANIK: I'm not complaining, mind you. I think it's just wonderful how simply the people live, but where I come from ...

SECOND ROAD-BUILDER begins striking his hammer over stone, in cadence to his words.

SECOND ROAD-BUILDER: Si. The pig don't shit ... neither do the cowboys or their horses. Lots of times I go to pictures, but never do I see a cowboy stop behind the bush when he's on the trail of banditos who have stole his cows and raped his daughter!

MRS STEFANIK: What I meant was, you see, we're only here until April ... and then we're driving back through El Paso.

FIRST ROAD-BUILDER: Si. My father was a big man in El Paso ... poor, but a big man!

The ROAD-BUILDERS begin to laugh softly.

MRS STEPANIK exits.

Enter an AMERICAN MAN, dressed in dark, heavy winter clothing. He is upset. He holds a sheet of paper in his hands, on which he has drawn a pencil sketch of a cat.

AMERICAN MAN: Pardone me, senoras ... but have you seen this kind of el gatto? A cat is called el gatto ... no?

FIRST ROAD-BUILDER: Si, is called el gatto.

AMERICAN MAN: He's grey all over except for his derriere, which is white.

SECOND ROAD-BUILDER: Si ... el gatto is a cat in Spanish.

FIRST ROAD-BUILDER: And what you have drawn there is a good likeness of a cat.

The ROAD-BUILDERS take and pass the paper back and forth, examining it critically.

FIRST ROAD-BUILDER: Si ... it *is* a cat! I would say to my friends, *that* ... is a *cat!*

SECOND ROAD-BUILDER: The legs are longer here in front than back, but then perhaps it is a mountain cat, no?

AMERICAN MAN: That is my cat. It got lost on Monday. I am prepared to pay five hundred pesos in reward for its return!

The ROAD-BUILDERS are poised to strike the cobbles they have laid, then turn to face him, their expressions puzzled.)

FIRST ROAD-BUILDER: Five hundred pesos ... for a *cat?* Senor, you must avoid the sun!

AMERICAN MAN squats before the men, confident he has won their trust and cooperation.

AMERICAN MAN: I called him Louie, after Louisville, Kentucky ... that's where I'm from! If you see him and call him "Louie," he'll come runnin' to you, just like that!

He indicates with his fingers on the floor how the cat would trot towards anyone calling him.

SECOND ROAD-BUILDER: (*nodding dumbly*) Si.

AMERICAN MAN: I sure would like him back, senoras. He was family to me, you hear ... used to sit on the dashboard an' talk to me while I drove, an' when I'd get around to eating, he'd be right there on the table having his dinner with me... just like a small son!

FIRST ROAD-BUILDER: (*also dumbfounded*) Si ... like a small son ...

AMERICAN MAN folds up the sketch and rises from his squat.

AMERICAN MAN: I'll make it worth your while, gentlemen, if you'll pass the word around. Or find him *yourselves.* Five hundred pesos to the first man who brings Louie back, dead or alive! I'm in apartment four, across the street.

The ROAD-BUILDERS nod. The AMERICAN MAN exits.

Sounds of mariachi music. Recorded.

The ROAD-BUILDERS begin laying cobblestones furiously, their heads bent low. Then, suddenly, they both look each other in the eye, and lower their tools slowly.

FIRST ROAD-BUILDER: Ahora ... *senora!* ... If you see him and call him Louie, he will run to you like this ... (*mimics AMERICAN MAN*). Cichi-cichi-cichi!

SECOND ROAD-BUILDER: Si ... like a small son!

FIRST ROAD-BUILDER: He is like familia to me. (*shakes his head*) Five hundred pesos for a cat! ... That talks in a car and eats from your dish ... we should save our money and go to Louisville, Kentucky, amigo. They have crazy people there who make you rich!

Quick spotlight to a separate playing area of stage on sound of a baby's cry.

Mariachi music out quickly.

MRS STEFANIK, in spotlight, is peering into a doorway, her arms laden with the usual daily tourist accumulation of baskets, shawls and bananas.

MRS STEFANIK: Oh, you poor little thing! Nobody's taking care of you ... nobody's with you except your little sister, who's hardly older than you!

MRS STEFANIK begins to coo childishly and gesture with her parcel-laden hands.

MRS STEFANIK: Come to me ... come on! Come to your Canadian auntie! You're so cute, you little monkey ... I could just steal you and take you back home to Saskatoon with me!

Mariachi music up loudly, then down and out over laughing ROAD-BUILDERS and the cooing, gesturing MRS STEFANIK.

All lights to black.

Curtain

ACT 2

On sound of hammering, lights up on DANNY in the town square, at his table, writing.

The two ROAD-BUILDERS are in another area of the square, repairing cobbles.

DANNY: In Angelica, Mother, a man cuts sugar-cane from dawn to dusk ... for wages of three, maybe four dollars daily. The price of milk is forty cents a litre if you're Mexican, and seventy-five cents if you're not. A horse for rent carrying a gringo on its back for seven hours earns more money than a Mexican labourer earns in seven days. An enterprising citizen can trade a wrist-watch or a bicycle for a comfortable small home, while beside him, an American will pay as much for land and housing as he would in downtown Los Angeles or Montreal.

JOSE strolls onstage, carbine on his back, his hat pulled low, rubbing his stomach after the content-ment of a meal. He moves to the ROAD-BUILDERS and rolls their cobbles this way and that with the toe of his boot while he speaks.

JOSE: In the month of January, we predict the temperatures and rainfall of each month within the coming year ... what crops to plant and when ... what water we shall have ... according to a Mayan calendar of observations that has never failed us ... and never will.

The FIRST ROAD-BUILDER rolls back the cobbles JOSE has dislodged. He taps JOSE'S boot with the end of his hammer.

FIRST ROAD-BUILDER: (*to JOSE, who moves away to his post*) The government pays us to repair the cobbles, and not to carry stones for your amuse-ment!

DANNY: There is magic in the masks and sounds of people from the hills that both delights and frightens me.

FIRST ROAD-BUILDER: One of them asked me, through the window of his car, why I keep a cow and plant my field to corn when I earn wages.

SECOND ROAD-BUILDER: Another said, when he had drunk too much, that life is cheap in Angelica. He saw Jose shoot a gringo by the fountain.

DANNY: On the twenty-third of August, one shot—through the chest and coming out the back. That sad-faced, dark-eyed mother standing guard beside the wall ... can kill!

JOSE: (*snapping to attention, as if delivering a report to his supervisors*) He wrecked a mirror in a bar, then hurt a woman asking him to leave. I was summonsed ... arrested him and was taking him to prison. Near the fountain, he swore no dark man was taking him to jail, no sirree! He hit me with his fist, knocked me against the fountain ledge. I took my carbine off and warned him I would shoot to kill. He ripped up a paving stone and rushed at me. I shot him through the chest and left him there beside the fountain, for I had to vomit. His pale eyes ... sober now with surprise and fear ... staring at the mauve sky of the tropic night until they died with him and turned to glass.

DANNY: We, the community of shocked and chastened whites, stayed away from bars and par-ties for a month, for Jose, whom we considered a village character with a rusty carbine on his dusty back, turned out a vengeful, death-spitting angel of the south, in whose gloomy eyes, had we but looked more closely, was the burning history of conquest by the Mayans, Aztecs, Spaniards, French and Yankees, that is not yet forgotten ... or forgiven.

The ROAD-BUILDERS pick up their basket of stones and tools.

FIRST ROAD-BUILDER: The long highways of Mexico must be maintained to bring and take away whatever comes to us or leaves.

The two ROAD-BUILDERS exit.

Rock music is heard. Recorded.

Two MEXICAN GIRLS enter, led by a DANCER, and followed by a few other younger people. The DANCER dances in centre of stage, forcing back the group in a widening circle.

The TWO GIRLS clap their hands and chant in time to the music.

FIRST GIRL: On the feast of Lupe
I will write a message for him
On the chapel wall
And if he reads it
He will send me mangoes

From the hills
In a woven basket
Of coco mats and reeds
And covered with his shawl ...

SECOND GIRL:
When the horsemen come to town
My heart turns to fire
Like the scarlet tunics
That they wear ...

FIRST GIRL: On the feast of Lupe
I will tell the desert wind
To bring him to me
As a scorpion or lizard
So he can visit me at night
By sliding silent underneath
My father's door ...

SECOND GIRL: Give me music, light and fire
With a man who doesn't tire ...
Danger in his wild eyes
As through the night
He rides ... and rides ...

A DRUNK enters and tries to catch the DANCER, who giggles and lightly dances out of reach.

DANCER moves to DANNY'S table, inviting him to join her. He pushes his papers aside and jumps on top of the table. The crowd cheers as he clumsily tries to imitate her steps, then gives up.

The DRUNK moves from person to person, embracing and greeting each in turn. DANNY watches him as he comes down from the table.

DANNY: The drunks in Angelica, who manage to survive, are a gentle and a loving lot of men, well primed before the noon, their breath scented with tequila, which smells and tastes like northern moonshine. Standing in the square at a tilt of forty-five degrees, shouting salutations to all things that move—passing strangers, dogs in search of dinner, clattering Volkswagens, children throwing rope or skipping, Jose frozen in his duty, sweepers, carpenters and herdsmen ... All the world's a lover to a southern man struggling with gravity!

Sound of bell ringing sharply over music. DANNY is excited by the sound. His voice rises.

DANNY: In Saskatoon, Edmonton, Fort Saint John, we are taught to endure in silence heat, cold ... poor health ... taxes ... a wrong choice of government or marriage ... and our reward for this stoicism is an ulcered stomach, heart disease, brutality between the young and old. We drink like horses at the trough. Screw out of duty and work for generations to erase laughter, music and a purple curse out of our minds and souls. In the dead of winter, Angelica's great fiesta lights the night with song, laughter, dance and fireworks that dazzle and defy the night. For death is an enemy that fears colour, light and sound!

TWO GIRLS, DANCER exit, followed by the others.

ELENA enters, dressed in scarlet, with a shawl over her head and shoulders, moving to a point between JOSE and DANNY.

Music dies out. Bell sound becomes a steady beat that echoes the rhythm of the previous music.

JOSE and DANNY move to ELENA and take her by each arm.

ELENA: In the dead of winter, when the fields are dormant and the dust hangs like a grey cloak over eucalyptus, limes, banana palms and the tulip trees ... when the children's eyes turn gloomy, and the old ones die of slight diseases, it is time to defy ...

JOSE: The spirits of the frosty winds that circle our moon with particles of ice. We are Children of the Mountains and the Light!

ELENA: In the dead of winter, when the birth of Christ is the death of seasons, when the bones of our ancestors stir and shift within the soil ... and their moans are heard in the sad, far cry of the wild grey dove ...

JOSE: It is time to wear clothes dyed in the colours of the flames ... blood and rising sun!

DANNY: In the winter evenings, I write to my mother. And in the evenings I go to the post office of the fascist colonel for replies to letters which I never wrote.

ELENA: It is time for men to think of autumn babies ... and to plan new hatchings from the winter eggs!

JOSE: It is time to dress our heads in the old carved masks of demons ... which frighten death and sadness out of town!

ELENA: Eat boiled green garbanzos in the shelter of the wall and exchange wisecracks with the passing people!

DANNY: Season now of flu, and jingle-bells without the snow ... I get lonely so far from my natural home!

JOSE: Those who came to die, or write a book ... are at their worst.

Procession of AMERICAN TOURISTS and RESIDENTS enters and passes before DANNY, ELENA and JOSE, shaking them by the hand and leaving.

JOSE: Grey-faced and with eyes that are trapped and frightened ... they buy things for other people's children ... wish the postmaster, mayor and myself a happy Christmas. But when we reach out to embrace them ... to assure them that man can make even the short days happy ones ... they stand like pillars ... their hands frozen to their sides ... I feel sorry for the norteamericanos when I wish him Merry Christmas in his language!

ELENA laughs, watching DANNY stiffly facing the procession. Impulsively, she takes him by the shoulders and kisses him quickly on the mouth.

ELENA: (*almost desperately*) Merry Christmas, dear Danny! ... May everything you wish come true for you!

JOSE touches ELENA on her arm.

JOSE: Let him do what he has to do, Elena.

After the PROCESSION leaves, bell sounds die.

TWO CHILDREN enter and begin to play marbles in front of JOSE, ELENA and DANNY. JOSE moves to his post. ELENA moves slowly into exit, her head lowered. DANNY returns to his table.

DANNY: So I weathered Christmas and the new year coming and lived to see another white noon in the square of Angelica.

JOSE: The time of avocado blossoms is the time of my birth.

DANNY: My mother wrote to me—Danny, you must understand my health is not what it used to be. The family business would do better were you here. Were your father living, he'd be proud to know his work continues with his son ...

DANNY begins to laugh. JOSE peers at him and shakes his head.

DANNY: So I should return, to sell shoes manufactured by the better brand manufacturers to Canadians with icy feet! ... I should take an interest in the politics of property ... join the Junior Chamber ... dress like a businessman ... entertain ... contribute to Red Feather and United Fund ... run for the school board ... behave like a model citizen. Forget Elena and the dusty, populated seasons of the heart ... it would be an easy drift for me. I could never be a hippy or a rebel. I came to Mexico in my own Volkswagen bus and Samsonite luggage. I motelled all the way ... ate in the better restaurants.

ELENA enters with a burst of laughter, on the arm of GABRIEL. They pass the children, and stop. Under ELENA'S urging, they squat and mime a game of marbles, but with erotic gestures, private giggles.

ELENA: (*exclaiming*) Oh, but we will play!

DANNY: I first rented a small house in Angelica when I came, fully furnished and supplied with maid and laundry service. There was to be no hardship in this experience for me, for I was a white Canadian, holder of an M.A. in history and English, all paid for through insurance policies my father left at death ...

ELENA laughs, pushes GABRIEL over on his side.

ELENA: How can I play when I have no marbles? Give me some marbles, my dear Gabriel. I would trade my virtue for a sack of marbles!

GABRIEL remains lying on his side, laughing.

GABRIEL: I will give you marbles by the kilo ... a good woman should get what a good man can give her!

JOSE: (*muttering darkly*) This good man will get a haircut and six months in the camp, if he keeps it up!

DANNY smiles and turns to ELENA.

DANNY: I met her in the Grand Hotel. She brought me coffee when I went into the restaurant for breakfast, my clothes neatly pressed and a blue necktie wrapped around my heart and mind.

ELENA: What else?

DANNY: I would like two eggs, senorita … fried lightly and turned over once.

ELENA laughs again and rises to her feet.

ELENA: I will bring you eggs—fried, battered … boiled … whipped … nailed to the wall, if you'll only smile at me. You're a bad omen for a happy girl … the first man I see this morning, and he growls like a peddler's dog!

DANNY: I haven't seen you in the restaurant before.

ELENA: My cousin Julia left for the city on the morning bus. I am working in her place, but only for this day. Tomorrow, I will serve people that I know.

DANNY: Are you from Angelica?

ELENA: Angelica is the only town I know. There must be others … bigger, for the bigger people. I will bring your eggs, senor.

DANNY: I'm sorry if I seemed distant when I saw you.

JOSE swats at a flying wasp with his hat.

JOSE: Caramba!

ELENA: Don't apologize … just leave fifty pesos for a tip. I have shoes to mend, and my hair needs trimming. (*laughs*) I will bring your eggs, senor!

DANNY: A few days later, she moved in with me … quietly …for the stern eye of Jose seldom blinked where Elena was concerned. She brought me eggs and tea to bed each morning, arranged my books and opened all the windows of the room.

ELENA: They put glass in the houses built for gringos! It stinks in here! It stinks of wax and socks and tired sex!

DANNY: (*protesting*) Your voice is as gentle as a mountie's siren, my beloved.

ELENA: (*soaring*) Wear harachis like our campesinos do, so your feet can air! Make love in the mornings so I can hang the sheets to dry in the first heat of the rising sun! On the other hand, never mind … I am sick of you already, Danny Baker!

DANNY: (*smiling*) And with that, she dumped the soft eggs on top of my blankets. I swore at her and she picked up the pot of tea and poured it on my pillow, round my head. The first time we parted, I hit her with the handle of the broom as she fled down the stairway to the street.

ELENA laughs and, offering her hand to GABRIEL, lifts him to his feet. They move away, hand in hand.

ELENA: What you've lost, someone else has gained! But never mind—we will play again!

GABRIEL and ELENA exit, laughing.

DANNY goes to the CHILDREN, who rise now. He helps them collect their marbles and pocket them.

DANNY: (*thoughtfully*) We all manage to survive … even those of us who never have to fight for shelter and integrity.

FIRST CHILD: Mama sings in the morning
When she sweeps the cobwebs from the walls
Dust and feathers from the floor.

SECOND CHILD: My father picks his nose
And eats it while he thinks
Of places he will pilfer wood
To exchange for melons and for lard.

Woman's song up in background. DANNY responds happily to the sound. He moves across the stage, indicating places in the town.

DANNY: The streets are named for heroes of the revolution and the reconstruction: Juarez … Lopez Mateos … Pancho Villa … the Avenue of Children … In the heat of afternoon, the white, bright, cobble-scattered, water-speckled afternoon of an Angelica day … Raul, the keeper of the stable, rides the dunes beside the lake on Diablo, the white stallion belonging to a former presidente. The horse whinnies and Raul shouts. The earth rumbles underneath its iron hooves!

Stage lights slowly darken to half-light.

DANNY: A spray of sand and flecks of foam fly as Diablo and his rider become one—teeth bared, bent into the wind like arrows flying. Galloping over pale sands of Lake Chapala. Disappearing into eucalyptus groves and then reappearing. Galloping in water now … grey water beaten to a mist … by Diablo's iron hooves.

JOSE removes his hat and beats the dust from it. Then, taking out a cloth, he sits down at his post and begins polishing his carbine.

JOSE: In the afternoon, brother, the coffee has turned cold and tastes like sewage in the market. The girls in the restaurants sit in the shade and knit.

Slides are projected in diffused focus over darkened stage. Scenes of people occupied with various chores.

DANNY: And in quiet tones, discuss the coffee drinkers: Bell and her noisy children, whom she hits with a silver fork across the knuckles; Mercedes Perez, doctora who invites an illness with her languid eyes, delicious thighs and septic hands ... legendary healer of small dark children with dysentery ... and white gentlemen with clap ...

JOSE: Antonio, the fixer ... a hot lunch and four hundred pesos buys anything from Antonio—a two-year visa ... marriage license ... death certificate.

DANNY: Blind Santo, who plays one note on his harmonica beside your open window until he's paid to go away. Over coffee he listens for the addresses of all newcomers to the town, so he can serenade them at a later time.

JOSE: The pimp, Augustino ... hustling disease and brightly-coloured woven shawls of finest mountain wool.

DANNY: The soldier, Gus ... ancient remnant of an ancient war.

Slides out.

JOSE snaps to attention and brandishes his rifle in imitation of Gus in battle.

Spotlight in two separate areas, on JOSE and DANNY.

JOSE: There was enemy to the left of me! Enemy to the right of me! Enemy in front ... and five hundred krauts back of me!

DANNY: I jumped upon the sorrel's back, and rode full gallop into that misty valley filled with death. When I reach the swirling cloud, my horse coughed once and fell beneath me.

JOSE: I saw a bicycle, and a dead hun lying near it!

DANNY: I took that cycle, lads ... and rode it ... a sturdy, German-made machine it was, that took the cobbled roadway like a dream.

JOSE: But the mist was thick as soup, settling on the eye-pieces of my mask.

DANNY: Soon, I could no longer see, and fearing an encounter with a wall or fallen cow ...

JOSE: I ripped that blasted mask away and cycled on until I fell. But by then, I had reached our lines, and the day was saved!

A loud, distant cheer that is wheezy and plaintive offstage.

Full lights onstage.

DANNY: Old Gus was pensioned by the government of His Majesty, the King of England, to sustain him for what months of life remained for him.

JOSE: He turned eighty-six in Angelica last July.

DANNY: He fights his morning war for an audience of one or twenty, punctuating his great ride with hammer blows of fist upon the table ... spitting blood and sputum out the door and cursing his contempt for lesser men than he.

JOSE: Every inch a gentleman. He salutes me like a soldier when he passes ... in tennis shoes and English sweater, white pants stained with urine ... and the hard eyes of an English sparrowhawk. I return his salute, the only man I honour in this way, for he is an honest and a dedicated fool!

ELENA enters, a metal bucket of bean cuttings in her hand.

ELENA: (*shouting*) Garbanzos! Who will buy garbanzos?

JOSE brightens and waves to her, gesturing for her to come towards him.

JOSE: (*chiding*) Elena ... Elena—think! The wife of a constable need never eat the peasant beans again! You must soon decide, my flower ... for you are growing older!

ELENA: Our kings fed upon them on the eve of battle! Lovers eat them on the mountains, when they tire of the other things that lovers do. Garbanzos! Who will buy garbanzos?

JOSE: The revolution promised us that we could strive to rise above our past, Elena! Open sewers and garbanzos are as reactionary as secret wishes for return of slavery!

ELENA: There is no dark bread to be had in Mexico tonight. The revolution gave us Coca Cola and white bread. We may fart our way to freedom on such food, who knows? But I'll take my chances with the older, stronger stuff of which my mother's bones and mine were made … Garbanzos! Who will buy garbanzos?

JOSE is exasperated.

JOSE: Elena! I *order* you to stop shouting like a country tart!

ELENA stares at him, then laughs.

ELENA: You? … Order me? Hero with the rusty yankee rifle and pants cut for a wider arse than yours! Protector of a revolution remembered now by old and toothless men. *You* … would order me? Kiss my ass!

JOSE: Elena … my uncle was a mayor once … a leader of the people. I have obligations I cannot forget, even for you!

ELENA: Piss on your obligations … and piss on your uncle's grave for inspiring a fool! I am a woman of my time—if my thigh itches me, I scratch! If I wish to be a doctor or a field hand or a whore, I will be all that and more! … And heaven help the revolution that has made millionaires of petty bureaucrats who walk upon me as if I was a paving stone! (*loudly, defiantly*) Garbanzos! Who will buy garbanzos from me?

JOSE is very upset now. He begs with a gesture of his hand for her to desist. She flips her skirt about her in a gesture of derision.

ELENA: I am nothing in this town except a body and a mouth that is known to amuse.

JOSE: That is not so, Elena!

ELENA: The role fits well and is easy to maintain. I have dogs and horses that obey me. You have people … and I am not a dog or a horse. Sometimes I think the revolution has forgotten this. There are open sewers in the streets, Jose, my flower with a gun and dark, forbidding eyes.

Old women beg for food, and children sleep on floors made of earth. I beg and sleep with them sometimes, and if I please my cunt at other times, that is my affair. Good things have been known to come of that as well! (*loudly, in a shout*) Garbanzos! Who will buy garbanzos?

She throws her bucket across the stage into the wings, and exits in the opposite direction.

DANNY looks sadly at JOSE.

DANNY: Neither he nor I saw Elena after that … and our loneliness and loss brought us closer than we would both admit. I pass him in the evenings … and if the square is empty for a moment, he lifts his eyes to mine and we recognize within each other the same tyranny … the same victims of forces larger than ourselves.

JOSE turns away from DANNY and busies himself with tacking a public notice on the door of the municipal hall.

JOSE: She left, some say, to train herself for singing opera. I wish her well, but no one from Angelica has been known to rise above the town. It is a simple town with simple ways, and all things cannot be achieved in one lifetime … or two. Yet, I wish her well … and if ever she returns, I will care for her.

Light deepens into gloom, with two spotlights on DANNY and JOSE.

Woman's song in background.

DANNY: Twilight falls like purple petals on the streets of Santa Angelica … the lemon-blossom-scented air is like a sleep-inducing drug.

JOSE: The grey waters lap the shore … and in the mountains two kilometres away, the gentle wind stirs dust in clouds that resemble evening mist in cooler places.

DANNY: Fishermen, silhouetted in the dying light, haul nets into boats designed ten thousand years ago. The women gather laundry left drying on the stones, their dusky faces and their eyes haunted by memories of long ago … of kings who rode this valley, their glowing helmets ablaze with quetzel plumes gathered from the places of the dead.

JOSE: Their shields emblazoned with the crests of gods!

Sound of bell tolling over song.

PADRE EDWARDO enters, dressed in priests' robes. He makes the sign of the cross when he enters JOSE'S pool of light.

PADRE EDWARDO: May the evening find you peaceful, senor.

JOSE: There is no peace, padre! Behind the kiss, I have visions of the grave. All this is nothing. We must rise on the ashes of our former glory if we are to survive at all.

PADRE EDWARDO: What former glory do you remember now, Jose?

JOSE: (*animated*) The mountains trembled once and flashed with fire. We were heroes—every man, woman and child—and not smiling, tolerant, forgiving, poor people biding our time for God knows what destiny to smile on us once again! Great industry once split our mountains … machines of the gods once moved boulders through our lands! We built heroic monuments that still stand to puzzle and defy us to this day.

PADRE EDWARDO: The earth is a puzzle, and everything that grows and dies upon it is a puzzle. It is enough to bide and trust some providence wiser than ourselves.

PADRE EDWARDO blesses JOSE once more and slowly moves into the darkness. JOSE watches him exit.

DANNY: The padre is mistaken. Had he taken a moment more to study Jose's face, he might have realized how wrong he was …

JOSE: This is the land of silver, gold and jade, of fields winter-scorched with heat and dust … of yellow acacia whose scent can deaden hunger … of pathways beaten a metre deep into rock and soil by footsteps of a thousand generations … land of the condor and the raven and the fleshy cactus whose blood is life to us in times of famine.

DANNY: Fields of sugar-cane and citrus border Angelica like primeval forests, whose fruits burn the throat like fire. The evening deepens … the lemon sky deepens into purple of the tropic night.

Woman's song dies out.

Sound of crickets. Recorded.

JOSE: Cicados begin their nightly serenade … it is time to check the highway for accidents and poachers of mesquite returning from the hills!

Shouldering his carbine, he turns and exits. Light dies out in his playing area.

Rock music up faintly in background. Recorded.

Spot light on TWO MEXICAN GIRLS, embroidering shirts, seated back to back, facing away from each other. They chant their speeches in time to the music.

FIRST GIRL: On the feast of Lupe
I will drop my baby brother
On his head
So I might be relieved of caring for him
And return to school …
I will learn to be a nurse
Treating children for diphtheria.

SECOND GIRL: When evening comes
I stand beside my father's wall
Knitting shawls of black and crimson
Waiting for the passing horsemen
Waiting for the mango seller
Waiting for the blind beggar
Waiting for the laughing woman
Waiting for the smelly herdsman
Waiting for the toothless cobbler
Waiting for the English teacher
To tell me of the presidente's visit
To London and to Moscow.

FIRST GIRL: On the feast of Lupe
I will visit our padre
And ask him for forgiveness
Then I'll go into the graveyard
And tell my great-grandfather
I have ample food and clothing.
Sulfa cures the wounds that killed him
Death and fear no longer shade me
Which changes how I think and function
I will kneel and ask forgiveness
For changing all that he remembered.

Rock music dies abruptly.

The TWO GIRLS instantly drop their handiwork, and, turning into a side-by-side position, lift ancient godmasks to their faces.

DANNY: I walk home through Angelica in the night, my nostrils wakening to the scents of time and places distant from my prairie home three thousand miles to the north. The land of my mother's letters deep in snow and frost, grey poplars frozen on the landscape, footsteps squeaking through the night that overcomes us both. I walk through odours of lemon peel ... scalding peppers ... steaming beans ... the wild smell of roasting beef, newly slaughtered ... pungent tortillas and the ever-present scent of earth and stone washed a thousand years with the urine of people and the animals they bred and ate.

The TWO GIRLS rise slowly to their feet, masks held over their faces. Light changes to colour on them.

DANNY begins to pace.

Sound of drums beating.

DANNY: Passing my apartment, I look up at the darkened windows, a dead chamber built for dead souls to inhabit. A chill passes through my body, though the night is warm and scented now with blossoms of the orange and the lemon trees, open-petalled like a loving woman in the darkness.

The TWO GIRLS move towards him in frightening movements.

DANNY: I am afraid now ... helpless! Isolated from furniture and faces that I know, the anecdotes and illusions of a younger race, I listened to the sound of cities buried by volcanoes centuries ago, voices of singers long returned to earth. Kings, slaves, warriors, fleeing refugees streaming down the mountainsides in shame and triumph, the copper in their skins aglow. The must of love and combat on their lips. Vultures crowding them against the rocks, their Egyptian vessels filled with corn, lentils and oil cutting deep into their skulls and backs.

Drum beats stop.

FIRST GIRL: Welcome to the house of light! There is nothing you must fear but yourself. Once the glare of our light burns into your eyes, you will be blind to all things of which you have no further need!

DANNY shields his eyes with his hands against the voice and mask of the girl.

DANNY: Elena? ... Is that you?

SECOND GIRL: No ... I am the sound and sight of all women, so listen carefully to me. You will not know the texture of this sand, the taste of life and death so far from home until you know my songs.

DANNY: Where can I meet you? How will I know you?

FIRST GIRL: I am the night which ends the sunlit day... I carry secrets of the morning in my ancient hands, and give them to you. One by one. Emeralds, bracelets made of purest gold, adorn yourself with them. Flowers are your riches, stranger to my house and womb. Dress yourself in green plumes, in plumes of the sunbird, gold and black. In the red birds' dress, red as light. Weave them in the song of drums ... for flowers are your riches!

Sound of dogs barking, people shouting.

Light up on full stage. TWO GIRLS have dropped their masks and settled to their embroidery work.

JOSE is at his post, watching DANNY and laughing.

DANNY is bewildered and looks around himself.

DANNY: I learned nothing from the songs ... there can be no pretence to learn the secrets of the centuries in what appears to me as one short day and night. If we did, how difficult it would be to wage a war!

DANNY suddenly salutes JOSE, as a soldier saluting a commanding officer. JOSE stiffens to attention, his expression suddenly grave and severe.

DANNY: What sir? ... Fight them, sir? ... No, I'm afraid I cannot ... I'm ruined for that ... I've embraced their men and made love to their women. Well, you see, sir, to kill people like that would be like killing myself, or my grandfather. I heard their old songs, once, and they were the soul and spirit of ... of members of my own family! Huh? ... Stick their old songs up my arse, you say, sir? ... You don't understand ... no, no! You really don't understand ... that you are a strange, perverse dinosaur ... Sir!

DANNY drops his salute and laughs. JOSE also relaxes and, leaning back against the municipal office door, also laughs.

DANNY returns to settle at his table, picks up a sheet of paper and resumes writing.

DANNY: It is always morning in Angelica, dear Mother. Yesterday, Ignatio, the thief, sold me the mirror he'd stolen from my car last Thursday. His wife had another baby, and his brother, Jesus, broke an ankle falling from the Pepsi truck ... so Ignatio's lapse of memory is forgivable this time. Elena ... who guided me when first I came here ... is gone now, Mother. In Canada, she might do profitable and interesting things, I think, but in Santa Angelica ...

He hesitates, his face showing strong sorrow. He suddenly rises and, gathering his papers, rips and scatters them.

Sound of rock music in background. Recorded.

The TWO GIRLS rise and begin folding their work. They chant as they work, in cadence to the music.

FIRST GIRL: On the feast of Lupe
A stranger came to town
With flare-bottom trousers
That almost touched the ground.

SECOND GIRL: We heard stories from Elena
Of bedding him at night
But when she told him that she loved him
She said that he cried.

DANNY turns on them angrily.

DANNY: That's a lie! (*considers*) No ... it's true ... it's true. I said to her that I was afraid of her having a baby by me. She laughed and then took my head in both her hands, looked into my face and told me ... when she was a child, an earthquake destroyed her father's home. When her father pulled all the children and their mother from the dust and rubble and found them unhurt, he said, "Thank God, the people have been spared again!" And before the dust and smoke had settled, he was pulling bricks and tile from the wreckage, discarding broken pieces, saving ones that were still intact. Her father sang as he stirred mortar and began rebuilding a new home.

FIRST GIRL: I carry secrets of the morning in my ancient hands and hand them to you ... one by one ... emeralds, bracelets made of purest gold.

DANNY: Singing his joy at being spared to live on.

SECOND GIRL: Flowers of the desert are your riches. Dress yourself in green plumes ... in plumes of the sunbird, gold and black.

DANNY: Then, the entire town in song, each man and his family rebuilding what had been destroyed! She explained to me, a child was no

curse ... it was the greatest blessing ... for as long as people made people, Angelica in the sun lives forever, with her gleaming cobbles.

Projected slides, projected randomly off lit stage, through theatre auditorium, scenes of buildings, people, colour of Mexico.

Rock music up in volume.

DANNY: The fools who come to visit ... old women with baskets on their heads ... copper-glowing maidens drowsing in the doorways ... heroes riding horses by the water's edge ... the white burst of lemon blossoms on the boulevard ... the pain of birth and death in the singing, scented night ... dogs with human wisdom in their eyes ... the cobblers ... beggars ... herdsmen ... masons ... merchants ... singers ... talkers ... taxi drivers and lame walkers ... priests and whores all out of doors ... peddlers who tell lies ... maids with slavery in their eyes ...

Slide projection tempo speeds up now.

DANNY: Gleaming sun and languid rhythms ... blazing gardens so well hidden. Night and day the city hums ... to the beat of ancient drums ...

JOSE begins to clap to the tempo of the words and music.

The TWO GIRLS have now moved to either side of DANNY. He puts his arms around their shoulders and leans over to kiss the SECOND GIRL on the cheek.

Sudden stop to rock music.

Once the music is cut, all activity is frozen. The scene must have the effect of a three-dimensional holiday photograph in colour.

Slowly, the light dies, going into black.

Woman's song in background. Recorded.

SONG: Subi à la sala del crimen
Le pregunto el presidente
Que sies delite el correrte
Que me sentencie la muerto
Ah-Ah
Corazon porque no amas ...

End

PLOUGHMEN OF THE GLACIER

Ploughmen of the Glacier marks Ryga's return to and his celebration of his adopted community of British Columbia. In it he pits two men, polar opposites, against each other in an ongoing mental and physical combat, each man echoing the roughhewn parts of an often divided and contentious land, and a synthesis of their positions becomes what, for Ryga, amounts to the raw heart of Canada's westernmost province. One is a cultured, cynical writer, the other a rough, idealistic miner. Both are broadly drawn, the stuff of myth, each based on figures historical as well as legendary, while the setting, although tied to actual geographic locations, is also specified in the stage directions as being "surrealistic," a literary form later to be dubbed "magic realism." The play attempts to further mythologize a people in a specific time and place through what Ryga called "telepathic drama," a shorthand language of gestures and locutions which would be deeply familiar to local audiences, wherein commonly shared sounds and values are intended to trigger associations, producing a harmony of recognition between the actors and the audience. In the wiles and exclamations of Lowery and Brown, in their dashed dreams and warm regrets, and in the familiar sights and sounds of their environment, the audience is meant to identify something of the emerging collective unconscious of British Columbia.

As with many of Ryga's plays, this was another commission, this time initially from a group attempting to organize an "Okanagan Images" festival of the arts. For his story Ryga returned to a radio play he had written in 1973, *Dreams Are Made of Gold Dust*, which he had written while collaborating with BC historian and folklorist Bill Barlee, editor of *Canada West* magazine. It was in *Canada West* that Ryga had read Barlee's article, "The Lost Mine of Pitt Lake" (Winter 1970), which he tells the tale of "Volcanic" Brown, a longtime grizzled miner from Grand Forks, BC, who for years had attempted to discover the infamous Slumach mine. (John Slumach was a Salish Native who turned up in New Westminster with an impressive poke of gold. He kept the secret of his "lost mine"—right up to his death by hanging in 1891 after being convicted of murder). After seven years of trying, Brown never did find the mine, and simply disappeared in the rugged mountain wilderness. Robert Lowery was a thirty-year-long editor of Kootenay area newspapers: a colourful, feisty man, he was not afraid of controversy, eventually being boycotted by both the CPR and the Post Office!

Ploughmen of the Glacier was officially commissioned by the Okanagan Mainline Regional Arts Council. It was staged by the Western Canada Theatre Company of Kamloops, directed by Tom Kerr, and featured Richard Farrel as Volcanic, Eric Schneider as Lowery, and Keith Dinicol as Poor Boy. On provincial tour during April and May, it opened in Vancouver at the David Y. H. Lui Theatre on May 10, 1976.

Having clearly missed the fact that Ryga's characters in this play were embodiments of pre-existent folk heroes, themselves already much larger than life in the minds of their own contemporaries, and whose fates had remained unresolved and mysterious, many critics faulted the play for what they perceived to be its "lack of action," "thematic floundering," an "uncertain ending," and even, occasionally, its use of "cartoon-like characters"! Some, however, lauded the play's attempt to use poetic folk forms to capture the frontier spirit of British Columbia. Max Wyman of the *Vancouver Sun* (May 11, 1976) concluded, "The play ... is not Ryga's greatest, but it does give us an interesting sidelong view on the origins of Lotusland."

PLOUGHMEN OF THE GLACIER

CHARACTERS

VOLCANIC
LOWERY
POOR BOY

SET

The setting is possibly surrealistic to suggest a mountainside, up and down which POOR BOY struggles in his eternal, groping quest. There is a mine shaft, the edge of a cabin, but all is staged and designed to highlight the elemental loneliness of the protagonists. The setting must also be flexible enough to allow for a momentary escape into another time, another place, in part of Act 2.

ACT 1

A harmonica is heard sounding a tuneless, repetitive few phrases of music played by POOR BOY as he struggles with his leaking water buckets.

The lights go up.

There is the sound of a pick from inside the mine shaft, plus the sound of wind. LOWERY is in front of the mine shaft. POOR BOY is crossing an inclined riser.

LOWERY: (*shouting*) Volcanic! Volcanic, you in there? Is Volcanic in there, Po' Boy?

POOR BOY shrugs.

Volcanic, you in there? Goddammit!

VOLCANIC: (*his voice muffled, the pick axe sound stopping*) Who wants to know?

LOWERY: It's me, Lowery!

VOLCANIC: (*roaring with laughter*) Go to hell, Lowery!

LOWERY: You perverse, argumentative old son-of-a-bitch! There was nothing funny about that. Get your ass up here. I wanna talk to you!

There are a few more pick strokes, then silence. The flap of the mine shaft entrance opens showing a flicker of flames from within. VOLCANIC emerges quickly as if expelled from the shaft by some force. He walks awkwardly, for he is without toes on his feet.

VOLCANIC: (*heartily*) Lowery! I'd heard you'd died ... choked on your own bile, someone said. Happened while you slept, dreamin' of mine managers ... railway superintendents ... a high-steppin' whore or two!

LOWERY: (*sardonically*) Bein' nice to me won't help now!

VOLCANIC laughs and dusts himself off in such a way that dust flies in LOWERY'S face. LOWERY coughs.

Constable Long Alex came to see me. You know why, don't you?

VOLCANIC: (*laughing*) I was only funnin', Lowery. Same way you fun with me sometimes!

LOWERY: (*annoyed*) Well I didn't think it funny!

VOLCANIC: It sure was somethin' to see ... that flat-faced Indian constable, blinkin' like he'd been pole-axed when I told him ...

LOWERY: ... that I'd been raped by a brown bear!

VOLCANIC: Yeh ... while you was sittin' by the creek, readin' a book. Musta been the old brown overcoat you wear reminded the bear of his widow!

LOWERY: You make it difficult to believe there is some redeeming virtue in all of us ...

VOLCANIC: That constable sure stood up an' took notice when I told him.

LOWERY: You make it difficult to remember that man has mastered the skills of printing an' binding poems ...

VOLCANIC: It sure was funny.

LOWERY: ... that great music was composed and performed as a tribute to the human will.

VOLCANIC: I bet he's been tellin' everyone ... that Lowery got raped by a brown bear.

LOWERY: (*in frustration*) You're a savage! This country is overrun by savages ... burning trees off the mountains an' drillin' holes through them ... all for a handful of gold ... a wheelbarrow of galena! You break your health finding fortunes ... an' overnight it's gone ... in a card game ... or in a mining swindle at the hands of a bandit from Ontario, where every woman who bears a child brings yet another bandit into this world!

VOLCANIC: (*with elation*) Lowery, you old sack of bones ... that's all there is to life, don't you see?

LOWERY: Hah!

VOLCANIC: There's nothin' more!

LOWERY: Talkin' to you is like conversing with a windmill. You don't listen ... you don't read ... you don't hear nothin' ...

VOLCANIC: (*pausing before he answers*) In my heart ... there's a different drum a-beatin'!

LOWERY stares him in the face, incredulous.

LOWERY: In your heart ... there's *what*?

VOLCANIC: Lowery, inside of me is somethin' like the innards of a mountain. When I go into a mountain, I can smell its guts! I can smell its liver ... its heart. Gold! Everywhere I turn to break stone, I smell gold!

LOWERY: So you hack an' butcher ... spewing everything out the hole you've made.

VOLCANIC: It keeps me livin' ...

LOWERY: It's not life, Volcanic ... Nothing you earn goes into making your life better or more meaningful. Slaves in ancient Greece worked shorter hours for better pay than you. The same with men in jails. You're not even doin' it out of greed anymore. You're a lunatic now ... the rock dust's made you crazy.

VOLCANIC sighs deeply and painfully, tries to straighten his back, but the effort required is more than he can manage. He sits down and taps his boots with a short stick.

VOLCANIC: See my feet, Lowery? See 'em?

LOWERY: Yeh, I see them. What the hell has that got to do with anything?

VOLCANIC: You know why the front of my boots is turned up like that?

LOWERY: Have you thought ... that Chinese miners never complain? ... They save all they earn, do the foulest work, but never complain ... One day, the white race may work for them the way they work for us. When all the mountains are blasted, crushed, an' all that's worth anything taken by the Yanks, what will remain? Will we find work as gardeners for the children of the Chinese miners? Have you thought about that, Volcanic?

VOLCANIC: No toes!

LOWERY: Huh?

VOLCANIC: I got no toes on my feet.

LOWERY: (*staring at VOLCANIC'S boots*) No toes? I've often wondered ... You born that way?

VOLCANIC: (*proudly*) Nope. I froze 'em an' had them cut off ... to save the rest of my feet. But it don't bother me. Even without toes I can walk straighter than you because I got somethin' to live for ...

He points at the burlap-covered mine shaft.

... in there!

LOWERY: In there! ... You're stoking the fires of hell for the man you killed! You're dead, Volcanic!

VOLCANIC: An' you! ... You walk hunched over like a moose with kidney stones! I take a hammer to the goddamned mountain an' I'm livin'!

The sound of a harmonica played by POOR BOY is heard.

You're bent over a piece of paper shakin' like this ... shakin' all over ... shakin' from drink, squintin' at words you've written but can't read no more, because your paper's been rained on. What kind of way is that for a man to live? ... Or die?

LOWERY: (*shaken*) Where did you hear all that, Volcanic? Have other men said that?

The harmonica music dies. POOR BOY crosses the stage, whistling now, a water bucket in his hand.

You been hearin' people saying things about me, Poor Boy?

POOR BOY exits.

VOLCANIC: (*shuddering*) Every time he passes through my life, Lowery ... the seasons change.

LOWERY: Carryin' water up his mountain. Like Sisyphus ... always carryin' water to the high, dry places ...

VOLCANIC: Like a dream, carryin' water to his shack. Fillin' this big trough that leaks, same's his bucket ... So he'll have water to save his shack ... for when the mountain starts to burn.

LOWERY: But he'll perish?

VOLCANIC: Yep. He'll die, an' then he'll rot ...

LOWERY: Each time a crow flies over me, throwin' a big shadow over my head, I look up, hunching in my coat, thinkin' it's a vulture. I don't want to spend the rest of my life doin' that ...

VOLCANIC: (*laughing*) That's because you're on the dark side of things, snarlin' like a dog with yellow, worn-out teeth!

LOWERY: There's been an eclipse on reason down below ... The poor I tried to help can't help me in return. I can write and publish the finest newspaper in America, but it's the money of advertisers keeps me goin' ... The men I fight pay for my paper, my clothes ... my food.

VOLCANIC: (*strutting*) Me? I walk on the sunny side! I walk on what's left of my two feet ... throw out my chest an' I'm crowin' so the whole mountain hears me! I'm crowin', Lowery ... an' everything younger an' weaker than old Volcanic gets the hell out of the way!

LOWERY: (*also laughing*) An' I cringe each time a crow flies over me ... But we both lived this long, so what the hell!

VOLCANIC: You never lived at all, Lowery! Your mother had a still-born baby she forgot to throw out with the slops! ... Look at you ... hunched over ... sniffin' the earth for a piece of gossip an' a free drink! What are you?

LOWERY: (*grinning*) An honest man surrounded by thieves stealing a country I meant to save once!

VOLCANIC: You're a drunk ... a walking disaster! Ever hold a pick like this in your hand? You ever cracked into a mountain to find what's been buried there a million years, waitin' for you to take?

LOWERY: Nope. But I have a brain which tells me all I ever need to know about such madness. One day, I'll buy a small house somewhere ... plant a flower garden ...

VOLCANIC: Goddamned deer will eat it up! ...

LOWERY: Yeh. I suppose ...

VOLCANIC: Trouble with you, Lowery, is you don't eat right ...

LOWERY: Don't start on that ...

VOLCANIC: Someone's got to tell you ...

LOWERY: I didn't come all this way to hear you pontificate about where you went right and everyone else went wrong. But I was interested in writing an article on edible herbs growing wild in these mountains ...

VOLCANIC: So?

LOWERY: So ... remembering you would eat just about anything under or above ground, I had intended to get some information from you.

VOLCANIC: About what?

LOWERY: Well, like why you do it? Did your mother beat you for doing something to the meat on the dinner table?

VOLCANIC: (*threatening*) Eh? ... Eh!

LOWERY: (*laughing*) Why else would anyone eat armloads of hay an' weeds when there's food around?

VOLCANIC: (*angry now*) Say it! ... Go ahead an' let me hear you say it!

LOWERY: Say what?

VOLCANIC: That the only food fit for a man is the flesh of a pig!

LOWERY: Of course I'll say it. I like bacon ... ham ... boiled hocks and beans.

VOLCANIC: That only proves what a goddamned savage *you* are! Don't ever put on airs with me about my manners ... or what I don't know about books! I know a lot more than you about some things … you remember that!

LOWERY: (*goading*) Now what in hell is wrong with the way I eat?

VOLCANIC: (*snorting with derision*) I could walk down my path an' whistle at magpies … They'd know what I'm sayin', but not you … Why talk to you? Why waste my time jawin' with someone like you?

LOWERY: Come on, Volcanic …

VOLCANIC: (*with passion*) Somethin's got to die to feed *you*! That's not right … The Almighty didn't intend it should be that way. No sirree … everything I need to feed myself is out there, growin' outside my door like the Almighty Himself said it should be.

LOWERY: Now how in hell would God know where you'd put your front door?

VOLCANIC: No sense talkin' to you …

LOWERY: And as for food living and dyin' … the carrot pulled out of the ground … or an apple off a tree … dies when a man gets his paw on it.

VOLCANIC: No use sayin' anythin' to you …

LOWERY: Everything dies so something else can live. A *pig* gets the knife when I want bacon. Same's a fish dies when I order trout for supper. Wheat dies an' gets crushed an' cooked when I ask for bread. A whole vine of grapes gets to meet its maker so I can have wine …

VOLCANIC: Shut up! I don't wanna hear your stupid arguments … I know what's right even if you don't!

LOWERY: Dead horse manure … the deader the better … makes a cornfield live and grow. When I die, the coffin worms will have a picnic …

VOLCANIC: Now you done it! … For a man worried about other people's manners, you sure got a lot to learn about yours, Lowery!

LOWERY: (*curious*) What has my point of view got to do with manners? You say one thing, I say another …

VOLCANIC: You talk like you'd never learned manners. Talkin' about them worms makes me want to vomit.

LOWERY: You killed a man once, Volcanic. I was at your trial …

VOLCANIC ponders this comment, then grins with pride.

VOLCANIC: Yeh, I did … yeh.

He lifts up his arms as if sighting down a gun barrel.

Boom, an' down he went. One more boom to make sure he don't get up no more … But they found me innocent, Lowery … self-defence, you know.

LOWERY: Self-defence indeed! … The judge at your trial reckoned you was about half the value of the man you'd killed, so hangin' you for it was a waste of rope an' a hangman's time!

They both laugh and stretch wearily in unison.

VOLCANIC: You et yet, Lowery?

LOWERY: No. But I'll be goin' back into town …

VOLCANIC: Naw …

LOWERY: Watching you eat your evening rations of hay is one thing. Being invited to partake of same is … out of the question.

VOLCANIC: (*becoming angry*) Don't start on that, Lowery … I'm warnin' you! Enough's enough … I don't eat anything that's got to die.

LOWERY: Then why kill a man if you don't intend to eat him?

VOLCANIC: (*threatening*) Lowery!

LOWERY: Seems like a waste of good flesh which might still be out punching holes in mountains, same's you're doing!

VOLCANIC glares at him. LOWERY grins back.

VOLCANIC: You're a good example of where a bit of schoolin's a dangerous thing, you know that?

LOWERY bows to him.

LOWERY: (*sardonically*) I've often wondered where I went wrong.

VOLCANIC: Thought you should know. I've heard others say it, too.

LOWERY: Volcanic, you're like a friendly priest when it comes to giving advice. I'm going back an' get a hotel room for the night before the billies hit town with their gold pokes looking for booze, whores, an' a place to sleep.

Harmonica music is heard faintly in the background.

VOLCANIC: You're not goin' anywhere tonight, Lowery. You're stayin' right here with me. I see you twice a year ... We got some talkin' to do ... lots an' lots of talkin' ...

POOR BOY enters, playing his harmonica and carrying a bucket of water. He struggles thoughtfully to an elevation. Then, as if talking to stones, he utters his monologue in a tortuous way.

POOR BOY: Them Hennessy boys got themselves a million findin' one silver mine ... They got crazy doin' that ... They leased a train to Toronto 'n' New York ... a whole train ... one car to eat in ... one car to sleep in ... one car to play cards in ... an' one car to carry Bill Hennessy's minin' boots so he ... don't forget ...

He appears puzzled.

So he don't forget what? That he's gone crazy? ... What's wrong about forgettin' that?

POOR BOY exits slowly.

The atmosphere of the scene changes. LOWERY has become weary. VOLCANIC is agitated. He lights a storm lantern and hangs it on a post by the mine shaft.

LOWERY: How many hours before daylight? Before I can leave this place?

VOLCANIC: *(laughing)* Four hours to daylight, Lowery. I just heard me a loon sayin' that ...

LOWERY: Four hours? ... Oh, my God!

VOLCANIC: This hour of the night, I hear night birds talkin' to me. An' the aspen leaves in the wind ... kind of a sweet water sound in a big garden I never been to myself ...

LOWERY: What the hell did I hear you say?

VOLCANIC: *(a bit self-consciously)* I feel good ... talking to you like this ... about this an' that. Don't spoil it, Lowery, or I'm gonna have to teach you how to live!

LOWERY: Oh, no you don't ...

VOLCANIC: There's God puttin' stars in the sky ... for the likes of you an' I! You hear how I said that?

LOWERY: There's a chance I did ... Let's leave it at that ...

VOLCANIC: Listen ... there's God putting stars in the sky, for the likes of you an' I ... I sometimes have things like that runnin' through my head ... comes kind of natural an' unexpected ...

LOWERY: I want to sleep ... You talk too much. Your mouth never stops working! I want to sleep, but you won't stop talkin'. An' there's fleas in your shack!

VOLCANIC: You love this life, admit it, Lowery. You growl like an old dog about what minin' does to the country an' to men, but it's the only life for you, too. You get as excited as me ... your blood heats up ... heart pumps faster ... the hearin' an' seein' gets clearer when a prospector finds a paystreak of gold or silver!

LOWERY: The walls and ceiling are crawling with fleas!

VOLCANIC: Not so much here. My friend, Emile Voight's got fleas. He says to me once, if he took the time to talk nice to them, they'd bring his pick in off the porch ... or carry his woodpile into his cabin ... That's fleas! What I got here's misfits ... the sort of fools you'd find tryin' to set up house in a new shirt sittin' in a store ...

LOWERY: Look around you ... They got your house ... they're movin' out to take over the world!

VOLCANIC: You're confusin' them with wood lice ...

LOWERY: On the topic of fleas, my friend, I am an authority. I've travelled the length and breadth of this continent, always in the company of fleas. There's as many varieties of fleas as there's days in summer ... from the genteel breed found in the armpits and genitals of mining superintendents, railroad dignitaries to perfumed ladies of pleasure ... languid as their owners ... jumping from here to there an' no farther ... Then there are fleas toughened by winter, sweat an' smoke ... who travel on the backs of prospectors and trappers ... like government tax collectors. These *work* for their food, but when their host eats, they eat. And then there's fleas as hungry an' depraved as sin ... living in the red beards of demented hill preachers. A man with such fleas becomes a fanatic ... *has* to become a fanatic ...

because he is driven by the hungers of a multitude!

VOLCANIC considers this information thoughtfully.

VOLCANIC: Emile Voight's got them kind ...

LOWERY: (*laughing*) So have you, Volcanic. So has every aging bone-sack clawing at the granite of these mountains!

VOLCANIC: Emile's got them because, like you, he don't live right. Eats salt pork like a cannibal. I'll feed you proper ... cook you up some fiddle-heads!

LOWERY: Huh?

VOLCANIC: Fiddlehead ferns. You et them once before ... last summer.

LOWERY: Yes, I remember. An hour after I swallowed a mouthful down, I got the most painful stomach cramps. You said it was okay ... the pain would last another six days, an' on the seventh, my eyes would get better!

VOLCANIC: (*laughing and reaching for a frying pan*) It's good for your health, Lowery. There's signs of scurvy in your face ... an' you're shrinkin'. You're shorter this morning than you was last night.

LOWERY: Good health, my ass. Look at *you*! Teeth going ... chest caved in ... toes cut off ... pants hanging at your butt like a bladder with no air ...

VOLCANIC throws down the frying pan and rages at LOWERY.

VOLCANIC: Same's you, boy! Same's you! Go look at yourself first ... Hands tremblin' for booze ... Eyes like I seen once in the head of a snake ... never blinkin' ... When's the last time a woman looked at you without yawnin'?

LOWERY: (*thoughtfully*) Seven years ago, Volcanic ... seven years ago.

VOLCANIC: (*viciously*) You lie! Don't lie to me!

LOWERY: I'm not lying.

He is embarrassed.

A woman came to see me. I was asleep, covered with a horse blanket in the shed I'd rented for an office. I was hung over ... sick ... bitter ...

VOLCANIC: I seen you sleep like that once or twice ... but there was no woman then. You lie!

LOWERY: My door was unlocked. Why lock a door? I never owned anything worth stealin' ...

VOLCANIC: I lock my door even out here. The earth's crawlin' with thieves who'd take anythin' not nailed down!

LOWERY: She just walked in ... shook me. I swung at her with my fist an' she laughed ... That's when I knew my visitor was a woman. I sat up ... She was young, beautiful ... with large, soft eyes, Volcanic ...

VOLCANIC: If there *was* a woman, she was a whore. No proper woman would walk in on the likes of us, Lowery.

LOWERY: She was real. Volcanic ... young, beautiful, alive.

VOLCANIC: You're making it up. The way you make things up when you write that fool news-paper of yours ...

LOWERY: I'll never forget what she said the first time ... "Mr. Lowery?" Yes, I says ... "Mr. Lowery, men are being worked like animals in the Kootenay mines and smelters. They've killed my husband ... They're bringing in prisoners from Missouri jails to strike-break. Get up, Mr. Lowery ... you've got to help!"

VOLCANIC begins to get morose.

VOLCANIC: (*snorting*) A widow, eh? ... A second-hand woman ... Well, that's different. Never go near one of 'em. They let you touch their skirts an' whamo! They hang you for it!

LOWERY: She was like morning air, Volcanic ...

VOLCANIC: Once a woman's been used by another man, she's not much good to anyone. If you're crazy enough to get aroun' them, they call you by the name of the first man they knowed ... What the hell's that worth?

LOWERY: (*laughing*) A woman's not a bucksaw that wears down, you old bastard! A woman's like a violin ... the more she's played with, the sweeter the music!

VOLCANIC paces back and forth clumsily, his face tortured.

VOLCANIC: You're starting to talk dirty, you know that? You're makin' me mad. I don't allow that kind of talk on my claim ... not from you or anybody!

LOWERY: Why get mad?

VOLCANIC: Dirty talk's like smokin' opium ... once you start you can't stop.

LOWERY: Volcanic, look at us ... think of what we've lost. How many women have you and I known and loved?

VOLCANIC: Lots ...

LOWERY: I only knew this one ...

VOLCANIC: Well, I've had lots ...

LOWERY: Her breeding an' speech was that of a southern belle. But the words she spoke were of revolution. Do you know what that means?

VOLCANIC: Don't wanna know, an' don't wanna hear that kind of talk! *Everything* ... this country's gonna become ... everythin' important ever gets done here, will be the result of men like me, Lowery. Come back fifty, a hundred years from now, an' I'll bet you all I ever seen or knowed that the virtues everyone will look up to will be thrift, hard work an' loneliness. Because for them virtues, God forgives everythin'!

LOWERY: Even murder ... like you done?

VOLCANIC: Yes, even that!

LOWERY: A wild coyote's got more reason to live than you, if you believe that ...

The sound of a harmonica is heard in the background.

VOLCANIC: I do ... an' if your wild coyote wants to take me on, Lowery, let him! I'll tear him open from asshole to throat with my bare hands!

LOWERY: You shouldn't go back into civilized towns with that attitude, Volcanic. The first workin' man who sees you is bound to shoot you down, mistakin' you for some wild game ...

VOLCANIC: (*laughing fiendishly*) But he couldn't eat me, eh? Even a cannibal like you couldn't eat me, Lowery ... I'm too tough!

He flexes his arm muscle.

Feel this, Lowery ... feel it!

LOWERY: Go away ... You're crazy ...

VOLCANIC: First dog bites me loses a tooth. Tough as a miner's boot, that's me, old Volcanic!

He whoops and dances bizarrely, then becomes pensive. The harmonica music dies out.

This woman, Lowery ... did you ... ever do it with her?

LOWERY: Do what?

VOLCANIC: You know ... touch her where you're not supposed to ... and ...

LOWERY: You mean, sleep with her?

VOLCANIC: (*irritated*) You know what I mean ... No! Not sleepin' with her after you done it ... just doin' it and goin' away ...

LOWERY: Now what in hell does that mean ... "doin' it an' goin' away"?

VOLCANIC: I'm gonna punch you in the nose if you keep that up! Men who're not married don't sleep beside a woman after they done it ... you know that!

LOWERY: (*amused*) Why not? The French call it the short, sweet death ...

VOLCANIC: There's your reason, you said it yourself ... you can die. The other reason is ... well, you get a disease doin' that!

LOWERY: (*laughing*) You're just a walking sack of useless information ... Don't eat meat ... Don't sleep with women ... Where do you hear all this wisdom?

VOLCANIC: I've been told by lots of men.

LOWERY: Men who had the disease?

VOLCANIC: Yes, goddamnit!

LOWERY: An' they said they got it from hangin' around too long?

VOLCANIC: Yes. You never see a moose or a buck or a male wolf who goes around with the thing drippin' like a nose cold, do you?

LOWERY: No. But then, I've never made a study of the ... matter.

VOLCANIC: That's because they're in an' out an' gone!

LOWERY: I see ... How do you reckon it is with married men?

VOLCANIC: They must have problems ... That's why I'm not interested in that kind of thing myself ...

There is a long pause. LOWERY tries to hold back his laughter. VOLCANIC turns to him, his gaze sober and questioning.

LOWERY: No, Volcanic ... I didn't do it.

VOLCANIC: Good ...

LOWERY: Not that I didn't want to ... God, I wanted to so badly. When she left me ... when I ordered her to go away from me ... an' she did ... I went into a bar an' as I got roaring drunk, I cried ...

VOLCANIC: Yeh ... yeh ... well ...

LOWERY: One night, we'd worked late on an issue of my paper. After we finished the layout, I sat back, and shut my eyes with weariness. She sat beside me, an' put her hand across my chest ... then her head ...

VOLCANIC: You'd locked the door this time? Nobody to bother you?

LOWERY: She was so young ... the smell of her hair like sunlight an' fresh hay in a summer meadow ... She reached up and touched my face with her hand ... The touch was cool, gentle, like soft rain ...

VOLCANIC: (*squirming*) You lied again ... you did it to her! Hell, it wasn't your fault. She was askin' for it.

LOWERY: Nope ...

VOLCANIC: Nope?

LOWERY: (*smiling sadly*) No. I didn't do it, Volcanic. I was too ashamed.

VOLCANIC stares at him in disbelief, then reaches out and shakes him. LOWERY does not resist.

VOLCANIC: All my life I couldn't trust you ... never could I trust you.

LOWERY: (*painfully*) I ... suddenly ... thought of what I must look like ... wasted by years of sleep-lessness an' booze. Kidneys failing ... eyes running. The wretched, dirty clothes I wear ... I didn't have a bath ... haven't shaved with a razor

in years ... But the thing I was most ashamed of was how my naked body would look to her. I was so humiliated with myself I couldn't do it. I felt so sorry for her I just stood up an' held her in my arms, both of us cryin' and sayin' ... "It's alright" to one another over an' over. But it wasn't alright ... I wasn't there anymore. In my place was another person ... someone watching sadly.

VOLCANIC: Oh well, there'll be another time ... Always is, you know Lowery ...

He pats LOWERY on the shoulder comfortingly and sits beside him.

LOWERY: Yes ... there's always that hope ...

POOR BOY enters and crosses the stage purposefully.

POOR BOY: When the fire comes ... my mother said ... to fill the trough ... for when the fire comes ... She said ... Sally Jane's a widow ... to court a widow, she said ... is to eat ... with another man's spoon ... That's no good ...

He laughs gently, then ponders.

Heard a man say ... the valleys would fill up with water. That's no damned good ... people who stay don't live on mountains ... got to have valleys like they always been ... Can't grow good carrots in water ... I don't care, I'm gone tomorrow ... but the others ...

POOR BOY exits. LOWERY doubles over with a wheezing cough. He bundles into his coat. VOLCANIC rises, his teeth bared in anticipation of something.

The wind sound rises.

LOWERY: I'm cold, Volcanic ... the wind's as chilly as the breath of a glacier.

VOLCANIC blows out the storm lantern by the mine shaft. He rolls up his sleeve and removes a hunting knife from his belt. He examines his arm.

The wind sound dies.

LOWERY: What're you doin', Volcanic?

VOLCANIC: Gonna bleed myself a little ... got to get rid of this bad winter blood. You should do the same.

LOWERY: Come on, Volcanic. I've got enough problems without interfering with my blood supply ...

VOLCANIC: I been dreamin' bad dreams lately ... wakes me up. I'm sweatin' an' cryin' when I wake up.

LOWERY: I'm not sleepin' too good myself. It's my lungs ... every winter that passes, my lungs give out a little more. One winter, they're going to give in an' all the steam kettles and camphor in the world won't help me anymore.

VOLCANIC: Yeh, that can happen ... Lowery, you know anythin' about how blood runs through the body?

LOWERY: A little, why?

VOLCANIC: There's tubes called arteries an' others called veins take the blood around ...

LOWERY: That's right.

VOLCANIC: Them blue things in your arm ... them arteries or veins?

LOWERY: They're veins, Volcanic. Arteries are supposed to be deeper in the body, where you don't see them. They say if you cut an artery, it spurts out blood, but a vein don't.

The wind sound rises.

LOWERY shudders.

It's so cold up here, Volcanic ...

VOLCANIC: What the hell ... don't suppose it matters ... comin' or goin', blood's blood.

VOLCANIC holds his head in his hands. He sways, as if in weakness.

Hear them cowbells, Lowery? Somebody's keepin' cows by the creek now. They're not supposed to. That's on my claim.

LOWERY: (*listening*) I don't hear any cowbells. The rest of you is fine, but your hearing's going. But what do you expect ... eatin' hay like a horse ... bleeding yourself in spring like some pagan savage? ...

The wind sound dies.

VOLCANIC: In my dreams, he keeps comin' to see me ... dead eyes starin' ... a hole in his throat ...

LOWERY: Who?

VOLCANIC: (*looking up sadly*) The man I killed, Lowery. The man I killed.

LOWERY: I thought you'd forgotten about him long ago ... didn't consider him worth rememberin' ...

VOLCANIC: I had ... but now he's come back to me. Only ... it's not the man I killed then ... He's older now ... an old man.

LOWERY: The stuff you eat is backin' up on you ... givin' you bad dreams.

VOLCANIC: I caught him on my claim an' shot him ... had to. He was a poor bastard, same's me ... harmless enough. Used the same kind of worn-out tools I work with. I claimed self-defence ... I had to so's to avoid hangin' for it ...

LOWERY: Yes, I remember ...

VOLCANIC: But every night he's comin' to see me, like he wants me to help him find somethin' he can't see, because there's only holes where his eyes once was. He's an old man now ... old like me.

LOWERY: Are you ... afraid of him?

VOLCANIC: Naw ... nothin' scares me. But he's gettin' to me, Lowery. He's so hang-dog ... his pants torn ... the hole in his throat full of dried blood ... an' with them eyes that can't see ... I ... I feel kinda sorry for him. I feel sorry I killed him. Do you think God knows how sorry I feel I done it?

The sound of the wind is heard.

LOWERY: I don't know. I'm not much for religion ...

VOLCANIC: Hear them cowbells now, Lowery? Eh? ... They're comin' nearer. Maybe it's some claim-jumper usin' cows for a decoy ... what do you think? I'll scare him off ... I still got my rifle ... but ... the shells got left out in the rain an' won't fire no more.

LOWERY: (*listening*) You're hearing things again, Volcanic. There's no cowbells out there.

VOLCANIC: Funny. I could've swore I heard them again ...

He turns away suddenly and stabs his arm. He then turns, grinning triumphantly as he shows his bloodied arm to LOWERY.

LOWERY: Good God! You've made a hole in your arm!

VOLCANIC: (*proudly*) Look at it come out … thick and dark … all the filth an' corruption of winter's in there. All the chill in the bones … goin' away … makin' room for spring!

LOWERY: You can't afford to lose blood, Volcanic … here, let's get you bandaged up!

LOWERY starts to tear his shirt open to make a bandage. VOLCANIC dismisses his offer of help with a gesture.

VOLCANIC: Naw … let it run for a while. Got to get rid of the sickness an' corruption.

LOWERY: You haven't got enough blood in you to do that. Lie down, Volcanic. Let's put a dressing on that cut.

LOWERY breaks into a fit of coughing which immobilizes him.

The wind sound dies.

VOLCANIC: (*growling*) You keep away from me, Lowery. I'm gonna be healthy, not like you! … Look at you … coughin' … wheezin' …

LOWERY: (*breathless*) You're a madman!

VOLCANIC: Come on … wrestle with me, Lowery! Come on! Even with half my blood gone, I can still throw you over the woodpile … Come on, Lowery, wrestle me! … Wrestle me!

He pushes at LOWERY with the palms of his hands. He struts and dances, inviting a fight.

LOWERY: Sit down, Volcanic. Sit down before you fall down!

VOLCANIC: (*still trying to provoke him*) I eat right, work hard … bleed myself … see! I'm as good as new … If that widow had come to me, I'd have done her right! You're cold, I'm hot. You're coughin' … I got all the air I want. Twice a night you get up to piss. Me? I've got me a bladder like a Kentucky likker crock … I can go two days without makin' water … How's that for good health?

LOWERY: (*angry*) You're filled with it … up to your eyes! You're nothing more than a walking piss-pot! You an' all the others … Where in hell's your dignity gone? … It takes men of substance to build something more than shacks an' holes in the ground, yet the best we can manage is bums an' hardware merchants … An' as for the widow,

you asked me an' I told you, so leave her alone … Leave her out of this!

VOLCANIC: I killed a man for a claim once an' I'll do it again, goddammit! So if you see him, tell him for me that cowbell trick won't work. You hear what I'm sayin', Lowery?

LOWERY is racked with another coughing fit.

LOWERY: Yes … I heard. I wish I hadn't …

VOLCANIC stands up, swaying but furious.

VOLCANIC: Why in hell not? … You never let up … like a travellin' preacher, you never let up pickin' sores open … savin' things up for the future. To hell with the future, I say!

LOWERY: Dress that wound in your arm. Your mind's leaving you as well as your blood.

VOLCANIC: Never stop to help the weak, Lowery … if they fall, let 'em die. You're wastin' your time. Who made them weak in the first place?

LOWERY: Tell me, an' we'll both know!

VOLCANIC: God did, that's who!

LOWERY: For Christ's sake, Volcanic … stay with prospectin' …

VOLCANIC: (*chanting*) God did! … God did! …

LOWERY: Leave interpretation of Scriptures to those who can read …

VOLCANIC: God made some of us strong so as to find what He'd left for us inside of mountains …

LOWERY: (*sarcastically*) And He made the weak to help with the digging an' carting away of tailings!

VOLCANIC: That's right!

LOWERY: Bleed to death, you sonofabitch, see if I care! … Die! Who's gonna care anyway? Just one scavenger less on the landscape when you drop!

He goes into another fit of coughing.

VOLCANIC: (*upset*) Okay, Lowery … I'm sorry. You're sick. I can see that … I'll make you some pine-needle tea.

LOWERY: You'll drink it all if you do. I've smelled it cooking on your stove … it's the poison they boiled up to kill Socrates!

VOLCANIC: Oh? ... Who's he?

LOWERY: Forget it!

The sound of the wind is heard.

VOLCANIC: Them cowbells are back at it, Lowery ... comin' nearer now ... I shouldn't of killed that man. He was grubbin' same's me to make a livin' ... was a mistake doin' that ...

VOLCANIC keels over backwards and vanishes off the porch platform into the mine. LOWERY in a half-crouch moves after him, but begins to cough violently.

LOWERY: Volcanic? ... You alright, boy? ... Of all the damned stupid things I've seen you do, this is the worst. You're bleeding to death, you old toad ...

The wind sound dies.

POOR BOY enters, measuring the path he uses with a length of stick.

POOR BOY: (*as he measures*) Grass that's dead's grown green again ... Lots of trees, but lumber's scarce in New Denver, says Mr. Lowery in his newspaper ... Rivers are runnin' full ... leaves are out ... summer's come already ...

He exits over the top of the mine shaft, humming his tuneless melody.

There is the sound of VOLCANIC breaking rock with his pick inside his mine.

VOLCANIC: (*to the rhythm of the pick*) Hep! ... Hep! ... Fall, goddammit! ... Fall, 'cause I'm out of powder!

The sound of crashing stones is heard.

LOWERY moves to a slight elevation. He crouches forward, his hat pushed back. He resembles a dog barking at a gopher hole.

LOWERY: (*loudly*) Fool! Rocky Mountain crazy man! ... You hear me?

VOLCANIC: (*from the mine shaft*) Go away, Lowery!

LOWERY: They're laughin' at you in town! ... You hear? ... Even Long Alex, who's never laughed ... I seen him laughin' when Short Charlie spoke your name.

VOLCANIC: (*still in the mine shaft*) Good! I'm glad someone else is laughin' ... I'm laughin' ...

There is wild laughter from the mine shaft. The picking sound resumes.

LOWERY: (*still speaking loudly*) Hey, coyote! ... Who are you doin' this for? ... For the wife and children you'll never have? ...

He laughs tauntingly.

You're old now ... old as the rock you're molesting!

VOLCANIC: (*from the mine shaft*) For me! ...

LOWERY: It's not enough ... an' it's too late now! Who's gonna remember you, an' why?

VOLCANIC: (*from the mine shaft*) Fuck 'em then!

LOWERY: Come out of there, Volcanic ... you're nothin' now but a man-rat with a pick! One day a rock will break loose an' fall on your head, and the mountains will be happy again to have done with you ... They're laughin' at you in town. Don't you care?

The picking sound stops.

The flap on the mine shaft opens violently.

VOLCANIC is thrown out, covered in dust. He picks himself up, adjusts his hat and stares back at the entrance to the mine shaft, over which the flap has fallen.

VOLCANIC: So they're laughin' ... are they, Lowery?

LOWERY: Yep, they're laughin' ... hee ... hee ... hee ... they're laughin' ...

VOLCANIC: In there ... I heard laughter in there for the first time ... I'll show them who's laughin'!

LOWERY: You want a smoke?

VOLCANIC: Naw ... They'll laugh ... give me six months an' they'll be laughin' out their windpipes when they see what I got in there ...

LOWERY: What've you got in there to excite such mirth, a lame mare?

VOLCANIC: A mountain of gold, that's what I got me! It's in there so strong I can smell it!

LOWERY: In 1896, there were a hundred cases of typhoid and mountain fever in Rossland. But there was an epidemic of gold fever ... over a thousand men came down with it ...

VOLCANIC: You laugh if you want to ... but it's comin' out of the pores of the granite in there ... I know that smell. I can plug my nose an' still smell it!

LOWERY: It's the sulphur from the fires of hell you smell in there, Volcanic. Give up, for the love of God!

VOLCANIC: (*strutting*) Me? Give up? Never, Lowery! Never give up, boy! Why, when I open this here mine, it'll have more gold than anythin' ever discovered by man in all of history. When I open 'er up, all the pencils in Grand Forks won't be able to tally up the value of what's in this mountain!

LOWERY: (*grinning*) When you've uncovered ... all this great wealth, what'll you do with it, Volcanic? Buy yourself a feed of roast beef an' pickled alfalfa? ... New clothes?

VOLCANIC: Roast beef? ... New suit of clothes? ... You was born crazy an' you'll die crazy. Crazy an' small. I don't look for my name on a scrap of paper like you. It's gonna be engraved in stone, Lowery, so it'll keep! I'm gonna use the wealth of this mine to build me a *city*!

LOWERY: You're ... gonna build a city?

VOLCANIC: I'm buildin' a city on the plateau top of this mountain. I'm gonna call it Volcanic City, so the whole world knows who done it!

LOWERY: But what about Poor Boy? He's got a shack up there ...

VOLCANIC: To hell with Poor Boy ... his shack gets pushed down the mountain. He's a fool. I don't want no fools in my city.

LOWERY: You're sort of like God on the fourth day of Creation ...

VOLCANIC: Better even ... Sit down, Lowery. I'm gonna show you ...

Both VOLCANIC and LOWERY squat in the dirt. VOLCANIC takes out a crumpled piece of paper from his shirt pocket and flattens it on his knee. It is a map.

See this? That's what the city's gonna look like ... Houses, hotels, businesses ... but only this far. City ends here an' here ... beyond, that's bush.

LOWERY: Everything you need to make a city's in there?

VOLCANIC: Everything. But there's not gonna be no schools, banks or churches in Volcanic City, Lowery.

LOWERY: No?

VOLCANIC: No sirree, Lowery.

LOWERY: Well, I can sympathize with the part about banks and churches. Although if your city gets prosperous, people carrying their money in their pockets run a risk of breakin' their suspenders an' losing their pants from the weight of all they own. What've you got against schools?

VOLCANIC: No schools ... no sense confusin' children with useless learnin' ... They don't teach a kid in school how to find good food, or how to smell out a gold mine. Until they do, no schools!

LOWERY: Hold on now, Volcanic. I went to school. What little I learned about reading an' writing has given me a living of sorts as a newspaperman.

VOLCANIC: (*snorting derisively*) You call that livin'?

LOWERY: Yes, I do ...

VOLCANIC: You would've done better sellin' likker an' tobacco from a two-by-four store!

He laughs with contempt.

Think how good you'd of lived if you'd *worked* instead of pretendin'!

LOWERY: (*hurt*) I've worked, boy ... How I've worked ...

VOLCANIC: No schools, Lowery. An' no banks. Never met an honest banker yet, never will. An' no churches ... I've done a lot I shouldn't of done, but I'll be damned if any sky pilot's gonna tell me where I went wrong. I'll face Long Alex, the constable, over that one. So to hell with churches!

LOWERY: I still think schools are ...

VOLCANIC: (*sharply*) Who wants to know what you think? *I'm* buildin' Volcanic City, not you! If you want to open a newspaper in it, I'll give you a place rent-free. I've known you a long time an' I owe it to you. Even send some booze your way once in a while. But it's the gold I find in this mountain that'll keep it alive as a city, so don't tell me what my city's gonna have in it an' what it won't have …

LOWERY: I've heard identical sentiments from railroad and mining companies all my life!

VOLCANIC: A man talks with his wallet, Lowery. If you was me, you'd be sayin' the same thing … that's never gonna change!

LOWERY: Go to hell! I don't want your rent-free office. If I couldn't pay, I wouldn't take it!

VOLCANIC: The same to you! … The ones who got nothin' can afford to give it away, don't cost them nothin'! But once you got more than you can eat, there's a million Poor Boys out there … wantin' what don't belong to them! Well, I'm not givin', Lowery!

LOWERY: Oh, you're a tough, mean man when you're shouting at your shadow, Volcanic.

He studies the map.

What are all these lines you've drawn here, cutting up your city like a pie?

VOLCANIC: Them's railroads, Lowery. Volcanic City's gonna have four railroads comin' from the four corners of the world, all meetin' right here in the middle, where I'm buildin' a big railway station for all of 'em. In that way, if we can't do business with the folks to the east an' west of us, then to hell with 'em. We still got business to the north an' south!

Both men break into laughter.

LOWERY: That's quite some dream you've got there, Volcanic. Quite some dream …

VOLCANIC: All, well … a man's not a raccoon, livin' with his nose to the ground.

LOWERY: But … it's only a dream …

VOLCANIC: What's that mean? … Come on, spit it out!

LOWERY: It's based on nothing. You only *think* there might be gold in that hole.

VOLCANIC: You rest easy about that one … when it comes to a gold mine, I'm a genius.

He withdraws another tattered piece of paper from his wallet. It is a list of his mining claims.

Look, see this?

LOWERY: Yeh, I see it … What is it?

VOLCANIC: All the mines I've discovered that paid … count 'em yourself. Nobody told you about them, eh, Lowery?

LOWERY: (*impressed*) Well, I'll be damned. That's a fine record, Volcanic. An' what's this?

VOLCANIC takes away the paper and stands up. He is embarrassed.

VOLCANIC: Them … them's the mines that didn't pay … claims I've abandoned …

LOWERY: But there's as many of them as there is of the others …

VOLCANIC: Not so … there's two less on that list …

LOWERY: It's a fifty-fifty chance then, Volcanic. You're good … hard-workin', obstinate … but I wouldn't say you'd qualify as any kind of mining genius. Not by a long stretch …

VOLCANIC: That's alright … a man's got to dream or he dies from the inside out, same way a sore heals … Think of it … Volcanic City … named after *me*! You ever have dreams like that yourself?

They sit beside each other. They are almost look-alikes. Both become pensive.

LOWERY: Yes … yes, I do. But in my city … my city will be filled with books and music. You see, Volcanic … the city I dream of is run by wise, compassionate people … not illiterate bandits like you.

VOLCANIC chortles over this remark.

VOLCANIC: (*deceptively cheerful*) Keep talking like that an' you'll end up with a pick handle where your teeth once was …

LOWERY: (*thoughtfully*) It won't happen, will it? It will always be a fight between you and me …

VOLCANIC: Yep … an' I'm gonna keep winnin', Lowery, because I'm tougher an' meaner. If your books or dreams get in my way, I'll beat 'em to rat shit with a pickaxe or hammer. I'll walk with these here toed-up boots all over your schools an' your music! If what you stick up don't make money, it's got no goddamned right to be! The only way you'll win is by killin' me ... but you can't. You're scared of me ... an' you're scared once I'm gone you won't know how to get by!

LOWERY: In a pig's eye I'm scared!

Both men rise and square off pathetically with one another. VOLCANIC pushes LOWERY sharply. LOWERY stumbles backwards, surprised at VOLCANIC'S intensity and rage. VOLCANIC follows and pushes him again, laughing now.

VOLCANIC: It's Volcanic City or nothin', Lowery! ... You'll come askin' me, not tellin' me! ... What do you say to that, eh? ... What do you say, you Wobbly sonofabitch?

Over the action of the struggle, POOR BOY crosses the stage with his dripping water bucket. He is singing in a tuneless, wild voice, searching for a melody.

POOR BOY: (*singing*)
My left arm is leather,
My right arm is straw,
My teeth are of marble,
An' there's spit on my jaw.
My left eye is granite,
My right eye is water.
They say when I die
They will meet one another ...

The lights go down slowly on his exit, with VOLCANIC and LOWERY in the background, poised in a battle stance.

ACT 2

The lights go up.

Harmonica music, tuneless and persistent, is heard, played by POOR BOY as he enters from a higher elevation to where LOWERY stands. LOWERY is leaning towards the mine shaft opening as at the beginning of Act 1.

LOWERY nods to POOR BOY, who stops and speaks to him and past him, as if addressing the landscape.

POOR BOY: (*amused*) There was a man ... lived in Greenwood ... took his sister's boy ... who was only four ... took his sister's boy into the mountains one day. Be quiet, he says ... look there ... way over there on that bare ridge ... what do you see? ... Nothin', says the child ... Look again ... carefully ... what do you see? ... Nothin', says the child again ... Look! See, there's a deer on that bare ridge! ... The kid stares an' stares ... for a long time he stands there, starin' ... his bare feet on the ground ... little pants droopin' on his hips ... then he grins. Yes, Uncle Joe ... I see! ... There *is* a deer ... a *mother* deer! ... How in hell you know that, the man says ... Because it's got a baby with it! ...

VOLCANIC: (*in a howl from inside the mine shaft*) There's nothin' here!

POOR BOY: ... An' if you listen, you can hear the mother deer an' baby eatin' grass, the kid says ...

VOLCANIC: (*from the mine shaft, pained and furious*) There ain't a goddamned thing here!

POOR BOY: ... Uncle Joe grabs the kid by the arm, kicks his butt an' turfs his sister's kid down the mountain back to Greenwood ... I took you up there, he says, to teach you the art of bull-shittin', not to improve on it! You stay in the house an' grow some before I take you out again. An' keep your mouth shut ... until this town grows bigger, there's only room for one of us!

Laughing, shaking his head, POOR BOY exits partially up the elevation, where he seats himself in dim light and proceeds to eat bits of food that he carries in his pockets.

The sound of the wind is heard.

A picking sound is heard from inside the mine shaft.

VOLCANIC: Goddammit!

LOWERY: (*loudly*) Volcanic!

VOLCANIC: Cheez!

The picking stops. VOLCANIC emerges from the mine shaft, dusty, upset.

He speaks plaintively.

There was nothin' there ... dead stone an' fire leadin' me this way an' that ... What went wrong, Lowery?

LOWERY: Your instincts were wrong. But what use is it my saying so now? ...

VOLCANIC: Yeh ... true ... nothin' gained by worryin' about it. Oh well, to hell with gold, Lowery! Gold is the metal of fools ... the blind bitch no man should follow. That's it! ... I'm through with gold for good!

He heaves his pick against the burlap flap of the mine shaft.

LOWERY: What will you do now?

VOLCANIC: Gonna team up with my friend, Emile Voight ... go to the Princeton area. Got to raise some money quick, Lowery ... I'm too old for this.

LOWERY: What's in Princeton?

VOLCANIC: (*with growing excitement*) Copper, Lowery!

LOWERY: Copper?

VOLCANIC: Good red copper just lyin' there inside a mountain ... waitin' for me to find it! When I turn my face towards Princeton like this, I can *smell* the goddamned copper, there's so much there!

LOWERY: There's only so many heartbreaks an old man can ...

The wind sound dies.

VOLCANIC: Shut your mouth, Lowery! I don't want to hear what you're gonna say! I'm comin' to life once again ... Almost got done in by the gold bitch, but never again ... This time it's gonna happen ... in a bigger way than you can imagine.

LOWERY: Volcanic!

VOLCANIC: Get out of my way, you hunchedback pen-pusher ... You depress me!

Retrieving his pick, VOLCANIC exits jauntily, whistling POOR BOY'S tuneless melody.

The sound of POOR BOY'S harmonica is heard.

LOWERY withdraws a notebook and writes furiously. The harmonica music stops abruptly.

POOR BOY: (*in slow recitativo*)
There's some men who holler,
An' others do whine.
An' some men do labour,
Way down in a mine.
The ones who are useless,
To me it so looks,
Is the ones who get blinded
From readin' big books.

LOWERY, listening to POOR BOY'S recitation as if it were coming from some sardonic corner of his own being, begins to laugh. He puts his notebook away and dusts off his hat, still laughing.

VOLCANIC enters. He is dressed in a new suit of clothes. He wears a hat that is placed rakishly on his head, a clean shirt and tie, but the same old boots on his feet.

VOLCANIC: Lowery!

LOWERY turns quickly at the sound of VOLCANIC'S voice.

LOWERY: Volcanic, you smelly old bushcat! How are you?

VOLCANIC: Never been better, me boy. But you ... you ... hunch over anymore an' you'll need a wheelbarrow for your backend to carry your front end in! ... Lowery, you're gettin' old ... you're walkin' into things ... when you gonna lie down and die?

LOWERY laughs, almost a continuation of his previous laughter.

LOWERY: One of these days, Volcanic ... I'm gonna start living right ... and when I do, you get ready to run me a race up a mountain an' back down again!

VOLCANIC: The furthest you'll be runnin' is to the outhouse when you've drunk too much ... Well, what do you think of me?

VOLCANIC lifts up his arms and turns on his heel to show off his appearance. He resembles a rooster in doing so. LOWERY laughs.

LOWERY: Hold on ... hold on, now. What am I supposed to be looking at ... your ability to still half-raise your arms?

VOLCANIC: My get-up, Lowery. Tell me what you're lookin' at ... an' say it's good!

LOWERY: What in hell's all this? ... New jacket ... waistcoat ... tie. The same face, though ... mean as a cobra in the wind ... Hair needs cutting an' the beard needs a shave ... or a wash. There's traces of things you ate yesterday in your moustache, Volcanic ...

VOLCANIC: Don't josh ... I wanna know ... how do I look?

LOWERY: You look like Hennessy's mare goin' to the races ... But there's something I want to know ... hold still.

LOWERY reaches out and opens VOLCANIC'S shirt to examine his underwear.

Like I suspected ... new jacket, waistcoat ... but underneath it all you're still wearin' the same filthy old miner's underwear you've worn the past seven years!

VOLCANIC: What in hell's wrong with that? It don't show.

LOWERY: An' the same socks ... boots ...

VOLCANIC: (*grinning*) But if you stand back an' see me for the first time, you'd think I worked in a bank, no?

LOWERY: (*squinting, thinking*) Well, maybe one of those banks that operates from a tent in the summer ... How'd you do it ... rob someone?

VOLCANIC: I struck it rich, Lowery. I found me the biggest mountain of copper in this country. Copper Mountain, I called her!

LOWERY: Come on, you've never had the money to develop a copper mine.

VOLCANIC: Nope ... so I sold the claim. Got me forty thousand for it. Let someone else develop it ... I gotta live now!

LOWERY: (*whistling with surprise*) Forty thousand!

VOLCANIC: Forty thousand, boy ...

LOWERY: (*bemused, grinning*) My, my ... what about food? You gonna buy yourself something decent to eat now, or you still scrounging rubbish among the packrats an' brown bears?

VOLCANIC: (*testily*) Don't you start in on that one, Lowery ... just don't start that again. My temper's gettin' shorter the older I get ...

LOWERY: Then keep walkin'. I was on this street first ... goin' that way. You go the other way ...

VOLCANIC: (*startled, then suddenly becoming cheerful*) Look there, Lowery ... somethin' else I got me ...

He points offstage.

LOWERY stares reluctantly, then pushes back his hat for a closer look.

LOWERY: Two matched black horses and a new buggy. Yours! ... I'll be damned!

VOLCANIC: Yep ... paid for 'em with cash! Them horses ... perfectly matched ... switch them around in harness an' even I don't know which is which ... But the buggy, Lowery ... the buggy ...

LOWERY peers offstage again.

LOWERY: It looks good and sturdy. Springs on it, too ...

VOLCANIC: Better than good, Lowery ... there's not another one like it in the country! I had it hand-made ... everything on that buggy's one of a kind ... never buy another like it for any money. I told the man what I wanted. He asked if I could pay. I pulled out a wad of bills this thick from my pocket an' waved them in front of his nose. You shoulda seen his face, Lowery ... man about my age ... I called him "boy" after that, an' he calls me "sir" ...

LOWERY swats at the air, as if driving away some irritating insect.

Here's your money, boy, I says to him when I came to pay an' collect my buggy. Thank you, sir, he says to me. As I'm leavin' his shop I drop an extra five on the floor sayin' that's for gettin' the buggy finished on time, boy ... I stood around to watch him kneel down to pick it up, an' hear him say again, "Thank you, sir." ...

LOWERY: I'll bet you did, you unrepentant old bastard. Remind me never to ask you for a favour ...

VOLCANIC: That's alright ... don't intend to give none ...

LOWERY casts a few more glances at the buggy off-stage. VOLCANIC thoughtfully picks at his teeth with his thumbnail.

LOWERY: So you're feelin' pretty good, eh?

VOLCANIC: Well ... I'm not eatin' too good these days, Lowery ...

LOWERY: Your stomach's died ... the things you eat, it's an overdue demise.

VOLCANIC: No. Stomach's alright ... It's my teeth.

LOWERY: Well, mine are still sound. And so long's the teeth still bite, the food goes down an' the carcass lives on ...

VOLCANIC: (*preoccupied*) What're you doin' for a livin' these days, Lowery?

LOWERY: Still publishing my newspapers, writing my editorials with courage that's not as convincing as it was years ago, because when I walk down the street now an' stare into the windows of banks, mining companies an' railway stations, I feel an icy chill creepin' up my spine ... and I feel my hands an' my insides trembling with frustration. My advertisers push aside my statements because in an hour they'll see me on the street, drunk an' ravin' with impotence! I wrote a poem about that ... remember it by heart. Want to hear it?

VOLCANIC: (*reluctantly*) Well ...

LOWERY: I looked at your clothes ... an' your damned buggy!

VOLCANIC: (*grinning*) Alright ... but it's got to be no longer than you looked!

LOWERY: (*reciting*) If I should die tonight
And you should come to my cold
Corpse an' say,
Weeping and heartsick o'er my
Lifeless clay—
If I should die tonight
And you should come in deepest
Grief and woe—

And say—Here's the ten dollars
That I owe ...
I might arise in my large
White cravat
And say, "What's that?"

VOLCANIC laughs.

If I should die tonight
And you should come to my cold
Corpse an' kneel,
Clasping my bier to show
The grief you feel,
I say ... If I should die tonight
An' you should come to me
An' there an' then
Just even hint 'bout
Paying me that ten,
I might arise the while
But I'd drop dead again ...

Both men laugh and, reaching out, embrace each other in a hug. They separate. VOLCANIC becomes thoughtful.

VOLCANIC: I got a lot of money now, Lowery. No need for you to work anymore ... Why don't you an' I take off for the hills together ... in my new buggy with them matched black horses ... There's places I still want to see.

LOWERY: Not with you, Volcanic.

VOLCANIC: Why not? I never done you wrong ...

LOWERY: Being alone in the forest for a week with you would turn me into a lunatic ... or a murderer!

VOLCANIC: Well ... yeh ... never mind. I thought I'd ask all the same ...

He cannot disguise his growing anxiety anymore.

You ... you ever had to go to a dentist, Lowery?

LOWERY: From time to time ...

VOLCANIC: Did it hurt like they say?

LOWERY: Depends on the dentist. Some labour like they were virgins an' your mouth was a Persian garden ... Others go in like they were layin' CPR track in the Crowsnest Pass! ...

VOLCANIC: I only asked if it hurt ... no need to bring blastin' powder an' pickaxes into it!

LOWERY: (laughing) So ... your teeth are goin', Volcanic?

VOLCANIC: They been givin' me hell, lately. I've got money to pay for what I need ... I'm not gonna grow old lookin' like them other prospectors who don't have a nickel to their names ... mouths pooched like the manure end of a horse!

He laughs.

Lowery, I want you to come with me ... I'm gonna put my money where it shows ... in my mouth!

LOWERY: You gonna use your mouth for a wallet now?

VOLCANIC: Naw ... come on! I'll show you!

The sound of POOR BOY'S harmonica is heard.

POOR BOY enters, his cap pushed back, his brow knit in concentration.

VOLCANIC, in a counter movement, turns his back to the audience and slouches into a sitting position, as if he were in a dentist's chair, where he contorts in silent agony over POOR BOY'S and LOWERY'S monologues.

POOR BOY: Mister Lowery writes an' says ... the new gov'ment's good for the people ... Others say the gov'ment's no good ... gonna take away my house ... They say that ... they say the gov'ment's gonna take me away, too ... I don't think I like a gov'ment would do that ...

He plays a harmonica interlude as he peers about for good government or meaning to his life.

LOWERY: If there is a God ... I'd say He was a laughin' God ... tough as boot leather and laughing a lot of the time. He must have laughed when he made me short an' gave me tall wants ...

VOLCANIC groans and writhes with pain.

There is a harmonica interlude from POOR BOY.

God's a joker. He encourages wealthy men not to pay me my printing bills. And ... when I die, I will ask Him to send me down to hell, so I can spend eternity stoking fires under the asses of my enemies, for they will all be congregated there, like pimps in a steam bath. An' God will oblige me, for He's a laughing God ...

There is another groan of pain from VOLCANIC.

There is another harmonica interlude, more rasping now, from POOR BOY.

The strangest joke the Almighty played was giving money to the likes of my friend, Volcanic. I accompanied the old fool ... saw him into the dentist's chair, the throne of the devil's mercy ... an' then watched that tooth miner go to work on old Volcanic ... Hacking, scraping ... chipping away at the stumps passing for teeth Volcanic still had in his mouth. No pain-killer ... nothing but hard steel against raw, decaying pulp ...

There is a howl of pain from VOLCANIC.

There is another harmonica interlude from POOR BOY.

About an hour into the job, Volcanic's soaking in pain sweat ... He turns to me an' grins ... Only it's not the grin of a man ... it's sort of a soundless snarl, like you'd expect to see on a dying old wolf! The brown rot an' stains are gone now ... so are most of his teeth. What's left are ground-down remnants of bone, some hardly more than slivers that would've cut his tongue to shreds if he bit down ...

There is a pained laugh, like a burst of sobs, from VOLCANIC.

The dentist returns then, asks Volcanic to open his mouth wide. Volcanic obliges, and that sadist wipes the inside of Volcanic's mouth with a horse towel which he'd wrapped around his fist. That bit of hygienic detail dispensed with, he starts packing fine gold leaf into the hollows an' around the stubs of Volcanic's teeth. It must've hurt like hell, because he heated the gold leaf to melting over a burner, then transferred the hot gold to Volcanic's mouth ...

There is a prolonged howl of agony from VOLCANIC, accompanied by a lurching, frenzied twist of his body.

A harmonica interlude is heard over the howl. As he plays, POOR BOY flees in terror to his position in the dim light over the mine shaft entrance.

LOWERY laughs, as he continues ...

I promised Volcanic I'd stay over in Princeton until this demonstration of respect between the torturer and the tortured was completed, but I refused to accompany him to the dentist again, even if it meant losing the privilege of another free ride in his buggy. On the third day, Volcanic came to see me in my hotel room ...

VOLCANIC rises and approaches, his hand over his mouth. He is happy.

VOLCANIC: Are you ready?

LOWERY: Ready for what?

VOLCANIC: The greatest miracle since the construction of them pyramids!

LOWERY: The only miracle possible now, Volcanic ... is some arrest in the advances of pestilence, venereal disease an' the remnants of the earth's insane ...

VOLCANIC: I'm happy ... so ... I'm smilin'!

He removes his hand from his mouth and smiles. His mouth is a dazzling mass of gold—incongruous, ridiculous, pathetic.

LOWERY: Well, I'll be goddamned! Shut your mouth, Volcanic. You're hard to look at, that way ...

VOLCANIC: (*disappointed*) Somethin' wrong with 'em? I seen 'em in a mirror an' I liked what I seen ...

LOWERY: What in hell did he do? ... Gold plate every tooth?

VOLCANIC: I asked him to ... except the back ones. They don't show unless I yawn ...

LOWERY: (*agitated*) You're insane! You're a sick old buzzard ... a fool ... the kind children throw pebbles at!

VOLCANIC: Is that so?

He laughs.

The trouble with you, Lowery, is lack of style!

LOWERY: If my tooth hurts, I have it pulled ... not this! What're you gonna do next ... dye your hair? ... Pretend the years you wasted never happened? ... God is merciful ... He kills off the few good men this earth is sometimes blessed with. But He doesn't spare the greedy bandits, either. In the end, death gets them as well, an' no arguments or wealth will postpone that welcome judgment.

VOLCANIC: When I face the sun an' smile, everybody in Princeton sees me! Even the horses them

cowboys ride into town stop an' shy away in surprise ... Dogs start to bark from one end of town to the other ...

LOWERY: (*in despair*) Yes ... Volcanic's comin' through again ...

VOLCANIC: Dreams are made of gold dust, Lowery ... I'm too old for chasin' fancies now ... So are you. What might've been's behind us now. Today, my dreams go where they'll keep ... into my mouth. An' they'll stay with me even when they lower me down the hole. I never built me a Volcanic City ... but look at this!

He bares his teeth at LOWERY, who backs away a pace.

LOWERY: Don't do that! ... The way you're goin' through money, you'll be pulling out a tooth at a time to pay your rent before next winter's over ...

VOLCANIC: Yeh ... well, maybe I will, maybe I won't. But today I'm feelin' good. When I smile into the sun, the whole town stops to look! You ever had a moment like that, Lowery?

LOWERY: No, I haven't. I've always been a man of humble tastes.

VOLCANIC: But you wanted to. With the widow you wanted to ...

LOWERY: Yes, yes ... I've wanted to ...

VOLCANIC: Then you're no different than me. Nobody is!

LOWERY: You're right. It's no great joy goin' through life looking like me. I look at myself in a mirror on a cloudy morning, an' I see a cretin of a man ... wild-haired ... disorderly beard ... wearin' worn-out, filthy clothes ... his eyes sick with worry about unpaid accounts, and surviving in a world where everything costs more today than it did yesterday!

VOLCANIC: (*thoughtful*) It was no good ... the minin' company givin' me all that money at once ...

LOWERY: It's made you crazier than you were. Would've done the same to me.

VOLCANIC: I got to spend it then. If I don't, it'll kill me ... or put me into irons in a crazy house.

LOWERY: And what will you do when it's all gone?

VOLCANIC: Go back to prospectin', Lowery. It's the only way to live.

LOWERY: (soberly) Yes ... the only way to die, too. I'm leaving town, Volcanic. I've wasted so much time ... Watching you get your gums gold-plated ... your Volcanic City ... your interpretations of Scriptures ... I'm gettin' out of here!

VOLCANIC: Hey, Lowery ...

LOWERY: What?

VOLCANIC: Forget all that, why don't you? ... I ... I want you to stay with me now. This last month ... I've been sleepin' bad ... been havin' a dream about the last prospect I'll be makin' ...

LOWERY: Nope. You go wherever you're goin' by yourself. Do what you have to do. But not with me. You're not now ... never were ... the kind of friend I'd choose had I a choice.

VOLCANIC: Yeh ... I understand.

LOWERY: Good.

VOLCANIC: I don't think I ever want to see you again either, Lowery.

LOWERY: Fine ... that's fine with me.

VOLCANIC moves quickly to LOWERY and, grabbing him by the collar of his coat, shakes him violently. LOWERY takes VOLCANIC by the throat and shakes him in return. Both of them get winded quickly and separate, gasping for breath. LOWERY is coughing. They have kicked up dust which rises around them.

VOLCANIC: You're worn out by poverty ... you depress me! ... You're like a preacher in a whore-house. I want to dress up like a monkey to show the world I'm livin' ... I want to bleed myself ... show God I can do without Him ... that I can spill my life on the ground an' still have more left in me than men like you! ... I want to smell out a claim an' go after it ... all alone ... just my body with a hammer an' chisel against the whole god-damned mountain! To eat what nobody's ever cooked for me ... to stand on a cliff, pants aroun' my ankles ... an' shake the sperm in me over the cliff into the valley ... an' laugh to see a gull scoop down an' swallow it before it hits the ground below ... Hah! The seeds for children I could've had ... eaten by a seagull!

He laughs harshly, shaking his fist in LOWERY'S face.

An' here's to you ... with your widow ... your widow ... your *widow*!

LOWERY: (icily) Don't you touch me, you brain-less savage!

Both men separate in slow motion. VOLCANIC vanishes at the edge of the stage. LOWERY with-draws his notebook and writes in slow motion, turning away from the scene.

The sound of POOR BOY'S harmonica is heard.

POOR BOY comes down in normal motion, his water bucket in hand. He arranges elements of the set, then pauses in his work.

POOR BOY: Was a rumour goin' round ... that some miners found a vein of gold ... somewhere back of Pitt Lake ... began bringin' back chunks of samples ... some big as a fist ... An' each man died in strange circumstances until none was left ...

He ponders on this a moment, then smiles as he loses the trend of thought.

My Uncle Willie ... who never told a lie ... said once he threw a small stone up as hard as he could an' it never come down ... He waited all day, but it never come down ... all he seen that day in the sky was a sparrow hawk ... Maybe small stones thrown at the sky by big men become hawks ...

Playing his harmonica raucously, he exits.

There is the sound of picking from inside the mine shaft.

LOWERY moves to the mine shaft, pushing his hat back on his head jauntily.

LOWERY: (loudly) You in there, Volcanic?

The picking sound stops.

VOLCANIC: Who wants to know?

LOWERY: It's me, Lowery.

VOLCANIC emerges, more stooped and aged than ever.

VOLCANIC: Well, goddamn if it isn't!

LOWERY: How's your winter been ... lots of snow? You still hearin' cowbells down below?

VOLCANIC: Yep …

LOWERY: And your dream …

VOLCANIC: (*sharply*) Forget my dream!

LOWERY: In your dream …

VOLCANIC: I said forget that, Lowery!

LOWERY: The cowbells … always gettin' nearer. The dream you never told me … that was botherin' you … is botherin' me now. Bothered me all winter, Volcanic …

VOLCANIC: Why keep askin' me?

LOWERY: It's the last time I'll be listening.

The wind sound rises and dies slowly.

VOLCANIC: (*shuddering*) I go to sleep … but I know I'm not sleepin' because I'm up in the most rugged mountains I ever seen. All around me I can smell gold. Other men were supposed to have found it … in big chunks which they brought back … an' they died. Never tellin' others where or how they got it. So I … the minin' genius … take off into these mountains in my sleep. An' the odour's in the air … so strong it makes my mouth dry.

LOWERY: The gold smell?

VOLCANIC: Yeh.

LOWERY: How does gold smell, Volcanic?

VOLCANIC: Can't describe it if you don't already know, Lowery. I'm up in these mountains … walls of solid rock … goin' up in every direction … the air is cold an' damp … clouds have closed in … no way of tellin' the time of day … which is north and south … nothin' but darkness an' grey light …

LOWERY: Nothing very real about it … like any other dream …

VOLCANIC: No, Lowery … it was more real than anythin' I've ever known … it's like … I was *there*, but sometime in the future.

LOWERY: Were you nervous or afraid? … How did you feel?

VOLCANIC: Hell, no … I was excited. But also … very tired … like there'd be no goin' back … an' I didn't care about goin' back. In the dream I was out of supplies … my grub ran out … nothin' to eat. The stuff that grew in the canyons was bitter an' watery … Then, just before darkness one evenin', I turned a corner where a dried-up stream bed had cut right through the mountain … an' there it was … exposed … a two-inch seam of pure gold … glowin' like a dull light in the fallin' darkness!

LOWERY: (*withdrawing his notebook and writing*) You were … out of your dream? … Aware that you were not really dreamin'? That it was somehow an actual event that you were seeing?

VOLCANIC: Yeh, that's it … I even seen the nicks where the gold had been cut out of the seam by others in lumps … An' now it was mine! More gold than any man ever claimed before!

LOWERY: The dream ended like that?

VOLCANIC: No … it went on an' on … the most important thing ever happened to me … My stomach turnin' over … head goin' dizzy.

LOWERY: You're a good sleeper. That kind of dream would sure wake me up in a hurry …

VOLCANIC: Me, too … me, too …

There is a long pause. LOWERY watches VOLCANIC. VOLCANIC is wrestling with the memory he has evoked. A flutter of feeling crosses his face: from a strange, demented happiness, to fear which makes him hunch his shoulders, as if against a great cold.

But I kept goin' back … I keep goin' back, night after night … At first, I broke a chunk of gold the size of my fist, off the vein, an' stitched it in the linin' of my jacket, intendin' to break it down when I reached civilization an' could return with supplies an' tools to stake my claim. I left then, tryin' to work my way out of the mountains. But … I couldn't … Every time I moved to get out … I ended up against a canyon wall I couldn't climb, not havin' any toes left … I'd turn around … an' there'd be another canyon facing me … higher than the other … Pretty soon I was in snow … I'd climbed that high, followin' small ravines …

LOWERY: So you returned …

VOLCANIC: Naw, I couldn't … Once I was up in the snow line, I couldn't find the canyons I'd come up through … You got to remember I had no food … My clothin' was thin … I'd found the gold in warm weather ... I didn't have clothin' for frost an' snow.

LOWERY stares at him for a long moment, a flicker of realization dawning.

LOWERY: So ... you ...

VOLCANIC: (*nodding*) Yes, I died.

LOWERY: Was the death as violent and painful as the life preceding it had been?

VOLCANIC: No ... not at all. Not a fast death ... but slow ... a little at a time. First the deliriums of starvation an' exposure ... then realizin' that my fingers had froze, like my toes done on me a long time ago ... An' my eyes were doin' strange things ... The man I'd killed long ago came to stand in front of me once or twice, snow gathered on his nose an' shoulders, an' packed into the hollows where his eyes had been ... But when I reached to him, he kind of disappeared ...

LOWERY: (*frightened*) Hell *must* be hot ... all faith an' reason says it's so. Not a glacier ... not after all this cold I've endured ...

VOLCANIC: No pain ... only a terrible tiredness an' the feelin' that all my body juices were dryin' out of me ...

LOWERY: No! A man can't take that ... a man fights back!

VOLCANIC: Who was there to fight? A man can't fight God, can he?

LOWERY: (*groaning*) I've wondered ... at times I've wondered.

VOLCANIC: No, I tried to keep movin', but there was never any sun ... no way to find me bearin's ... I tried to retrace my steps, but my eyes played strange tricks on me. I'd see this track I'd made ... I'd see blood on it ... but when I bent over to make sure, it vanished ... An' lookin' around me at the mountains I thought I seen them movin' ... closin' in ... re-arrangin' themselves, like in a dance ...

Notebook close to his face, as if short-sighted now, LOWERY writes in a trembling hand.

For a while I kept feelin' the large nugget in my jacket, but after my hands froze, the feelin' went out of them. An' I couldn't tell if it was still sewn into the cloth, or if I'd lost it ... made me very sad ... The dream always ended the same way ...

LOWERY: You ... died ...

VOLCANIC: I died. In a small ravine with towerin' walls of grey granite an' an icy wind blowin' through so hard it whistled in my ears, I just sat down an' never got up again ...

LOWERY huddles deeper into his coat.

LOWERY: That's ... one hell of a thing to live with every night you go to sleep, Volcanic. It would drive me to more drinkin' than I'm doin' now ...

VOLCANIC looks at LOWERY, aware of LOWERY'S fear of greater chill in his declining life. He grins fiendishly.

VOLCANIC: It's like writin' a newspaper nobody buys ... or losin' a young widow who *asked* to stay!

LOWERY: (*breaking*) She was so young, Volcanic ... the smell of her hair like sunlight and fresh hay in a summer meadow. She reached up to touch my face with her hand ... The touch was cool and gentle ... so cool and gentle ... like a spring rain ...

LOWERY lowers his head in defeat. VOLCANIC laughs.

The wind sound rises.

VOLCANIC: But that's not the end of it, Lowery ... In my dreams I always seen two big cougars approach me from opposite ends of the ravine. An' when they got to where I sat, they slowly tore my clothes off ... except for the boots ... couldn't get the laces loose. Old Volcanic ... forty thousand dollars in his ass pocket ... et up by two cougars!

VOLCANIC goes off into loud, insane laughter. LOWERY stares at him with bewilderment and disbelief.

Yeh! Old Volcanic ... et up by them two big pussy cats ... You know what was funny about that?

LOWERY: (*wearily*) No, but you tell me, and I'm getting the hell out of this ... out of your presence! They killed you givin' you all that money ... An' I have this raging thirst comin' on ... my mind's beginnin' to go ...

But he doesn't leave. He dies where he is, the notebook and pencil falling out of his hands to the ground.

VOLCANIC begins to hobble in a crippled, bizarre, reeling sort of death dance.

VOLCANIC: As they was eatin' me ... the part of me that died last started grinnin'! When them two cougars seen my gold teeth startin' to gleam, they both sprang back an' kept their distance ... they sure did ... a long time they did ... weeks it seemed like ... growlin' with hunger, waitin' for my lips to cover these teeth so they could resume their dinner!

There is more laughter, insane, defiant, the body action turning into a wrestling and boxing match with death. Then, suddenly, he trembles and falls.

LOWERY and VOLCANIC are still, dead.

An echo of VOLCANIC'S laughter is still heard, becoming softer, more distant.

POOR BOY'S harmonica plays. POOR BOY enters, carrying two wooden crosses and a shovel under his arm. He stops playing the harmonica and surveys the two dead men. He looks down at the death grin frozen on VOLCANIC'S lips. He reaches down with the handle of the shovel and forces VOLCANIC'S mouth shut. Laying two crosses upright beside the mine shaft, POOR BOY turns over a shovelful of earth from the graves he is about to dig. He pauses and pushes his cap back on his head.

POOR BOY: Livin' men work ... fight ... take an' sell everythin' that's not tied down. Dead men ... they got no rights. They don't eat ... they don't vote ... don't need roads or windows. They got nothin' to say. No use rememberin' them ... unless ...

He laughs.

... unless you can forget them ... that's different then. It's like they never died at all!

He laughs again.

The wind sound comes up as the lights go down.

A few more bars of harmonica music are heard until it is completely dark.

All the sounds end.

End

SEVEN HOURS TO SUNDOWN

In the mid-1970s, Ryga travelled to Edmonton to watch a play being staged by a new theatre company, Theatre Network, the creation of a group of University of Alberta graduates, one of whom was his daughter, Tanya. She had invited him to watch their production of *Two Miles Off*, a play the group had put together working as a collective, which dramatized the efforts of a small community, Elnora, Alberta, two miles off the main highway, to preserve its local identity. Ryga was impressed with the group's work and later wrote them a letter of support: "I was … impressed by the clean separation made away from derivative and colonial drama into exploration of experiences, language and mythology of Canadians living in rural communities" (July 5, 1975). He had also discussed the possibility of writing a play for them—and when he returned home a subject was waiting for him: his own community was in turmoil over the fate of one of its heritage buildings.

In Summerland there was an old hospital made of three storeys of solid concrete, which had served the town since the early 1900s. By the mid-1960s, especially as the Summerland townsite moved further away from the hospital's lakeside location, it was decided to erect a new hospital closer to the new town centre. The old hospital was renamed Century House and functioned for a while as a geriatric facility—until the venture closed in the mid-1970s, leaving the building sitting empty.

Ryga, with his wife Norma and his friend Ken Smedley, had an idea: they saw the forty-room facility as a potential community arts centre, including a two-hundred seat theatre, something Summerland lacked. Forming a committee, the Summerland Theatre and Arts Foundation, with Ryga as an executive member, they first met with interested community members in Bookstore and Bazaar, George's and Norma's bookstore, then developed plans to prepare a feasibility study. Afterwards, they approached town council—then in the midst of elections. What happened at the council meeting when the committee's report was presented was a shock to Ryga, as he describes in his reminiscent book, *Beyond the Crimson Morning*: " … a seconder emerged who then moved that the documents be rejected without further study or discussion." Not only did council reject the proposal, but it voted to demolish the building at the same meeting. Unbeknownst to many people, the land was in the process of being sold, along with other parcels of town land, to pay off municipal debts.

Ryga's group was infuriated. They immediately applied for a court injunction to halt the demolition of the building, held petition signings at the bookstore, and began an occupation of the building itself. The occupation, which lasted some weeks, had its moments of high drama, as when an occupier jumped onto the wrecking crane's cable, rode it to the ground, and unhooked the wrecking ball, and when a defiant Ken Smedley directed a fire hose at the operator of the crane. All of this was duly reported in the town newspaper, the *Summerland Review*, until there was a putative "complaint," apparently a highly-placed one, and the newspaper's reporting of the affair promptly ceased. The town council finally agreed to cease and desist with its efforts at demolition and board up the building pending litigation. But, in the end, the court's decision went against the community group and Century House was finally torn down—although, ironically, the land was not sold and the plot sat empty for years afterwards.

Ryga used much of this real life material in *Seven Hours to Sundown*. The play's major action concerns similar attempts to turn a municipally-owned building, in the case of the play a former church, into an arts centre. The antagonistic mayor in the play is named Kiosk—a synonym (in real life the Summerland mayor's name was Booth, and his father was a carrot farmer). The fitfully waffling participation of the local newspaper is depicted through the shenanigans of the characters Janice and Jeff.

At the same time, as was his wont, while the play is based on very real local events in his own community, Ryga could not resist elevating the drama to the level of myth-making, which unfortunately, in this case, drifts dangerously into the realm of parody. Ryga portrays Kiosk in the play as more than just a hard-working man who succeeds in becoming mayor: the son of immigrants, he also struggles, as did his gruff, overbearing father, to maintain personal pride in a conservative community that regards them as "low level scruff." Even in public office Kiosk fails at "holding up my goddamned head among men!" Doomed notes of family tragedy are struck as, one by one, his relatives suddenly leave him or are killed in accidents, his father being impaled, martyr-like, on a fir tree—all of which sits uneasily with the documentary, agit-prop, realpolitik thrust of the play. At the end of the day, when all the (negative) reviews were in, Ryga himself admitted, "I blame my faltering discipline: I got swept up by the events … I was too close."

Seven Hours to Sundown was commissioned by Theatre Network and the University of Alberta, and opened at the Studio Theatre at the University of Alberta on May 27, 1976. The play was directed by Mark Manson, with Dennis Robinson as Sid Kiosk, Tanya Ryga as Irma Kiosk, Shay Garner as Janice Webber, Juergen Beerwald as Jerry Goyda, and with Jonathan C. Barker playing Tom Rossini, Del Kiosk, Jeff Dolan, and The Man.

SEVEN HOURS TO SUNDOWN

CHARACTERS

SID KIOSK, *the mayor*
TOM ROSSINI, *an alderman*
IRMA KIOSK, *a young woman*
JANICE WEBBER, *a newspaper woman*
JERRY GOYDA, *an ex-schoolteacher and craftsman*
DEL KIOSK, *the father of the mayor*
JEFF DOLAN, *the newspaper publisher*
A MAN

SET

A non-set stage.

Scene and location changes are accomplished by movement of coastered hardware. Two chairs, a desk and a telephone bring the mayor's office onstage. A workbench for leather tooling brings the environment of JERRY GOYDA on the set. A metal typing desk, through physical activity around it, becomes the offices of the newspaper.

Entry positions of these various elements of the set, once established, are maintained, such as: stage right for the mayor's office; stage left for GOYDA'S workshop; centre backstage for the newspaper office. Scenes which are imagined or which come out of the past are played centrestage forward in an area isolated with light.

ACT 1

The lights come up slowly.

Drum and harmonica music are heard, played in a driving rhythm.

JANICE WEBBER enters, singing, bringing on her part of the set.

JANICE: (*singing*)
In our town
The grass grows green

The air is fresh
The water's clean
No one's poor
An' no one's mean
At seven hours to sundown ...
In our town
Seven hours to sundown ...

There is a drum and harmonica interlude before the next stanza.

JANICE: In our town
There is much to do
The bus an' transports
Drive right through
We all grow beans
An' lilacs, too
At seven hours to sundown ...
In our town
Seven hours to sundown ...

The music continues for another interlude. JANICE picks up and opens a back issue of the newspaper that she writes for. The music ceases. She reads aloud from the paper.

Last week's civic elections in Woodlands were no surprise to this newspaper or to seasoned political observers in this community. A low-keyed, lack-lustre campaign ended in a low-keyed, lack-lustre election of members to town council. Less than thirty percent of eligible voters cast ballots, in an election which saw the victory of Sid Kiosk as mayor, winning by a margin of eight votes over his opponent, hardware merchant John Henderson.

KIOSK enters with his portion of the set. He is studying the newspaper as well. He is annoyed with what he reads in the paper and, using the telephone on his desk, dials a number.

KIOSK: Hullo, Dolan? Sid Kiosk here ... I'm not happy about your damned editorial ... not one bit! ... How come Henderson gets identified as a hardware merchant an' I just get named? ... I've advertised farm produce with you. I don't like it when bigger advertisers get free plugs for their businesses out of an election campaign. An' I don't like that insinuation that deadbeats got elected this time ... Running the town is a big job these days ... I ran a good, vigorous campaign ... Yeah? Well, you tell her then!

KIOSK hangs up the telephone and reads on in the paper.

In the following dialogue, DOLAN might speak through an intercom.

DOLAN: (*offstage*) Janice!

JANICE: Yes, Mister Dolan?

DOLAN: Ease up on that goddamned new mayor, will you?

JANICE: (*smiling*) Yes, Mister Dolan.

DOLAN: Maybe you could run a two-column photo of him cutting some ribbon ... or petting a carrot ... or kissing a kid. Something to make him happy.

JANICE: Yes, Mister Dolan.

DOLAN: You're a good kid, Janice. Learn and listen ... and in twenty years, who knows? You might leave home, go twenty miles down the road, and work for the *Highlands Herald*!

He laughs.

Even Randolph Hearst started small!

JANICE laughs, then reads on in her copy of the paper.

JANICE: (*reading*) The election also saw the return of Tom Rossini as alderman. It is hoped that this alderman, who has shown strong initiative in the past as a developer, might demonstrate an equal vitality in the public office to which he was elected, a quality noticeably absent in his previous term in office.

ROSSINI enters KIOSK'S area of the stage and offers a handshake to KIOSK. He then settles back comfortably in a chair.

ROSSINI: (*warmly*) Congratulations, Sid ... I voted for you, in case it matters.

KIOSK: If everyone who's come forward since the election to say they supported me *had* voted for me as they claim, I'd have come in on a landslide.

He points to the paper in front of him.

See what they've written about you?

ROSSINI: Yes.

KIOSK: Sue them!

ROSSINI: What for? ... I got in, didn't I? ... Any publicity is better than none. People remember reading about a man. They soon forget whether it was good or bad.

DOLAN: (*offstage*) Janice!

JANICE: Yes, Mister Dolan?

DOLAN: Keep a low profile on that bastard, Rossini, will you? ... He doesn't need any help taking over the town.

JANICE: He's not exactly a ball of fire, Mister Dolan. At most council meetings he doesn't even bother voting.

DOLAN: He doesn't have to. He fixes things so the voting goes the way he wants, whether he's there or not. Look at his investment record sometime ... I've got it here in my office. His assets doubled during his first term as alderman.

JANICE: (*surprised*) I didn't know that.

ROSSINI: (*speaking to KIOSK*) Nobody knows much about the inner workings of civic government ... an' they care less. So ... I came to congratulate you, and to offer any help I can give, in ... showing you the ropes, as they say.

KIOSK: (*coldly*) Appreciate that, Tom. But the outgoing mayor has given me as much help as I'll need.

ROSSINI: Well, in case ... I offered.

KIOSK: No need, but thanks all the same, Tom.

JERRY GOYDA enters with his portion of the set. He is followed by IRMA KIOSK. She is agitated.

IRMA: Let's give Rossini his notice ... The church will cost sixty dollars a month, and we'll have three times the studio space to work in!

GOYDA: Hold on, Irma ... nothing is quite as simple as it appears at first.

IRMA: I've checked it out ... look!

She takes out some scraps of paper from her handbag and spreads them in front of GOYDA.

ROSSINI: (*speaking to KIOSK*) So ... you made it as mayor.

KIOSK: Would appear so.

He tries to make himself busy with his paperwork.

ROSSINI: I never had any desire for that ... Too much like being a foreman of a work crew. You get all the responsibility. If anything goes wrong, it's you who gets the blame.

KIOSK: (*irritated*) Somebody has to.

ROSSINI: It's been a long time since we worked together ... or had any dealings.

KIOSK: You've done alright without me.

ROSSINI: Your family, are they well? ... Your daughter, Irma, was it? ... Where's she now?

KIOSK: (*struggling to be civil*) My wife had an operation on her shoulder, but she's fine now. Irma went to Winnipeg, but came back last summer ...

He becomes thoughtful.

IRMA: (*speaking to GOYDA*) Heat, light and water ... a total cost of nine hundred a year ... including a trade licence if we were to set up a retail store in the lobby.

GOYDA examines the papers more closely.

ROSSINI: Is she living at home, then?

KIOSK: (*sharply*) Yes, she's livin' with us!

ROSSINI: I'm sorry if I said something ...

KIOSK: Dammit, you had no kids! ... She's a good person ... helps out with work, pays her room an' board ... A bright, beautiful girl ... but ...

GOYDA: (*speaking to IRMA*) Where did you get these figures?

IRMA: At the municipal office.

GOYDA: It doesn't mean anything. That old church has been vacant for five years.

IRMA: I took the volume of services used in the past, multiplied it by two, then calculated charges on the current cost of services ... added a trade licence ... two hundred dollars for maintenance an' repairs and ...

GOYDA throws up his arms.

GOYDA: Okay, Irma ... right, love ... I've got it! What shape's the church in?

IRMA closes her eyes and recites the facts.

IRMA: It's seventy-two years old ... frame construction ... stucco exterior and three-quarter inch plaster interior ... hot water system installed in the parish hall next door ... good roof ... some windows cracked ... seven rooms ... pine floors ...

KIOSK: She's got no ambition ... doesn't go out. Lots of nice young men have phoned or come around to the house ... but Irma looks right through them. Spends all her time ... even Sundays ... in that grubby little leather shop on Elm Street.

ROSSINI: The place run by Jerry Goyda?

KIOSK: Yes ... Goyda.

ROSSINI: Ah, but maybe Goyda is ...

He leers at him.

KIOSK: I don't want to hear what you gotta say about that ... not a word! I brought my child up good ... That's not a man ... I told him that myself once when I was on the school board an' saw to it he wasn't teaching in our schools no more. To cut leather and sew buttons is not a man's way of making a living, an' nothing's ever going to change my way of thinking!

Both men stare at each other.

GOYDA: (*speaking to IRMA*) Who owns it now?

IRMA: When the parish dissolved itself, the church reverted to the municipality for back taxes.

GOYDA: But wasn't there a service club ... or some lodge leasing parts of the complex?

IRMA: The Masons lease the parish hall one night a month. It can all be cleared up at the municipal offices ... my dad's mayor now ... and Alderman Rossini is the contact for the lodge holding partial lease.

GOYDA: Don't jump to any conclusions where those two are concerned.

IRMA: They're good men ... everybody does what they have to do. Sometimes we don't understand ... I don't like to see us gouged for rent by Rossini, but other than that ...

GOYDA: Stop being a child, Irma. I've been up and down that whole route ... from the Teacher's Federation to part-time helper in a village mortuary.

IRMA: And what did you learn from it all?

GOYDA: (*considering his reply*) That it takes a lot of effort to stay out of fights. That the serenity of a small town is nothing more than a slower-witted killer stalking his prey!

During the last speech, JANICE has pushed her newspaper aside, stretched languidly and, gathering her handbag and notebook, gone to where KIOSK and ROSSINI are.

JANICE: Have you gentlemen any statement to make for the next issue of the paper?

KIOSK: (*foolishly*) Why should we?

IRMA: (*addressing GOYDA*) That's an awfully suspicious attitude to have.

GOYDA: Never mind my attitudes ... hold this. I need to cut a yard of lacing.

IRMA holds the leather for him while he cuts.

JANICE: You're the politicians. I merely report on your deliberations.

ROSSINI: Nice girl, eh, Sid?

KIOSK: I don't know about that. I don't like what she writes. But I don't suppose many people read the paper, except for the ads an' help wanteds.

He grins at his own witticism. ROSSINI is watching JANICE closely.

JANICE: I was passing by ... saw two heads through the window. Thought maybe some startling new civic development was under consideration by the two crackerjacks on town council.

ROSSINI: Like hell you were, Janice. We're both old enough to be your father ... I wish you'd remember that.

JANICE: Then I've come as an enemy of the people ... looking for information to ridicule the choices of the electorate ... thirty percent of the electorate, but who wants to know?

ROSSINI: (*speaking to KIOSK*) Mouth like a garage door, but a nice girl! Like Mussolini ... When my grandfather was fading, he began to admire Mussolini ... for the same reasons I admire her!

KIOSK: I don't know anything about that ...

He addresses JANICE.

What can I do for you, young lady? I'm busy getting into harness, as you can appreciate. But you can count on my co-operation ... if for no other reason, than to keep information you write a bit more truthful!

JANICE: (*smiling sweetly*) That's nice!

KIOSK: Think nothing of it. Now ... I have work to do.

JANICE rises and, nodding to ROSSINI, leaves. She moves back to her office.

KIOSK and ROSSINI go into a soundless discussion.

IRMA: (*speaking to GOYDA*) I think *you* should write the letter of application for a lease. Coming from me ... well ... my old man's the captain now, and it would look a bit ...

GOYDA: Embarrassing?

IRMA: It's a small, conservative town. The idea of converting the oldest remaining church into a workshop or business premises ... I *like* him ... the idea may not rest easy with people who supported him. You know ...

GOYDA: Be decisive, for God's sake. You came in with everything, including a business licence ... now what?

IRMA: (*confused*) You don't understand. I was born and raised here. You're an outsider.

GOYDA: I've lived here fifteen years ... my teaching career began and ended here ... thanks to your father. I've developed a business here ... most of my friends are here.

IRMA: You're still an outsider.

GOYDA: What makes an insider? The ability to see every point of view three different ways?

IRMA: No. It's the inability to see one point of view, Jerry!

GOYDA: So it's screw Rossini and his rent rip-off one minute, and be nice doing it the next. I enjoy doing what I do, but sometimes I would like a break. You came in with an idea, and I say, "Fine!

Let's move on it." But I don't like having it left in my lap. Your father and I have a grudge going back many years ... You've got a share in this shop. It would be easier for you to approach him.

IRMA: Alright, I will. But you write the letter.

GOYDA: Why?

IRMA: (*floundering*) Because ... you're in charge ... here.

GOYDA nods. The lights go out on the scene. GOYDA exits.

When the lights come up, IRMA is seated in front of KIOSK. The setting around them has lost the officious appearance of the mayor's office. The setting could be the mayor's home, or might indicate a closeness between two people who are in reality separated by a failure of communication.

KIOSK: No!

IRMA: No, what, Dad?

KIOSK: I said no, and I'll say it again.

IRMA: The proposal is reasonable ... the church has been empty a long time now.

KIOSK: He could come in person to ask me. Why does he write a letter as if I lived in another country? When I told him I didn't approve his lack of discipline in the classroom ... that his contract would not be renewed ... I called him into the school board office and told him face to face. Goyda, I said, we need children who can learn to do things, not just vote. They vote or not once every three or four years ... but every morning, they'll be getting up to go to work.

IRMA: I still hear people say he was a good teacher.

KIOSK: Then let him teach somewhere else. I didn't stop him teaching. I only stopped him teaching *here*! He had no right getting his hooks into you ... opening up a useless shop ... looking poorer an' poorer. He did it to bother me ... everything he's done was for that reason.

IRMA: He didn't get any hooks into me. I would rather do crafts than work at a nine-to-five job.

KIOSK: If you'd said that, I could've opened a shop for you.

IRMA: I don't want a shop ... I only want to do what I like doing.

KIOSK: (*thoughtfully*) Is there anything ... between you and him?

IRMA: Do I like him?

KIOSK: There's not much of a man there ... a knitter ... a shoelace tier!

He is angry now.

Whatever you call it! ... You're with him half the night sometimes!

IRMA: Yes ... I like him.

KIOSK: What about *him*, eh?

IRMA: He's not like that ... He works very hard ... reads ... takes long walks by himself ... listens to music on Sundays.

KIOSK: He doesn't work hard. He amuses himself ... like a professional card player, or piano tuner. I don't understand why a child of mine can't see through all that nonsense.

IRMA: He works hard ... long hours. He reminds me of my grandfather, Dad.

KIOSK: The old man would turn over in his grave if he heard you say that, Irma! There was a man for you ... took on the world with two hands. Always said the Kiosks would become people to look up to ...

DEL KIOSK, IRMA'S GRANDFATHER, enters, an old, beaten man out of the past.

Tell them, Pop! Tell 'em how it used to be!

The GRANDFATHER peers uncertainly into the gloom. He throws back his shoulders irritably.

GRANDFATHER: The carrots ... one helluva poor job you done hoeing them carrots, boy!

KIOSK: (*disturbed*) Tell 'em how you told Williston to get his goddamned truck off the yard when he delivered a load of twisted lumber for the new greenhouse! You told that deaf old bastard off good, I remember that!

GRANDFATHER: 'An the Deering girl ... you were the one got her in trouble ... Joe Deerin's come to see me about it.

KIOSK: (*plaintively*) I don't love her, Pop!

GRANDFATHER: Damn the lovin' … you're gonna do what's right by her. If she leaves you, that's another thing. But you're gonna do the right thing an' marry her!

KIOSK is shaken. IRMA rises to her feet. She is a small girl, frightened.

IRMA: Dad?

KIOSK: He was tough as nails, runnin' that carrot farm single-handed … morning to night. I helped him when I could … after work … on weekends.

GRANDFATHER: All alone … in sickness or in health … all alone I worked them fields, growin' carrots for shoe salesmen, the blacksmith an' his family … Slippery Jess, the lady with the board-inghouse … Slippery Jess, they called 'er!

KIOSK grasps at what small details he can to sustain himself.

KIOSK: But you never let anyone have a free ride on a Kiosk, Pop! You sure told that Williston off when he tried that trick with bad lumber …

GRANDFATHER: Five o'clock in the morning, frost on the ground, my back achin' so I could hardly stoop … but there I was, haulin' sacks of carrots to the railway station. Had to be in when they was still cold … People who don't grow their own food don't buy anythin' which don't taste or feel like it just come out of the ground. Five o'clock in the mornin', and I'm out there workin'. The Chinaman in town, he don't work half as hard … sits in his store all day an' sells chewin' gum an' French safes to boys like my son.

KIOSK: I told you and I meant it, Pop, that one day a Kiosk would be on top in this town!

GRANDFATHER: (*leaving*) Five o'clock in the morning, an' I'm hauling sacks of cold carrots like I'm some coolie movin' a rock pile. My son's asleep … his overheated wife's asleep … they're all sleepin' still.

The GRANDFATHER exits.

IRMA: Dad … I'm sorry about Grandfather. And Mom leaving … I feel like I'm to blame for a whole lot of things that went wrong.

KIOSK: (*wiping the tears from his eyes*) It's nothing. We've still got our health. An' people respect your old man, Irma. With the newspaper against us, we showed them! Your old dad is

mayor of this town … from a carrot farm to mayor … and if I do well, I'll run again and do it twice!

IRMA: We … didn't do it. I never supported your campaign, Dad.

KIOSK: (*momentarily hurt*) Others did, so what the hell? Wish the old man had lived long enough to see it happen … In his lifetime, you know, we were treated like low-level scruff in this town.

IRMA: Don't talk about it if it hurts you. It's not important to me.

KIOSK: But it's important to me, young lady!

He is growing annoyed and restless.

I wanted to be an engineer, but I couldn't get away from that goddamned farm. Then there was the business with your mother … and her going to live with that bone-headed rancher, Stark. You know what he does when he should be repairing fences in the spring?

IRMA: No, I don't.

KIOSK: He flies kites! She told me once he's even won awards for it … Like a kid, he flies goddamn kites!

IRMA: But … what difference does it make now, Dad?

KIOSK: What difference? Somebody has to care if our world's to survive from one day to the next. Do you think life goes on as if by accident? No damned way … There are people everywhere making sure roofs don't leak … that machinery is oiled an' ready to go … that food reaches the tables … that roads get repaired an' cleared. I resent people like your friend, Goyda, who hangs on to the system with one hand an' thumbs his nose at the stars with the other! He's not the first … There were others before him in this town!

IRMA: I don't know what you're talking about.

KIOSK: Remittance men … Lazy, insolent Englishmen who came to this country with a monthly retainer of money to keep them here. My old man came over as a working immigrant. *They* came like royalty … bought up the best farming land an' left it in bush. My old man wants to farm, but he gets the gravel to farm on. They bring their relatives over on holidays … drive up to our farm an' show us off as if we were their hired labour! They never learned to say my old man's name, even though he emigrated from the same country they did ... "Hey, chappie," they'd call him, an' wag their forefingers as if they were calling a dog ... "Hey, chappie, come over and mow my lawn tomorrow." ... an' he did. Goddamn him, but he did!

IRMA leaves while KIOSK is deeply preoccupied with his thoughts. Slowly, he mobilizes himself and begins to sort through the papers on the desk in front of him.

ROSSINI enters and paces about in front of KIOSK'S desk.

ROSSINI: Still working, Sid?

KIOSK: Yes.

ROSSINI: Come on to the Legion. I'll buy you a beer.

KIOSK: I don't drink beer. It makes me drowsy.

ROSSINI: You doing work, or making work?

KIOSK: What the hell does that mean? I spend a lot of time in here ... I was elected to spend time here. Sometimes I'm in this office until midnight ... thinkin'.

ROSSINI: Thinking what?

KIOSK: Thinking for the rest of you ... You guys come into council meetings Monday nights ... Bert Jones is pissed ... Some of you sleep here ... I seen Will McIntyre dozing last week ... an' voting away eight thousand for road repairs. He votes, but he doesn't know what for. The bastard comes to council meetings to sleep, so he can be in shape for his night job at the trailer plant after he leaves the meeting!

ROSSINI: You worry for all of us, is that it?

KIOSK: You damned right I do!

ROSSINI: I'm glad I'm not mayor.

KIOSK: I wish you'd all start to shape up ... Water mains breaking like they were made of glass. Dinners to attend, speeches to make ... for what? To keep the town from falling apart, that's for what!

ROSSINI: Stop campaigning ... you're elected now.

KIOSK: Then don't provoke me.

ROSSINI: Your daughter came to see me at my office today. She wants my support for her partner's application to lease the old church.

KIOSK: (*annoyed*) Why did she do that?

ROSSINI: I don't want to lose the rent they pay on the shop they're in. But ... I don't want that thrown in my face if it comes to a vote in council.

KIOSK: So you promised you'd support Goyda ... after I'd already told her I'm opposed?

ROSSINI: (*grinning*) The art of politics, my friend, is the art of kissing a homely woman ... as you push her out the door into the street. Your daughter spoke to me. I listened sympathetically, nodded and promised her nothing.

KIOSK: Yeh ... I see.

He is thoughtful.

You figure my daughter's homely?

ROSSINI: (*coughing into his fist*) No. I was only explaining how I deal with life.

KIOSK: Get this straight, Rossini ... I don't want Goyda getting into that church. I know it's personal ... if I wasn't mayor ... if I hadn't had dealings with him in the past, I'd be the first to support his application. But that's not the case ... I don't like the guy or what he does an' thinks. So if he gets in, it's over my objections ... and my loss of face. That's the way I read it, an' I'm too old to change. That sonofabitch stays where he's at!

ROSSINI: That's fair enough with me. He's a good tenant. And it may complicate the lease our lodge has with the community. But we have to come up with something reasonable for council to make its decision on.

KIOSK: What do you mean?

ROSSINI: You can't face the other aldermen and say that sonofabitch stays where he's at ... I don't like him personally, and Rossini, his landlord, doesn't want to lose rent!

KIOSK: I'm new to the job. Can't you come up with something?

ROSSINI: My suggestion is to wear him down by asking for further information ... more presentations. Give him encouragement, but not a commitment. In the end, we can always hang him on a technicality.

KIOSK is confused by this explanation.

KIOSK: I'm a farmer, not a manipulator in real estate.

ROSSINI: Don't start weighing in what you do for a living against what I do ... You want a problem resolved, I'm offering a suggestion, that's all.

KIOSK: I don't like telling lies to people. It's either yes or a no ... What you're saying bothers me. I remember your old man tried to punch out my old man for a piece of his farm ... That's in the past, but I don't forget. I'd prefer some way of refusing Goyda's application.

ROSSINI: There is no way. Any short cuts through the system means somebody ends up with a bloodied nose. In this case, it'd be your nose. I won't support you. Neither would the riff-raff passing for aldermen in this town.

KIOSK: I see what you mean ... Okay ... we got to think.

They huddle into a wordless conversation.

GOYDA and JANICE enter into GOYDA'S stage area. GOYDA brings with him a parcel and drops it on the floor at the back of his table.

GOYDA: The smaller the supply order, the higher the mailing charges. Also, my discount percentage drops. A business can't stay small anymore. You *pay* to maintain a shop this size.

JANICE: You're undercapitalized ... marry a rich widow.

GOYDA: I don't want a crafts supermarket. Is there no other option?

JANICE: Not for a man. They're on the downslide. The day is coming when men will be hiring out to houseclean and mend clothes for working women. Of course, they'll be eligible for alimony support from wives who divorce them, so the picture is not altogether desperate.

GOYDA laughs.

GOYDA: You're a joy to see first thing in the morning, you know that? Cheerful, wise, consoling ... a mother hen to a worried man ... Get out of my shop!

JANICE: *(laughing)* Has Irma been by yesterday?

GOYDA: She's on a mission. I've got seven hand-bags to bead and three leather vests to lace, but everything slows to a crawl when Irma's on a mission.

JANICE: *(holding up a handbag)* I'd like this one ... when it's finished.

GOYDA: Not until you've paid for the last one you took.

JANICE: But I've explained ... I left it on a seat at the movie when I went to get a drink. When I returned, it was gone ... I haven't got it.

GOYDA: I'm in the business of selling handbags, not theft insurance. You owe me fourteen ninety-five!

JANICE laughs.

JANICE: That's the retail price, for Christ's sake, Jerry.

GOYDA: You're not a wholesaler. Buy twenty and I'll give you a discount by jobbing. Otherwise, you owe me fourteen ninety-five.

JANICE: You're serious, aren't you?

GOYDA: Yes, I am. There are too many things in this shop getting carted away by my friends.

The lights go out on KIOSK and ROSSINI.

JANICE: *(whining)* When I've paid my rent from what I earn at the newspaper, there's almost nothing left.

GOYDA: So what am I supposed to do? Subsidize your income with hand-tooled leather handbags? ... Go away, I'm busy.

JANICE: *(holding the handbag lovingly)* It's beautiful ...

GOYDA: Alright, I'll make you a proposition, Janice. If we get space in the old church, I'll expand business. You can then put in some part-time work here. I'll talk to Irma about what we can afford to pay.

JANICE: You're putting me off. Irma doesn't know business from her asshole ... What's the latest on the church?

GOYDA: Kiosk is cold. I knew he'd be. Irma's working on the others.

JANICE: You're too small to take on such a large building, Jerry.

GOYDA: Well, I'm suffocating in this place. It's cluttered ... it's a pressure-tank of contradictions. I work with leather and bone all day ... but each time I look up I get an accusing eyeful of Greenpeace *Save the Whales* posters. Blubber's bad this season, but every ecologist I know is working leather. When I mention this paradox, I get a dead stare.

JANICE gives him a long, dead stare. GOYDA grins.

JANICE: Under that long hair ... under the skin ... you're really a law and order type.

GOYDA: (*still grinning*) That's right ... and I believe in justice, and in an honest day's wages for an honest day's work!

JANICE: (*caustically*) And in marriage ... and retirement fund contributions!

GOYDA: As a matter of fact, that, too ... When I was at university, I lived with a woman ... for three years we stayed together. She had my child ... a son. Stephen, we called him.

JANICE is startled. GOYDA turns away from her. A MAN in a bizarre costume enters and stops a short distance from GOYDA. He avoids looking at GOYDA, his face shaded by a large dark hat.

MAN: She's not comin' back ... She told me to go see you and tell you that she's not comin' back.

GOYDA: Marlene met some charlatans with yet another religious vision of how to save the world. She took Stephen with her ... When the prophet finally came to lean on my door-frame to tell me, she had been gone three months.

MAN: I'll tell you so you'll know, the brothers and sisters will kick your ass if you try comin' around makin' trouble ... She's happy with us.

GOYDA: Filthy scruff dressed in rags ... elementary school drop-outs too weak and stupid to make it in petty crime ... Tuned in to Christianity with jackboots!

MAN: You got to speak to me sometime, man ... You can't just stand there lookin' at me like that ... I don't like anyone lookin' at me that way!

GOYDA: (*turning away from him*) Ignorance has an odour ... a sauerkraut barrel stench. It was beginning to fill my room, my eyes, my life ... with him standing there only a few minutes.

MAN: The kid's been christened Ezekiel ... that's his name now. She's been christened, too. Her name's Diana. If you ever see them, you're gonna call 'em that, you understand?

GOYDA: Ignorance not only stinks. It inflicts pain.

MAN: (*gloating*) Your kid's my kid now! He's never goin' to any school. I'm gonna teach him everythin' ... how to be a high priest. When he grows up, he's gonna punish her ... I'm gonna teach him how ... He's gonna punish her an' any sister who smokes, drinks, eats meat or fornicates!

GOYDA: Ignorance inflicts pain by breaking your ribs when your back's turned ... bruising your liver ... breaking a tooth with the toe of a boot ...

Almost as if it were in slow motion, the MAN attacks GOYDA from behind. He knocks him to the ground, then kicks at his ribs, face and back with his booted feet. GOYDA makes no effort to protect himself. He rolls and twists with the blows.

The MAN leaves. JANICE stands frozen, staring away from GOYDA, who rises slowly, painfully, to his feet.

JANICE: (*coldly*) I don't know what you're talking about ... I'm not interested.

GOYDA: That's fine. So long's you remember that you heard it all before once.

JANICE: If you get the church, you plan to lease it all for yourself?

GOYDA stares at her, surprised.

GOYDA: I certainly wasn't planning to invite the congregation back, if that's what you're asking.

JANICE: You've been bent over that table a long time ... withdrawn, embittered ... trying to convince yourself and Irma there's some great value in diligence. She's probably convinced of that herself ... Irma convinces easily.

GOYDA: (*darkly*) Leave Irma alone. The last thing she needs is you riding her back.

JANICE: I could help you ... turn your shop in the church into something of a tourist fixture in town with regular stories and photo coverage around the shop and around yourself. But only if you stop thinking selfishly.

GOYDA: (*staring at her*) What in hell are you talking about?

JANICE: There are people I know in town who work in coloured glass ... macramé ... Two kids I know would like a place to set up a bakery ... for production and sale of whole-grain breads. Then there's a couple who would come back to build a vegetarian kitchen!

GOYDA: (*angrily*) Oh, sure ... hangers-on ... wilted apple merchants ... incense-burners ... all the screwed-over offsprings of the affluent middle class searching for voluntary poverty! Out!

JANICE: You're a weak, selfish man!

GOYDA: Out!

JANICE: You're a cop-out ... a self-seeker ... a prick!

She leaves. GOYDA picks up some leatherwork and tries to hand-stitch it. He drives a needle into his finger and sucks on it.

GOYDA: Goddammit!

The lights go out on GOYDA'S area.

The lights come up on KIOSK talking angrily on the telephone.

KIOSK: Yeah ... well, why put it on the agenda at all? ... Listen, Homer, your job as town clerk is to work for me an' members of council ... an' we've got enough to do without goin' over this thing another time! Eh? ... What in hell makes you think *that?* ... Then screw your union. When I decide to get rid of you ... or anyone else in the front office, I'll get rid of you! You think so, eh? ... Don't push it, alright? ... That letter from Goyda doesn't go on the council agenda this week ... Alright, so it's from my daughter ... it doesn't go! ... You've what? ... Copied an' sent it out already? ... That does it, Homer ... you'll be back in the lumberyard countin' two-by-fours for a living!

He slams down the telephone angrily. He then punches the intercom and yells into it.

Front office! ... Who's the municipal lawyer?

He waits for a reply which doesn't come. The intercom only burps and crackles back at him.

Front office? You deaf? ... It's the mayor here!

He gives up on the intercom and leans back in his chair, glowering.

KIOSK: Bitch has turned the machine off ... stands in the window watching the big boys in the school grounds playing football ... towels bundled up on their crotches so they look like what they got there could hang on a stallion! ... I've seen her do that ... her mouth open ... eyes glassy ... It's the vitamins that do it ... too many vitamins while they're growin' up!

He rises and prepares to leave the office.

JANICE enters. For a moment, he doesn't see her. When he does, he is startled by her presence.

Did I have an appointment with you, Webber? ... I don't remember having an appointment with the press!

JANICE: (*laughing*) For a novice in office, you're taking yourself altogether too seriously, chum.

KIOSK: The proper address for a mayor during business hours is "Your Worship" ... not "chum."

JANICE: (*curtsying mockingly*) Yes, Your Worship! I'm sorry, Your Worship! May I have a word with Your Worship?

KIOSK: Cut it out ... I've got serious problems to consider. This office is not a circus!

JANICE: You wanted to be worshipped ... How shall I worship an eight-vote lead ... on one knee, or on two?

KIOSK: Bitch! ... Same as your mother!

JANICE: Watch it, Kiosk!

KIOSK: Your mother, the accountant! Well, let me tell you, I once took my farm accounts to her an' ended up paying three hundred dollars tax on income I never made!

JANICE: I work for a one-woman newspaper. You push it far enough and I'll tighten the vice on your balls until you cry uncle!

KIOSK: (*startled, dismayed*) Shame on you, talkin' like that to a man old enough to be your father! Have you no shame, girl?

JANICE: None whatsoever.

KIOSK sighs deeply and sits on the edge of his desk.

KIOSK: Did Dolan send you here to queer me around, or you doin' it on your own?

JANICE: I find my own stories ... For next week's paper, I want to write a history of an old church. I know all about Goyda's wish to turn it into a crafts centre.

KIOSK: You talked to him ... He sent you!

JANICE: Yes, I talked to him. But he didn't send me anywhere. Why did you destroy his teaching career?

KIOSK: That's crap. He could've gone someplace else to teach.

JANICE: He couldn't, an' you know it.

KIOSK: Alright, I'll tell you. A man serves the company or employer who pays his wages. Men don't vote if they should go to war ... no more than they have a right to vote if they should go to work. I'll never quarrel with that, otherwise, nothing would get done. I was chairman of the school board when he sued the board ... and won. Keeping a man like that around is a poor example to other teachers ... I did what I had to do.

JANICE: Even when he's right, and you wrong?

KIOSK: Even then.

She stares at him.

JANICE: You know something? ... You're more of an ignorant bastard than I first thought you were.

KIOSK turns his back on her and picks up his papers, preparatory to leaving.

The lights go out on KIOSK'S office.

The lights come up on GOYDA seated, his feet on his table, a bottle of beer in his hand. IRMA sits on the table opposite him. She is excited.

IRMA: I've been asking people all over town ... Nobody objects. One older woman said a church is a bit like a crafts centre anyway.

GOYDA: The opinions of ten people don't matter. This is a village ... suffering a bad case of time-warp.

IRMA: The aldermen are waiting to see what my dad says. But they were interested ... every one of them.

GOYDA: But they'll have to wait and see ... Then they'll vote.

IRMA: Yes. It's the right way to do things.

GOYDA: Irma, listen to me ... I once proposed to a parents-teachers meeting that Canadian history should be taught in the local schools. Your father chaired the meeting ... He called for a vote on the proposal ... People were being asked to *vote* on whether their history should be taught to their children! ... Twenty parents voted for ... eighteen against. The issue was tabled to die, because it was too controversial.

IRMA: What was wrong with that?

GOYDA: We're the only goddamned country in the world where a study of national history is not mandatory in the schools. One day we'll vote ourselves into extinction!

IRMA: I don't know anything about politics ... It bothers me that people get angry talking about politics.

GOYDA: You are your father's daughter ... right to the finishing line!

IRMA bows her head in humiliation.

IRMA: I wish I had money or a job I could go to ... so I might leave this town. Life is so complicated and confused here.

GOYDA: Sorry, baby. I can't help you.

IRMA: That's not true ... You don't want to!

GOYDA looks sadly at her and shrugs.

The lights go out on GOYDA and IRMA.

The lights come up on JANICE at her desk typing. She is humming the theme song from the opening scene of the play. She pauses in her typing as DOLAN speaks.

DOLAN: (*offstage*) Janice!

JANICE: Yes, Mister Dolan?

DOLAN: You've been typing non-stop for forty-nine minutes now. I get suspicious when you're not dodging work by going to the john, or trickling the water fountain.

JANICE: I'm on a good story, Mister Dolan.

DOLAN: Is it going to get us into trouble, Janice?

JANICE: No, Mister Dolan.

DOLAN enters in a wheelchair, his eyes shaded by dark sunglasses. A hat of great age and deformity is on his head. He is blind. JANICE talks to him as if he were still in another room.

DOLAN: They're building a wheelchair ramp leading into city hall, they tell me ... Maybe one day I can ride this thing into the dizzying seats of our town power, eh?

JANICE: Sure, Mister Dolan.

DOLAN: They're not doing it for me ... they've got two cripples on staff, and a third got elected to council. We're gaining power and influence, Janice. To ride a wheelchair is as politically volatile these days as being an Indian militant!

JANICE smiles.

You seen the ramp yet? Is it steep?

JANICE: Yes, Mister Dolan.

DOLAN: Good. Maybe one of those bastards will have a failure of the wrists half way up the ramp. That should bring him down into street traffic at about thirty miles an hour, coming in at right angles to the passing cars. If that don't get him, the concrete wall the other side of the street should do the job ... By that time the little buggy ... if well greased ... would be doing around forty-five miles an hour. Which might open a job for the young and needy.

JANICE: That's very thoughtful of you, Mr. Dolan.

DOLAN: (*wheeling himself away*) I'm through for the day, Janice. You lock up. And don't push too hard, you hear? ... You'll get where you're going, but wait your turn. You need friends in life, Janice ... as much as you need enemies.

He exits.

JANICE ponders what he has said.

The lights go out slowly.

ACT 2

The light value at the opening of this Act is different. The light is unworldly, the Act a journey into dreams, recollections and projected fears of the major protagonists in the play.

The music at the opening of this Act is reminiscent of the previous theme, but the rhythm and melody of the theme song has changed tempo and pitch. A male voice sings the song.

MAN: (*singing*)
In our town
The demons crawl
Within the darkness
Of the skull
Like gliding hawks
The shadows fall
At seven hours to sundown ...
In our town
Seven hours to sundown ...

KIOSK and GOYDA are in their respective playing areas, but the settings they occupied in Act 1 are stripped down. Each man is isolated. The lights come up on KIOSK and GOYDA, each in a separate pool of light.

KIOSK: One morning, she says to me she wants an automatic washer ... What the hell for, I says? ... We've only got one kid ... the old wringer machine is good enough.

The GRANDFATHER enters, an old shirt in his hands. He squats down and, with a needle and thread, repairs a tear in the shirt.

GRANDFATHER: Damned fertilizer's gone up in price! ... If we cut back anymore, them carrots is gonna be an inch short!

KIOSK: I says to her ... the old wringer machine's good enough!

GRANDFATHER: Jews 'ave set up things so an honest man never gets ahead of the game.

KIOSK: I bought her the washer like she wanted. But we had to buy tractor gas on time that year.

IRMA enters GOYDA'S playing area. She is nervous.

IRMA: I walked ... He'd hear the car otherwise ... You asked me to come.

GOYDA: Autumn's arrived. So early this year, Irma … Yesterday it was still summer … Today, the north wind has started to blow.

IRMA: You've lost buttons on your jacket … Did you lose them, or are they in your pockets?

GOYDA: What the hell's a button? … Nothing changes here.

IRMA: Things grow an' blossom … People I knew as kids are doing interesting things. Peggy Goddard could never learn to read or write … She's teaching music to children now.

GOYDA: Peggy Goddard can't count to five on beat … The incompleteness of it all sits like a dust cloud over the streets and houses.

IRMA: You ask for too much.

GOYDA: And you … ask for so little that what you get means nothing.

IRMA: (*suddenly agitated*) That's not true, Jerry! … That's not … true.

GOYDA: The man in Winnipeg …

IRMA: … had three children.

GOYDA: You didn't love him … Nobody loves anymore … They negotiate the best arrangements and then settle into a slow, sullen death.

GRANDFATHER: She's gettin' fat … sleeps late, boy. I was wrong … the kid's not yours. I wonder if old Joe Deerin' himself did it to his daughter?

KIOSK: What shall I do, Dad?

GRANDFATHER: She stands at the front gate, a rake in her hand. But she's not doin' anything … She's starin' down the road … after other men.

KIOSK: Maybe if I borrowed some money … took her an' Irma on a vacation somewhere … like Victoria.

GRANDFATHER: You get her in the family way … get a boy out of her quick. The land's got to go to someone … Without a boy, there's no more Kiosks left.

KIOSK: She asked for ten dollars to pay for a ride in an airplane.

GRANDFATHER: My boots need new soles … Two teeth need pullin'.

He rises and exits, a forefinger prodding into the side of his mouth.

GOYDA: You didn't love him … or else, how could you have left him?

IRMA: I loved him, but he didn't love me. There was bitterness … The children woke up screaming at night.

GOYDA: (*disturbed by this*) Why do people have children … when all they give them is food and nightmares?

IRMA: When I left … I came here. I was looking for a place to hide, where I could have time to think and understand …

GOYDA: Understand what, Irma?

IRMA: Why I'm not loved. Why I'll never be loved.

GOYDA goes slowly towards her and puts his arm around her. They sit down side by side.

GOYDA: One rides a glider through life … avoiding the dark places and the high places … hanging on to the edge of the sun … but mostly circling familiar places where it's safer to land when the time comes.

IRMA: Do you think two people can make a life happen … no magic … no help … just two people working to make it happen?

GOYDA: I don't know. I tried once … lost … and ended up in hospital a week for having tried.

IRMA: Could we … try?

GOYDA: I don't know, I've become a lot like this town … content with very little … working to the routine of changing days and seasons.

IRMA: Nothing else?

GOYDA: My books … recordings.

He laughs.

Like yourself, I also don't believe I can be loved by anyone!

They both laugh. The lights go down on them.

KIOSK: Blasting powder! I could take any rock around into four pieces with a handful of blasting powder. Men working on a three-foot thick pine stump would call for me … Get Sid Kiosk here with a stick of dynamite, they'd say, an' he'll blow the things to hell!

The lights come up on DOLAN in a wheelchair. He is grinning sardonically.

DOLAN: You can hear, if you listen, flies walk across the ceiling ... or mountain storms building two hundred miles away. Sometimes I'm thinking, as I listen at my window to street sounds ... that one can hear the inner workings of a foolish mind ... It sounds like a jar of nuts being tumbled.

KIOSK: Bills always got paid an' every item of earnings an' expenses put in a book. Farm has account books goin' back forty-five years now ... Otherwise, how does a man know where he's goin', if he don't know where he's been?

DOLAN: Around the world seventeen times in my lifetime ... Been everywhere without going further than four miles from the building where I live and work. I know all about African grass plains ... can even smell the scorched vegetation if I concentrate. Wrote a small book on Argentina once ... It got published in Australia.

KIOSK: When I work with blasting powder, I know the place for everything. My old man wouldn't go near the stuff ... It scared him. But not me ... They'd call for me on the difficult jobs.

DOLAN: Sports track on a Sunday morning ... cinders hammered by two hundred pairs of feet ... odour of sweat ... runners panting past me where I sat and stared through them ... beyond them ... to the creeping edge of the Sahara Desert.

KIOSK: Yes, I belong to the two service clubs ... I've got opinions about how things should be done ... What? No, I'm not a member of a church. But I took flowers to my mother's grave last summer.

JANICE enters DOLAN'S playing area.

DOLAN: Janice?

JANICE: Yes, Mister Dolan.

KIOSK: Had a five dollar order of flowers made up nice, an' I drove down an' put them on her grave. The only other person there that morning was Dolan, sittin' in his chair like he'd been made into a headstone.

DOLAN: Kiosk took flowers to the cemetery. I think they were intended for his mother. But he made a mistake ... put them on Bess Henderson's grave instead.

JANICE: Should I report on that, Mister Dolan?

DOLAN: How well you write ... I listen to your work and it warms the room around me ... But I'll lose you, won't I, Janice?

JANICE: Where would I go?

DOLAN: If you stay, I'll teach you everything ... I'll teach you to use words as songs to captivate, enchant ... Physical beauty is only transitory, Janice. Don't preoccupy yourself with it ... The lasting beauty is in the language of the mind.

JANICE: Yes ... I understand.

KIOSK: Hell, I never thought of it ... but if there's some people who feel I should run, I'll run ... Is that right, Dad?

He listens. Hearing no reply, he is puzzled.

DOLAN: Good! ... What you have is also a weapon, Janice. Use it to attack and demolish stupidity!

KIOSK: Empty the swimming pool at harvest time! ... No one should be swimming when there's work to do diggin' out potatoes an' shellin' peas!

JANICE: Shall I write something on Bess Henderson's grave?

DOLAN: Find your targets first ... then move slowly forward ... dismantle their defences ... give no ground ... but don't take more than you can handle! It's war, Janice ... a bloodless war of nerves and talent against the darkness!

KIOSK: If I do right, will I be remembered? Will all the bad things that've happened be forgotten?

JANICE: Everything they do ... in public and in private ... all is game, is it not, Mister Dolan?

DOLAN: All are pieces in a game of chess. If you stay, I'll teach you all I know, Janice.

JANICE: There's so much to learn.

KIOSK: A town is like a farm ... only bigger!

JANICE: But I will!

KIOSK: Yes ... I can an' *will* do it! I'll be mayor ... I can do it myself! Nobody's ever goin' to tell me what to do an' how! I'll do it!

DOLAN: (*hissing*) Get him, Janice!

JANICE: Yes, Mister Dolan.

The lights go down on DOLAN, JANICE and KIOSK.

The lights come up on GOYDA and IRMA. She is crying.

GOYDA: It takes time, Irma! Everything takes time!

IRMA: How long is that?

GOYDA: I don't know. Even with your help, I almost lost it all last month.

IRMA: Then what can I do to help?

GOYDA: Nothing. I have a style and a pace for doing the work and the marketing ... It's nothing I can delegate or share. It's only an instinct.

IRMA: What about us?

GOYDA: We agreed to try ... a step at a time ... starting here. It's still here. I'm sorry, but I can't do it!

IRMA: At least you're honest.

GOYDA: Will it help you if I said I was insane? ... That pieces of me are spread over twenty years in twenty different places? ... Like luggage I'll never go back to recover, there are things I need left with other people whose whereabouts I can't locate?

IRMA: It's Marlene and your son, isn't it?

GOYDA: Yes ... goddamn them both!

IRMA: But they'll never return, and if they did ... how will you know them? I'm like my father ... there's not much to know, an' it's not likely to change!

They both laugh.

You're not insane, Jerry.

GOYDA: Then why am I here? I step outside ... look down the streets ... and know this is a forgotten, receding world, yet I stay ... and the madness of the social and political activity even makes sense.

IRMA: My father's running for mayor.

GOYDA: I know. He'll win.

IRMA: It bothers you.

GOYDA: No. Not anymore. It's the way things are done, I guess. I got a collie pup once, and swore off getting involved in such things ever again in the town. The pup got run over by a motorbike ... and ... I'm still around.

The lights go out on IRMA and GOYDA.

The lights come up on ROSSINI. He is speaking on the telephone.

ROSSINI: Sell you a house, Dolan! ... No sense you paying rent forever on this place ... I'm kind of worried about renting this to you any longer. You've got a lot of hardware an' filled-up filing cabinets ... building wasn't meant to hold up that much weight ... floors are sagging ... the roof line's dipping ... Well, Dolan, what the hell difference would it make reducing your rent? Won't make the building stronger, will it now?

He laughs.

Damn right it won't ... Shore it up? I can't get workmen goin' down in the basement to do that ... Basement's half full of water! ... No, let me sell you a house. What? ... Naw, I won't sell you a place where there's water in the basement ... That's why I never put this place up for sale. Got just the place for you ... One an' one-half storeys ... your girl can work up on top, an' your place for workin' and living in would be below ... I could get my men to lay a couple of two-by-six stringers out the back door to build you a ramp for your chair ... That way you can ride out into the back-yard an' do your thinking when the sun's out ... Eh? No, there's no trees in the backyard ... lots of old grass, but it can be burned out ... Better that way ... You don't want yourself runnin' your wheelchair into a maple tree, do you? ... I'll let you have it at a discount ... a quick sale for cash! ... No, no, it's not downtown ... but your girl has a car, she can drive. It's four miles out of town, where the air's clean ... Think of it, Dolan, clean air, country livin' ... You'll live twenty years longer out there!

He listens.

Don't you say that to me!

His face hardens with anger. He hangs up the telephone receiver hard. He exits.

Goddamn cripples ... try to do them a favour an' they throw shit in your face!

The lights go out on ROSSINI.

The lights come up on KIOSK. He is pacing back and forth irritably.

KIOSK: The school board ... made it on the school board in one try. What a mess I found there ... you wouldn't believe. They had one teacher on staff ... a woman called Del ... That's a man's name ... She wore pants, but she said she was a woman ... She worked only an hour an' a half a day teaching painting to small kids. What the hell can a kid that age paint? Desks an' walls is what they painted! Never seen such a mess made of public property. I says to the board, "Either that woman starts workin' for a living, or she can hit the road selling Fuller brushes!" Well, that started it ... all the lay-abouts on school staff came at me ... That was the first time Goyda an' I locked horns.

The lights come up on GOYDA. He is cold, distant.

GOYDA: The chairman's a joke ... an ana-chronism.

KIOSK: A town's like a farm. Anybody crossing the fence or comin' through the gate uses the paths that're there to walk on!

GOYDA: Let him start picking off individual teachers, and soon he's running a school that's next to useless.

KIOSK: I've taken hell long enough from junk dealers an' smart talkers. The day my old man ordered Williston's lumber truck to turn around an' drive out, the credit limit for our farm got lowered in town. The Chamber of Commerce was against the Kiosks ... so were the holies on account of my wife leavin', but we made it!

GOYDA: If Del gets fired, we sue or we walk out!

KIOSK: I talked it over with my old man ... He was a tough one! "Get any sonofabitch who's out to get you," he says to me. So I went after Goyda.

GOYDA: I stood up for Del ... Who's standing up for me? ... Nobody? ... Are you sheep? ... The man's illiterate, a village fool! ... This is my first contract ... I can't afford to be dismissed ... What are you afraid of? ... Ah, the homes and second

cars you've bought here! Is that it? ... Del and I never bought anything.

The lights go out on GOYDA.

The lights come up on DOLAN.

KIOSK: I didn't like doin' it ... But the young punk was asking for it right from the start.

DOLAN: The man is a threat, Janice ... but hopefully he'll never rise beyond the school board. To do that, one needs to have mastered the ability to read.

KIOSK: She liked it those first months when my name and picture was in the paper ... "Sid," she said, "you're flyin' high." "It feels good, don't it?" ... Sure, it felt good! ... One night, we had a ribbon-cutting ceremony to open a two-classroom addition to the school. She'd had a bit to drink that night ... somehow got her green skirt snagged and torn ... Going up the steps to the stage so she could stand beside me, she tripped an' fell, spraining her elbow. I gave her the car keys and told her to drive the old man home.

DOLAN: (*singing idly to himself, his face straining with concentration*) What shall we do with the drunken sailor? ... What shall we do with the ...

KIOSK: I didn't know how much she'd drunk ... I didn't know at all.

DOLAN: Kiosk's wife took the car down the road to his carrot farm. At Wilbur's corner, she couldn't manoeuvre the turn because of her sprained elbow. She went off the road and down a sharp incline ... the car striking a hundred-year-old fir tree growing in the field below. She came out of the accident without a scratch. Old Del Kiosk died ... thrown out through the windshield and impaled on a dead fir limb. He hung there ... forehead, hands and tips of his boots touching the tree ... his grey hat still on his head.

KIOSK: They had to cut the branch off with a chainsaw to get him down ... What a goddamned way to go!

DOLAN: He's a dangerous man, Janice!

KIOSK: Soon after that, the business with the kite-flyin' rancher an' her started.

DOLAN: Study the man ... find his weaknesses ... work on them ... Wear him down with ridicule!

KIOSK: (*with anguish*) It hurt me ... seein' her in town ... having Ella come for a month or two, then go away ... knowin' that at night she was doin' with that bone-headed rancher, Stark ... what she did only a half dozen times with me ... before she started havin' headaches an' things.

DOLAN: He's stupid and frustrated ... like that paperhanger in Germany who started it all once before. Hit him, Janice ... I'll tell you when to let up!

KIOSK: Never once did that blind cripple, Dolan, come to me like a man an' say what was bothering him! There's others who didn't like me ... but I knew why!

DOLAN: (*singing*) Put him in a longboat till he's sober ... Put him in a longboat till he's sober ...

KIOSK: His father ran the drugstore ... Teachers were hired to go where they lived, back of the store, to teach the blind little bastard ... At noon, they'd wheel him out front, where he sat in his wheelchair, wrapped in a blanket ... starin' through them black glasses like a zombie into the street! I'd walk past him sometimes, but not often ... He gave me the creeps as a kid.

DOLAN: (*calling boyishly*) Hey, Kiosk ... the left heel on your shoes is worn down ... You're limping!

KIOSK: How'd he know that? ... The edge of my left heel *had* broken off ... I'd been digging with a shovel and broken it ... I couldn't wear my farm boots to school ...

He calls back loudly, replying to DOLAN'S taunt.

It's better'n what you got, Dolan! At least I got feet that work! My father said you shoulda died!

DOLAN: (*laughing grimly*) He said that, eh? ... He could die for saying that ... I could make him die if I wanted, Kiosk! I make people like that die just sitting here!

KIOSK: I was afraid ... He was weird ... a hot day ... middle of the day, an' he's wrapped up like that in a woollen blanket saying he could make people die! Kids get scared of such things.

DOLAN: I can have a wooden stake driven through your heart ... How does that grab you?

KIOSK is visibly shaken.

KIOSK: If I'd hit him, all hell would've broken loose. They had a lot of money ... Everybody said so ... to afford teachers goin' into the house to teach him like they did.

DOLAN: (*still shouting*) Kiosk, what's in your head?

KIOSK: Brains, same's everybody's!

DOLAN: Not in yours. Yours is a farm turnip. Do you know the chemical composition of a turnip?

KIOSK: No.

DOLAN: Cut a spot open between your eyes. You'll see for yourself!

KIOSK reaches up with his hand and rubs his temples and between his eyes.

KIOSK: For five years I never walked down that street when they wheeled him out an' left him on the sidewalk to sun. After that, his folks had him sent to some special school ... People who look like that get crazy, I guess ... I've spoken to lots of people about that an' they all agreed.

DOLAN laughs and exits, wheeling his chair off the stage.

I'm sure cripples like him get a government pension ... You'd think gettin' a pension like that would make them obligated to being respectful to those of us doin' all the work an' payin' taxes! ... At least, it shouldn't give them any rights meddlin' in politics! ... I said it to him once over the telephone, an' the bastard had the rudeness to laugh an' hang up on me!

The lights go out on KIOSK, looking worried and confused.

The lights come up on GOYDA. IRMA stands forlornly on the outer perimeter of the scene.

IRMA: He offered to buy all twelve vests ... I didn't see anything wrong in discounting them ten percent! You said we needed money.

GOYDA: They're on sale twelve miles down the road this morning ... in a chain clothing store ... at forty percent above our retail price!

IRMA: What's wrong with what someone else does?

GOYDA: We're competing against ourselves doing that, Irma! ... If somebody wants a handmade vest, they have to come here ... where they'll see matching gloves and bags and belts. I'm not a mill running assembly line products ... If I was, then why keep this shop?

IRMA: I'm sorry ... You didn't explain.

GOYDA: It wasn't your fault ... I've got a lot on my mind.

IRMA: I could take my things and work at home, if that would help.

GOYDA: A few years ago, I was doing very well ... grossing over twenty thousand a year. And rising ... There were people coming around by day at first ... then by night. Wives of doctors ... doctors, dentists and architects ... perfumed, overpaid, jaded people looking for kicks and investments. They were buying Group of Seven sketches, hoping the price on what they bought would rise quickly ... They began buying out my stock. Then one day, one of them offers me forty thousand dollars ... for my name!

IRMA: I don't understand.

GOYDA: I could put my label only on items he'd buy ... which he'd hold a few years and re-sell to his wealthy friends at three times the price. Anything else I made to sell here to street trade was no longer to carry my label! Each year, I was expected to dress out his wife in a new outfit ... and the wives of his friends.

IRMA: But ... nobody can buy another person's name!

GOYDA: Oh, yes, they can ... Attached to the forty thousand dollar cheque was a four page contract ... If I signed it, I sold everything ... what talents I have ... my name ... my reputation ... even what I said privately or publicly. It was servitude for the rest of my life! ... Irma, I grabbed a chair and smashed it over the back of that man. He sued ... I had to pay for his broken glasses and for assaulting him. I let my hair and beard grow ... and I've remained anonymous behind my mask ever since. I don't trust people anymore, honey!

IRMA: I'll ... put some coffee on.

GOYDA: I wanted to see my son after that ... Stephen's nine years old then ... I wrote a letter to his mother, then drove out to a remote, Godforsaken little valley between two ranges of towering mountains which almost met overhead.

The MAN appears on the periphery of the scene, opposite IRMA. He has a rifle in his hands.

MAN: I told you long ago to stay away ... You remember that? ... The devil's not welcome into the family.

GOYDA: He met me at the entrance to the small farm ... It was fortified with walls of piled and broken stones ... Beyond it, in a small field, children and women were bent to the ground, tilling the gravelly soil with their bare hands ... Goats had eaten all the bark and foliage off surrounding trees and stood bleating on outcrops of rock, their eyes wild ... stomachs distended with hunger ...

The sounds of bleating goats is heard.

MAN: There's an aura of the devil around you, buddy ... So turn around an' keep walkin'.

GOYDA: The women and kids were pale and thin ... One or two of them looked up at me, but they didn't see me ... their eyes were dead ... lips dry and crusted with blood.

MAN: Why don't you say somethin' to me? ... You never say nothin' ... treat me like I wasn't here! You can't keep doin' that or God will get you!

GOYDA: The day was hot, but a cold sweat started trickling down my face ... It smelled like ammonia around my face.

With a sudden motion, GOYDA whips out his elbow into the face of the MAN, who ducks and strikes GOYDA in the back with the gun butt. GOYDA rises, gasping for breath. The MAN places the gun barrel to the back of GOYDA'S head.

MAN: (*speaking quickly, excitedly*) In your eyes I seen somethin' I seen in the eyes of others before they come here ... But you've got the wrong aura ... You can't stay. You're lucky for that ... that there's still hope for you ... or I'd of killed you like I done two others who come around here from the devil, tryin' to make trouble ... You get out of here ... You come back when you can talk to me ... When you can ask to join the family ... When the devil's gone from your heart ... You hear me? ... Now git!

The MAN pushes his gun hard against the back of GOYDA'S head. GOYDA falls down. The MAN retreats from the scene. IRMA comes up to GOYDA and shakes him.

IRMA: Jerry, wake up! You've slept here all night with your clothes on. I've brought a thermos of coffee … Wake up!

GOYDA: (*rising slowly, painfully*) For Christ's sake, stop being a missionary, Irma! I've never cared for missionaries.

The lights go out on the scene.

ACT 3

The lights come up slowly on KIOSK and ROSSINI standing in an animated, soundless discussion.

There is the sound of a drum and harmonica played in a driving rhythm. JANICE sings offstage, possibly with other voices.

JANICE: (*singing offstage*)
In our town
The houses stand
Back to back
On squares of land
One in front
An' two at hand
At seven hours to sundown …
In our town
Seven hours to sundown …

There is a drum and harmonica interlude before the next stanza.

JANICE: In our town
The lines are drawn
No fight is lost
And none is won
Each mother wants
Her neighbour's son
At seven hours to sundown …
In our town
Seven hours to sundown …

The music and song die abruptly as ROSSINI speaks.

ROSSINI: Then learn to keep your mouth shut!

KIOSK: Don't you talk to me like that!

ROSSINI: I didn't get to own half the town by being a nice guy. If I had to, I'd get your land … same way another man got your wife. Kiosk, you're a walking failure … a joke … a self-right-eous buffoon. So is Goyda … The old church is only a piece of vacant real estate … The land the building stands on can be sold. The church is nothing to the rest of us … but for you …

KIOSK: (*breaking*) Why are you doin' this to me? … What have I ever done to hurt you?

ROSSINI: Nothing … I'm only trying to tell you, Sid … that politics, like finance, is a cold-blooded art. You're not equipped … you're makin' mistakes.

KIOSK: What mistake have I made?

ROSSINI: Running for mayor … and winning.

KIOSK: An' why not? … I was born here! I believe in this town. I want to leave something of myself … a plaque on a new building … some kind of reputation. I haven't exactly gone anywhere in my life. Now my kid's back to stay. A few years from now, she's gonna marry someone … badly. The same thing repeating itself.

ROSSINI: That's another mistake … passion.

KIOSK: But I believe … an' I want things for myself and others.

ROSSINI: Fine, but don't go showing it! You'd of made a good alderman, Sid. But as mayor, you're in trouble. So don't count on support if it means getting the rest of us in trouble. Otherwise, the council will vote you down … and when that happens …

KIOSK: Are you threatening me, Rossini?

ROSSINI: I'm the only friend you have, don't you realize that?

KIOSK: You're a goddamned sneaky little Italian!

ROSSINI: (*coldly*) I could break your back for that … turn all your little dreams into so much crap.

KIOSK: Okay, I'm sorry I said that, but you pushed me!

ROSSINI: I could buy and sell you three times over! … I can do that with anybody on this council … so why in hell do I come into your office when nobody else does? Because I'm your friend. You lose that an' you might as well resign, buddy, because you'll only get what we allow you. Is that understood?

KIOSK shakes his head feebly.

KIOSK: (*quietly*) Yeh … I understand.

The lights go out on KIOSK and ROSSINI.

The lights come up on GOYDA, IRMA and JANICE.

IRMA: (*speaking to JANICE*) I'm not interested in what they do at city hall. All I want is to move this shop out to where we'll have more space!

JANICE: Then why haven't they accepted Jerry's application?

GOYDA: The same reason a pothole in the street takes a year to repair … nobody gives a damn, and the one person who could move that procedure along doesn't like me.

JANICE: You did wrong, you know. The way to have gone about it was to visit each alderman and discuss your plans before writing an application for lease. They like to feel wise and important … and since you're not exactly a favourite of any of them, they would've appreciated the opportunity to give you hell … see you crawl a little.

GOYDA: Who in hell's been laying that crap on you … Sid Kiosk?

JANICE: I know what goes on … I've covered more council meetings than I care to remember. There are two ways of getting city council decisions quickly … go in like gangbusters or crawl.

GOYDA: Sorry, Janice … I do it my way or not at all.

JANICE: Fine. But you're in a fight whether you like it or not. So you'd better plan your next step or start looking silly. I've run a story on your problems in today's paper.

GOYDA: Who asked you to do that?

IRMA: We both thought it would be a good idea if people knew.

JANICE: The next step is to increase public interest … get more people involved.

GOYDA: Involved in what?

JANICE: An organization … a society for setting up a new crafts centre in town … in a vacant, civically owned building!

GOYDA: What has this got to do with this shop? If I was in the business of selling hamburgers, I'd be interested in the best shop deal I could get … but I wouldn't be inviting the fried chicken place to come in with me!

IRMA: You're being difficult, Jerry.

GOYDA laughs and throws up his arms.

I think Janice is right … we should get up an organization, with Jerry as chairman. You could be the secretary, Janice.

JANICE: I can't be signing letters, then reporting on them for the paper. My boss can sympathize with many paradoxes, but not that one.

IRMA: Then I'll be secretary. You be the treasurer.

GOYDA: In case you two have forgotten, I own a controlling interest in this shop!

JANICE: You're such a dear when you're cooperative, but a bastard when you put your mind to it ... This is in your best interest. The three of us leading an organization can put them back on their ears.

GOYDA: Three of us ... with equal voting power?

IRMA: Of course.

JANICE: (*sweetly*) I'm sure we'll never disagree.

GOYDA: (*sarcastically*) I'm sure we never will!

IRMA: It's settled then? We can call ourselves the Crafts Centre Committee.

JANICE: Fine. I'll look into getting a charter. Jerry doesn't follow through on his application. *We* go after a lease on the old church, right?

GOYDA: (*speaking to IRMA*) Do you really know what you're doing?

IRMA: Janice wants to help. I'm sure my father will be happier dealing with an organization ... It won't hurt his pride. I think it's time we started considering the community more ... This shop was a good beginning ... but ... it looks and feels like ... it's old ... dying.

GOYDA: I go along or I buy you out, is that it?

IRMA: I'm afraid so, Jerry.

The lights go out on them.

The lights come up on KIOSK and ROSSINI. KIOSK is now confident; ROSSINI, upset.

KIOSK: A *what?*

ROSSINI: A crafts committee, but it's the same bunch ... your daughter, Goyda and our friend at the newspaper. On top of that, I get a lease termination notice from Goyda, effective in sixty days.

KIOSK: Evict him tomorrow. I'd do that!

ROSSINI: If he's going, I'll need sixty days to find someone new for the building. If this is some-

thing Goyda has figured out, why didn't he do it before?

KIOSK: He's capable of anything ... an' he's bound to take my girl with him. I've said no to him already ... I'm not backing down to his tricks.

ROSSINI: Town secretary has duplicated and sent the new application to all the aldermen.

KIOSK: What does it take to fire that Homer?

ROSSINI: He's doing what he's been hired to do.

KIOSK: How are you treating this ... this new application when it comes up on the council agenda?

ROSSINI: I'm losing Goyda's lease ... I don't like it, but he's in his rights ... If he gets the church, I'm out of rent, but ...

KIOSK: You'll vote to let him lease?

ROSSINI: Why not?

KIOSK: Sure ... why not? He hasn't got a home or obligations to this town ... People build a church an' he gets it for the asking. Times get rough an' he'll go on welfare ... so would my daughter ... There's no pride left. Is that what property owners elected us to do? Other men *build* new buildings for their businesses.

ROSSINI: He asks for a lease, not expropriation.

KIOSK: I don't trust people who own nothing ... they have a thirty-day outlook on everythin' they rent ... We have to look after the years for better or worse. Why is it that way? ... Who says it has to be like that?

ROSSINI: I never thought of it. All the same, it works.

KIOSK: So does Communism.

ROSSINI: Well, I have an idea ... you may not like it, but it may save me rent loss and give you peaceful sleep by spreading responsibilities around a bit.

The lights go out on KIOSK and ROSSINI.

The lights come up on JANICE who is at her desk preparing newspaper layouts.

DOLAN: (*singing offstage*)
What shall we do with the drunken sailor?

What shall we do with the drunken sailor?
What shall we do with the drunken sailor? ...

He calls loudly, so that JANICE can hear.

DOLAN: Ask Constable Radomsky to apprehend his driving licence before he drives into a light pole, that's what we do ... Janice?

JANICE: I'm here.

DOLAN: How many obituaries are going into this week's paper?

JANICE: Three ... two old-timers and Jimmy Hessler, who drowned.

DOLAN: And how many help wanteds have we got?

JANICE: One ... for a part-time bricklayer's helper ... Why?

DOLAN: Just wanted to know how the town economy was doing.

He laughs offstage. JANICE laughs with him and continues working.

The lights come up on the remaining areas of the stage.

KIOSK is at his desk, squinting at the paper work before him.

GOYDA is also examining some papers. He dials a number on his telephone. The telephone on KIOSK'S desk rings. GOYDA gets a busy signal and hangs up.

KIOSK: (*officiously*) Hullo ... No, this is not Hogarth's Welding ... This is the mayor's office! ... No, I'm not kidding ... Who in hell are you?

His caller hangs up as GOYDA dials again. KIOSK drops the telephone down hard and scowls. The telephone immediately rings again.

Why don't they leave me alone?

He answers the telephone.

Hullo!

GOYDA: This is Jerry Goyda calling, Mr. Mayor.

KIOSK: (*surprised*) Yeah ... well ... how you doin', kid?

GOYDA: I'm calling about ...

KIOSK: (*speaking officiously, the mayor now*) Well, council decided to table your request, boy. We felt we needed more information.

GOYDA: Information about what?

KIOSK: Information ... that's all. Listen ... did you call this number just a moment ago?

GOYDA: No, I didn't ... How was the council decision arrived at, sir?

KIOSK: Why do you wanna know?

GOYDA: The newspaper report on council meeting made no mention of a discussion on my proposal.

KIOSK: Who was there to discuss with? You didn't appear before us ... Anyway, things like that are decided in committee now.

GOYDA: I've given my rental termination to Mr. Rossini ... I didn't see any difficulty acquiring a lease on the old church ... yet ...

KIOSK: You shouldn't count your chicks before they're hatched, should you?

GOYDA: What further information is it you need?

KIOSK: Something more on the nature of ... your ... what you call it? Committee? I never heard of that before. Your ability to pay ... an' all the rest of it.

GOYDA: (*angrily*) Dammit, I've been around long enough to be known in the community!

KIOSK: (*trapping him*) Ah ... for me ... no! But there's other members on council who never go near a shop like yours. They might see the old church being reduced to a flophouse an' then abandoned. You've got to see other points of view, Goyda.

GOYDA: Nobody on council has a right to feel that way!

KIOSK: I agree, but life is life, boy. We need a ... a feasibility report on the state of ... the mechanical condition of the building. Who knows what shape the roof's in ... or if the wiring won't burn out!

GOYDA: I'd have to hire a professional engineer for that ... and that costs money. Since town hall is the landlord in this case, would you be prepared ...

KIOSK: Nope … I don't see why we have to pay when it's you who wants the building. As it is, I don't think the building's worth anything. The land it stands on should of been sold off by the previous administration to offset municipal operating costs. They should of done that, if they'd been worth a damn … which they weren't … but that's between you an' me.

GOYDA: I'll see about preparing a report on the condition of the building. Would this mean the building is available to me if the report is favourable?

KIOSK: As far as I'm concerned, you could move in today. It's the others who are worried.

GOYDA: Yeh …

They both hang up their telephones. KIOSK jiggles the telephone cradle.

KIOSK: Marge? … Give me the building inspector … quick! … Joe? It's me. What's with the heating system at the old church? … It's totally dependent on the furnace in the parish hall? … Good! … An' the guys with the funny hats still got a lease on that building? … Thanks … Oh, nothing … I just wanted to know.

During the last speech, JANICE collects her papers and goes to GOYDA'S area of the set. IRMA enters to join them.

The lights go out slowly on KIOSK.

GOYDA: (*looking with surprise at the papers that JANICE gives him*) Forty members? … There actually *is* an organization!

JANICE: Sure. You ask people to sign up and they sign up.

GOYDA: But … at least a dozen of these people have nothing to do with crafts in this community. I know everybody who's active … These people aren't.

JANICE: You're not the crafts centre, Jerry. What form a centre takes is up to the membership.

GOYDA stares at JANICE, then at IRMA, who looks away.

GOYDA: I am supposed … to have my work and livelihood left to the decision of outside people … who've got no experience or understanding of what I do … or how … or even why? Every

organization I've ever belonged to reserved the right to accept or reject membership applications … Who are these people? What am I chairman of?

IRMA is hurt and moves away. JANICE becomes annoyed.

JANICE: We have an objective to accomplish … We need people … numbers of people!

GOYDA: Not this way … No way!

JANICE: There is no other way!

GOYDA: On two occasions in the past, I've come within an inch of losing this place and all inventory. It was my knowing what to do … and doing it … that saved me from closing down.

IRMA: This shop is only a small part of it, Jerry!

GOYDA: (*rising to his feet, facing them*) This shop … my work … is it supposed to catalyst something else? Is there something you haven't told me?

They do not reply.

I'm asking you?

He speaks to IRMA.

You've invested some money and a lot of voluntary work … I've got twenty thousand dollars in here!

IRMA: As Janice says, this should only be a small part of the project.

GOYDA: There is no project … there's only my application for a lease … I'm applying for a lease of the church for this shop … Period!

JANICE: Other people have other plans for the building.

GOYDA: Then take your non-existent people and plans and get yourselves out of here so I can get on with what I'm doing!

IRMA: I don't like hearing that from you!

GOYDA: Fine … I'll buy you out and find someone else to help!

JANICE: You had helpers once before … two stand out in my mind. Roger, who stole leather and polished stones … and Nick, the alcoholic … They brought on the first of your two crises … Right?

GOYDA: I don't think that's any concern of yours, Janice.

JANICE: Irma and I have done a lot for this community ... and for you. Any change now is not going to be only a change in location. There's got to be a change in attitudes.

GOYDA: What does that mean?

JANICE: Group decisions on everything.

GOYDA: Ah, the workers taking over the factory! You're welcome to it ... the tools, the supplies ... the accounts payable which, when paid ... would leave me with earnings of one hundred and eight dollars for this month!

IRMA: That's not what Janice said, Jerry.

GOYDA: Good ... from now on she doesn't interfere with my work, or I with hers!

JANICE: (considering the situation) Either we agree as a committee, or this shop's application for a lease on the church is not the only one going to town council.

GOYDA: You ...

JANICE: Yes.

GOYDA smiles coldly and sits down in exasperation.

GOYDA: I see ... I pay the rent. In a week, you're baking unchewable bread to sell on the doorstep ... Then comes the hookah pipe carvers with shaven heads.

JANICE: (angry) Do you want a vote now ... here? Or shall we call a membership meeting? ... In both places you'd lose out, and you know it!

The lights go out on GOYDA'S shop.

The lights come up on KIOSK'S office. KIOSK and ROSSINI are seated on the same side of the desk.

KIOSK: They're comin'?

ROSSINI: They asked to come. You let me handle this ... you tend to lose your temper quickly.

KIOSK: Me? ... What in hell you talking about?

ROSSINI: That's fine ... just keep your voice down. Everything's alright.

GOYDA, IRMA and JANICE enter.

ROSSINI is expansive, smiling.

Ah, representatives from the Crafts Centre Committee, Your Worship! Come on in!

KIOSK: (under his breath) Shit!

ROSSINI: His Worship and I are pleased to receive you on behalf of town government.

KIOSK: Get on with it, Rossini ... I've got an appointment with the dentist.

ROSSINI: We've examined your feasibility study carefully and wonder how your technical findings were made?

GOYDA: We employed the services of a mechanical engineer. If you'd read the report, his signature appears at the end of the findings!

JANICE grins and begins writing.

Both KIOSK and ROSSINI turn to the last pages of the report before them. KIOSK glances up and stares at JANICE.

KIOSK: What's she writing there? You came to talk, not to write!

JANICE: I'm here as a news reporter, Mr. Mayor. This interview is being covered by the press. Is there some objection? Or a new regulation prohibiting me from doing what I'm employed to do?

KIOSK: Goddammit, but you can't take a crap anymore without the press being around!

He turns and speaks to ROSSINI.

Does she have to be here?

ROSSINI: Everything we do is public, Your Worship ... even the thing you just mentioned.

He grins at his joke.

I see no reason why she can't report on this meeting.

KIOSK loosens his tie angrily.

KIOSK: (speaking to the delegation) Alright ... what else?

GOYDA: (staring him down) We did have an appointment, did we not? If so, why are we being met with this hostility?

KIOSK: What in blue tarnation do you expect ...

ROSSINI: (cutting in) No, Mr. Goyda, there's no hostility. Both the mayor and myself, as chairman of the public buildings committee, are delighted you were able to come ... accompanied by your friends. Now ...

GOYDA: Do we, or do we not, get a lease on the old church?

ROSSINI: Nothing can be rushed ... I must say you provided a thorough report on the condition of the building. However, I'd question some details of the findings ... such as the condition of the roof. Young Billy Myers climbed up the attic to ring the bell last summer, when he had no right being there ... When the firemen got him down, he said he'd seen through the shingles of the roof.

GOYDA: A divine revelation ...

ROSSINI: What?

The women laugh.

GOYDA: Young Billy Myers is doing two years for car theft. We didn't consult with him. We consulted with a mechanical engineer!

ROSSINI: The point is well taken ... Now, the electrical wiring ...

GOYDA: Again, we're not applying to establish an electrified cement mixing plant. You requested a report on whether the building was serviceable for our purposes. If you'd read the report, you'd find the answer is affirmative.

ROSSINI is becoming visibly unsure of himself. He keeps his temper in check but his speech is becoming more rapid.

ROSSINI: Parking ... there's only room for thirty cars in the lot, it says here.

KIOSK: I'm not allowin' any street parking from now on except if the building re-opens as a church.

IRMA: But Dad ...

GOYDA: (*cutting in*) Again, thirty parking spaces are more than adequate. If not, there's a super-market parking lot within two blocks.

KIOSK: (*eagerly*) That's private property. You're not leasing the supermarket parking lot!

He turns and speaks to ROSSINI.

Tell them an' let's get it over with.

IRMA: Tell us what? Can someone please explain why this meeting feels like a fire fight?

KIOSK is distressed.

ROSSINI: We see the merits of your proposal ...

He turns to scowl at KIOSK.

... but unfortunately ...

GOYDA: We don't get the lease!

ROSSINI: There's no heating for it, Jerry. As land-lords, we can't rent a building without heating facilities.

GOYDA: The one I rented from you got around that one.

ROSSINI bites back his anger.

The furnace to the church is in the parish hall.

ROSSINI: (*his voice rising*) True, in the parish hall, but not the church. The hall is leased by someone else.

GOYDA: They never use the place. The heat can be left on and billed to us.

ROSSINI: No, it's against municipal building by-laws.

GOYDA: Then arrange for a waiver, for God's sake. This is not a federal constitutional question!

JANICE: (*muttering*) That's a good lead line for the story.

KIOSK: (*exploding*) Screw your story, lady!

GOYDA: I protest! His Worship made an abusive remark. We are members of a responsible organization and we demand an apology.

KIOSK: No bloody way, boy.

ROSSINI: Young man, you are also being abusive. Yesterday you make up an organization and today we're called upon to apologize for things said in dispute ... Do you think yourselves equal to the Chamber of Commerce?

GOYDA: As a member of that organization as well, I can ask the Chamber to respond to your question, if you wish.

ROSSINI: I'm sorry ...

IRMA: Please ... can't we just talk this over like civilized human beings?

ROSSINI: (*addressing IRMA*) I can only apologize.

He turns and speaks to GOYDA.

ROSSINI: No, you can't have the old church. Nobody can have it. The committee of which I'm chairman reviewed your request, and we've decided to propose to council the building be demolished and the land on which it stands sold to pay off municipal debentures.

There is a stunned silence. JANICE slowly raises her hand.

Yes ...

JANICE: Has council already voted ... or decided in committee that the old church is to be demolished?

KIOSK: Hell, no ... but they will.

JANICE: They will?

KIOSK: You're damned right they will! Who's runnin' this town, you? Or I?

JANICE: Thank you, Your Worship.

She rises quickly and leaves. ROSSINI watches her go. He is worried.

ROSSINI: (*addressing KIOSK*) I think you'd better phone the publisher of the paper and get that story straight.

GOYDA: That's fast thinking, Alderman!

ROSSINI: (*impatiently*) Alright, the meeting's over.

IRMA and GOYDA leave. ROSSINI paces back and forth in the office area.

KIOSK: Relax ... I wonder what makes my daughter get involved with characters like that?

ROSSINI: Never mind your daughter ... One of two things had better be done fast, Kiosk.

KIOSK: Like what?

ROSSINI: Like you get on that telephone and call the others with a deal to close ranks around you ... promise them your vote on their pet hang-ups ... anything. Or you get ready to resign and get your ass out of municipal politics for good in this town!

KIOSK: Who in hell you think you're talkin' to, Rossini?

ROSSINI: If I know Goyda and his two lady helpers, we're in trouble ... bad trouble.

The lights go out on KIOSK and ROSSINI, with KIOSK staring vacantly at ROSSINI.

The lights come up on GOYDA'S shop. GOYDA is at his workbench. IRMA is folding handbills at the other end of the table. JANICE is preparing to interview GOYDA for a radio show. She checks her cassette tape recorder and holds the microphone before his face.

GOYDA: Come on, Jan ... This is ridiculous.

JANICE: People need information ... they're demanding it. Trust me.

She adopts a radio voice.

Mr. Goyda ... you operate a crafts shop in Woodlands, is that true?

GOYDA: Yes.

JANICE: And how long have you done this?

GOYDA: For six years, and some years prior to that on a part-time basis.

JANICE: You were also a founding member of the Woodlands Crafts Centre Committee ... an organization of concerned and responsible people. What is your role presently in this committee?

GOYDA: I'm the interim chairman.

JANICE: It is widely recognized that you have contributed much to this community in exhibits and crafts development ...

GOYDA grimaces at her. She ignores him.

Your recent decision to revitalize a historic community building now vacant and neglected is also drawing wide community support.

GOYDA: That's a question I'm not prepared to ...

He motions with his hand to cut the interview. She ignores him.

JANICE: Concerned people in Woodlands are now looking to you and your committee as standing between the first church built in this town ... and the demolition hammer threatening it now as a result of city hall decisions!

GOYDA: (*sharply*) The decision to demolish this building was arrogant and came as a surprise, but ...

JANICE: (*closing hard on him*) You went before the mayor and representatives of council to argue for saving a historic building. What was their response for an alternative plan of renovation and public use?

GOYDA: I never argued for saving the church ... merely for leasing it to us as a crafts centre! The decision to demolish was announced at my last meeting with them.

JANICE: (*feigning surprise*) You had no previous indication of this decision?

GOYDA: (*with exasperation*) Yes! Look, I don't care if they turned the place into a hamburger take-out business!

JANICE: Yes, your anger is understandable ... You were informed at this last meeting with the mayor of a plan to demolish the historic church and sell the land it occupies for development, is that right?

GOYDA: The question of development didn't come up.

JANICE: But one can assume that was the intention of the Woodlands civic government.

GOYDA: One can assume anything, I suppose.

JANICE: Thank you. That was Jerry Goyda for evening radio news from Woodlands.

The lights go out on the scene with GOYDA.

The lights come up on KIOSK and ROSSINI. ROSSINI is seated, glum. KIOSK is pacing back and forth. The telephone rings. He stares at it, but does not answer it.

ROSSINI: You going to answer it?

KIOSK: It's another call like the ones I've been gettin' all morning. Can't we sue that bastard?

ROSSINI: I heard the interview. There's nothing we can sue for.

KIOSK: Daughter or not, I told Irma to find herself another place to live ... I can't have her around my home now ... My own kid ... When I told her that, she just looked at me like I wasn't there an' said, "You can't see beyond your feet ...

I feel sorry for you." What a helluva thing to say to your old man! ... An' Tom, if that bitch from the newspaper ever shows her nose in here, I'm throwin' her out!

ROSSINI: You've got to cool down, Sid ... your health won't take too much of this.

KIOSK: There's nothing wrong with my health ... I've never felt better.

Speaking sadly.

What's happened to respect for public office? It never used to be like this ... One disagreement an' they're on the radio making hay of the whole damned business ... ridiculing, undermining confidence.

ROSSINI: Things started off wrong. Positions were too severe ... Things from the past got in the way.

KIOSK: I thought the older a man gets, the more respect he earns from things he did ... It takes a long time. I don't want to be laughed at, Tom.

ROSSINI: Neither do I.

KIOSK: What do we do now? If you think calling on them ... asking for another meeting would ...

ROSSINI: (*angrily*) Do that ... and sink yourself good! You should've thought of all that before the role of mayor got into your head!

KIOSK: (*feeling helpless*) That doesn't help me ... I need someone who knows how to put things together again.

ROSSINI: Give an inch now and you can call a new election for mayor! Because if Goyda doesn't ... that Webber girl will ... call for your resignation!

KIOSK: But not yours?

ROSSINI: (*smiling coldly*) Nope.

KIOSK: If I go down, I'm takin' the whole council down with me ... You'd better understand that! You all voted on the position I took.

ROSSINI: Why not take the whole town, while you're at it? You really can't see beyond your feet, you know.

KIOSK: When I was a kid ... it was the English remittance men an' their kids who did it to us. Next, it'll be you ... As a kid, if I invited their kids to my birthday party, they never came ... I stood behind trees, watching them ... a goddamned second-class citizen in my own country ... I'm never gonna forget that!

ROSSINI: What's it got to do with me? You don't hear me crying about things like that ... It doesn't bother Goyda ... or your daughter. Certainly not the newspaper lady. Nobody cares about the dreams of old men, Kiosk! You pay for what you need, that's all that matters. If you can't pay, that's another thing ... then you're a bum.

KIOSK: They call you the Italian behind your back. You want to be called that all your life?

ROSSINI: (laughing) I don't care what in hell they call me. I own more than I can eat ... putting my kid through university ... I've even had enough friends to elect me to town council. So, do I worry? If I was an Indian or a cripple, maybe I'd worry ... but I'm not.

KIOSK: No pride at all, eh? ... I've got pride, Rossini. I don't take crap from anyone no more ... not even from my daughter. An' certainly not from an educated bum who can do better things, but goes into a business a woman or somebody with less education could do. He's takin' away someone else's work!

ROSSINI: That's his problem ... We've got ours.

KIOSK: What do we do now?

ROSSINI: Council will support you ... they have to so's not to lose face. We all made a mistake. It doesn't mean much, but we've got to prevent Goyda winning.

KIOSK: He won't, then.

ROSSINI: He'll win ... if he's willing to go after us. With that radio interview, he's got the first jump. There's two options open to us.

KIOSK: What's that?

ROSSINI: You go on radio ... be nice ... but accuse him of making a big issue out of nothing. Make our position look responsible.

KIOSK: I don't like it.

ROSSINI: While you're being reasonable, the rest of us move like hell with a demolition tender ... find a quick buyer for the church land so it's sold soon's the building's down. Nobody argues long with something that's done and over with ...

because even if we lose the argument, it won't change a thing!

KIOSK begins to realize what ROSSINI is proposing. He straightens up resolutely.

KIOSK: Alright ... if that's the way it has to be then that's the way it is. When I go on radio, what'll I say?

ROSSINI: (rising, facing him coldly) You'll say what your political instincts tell you to say ... nothing more ... nothing less. If you don't, you're dead!

Mechanically, like robots, KIOSK and ROSSINI move from their office to the newspaper office. JANICE, dressed in cold colours, holds up a microphone as they approach. KIOSK goes to the microphone and begins to speak into it.

KIOSK: My colleagues and I respect the people in the Woodlands Crafts Centre Committee an' welcome all they've done for the community. It's helped to develop an image for our town as a good place to live. But, we are elected to be responsible for problems which the committee has not satisfactorily helped us resolve. We asked them for hard information on the old church. Much of their information was idealistic. Our own assessment was that ... regretfully ... the building is in bad repair and must be demolished for public safety. Should the committee bring a proposal to *build* a new centre for their needs, we'd be more than happy to consider their proposal.

JANICE cuts the mike.

JANICE: That's the position you're staying with?

KIOSK: What does it sound like, lady?

KIOSK looks to ROSSINI for approval. ROSSINI is cold and distant, the general on the battlefield. JANICE is a mirror image of ROSSINI.

JANICE: It sounds like something I've heard elsewhere ... on other issues. From Alderman Rossini.

KIOSK laughs loudly. He continues laughing as ROSSINI escorts him from the newspaper office to the mayor's office. ROSSINI slaps him across the face. KIOSK blinks, his laughter dying abruptly.

ROSSINI: Stay with what you said ... no matter what happens ... You repeat what you said over and over ... Do you understand?

KIOSK: (*woodenly*) Count on me, Tom. You know you can count on me.

During the above exchange, JANICE moves her tape recorder to GOYDA'S shop. While JANICE briefs him soundlessly, IRMA paints signs reading "Heritage, Yes—Bulldozers, No!"

DOLAN: (*from offstage, in the newspaper office*) Janice? ... Are you there? ... Can you tell me why the only bastards in town who don't subscribe to the paper are coming and going through here like I was a bootlegger in a dry town?

GOYDA: (*speaking to JANICE*) Is that all he said?

JANICE: Yes ... you're on.

GOYDA: The issue is no longer a dispute between our organization and members of town council. The arrogance of Mayor Kiosk ... the decision to demolish the only building remaining from the original town site ... must be stopped! Our membership is canvassing with petitions. The ministers of three active churches have given us support. Protest posters are available at the leather shop!

The lights come up on KIOSK and ROSSINI who are listening to a radio.

We request the town fathers turn the decision on the church to a citizens' committee for further study and recommendations!

ROSSINI: Goddamn him!

KIOSK: Over my dead body!

GOYDA: We ask the city council to revoke the demolition order as of today!

ROSSINI: (*addressing KIOSK quietly*) No.

KIOSK: (*loudly*) No!

GOYDA: (*angrily*) We demand members of council come to their senses and stop behaving like village fascists!

ROSSINI AND KIOSK: Like hell!

KIOSK and ROSSINI huddle in silent conversation. KIOSK dials a number on his telephone and begins a soundless conversation.

GOYDA: (*pushing the microphone away and rising to his feet*) How are the petitions doing, Irma?

IRMA: (*upset*) Six hundred signatures ... You're after him? You're out to get him, aren't you? This issue is not as important as breaking my father down!

JANICE: (*moving towards her*) Irma ... you're tired.

IRMA: Don't touch me! You're both out to get him! You are moving headstones in a country graveyard ... dead ... no feeling ... no tears ... no remorse ... no hope. You're no different than he was! It's just a killing game ... Nobody cares for anybody!

JANICE turns away from her.

JANICE: (*speaking to GOYDA*) I'll take her to my place ... There's a demonstration being organized around City Hall.

GOYDA: (*startled*) What demonstration? ... When?

JANICE: Friday evening.

IRMA: (*in great frustration*) I'm going by myself! I'm going home. There's nobody left. Everything is dead. Frozen. It was a lie! ... You both lied to me ... to yourselves! ... I'm going home.

She runs out of the shop.

JANICE and GOYDA look after her, briefly, but their minds are on other things. GOYDA turns on JANICE.

GOYDA: Who in hell gave you authority to do that? We never discussed a demonstration as a tactic!

JANICE: I've canvassed some of the members who agreed.

GOYDA: What members? ... There's never been a membership meeting!

JANICE: The members I brought into the organization.

GOYDA: A public meeting would've been fine ... but not a demonstration ... not in this town!

JANICE: (*sneering*) Why not? It's time Woodlands joined the twentieth century along with the rest of the world.

GOYDA: I agreed to chair the group ... I expect to be consulted before action such as this is considered.

JANICE: Listen, baby, you're a shopkeeper. In the end, you'll be influenced by that consideration. The demonstration's on.

The telephone rings, as KIOSK hangs up his own phone. JANICE answers the phone.

Yes? ... Great! ... Bring them in ... No, send them over by cab!

She hangs up the telephone and turns to GOYDA happily.

Petitions have topped one thousand signatures ... By tomorrow, more people will have signed than voted for the mayor! You should announce that, Jerry.

GOYDA: (*stonily*) Announce it yourself ... Get your bread bakers and prune eaters together and announce it with a bullhorn down Main Street. If you run into the mayor while doing it, you might give him a flower and then break his legs with a club! Get out of here!

Ignoring him, she holds up the microphone. She smiles warmly at him.

JANICE: Just make the announcement and then go have yourself a coffee, Jerry.

GOYDA: I want you to clear out ... and stay out of Irma's life as well!

JANICE: It's not some diabolical scheme ... It's the end of a time in this town. Win or lose, the town fathers will have to reverse gear ... under pressure.

GOYDA: But you won't stop there ... No way! The taste of power is too heady for our Janice ... No small town paper is going to tie you down *now*!

JANICE: Look at it this way then ... our membership didn't elect you ... or Irma ... or me. We elected ourselves ... to get a new location for Jerry Goyda's shop. It's not quite true, but that's what people will be saying. Pulling back now makes you a mark ... Announce the petition results.

GOYDA: No.

JANICE: (*annoyed now*) You'll do what has to be done. Just as Kiosk reacts to what he's told to do

... Kiosk is nothing ... a piece of cardboard. It's Rossini we're fighting!

GOYDA: It's the same over there?

He points in KIOSK'S direction.

JANICE: Yes.

GOYDA: And I'm ... also ... made of cardboard? You knew how it was going ... right from the start!

JANICE avoids his eyes.

The lights come up on DOLAN'S wheelchair. His phone is off the hook.

The telephone rings in KIOSK'S office. He answers it.

KIOSK: Yeh ... speaking ... What? ... When? ... How bad is it?

KIOSK hangs up the telephone, his face frozen.

JANICE hangs up DOLAN'S phone.

ROSSINI: Someone find a new pothole in the street?

KIOSK: Irma's car ... went off the highway overpass ...

ROSSINI: Is she ... alright?

KIOSK moans and covers up his face with his hands. ROSSINI rises and goes upstage from him. He stands rigidly, opening and closing his hands.

GOYDA: If I was to walk out that door and go talk to Kiosk directly ... explain how both of us were being worked over ...

JANICE: I wouldn't recommend it. It would give him the kind of advantage you'd get if he decided to come here and see you first ... for the same reason.

GOYDA: (*savagely*) How does the remainder of the scenario read? ... Let's get it over with so I can see Rossini about recovering my lease before someone else picks it up and I'm out on my ear in the street!

JANICE puts away her microphone and hands a paper to GOYDA. He reads it, then moves to KIOSK'S office, followed by JANICE, who takes out her notebook.

KIOSK drops his hands from his face as GOYDA enters. KIOSK'S face is dead, his words wooden and without feeling.

KIOSK: Is it the resignation of council you want? ... Or mine?

The sound of human voices offstage growing slowly in volume is heard. ROSSINI turns to stand behind KIOSK.

GOYDA: We are not here to waste Your Worship's or our own time. Fourteen hundred signatures on our petition demand a reversal of demolition order on the old church.

GOYDA hands over the sheaf of papers to him. KIOSK ignores them.

KIOSK: Tenders have been given ... We have a buyer for the church lots.

GOYDA: The petitioners demand a reversal of that decision!

The crowd sounds grow louder.

KIOSK: Whatever you want.

GOYDA: (*surprised*) I beg your pardon, sir ...

KIOSK: Tell Rossini what you want, Goyda ... Someone will look after it.

The crowd sound becomes a cheer.

ROSSINI: (*groping now*) What His Worship means is that ... the entire question of your lease application ... will be reviewed by a committee ... made up of representatives from our side ... an' from your side ... as well as members from the community at large. Is that agreeable?

KIOSK rises and turns away from them.

KIOSK: Irma died ... in her car ... She's dead, Goyda ... What do you think of that?

GOYDA looks at KIOSK, speechless. ROSSINI nods to JANICE. They leave in separate directions.

The lights tighten on GOYDA and KIOSK.

GOYDA: I ... didn't know. Nobody told me.

KIOSK: (*speaking over the noise of the crowd off-stage who are chanting, "Goyda, Goyda"*) First my wife ... then her ... I lose them both ... You know what that means, Goyda?

GOYDA inhales sharply, as if sobbing.

GOYDA: Yes ... yes ... yes ...

He is shouting now.

Yes!

KIOSK: In thirty years ... I never once took a holiday ... I only went to grade eight in school ... It's been ... such a job ...

He speaks with effort, continuing almost in a howl.

... just holding up my goddamned head among men!

The lights go out slowly on them as DOLAN sings.

DOLAN: (*singing*)
In our town
The roses fade
And one by one
The stones are laid
To trim the grass
Around the grave
At seven hours to sundown ...
In our town
Seven hours to sundown.

There is a short music interlude, then abrupt silence and a blackout.

End

JEREMIAH'S PLACE

After the relative success of *Compressions*, his first play for young audiences, Ryga encountered production problems with *Jeremiah's Place*, written in the late 1970s for Kaleidoscope Theatre of Victoria, a fairly new company specializing in public school performances. There was a brief discussion during the initial phases of the commission of a possible theme of racism (vestiges of which can be found in this play in the character of Wanda), but the topic was finally left open to Ryga. The production was slated for secondary school performances during 1978–1979, but was withdrawn before Christmas after there were negative comments from the schools where it had played. In the end, both Ryga and the company's director, Elizabeth Gorrie, admitted the play would not work within the school system. Despite the best efforts of Kaleidoscope, a company known for its energetic, highly creative use of movement, masks, and properties, the work, it was felt, remained too "talky" for their young audiences, and raised issues that educators were both unwilling and unable to discuss with their students.

Jeremiah's Place has a familiar Ryga theme: the anguish over the loss of a homestead, especially as family relationships are seriously disrupted and questions are raised about the best use of the land. The play is set in the autumn, on the day when Don has sold the family farm to the faceless buyers of a holding company who have plans for building a lodge as a "destination resort" for tourists. As coyotes howl and overgrown maples threaten, members of the family respond to the change, most notably Jeremiah, the aging patriarch, who can no longer work the land and feels betrayed by his offspring: "It was given to you to farm, not to sell!"

Grandpa Jeremiah's passionate reaction, alternately prophetic and vitriolic, echoing his biblical namesake, provides a harshly critical counterpoint to the family's rationale for selling the farm. In the end, however, he is helpless to stop the inevitable: despite his memories and dreams, the man who built the farm is simply consigned to sickness and approaching death, while none of his descendants seem to have much of a future anywhere else either, at least not from his point of view. The setting for this tale of cultural loss is central British Columbia—or any place in the world, really, where the failure of family farms in a context of rapidly accelerating urbanization present an increasing social problem. It is instructive to recall that Ryga lived among the orchard farms in rural Summerland, a major fruit growing area on the west side of Okanagan Lake in south central British Columbia, where, since the 1890s, there have been numerous commercial family fruit growing and packing operations. Ryga knew some of these families, occasionally working for them at harvest time. He also witnessed first hand the beginning of the end of this culture based on life on the land and his dramatization of this cultural shift in *Jeremiah's Place* is not only darkly prophetic, but also devastatingly critical of the spread of the growing, professional urban class culture world-wide, which, primarily through its control of both capital and technology, continues to undermine and replace, often at a far-removed distance from the communities affected, Canada's older, formative agrarian and working-class settler culture.

The *Oxford English Dictionary* defines the symbolic and biblical character "Jeremiah" as a "doleful prophet or denouncer of the times." There is no doubt that Ryga's character Jeremiah is doleful, begging the question of the audience as to what he is denouncing. The answer lies almost entirely in Ryga's introduction of the Guatemalan woman character Wanda, the diametrical opposite of his picture-postcard

Central-American women characters we see in *A Portrait of Angelica*. In *Jeremiah's Place*, the character Wanda becomes, successively and by inevitable degrees, first an objectification of the social conscience of the emergent First World's growing professional class; then its exploited subject; and finally a disposable inconvenience, rejected and left to her own devices as a stateless person, packaged and commodified with the farm and its elements of agrarian culture—displaced by this new urban professional class as part of what it considers an outdated lifestyle. Wanda, and the cultures she (in terms of space) and Jeremiah (in terms of time) represent in the world, have become an impediment to the new transnational "professional" generation's singular goal of "development" of the land for absentee landlords' profits, rather than the use of the land to sustain a resident life and legitimacy for those who live on it generation after generation. Given Canada's explicit and complicit participation as one of the G-8 nations in the rapidly accelerating globalized exploitation of the Third World, it is hardly surprising that educators in Canada's public school system found the play "difficult," and "unsuitable" for discussion with their students.

At an international conference of populist theatre companies from around the world in Thunder Bay, Ontario, in May 1982, Ryga was to explicitly articulate his frustration with the seemingly insurmountable task of introducing the kinds of social and cultural issues he addressed in *Jeremiah's Place* (and elsewhere in his work) to the official public agenda in his own country. It was characteristically generous and modest of him that, despite his tireless and ongoing work as a social activist in all of the many causes of the oppressed throughout the world and especially in his own country and community, he chose to bear the public burden of this "failure" on his own shoulders: "I am aware our country is an economic exploiter in areas of the Third World—that as an artist in resistance I have not done enough to catalyse public concern around this issue."

JEREMIAH'S PLACE

CHARACTERS

STANLEY, *a young high school graduate*
PEARL, *his older sister*
DON, *their father*
GRANPA, *old Jeremiah*
SINGER/ACCOMPANIST/DANCER, *a female*

SET

The front porch of an old farmhouse in central British Columbia or any farming community where similar stories occur. There is a separate playing area below and around the porch. The play opens on the SINGER leaning on a railing of the porch, as far as possible from the centre of the stage.

SINGER (*singing harshly*)
Go bring the buryin' coffin 'round
Ol' Jeremiah's goin' down
Ol' Jeremiah's goin' down
To meet the darkness underground ...

Driving musical interlude of theme.

Go tell the magpie in the sky
That Jeremiah's passin' by
That Jeremiah's passin' by
Don't know where an' don't know why ...

Driving musical interlude of theme.

Oh, don't you weep an' don't you cry
'Cause Jeremiah's gonna die
'Cause Jeremiah's gonna die
All I can do is say goodbye ...

Music dies out.

GRANPA enters, stumbling and peering as if he'd just been awakened from a bad sleep. The SINGER retreats from the scene. GRANPA stumbles and falls.

GRANPA: Goddamnit!

Struggles to rise, breathing heavily. DON enters, alarmed.

DON: Here, Pop ... I'll help you. Didn't see you go past me.

Reaches down for the OLD MAN, who repels him with an angry motion.

GRANPA: Get away from me!

Struggles to his knees and rises with the help of a nearby bench.

GRANPA: If I can't get up by myself ... then maybe I shouldn't!

DON: Sit down ... here ... that's it ... that's better.

GRANPA: You hear what I said?

DON: Yes, I heard.

GRANPA: Like a blade of wheat. Once it falls it don't ever come up ... same way with a man. You think about that.

DON: Yes, it's something to think about. You sleep good?

GRANPA: Naw. I just lie there, dreamin', not quite awake, not quite asleep ... dreamt of my woman. Why's them bushes not changin' colour? Summer's ended ...

DON: Summer's ended, but it's been unusually warm this past season, Pop. The trees are green and dark, especially along the creek.

GRANPA: Summer's ended, but the livin' branches keep reachin' out for somethin' ... like a blind beggar they keep reachin' ... makes the fields dark. Keeps sun off the pumpkins. Them trees got to be cut, fella ...

DON: Yes, Pop. Do you feel okay?

GRANPA: They got to be cut an' milled into lumber. House is still good, but barn needs repairin' ...

DON: Don't worry about it. You just get yourself better.

GRANPA: Fifty years this summer—you know that?

DON: Huh?

GRANPA: This house—fifty years old this summer. Barn's only forty-nine ... built that a year later. Funny how the barn's aged ... ever since we went out of cattle ... it's gotten darker ... moss growin' on the roof.

DON: I never noticed that before ... but you're right. Seems like it ... started to die once it wasn't used.

GRANPA: Seems that way, don't it?

SINGER begins to play music softly in the background. Both MEN stare thoughtfully away in the direction of the barn.

GRANPA: Barn's aged, but the house is still good ...

DON: It's not, you know.

GRANPA: (*still staring*) What?

DON: The house ... it's sagging in the northwest corner.

GRANPA: Bullshit!

DON: Well, you haven't looked lately, that's all.

GRANPA: You go to hell, fella!

DON: It costs a lot to heat now—it was never insulated right.

GRANPA: Them walls is packed with sawdust an' lime right up to the rafters. Remember well how it was done ... she mixed it all in a wooden box an' handed it up to me with a bucket an' I rammed it down between the walls ...

DON: Marge and I talked a long time ago about building a new house once the kids grew up, but ... the way things happened ...

GRANPA: This here house is as warm as any damned new place you'll find ... better even ...

DON: She liked the creek ... wanted to be nearer to hear water tumble over stones, especially in summer ...

GRANPA turns on him.

GRANPA: Who you talkin' about? The half-breed gal?

DON: What half-breed girl?

GRANPA: (*nods to house*) Her ... Wanda.

Music fades out.

DON: (*laughs incredulously*) What a strange thing to say. Our Wanda is Guatemalan.

GRANPA: Same thing ...

DON: It's not the same thing, Pop. She's from another race, another part of the world ...

GRANPA: I know what I see, an' I see what I know. She's a half-breed. Look like one ... moves like one.

DON: (*to himself*) What a foolish thing to say!

GRANPA: Marge ... she liked this house. Same's her mother. I dreamt about her ... I tell you that?

DON: Yes. I think you did.

GRANPA: Not as she was before she died ... but as a girl. Younger even than when I married her.

Music builds slightly for background.

GRANPA: Never knew her that young, but there she was in my dream ... brown, shiny skin ... eyes you never forgot.

He becomes disturbed, his body shuddering. Music picks up tempo.

GRANPA: She ... she was drivin' a wagon in my dream ... a wagon pulled along by one old cow! An' in back of the wagon was this jesus big vacuum cleaner which was plugged into somethin' because it was hummin' an' suckin' up road dust ... an' leaves off the trees. She just kept drivin', pulled along by this old cow! It sure scared me, fella. You know anythin' about dreams? You know what it means dreamin' like that?

DON: No, but did Wanda give you your medication this morning?

GRANPA: Sure ... yeh ... she did.

Music fades down and out.

DON: Are you certain of that, Pop?

GRANPA: Get off my back, eh! I'm alright ... rememberin' that dream kinda put me out of sorts. I'm alright now.

DON: What a strange autumn this is. Leaves haven't turned—they still have their growing colour.

GRANPA: Don't let that fool you. Never trust a thing you see goin' on out there …

DON: Day after day the weather stays warm …

GRANPA: I've been cold a month now! Only thing I'll have between me an' the weather is this here house … built solid of eight-by-eight timbers. Built to goddam well last!

Strikes backwards at the wall with his fist, as if to confirm its steadfastness. The pain he inflicts on his fist makes him blink. He turns away from DON to suck at the cut he has made on his knuckles.

DON: (*suddenly annoyed*) It's only worthy of being a summer home! It's too costly to maintain. It needs repairs.

GRANPA rises painfully, angrily, to his feet.

GRANPA: While I'm alive … it's alive!

DON: So what do we do? Heat one room? Sit staring at TV during the cold winter nights like two brainless paralytics?

The tension evaporates between them. Each dismisses the other with a gesture and they turn from each other.

GRANPA: You keepin' an eye on them kids of yours?

DON: They're around somewhere. They're both here.

GRANPA: Notice the dark-skinned one's been gone this afternoon. You seen her?

DON does not reply.

GRANPA: First time she's done that, just left the house. Usually she bothers the hell out of me with hot tea, blankets … all them pills an' needles I seem to need to stay alive these days.

DON: You remember after the kids' granny died … signing over the farm to Marge and me?

GRANPA: Can't say I do, but it would've been the thing to do considerin' Margie was my flesh an' blood. (*harshly*) Damn that kid doin' what he did!

DON: He was not responsible! The road was icy and the car had bald tires. It's lucky he came out of it alive!

GRANPA: I don't see him cryin' about it. Your hairs turned greyer an' I'm carryin' that day like a stone in here. (*strikes his fist over his heart*) But … nothin' shows on him. He's not a man!

DON: How can you say that? The car needed new tires, and it was I who kept putting off getting them.

GRANPA: Don't cover for the boy. He's got to learn to take his lumps … be tough if he expects to get along.

Music up gently. Both men remain silent. GRANPA checks his pulse, silently lipping the pulse beat, which is rapid.

GRANPA: Why you ask about the deed to this farm? Don't remember you ever askin' that before?

DON: No reason … it's been on my mind, that's all.

GRANPA: You reckon I'm dyin'? Is that it?

DON: No, Pop. We'll talk about it later. You should get your rest now.

DON is troubled. The OLD MAN notices and frowns at him with displeasure.

GRANPA: Is there somethin' I don't know? You keepin' somethin' from me, fella?

DON: We'll talk about it when you're feeling better, Pop.

GRANPA: That wind … movin' slow an' gettin' colder … you get them kids of yours pickin' the tomato crop.

DON: Tomatoes are still green. Everything is green and succulent like it was mid-summer …

Music up, gently.

DON: How times passes … I was thinking just now when the kids were both young how much they enjoyed bringing in vegetables … doing canning. Margie in the kitchen … the smell of spices and herbs so strong I could smell it all the way down to the creek …

STANLEY and PEARL enter the lower playing area, carrying a large bucket between them. They are children, laughing, pulling each other this way and that in a game dance. GRANPA grunts and slouches in his seat, staring grimly ahead of himself.

PEARL: I think it's funny!

STANLEY: You say you think it's funny. Why do you say you think it's funny?

PEARL: They way you repeat every question I ask you. I heard you doing it in school.

STANLEY: I don't repeat every question you ask me. And you didn't hear me doing it in school!

PEARL: There—you're doing it again!

She laughs. STANLEY stomps along beside her, upset.

DON: It was so good watching them being children … watching them grow up together.

GRANPA: I remember them fightin' more times than not.

The atmosphere between STANLEY and PEARL changes. They are suddenly older, hostile.

PEARL: Stop it! Stop repeating everything I say!

STANLEY: I don't repeat everything you say …

PEARL: Grow up, will you? Stop being a dumb asshole!

STANLEY: I'm not a dumb asshole …

She yanks the bucket out of his hands and flounces offstage, with STANLEY following belligerently.

GRANPA: Remember them fightin' a lot. Worried me … used to take the boy fishin' in the creek to keep him out of Pearl's hair. Wish somebody'd done the same for Pearl.

Music stops. DON slowly turns to face GRANPA.

DON: Pearl was well looked after. You know that.

GRANPA: So's the dark-skinned one we got us now …

DON: *(annoyed)* There are times I don't know if you're serious or not.

GRANPA: I'm serious!

DON: Marge and I always looked after our kids good. Pearl had a good time here … grew up better than most kids. Sure, there were times when she had to put her back into some hard work, but that was only natural … also part of growing up.

GRANPA: It's not the work, fella … it's them other things. The way the eyes open in the mornin', if you wish …

DON: You're not making sense.

GRANPA: You wonder why she's here again? Been married one year an' this is the third visit she's makin' … each visit lastin' longer an' longer.

DON: It's her home! What's wrong with that? Or are you suggesting …

GRANPA: Suggestin' nothin' … I'm telling you. That bastard lawyer-man is givin' her the boot! Or you too blind to see that? First year of marriage, too … the best part. Never trusted that man from the first time I seen him. He's cold, like the air that's movin' up from the hollow.

DON: I don't believe that! You're unwell and you're saying such things because you can't help yourself!

GRANPA: Alright … then I never said it.

DON: *(worried)* Can I help you back to your bed, Pop?

GRANPA: I want to stay here a little longer. Bed's a bad place to be by yourself when you're dyin' …

Music up softly.

DON: You're not dying, Pop. All that medication's working. You're looking better today than you were yesterday.

GRANPA: There was a man in a big new car came to get you day before yesterday. I seen him an' you from my bedroom window. What did he want?

DON: *(uncomfortable, reaching in his shirt pocket)* Just … somebody I knew …

GRANPA: An equipment salesman?

DON: No.

GRANPA: Somebody about insurance?

DON: An acquaintance. You wouldn't know him.

GRANPA: I thought everybody you knowed, I knowed. Never seen that sport before … now about our Pearl …

DON: (*irritated*) Pearl's married and has a good life. Nothing's going to change my mind about that, so why don't we leave her alone?

GRANPA: (*peering*) Them maples got to come out ... they'll be reseedin' themselves over half the meadow by next summer. You get that boy of yours out there with a chain saw ...

DON: It's good to have her come back this way. If something was wrong she'd say so.

GRANPA laughs dryly, then doubles up with coughing.

DON: Are you alright? Why are you laughing?

GRANPA: (*struggling for breath*) You tell that boy ... to get out there with a chain saw!

DON: Now? This afternoon?

GRANPA: Yes.

DON: Stan does what he's asked to do. I don't understand why ... since Marge died ... he's shouted at ... ordered to do this and that.

GRANPA: (*fiercely, half-rising*) He's got to make up for killin' her, his own mother!

DON: (*startled*) You can't mean that! He's hardly more than a kid.

GRANPA: Then he's got to grow up, quick. When I was his age, I was five years on my own already.

DON: (*arrested by the primordial rage of the OLD MAN*) It was an accident ... car was in bad condition ... Stan did the best he knew how ...

GRANPA: Wasn't good enough. He come out without a scratch.

DON: (*furious*) If he's lost an arm, or an eye, or a leg. You'd feel better then? Is that what it is?

GRANPA: (*becoming subdued*) At least he'd a paid somethin' for livin'.

DON: We're talking about our own child ... our flesh and blood.

GRANPA: We've driven cars an' trucks in worse shape on this farm.

DON: I've never heard this before. Never thought anyone would have such things to say ... especially about one's own family!

GRANPA: He coulda driven safe ... if he'd been trained right.

DON: I was teaching him to drive. He'd passed his driving test and ... (*stares at GRANPA, who peers past him*) ... I see ...

A long moment of silence between them, charged by many years of differences. Music, slow and haunting, up briefly, fading slowly into silence on dialogue.

GRANPA: Them trees gotta be chained down, or half the meadow's gone next summer.

DON: It doesn't matter ...

GRANPA: It always matters. Every bit of land matters.

DON: Whatever you say, Pop.

Turns as if to leave the OLD MAN.

GRANPA: Them two'll need every bit of this land to survive ... same's I did ... same's you did ...

DON: Just between you and me, Jeremiah's place is the last thing on the minds of either of my kids, Pop. And I'm kind of hoping it stays that way.

GRANPA rises slowly and makes his way to the railing.

GRANPA: Never expected to hear that from you. 'Specially now, when the livin' part of me an' the dyin' part of me is keepin' such close company ... never expected to hear that.

DON: Do you want to come in and lie down now?

GRANPA: Them two'll need this to survive ... every tree I cut down, every shovelful of ground I turned over the first time ... they'll need it all.

DON: Come on. I'll help you indoors.

GRANPA: I don't need your help! You're the one needs help!

DON: What help?

GRANPA: Teachin' them! I spoiled him. Liked to see him laugh. Showed him good things I knew about, like them grandfathers on television. Never showed him bad things. Nobody did. Never saw that kid cry, not once, after the accident that took me Margie's life!

DON: He's suffered. I've seen him suffer.

GRANPA: That's more than I've seen!

DON: That's a damned lie!

GRANPA: Show him ... work him hard! But with her it'll be different ...

DON: Pearl?

GRANPA: She's heated up ... brushed bare skin with the devil more'n once an' wantin' more ...

DON: Leave my children alone!

GRANPA: It's my land, so it's my children, too!

DON: Not anymore!

GRANPA: Like hell you say!

DON: You turned the land over to me.

GRANPA: It's mine as long's I'm able to stand on these two pegs ... an' I'm standin'.

DON: I won't allow you to eat up my family! It's all over with, except for the shouting!

GRANPA: You can say that when I'm dead. Until then, you'll hear me out.

DON: (with exasperation) Hah!

GRANPA: Don't "hah" me! You look to her, fella. She's heated up an' burnin' the only way a fool kid woman knows how, with them tight jeans an' sweaters holdin' up her tits. No love, no pity, just a walkin' Jezebel turned that way by the first man she knowed!

DON stares at GRANPA'S back. He opens and closes his fists, a glimmer of uncertainty darkening his face.

DON: (with control) The man she married, Pop, ... Ron ... is okay.

GRANPA: He's a piece of shit wearin' a fancy suit.

DON: He's not our kind of people, I agree, but she hasn't complained. So we've no reason to interfere.

GRANPA: Then why's she home again? Why's she always comin' home? You forget I've also raised a girl once.

DON: She's home to visit ... see us ... help take care of things.

GRANPA: You get her divorced an' back in this family before it's too late. Sell some cows to pay for it ... sell anythin'.

DON: You're wrong, Pop. I think you're very much mistaken.

GRANPA: An' if I'm not? You prepared to live with that? An' not much chance for a second try ... you're pushin' old age yourself an' with no woman to help you ... an' speakin' of women, you tell that damned Wanda I wanna see her when she gets in. She's gone an' hid my vitamin bottle.

Over the scene about PEARL, the SINGER can dance an interpretation of PEARL in a struggle with her own oppression and her own nature, followed by the SINGER coming down to the lower playing area and being joined by PEARL who dances identically, ending in the DANCER vanishing behind PEARL and freezing into the end of this pre-act of the play.

GRANPA leaves the stage slowly.

The SINGER and PEARL separate and move apart—PEARL leaves offstage, SINGER goes to her own area.

During this action, DON exits and returns with a cup of coffee. He sits on a bench and takes out legal papers from his hip pocket. He studies them in silence.

STANLEY: (offstage, shouting) Pearl!

DON glances up in the direction of STANLEY'S voice, then returns to his papers.

STANLEY: (offstage) Why in hell is it I put two socks in the wash and only one ends up in the dryer? Pearl!

Long silence.

STANLEY: (offstage) Pearl!

Another silence. PEARL enters and leans against the wall back of DON. She yawns and brushes back her hair with her hand.

STANLEY: (offstage) Boy, will I be glad when I leave for college!

DON: (without looking up) He's calling you, girl.

PEARL: I heard. The dead in the cemetery can hear him.

DON: Then see what he wants and stop him yelling.

PEARL: He doesn't have to yell. I'm not his maid. He's a spoiled creep. I don't understand why you don't speak to him.

DON: About what?

PEARL gestures in frustration.

DON: Well?

PEARL: Anything. You can start with him learning to take care of his needs. Or helping with chores. It was his turn to do breakfast dishes this morning. They're still in the sink.

DON: (*tolerantly*) Come now, Pearl …

PEARL: And don't you use that tone of voice with me!

DON: If you persist in being childish.

PEARL: I'm not a child and neither is he. But it would help everyone if someone around here showed some authority.

DON: Meaning what?

PEARL: (*exasperated*) What's the point in talking about it? Maybe it's less hassle just to wash, cook, and pick up for everybody in this house. Where's Wanda? She's nowhere to be found this afternoon.

DON: I'm not asking to bug you, but, have you ever done those things for Ron?

PEARL takes a moment to reply, a moment to recover her self-control.

PEARL: What is it that you're asking me, Father?

DON: Just trying to tell you that Ron might care for you more if you did the same.

PEARL: Did I, or Ron, come to you for advice on how we are to live?

DON: No. But maybe if you had, things would be better now.

PEARL: Who said there's anything the matter? The old man?

DON: I can see. I can feel when things are not right. But don't feel you're alone, because you're not, Pearl. I always felt he was too ambitious, always there with answers to questions nobody asked.

PEARL: I don't care what you think you see or feel. If you're asking me to leave, then say so and I'll take the night bus out.

DON: No. Please don't go, Pearl. I'm sorry.

PEARL: (*pacing*) And where's that damned Wanda gone? She never told me what she planned for supper. It'll be getting dark soon.

DON: How green are the maples this summer. As if they were sucking some nourishment I never knew was in the earth.

PEARL: (*still pacing*) She doesn't talk to me … makes me feel I done something wrong.

DON glances at his papers again, but his hand is trembling. He avoids looking at PEARL.

DON: (*quietly*) I … I sold the farm today, Pearl.

PEARL: (*still pacing*) She's left a roast out … but also some hamburger …

Music up softly.

DON: The price they paid for the land was a good price … I think.

PEARL slows in her pacing. She is agitated, but does not look at her FATHER.

PEARL: It'll be dark soon and too late to make a full meal.

DON: Feed yourselves—don't make nothing for me. I ate a good lunch. The real estate agent bought me lunch in town after we closed the deal on the farm …

PEARL: (*turning on him*) You … sold the farm?

DON nods, his eyes still on the papers in his hand.

STANLEY: (*calling offstage*) Pearl?

PEARL: (*nods to house*) Have you told him?

DON: Not yet, but it's alright …

PEARL: Oh, this is one I won't wait to see …

STANLEY enters. Music dies out.

STANLEY: How come she don't answer when I call?

PEARL: What in hell do you want now?

STANLEY: Nothing. Just wanted to know where you were.

PEARL: (*angry*) I'm not your damned mother!

STANLEY steps back from her, shocked. She reaches out to him and presses his shoulder assuringly.

PEARL: It's not your fault. There's just too much going on at once. Dad sold the farm today ...

STANLEY misses a beat as the news sinks in.

STANLEY: Oh, yeh?

DON: Five hundred dollars an acre is not bad. Especially when it's all in cash.

STANLEY: Really? It's not ours no more?

DON: You kids think I done right in selling out?

There is no reply. STANLEY fidgets. Music up gently.

DON: What do you say, Stan?

STANLEY: I ... don't know. That still mean I'm going to college next month?

DON: Sure, no problem. But you did expect to come back?

STANLEY: Yeh, this is home. But that don't matter. Whatever you say is okay with me!

DON: You kids ever seen the maples so green before? Almost like they were saying something ... to me.

PEARL: I'll be leaving next Sunday, Dad.

DON: Ron write you ... or phone?

PEARL mimics a young divorcee out to conquer the world. Music ends. SINGER on the far end of the stage mimics the world out to receive her, reward her for her singular mind, then break her.

PEARL: (*coyly*) Oh, for gosh sakes, Daddy, don't worry! My old job in the transport company office is waiting for me. Mister Steiner said when I got married to come right back first time Ron got nasty!

DON, turned away from her, misses her mockery.

DON: Promises like that don't mean much, Pearl. A year's a long time.

STANLEY: (*troubled at his father's ridicule*) Pearl!

PEARL: Hush your mouth, child. (*to DON*) But Ron might call tonight—or tomorrow. He's pretty

busy all day at his office. If he says "Please, Pearl, come back" I might think about it until Sunday.

DON: I thought of him when this sale offer come up.

PEARL stops mimicking. SINGER fades down.

PEARL: There's no law office in town no more. Who was your lawyer?

DON: Did it all myself. Nothing to it. (*holds up papers to her*) Their lawyer drew this up ... legal description of land, terms of payment, and all this here about my staying on if I wanted.

PEARL: Staying on where?

DON: Here. (*shows her the sale document*) See this? You see yourself Granpa and I can live out the rest of our lives if we want here.

PEARL: I don't understand how or what you've done. But it scares me, Dad!

DON: Nothing to be scared of, girl. I had no choice, you know. Both of you gone soon, Grandad getting more frail. Not much I could do without help. And I could sure use the money. If for no other reason than to afford a safe car at last for these damned roads ...

PEARL: I haven't been this scared since Mom died.

DON: Everything will turn out fine ... you'll see.

STANLEY: Never thought when I cut the alfalfa last week that it'd be the last crop off that meadow.

DON: I ... should've asked you, I guess.

PEARL: If you think selling was right, then it was the thing to do! Besides, if you stay on, no reason we can't help out with hay and gardening for whoever farms this land whenever we're home!

DON draws away from them, shaking his head.

DON: Can't do that, Pearl.

PEARL: Depends on the people. They may be like us and need help.

DON: It's in that agreement—can't be done. And they told me a couple of times so I understood. The land's not to be touched. No cattle. No honey-hives, nothing. House is ours to live in, but ...

PEARL: Then how will they be farming it?

DON: Not even a garden, they said to me. Can't shoot a deer or partridge, not even a coyote. So anything we need we buy in town.

STANLEY: But it'll all grow back in trees! The garden space is too small for them to run machines through.

DON: That's what they want to happen …

STANLEY: The garden soil's been worked over good, no sense losing it that way.

DON: (*anguished*) It's not the garden I'm talking about! It's the whole damned farm!

PEARL and STANLEY stare at him, not comprehending.

DON: The garden … the fields … meadows … everything's to be allowed to grow back into bush.

PEARL: (*fearful*) Who are these people you sold out to, Dad?

DON: I don't know.

PEARL: What do you mean you don't know?

DON: It's a company … call themselves Golden West Holdings. Only person I met was their lawyer, a young guy with a funny accent.

PEARL: Did he come out to see this place?

DON: No.

PEARL: Did anyone?

DON: I don't know, but what difference does that make? They bought it, didn't they? Same way as they're buying out Alf down the road, and Thorensen's place up the creek.

PEARL: (*shivering*) Are you saying the whole community is being sold the same way?

DON: That's right. Only this place was the first, which paid me five hundred dollars an acre. The others are getting four, the lawyer said.

PEARL moves resolutely towards the house.

DON: Where are you going?

PEARL: I'm calling Ron and asking him to look into this. There's something scary about what you've got us into.

DON: No need for that. I signed the deal and took their cheque. Bank cleared it. It was good. A deal is a deal.

STANLEY: It's killing the land, sounds like!

PEARL returns to DON'S side and stares at him, searching for some other explanation. A distant howl of a coyote to which all three respond. GRANPA enters dressed in a heavy dressing gown and slippers. He stands apart, unobserved.

PEARL: Why would anyone wish to buy this farm and then want to kill it?

DON: That creek at the bottom of the meadow, the way the maples are growing, as if they knew.

PEARL: I don't understand what you're saying!

DON: They're counting on deer coming back once the trees grow in through the fields.

PEARL: Deer?

DON: Yeh. First they'll shoot grouse and partridge. But once the deer are back, there's plans for a hunting lodge …

PEARL: This land—to be hunted on?

DON pockets his sale documents disconsolately and sits down.

DON: They asked and I agreed that if some hunters were to come up next month, and we decided to stay on, we'd see to putting them up and making their meals.

PEARL: Hunters staying here? That's impossible!

DON: I thought your room and Stan's would be empty … that's good for four men.

PEARL: I don't believe this!

DON: We'd be paid, of course …

PEARL: (*bitterly*) Oh, sure, I mean, how else could it be …

DON: (*defensively, hurt*) Seemed like a good idea. If for no other reason than for Wanda to make some money. But now that she's gone …

GRANPA: She'll be back!

He enters the playing area aggressively, as if to confront some other force not visible to the others.

PEARL: Granpa, you should be in bed! The doctor said you were to lie still until your pulse stabilized. Have you taken your medication?

GRANPA: (*ignoring her*) She'll be back, boyo! Little brown girl got no place to go now except where she's supposed to be. Same's the rest of us!

DON rises and goes to him, touching his shoulders.

DON: Let me help you back to bed, Pop ...

GRANPA pushes him away sharply.

GRANPA: I was dreamin'... I heard talk ... of this farm bein' sold!

DON: You'll make yourself sick again.

GRANPA: Nobody sells this farm while I'm aroun'! You hear?

DON: Yes, we hear you.

GRANPA: I cleared an' turned every inch of it with these here hands for you an' the kids. It was given to you to farm, not to sell! You hear that?

DON: It's alright, Pop, take it easy. I'll take care of everything.

GRANPA: I lie in bed an' dream a lot ... while you're takin' care of everything. Can't sleep, can't wake up, it seems.

DON gently edges him to the bench.

DON: Sit beside me, here.

The OLD MAN obeys, as if confused.

PEARL: We'll get you a hot drink. (*to STANLEY*) Go put water on to heat for tea.

STANLEY exits.

GRANPA: I lie there an' dream the creek bed's chokin' up, water backin' up, turnin' garden into slime. I hear night owls in the sky scoopin' flies an' the yelp of coyotes comin' nearer, like a winter frost. Them yelpin' coyotes always made me feel cold inside ... they're the wilderness comin' back ...

PEARL: I heard them, too. The last time I heard them I was a small girl. I felt cold and scared inside of me.

DON: Are you warm now, Pop? Stan will bring hot tea for you.

GRANPA: I want Wanda to make an' bring it for me!

PEARL: She's not back yet.

GRANPA: Make her come back, then! That girl's got to learn how to earn her keep. No one rides free no more, not even the children. I hear her sing in her room at night, singin' in Spanish so's I can't tell if she's serenadin' a man or a mud puddle ...

DON: I've heard her, too.

GRANPA: Probably a man. Them southerners got hot blood, you know. Not much they live for that don't start where their pants is buckled!

PEARL: That's nonsense.

GRANPA: I says to her once—what's your singin' about? An' she says I heard wrong. That she don't know how to sing no more. Wonder why she said that to me?

PEARL: Here's your tea now Granpa.

STANLEY enters, teacup in hand. PEARL takes it from him and helps GRANPA take a clumsy sip. Music softly.

PEARL: That feel better?

GRANPA: Yah. I heard your dad sing once ... bet you kids don't know about that!

DON: It's not important, Pop.

GRANPA: Sure it's important, like my dream about the land you wasn't gonna sell was important. It was the day of your mother's funeral. He came home in his suit, started up the tractor an' cultivated twenty-five acres of summer fallow, right into the night he worked. An' I heard him singin' one long sad song about things that's been an' gone.

Music dies. DON moves away from him irritably.

DON: Why does that have to be brought up?

GRANPA: So you don't forget what that girl's got to learn. You're all too soft on her. Cleanin' up house, cookin' and doin' the washin's not enough. Not enough to keep her mind off the men in the songs she's singin'.

STANLEY: Maybe she was singing the same way Dad sang.

DON turns on him angrily.

DON: I don't want it discussed anymore!

GRANPA: (*shivering*) There's cold air movin' up from the creek. Too soon for that.

STANLEY: It's a warm evening, Granpa. I'll bring your medicine for you.

GRANPA: Not you! The brown-skinned girl gives it, or I'm not takin' it …

DON is startled.

DON: I've never heard such nonsense, Pop.

GRANPA: Then there's always a first time. I'm holdin' her responsible if she don't do what she's supposed to do.

Coyote cry again. GRANPA half rises to it, then sits down, wrapping his gown tightly.

GRANPA: That's the new winter comin' I won't live to see the end of!

PEARL tries to dispel the gloom which deepens on them.

PEARL: (*cheerfully*) The village in Guatemala where Ron and I spent our honeymoon last year had this cobbled and whitewashed square. In the middle of the square, an old mango tree grew, its roots pushing at the cobbles …

GRANPA: There's cold air comin' up from the creek an' the tomatoes haven't been picked. Why aren't you out there now pickin' them tomatoes, boy? You young people sit aroun', watchin' danger comin' right for your nose!

PEARL: In the afternoons we'd walk around this square, and we'd see Wanda's family doing washing in their doorway. They always smiled and waved to us …

STANLEY: I can pick them, but what'll we do with them? Wanda planted enough tomatoes to last us five years!

GRANPA: Do I have to try pickin' them myself?

PEARL: We got to know Wanda. And then one day she asked if she could return with us. She said she'd do anything to earn some money to put her younger sister through school she herself never had …

DON: (*harshly*) You weren't thinking too good when you said you would, Pearl!

GRANPA: Can't let food spoil! Keep one hand on a full sack of potatoes an' you've got it made, I say. Go bring me my jacket, boy, an' a couple of buckets!

STANLEY: I'm not a boy anymore! I'm a man! Been that a few years now! Even when the accident happened!

GRANPA stares at him, blinks, laughs with contempt, and spits on the floor. Then he turns and goes into the house.

DON: Didn't have to do that, Stan.

STANLEY: (*upset*) I'll pick his tomatoes, do anything, but he's got to …

DON: (*to PEARL*) There was nothing you could do for Wanda, with Ron in university, and you all living in a small apartment …

STANLEY: Dad!

PEARL: (*distantly*) I'm glad you took her in when I asked.

DON: What's done is done. Anyway, I've no complaints then or now.

PEARL: When she gets her papers and social insurance number, she'll be fine.

DON: Nothing to worry about there.

STANLEY: (*urgently, walking between them*) I don't want him to be angry at me all the time.

DON: Stay out of his way. A few weeks more and you'll be gone.

STANLEY: When I was small I thought he was the best granpa any kid ever had. We used to fish the creek together. He knew where the fish were, what time of day they'd bite. And when he'd go into town for groceries or spare parts, he always remembered to bring me something. Sometimes it was candies or a can of roasted nuts. Other times it was a basket of black grapes.

DON: That's right—we all owe him something. Can't forget that.

STANLEY: (*suddenly trembling*) The day of the accident, it was he told me it was alright for me to drive the car into town with Mom!

DON and PEARL are shaken by this statement.

PEARL: Oh, my God!

DON: (*harshly*) I don't ever wanna hear about that—ever! You hear?

He approaches STANLEY and glares at him, breathing hard.

STANLEY is frightened, but unable to draw back. DON reaches for his lapels, but PEARL intercedes and forces them apart.

PEARL: (*sadly*) It was nobody's fault. Just an accident. A dumb accident. Happens every day of the year to someone, somewhere …

STANLEY: Then why can't I tell about it? There was nobody I could tell I couldn't stop the car, tried to miss the pole, but the brakes caught an' turned us so we hit where she was sitting.

PEARL embraces and holds him to herself, as if he were a child.

PEARL: Don't talk … it's alright now. Relax … take a deep breath.

DON: Can I do something for him?

PEARL: Nothing.

STANLEY: From that day, I became "boy," like some hired hand. I couldn't tell what happened because nobody'd listen. I was just a boy again, pulling at everybody's sleeve.

PEARL: I know.

STANLEY: Nobody would listen to me, Pearl, not even you! I tried but couldn't tell anyone that it was my fault and that I was going to make up for it the only way I know … by coming back here after college and taking care of this place!

DON: (*shaken*) Damnit, Stan.

PEARL: Don't talk or think about it. It's impossible now. Nothing as we knew it once is possible again.

STANLEY: So what's to be done? Leave, and never come back? Like you've done—or tried to do?

DON: She came back—we're still a family. She'll keep coming back. So why talk this way?

PEARL turns to him, her expression pained.

DON: Tell him, Pearl.

PEARL: (*quietly*) Tell him what?

DON: That nothing's what we expected … whether for better or worse. Whether it's us, or Wanda.

PEARL: I'm not sure I know what you're talking about.

GRANPA enters, jacket over his dressing gown, two plastic buckets in his hands. He is agitated, staring from side to side, then into the distance.

DON: About Ron and yourself … I know. I've known for most of the year. Since the first time you came to visit by yourself. The phone call that never came … letter that never arrived.

PEARL: (*guarded*) Ron is busy at his law office. He'll call. Maybe even tonight.

She glances at DON, then looks away.

PEARL: (*softly*) It's possible he's even tried to call while we've been out here.

GRANPA: (*hoarsely*) Nobody called. Phone hasn't rung all day. Hasn't rung all week. Can't do it no more.

DON: What's wrong, Pop?

GRANPA: Can't do this … (*holds up buckets, looks at them, then drops them to the floor*) Damned heart, can't even walk down to the creek no more without runnin' short of air.

DON: Stan and I will do it later, Pop.

GRANPA: Guess you'd better …

He goes to lean on the rail.

PEARL: What Ron and I do is our own affair, Dad.

DON: I'm not blaming you, Pearl. My God, girl, I'd do anything to make it different, the way you'd want it to be. But dreams are dreams.

PEARL: Dad!

DON: Dreams are dreams, and this is Jeremiah's place where the sun comes up and the sun goes down and things keep growing and dying between the light and darkness.

PEARL: (*moves from him quickly*) Where is Wanda? What has happened to her, anybody know?

STANLEY: She'll be back. She'll be back to make supper.

GRANPA: It's past supper makin' time. Soon it'll be dark again. Days are gettin' shorter … the long night's comin' on …

PEARL: (*to DON*) What did you do to her?

DON: Nothing. We did nothing.

PEARL: (*to GRANPA*) Where is she? Did you do or say something to her?

GRANPA: (*shrugging, avoiding her*) Why should I? She got enough troubles bein' dark-skinned in a white man's world. I got nothin' to say to her, so long's she does what she's told. An' that's somethin' else now. She's singin' too much, an' thinkin' without talkin', though half of what she says I can't understand anyway …

He shuffles down the railing away from PEARL.

GRANPA: Them damned maples got to be cut out! They've gone black an' rank an' are chokin' up the creek. Can't see the creek nowhere for maples now.

PEARL: Was she treated well? Will anybody tell me?

STANLEY: Sure. As far as I know …

DON: Yeh. I saw to it she had clothes. And them napkins, like you said I should do the time you wrote it all down.

PEARL: But you gave her money for that. Men don't go buying such things for a woman.

DON: Why not?

PEARL: It's awful … it's humiliating …

DON becomes uncomfortable.

DON: I … I never thought of that. You see, with Granpa being unwell since winter Wanda had to be around him when Stan and I left the farm …

PEARL: But there were times she went into town to do things for herself. She could've done her personal shopping then!

DON: With Stan not being able to drive, it was difficult.

STANLEY: No, Sis. Wanda hasn't been in town for months.

PEARL: (*surprised*) You're kidding!

DON: I intended she should have time for herself, but one thing led to another and …

GRANPA: (*gripping the rail hard*) Why am I sick an' not getting' better? There's things I got to do!

PEARL: But she did get paid …

DON: No, Pearl. I'm sorry.

GRANPA: What in hell would she do with money anyhow? I never had any money an' I never starved.

PEARL: I'm scared to ask this—but what about immigration proceedings? We promised her help with getting landed and starting a new life for herself …

DON: (*desperately*) It was all going to be looked after, when I had the time!

GRANPA: I ask again—what's she need money for?

PEARL: (*angry*) To send something home to help a family who can't afford food, Granpa!

GRANPA: Anybody can't support himself shouldn't be! Them that wants to work don't need charity.

PEARL: I … we … promised her wages and help with legal entry into this country!

GRANPA: What about our own that's unemployed? What're we gonna do about them—send them to Guatermaller?

DON: It's my fault. I did promise her certain things and I let her down. She worked hard and deserved better …

GRANPA: Prices goin' up, money worth less every day. White men built this country an' along come the Hindus an' Mexicans to eat it up. Pretty soon we'll be sellin' our land an' houses from under us just so we can eat! Or to support them dark skins who ain't never learned to speak English proper. Never will, to my thinkin'…

PEARL: Somebody must know where Wanda went … when she's coming back!

DON: She's … not coming back, Pearl.

STANLEY: Who said so? She never said anything at breakfast this morning.

DON: Believe me, son, she's not coming back. She's gone, and that's all there is to it.

GRANPA turns to them.

GRANPA: Who's givin' me them injections I need? None of you's doin' it, no sir. That one was tryin' hard, so she was sure not to make a mistake.

DON: I'll drive you into the hospital, tonight. Tomorrow, we'll see. Don't worry, Pop. You'll be cared for.

GRANPA points angrily at DON.

GRANPA: Like everythin' else that's been cared for? Trees crowdin' the land, tomatoes rottin' in the fields, house an' barns dyin', machinery startin' to rust. Women gone an' kids hangin' to a rope that's tied to this railin'! How you gonna turn that aroun', fella?

DON shakes his head in confusion.

GRANPA: By sellin' this land? It's my land. I gave it to you to farm an' keep it lookin' green an' young!

DON: I think we should talk about that now, Pop.

GRANPA: I don't wanna hear what you've got to say. I'm goin' in to die ... or get better quick!

He stomps indoors. PEARL moves after him, but DON restrains her.

DON: Leave him be, Pearl. I know how he feels.

PEARL: What happened to Wanda?

DON: She ... didn't want to stay here anymore, I guess.

PEARL: That doesn't surprise me.

DON: (*SINGER mimes this story of WANDA*) She somehow figured out I was selling the farm. I don't know how. After you both left the house this morning to bring in the hay bales, she told me she was leaving. I explained I owed her money, but couldn't pay her until the cheque cleared the bank. I don't think she understood that. She must've felt I was delaying, had no intention of ever paying her. At first she got angry, and then went into her room. I heard her sobbing, saw her packing through the open door. Then, with her small suitcase in her hand, she walked out without saying goodbye to any one of us.

PEARL: She left on foot?

DON: On foot.

PEARL: This is worse than what happened in her own village! I'll take the truck into town and find her and bring her back.

DON: No, Pearl, don't.

PEARL: Why not? What can she do without documents?

DON: I can't handle it, honey. I can't do anything for her. Caring for the old man, doing what chores are left, it's something I've got to do by myself.

PEARL: But she's in the country illegally.

DON: She'll figure out a way—she's bright. Meet friends who are better at this than we are. I'm not a bad man. But I'm alone now. And there's things I can't change. We got to learn to care for each other first. Maybe then we can find Wanda and help her, if she still needs help.

PEARL embraces him.

DON: Is there ... is there a chance Ron will phone? Or drive out to get you?

PEARL: You know the answer to that question.

DON: I was hoping ... I was wrong.

PEARL: Nope. It's over with—kaput. But I'll be alright.

DON retreats from her, blinking back his tears. He shivers. An owl hoots and a coyote yelps.

DON: I better go in and help Granpa with his medication. There's leftovers in the fridge which you might warm up for dinner. It's not much of a meal, but we'll do better tomorrow.

PEARL: I'm not hungry.

STANLEY: Me, too ...

DON leaves. PEARL and STANLEY move to the railing. Both stare offstage. Light darkens into late evening. The SINGER begins to play music and hum gently in the background.

STANLEY: Over with ... kaput ... just like that?

PEARL: Just like that.

STANLEY: I don't believe you. A year of marriage means more than that. It's got to!

PEARL: I'm glad you feel that way.

STANLEY: Why?

PEARL: It renews confidence in myself, your not believing me.

STANLEY: I don't understand.

PEARL: You will. What about you? Has there been a girl in your life?

STANLEY: No. Not really.

PEARL: I'm surprised. And you're older than I thought. I liked the way you stopped the old man in his tracks.

STANLEY: (*laughs bitterly*) Since the accident I haven't been very mobile. I was thinking as I was listening to Dad and you that maybe I know what it feels like to be Wanda better than both of you.

PEARL: What about her? You liked her, didn't you? She was very pretty …

STANLEY: Sure I liked her. Only …

PEARL: Only what?

STANLEY: I never felt she liked us or this place … that she was just waiting for something to happen. She was always busy … helpful … cooking … washing. But if I tapped her on the shoulder, or brushed by her, she'd give me this icy stare which I never forgot.

PEARL: Poor Stan.

STANLEY: I'll get by. But what will happen to her?

PEARL: I don't know.

STANLEY: If we both went into town after supper and looked for her …

PEARL: Can't do that, Stan. There's nothing left to come back to.

Sound of a coyote yelp. Both of them draw closer to each other instinctively.

PEARL: They're coming closer again. They did that once before when I was small. That was the autumn Granma died.

STANLEY: I heard them the night before the car accident. The same way, getting nearer and nearer …

PEARL: They scared me then and they scare me now. It's like the wilderness coming to take over …

STANELY: Like a long night coming to close all the days …

PEARL: Like the wilderness coming to take over everything we once seen and knew. The paths in the fields, the garden furrows, the barns and buildings …

STANLEY: (*childishly*) Pearl! You're not gonna die, are you?

She laughs and brushes tears from her eyes. Then she pats him gently on the arm.

PEARL: Don't be silly. What made you think that?

STANLEY: I thought … the way it is between you and Ron, that maybe …

PEARL: Don't worry for me—I'll survive. And I want to apologize for treating you like a kid this past year. You're not a kid. Nobody's got a right to do that no more.

STANLEY: He might still phone …

PEARL: Don't, Stan! Please don't talk about it!

He nods. Music rises slightly. She holds out her arms to him.

PEARL: Dance with me, Stanley! I've never danced with any man I knew, not even my own brother.

STANLEY: With Ron living in the city, I thought there was lots of …

PEARL: I saw a bumper sticker which said: Hire a cripple—they're fun to watch! I'm that cripple, Stan. I was fun to watch by a bright, up-and-coming lawyer and his friends. A bit of a cow the way I got into conversations which I knew nothing about sometimes.

STANLEY: That's not fair to say that.

PEARL: The parties I didn't get invited to. Oh, things were pretty good in bed. But a young lawyer on the way up doesn't spend that much time in bed with a clumsy woman!

She laughs. They draw apart. She reaches out to him and they continue dancing.

PEARL: When Wanda came back with us she stayed in our apartment. It didn't work out … not enough privacy or room.

STANLEY: I thought that's what happened.

PEARL: I spoke to Ron about it one night. He had an answer to that right off. "Send her to live with your folks," he said. "They're country people same as her. They'll know what to do."

PEARL pulls away from STANLEY and stares down at her feet. Another coyote yelp, nearer now.

PEARL: I suddenly realized who and what I was: a nigger in my own country. Only some unusual talent would make me equal. And I'm not talented. I'm just pretty! And in a few years even that'll be gone. By which time I'd be on the way out of a marriage with a few kids he'd see he got custody of, because he's a good lawyer …

She pauses and stares at the house.

PEARL: Dad and Granpa—they think Ron is leaving me. They won't say it, but I know what they're thinking. They're wrong, you know.

STANLEY: It's okay, Sis. It doesn't matter …

She smiles quizzically at him.

PEARL: You don't understand, either.

STANLEY: Understand what?

PEARL: I'm the last thing Ron worries about. As far as he's concerned, I've just gone back to see family and will return before the end of the month. Feeling that way, I'm out of his mind until the end of the month.

STANLEY: But …

PEARL: I'm not going back to him. I've been writing a long letter every day I've been here to tell him why. But I'll never mail it. Do you know why not?

STANLEY: No.

PEARL: (*laughing, but on the verge of tears*) Because my spelling's lousy! I charmed my way through high school here. It was easy, but I never got an education. (*severely*) Stan—when you leave this farm for college, don't you ever come back! Don't ever think about what was here once …

Sounds of a coyote howl, very near now. PEARL listens intently.

STANLEY: That accident and Mom dying … I didn't know enough not to have it happen … wanted you to know that.

PEARL: (*quietly*) Don't think about it anymore. It's gone for good … like everything's gone—the living and the dying. Black maples will swallow the creek and willows will sprout and grow in the fields …

She glances towards the house.

PEARL: He'll bury Granpa and sit here on this porch watching the wilderness take back the land and his memory. Watch the barn roofs buckle and fall, with the coyotes and north wind for company. And every September, men like my Ron will come out to shoot things and talk business in the bush …

STANLEY: (*turned away from her*) An hour ago I would've felt very sad hearing you say all that. But now … I'm not sure. I'm not sure …

She takes his arm and leads him down to the lower playing area and exit.

PEARL: Come, let's find a few ripe tomatoes for a salad.

They exit on the SINGER'S song.

SINGER (*singing*)
Go bring the burying coffin 'round
Ol' Jeremiah's goin' down
Ol' Jeremiah's goin' down
To meet the darkness underground …

A musical interlude into abrupt silence.

End

LADDIE BOY

In the late 1970s Ryga was once again living for occasional periods in Vancouver, and, as the next two plays in this collection demonstrate, his work continued to take a more urban, apocalyptic turn. *Laddie Boy* is a short sketch of what Ryga called (in his introduction to the published play) "failed human beings," the inevitable consequence of living in "a decaying social order." As writer in residence at Simon Fraser University, Ryga was becoming a vocal social critic, giving a number of lectures, speeches, and readings to various groups, often sounding the alarm about the desperate need to re-examine Canadian culture closely—especially as it continued to be threatened by imported, neo-colonizing cultures. He stressed the need to study his country's history and lore, to discover those deep mythologies and preoccupations that ultimately reveal "a popularly agreed-on interpretation of who we are and how we got that way." He wanted tough, fearless writers, "raging, possessed poets and novelists," who would speak authentically, vibrantly, about the soul and stresses of the ordinary person, and roar defiance at all forms of political oppression. While this led to his eventual adaptation of Aeschylus's *Prometheus Bound*, it also steered him, in a much different way, to *Laddie Boy*.

At this time Ryga was busy writing mainly for the electronic media. One of his projects involved the creation of several scripts for the CBC-Radio series *Advocates of Danger*. His plan was to chronicle the adventures of a lone character, Dan Kubrick, moving through different areas of Canada where, in each specific locale, this man's presence, his interaction with the local people, was to catalyse authentic folk-lore, with the intention that the finished series would create a patchwork fabric of a regionalized Canadian culture. Like Duke Radomsky of *Nothing but a Man*, Dan Kubrick is a modern, post-agrarian Canadian "everyman." In the opening scene of *Laddie Boy*, he has just arrived in Halifax and finds himself, allegedly mistakenly, in jail. There he engages in banter with his cellmate, Jess, a local "rounder" (Ryga's term), and Bell, a cleaning woman. While each of these two "locals" have honest tales of their parents, their work and their dreams to tell, and both of them exhibit folk instincts for wisdom and survival, even, in Jess's singing, for celebrating life, Kubrick keeps the details of his own life hidden behind a veneer of fancy dress and a dissimulating, disarming, opportunist manner.

The play also, however, subverts the original conception of the series: in Ryga's own words, it "begins to dredge up the third-world aspects of our country." Each of the three characters, in varying ways, is portrayed as a victim of a dominant society content to marginalize too many of its members in conditions of poverty and unemployment, while too often vaunting those who have "risen to the top" by questionable means. It is Jess who most readily (and literally) slips into fully accepting the emerging criminal values of an increasingly slick, anonymous and transient Canadian society by putting on Kubrick's fancy yellow shoes, having traded his own work boots to Kubrick, who intends to use them as a disguise the next morning, hoping therewith to evade the (obviously metaphorical) community's charge of "exposing himself" against him.

Laddie Boy was first performed on the stage by Kam Theatre Lab of Thunder Bay, Ontario, in 1981. This company also staged Ryga's *Ploughmen of the Glacier* and *A Letter to My Son* in the early 1980s.

LADDIE BOY

CHARACTERS

JESS, *a middle-aged man of no visible means*
KUBRICK, *a man in his prime*
BELL, *a middle-aged cleaning woman*

SET

A prison cell: two cot beds. A hallway behind and to one side of the prison cell. JESS is seated on a cot. KUBRICK paces and rattles the bars of the cell.

JESS: Hey—laddie boy! When did you come in?

KUBRICK: Five minutes ago.

JESS: You must've flied in like a swallow. I didn't hear you.

KUBRICK: You sleep like the dead.

JESS: The dead don't sleep. The dead ... are dead. What time is it?

KUBRICK: I don't know. They took my watch away.

JESS: An' your wallet ... an' your belt ... necktie an' shoelaces. I tell you, laddie boy, a man without his shoelaces an' a necktie is helpless. Or so they think ... I'd feel undressed without me cap. Lucky for me, I always get to keep that ...

KUBRICK: Why don't you shut up?

JESS: Now, now ... that sort of talk's not sociable.

KUBRICK: I don't feel like socializing. If this was a hotel, I would have booked a private room and not had to listen to a fisherman's logic about why a cloth cap is more desirable than a wristwatch!

JESS: Jess is the name ... an' I'm not a fisherman. I'm a town boy myself.

KUBRICK: My name's Dan Kubrick. What're you in for?

JESS laughs.

JESS: I like a pint once in a while ... same's any other man. An' when I get a gullet-full, crossing a street is enough to get me in trouble.

KUBRICK: What sort of trouble?

JESS: Well boy, there was this police car parked beside a café on the waterfront. I was tired ... so I got in an' drove it home! An' what did you do, laddie boy?

KUBRICK: Nothing ...

JESS: Nothing?

KUBRICK: ... Nothing ...

JESS: Be an interesting thing to see the judge read out charges against you in the morning ... (*mocks a judicial tone of voice*) Mister Kurbick ...

KUBRICK: Kubrick's the name, goddamnit!

JESS: (*in judicial tones*) Mister Kurbick ... you are hereby charged with ... doin' nothing. How do you plead, sir—guilty, or not guilty?

KUBRICK: Let's cut the crap, Jess ... This place is awful. What do they do—hose it down with carbolic acid twice a day?

JESS: It's in the walls an' floor ... when Bell comes in to clean up she just wets it. That's when it really stinks.

KUBRICK: Yeh ... do you know the name of a good lawyer?

JESS: Nope. I don't believe in lawyers. I just takes what I get. Maybe I get thirty days for this caper ... so what? I've got nothin' to do with my time anyway.

KUBRICK: Something wrong with my feet?

JESS: Your shoes, boy ... you're wearin' yeller shoes! Well I'll be go-to-hell!

KUBRICK: And you're wearing old boots—so what?

JESS: (*sings*) ... See her comin' down the stair
Combin' back her yeller hair

See her comin' down the stair
Pretty Peggy-O ... !

KUBRICK: (*with exasperation*) Carbolic acid and a singing drunk! ... Do they feed a man in here? ... How does one get a cup of hot coffee?

JESS: Bell, she comes in to clean up later on. Otherwise, that's it for the rest of the night ... most nights of the year.

KUBRICK: And those two mattresses—is that all we get to sleep on?

JESS: Yep ... them yeller shoes ...

KUBRICK: The blanket smells of fungus!

JESS: I had an uncle who wore yeller shoes like them once. He bought them when he went to see his niece in Boston ...

KUBRICK: Jess, I'm not really interested in your uncle who went to Boston ... or, for that matter, in any other member of your family—no matter where they went!

JESS: He'd seen his niece, an' another time he went to Boston to find work. First place he applied for a job, the foreman asks him—"Are you a carpenter, boy?" "No," says my uncle, "I'm a McIntyre, sir ... Did you thought you knowed me?"

JESS laughs. KUBRICK also begins to laugh.

KUBRICK: You've had your sleep ... You've got a sackful of yarns, and I'm going to have to listen to every one of them, right?

JESS: That you will, boy ...

KUBRICK: Living with you through the night is going to be one long Nova Scotian riot, right?

JESS: Right!

KUBRICK: It's going to be one haw-haw party full of windy, long-whiskered, salty stories about lobster pots ... and dim-witted sailors at sea ... and moonshiners the Mounties never caught—right?

JESS: (*loudly, joyfully*) Right, boy!

KUBRICK: (*rattling the bars*) Oh, God! What did I do to deserve this?

JESS: (*laughing*) They look soft as a new baby's ass, them yeller shoes ... Wonder how they feel to wear?

KUBRICK: Keep wondering. These shoes stay on my feet, even if I have to stay awake all night to make sure they remain where they are!

JESS: (*sings*) See her comin' down the stair ... (*speaks*) What part of the country you come from, laddie boy?

KUBRICK: From all over.

JESS: Where's that?

KUBRICK: The rest of this country's a bit different than the east coast, you know. For example, where I come from we don't consider going two miles down the road to a country store as a major adventure in travel ...

JESS: A cheeky bugger, eh!

KUBRICK: ... In fact, I know men who've travelled as much as forty miles one week alone! How's that for an expanded vision of the world?

JESS: (*sings*) Combin' back her yeller hair ... (*speaks*) What did he pull you in for? ... Dead-eye Murphy don't make many mistakes when he provides a man with a place to sleep at government expense, you know ...

KUBRICK: Then he's made his first mistake ...

JESS: I told you how it was with me when you asked ... Now be a good laddie an' tell me what you ...

KUBRICK: If I was to tell you ... you wouldn't laugh? Or spread it around?

JESS: May lightning strike me dead if I was to think of it!

KUBRICK: (*laughing*) You lying flat-faced bastard!

JESS: It's the truth, Kurbick. I'm a man of my word. Don't trust me with nothin' else, but me word's a contract written in blood!

KUBRICK: The name's *Kubrick*! You're mis-pronouncing it on purpose to get my goat, aren't you?

JESS: Did I do that? ... I'm sorry ... Now what's the story?

KUBRICK: Indecent exposure.

JESS: (*startled*) Huh?

KUBRICK: Like I said ... indecent exposure.

JESS: (*laughing*) You ... doin' *that*? Get off it! Wait 'til Bell hears of this!

KUBRICK: I thought you swore to keep it secret!

JESS: That I did ... Then she'll never hear it from me. How'd it happen?

KUBRICK: ... I'm staying at a downtown hotel. About an hour ago I felt like the best thing for me would be a brisk walk ... a few deep breaths of your bracing Atlantic wind. I'd have done better buying the wind in a can ... I ended up admiring some flowers in front of a house. I got day-dreaming ... thinking of other flowers in other places where I've been ... Vancouver ... Holland ... a tiny park in a small town on the west coast of Mexico.

JESS: ... The dreams men get lookin' at beauty— I know! I've had them dreams myself, watching a sunset in a crimson herringbone sky ... Or a beautiful woman on the docks who's seein' a boat off to open seas ...

KUBRICK: ... Or a jet aircraft, rising like a gleaming arrow over jagged mountains! ...

JESS: ... Or a storm, dashin' white spray over glowin' rocks ... frozen as death itself on a winter shore, boy!

KUBRICK: ... Then ... your constable Dead-eye Murphy has me by the shoulders ...

JESS: His stubby fingers diggin' into your collar bone ... I know that hold!

KUBRICK: I'm propelled into his car ... my feet only touching pavement on every second step ...

JESS: Ah, yes ... Me ... with me it's a fight all the way! I keep fallin' ... holdin' back ... I make him earn his wages!

KUBRICK: And then I'm charged with indecent exposure!

JESS: (*laughs*) I've reached for myself that way, too ... on occasion, laddie boy. But I've never gone through with it ...

KUBRICK: Neither did I.

JESS: Oh ...

KUBRICK: I did nothing to provoke him or anyone else. I've been arrested only once before ... for not paying three jaywalking tickets. This time ... somebody in the house in front of which I stood saw me. Apparently there had been incidents in that neighbourhood of a man bothering people by exposing himself. He or she ... whoever it was saw me ... thought I was the same man, and Murphy was called.

JESS: No, I couldn't do it, drunk or sober ...

KUBRICK: I didn't either ... I've only been in Halifax a day and a half. I don't know anyone here.

JESS: Then why'd you come? It doesn't seem right to me a man should go where he's not known ...

KUBRICK: Said who? Your uncle who went to Boston?

JESS: I wouldn't go where nobody knows me, an' that's for damn sure.

KUBRICK: That's because you're a bumpkin ... a man who'd walk down the streets of a modern city carrying a pitchfork over his shoulder!

JESS: Jesus ... I knew a man who done that once ...

KUBRICK: (*to himself*) My God ... I'll plead guilty ... I'll plead insanity ... take a fine ... thirty days ... anything! So long's I don't have another night like this ...

JESS: ... Charlie Martingale they called him ...

KUBRICK: You don't have to tell me, Jess ...

JESS: Charlie Martingale drove to Sydney with a hay-wagon, lookin' for someone to sell him hay for his horse. He had a pitchfork on his hay wagon ... I remember it ... two prongs glowed an' the third was rusty. I wondered why ... the third one was rusty ... an' two glowed like he'd spiked hay that very morning. If he'd done that, all three prongs should've looked the same ... Hey, Kurbick ...

KUBRICK: What?

JESS: They say the devil goes huntin' for souls with a pitchfork ... You think there's somethin' in that?

KUBRICK: Jess, I think before long I'll believe anything is possible.

JESS: How about you and me swapping shoes for a bit ... come on.

KUBRICK: Go to hell ...

JESS: You had them made to fit you, I bet.

KUBRICK: Yes, Jess ... they were custom made.

JESS: Bet they fit like they was your own foot skin!

KUBRICK: They're comfortable ...

JESS: Bet they cost plenty, too ... Bet you had to work a couple months to save up enough for shoes like them ...

KUBRICK: (*mocking*) I'll tell you, and this is the truth, Jess ... When I set my heart on buying them I loaded cement blocks on a truck ... I stood in boiling tar paving streets ... I worked by moonlight washing windows in a tall building ...

JESS: (*sings and stamps his foot*)
See her comin' down the stair
Combin' back her yeller hair
See her comin' down the stair
Pretty Peggy-O ...

(*speaks*) ... You're a lyin' bastard from Ontario. An' you been here before ... all the times they seen you do it ... an' you did it again tonight when Murphy caught you! If Dead-eye Murphy took you in ... you done it, boy! He don't make no mistakes, that one ... Mind if I touch them shoes once?

KUBRICK: Screw?

JESS: Who'd you say that to?

KUBRICK: Where have you been in your life, Jess? Who do you know?

JESS: I been here. Went to Sydney once for a funeral.

KUBRICK: One day, somebody like yourself from Sydney will come here for your funeral ... and that will be it!

JESS: (*sings loudly*)
 ... If I had the wings of an angel
Over these prison walls I would fly ...

KUBRICK: (*slamming prison bars hard*) It's like talking to a flywheel!

JESS: (*sings loudly*)
 ... I'd fly to the arms of my loved one
And it's there I'd be willin' to die ...

KUBRICK: A flywheel—that's what you are, Jess! A goddamned flywheel going round and round ... propelled by cold winds off the Atlantic!

JESS: (*laughs*) The man from Ontario ... showin' it to the local people! ... The man who's got everything ... yeller shoes ... an electric razor ... wristwatch. But what does he come to show us? Not those things but somethin' else he's got! Shame on you, laddie boy!

KUBRICK: (*angrily*) You stop calling me that! I'm not a boy to you ... not by a long shot!

JESS: Well, it don't matter what you're called. You're just a number to Dead-eye Murphy ... an' the judge who'll do you in. Consider yourself lucky you're important enough to someone like me.

KUBRICK: To hell with this noise. I've got a right to a private cell if I'm to stay in here overnight! I pay taxes to keep these places going!

KUBRICK starts to shout and rattle bars of cell.

KUBRICK: (*shouting*) Hey! ... Anybody out there? Murphy! ... You come over here! ... I want to talk to you!

Sound of distant door opening and clatter of metal containers.

KUBRICK: (*surprised*) You hear that? Someone's coming!

JESS: It's only herself ...

Sound of nearby door opening and shutting.

BELL enters.

BELL: (*approaching*) Good evenin', boys. You're sure a noisy lot tonight.

JESS: Hullo, champ. It wasn't me makin' the noise. It was him.

BELL: You in here again, Jess? That's the second time in a month ...

JESS: (*laughing*) I took Murphy's car an' drove it until the gas run out! ... This here is Bell, laddie boy ...

KUBRICK: How do you do, ma'am ...

JESS: I drove it with me foot to the floor, Bell ... There's more gears than one, but I didn't know where they was I was that tanked. Took out a couple of hedges an' one front fence, so Murphy's got me up for damages this time, Bell.

BELL: It'll go hard on you this time, Jess ... an' you deserve it.

JESS: There's nothin' they can do to me. Nothing at all!

BELL: My sister cooks in a restaurant where she says she's seen Murphy havin' dinner with the judge an' his wife on Sundays. That means they're friends, Jess. He'll tell the judge how to deal with you.

JESS: (*defiantly*) Murphy can shove it! Judge can shove it, too! ... I'm not afraid. If the worst comes to the worst, I still got me brain an' two fists an' two feet. I can get out!

BELL: If they put you in for good, you'll stay in ...

JESS: (*sings defiantly*)
See her comin' down the stair
Combin' back her yeller hair
See her comin' down the stair
Pretty Peggy-O ...

KUBRICK: You haven't the brains or friends left to take you around the block on a foggy day! ... Bell, I want to see the constable in charge of this place ... Would you call him for me?

JESS: ... This one's got home-made yeller shoes Murphy took the laces away from ... an' he's in for exposin' himself near Citadel Hill! What do you think of that, Bell?

KUBRICK: Call me Murphy, or whoever's in the office!

BELL: Is that what he's in for? ... Bloody animal, isn't he?

JESS: Isn't he, though!

KUBRICK: I demand to be moved! I have that right!

BELL: Sorry, lad ... The two cells next to you have no keys. The other cells are behind that door, an' that's not been opened since the night of Ritchie Harris's weddin' ... when twenty drunks burned down Sandy McPherson's barn an' garage to the ground ... What a noise that was! Five Mountie cars were used to bring 'em in ... All night long they stamped their feet an' sang ... I thought they'd take the walls apart!

KUBRICK: You're all animals! ... I want to talk to a civilized human being ... a police officer ... court clerk ... a minister of the church!

JESS: (*laughing*) You'll be hard to take for the night if you keep this up, lad. Relax ... the government's takin' care of us ...

BELL: Governmen's takin' care of everything now ... I get five hundred a month cleanin' up this place an' that's enough to get by on ...

KUBRICK: But you've only got a job so long as him and me are in here. The government has to put men in jail so you can work!

BELL: I don't care about you ... him I worry about. He's makin' it a habit.

JESS: No need to worry about me, Bell. I'm alright ...

KUBRICK: Both of you—let me tell you something ... I earn between twenty-five and forty thousand a year. I'm not married ...

BELL: Thank God for that ... after what you done to get yourself in here!

KUBRICK: I'm in here by accident.

BELL: Huh!

KUBRICK: That's beside the point now ... what I wanted to say was that I pay a lot in taxes on my earnings. Some of my taxes go to maintaining government agencies ... road building ... for hospitals, schools and child care. Tonight, I'm in a cage—and what do I learn?

BELL: I could tell you what you should've learned!

JESS: Me, too! ... Yeller shoes with no laces! (*chuckles*)

KUBRICK: I find you, Jess ... a bum ... fed and looked after by the state.

JESS: Don't you call me a bum, sunnyboy! Or you'll get your teeth loosened by this!

BELL: An' when he's finished with you, you'll be gettin' a faceful of mop from me ... an' that's no lie! I've got two kids and a man with bad lungs to look after, so never mind yappin' off at me. Especially when I'm workin' an' you're behind bars doin' them things to women!

KUBRICK: What things? What in hell are you talking about?

BELL: I read the papers.

KUBRICK: You don't know what the hell you're talking about. Because a man's in jail doesn't mean he's guilty of anything ...

JESS begins humming "Pretty Peggy-O."

KUBRICK: (*quietly*) There's other places to clean up, Bell ... useful places, where people grow into something instead of rotting in the stench of disinfectants.

BELL clatters her equipment noisily.

BELL: (*angry*) Never mind that ... The money they're payin' me comes from the same bank!

KUBRICK: Okay, Bell ... okay. Could I have a cup of hot coffee?

BELL: I don't know ... I'm only supposed to wash this place an' get out.

KUBRICK: I'm tired and dehydrated.

JESS: I wouldn't do him no favours, Bell!

BELL: And why not? What makes you so damn smug and uppity all of a sudden?

JESS: (*laughing*) With them gangster shoes he's wearing, who knows what he might do next? ... Maybe throw hot coffee in your face, thereby blindin' you long enough to steal your keys ... I'd fight to keep him in here, so I would.

BELL: Oh, hush your face ...

JESS: ... But he'd overpower me for sure an' break out. With the doors open, there'd be nothin' for me but to leave, also ... Murphy would have your job for bringin' coffee to a prisoner, an' I'd be charged with escapin' lawful custody!

BELL: Both of you—enough ... shut up! Listenin' to you has given me a headache ...

KUBRICK: For God's sakes, woman ... it's only a coffee!

BELL: Okay ... okay ... I swear I'm losing my mind. (*loudly*) It's you, Jess! You're a disgrace to your mother, poor woman ... Why am I findin' you here at least once a month now?

JESS: Somebody's got to keep you company, Bell! There's no fish left in the sea ... woman ... We'll only live now by puttin' each other where we can make money carin' for them! The man from Ontario's right ...

BELL: I'm not listening to this crap ... I'll get your coffee.

BELL leaves. KUBRICK and JESS break into laughter.

KUBRICK: Poor woman ... You know her well, eh?

JESS: My mother an' she were just like that.

KUBRICK: Your mother's still alive?

JESS: Yes. But Bell's in better shape than her.

KUBRICK: And your father?

JESS: He's dead ... Been dead a long time now ...

KUBRICK: So's mine ...

JESS: I seen him take out to sea ... just him an' his fishin' gear. Beyond the harbour, the sea was boilin' ... great flecks of foam bein' ripped off the breakers by a high wind. She'd said that morning—don't go out there, Chuck. But he was mad ... roarin' mad 'cause only two days before a boat had capsized an' taken his best friend to the bottom.

KUBRICK: That's sad ...

JESS: ... I seen him go out there ... I was only a kid then ... I seen him hit the storm like it was the furies of hell itself. I seen the boat clean leave the water over the crest of a wave, the propeller gleamin' a moment in the sun ... then ... it fell in a trough between two waves. That's the last I seen of my old man ... the very last.

KUBRICK: You didn't go to sea yourself?

JESS: I did. But I wasn't much good at it. Too scared ... After seein' him die like that I was this high. Maybe I'd of turned out different if he'd lived ...

KUBRICK: My father also died at work. I never knew him … It happened when I was a baby …

JESS: You think it's because of that we're here together tonight?

KUBRICK: (*pacing*) It's got nothing to do with what we become, Jess!

JESS: Bell will tell you different if you ask her …

KUBRICK: I'm not about to ask Bell for her advice … We're grown men.

JESS: Your mother get mad same as mine about gettin' in trouble with police?

KUBRICK: (*irritated*) I don't get in trouble! This is the first jail I've spent a night in … and hopefully the last. I've more things to do than I have time to do them in! Man, we're here tonight, but we come from different places. We're suns and moons apart, you and I!

JESS: There was a parson here once who spoke just like that …

KUBRICK: What parson? What're you talking about?

JESS: He was smart … oh, he had brains, that one! He had one hand in your pocket, an' the other up the skirts of the widows. They caught him out … an' the last sermon he preached, everybody was there to see how he'd talk himself out of trouble. "You judge me by yourselves," he says, "But I am not of this world" … same's you just said. An' a stevedore sittin' next to me says, "If he lays his hands on Betty Jane again, I'll send him back there with a blow of me fist!"

KUBRICK: Does Bell have to go across town for a cup of coffee?

JESS: She'll be back … You want to tell me how you do it?

KUBRICK: Do what?

JESS: Make money to buy shoes like that … nice clothes.

KUBRICK: I work.

JESS: Come on, Kurbick … I'm no stool-pigeon. You can tell me. What you've done, you've done. To have yeller shoes made just for you, that's somethin' …

KUBRICK: You really take me for a gangster!

JESS: What's wrong with that? … They're comin' every day now … especially when tourists drive around in summer … takin' pictures. But the gangsters are different … They got oil on their skins … silk shirts … black glasses. Women come with them smellin' of cinnamon an' wild roses. They tip you for parkin' their cars, even if you can't drive good. They tip you for carryin' their bags. An' if you've got a boat, you've got it made. They'll hire you to take them out to sea, but they don't fish. They take pictures of the city from the harbour … like spies do in the movies …

KUBRICK: It doesn't take much to impress you … or scare the hell out of you.

JESS: … But it's the shoes they wear … soft leathers, with the toes open to the wind. No sock smell there, laddie boy … Not like in my old boots. I seen one gangster wearin' alligator slippers … an' another who didn't wear shoes at all—just straps riveted together. But what you're wearin' is the best I've seen yet …

KUBRICK: Maybe that's because I'm tougher … is that it?

JESS: I'd like to live like that, laddie boy … I tried it once.

KUBRICK: Oh.

JESS: I lifted some of Molly Hemsworth's weaving … she's blind, you know.

KUBRICK: No, I didn't know …

JESS: I sold it to a gangster for thirty yankee dollars … but Murphy got me before I saw the guy again …

Sound of BELL opening door and approaching. BELL enters carrying two coffees on an old tray.

JESS: Here she comes … pushin' poison to the helpless victims of the law!

BELL: Helpless indeed! There's the two of you, strong as plough horses … an' an old woman has to wash around you an' carry coffee for you. There's sugar there, but Murphy's drunk all the cream.

JESS: Murphy would eat a baby's pablum if it came his way for nothin' …

KUBRICK: Thank you, Bell.

BELL: Oh, it's nothin', boy. I needed the walk …

JESS: (*laughing*) How's me mother, Bell? Does she know her poor boy is sorry for what he done?

BELL: Don't you laugh at her, you worthless good-for-nothin'! You'll be laughin' one day as they carry her off to her grave because of you!

JESS: Naw ... one day someone like my buddy here will take me on as his partner. Then I'll go someplace else, Bell ... an' make good money. An' I'll send me mother things she's never had. You, too!

BELL: This one—that scares women by showin' his thing? I think you'd better stay where you're at, Jess ... Just stay where you're at, even if it's nothin' to be proud of. He's got less to be proud of than you!

KUBRICK: If ... we were to swap shoes, Jess ...

JESS: (*sings loudly*)
See her comin' down the stair
Combin' back her yeller hair
See her comin' down the stair
Pretty Peggy-O! ...

KUBRICK: I mean it. You can have my shoes, if you want them.

BELL: Don't take them, Jess! You don't want anythin' to do with that business!

KUBRICK: I'll take your boots in return, because I can't walk out of here tomorrow in my socks ...

JESS: You mean it ... for sure?

BELL: (*angry*) Jess McDonald ... don't you dare take them!

KUBRICK: Yes, I mean it ... here!

JESS: Yeller shoes of my own! ... Soft as rain, Bell ... I could walk half-way 'round the world before the soles wore out!

BELL: (*threatening*) Jess! I'll tell Murphy if you take them!

JESS: ... With shoes like them, I could walk into places I never been into! ... A high school, or a bank ... An' nobody would think I was the same Jess McDonald!

KUBRICK: Alright ... now give me your boots ...

JESS: Will you look at that! ... They fit like they was made just for me!

BELL: You're an outsider—you don't know him or what he thinks....Why did you do it, you bastard?

KUBRICK: Because ... just possibly ... he's right. Until the court convenes tomorrow morning ... this place and the three of us are all that matters. I dream of leaving ... while he dreams of yellow shoes ...

BELL: Nobody's leaving ... not any of us! Once we start this way, we're here for the rest of our lives! You're nothin' special ...

KUBRICK: (*laughs*) You're wrong, Bell. I don't think I'm here at all. This is one night when I feel I've vanished ... They've arrested someone in my place ... someone I've never met, for an offence I know nothing about ...

BELL: You're lyin'!

KUBRICK: Why should I lie? ... This is good coffee, by the way ...

BELL: Oh, but you're smug as a barn cat, you are! ... But the judge will take that grin off your face soon enough!

KUBRICK: Whatever you say. But I won't be seeing you again.

BELL: Yeh ... well, tomorrow night you'll have a different story. I got to get on with my work ...

KUBRICK: (*laughing*) I got brought in here and locked away with Jess. He can't pronounce my name ... and no matter what I tell him ... or you ... tonight's the night for a high-living gangster to pass the time with. And I'm it ... like in a tag game. So ... the only real thing left ... is my shoes. Mind you, they're good shoes ... he'll get a lot of wear out of them yet. But they're only shoes—not enough to spend the night talking about. Now I've got to get some sleep, or I'll start feeling hungry next ...

BELL: Lies! Nothin' but lies from a fast talker, Jess!

KUBRICK: Whatever you say. Goodnight, Bell ... you, too, Jess. If your cloth cap's for sale after court tomorrow, I'll give you five bucks for it! (*laughs*)

JESS: Look at them, Bell ... aren't they beauties?

BELL: You gonna wear them to sleep?

JESS: Yep. I'm wearin' them day an' night!

BELL: That does it ... You can both sleep with stinkin', dirty floors. I'm goin' home!

KUBRICK and JESS laugh over clatter of BELL removing herself and her cleaning equipment.

JESS: (*singing slowly and happily*)
... Combin' back her yeller hair
See her comin' down the stair
Pretty Peggy-O ...

Lights out slowly.

End

PROMETHEUS BOUND

As a young man Ryga developed a strong interest in Marxist ideology, not surprising for someone who grew up on the Canadian prairies in the mid-twentieth century, in an area that had seen the progressive agrarian politics of the United Farmers of Alberta, then the radical economic program of the Social Credit Party under William Aberhart. By the time he had moved to Edmonton, in the early 1950s, Ryga was reading numerous left-wing materials, whatever books and pamphlets of Marxist-Leninist writing he could find, including *New Frontiers*, the Canadian journal of left-wing opinion. For this publication he submitted poems, two of which were published, "Federico Garcia Lorca" (See *Just an Ordinary Person*) and "They Who Suffer." A stanza from the latter (published in fall, 1955) focuses on the disquieting presence of the working person in a political economy:

> But mark my words, John;
> A people bled white
> By those who own all, John,
> May awake overnight!

At the same time Ryga remained the romantic, passionately interested in recording the colour and vitality of nature, and in celebrating the life of the common people of the land—he would soon make a pilgrimage to the countryside of Scotland in search of his poetic muse, Robert Burns. For a while he actively worked for the Communist Party in Alberta, not as a theorist or political strategist but as a cultural worker organizing rallies and meetings and he was a member of the singing group, Tamarack, who performed at peace marches, ban-the-bomb demonstrations, and union rallies. By the mid-fifties, as a member of the National Federation of Labour Youth, he travelled to Europe to attend Peace Festivals sponsored by communist countries—Finland and Bulgaria. While there he invariably gravitated toward the poets and writers who were in attendance, rather than the political activists.

Prometheus Bound is George Ryga's "modern adaptation of the drama by Aeschylus," as he wrote on the manuscript he completed in November of 1978, and is in a very real way a return to his roots in a more radical politics embedded in a literary form, after the disastrous failures of the so-called "counter-culture revolutions" of the 1960s and 1970s in the Western world. The idea for this work came to him from a collaboration with Brian Richmond, who was planning to direct a play for Toronto's Open Circle Theatre, a company known for its collective approach to the creation of plays and for its radical politics—earlier successful works had dealt with issues of welfare, unemployment, and the misuse of police powers. But when its funding sources started shrinking in the late 1970s, Open Circle began to look for scripted shows. Ryga's commission, however, finally disintegrated with the Company's worsening financial problems and its subsequent sudden closure in 1982. The play, although well published—first in *Prism International* (Autumn 1981) and then by Turnstone Press (1982)—remains unperformed to this date.

Richmond and Ryga agreed that the figure of Prometheus, the legendary bringer of fire and hope to primitive mankind, was the perfect icon of the true revolutionary. Placed in a modern setting he could be used to interrogate the state of contemporary human progress—especially in left-wing countries. *Prometheus Bound* is unique in the Ryga canon in that it constitutes his specific critique of socialism. He stated: "As a Marxist, 1978 was a crucial time for me in the relationship of democracies to the various national liberation struggles—I found that expediency was displacing commitment" (Hoffman, 278–9). In short, he found that, rather that long-range, progressive development, countries that had made promising beginnings through revolution had suddenly dropped or modified their ideals in the name of immediate gains, often to the extent of becoming mere tyrannies. Ryga was mindful of recent events in Africa, where democratic governments were being overthrown in the continent's many shifting, post-independence, cold war alliances, as well as in Russia, where Leonid Brezhnev took on despotic powers by combining the roles of both Communist Party Chief with that of President, while human rights activists, such as Yuri Orlov, Anatoly Shcharansky, and Alexander Ginzburg, were being confined, like Prometheus in his cavern, to prison camps. Like these imprisoned and exiled revolutionaries, Ryga's Prometheus, to the end, remains both an unwavering ideologue and a passionate man of the people.

PROMETHEUS BOUND

CHARACTERS

PROMETHEUS, *a man*
POWER, *security agent, a man*
FORCE, *security agent, a woman*
HEPHAESTUS, *Security Director, a man.*
OCEANUS, *Admiral of the navy, a man*
FARMER, *a man*
WORKER, *a man*
IO, *a woman*
HERMES, *courier and expediter, a man*
ARGUS, *a dead man*

Notes: Re: music and songs—The melody of IO'S SONG establishes the precise beat for the drum sounds. To establish this, four or eight drum beats should be used between verses of the song at the top of the play. That beat then occurs where drums are indicated. Music of IO'S SONG is to be played on clarinet or flute where music in background is indicated. SONG OF PROMETHEUS would be better sung unaccompanied, if possible.

Drums beats in darkness.

IO'S SONG: I walk the burning streets
A lantern in my hand
And no one knows me …

Ten thousand hooded men
Have memorized my face
Yet look beyond me …

I board the screaming jets
And walk through tunnelled earth
A lonely stranger …

Now that Prometheus is bound
There's no freedom to be found
Except in danger …

Poor Prometheus is bound
There's no freedom to be found
Except in danger …

Lights up slowly. Drum beats continue.

Light up on a set which consists of two sleeping ramps rising to point in back centre stage. This suggests an emotional infinity.

Playing areas are on the ramps and in front of set. A third playing area is the nether world below the point where the ramps meet back stage centre.

The set should suggest an abandoned cavern under the earth where some military or isolated techno-logical facility had once functioned, but has since been stripped away leaving torn piping, gathering moisture and decay, burning gas fires from poorly sealed cut pipes, etc. An enormous tomb for debris and dead things of the world above.

Enter POWER and FORCE with a chained and gagged PROMETHEUS between them. PROMETHEUS is dishevelled and showing signs of fatigue and much physical punishment. They handle PROMETHEUS roughly as they escort and force him to the position of his final incarceration. They then kick the feet out from under PROMETHEUS in a graceful and cruel choreography and turn to wait at attention for HEPHAESTUS, who stumbles up to them. He is breathless and fearful.

Drum beat sounds heighten then die abruptly.

POWER: This is it.

FORCE: (*rapidly*) We've done it!

POWER: No interference—not a sign of protest from the people …

FORCE: No fanfare or debate in the press or on television …

POWER: The Deputy was captured, sentenced and delivered here in the back of a sanitation truck …

FORCE: He's come down a bit …

POWER: That he has … how much smaller he seems now.

FORCE: No more rides through the cities in open state cars. No more speeches to the people or debates in government to confuse every issue.

HEPHAESTUS: Enough! You've done your work well. I'll see you're commended to the ministry.

POWER: Shall we prepare the usual report on how the prisoner was found ... that he resisted?

HEPHAESTUS: I'll look after the paperwork. Our mission is not yet completed.

POWER: No problem with that. Now that we've got him here and no one the wiser for it, the last chore is just technical.

FORCE is suddenly agitated.

FORCE: He betrayed our homeland—sold military and security secrets—yet he lives.

HEPHAESTUS: (*sharply*) That was the decision of the tribunal. It has nothing to do with us!

FORCE: A confessed traitor deserves to die!

HEPHAESTUS: (*more sharply*) He confessed to nothing. The tribunal verdict is all we are assigned to execute—nothing less and nothing more!

FORCE: If he'd been shot trying to escape ... or trapped here by some explosion, I know our First Minister would be much happier than—

HEPHAESTUS: One more word, lieutenant, and I'll have you cited for insubordination!

She snaps to attention.

FORCE: I'm sorry, sir!

HEPHAESTUS: (*wearily*) I would've given ten years of my life to be a thousand miles from this place today ...

POWER: Are you well ... is something wrong, sir?

HEPHAESTUS: I can't release you from your manacles Prometheus—never again ... But can we get you some water?

FORCE: Sir ... the regulations forbid ...

HEPHAESTUS: Damn what the regulations say! The man is dying! (*stares at each of them*) For how long, and how many of you did it take to do this before he was brought to me?

FORCE: He ... resisted, sir.

HEPHAESTUS laughs bitterly and shakes his head.

HEPHAESTUS: As the hundreds of others over the past twenty years resisted!

POWER: Sir?

HEPHAESTUS: I have seen men with broken skulls brought before the tribunal and asked to recite confessions of treason and betrayal. Most would have difficulty remembering their names ... (*motioning to PROMETHEUS*) He knew. He even sanctioned many arrests and convictions of those who questioned the direction of our affairs ... How badly hurt do you think he is?

POWER turns away, uncertain of his answer.

POWER: He ... might as well be dead.

HEPHAESTUS: Because of injuries sustained? Or injuries to come?

POWER: Both, sir.

HEPHAESTUS: Let him rest a moment before he is administered the final tender mercies of our judicial process.

POWER: As you wish, sir.

HEPHAESTUS moves away and POWER and FORCE follow.

HEPHAESTUS: He and I ... we were both elected deputies by the people in our region. Did you know that?

POWER: No, sir. I didn't.

HEPHAESTUS: We were deputies from the same region, but beyond that, we had few similarities. He was returned time and again as a deputy, while I found and accepted work in the civil service. What a man he was! (*laughs*) Thoughts came to him like that! (*snaps his fingers*) No matter how complex the problem, he saw resolutions days before they occurred to others. But when he lost his temper—get out of the way and hide! Never saw a man could get that angry ...

POWER: Excuse me, sir. But ... are you afraid to do what must be done?

HEPHAESTUS turns and stares at him, his face saddened.

HEPHAESTUS: No. After all these years in the security service I have learned not to be afraid ... only cautious.

FORCE: I don't understand. Tell us what's to be done and we'll do it. Gladly, knowing that what we do is ...

HEPHAESTUS: Never be glad of anything you must do! Do it with as little passion as you would if you were adjusting a troublesome machine. Or preparing food for a picnic. The winds of our country change from time to time ... and when they do, those with passion this morning become victims of their passion by nightfall. Remember that, if you wish to live a long life.

POWER: You make decisions you must feel strongly about.

HEPHAESTUS: My decisions are forced on me, young man.

POWER: By our superiors—the ministry?

HEPHAESTUS: By our beloved First Minister. And others like him. A God without disciples would be a nobody.

FORCE: I don't like hearing such talk ...

HEPHAESTUS: (*unhappily*) That seems to be the majority sentiment of our times.

Turns to PROMETHEUS.

HEPHAESTUS: He was not like that.

FORCE: I'll say he wasn't. A confessed traitor.

HEPHAESTUS: Let us say there were two faces to Prometheus. What we have brought here is the condemned political leader.

FORCE: That is all there is, sir.

HEPHAESTUS: Oh, no ... there is more. There is also a man much loved and respected by the people. Else why was the trial and journey here conducted in such secrecy?

FORCE: Because ... (*uncertainly*) There might be other traitors around who would try to rescue him.

HEPHAESTUS laughs and shakes his head.

HEPHAESTUS: And to think it was I who trained you. That is some responsibility!

FORCE: Are you laughing at me, sir?

HEPHAESTUS: Would it make any difference now?

FORCE: (*confused*) I don't understand what you mean.

HEPHAESTUS: Understand this, then. (*points to PROMETHEUS, who groans with pain*) That wretch on whom you would be delighted to do legal murder was a hero, a god. Mothers named their first-born sons after him. Men followed him to the fields and through the streets to catch a word of praise from him, or some suggestion on how to do better. He criticized ... he inspired. Fine books and great pieces of music were created at his urging ...

POWER: And many were directed against the state and its lawful representatives. Eh—How many?

HEPHAESTUS: I am telling you things you should know and remember. I am not *debating* with you!

POWER: No offence ... I see your point. But ...

HEPHAESTUS: But what?

POWER: I think ... everything happened as it should've. Our government is strong now. The world is at peace. Our First Minister made that clear only last week ...

HEPHAESTUS: (*shouting angrily*) Damn what you think! Chain him to that rock—now!

Drum beats sound suddenly and continue. POWER and FORCE instantly jump at PROMETHEUS and raise him to his feet. They slam him hard against the wall. PROMETHEUS coughs and gasps. He stares at HEPHAESTUS.

HEPHAESTUS: (*furious*) Yes, it is I! I was always the silent one, yet I, too, am punished by carrying out their will! ... Damn you, anyway! Son of Themis, who never spoke without thinking—it has come to this—that I must have you chained to a rock like some wild animal. Say something—anything! Curse me ... or forgive me, I don't care ...

PROMETHEUS only stares at him, his expression frozen. HEPHAESTUS struggles for self-control and speaks more quietly.

HEPHAESTUS: Your mind will go first from thirst, hunger and loss of blood. You will begin remembering other times ... not for what they were, but for the false hope they will give you in your growing madness. And all the while, as the minutes of the endless night pass, this cavern with its flames and oozing water will erode you ... shrinking your painful eyes, bleaching your skin, bloating your flesh and intestines … turning the man of intelligence and sensitivity into a monster howling for air, sunlight and morning frost … Why do you not speak to me? Have you forgotten that I, too, was once a man of honour?

PROMETHEUS is silent. HEPHAESTUS writhes.

HEPHAESTUS: (*tortured*) There is no one alive who can save you now—don't you understand? … Of the millions of people on earth, only fifty protested outside the courtrooms during your trial. And these surrounded by militia, five hundred strong. That is why you were not condemned to death. Disarmed as you were, they could sentence you to torture in secrecy as an example to others who might find too much sympathy in your arguments for freedom and revolutionary transformation of both man and earth … We have now parted ways, old friend. Still capable of love … I think … I now have doubts about the holy destiny of people. They have shown themselves capable of selling their own dignity and the dignity of others for a pension plan, or a cool glass of milk on demand! … I speak the truth … and you must endure what I say in addition to physical pain. Our respected First Minister has decreed you be chained until death, standing on tip-toe!

PROMETHEUS laughs bitterly. FORCE and POWER advance on him, but HEPHAESTUS stops them with a motion of his hand.

HEPHAESTUS: The saddest sound I have heard today is your laughter, Prometheus.

HEPHAESTUS turns away from PROMETHEUS.

POWER: (*anxiously*) Why are we waiting for the final order, sir?

HEPHAESTUS: Because I choose to delay …

POWER: I thought our orders from the tribunal were to …

HEPHAESTUS: I know the instructions of the tribunal!

POWER: I'm sorry, sir, but …

HEPHAESTUS: But what? … I am an older man than you. We are not stringing up a horse-thief from the old American West here. Let us at least proceed at a dignified pace …

FORCE: (*urgently*) Sir—don't waste pity on him! He's hated by everyone now. They said he was an enemy of progress … a maker of wars and discontent.

HEPHAESTUS: He was once a friend.

PROMETHEUS laughs bitterly. As if on reflex, POWER jumps behind him and wrenches back his head. PROMETHEUS groans and shudders in pain.

HEPHAESTUS: (*shouts*) Leave him alone!

Drum sounds stop. FORCE and POWER release PROMETHEUS and retreat slowly. PROMETHEUS sways but remains on his feet. His shackles and bent body project both dignity and humility.

POWER: (*shaken*) I do have an obligation to report any irregularities while on duty. I'm not being disrespectful, sir, but I thought you should …

HEPHAESTUS: (*spits with contempt*) What agency of the state is responsible for you, boy?

POWER: Our First Minister was my superior in Internal Security.

HEPHAESTUS: Ah, yes … I should have known.

POWER: (*proudly*) He presented me with a medal once, sir. Pinned it here on my chest with his own hands!

HEPHAESTUS: You were rewarded for what? … Teaching small children to spy on their parents? … Demonstrating eye-gouging?

POWER: No, sir. For marksmanship!

HEPHAESTUS snarls with derision.

HEPHAESTUS: Old men and women tend the fields and orchards now, while youth shoots at things! Do you know the meaning of mercy? Or is hatred all you live for?

FORCE: I don't *hate* … He *knew* he'd get in trouble doing what he did, so he deserves what he's got coming …

POWER: It's nothing to do with me. I'm told what to do.

HEPHAESTUS: How fortunate you are.

POWER: I think I know how you feel, knowing him and all …

HEPHAESTUS: How compassionate of you! (*storming*) Your orders were to guard him in back of the vehicle. He has serious injuries which he did not have when he was turned over to me!

POWER and FORCE exchange guarded glances.

HEPHAESTUS: Do it then! I am helpless to change what is inevitable …

POWER pushes PROMETHEUS against rock wall. PROMETHEUS stumbles. FORCE takes his arm to support him while POWER puts his hands under the ribs of PROMETHEUS and turns his tortured entrails. PROMETHEUS screams in pain, moves helplessly into position. On scream HEPHAESTUS covers his ears and turns away.

POWER: That's better … now to hang this portrait!

FORCE laughs as POWER takes hammer and steel pegs from his waistband and begins to hammer the shackles of PROMETHEUS into the stone cavern wall. Seeing HEPHAESTUS turned away, he leans over and kisses the back of FORCE'S neck lasciviously, attempting to hammer without interruption. A hammer blow misses peg and hits PROMETHEUS over wrist. PROMETHEUS groans and settles as his knees buckle.

POWER: None of that! Lift him to his toes.

Hammering resumes and POWER and FORCE play a vocal game in cadence to hammer blows.

POWER: The work …

FORCE: We do …

POWER: Will hold …

FORCE: We must …

POWER: Take care …

FORCE: He has …

POWER: Been known …

FORCE: To …

POWER: Attempt …

FORCE: The …

FORCE & POWER: (*in unison*) Impossible!

HEPHAESTUS approaches and fearfully checks the binding on the arm of PROMETHEUS.

HEPHAESTUS: This clasp will last longer than the stone to which it is now anchored!

POWER: (*proudly*) That's right. Now the other arm … tightly. Look at him—how quickly all the cleverness is gone now that he's up against the power of our great First Minister of State! The *real* power of the man on top.

HEPHAESTUS: I should be grateful … that of all the things I learned in life … did not include such skills as these … You will age one day—find yourself helpless. Are you not afraid of memories that are shameful and without pity? You are a slave to what you do!

POWER: We are all slaves, then, sir. Only for the ones on top is there freedom.

HEPHAESTUS: Ah, at least we agree on that.

POWER: Shall we continue?

HEPHAESTUS seems momentarily transfixed at the gathering fate of PROMETHEUS as he looks up at him.

POWER: Sir?

HEPHAESTUS: (*startled*) Huh?

POWER: We have allotted time for this job. They will come looking for us if we take too long and it will go badly if there's a complaint!

HEPHAESTUS: We couldn't have that, could we? … Proceed. You have my order to proceed … Strange, but a moment ago I saw myself in the final seconds of my life. I was alone … abandoned, in a world I did not recognize … And he (*points to PROMETHEUS*) … he came through my door … *alive*! I was dying and he was alive, and he came to visit me.

POWER and FORCE exchange glances, then turn to PROMETHEUS.

POWER: Hold up his arm while I hammer this lock shut.

FORCE wrenches the arm of PROMETHEUS upwards with her shoulder.

FORCE: Like so?

POWER: That's it.

POWER strikes a few blows to the lock with his hammer.

HEPHAESTUS: How well your work goes. Cold steel over fevered flesh.

POWER: Help her—pull tighter!

HEPHAESTUS shudders as he touches the arms of PROMETHEUS who turns his head to watch him. He helps FORCE put the arm in place.

POWER: Against the rock ... hold it tight ... leave nothing loose. As a young revolutionary, this bastard has been known to escape where no escape was possible!

HEPHAESTUS: This same hand once initialled disarmament agreements and great production programs ... yet you call him revolutionary and bastard in the same breath. Revolutions are the mother of all civilizations—have you forgotten that in the heat of this ... this undertaking?

POWER delivers a few more blows of his hammer to the chaining device, steps back to survey his work with satisfaction. FORCE and HEPHAESTUS step back from PROMETHEUS.

POWER: Now the other arm. I think he understands now what a fool he was to contradict the wisdom of our beloved First Minister!

Fastens other arm.

HEPHAESTUS: I wish now I had been illiterate in politics and the arts of government.

POWER takes a small glittering dagger out of a compartment on his belt and treats it carefully with a chemical. Then with a quick, strong motion he stabs at the upper part of PROMETHEUS' stomach. PROMETHEUS shouts with pain and rattles the chains securing his arms. POWER steps back and wipes his dagger. Blood covers the stomach of PROMETHEUS.

POWER: (*a bit unsteady*) That's one procedure I don't care for. It's reserved for the most stubborn ones.

HEPHAESTUS: What is it?

POWER: It's called the Tongue of Jupiter ...

POWER: Blade is made of special alloy for this ... coated with chemicals which burn like fire, yet won't kill or let him faint. I don't care for it myself, but the lab in my unit is sure proud of this one.

POWER replaces dagger. HEPHAESTUS moves into shadows and retches. POWER turns on him angrily.

POWER: I said I didn't care for it! What more's there to say? ... It might even help him to die

quicker ... or bring out the sewer rats for the blood, which will be the same thing ...

HEPHAESTUS: What in hell are you saying?

POWER: Would you like to run out to the waiting truck and take off? Because this was once your friend? To me he's an enemy of the state and the people. Just remember that, or you might end up joining him here!

HEPHAESTUS: Don't you speak to me that way! We are dealing in horror now, not just politics!

POWER: I was never a Deputy so I know nothing about that, and I couldn't care less. I receive convicts and do what I'm told ... more even, so there's no complaints from anyone. To me he's just an uppity convict who lost out ... Now for the belt around his waist ... Here, pull!

He offers HEPHAESTUS one end of heavy belt which he carries over the mid-section of the writhing PROMETHEUS. HEPHAESTUS does not obey. FORCE steps forward.

FORCE: I'll help ...

POWER: Not you. (*coldly*) He helps!

HEPHAESTUS: Do it yourselves. I do not take orders from you.

POWER stares cruelly at HEPHAESTUS, then laughs sarcastically.

POWER: I have orders to take over in this place. Which means I get help when I ask for it. If not, I write out a report on what went wrong and why— I put an "urgent" sticker on it and it goes right up to the top in the agency ... You want that to happen, sir? ... Lock his legs with this!

With contempt, he throws a leg iron and chain towards HEPHAESTUS, who slowly picks it up, examines it, and clasps it on legs of PROMETHEUS.

POWER: Tighter! Lock them tighter!

Reluctantly HEPHAESTUS obeys.

POWER: I've never had a prisoner escape—did you know that?

HEPHAESTUS stares at him icily.

POWER: I've never had a prisoner escape because I know my job ... same's her. I do my job well. I was trained that way. 'Persist, but don't rush,' said our instructor in intelligence work.

FORCE: He also said, 'If you apply some imagination you can break the spirit.'

HEPHAESTUS: Imagination? What is imaginative about cruelty?

POWER: (*mocking him*) What a soft heart! ... How have you managed to survive to your age in this world? And in the security service of all places! Is this how you earned your big home in the country? Your servants? A staff car? Your pension benefits?

HEPHAESTUS: Enough!

POWER: It's not enough! (*sneering*) You're an aging whore with loose teeth, old man, sir!

PROMETHEUS laughs. HEPHAESTUS clenches his fists in fury, then turns away from his tormentors. POWER lunges at PROMETHEUS and strikes him across the face. FORCE jumps close behind POWER, as in a combat reflex, her hands clenching and unclenching.

POWER: Even now ... here ... he is still insolent! (*to HEPHAESTUS*) In the back of the garbage truck ... on the way here ... he sang ... wouldn't stop singing. So we worked him over a bit. I said I'd kill him if he didn't stop. He turned to me and you know what he said? ... He said that he could never die ... that he ... was beyond death!

HEPHAESTUS stares at PROMETHEUS and moves away in horror.

HEPHAESTUS: Oh, my god!

POWER: (*to PROMETHEUS*) But we've got you for bats and sewer rats to take apart! The tribunal called you Prometheus the contriver and the world spits on you! ... So contrive all you want— nobody knows where you are and nobody cares. Not now ... Not ever again! Make trouble and you get trouble!

PROMETHEUS tugs violently at his constraints. They hum and clatter. POWER laughs, then turns away and, taking FORCE by her arm, both exit in a military goose-step. HEPHAESTUS lingers, his hand over his eyes. PROMETHEUS groans and HEPHAESTUS shudders.

Drum beats.

PROMETHEUS: (*singing*)
Oh, winds from the icy mountains
And river waters enslaved by hills

Before the final roar of freedom
In the ocean waves—Oh, sweet earth
Beneath the ageless sun who sees
The sum total of all suffering.

HEPHAESTUS turns and exits at a run.

PROMETHEUS: (*raging in cadence to drums*)
See me and the tortures I am
Condemned to endure by those
Profiteers and false commissars
Who rose as flotsam to the top
Addressing each other by first name
Exchanging cars, suits and advice
On conquest of the earth and stars—
Who hears me now, entombed in the bowels
Of this raging planet? And from
What corner of the heavens
Shall deliverance come?

Not from peaceful deliberations
Shall the great changes come—
Not now—even were I blind
There would be no mistaking
The howling torment of the future
Built on betrayals of the past—
Built on rivers of spilled revolutionary blood,
These new perversions of the ageless game
Continue, and honest men cannot be silent
When human dignity is spat upon
And the very mention of a peoples' destiny
Is blasphemous unless it is
Officially approved ...

Over drum sounds, distant rumble of heavy traffic or disturbance above the cavern. One of the flames from broken pipe flares high momentarily, then dies back.

PROMETHEUS: In dark caves and secret places
I have, from the authority of high office,
Helped maintain the sacred flame of honour
And ongoing struggle for perfectibility
And resurrection of the human will
Against tired men grown old too soon
And burdened with their comforts
And fearsome acquisitions ...
Foremost among these is he
Who rose to the highest pinnacle
Of power on the yearnings
Of the people, only to betray
The masses with false fear
Of war and hunger—and the terrors
Of a long winter without heat—

He thus conspired to blunt and dull
The rightful wishes of the earth's poor
For bread, land and freedom.
Such decaying leaders fortify each other
And in time the rich grow richer
Than entire nations
While the poor—more numerous now—
Fade into a gray landscape of despair
Without voice or hope—all calls
For action now quickly savaged
With contempt, prison, long years
Of exile from events and family ...
The profile of slavery is this:
Deny protein to a man and feed him sugars.
Then withdraw these slowly—what remains
Is now a slave without mind or motivation;
A sluggard sitting by the roadside
Staring with unseeing eyes at wars, pillage,
Dismemberment of his own household
Which leave him unperturbed, untouched
In a dreamy world only troubled
By chill-spasms when the blood cries for
And is denied—more sugar!
What horror do I see in this
Reflection of the human spirit?
What horror do I hear?
The beat of dripping wings, the sigh
Of cavern winds, blowing from the deepest,
Darkest, most cold and melancholy
Depths of earth beneath the sea ...

Drum sounds stop abruptly. FARMER and WORKER enter, dressed in cave-explorers' apparel.

WORKER: The sounds came from here ... Look!

He lights the body and face of PROMETHEUS with a flashlight.

FARMER: It's Prometheus, the Deputy! Who in hell has done this!

PROMETHEUS: Go away! I have no patience
For killers and torturers
Sent into the bowels of this earth
To bury the mistakes of savages
Who've seized the helm of government!

FARMER: We knew nothing of this. There were rumours you'd been detained, and then nothing more.

WORKER: A great man of the people—and then this! Why? Who did it? ... We'll release you and treat your wounds, Prometheus.

PROMETHEUS: The sharpest chisels in the world could not cut me free now—go away!

FARMER: You were our second in command once ... I remember how good it felt to hear debates on every street corner about questions long suppressed in the interest of national security ...

PROMETHEUS: Why is it that every traitor
Hides first in the shadows
Of national security?
(*suspiciously*)
But you have come to gloat and taunt me!
You have come on his orders ... I know
The ruse!

PROMETHEUS struggles helplessly in his chains, then subsides.

FARMER: What orders? Had we taken another turn in the cave network back there, we'd never have found you here. Prometheus, is it true, this rumour of violence you planned against the state?

PROMETHEUS: Not the state ... but against
A certain military unit I had once
Voted to create as special protection
For key people in the government ...
But they exist! Foolishly, I created them and
Encouraged friends of good will to man them.
This
Cavern was their first research facility ...
Now, their guns and spies are turned on simple people
Who might have a question or a doubt
About where this new order and its leader
Plan to take this gentle land
And all who love it.

FARMER: I understand your anger and your pain, Prometheus. I understand. Somehow your love and care for all of us was subverted by enemies of the country, though how I'll never understand.

PROMETHEUS: Enough! I'll hear no more of this!
Sooner would I wither on this rock
Or be flung from one spearing outcrop
To the next in blind darkness
By a massive earthquake, or freeze
In dark winds which issue from some frozen
River under earth, than listen one more time
To such perjury!

WORKER: We are not perjurers, Prometheus. The laws we have made are the laws by which we live.

PROMETHEUS: They have become laws
Of vengeance and oppression!

FARMER: Your torment is a sad thing to accept.
And even if we don't speak about it, we suspect
the First Minister of State has overstepped his
limits a bit in recent times. And that is a sad thing
to accept.

PROMETHEUS: Overstepped his limits, you say?
He has gained a clawhold on an empire for it!
But that is not enough—not for him.
I saw him driven by fear
To sniff at the quality of love professed
For him—searching for doubt,
Mistrust—scribblings on the washroom walls—
Sensing plots to rob him of honour and his throne.
First, I am befriended by a heavy-breathing
Host of petty-thieves turned body-guards
For weekend visits to secluded villas
For urgent consultations on matters
Pertaining to the state.
These turned out nothing but excuses
For moody drinking and excessive eating—
I criticize, but keep my anger to myself.
Then I am threatened
For having knowledge of plots being devised
From the outside world.
I am charged in secret, tried and convicted
To this torture, which has stabbed his back
As well as mine, with fear of darker times
To come ...

WORKER: There is gossip now of a woman close
to you and the First Minister ... that a personal
argument has somehow become political. Is this
true?

*PROMETHEUS turns away from them, his face
tortured.*

FARMER: Is it true, Prometheus? The people will
forgive you if they know the truth ... I've served
my time in the armed forces ... I know second-
hand the horrors of torture and pain. What
they've done to you is more than that, and I'm not
afraid to speak about it to my friends and to
organizations of people. But your return will be
slow, acceptance of your blame and forgiveness
will take time.

WORKER: What he says is true. At this moment,
no land on earth would give you refuge and no
god forgive you until your good name is cleared.
I'm sorry, Prometheus, but that's the way it is ...

PROMETHEUS: The plotting of my personal
destruction
Has been more thorough than I thought ...

WORKER: Yes. And it's not helped by your defiance.

PROMETHEUS: (*anxious*)
Yet he, and those who planned it so
Are few in numbers—they fill a modest room!
Their ships at sea, aircraft in the sky,
Rocketry and chemistry of war
Makes nations tremble at their word
Or angry glance of eye—
They fill a modest room
These power brokers of the universe,
Small men obsessed with assurances
Of honours, medals minted in their names,
Finer food and clothing than their peers—
Mention of their prowess
On the holy days of state—
How fearful is their pride!

FARMER: Yet you were one of them—and until this
moment you were silent. Maybe it's too late ...

PROMETHEUS: I erred, but it's not too late.
For he, who is now First Minister
Must in time bow to the same adversities
Which overcome us all.
In times to come
I see him in my inner eye
Approach me, imploring friendship
And forgiveness ...

WORKER: If that happens, what will you do?

PROMETHEUS: I was tried and convicted of
subversion
On orders of the man whom I nominated
For the highest office in our land,
Of this early error I am guilty.
When our previous leader died
There was much discord and hostile nations
Fostered various factions of the masses into conflict
So they might at an opportune time intervene
In our affairs in the name of peace
And dismember our achievements and our wealth
For their own profit.

WORKER: We live with that threat ...

PROMETHEUS: Knowing this, and sensing factions
Even in our armed forces
I counselled as best I knew,
Coaxing the timid, holding back the headstrong,

Passing up great talents in politics
In favour of the weak—
All in the interests of internal peace ...

FARMER: For which the people thank you.

PROMETHEUS: Our present First Minister
Was a compromise in which I saw
Good merit and much to recommend him,
And so the new tyrant was awakened
From his fitful sleep—
It is not for this that I oppose him,
But for his brutal insolence
And his choice of council
From the dregs of criminality,
Futile, ineffectual beings,
Which began the process of creating
A strange new human in our midst—
Noisy adventurers, shouters of slogans,
Small minds viewing all the problems of commerce,
Culture and international affairs
Through the narrow window
Of a lowland village barn ...
For this I am condemned to lingering death,
The antidote to freedom!

WORKER: In the army and among the people, you are the symbol of the revolution, the living legacy of a better life to come. How sad to see this ending.

PROMETHEUS: (angry)
Return to your work, then!
I ask for soldiers, not pall-bearers ...
I will not be pitied!

FARMER: When I was a child, my father taught me that life conquers death, that light conquers darkness. That neither slavery nor despair are natural to living people. When I asked him how he knew this, he said Prometheus told him it was so.

PROMETHEUS: (struggling against his shackles)
Return to your work, I say!
I demand action, not blind hope!

WORKER: You're the only hope we have. We cannot turn against you, no matter what you've done. You gave fire to the spirit of us all.

PROMETHEUS: The same fire imprisons me now.
It was workers like yourself,
Who, without protest or question
Made the alloy for these chains I wear ...
Which a thousand others wore before me!

FARMER: Surely you knew of this ... did you protest? What were we to do, who knew nothing?

PROMETHEUS is startled by the question.

PROMETHEUS: Do the people still believe
In the resurrection of the spirit?

WORKER: Peasants, soldiers, workers in the mills ... they are still the same people you worked and moved among when you had time for us.

PROMETHEUS: And what have they learned?

WORKER: I don't understand.

PROMETHEUS: Where were the voices of the people
When these outrageous trials were held
With public charges and secret testimony?
Even nations who regard us
With contempt and hatred
For igniting skulls and human tallow
With new hope in a dying world
Regard such happenings with sorrow—
Such grief means nothing to me.
The indifference of my countrymen
Is the greatest torture I have yet endured.

WORKER and FARMER turn away in shame.

WORKER: We were afraid ... what can I say?

PROMETHEUS: Afraid? (snarling)
It was a grovelling act of shame
That lacked even the dignity of death-fear
Which I had trained you once
To overcome!

FARMER: I once thought I was a man of purpose, but not now. How long ago it seems that we all marched behind you, hungry, yet so happy in knowing we were changing history. We felt we'd never die so long as Prometheus was our leader. Now this god is chained ... a slave to the very thing we bled to save and give life to!

WORKER: If we said you'd asked forgiveness ...

PROMETHEUS: (sadly)
Thirst and pain plays havoc
With the mind ... I see before me now
Gentle fields and sloping valleys of my childhood
Where as a country boy I pondered
On the free flight of swallows
In the summer sky ...
How simple in such circumstance
To scold those tormented with adversity ...

WORKER: I suggested it because I worry for you.

PROMETHEUS: In the fever of reshaping destiny
I ignored this time, this place,
And the possibility I might occupy
The chains of others
Whose names and faces
Were unknown and of no concern
To me ... so return to work, friends,
And think of troubled days to come.
Have compassion but not pity for me.
No apologies or compromises
I once sanctioned ...
The years ahead are times of struggle
And remorse—such is our lot.

FARMER: There's little hope for my lifetime if
what you say is true, Prometheus.

WORKER: Is it you, or we, who are being crucified? (*with anger*) Tell us! I want to know what's
beyond this short life racing by me!

*A roar and shriek of some machine grows louder
and stops. The ADMIRAL enters. There is a flash of
white flame and a dying sputter. He turns in the
direction from which he has entered, a confused,
worried expression on his face. ADMIRAL sees
FARMER and WORKER, and becomes agitated.*

ADMIRAL: What in hell are you doing here? This
place is off limits to civilians—how'd you get in?
Never mind—get out or I'll have my pilot slam
you into cages so small they'll bend you four ways
to fit you in! Out!

WORKER and FARMER retreat and exit.

*ADMIRAL glances at PROMETHEUS and does a
bizarre and unexpected little dance, which might be
motivated by need for exercise or nervousness.*

ADMIRAL: Ah, Prometheus ...

PROMETHEUS: (*mocking*) Ah, Admiral!

ADMIRAL: I've come to see you ... come on this
new machine which travels under water, on land
and in the air as smooth as a limousine! You made
it happen, sir ... others have forgotten, but not
me, that it was you who said "without technology
we'll walk on one leg, like cripples!" Smart, very
smart!

PROMETHEUS coughs uncomfortably.

ADMIRAL: I heard about the mess you're in at the
Chiefs of Staff meeting. Twisted some arms to
find out where you were ...

PROMETHEUS: What for?

ADMIRAL: We've been friends a long time ...
knew each other as cadets—wasn't that where it
started?

PROMETHEUS: Such things escape my mind ...

ADMIRAL: This is bad business, Prometheus ...
and don't take that to mean I sympathize with
you. Not bloody likely. I'll speak to you simply, as
a common man ... because my eyes hear, my
ears can see.

*ADMIRAL hesitates, realizing it is not correct.
PROMETHEUS laughs.*

PROMETHEUS: As cadets, all of us surpassed you
In examinations for training of cadres
To which you responded—
"I don't think. I do."
It now seems your life has been
A vindication of this credo.

*ADMIRAL is puzzled by the barb he cannot locate.
Offstage machine flares and sputters again. It dis-
tracts the ADMIRAL.*

ADMIRAL: Why in hell can't he keep his hands off
the controls? I told him to park it and wait ...
Where was I?

PROMETHEUS: Heaven only knows ...

ADMIRAL: Oh yes, I speak simply and don't flatter, yet this uniform carries weight when it matters. (*startled by his own poetic eloquence*) How
was I going to put it? ... Our beloved First
Minister and I are just like that! (*holds up his hand
with two crossed fingers*)

PROMETHEUS: Which one of you is on top?

ADMIRAL: He's on top ... it's his right.

PROMETHEUS laughs.

ADMIRAL: If you want me to speak to him for you,
you just give the word. I don't turn my back on a
friend. Others might, but not this fella!

PROMETHEUS: What is this I look upon?
In your polyester uniform, tailored
To disguise the curses of advancing age—
Fat jowled, driven by machines of war

Like some primordial, dim-witted god!

ADMIRAL: Now you just hold on a minute!

PROMETHEUS stares at him, an expression of amazement on his face.

PROMETHEUS: You've a remarkable talent for the obvious.

ADMIRAL: What you think is not my business. I'd never agree with anything you say—officially. As far as I'm concerned, you're a traitor and deserve to rot here. Unofficially, you keep a watch on your tongue and I'll work to arrange another hearing for you to get out of this … this cesspool.

PROMETHEUS: (*hesitant, moved*)
I marvel at you,
Indeed I do … that you have known me
Yet kept your distance in the public eye—
A true soldier.
I advise you to remain that way.
Your petition for a new hearing
Might jeopardize the safety
You've enjoyed so long.

ADMIRAL: Appreciate that … always have, you know. I'm not the fool you think. I've got a common man's cunning. Our navy has sobered the leaders of more productive countries than ours. So my word goes a long way even with the likes of our First Minister. He may laugh behind my back at the way I look and speak … I know he does … but he's never sure which command I'll disregard. I'll be heard, be sure of that, and your freedom will come, give or take some time.

PROMETHEUS: Be careful, Admiral.

ADMIRAL: You be careful. War is my profession.

PROMETHEUS: If you knew as do I the other agencies of state
Who prowl by night, spying on those
Who labour for the common good—compiling dossiers,
Forcing dismissals, setting fires to hard-earned
Personal possessions—creating accidents on lonely roads,
Arranging disappearances
All for reasons nobody recalls—but our new tyrant
Knows the power of these forces
For he rose to power through them.

ADMIRAL: It strikes me strange that here you're at war, while I, the warrior, look for ways to end such violence … What you say and do in these times is dangerous for all of us. I hope things will cool down a bit when you're free again.

PROMETHEUS: There is not the remotest hope for that!

ADMIRAL: Prometheus—think before you speak! The land and people are so tired now. What's happened to the simple truth we had as youth? Was it not enough? Since the revolution we've been torn by schisms, which you helped create, I think. We've been preoccupied by real and imagined traitors. I understand and appreciate all you've done for technology and culture, but where's our joy gone?

PROMETHEUS: The joy is in the struggle!
The destination is infinite!
If you don't understand this
Then you've wasted your time
Seeing me!

ADMIRAL: (*angry*) You are chained like an animal that bites, Prometheus! Listen to what I say—I'm not a dog barking at the wind!

PROMETHEUS: You came with sorrow
And I give you bitterness.
That is not much of an exchange.

ADMIRAL: It's not my love or hatred for you that's keeping you hanging on the wall of a cave, goddammit! … It's something else which I don't understand.

PROMETHEUS: Then obey orders from those who do
If a natural death means anything to you.
What else can I say?

ADMIRAL: I guess … there's no more to be said.

PROMETHEUS: It was good of you to come.
Hearing what you think
Reassures me.

ADMIRAL: I wish times were happier … I'm going back in a machine that rides on air and water so smoothly I can sleep when I travel. I'll think of you … here … I wish the times were happier …

ADMIRAL departs quickly. Offstage, his machine roars to life. Sound recedes on his departure. Enter

FARMER and WORKER, passing before and around PROMETHEUS in a choreography of grief. They chant.

FARMER: He's been taken to hang below the earth, his flesh a damp banner—his eyes, a raging storm. And I, simple man of the earth and sun, weep helplessly for him—at the might and wealth these hands have helped to build.

WORKER: From Tehran to Buenos Aires, Washington to Vladivostok, the earth cries and shudders for Prometheus, friend of life and liberator of the spirit. Tyranny, once conquered, now sprouts like some rank weed …

FARMER: These hands have planted food. And helped build the instruments of war from which I cringe. Those who make a mockery of me exult in war—their gunbarrels placed and aimed in swamps, on oceans and among the stars …

WORKER: Soldiers! Think before you shoot! Listen to the groan of him who struggled to relieve you of the burden of warfare.

FARMER: Bent in toil on my fields side by side with my wife, who holds up half the heavens, he shares my suffering and I his, but here we differ. My concern is for an acre of this earth while his is for the black void of the universe …

WORKER: Earth, sky and dark places underneath the sea are struggling with his pain … Still his deepest anguish is the silence of the people forced to swallow half an argument. Give us ammunition for your defense, Prometheus!

PROMETHEUS: It is not because of insolence or pride
I kept my peace—I could have called
For protests and cries of outrage
Were it not for the guilt I carry.

WORKER: What guilt?

PROMETHEUS: It was my persuasion which swayed votes
In favour of the new tyrant, who,
In his first days in office
Dared rewrite the constitution.
I did not age growing older
But willingly accepted, too willingly,
The fast solutions of my youth
To complex problems centuries in the making.
Like the hunter, having killed something

I felt better. I did not
Become a pall-bearer to the past; instead,
I flung myself headlong into problems
Of the reconstruction.
Not all that fell was dead—some bodies
Healed and rose again, donned the dress
And manners of the revolution and proceeded
To exchange barnyard security of slaves
Against the chilly promise of a freedom
Only dimly understood …
To exchange death for life—
Ignorance for reason—prisons for debate …
To exchange dead gods
For unimaginative but living men …
Too much credence did I place
On human progress.

WORKER: What you say is true … Many changes shook our lives. At first, everything was debated in the streets and at places where the people worked. But with the passing years we were only told what had been decided by our leaders. Your name appeared on some of these directives.

PROMETHEUS: Yes.

WORKER: Truth, in which we took such pride once, became a matter of who spoke first. Debate became an unfamiliar language known only to a few. News of scandal was like a hidden bait. The morals of people we once worshipped were clouded—to this day there is a whisper of some woman you betrayed.

PROMETHEUS: Leave her out of this!
She will not be used
To shadow more serious
Matters which affect us all!

WORKER: I believe in you, will obey you. But I must know what's expected of me, and if I've failed in reaching expectations you had for me …

PROMETHEUS struggles with discomfort.

PROMETHEUS: Forgive me, but I've heard such sentiments
Before when it served their needs!

WORKER and FARMER step back, shocked.

PROMETHEUS: How much of the duplicity of which you speak
Did you willingly accept?
Did you really understand my undertaking

In creating love for learning?
My concerns for deep studies of medicine
And science to liberate simple people
From their fears of pain and insecurity
And harnessing their fascination
With mysteries of heavens
And the earth below their feet?

FARMER: Look at you ... a god among men,
dressed in rags, homeless ...

PROMETHEUS: My freedom is some years away
But I shall be delivered from this bondage.
As for other things ...

WORKER: (*interrupting*) Delivered by whom?

PROMETHEUS: By necessity. The men
Who welded chains
About my wrists feel
They have inherited a world
Where all can go into the deepest
Sleep. That machines will run machines,
To manufacture arms, shirts
And predigested foods,
With indifference to the raging storms
Brewing in the cosmos.

WORKER: Are these storms you speak of greater
than those envisioned by our present leaders?

PROMETHEUS: For a time he will rule
Guarded by armed forces,
The new constitution
And the silence of workers
Who confuse liberty with a well-stocked
Department store.
(*smiles*) Even as we speak this way
The earth has turned and aged.

WORKER: You know you can trust us. If there's
something we should know or do ...

PROMETHEUS: I will not speak of the time
Or conditions of release
From my outrage and humiliation.
The cage our First Minister
Forged for me
Will in time close around him.
Arguments he employed for my condemnation
Will return like ravens
Clawing at his face.

FARMER: (*angry*) I'm a worker in the fields,
producing food for philosophers, bootmakers,
miners, children, thieves, sailors and all others.
I'm a peaceful man, giving thanks to whatever

guards my health and the health of fields I
cultivate ...

WORKER: And I, a worker, thank heaven for my
right to labour, for my children and my precious
leisure. Yet I return to this place with danger to
myself, for the long, damp night of your fall,
Prometheus, is a turning point in my own fortune. I'm afraid of mighty men who rise from
troubled times ...

PROMETHEUS: What is there to fear now?

WORKER: Your faith in the final wisdom of
ordinary people. Men and women who fought
alongside of you ... many of these would now
turn against you out of fear.

PROMETHEUS: You lie!

FARMER: What courage have I, or my friends,
against the machines and power built in my name
and honour, and now turned against me? I'm
weak, blinded by my private dreams of peace.
Why do you not let me rest, even if my serenity is
an illusion for a short while?

*IO enters, her movements distracted, confused, as
she searches for a way out of the cavern. ARGUS
also enters and follows her woodenly, his face that
of a dead man. He makes notes of her activities.
When she draws near him, he becomes agitated,
excited. But she is conscious of this reaction, and
paces her movements away from him. ARGUS is visible only to IO.*

WORKER: Or me? ... You are dying, and a part of
me dies with you. I followed you to life. I did not
ask for death!

PROMETHEUS turns away from them.

WORKER: (*angry, disturbed*) Don't turn from me.
I left my place of work to dance with my wife and
children at your wedding!

*PROMETHEUS strains at his shackles, a moan of
pain rising from his lips.*

IO: (*in pleading tones*)
Who can tell me where I am?
What people live here
In this bat-infested, steaming cavern?
Why is this man chained like some beast?
What crimes are possible
For such a monstrous punishment?
Or is this a vision of my own
Final hours of my life?

Tell me, someone!

WORKER and FARMER turn away from her.
PROMETHEUS is torn between recognition and dis-
may. She turns to each of them, pleading.

IO: (*pointing to ARGUS*)
A dead spy
Working for God alone knows
What state or economic power
Has driven me across this earth and back!
He's dead ... I know he's dead
For with this hand
I killed him ... Twice shot him
Through the heart—him,
Who made of me a whore ...
Begged and paid me to haunt
Bedrooms of the world's powerful men,
Trading lust for information
On movements of commerce, secret research
And the private fears of statesmen.
I killed him, but the earth
Expelled his body, and now
He pursues me night and day
As does the banishment
By the leader of this country
Who forgives nothing ...
I wish to die, yet cannot.
I wish to sleep, but dare not
Close my eyes for fear his icy hands
Will brush my face, my breasts ...

She stares at PROMETHEUS, but does not recognize
him.

IO: I cannot see you for my tears
And the rank shadows of this place ...
Yet I sense a god in pain
Greater than my own.

PROMETHEUS is agitated.

PROMETHEUS: (*softly*)
Io ... it has come to this
For you?

A rumble of an earthquake. Burning lights flare
and sputter. IO screams and turns. ARGUS grabs
her and laughs mirthlessly as he tries to lock his
body against hers. She tears away and tries to hide
behind WORKER and FARMER, but ARGUS blocks
her escape. PROMETHEUS struggles against his
chains in rage.

IO: You know me? No one knows me now!

PROMETHEUS: How can I forget? ... I would
remember you
Even when all else had left my mind!

IO: No one knows me
Except torturers and paid assassins
Who at intervals place my body
On their racks, then fling it
To the far horizon in a speeding
Car or train, to be thrown
On brutal pavement of deserted roads
Or down the slopes of jagged hillsides
Where I choke and cry with pain—
I cannot die, I rise again.

She points to ARGUS and whimpers.

PROMETHEUS: It is I ... Prometheus.

She refuses to believe him. Backs away from him.

IO: No! ... Prometheus is at the capital
Absorbed in work which moves the earth,
I must not think of him ...
My mind is dying ... I've tried
Not to think of him ... it is
Seven years since I last saw him ...
I must not ...

FARMER: This is Prometheus, Io. This is
Prometheus in front of us, hanging from steel
pegs like some broken animal!

IO: No! When we were
Together, his health
Ignited all about him—his spirit
Was like some overflowing field
Rich with warm and splendid things!

PROMETHEUS: Those days and nights are gone,
Io.

She approaches him in growing recognition and
horror.

IO: You? Here? ... This way?

PROMETHEUS nods, unable to meet her gaze.

IO: Dearest Prometheus, who reduced you
To such wretchedness?

PROMETHEUS: It was done on command of our
illustrious
Head of state—executed by the blacksmith
Of the secret service—Hephaestus.
(*laughs*) In some previous life
Those two might have been farriers

In a smithy!

IO comes up to PROMETHEUS, and rising on tip-toe brushes his cheeks with her hands.

IO: Neither you nor I can die
Of pain or punishments!

PROMETHEUS: I wish you had been spared all this.

IO: I did not leave you, Prometheus—
I waited for you ... am prepared to wait
For all eternity ...
For what crimes are you so punished?

PROMETHEUS: My answer would change nothing.
Let us speak of other things.

IO: I did not plan this meeting.
I was travelling blindly, as I do,
Through nights and days, following
Dark lanes and tunnels in the earth.

WORKER: A good woman deserves pity for such torment ... but *her*? She was once your wife, Prometheus. And now she's branded as a whore and spy by all the nations! She has no allegiance to a man or place on earth ... What is to be done with someone like her?

IO: (*clutching her head*) No!

FARMER comes to her side and supports her.)

FARMER: We've seen too many easy condemnations. I'd like to hear her story.

PROMETHEUS struggles with anguish in his chains.

PROMETHEUS: I've denied such rumours
Knowing how easy it is to condemn
Yet you left me, Io.

IO: I did what I did out of love for you!

PROMETHEUS: Let them be your judges, for these men
Are brothers to us both.
Nothing is lost on such jurors,
Innocence will still draw
Tears in this icy desert
Of the soul!

The melody of IO'S theme song is heard being whistled in background.

IO: I did not leave you, Prometheus.
I only left the home we shared

And which I could not bear alone.
I tried to find you, but each hour and day
Made the distance to you greater.
Seldom did I see you after
The first whisperings of morning.

PROMETHEUS: It was only temporary.

IO: It was years, Prometheus!
Agonizing years of loneliness.
I was young ... green as meadowlands
Where my father tended cattle
White as first snows of winter.
When you walked the street of our village
Urging agricultural reform
You were a god to me—glowing
As the first light of day.
Honeybees crowded for your breath
And wild birds, dazzled by your eyes
And smile, dove above you like squadrons
Of love-dazed airborne guards
Protecting you not wisely
But with deepest love.
We met, and in my father's house
You stayed for dinner of the sweetest bread,
Red meat and wine from vineyards
Of the village ...

IO turns to FARMER and WORKER

We were comrades and lovers, he and I,
Wandering by day into remotest valleys,
Convincing the dubious, organizing
The distrustful into enthusiastic bands
Of men reborn!
By night we shared what crumbs we had
And lay side by side, his wondrous aura
Covering us with warmth ...

She turns away and sobs. FARMER and WORKER comfort her. She continues, but avoids looking at the tortured face of PROMETHEUS.

IO: The revolutionary council summoned him
To the troubled northern regions ... he left,
And I, crazed by his love, lonely,
Devoured by his touch and kiss, waited.
For three years I lived for his letters
And news of him from travelling emissaries,
Then went in search of him—
In search of him, to the deepest reaches
Of hell itself I went!
My face, glowing with the passions
Which I carried in me, excited
Battalions of men—saints and demons

Both ran beside me, panting their desires,
Lavishing their gifts at me—
Inviting betrayal.
The goat stench of men in heat
Was forever on the breeze
Which blew my way …

Points to ARGUS.

IO: (*in rage*)
He, the devil incarnate
Reached me with the most monstrous
Promise of them all! He promised me
Prometheus again, and I,
The country fool, believed him.

She hesitates, confused, as she stares at the grinning ARGUS.

FARMER: What happened then, child?

IO: What followed, the very rivers of the earth
Will never wash away—the degradation
Of the harlot, denunciation by my father
And my sister—
The sweaty labourings o'er my body
Of the man who at this moment
Commands all power in this nation.
(*with a self-condemning cry*)
Yes, even him! And when I fled
He unleashed the full fury
Of his vengeance with a roar,
"Prometheus a better man than I?
Heaven and hell together
Will not save him now!"
Argus, whom I killed
Was resurrected from his grave
To haunt me, and the whips of all states
Were bared to lash my back and buttocks
As I passed, until welcome madness
Numbed me.

She whimpers and withdraws like a child under the protective arm of the FARMER. PROMETHEUS throws his head in fury. Slowly, he subsides and looks down at her, his expression one of remorse.

PROMETHEUS: The village of your birth, in twilight
Was like burnished bronze.
Warm light rising from scant earth
And shadows like dark cloaks
Followed lowing cattle homeward bound.

IO: On such hours of the dying days
I gathered eggs for you.

PROMETHEUS: In times to come
Roads and rivers shall
Be named for you …

IO: Nightly I waited for you
In my father's garden
Crickets chirping in the trees
Children's laughter and music
Filling lanes and doorways
Each night I waited for you.

PROMETHEUS: But you are well? You hear my voice?

She laughs suddenly and dances away from FARMER and WORKER.

IO: Oh, this is the happiest of all times!
The changing of the seasons
Takes my breath away, and all the …

PROMETHEUS: (*forcefully*)
Say no more!
"This is the happiest of all times," she says,
Then turns away from me
As if startled by some sound
Or sudden stab of pain …

She hears him and retreats toward FARMER and WORKER, as if for shelter from what may follow.

IO: (*fearfully*)
Tell me it is not true!
That I have gone blind and see
Strange images in the mirror
Of the inner eye …
It is a dream and nothing more—
He is a great man still
Changing history, and not chained
In some damp, decaying cave
Like a savage beast!

PROMETHEUS: Speak no more
Of children's play times
Or flowers
In the wakening fields
When your mind and mine
Is still aglow
From the flaming shelter
Of the last April moon
We shared
In another world
Ten thousand miles
From this place …
Let us speak instead
Of how very, very civil

It is to meet this way
As strangers selling land
Or enquiring for the park
Without touch
Or unexpected joy …
Say no more
Of things we knew as children
In another life.
Let us speak instead
Of the passing of the days and hours
And sacrifices of the soul.

IO is stung and touched by what he says. She moves to him, past ARGUS, whom she now pushes aside.

IO: I would not have wished it this way,
Not for you—not for myself.

FARMER: It's sad to hear such words from her.

PROMETHEUS: You are given to quick sorrow, friend!

FARMER: *(stung)* How can you not feel pity for her here where the very stones weep for us all?

PROMETHEUS: I no longer have patience for submission!

IO: I would not have wished it this way …
Many days I dreamed of a simple life
Of few possessions, quiet thoughts
And hours filled with labour for others
And ourselves.
Letting others guide affairs of state
Even though they might be
Lesser men and women.

PROMETHEUS: Such is the doleful hymn of slavery!

IO: If so, what is this to me?
I have lost my honour and the man I loved.
Rather than live this lingering anguish
It would be better now to end my life.
If I could only find some way to escape.

ARGUS applauds silently. PROMETHEUS glowers at her.

PROMETHEUS: If our love meant anything
It means promise of my freedom, surely,
And an end to tyranny!

IO: You seem to think our First Minister
Will fall from power, Prometheus.

PROMETHEUS: If he does, will you rejoice?

IO: I, too, was abused by him
And denied peace and refuge.

PROMETHEUS: Then it shall happen!

IO: Who will remove power from his hands?
You? Hanging like a moist, torn
Banner from these rocks?

PROMETHEUS: The forces for his overthrow are planted
And in place. They merely wait
For the command to strike.

IO is confused. Turns to WORKER, who stares at PROMETHEUS.

IO: Will there be more years
Of hunger and upheaval?
Armies marching through my father's village—
Hillsides scorched by fire and neglect?

WORKER: Are you advising us to take up arms against those who've now risen from the revolution? Is this the only road for us?

PROMETHEUS: Weapons are the language of the hopeless.
From time to time the legacy of conflict
Must be resurrected
On more than the holidays of state.

WORKER: Arms or no arms? I don't understand.

PROMETHEUS: Arms and skillful knowledge of their use
Are arguments against small-natured
Architects of destiny—
Alert yourselves!
Redefine the tender love
Which knits you to the cosmos
And each other. Pass the banner
Of our struggle to her, she is worthy.
Do so in my name
And I shall be released!

WORKER hesitantly reaches into his shirt and takes out a rolled banner which he gives to IO. She unfolds it, then bends over it, shuddering. ARGUS retreats fearfully from her into shadows, buttoning up his tunic and brushing back his hair as if his personal appearance had to measure up to some standard.

IO: For the infamy and humiliation,
For the scorched harvests
Of my father's fields and life—

For the love of a god-man
Whose words and touch seared
This brain and heart to joy,
All scores shall now be settled!
Weak and frightened though I am
It is better to die
The mother of a hero-people
Than languish in my private pain
And lost illusions
For all that might have been.

She exits. ARGUS attempts to follow, then exits by a separate route. Drum beats sound, distant and ominous.

WORKER: I'm afraid of this wedding of the spirit, Prometheus. Once again I think I hear a trumpet calling for my blood to fuel the engines of history.

FARMER: I'm also afraid.

PROMETHEUS: More blemished is he
Who betrayed her and now hangs
Suspended from this painful wall—
The gods of the labouring poor
Are as scarred and tarnished, friend
As the street harlot
Or the thief stealing
Medications for his illness—
Like tormentors and murderers
Seeking salvation in the blood of others
Our gods are blemished,
As they grope upwards, eyes averted,
To the frozen slopes
Of their own redemption.

Drum beats sound louder, nearer.

PROMETHEUS: (*roaring*)
Think not of yourselves
And your puny dreams of warm hearth
And chirping, milk soured grandchildren
To lighten the heaviness of age!
Think of the burning skull
Nestled on the cruel road to paradise!

FARMER and WORKER reel under his denunciation.

PROMETHEUS: Think of the all-avenging god
His hands and garments bloodied,
His eyes grey and fierce as March gales
On lashing waters of the Atlantic.
Think of bracing gaunt bodies for battle
And the right to rule as you rise,
New men and women,
From the countless dead!

Think of surrender to the whip
And the harsh judgement of the weak
Who make it their affair
To learn the mastery of government!
Prepare yourselves!

FARMER: I'm afraid of something more. Perhaps the judgement of Prometheus is coloured by the personal harm he has suffered. I say this with respect, but still I must know, when does personal tragedy become the concern of everyone?

PROMETHEUS: No tyrant attacks an entire people.
He selects and isolates his enemies
One by one.

WORKER: You're not afraid of what may happen to you? To all of us?

PROMETHEUS: No.

FARMER: If I must resist, I will. But I'd like more time to weigh what is fact and what is rumour.

PROMETHEUS: (*sarcastically*)
It is rumoured I am chained
In an abandoned cavern.

Sound of drums stops. PROMETHEUS listens, turns his head and peers into side tunnel.

PROMETHEUS: I hear footsteps
Which have walked every hallway
In the corridors of power.
It is Hermes, the expediter,
Himself a holder of no office,
Yet able to enter unannounced
The dwellings of generals
And heads of states.
A man who, for a fee,
Will assume any face
Or point of view.
Today he must be
A lackey of our leader
Who comes to recite some new infamy
To the detriment
Of what health I have …

HERMES enters. Ignores FARMER and WORKER. Marches directly to PROMETHEUS.

HERMES: Good evening, Prometheus.

PROMETHEUS: Good morning, Hermes.
It is morning.

HERMES: (*checking his watch*)
It's evening. I watched the sunset

Before I came here.

PROMETHEUS: Counting the seconds
By my pulse, and adding these
To make the hours of the day
I swear it's morning!

*HERMES checks his watch again, listens to it.
PROMETHEUS laughs. HERMES turns angry.*

HERMES: I'm not here to be made a fool of!
The crimes you've committed
Make you no equal of mine!

PROMETHEUS: Can't you see I'm praying?

HERMES is flustered and retreats a step.

HERMES: I'm sorry. It wasn't my intention to …

PROMETHEUS: I'm praying for hangnails, warts
And slow death by cancer
For you and your masters!

HERMES: You cannot afford insolence now,
Prometheus!

PROMETHEUS: I'm happy to be told so …
I felt something had gone wrong.

HERMES: Our beloved First Minister's secretary
Sends a message for you.
Some provisions can be made
To facilitate your return to service
In some minor post yet to be determined.
Mind you, there will be conditions
With this offer.

PROMETHEUS: Take your message and insert it
…

HERMES: *(angry)* I'm not here to exchange
insults with you!

HERMES: Your anger comes from stress and
paranoia.
There are drugs for that …
If you should need these, I'd be happy
To arrange for such.

PROMETHEUS: What drugs have you for the
hatred
Which I feel at the sight of you?

HERMES: I don't understand …

PROMETHEUS: Time will teach you all you need
to know. Go away!

HERMES: You treat me as if my visit here
Meant nothing … as if I were a simple child

Who wandered in by chance.

PROMETHEUS roars with rage. HERMES is shaken.

PROMETHEUS: Do you not understand—
Do they not know there is no pain
Or torture which will bow my head
Before such scum as sent you here
With options for this village hoodlum?
They can bomb this place,
Poison every breath of air I breathe,
Infect me with disease
I will not betray the events
Which will destroy
This betrayal of our peoples' trust!

HERMES: You had a reputation for some wisdom
once.

PROMETHEUS: You will not live long enough
To make an assessment as to who I am!

HERMES: *(pleading)*
Think for a moment!
There's no need for stubbornness
You've lost—accept it
And take the best deal
That is offered …

PROMETHEUS: You're losing time with me,
Hermes.
Pilferers and thieves
Are waiting for your service
In the capital.

*WORKER and FARMER laugh. HERMES turns spite-
fully on them.*

HERMES: This is a private meeting!
An audience is not permitted!

*FARMER and WORKER stop laughing and face him
without moving. He attempts to push them away,
but his hands are struck aside. He is pained and
shocked.*

PROMETHEUS: This is the outer rim of hell
On which you stand, Hermes—such displays
Of petty power are a waste of time.
I will accept freedom—nothing less.
Go now—tell them what I said …

HERMES: My message … has another clause—
Should you reject the offer I have brought
Then instructions shall go out
To attack this cavern with fire and explosives.
When you are blinded, deafened, your flesh
Locked in the teeth of crazed rats,

The airforce will commence an operation
To reduce everything above and below
This cavern to smouldering rubble.
Nothing will be left of you.
Consider your decision.
I will wait a moment longer
And no more.

He consults his watch again. WORKER and FARMER are shaken.

WORKER: They plan to attack … to bury you! Prometheus … spare yourself … A dead martyr is not as useful to us as a living man who can lead us through this time!

PROMETHEUS stares at them. Music of IO'S SONG is heard playing for one stanza. PROMETHEUS tears at his chains and chants.

PROMETHEUS: He will not destroy me!
All his weaponry and rockets
May pulverize the earth—
May create great firestorms
Into which entire cities
Are sucked. An inferno …
May boil the oceans
So that mighty tidal waves reach
Beyond the driven clouds
And fall back moaning to a bruised
And aching world …
Still, he will not destroy me!
Even though he vaporize my body
And spread its atoms through the cosmos
The will to struggle
For a human order on this earth
Lives on! … In the final song
Of victory my name lives on!

HERMES: (*coldly to WORKER and FARMER*)
These are delirious cries you hear
Of a once fine mind unhinged,
Driven to betrayal by some disease
Or paranoia of which we have no knowledge—
Dreaming as he does of danger
And persecution
Which never did exist.

WORKER: Who then inflicted this horror that we see?

HERMES: His subversion—and your own.

WORKER and FARMER stare at HERMES with contempt and disbelief. Another verse of music from IO'S SONG is heard.

PROMETHEUS: I dreamed … I was hung and left to rot
On a rock in a cold, abandoned cavern …
What bastards has our revolution spawned!

HERMES motions WORKER and FARMER to leave.

HERMES: There is nothing you can do to help him.
The manner of his life and death
Are entirely of his choosing.
Let us leave, quickly,
For now the ear-shattering thunder comes
Which will destroy us all
Should we remain.

FARMER: Go by yourself, and tell them who sent you never to sleep again, for I am unpredictable. I did not leave as they planned I should … I chose to share his suffering, as he suffers for me. Only real traitors are afraid to die before superior arms!

HERMES: (*to WORKER*)
And you? Surely your skills
And discipline will not allow
For such ridiculous decisions?

WORKER: I'll stay with him. Tell them whom we elected to kill us, that they've wandered into a desert where a bitter harvest waits for them. Tell them to beware of every living thing which flies, moves or grows from the earth, for it now waits in ambush for them.

PROMETHEUS: No! … Go with him! You serve nothing
By remaining here!

WORKER: But Prometheus …

PROMETHEUS: In victory or opposition
I am still your leader!
I command you to leave
And take your place
In the new revolution!

The attack begins. HERMES flees. Booming thunder and lightning split the cavern wall to which PROMETHEUS is chained. His body is stretched sideways and a wind whips his clothes and hair. One arm chain breaks and PROMETHEUS, half-released, hangs shouting at FARMER and WORKER.

PROMETHEUS: Go!

FARMER and WORKER retreat from him and exit.
Another attack, and lights flare and die so that
PROMETHEUS is in silhouette, half kneeling, his arms
stretched upwards to remaining wrist shackle. Music
of IO'S SONG is heard over battle noises, which turn to
drum beats as background to his final speech.

PROMETHEUS: (*almost fearfully*)
They mean to terrify,
Such is their last bastion
Of contempt for all that once
Was decent and time-hallowed …

Another explosion, releasing debris over him.

PROMETHEUS: … They plan once more
To crush this earth,
Burn all the splendid books,
Silence songs of passion and of freedom—
Break the backs of upright men and women,
And look with pride on burning flesh
… I am afraid!
And tearful that my mind
May waver, and my voice
Cry surrender …
Help me, mother earth!
Help me, winds from the cooling
Restless sea!
Bring water to my lips,
Mother—for the flames
Reaching down towards me
Are more fearful
Than what god might wish us
To endure …

Another booming blast and flash of light. Scream of
PROMETHEUS over sound. Into sudden darkness
and silence.

End

A LETTER TO MY SON

A Letter to My Son marks a different, more personal return by George Ryga, this time to his cultural roots in Athabasca. It is a memory play about an aging patriarch, a loving portrait of a prairie homesteader in his declining days. Long past working his farm, Old Lepa has nonetheless lost nothing of his passion for the land and honest toil as he recalls his youth in the Ukraine, his jobs in Canada as an immigrant labourer, even a troubled situation within his own family. These are vital sources of identity and pride for him—he fulminates against those he deems timid or compromising, even as he works to settle accounts and seek reconciliation, particularly with his son, Stefan. In the end he achieves this—happily by finally receiving recognition from a government that literally believed him dead: he gets his pension. And in his concluding speech Lepa at last begins to find the right words for a letter to his son: "A man wants to be remembered for the good things he made possible … not the stupid things, but the good things." The play is completely focused on Ivan Lepa: it is presented entirely from his viewpoint (it was first titled simply *Lepa*) on a simple stage with only the barest suggestion of a kitchen, the people in his memory drifting in and out while his innermost feelings, some energizing, some troubling, emerge with each recollection. Overall, the structure is assured and the spirit is bright; *A Letter to My Son* is one of Ryga's most successful and warmest works.

The work began as a teleplay for CTV's *Newcomers* series and was aired in November, 1978, and Ryga was nominated for an ACTRA award for best dramatic writer for the series. The purpose of the series was to dramatize the experiences of ordinary persons who had experienced migration. For his subject material Ryga turned to his own family: the figure of Old Lepa is based on his father who was living nearby in Summerland at the time, and in the character of Stefan it is not difficult to read something of the playwright's own relationship with his immigrant father. The degree of undeniable autobiography which shapes the play, however, must be seen more in general terms than in its particular details. Despite his obvious familiarity with the subject matter, it was a play Ryga took a long time to write. In interviews he has stated that he believed he had only lately achieved the necessary distance ("you should be more than forty years of age") to write such a personal piece and that he had written the play positively, in the "brightness of day." Perhaps Ryga's most touching moment of personal satisfaction with his work came when the two of them, father and son, sat down to watch the broadcast: "My father wept through the whole evening. He recognized himself—I hadn't disguised it that well."

The creation of *A Letter to My Son* was an energizing experience, and Ryga returned to the script several times; indeed, it has enjoyed fairly wide publication. He rewrote it as a short story titled "A Visit from the Pension Lady," for publication in McClelland and Stewart's anthology, *The Newcomers: Inhabiting a New Land*, published in 1979. Two years later a German translation of *A Letter to My Son* was broadcast on South German Radio, for which it received an award from the German Academy of Performing Arts. The play appeared onstage in the fall of 1980, performed by Kam Theatre Lab of Thunder Bay, Ontario, celebrating the ninetieth anniversary of Ukrainian settlement in Canada. It was also published, along with photos of the Kam Theatre Lab production, in the journal *Canadian Theatre Review* 33 (Winter 1982) and by Turnstone Press in 1984, paired with *A Portrait of Angelica*.

A LETTER TO MY SON

CHARACTERS

OLD LEPA
STEFAN, *his son*
NANCY, *a social worker*
MARINA, *Old Lepa's sister*
DMITRO, *Marina's husband*

Doubles for the FANATIC, *ghost of* HANYA *and other incidental cameos*

SET

Interior of a farm kitchen.

A table, two chairs, overhead electric light. Some suggestion of cupboards and hanging cooking utensils in background. All this is only suggested, with isolations only of items necessary to the normal functioning of the old man. There are to be no specific mechanical visuals in this set. It must be a room as viewed through the eyes of its elderly, widowed, lonely occupant. He only sees what is useful and essential to him, all else flows out of focus. It has been many years since fine touches of another presence—or even his own expression of self through choice of paint, artifacts, design of kitchen furnishings—have mattered all that much to him.

The staging could be on two levels: the lower front level where most action in the play takes place, and a slightly elevated level to the rear where he encounters his memories in fading and indistinct surroundings. Should he have to move to this area to encounter his past, his frailty and thwarted optimism may be heightened in having to cope with the rise in levels.

NANCY, whose relationship with him is immediate and ongoing, would have her entrances and exits directly into his kitchen area. The others would enter only as indicated for extensions of memory.

ACT 1

The play opens on OLD LEPA at the table, seated. He is labouriously composing a letter in a scribbler, such as the ones used by school children as exercise books. Under musical opening, he labours for a long while over a phrase, then erases it. Tries again, ponders what he has written thus far, or is about to write.

MUSIC: Strains of a lively Ukrainian folk dance which segues into opening bars of "Solidarity Forever." On a head shake of discontent from OLD LEPA, music abruptly changes to portion of "O Canada" which segues into "Land of Hope and Glory" but abruptly cuts to opening bars of Soviet national anthem. OLD LEPA slaps scribbler on table and music cuts to "God Save the Queen," which almost immediately segues into "The Internationale"—cross-fading out into "Battle Hymn of the Republic" and lively folk dance at opening, with the folk dance music taking dominance and then dying out.

Sounds of crickets and distant dogs barking—sounds which continue in background of play, only to fade out as indicated.

OLD LEPA: (*to himself*) Dear Stefan: How is everything with you? I hope good. I wrote you the time I went to the doctor with my back. They know nothing ... the doctors ... so they found nothing wrong with me that time. If nothing is wrong, then how come it hurts so much? If they *found* something wrong, would it hurt even more? I tell you, Stefan, conversing with a man of learning these days is talking to the deaf. Whatever they know, they keep to themselves. Not like some others ... and I hope you will forgive me for saying so. I am writing this letter to say I am not happy with you ...

OLD LEPA stares at the letter he has written. He sighs and drops it on the table with exasperation.

That is a wrong way to begin—it is neither one thing nor another! Why is it when I write a letter, I am making a wallet out of wood? Lepa, you have lived a long time, but you have learned nothing ... not a damned thing. What way is this to write a letter to your son, eh? Don't dance around and hem and haw like a coward—say it! My son is an educated man and would laugh at this foolishness. You haven't started to tell him, and already half the page is used up. What has the doctor got to do with now and what happened?

He sits glumly staring at the scribbler, oblivious to the sounds of his fields and outside world.

OLD LEPA: (*beginning to write again*) Dear Stefan ... ach! What am I doing? The words fall like stones on the paper.

He pushes the scribbler away and drops the pencil on the table. Sits brooding.

I should tell him maybe how the fields look in the setting sun ... black trees holding up the sky, and between them and me, all them fields of yellow wheat glowing in a holy fire! Yeh ... tell him that, and then give him shit!

NANCY enters into perimeter of set, an overstuffed attache case in her hand.

NANCY: Mister Lepa?

OLD LEPA: She came by today ... in her little car that makes a tink, tink sound under the hood when she parks it in my front yard near the lilac bush ... and she walks to where I'm standing... looking at the fields.

Sound of outside world dies on remembered conversation with NANCY.

NANCY: Mister Lepa?

OLD LEPA: Yah?

NANCY: (*smiling*) Mister Lepa?

OLD LEPA: (*impatiently*) Yah? What is it?

NANCY: Mister Lepa—you've died.

Light dies on NANCY. Bird and barking dog sounds return in background. OLD LEPA rises and pours himself a hot drink.

OLD LEPA: That happened ... when? Yesterday? A year ago? ... It don't make no difference. She came that first time ... briefcase in her hand with "Government of Canada" written on it ... to tell me that I've died! And I think to myself—the government of Canada comes to an old man's farm in a small Japanese car to tell him that good news. I think some more, and I begin to laugh.

(*OLD LEPA chuckles at the memory*) If I was the government of Canada, I would at least listen for a heartbeat before I pronounced a man dead!

Sad musical bridge—an old mournful Ukrainian folk melody which fades slowly. OLD LEPA settles at the table with his mug and wipes his eyes with the sleeve of his shirt. He moves scribbler and pencil to himself and begins to write.

OLD LEPA: If only words were like feelings—free and simple as the rain and wind, how well would I write what I wish to say! But this ... this is the labour of the damned! I think words come easy for my Stefan. He is an educated man ... my Stefan. He speaks well ... now if only he knew more.

STEFAN: (*entering in memory*) I think you should leave this farm, Father. I can find you an apartment in town, with someone to come in and ...

OLD LEPA: (*writing furiously*) Words come easy for my son ... it's the thoughts that are difficult for him!

STEFAN: (*impatiently*) There's nothing for you here! There never was, you know. Look—you've sold the land, so why hang on to this house and garden? Where are your neighbours now? In town—in apartments and rest homes!

OLD LEPA: (*still writing, but glaring into distance*) My boy always had a way with words—especially when saying stupid things! There—I've said it, and I feel better already!

He sits back, momentarily content. But remorse quickly settles in.

Why am I like this—saying such things? I am old enough to have a pension. But I got no pension. It's time maybe to shut my mouth and not say everything that comes into my head. But ... I can't help myself. They bring it out of me.

He shakes his head in wonder at his follies and reaches uncertainly for his drink.

They bring it out of me—my sister, Marina ... and her Dmitro. The ones who did good. The ones the Angliki call "them good Ukrainians" ... I am sixty-five years old that day. An old man, no? (*sounds of outdoor world abruptly stop*) I'm cleaning the chicken coop ... pushing the wheelbarrow and putting manure in the garden. Stefan had sent me chocolates by mail the day before—

why, I'll never know. I still got my own teeth, but eating chocolates—even one small piece—makes them hurt now. I hear Dmitro and Marina's car drive up. And without looking, I know she doesn't like the smell of my yard. I know she will crinkle her nose in disgust, and I know she will say …

MARINA enters in periphery of upper level of stage, her arms out in a stylized and insincere greeting. And still in a stylized motion, she pinches her nose in disgust.

MARINA: Dear brother … Phew! What a stench!

OLD LEPA: (*laughing*) God provides so few opportunities to sing for her … but this is one that fell into my lap, so to speak …

OLD LEPA hits the table rhythmically with his drinking mug and sings lustily.

OLD LEPA: (*sings to melody of "Bringing in the Sheaves"*)
Bringing in the shit …
Bringing in the shit—
We shall come rejoicing
Bringing in the shit!

DMITRO enters and stops beside her, breathless with rushing to get there. MARINA winces and glances disapprovingly at her husband. Then she reaches with her arms to OLD LEPA again.

MARINA: Happy birthday, my brother! (*grinning, OLD LEPA half-acknowledges the greeting with a motion of his hand*) May Almighty God in his wisdom give you many more years of good health!

OLD LEPA: You asking him, or telling him, Marusha? Sometimes it's hard to know the difference with you.

MARINA: I *ask* God for mercy!

OLD LEPA: That's good to know.

MARINA: (*persisting*) I am a devout woman, Ivan. I pray whenever I have time …

OLD LEPA: So I hear. What about you, Dmitro? What do you think of all this praying business?

DMITRO withdraws into background so as to be scarcely visible.

DMITRO: It's like Marina says …

OLD LEPA: Never mind what Marina says! She speaks to … and often *for* … God, I think. Surely, she doesn't speak for you as well!

DMITRO chuckles nervously and awkwardly turns his hat in his hands.

DMITRO: You know how it is.

OLD LEPA turns to stare at him.

DMITRO: (*speaking quickly, eyes averted*) And so … how does it feel to reach the age of retirement, Ivan?

MARINA: Yes … how does it feel?

OLD LEPA turns away from them, brooding and distressed.

OLD LEPA: (*to himself*) My brother-in-law and my sister—when I think the worst of them I think the devil wore his way through a pair of boots finding them for one another—the clothing merchant and his wife. Dmitro speaks like a man, and he thinks. But all important questions about how he lives and thinks … are answered by Marina. She speaks for both of them … and when she has time, she speaks to God! But God must forgive me for such thoughts … these are good people. I owe them everything. To my death, I will owe them … for they raised my Stefan after Hanya died.

MARINA and DMITRO carry on a wordless conversation with him, which he ignores as he loses this memory. They retreat from him and vanish in gloom at far edge of stage. Sounds of outdoors are heard again. NANCY enters and pauses. He does not see her. She clears her throat. He ignores her. He begins writing his letter again, but her presence is distracting to him even though he refuses to acknowledge her. She is aware of this.

NANCY: What a beautiful day out there! …

OLD LEPA: (*grouchy*) How come they don't send a man to tell me?

NANCY: Tell you what?

OLD LEPA: About what you said the last time?

She laughs and takes a seat. That act of forwardness upsets him, for he did not invite her to sit.

Suppose I had glue on that chair—or fresh paint?

NANCY: (*startled, checks chair*) But there's no paint or glue.

OLD LEPA: (*with exasperation*) What's the matter? They afraid to send a man to talk to a man? Now I get the women! I dream when I'm sick my pall-bearers will be six women.

NANCY peers at him and reaches for his hand, which he draws away. She is upset.

NANCY: Oh, come now …

OLD LEPA: (*to himself*) Ivan, Ivan … why do you do this? She is doing what she is paid to do. You can live without this … you are an old man now … friends all gone … A pension would be good to have …

NANCY: I'm … I'm sorry.

OLD LEPA: (*angrily*) The goddamned pension—it didn't come!

NANCY: No. There have been problems.

OLD LEPA: Problems? What is—*problems*? When I was a young man and didn't do my job right, I had problems! Alright—I'm sixty-five years old, and I still got no problems. So give me my old man's pension!

NANCY is humiliated and angry now.

NANCY: I don't carry pensions in my pocket like sticks of chewing gum, sir! If I did, you'd have it.

OLD LEPA is taken aback by her anger. He stares blankly at her, his hands nervously tapping the table.

OLD LEPA: (*softly*) You don't have to shout. My ears still work.

NANCY: I wasn't shouting.

OLD LEPA: (*still softly*) Sure you were, but that's alright.

NANCY: I wasn't …

OLD LEPA: That's alright.

OLD LEPA: (*to himself*) I look her up and down. She's not dumb, not this one. Not very respectful to an old man, but not dumb. She opens her briefcase and takes out an old newspaper …

As if on cue, NANCY does exactly what OLD LEPA describes.

NANCY: Here … read this.

OLD LEPA: She hands it to me. My glasses are someplace in the cupboard with the spoons and knives. Even if I had them on my nose, I don't know how to read English too good from such small print.

NANCY: Here.

OLD LEPA: What does it say?

NANCY: Read it yourself!

OLD LEPA: You read it to me. I don't bother with newspapers. They only tell capitalist lies.

NANCY expects OLD LEPA to say more. With some amusement, she glances through the newspaper story.

NANCY: Jesus … this newspaper was published in northern Ontario in 1934. There is a short report here on page two of a mine cave-in in Timmins in that year.

OLD LEPA rises painfully to his feet.

OLD LEPA: So?

NANCY: You are among those listed as killed in the accident. You and a man named Olynyk.

OLD LEPA moves wearily away from her, almost into gloom in periphery of set. She stares after him, then begins replacing the newspaper into her briefcase.

OLD LEPA: (*dulled, distant*) Have some coffee, missus. And put some in my cup, too.

NANCY: Thank you.

She rises and busies herself with getting their drinks. OLD LEPA rocks on his feet, his back to her.

OLD LEPA: (*to himself*) Vladek … Vladek Olynyk with the bad bones. He used to limp after finishing a shift. Something was wrong in his hips. That morning … we went together down the shaft. I stopped to tie my boots—he went on … I never saw him again. For suddenly the earth groaned … stones exploded before my eyes … a cloud of stinking dust covered me. Ahead of me was the cave-in … but I couldn't hear it. If anyone shouted, I couldn't hear him. I was deaf now … I stayed deaf for three weeks after. I know Vladek is dead—nothing to do about that. So I got the hell out of that mine ... out of Timmins. Never once looked back.

NANCY carries his coffee to OLD LEPA. He is startled out of his reverie and momentarily unsure of who she is or what she is doing in his home.

NANCY: Your coffee. Well? What do you think?

OLD LEPA: Huh?

NANCY: The newspaper story ...

OLD LEPA: That time—yah. So they thought I was in there with Vladek Olynyk? That's what they thought?

NANCY: That's what they wrote. You can see for yourself.

OLD LEPA: You can't believe what they say in a newspaper—there's your proof!

NANCY: What *did* happen, then?

OLD LEPA: I never punched out—that's what happened! I never saw anybody to tell them I quit their goddamn job. Walked seventeen miles that day. Train came along ... I went west ... where you live longer with less worry about stones falling on your head!

They both laugh and share their coffee in momentary silence. From outside, sounds of distant diesel locomotive, followed by bird cries.

OLD LEPA: Hear that? That's a small hawk ... the day is ending.

She moves away from him and pensively stares out a window.

NANCY: Yes ... This farm—why did you sell it?

OLD LEPA: (*suddenly agitated*) It's a good life, lady! Lots of work, but a good life.

Sounds of music—a sad, melodic old Ukrainian folksong in background over his dialogue.

This time of the year ... sometimes I stand and look west into the setting sun ... trees, like black candles holding up the sky ... and between them and me, all them fields of wheat look like they was burning with a cold fire!

NANCY: But you sold it.

He struggles with his emotions, struggling for words to explain, justify. But his efforts break down into painful pacing, as music in background continues.

OLD LEPA: (*to himself*) How easy it is for her to say that! As she looks to the machine shed and the empty barn ... the barn Hanya built ... with the other man.

NANCY: When did you sell your farm, Mister Lepa?

OLD LEPA: (*to himself, anguished*) We needed money, so I went to the Crowsnest to work in a coal mine. We needed the money—that was all. Yet my heart still beats like a trip-hammer when I remember! How old must a man be before he forgets jealousy?

NANCY: You built this farm from a homestead.

OLD LEPA: (*harshly*) None of your business!

NANCY is startled and half-turns to him.

NANCY: What in hell is that all about—"none of your business"?

OLD LEPA tries to choke back his feelings, but is not successful.

OLD LEPA: Nothing ... forget it ...

NANCY: There are people I work with who get by very well by demanding, even shouting, at their clients to get information they need. I swore I would never do that ... if only because *I* don't like being shouted at. Am I wrong in thinking that? Well?

OLD LEPA: (*embarrassed*) I shout at you?

NANCY: Yes. You *shout* at me!

OLD LEPA: Sit down—I'll tell you! My wife is always in my mind ... not one day do I forget her ... hunched like a little girl in her big mackinaw, her belly big with Stefan. She's walking through snow from barn to house, barn to haystack ... I still see her like that. Carrying pails and forkfuls of timothy hay for the two milk cows ... and behind her ...

He freezes on the memory, his mouth slack.

NANCY: Is something wrong?

OLD LEPA: (*to himself*) Two waterbuckets in his hands—the man whose name I never knew! The fanatic—his eyes on fire ... soft lips set in a smile which means nothing to a sane man ... an idiot. Until you spoke to him—to ask, "What in hell you doing in my house when I'm away?"

NANCY: Here—sit down.

NANCY takes OLD LEPA by the arm and guides him to his chair. OLD LEPA moves woodenly, his mind elsewhere.

Take it easy ... I've got some brandy in the car. I'll be right back!

She exits hurriedly, leaving her belongings on the table. On her exit, vague form of a RAGGED MAN enters on distant area of set, almost out of light, his arms extended. All outdoor sounds die on his entry.

FANATIC: I served the Lord, brother. Your wife needed help ...

OLD LEPA rouses and stares at the apparition. He half-rises to his feet.

OLD LEPA: (*to himself*) What the hell is this? I go away for a month and another man takes my place. Her belly showed before he came, so at least the child is mine. That's for sure!

FANATIC: Your wife needed help, mister!

OLD LEPA: (*to himself*) I groan with doubt and guilt ... an anger catches flame and burns inside of me, sounds crash through my head ... my eyes go blind ...

OLD LEPA gropes around and finds a hammer. He raises it and begins a slow approach to elevation where the apparition stands.

And, through my blindness, I see the two of them like animals in my bed ... in the haystack. She sees the thoughts devouring me and shouts with pain ...

Recorded sounds of HANYA crying out in alarm. OLD LEPA advances slowly.

The man is afraid as I come towards him ...

FANATIC: (*whimpering in fear*) She *asked* me to stay and help!

OLD LEPA: (*roaring in rage*) Leave my land at once!

Another recorded cry of pain from HANYA. OLD LEPA wheels around at the sound, the hammer raised high. The FANATIC vanishes.

Begone, whore! Pack your things and go with him!

HANYA: (*recorded voice*) No, Ivan! No!

OLD LEPA drops the hammer to the floor and his shoulders slouch with regret.

OLD LEPA: (*gently, softly*) Through the years, I see it all still ... the man runs across the field to the bush by the railway embankment on the lower end of the farm. I point after him ... for her to follow. But she stays ... and she cries and cries ... Ivan, Ivan—will heaven forgive you for that?

NANCY enters with a small flask of brandy which she opens and holds out to him. Sounds of outdoors begin on her entry. Faint strains of the folk love song echo for a bar or two, and fade out in background.

NANCY: (*breathless*) You should be sitting when you feel unwell. Drink some of this—you'll feel better.

As if by reflex, he takes the bottle and swallows a mouthful, wipes his mouth with his sleeve and returns the bottle to her. She puts it into her briefcase.

Do you want a doctor?

OLD LEPA: Hah?

NANCY: Would you like a doctor to see you? Have you eaten today?

OLD LEPA rouses from his reverie and moves to the table.

OLD LEPA: Nothing wrong, lady. I'm alright ... same's you ...

NANCY: Now, Mister Lepa—you homesteaded here and this was your farm?

OLD LEPA: Sure ...

NANCY: (*delighted, picks up briefcase*) Good! Then it's in your name—which resolves whether you've been alive or not since that accident in 1934!

OLD LEPA stares balefully at her. She becomes confused.

OLD LEPA: (*to himself*) I like this young woman ... but I'm not going to show it. Long ago I learned the best way to deal with government is to stare at it ... and think of a toothache.

NANCY: (*uncertain*) Well? Why do you look at me that way?

OLD LEPA: No.

NANCY: No, what?

OLD LEPA: Not in my name.

NANCY: What are you talking about?

OLD LEPA: Not in my name. When I took out homestead papers, I wrote them in Hanya's name. The work I did ... places I went to ... I didn't know if I'd be living or dead one day to the next. So everything I put in her name. She willed it to Stefan ... like both of us wanted ... but Stefan, he didn't want farming.

NANCY: Everything—in her name? I don't understand ... here's you and ...

OLD LEPA: This house he had excluded from the farm ...

NANCY: That's not what I find odd ... it's leaving everything to your wife, who no longer lives.

OLD LEPA: That's the way it should be—has to be. To be a widow immigrant is bad. To be a widow with nothing is like being blind and deaf and having nothing to eat.

NANCY: (*amused*) That bad, eh?

OLD LEPA: Worse ... I don't tell things good.

NANCY: How in hell would you know what it's like to be a widow?

OLD LEPA has no reply. He stares at her, blinking elaborately.

NANCY: (*laughing*) Then maybe you *were* a widow ... in some other life!

OLD LEPA: (*coldly*) You laughing at me?

NANCY: No. I'm not laughing.

OLD LEPA: That's good. I thought you was laughing.

NANCY pulls out some forms and begins to review them.

NANCY: Okay—we have some forms to fill out ... You came to Canada ... in what year?

Wordlessly, he explains and they carry on a soundless discussion. She corrects the odd notation in her forms. He never takes his eyes off her.

OLD LEPA: (*to himself*) A floating Polish tub brought me here. I never had vermin and I was not Polish. But I was deloused and my head was shaved ... and I came on a Polish passport. I had to have a health certificate ... from the village doctor, who was drunk and stank of vomit. He said I had an ear infection. His open, trembling hand moved across the clinic table as he told me this. I put five zlotys in it, and the ear infection healed just like that. Twenty zlotys would have cured a cancer. He stamped my passport with good health, and all the time I stared at him as I stare at her.

NANCY: Everything in your wife's name, because you're worried about her.

OLD LEPA: To be an immigrant widow in Canada ...

Sees her smiling as she listens.

OLD LEPA: (*irritably, turning away*) To hell with you! Speaking with you is like speaking to a fence post!

NANCY: I ... I understand. I'm sorry. I know it means a lot to you.

OLD LEPA: (*his back to her*) You laugh—but if you are a widow and don't speak the language—eh? Who would worry for you? Your neighbours? The government? The cowboy in tight pants who sells you shoes? Bullshit! Nobody worries for the poor!

NANCY breaks into laughter, which she tries to choke back, but cannot. OLD LEPA turns and stares balefully at her.

That's nice ... I like that laugh. An honest woman. My Hanya laughed a little bit like that.

NANCY: Why, thank you. I didn't mean to ...

OLD LEPA: Yah ... I like that. What's your name?

NANCY: Nancy.

He leans forward and takes her face in his hand. Studies it intently.

OLD LEPA: Nancy? Nancy? ... Gimme the rest.

She becomes a bit anxious, but doesn't know what to do.

NANCY: My name was on a letter I wrote you.

OLD LEPA: I don't read letters. What's your name?

NANCY: Nancy Dean.

OLD LEPA: Hah!

Almost triumphantly, he releases her face and slaps the table.

OLD LEPA: (*to himself*) Just like that, I know! She's not one of the Angliki ... not with that face. Yet ... could she be one of ours? They changed their names—I heard of such things. I had a section foreman whose name was Dobush, but who called himself MacGregor because Scotsmen got the good jobs. *Meester* MacGregor, we would say to him, our caps in our hands ... give to me the good job. I have a prerwah ... (*he grins at the recollection*) A hernia down here! (*motions to his crotch*)

NANCY: Is there something amusing about my name?

OLD LEPA: I want to know your real name!

NANCY is startled and stares at him uncertainly.

NANCY: I told you ...

OLD LEPA: (*to himself*) Oh, my child ... if I was young again, we would find better things to do than talk of old men who lost their names.

Sound of cheerful folk dance music. Strains of melody begin softly, as if across open fields.

I was young once, you know. I didn't dance or play then ... or watch fields of grain at sunset, when the world seems to be on fire.

Music slows and becomes haunting and mournful.

NANCY: (*moved*) I know you were young.

OLD LEPA: (*interrupting her*) This homestead is where my youth came to rest ... right here. With a two-bladed axe, then out on the road, seeding and harvesting for others ... from Manitoba to the Rocky Mountains ... mining, railroading, cutting pulpwood ... through a depression. Youth started and ended here ... right here. We all danced at our weddings ... and after that ...

He rises heavily to his feet. Music ends abruptly. Sound of distant thunder.

What's your name? Your real name, Nancy Dean?

NANCY: (*distressed*) What difference would it make, Mister Lepa? Would that help me to help you get your pension?

OLD LEPA: To hell with the pension! In my heart I know this—there are no people called Dean in

Halychina. I could say more—but it is for you to speak.

NANCY: (*angrily*) It's for me to speak—and suddenly everything you needed to know will be self-evident?

OLD LEPA: Maybe yes, maybe no. I don't understand them big words.

NANCY slowly, methodically begins to replace her papers in her briefcase. Another sound of distant thunder. OLD LEPA strains to listen to it, as if judging whether it will bring good or troubles.

NANCY: I guess I should pack up and leave now. (*pause*) My grandfather's name ... was Odinsky.

OLD LEPA: (*with disinterest, still listening*) Ah ... I knew a shepherd boy named Odinsky in the old country. He had this growth on his neck, and because of that he walked with his head to one side ... like this.

NANCY: (*firmly*) Not this Odinsky. My grandfather was a Russian Jew, Mister Lepa!

OLD LEPA turns slowly to stare at her, then he breaks into hearty laughter which discomfits NANCY.

OLD LEPA: When he landed in Halifax, Odinsky was hard to spell by immigration. So they gave him the name Dean?

NANCY: I guess so ...

OLD LEPA moves to her and puts his arm around her shoulder reassuringly. He continues laughing.

OLD LEPA: How many names ... going back six hundred—a thousand years—of warriors, merchants, slaves ... died with the stroke of a pen in Halifax? Maybe one day we make a big monument of stone ... of a man standing looking into the country ... he's got hands, feet—everything. But no face. And we put that up in Halifax to remind us how we got a fresh start, no?

They both laugh and lean towards each other. Laughter continues under OLD LEPA'S memory. Another sound of thunder, nearer now.

OLD LEPA: (*to himself*) We laugh, but we are sad. There is much to forget before Halifax and all that business. I will not deny the pogroms, and you must know how poor I was. And that makes us sad.

NANCY: I have to go now.

OLD LEPA: So … after all these years, I have a Jew in my house. I'll make some tea for us.

NANCY: Not for me, thank you.

OLD LEPA: If I need tea, you need tea. So don't argue.

He busies himself preparing water for heating. She watches him with mixed emotions. Suddenly she shudders and pulls at the collar of her blouse.

NANCY: Winters … must be lonely here.

OLD LEPA: Was worse once. No woodpile, you freeze. Now they bring the oil even in the summer. Your grandfather was a good man, I think.

NANCY: (*with surprise*) He's never mentioned you. Where did you meet him?

OLD LEPA: Here … there …

NANCY: My grandfather lived in Winnipeg.

OLD LEPA: Sure, I know. He was the city man … the rag and bone man … the man who sold shoes for a living. I was a country man. We spoke the same language, he and I. So we told each other what could not be understood in silence. He was a good man …

NANCY rises and retreats to exit, her eyes fixed on OLD LEPA at the stove. A roar of distant thunder. OLD LEPA does not acknowledge her departure. When she is gone, he returns to his table with a cup in his hand and resumes work on his letter.

OLD LEPA: (*to himself, sadly*) She is gone. Didn't wait for tea even. Was it something I said? Naw. She'll be back. (*begins writing*) Dear Stefan … I say things the best way I know how. The woman I told you about was here—and I thought to myself—why are you a bachelor? I will never understand. But that is your business. If you was married and had a son… (*ponders*) … if you had a son, and he was old enough, I would tell him what I could not tell you. Sure, I would! I was not a good man to hurt your mother like I did, Stefan. Telling her to leave this house and follow a man who would die that night.

Distraught, OLD LEPA pushes the paper aside.

You cannot say such things, you crazy man! Stefan will not thank you for writing like that in a letter … yet someone has to know. I cannot die with that secret. No man should.

Ancient liturgical music begins, passionate and distant. OLD LEPA rises and turns this way and that, as if searching for something he has lost. Sounds of anguish, indistinct outcries of pain.

OLD LEPA: Hanya? Is that you?

HANYA, huddled and shawled, appears in dark periphery of memory stage. She faces him accusingly.

HANYA: (*pleading*) No, Ivan … it's not what you think!

OLD LEPA: How was I to know, when he left long ago, staggering away through the snow like a drunkard … that he would try to cross the railway at the bottom of the farm?

HANYA: Don't make me go with him!

OLD LEPA: I was mad … as men like me are … to see him here in my place. I was young, Hanya … young and crazy!

HANYA: (*frantic*) I am not guilty of what you think.

OLD LEPA tries to scale the elevation to reach her, his arms extended to her. But he stumbles and cannot rise. He speaks to her, but she retreats. In her place, the FANATIC appears, holding up a coarse wooden cross. He is ragged.

OLD LEPA: Oh, my God! Will he never leave me?

FANATIC: Let her stay. I only stopped by to help her plaster the walls of the house.

OLD LEPA: Leave my land! I wish to God I had never seen you!

The FANATIC retreats in fear. OLD LEPA slumps, clinging to the riser. The music fades and swells. Thunder crashes and echoes.

OLD LEPA: (*softly, to himself*) I was told later he carried a cross to my house. The cross he carried to the doorsteps of other homesteads. They told me he was trying to find converts to some god he had made up in his sad, simple mind. He walked across that field there through snowdrifts to the railway in the coulee beside this farm. A wind blew that night, covering fields and trees in a white cloud. He couldn't see where he was going. He might have fallen to the track … or tried to

walk on it until the train came. The train came …
it hit him and threw him into a drift. He was found
a week later when the section gang came along
and saw one of his legs sticking out of the snow.

*Offstage, sound of HANYA screaming in horror at
hearing the story for the first time. STEFAN crosses
memory elevation in shadows. He is in a hurry.
OLD LEPA tries without success to regain his feet
and run to him.*

OLD LEPA: (*crying out*) Stefan!

*STEFAN stops abruptly and turns to OLD LEPA.
STEFAN has the manner of an impatient professional interrupted in his thoughts.*

STEFAN: What is it, you foolish old man? Can't
you see I'm busy?

OLD LEPA: Just give me a moment to speak, my
son. I know you have much on your mind … it
must give you a headache sometimes to think of
so much.

STEFAN: Well, speak … go on. Be precise and to
the point. I have no time for animal grunts from
the ignorant!

OLD LEPA: Only a moment …

STEFAN: I am an educated and refined man, as
you can see. It's not all a blessing, you know. It is
a terrible responsibility, weighing on me like two
big suitcases on a hot day.

OLD LEPA: About your mother …

STEFAN: Or a carton of textbooks I have stupidly
agreed to carry, but cannot find a place to put
down.

OLD LEPA: I have never told you this, Stefan …

STEFAN: I have no interest in what you did or did
not tell me. Can't you see how terribly, terribly
busy I am? And may I ask who are you? Have you
children in my school?

OLD LEPA: Your father …

*Music and other sounds die. STEFAN yawns with
mock weariness.*

STEFAN: What a boresome days can be. Will the
girl never learn I can only see people by appointment?

OLD LEPA: Stefan … Stefan … Your mother was
the finest woman!

STEFAN: I keep telling her, but she behaves like
a peasant incapable of learning.

OLD LEPA: A thousand times I have seen this
nightmare of my foolish mind … wanting to tell
you, but afraid I would anger you.

STEFAN: Come, come, old man—state your business. I have work to do.

OLD LEPA: She was carrying you when I ordered
her out of my house. She didn't go, but something in her health and spirit died that day.

STEFAN: All this talk of death and dying is really
most unsettling—are you aware of that? Do you
really appreciate how much of a bother you are to
the educational system?

OLD LEPA: A year after you were born, she got
sick. I carried her in my arms down that road
there. Hoping for a truck or a wagon to come
along and drive her to the hospital. For two hours
I carried her before help came. I was out of my
mind.

STEFAN: That's impossible. Nobody leaves their
mind in one place while travelling to another, in a
manner of speaking. Therefore it is incorrect to
employ such a metaphor thoughtlessly. It is also
alarming to others.

OLD LEPA: Stefan—listen, please! She begged for
us to go back … because we had left you alone in
your crib. I ran all the way back to look after you.
I forgot to say goodbye to her, I was that worried.
She … never came back. She died. It was my fault
that I had broken her spirit when she was so
young and beautiful … that I had turned against
her … betrayed the love I felt for her. I am an old
man, soon I will die. I ask for your understanding
… and forgiveness. Stefan!

*Liturgical music sounds faintly. Also sounds of
storm. STEFAN stares at OLD LEPA, then knots his
hands into fists.*

STEFAN: (*in petulant rage*) Betrayed her? You
killed her, you ridiculous old bastard!

*He rushes offstage. OLD LEPA half rises and lurch-
es at the table, his face contorted with anguish. He
grabs the letter he has been writing and tears it out
of the scribbler and tears it to shreds. Hard crash of
thunder and sound of rain deluge on fast blackout.*

ACT 2

Same setting as in Act 1. OLD LEPA is at his table, laying out a hand of solitaire. NANCY appears and hesitates.

NANCY: (*calling*) Hello!

OLD LEPA: Come in. The door has no lock.

NANCY: And how are you today, Mister Lepa?

She moves towards him, but keeps her distance. He ignores her.

I'm sorry I couldn't come this morning as I planned to do, but something came up at the office …

OLD LEPA: She has no interest in how my day has been. She is not sure of herself … not sure how to take me … the government in my house. Why does she not come as a friend? Make some tea for both of us? Tell me I'm getting absent-minded … forgetting to shave and change my shirt? She insists on being nice … I don't like nice people, and that's for sure.

NANCY: Mister Lepa?

OLD LEPA: (*gruffly*) Sit down and don't bother me. I'm busy.

For a long moment he continues his game in silence. She becomes uncomfortable.

NANCY: But you're not doing anything. You're just sitting there …

OLD LEPA: I'm busy thinking …

NANCY: I spoke with my supervisor, Mister Lepa. He was not sympathetic. Nothing you have told me helps your case! Are you listening?

OLD LEPA: Sure I'm listening. What case? I'm a man, not a toolbox. What have I got to do with some kind of case where you put things into?

NANCY: It would help if you could tell me the names and whereabouts of surviving friends you once had.

OLD LEPA: This morning I went to town to get the mail. My pension cheque wasn't there … that's all I got to say to you!

NANCY: (*with irritation*) Come on, Mister Lepa … stop playing silly games with me. I'm here to help you.

OLD LEPA: Funny how everybody comes to help me … one more helper and I don't have time to play cards, take a crap, or go to sleep. So go away.

NANCY: You have reason to be angry. I'm sorry about all the problems. But if you could only tell me about some friend you have known from the early years.

OLD LEPA: How much money you make a month?

NANCY is taken aback. She takes a seat opposite him and stares at OLD LEPA disconsolately.

NANCY: What in hell has that got to do with anything?

OLD LEPA: (*angrily*) Maybe nothing for you … but lots for me. I'm old. I got a right to a pension. That's all I got to say. If you don't understand, turn your car around and get out of here. Tell your government to go to hell, too! No more talk! I play cards now!

He plays his cards angrily. She remains watching him. He glares at her. She returns his gaze. He lifts his chair and noisily moves to sit with his back to her. He rudely moves his arrangement of cards on the table to face him.

NANCY: You've got the four of clubs to go on the five of hearts.

OLD LEPA notices his oversight and angrily makes the change.

OLD LEPA: Shit!

OLD LEPA: (*to himself*) I *had* a friend. I called him *mazur*. He was Polish, and to me, every Polyak is a mazur. For the bishop of Warzawa, he would have given his right arm. As he would have for the Polish gentry, who exported him like so much meat to dig tunnels and lay railway track.

NANCY: Surely there was a friend.

Shadowy FIGURE in work coveralls appears, moving slowly through shadows of memory stage.

OLD LEPA: "Wake up, mazur!" I shout and shake him in the morning. "The bolsheviks have taken Warzawa and they're making babies in your sister and your mother!" He sits and crosses himself with this hand big as a shovel. Then he clears his throat and spits behind his bed, like the Polyaks do … scratches his ass through his long under-wear, and starts to speak to me.

MAZUR: You blaspheme all you want, hutzul. One day, you'll pay for it.

OLD LEPA: (*turning to memory, laughing*) How? I have no money. How can I pay without money?

MAZUR: Something will happen to your back. I've seen others with no respect for God or homeland get it that way. You'll learn … when it's too late …

OLD LEPA: (*still laughing*) When that happens, mazur, I go straight to a doctor.

MAZUR: Won't do no good. When that happens, you're a cripple until you die. No doctor living can heal the judgement of God, hutzul. Every Polyak knows that.

The shadowy FIGURE takes out a tiny pocket pouch and begins replacing torn buttons on his coveralls. OLD LEPA watches him wistfully for a moment, then turns to NANCY. Faint, pastoral music begins to play in background.

OLD LEPA: We work, argue about politics and God, make soup together. At night we play cards or smoke and talk of our families. Born a Polyak, he never learned to read or write his own language. I read Polish … I read his letters from his mother to him, and write back for him as if she was my own mother. "Dear Mother" I say, and it is like I am addressing my mother. When Hanya and I marry, he works both our shifts for three days. I offer to return the money he earned for me. But he won't take it … even though he is a mazur, and I heard it said in the old country that mazurs take anything that's not tied to a post.

Shadowy FIGURE on memory stage has lifted a block of wood upright and seated himself on it, as he sews.

MAZUR: Maybe one day *I'll* marry and go away for three days. Then you can do the same for me.

OLD LEPA: (*to FIGURE*) To which I said—how could that be? Who'd marry a mazur? You were born missing the thing you need for that. I tease him like that, and he just sits there, sewing his shirt, or his pants.

OLD LEPA at the table chuckles to himself at the memory. NANCY is amused, but withdrawn during his recollections. The FIGURE on the memory stage

ignores *OLD LEPA'S jibes. He continues mending his clothes. OLD LEPA looks away both from him and from NANCY. Music in background becomes more faint.*

OLD LEPA: We parted on a Spring morning long ago. A train of immigrants were discharged at the station where we worked. Frightened, tired people … with children holding on to mothers … woven trunks and cloth bags piled high on the station platform. We smile at the young women, who are older than they should be, their heads covered in tied kerchiefs. They smile back. The men stare into the wind … looking angry, like they were late for something. The mazur and I know what they are thinking. They are scared of failure and starvation.

MAZUR: (*loudly, waving*) Welcome to Canada!

Music remains soft in background, but becomes lively country dance.

OLD LEPA: And the immigrants start to laugh … talk about their long voyage … ask for a place to wash their children and cook their food.

MAZUR: (*loudly*) Please use our bunkhouse! You are welcome to it!

Music becomes even livelier. Recorded sound of happy people's chatter can be heard briefly.

OLD LEPA: So many of them the floors groan under their weight. The sound of their laughter inside the bunkhouse is like music to us … it has been so long since we have seen or heard our people in a crowd. Our hearts are bursting with joy! I wish for Hanya to be here with me instead of on the cold, lonely homestead away from people, where she is milking cows and plastering walls of this house.

On memory stage, the FIGURE rises and puts away his sewing pouch. He faces OLD LEPA.

MAZUR: I am leaving for northern Ontario, Ivan. The foreman said yesterday the railway is trans-ferring men.

OLD LEPA struggles to his feet and limpingly approaches riser to memory stage.

OLD LEPA: (*joyfully*) Good! … I'll go with you! I've had my fill of the bald, windy places. Maybe Ontario is better, and I can bring my Hanya out to start life all over. (*he turns to NANCY, his face elated*) I'm so happy at this thought I have to open the buttons on my tunic to cool off. The mazur turns away from me, shaking his head ... I can still see him like that.

FIGURE turns away, shaking his head.

MAZUR: (*sadly*) You don't understand, hutzul. Only *I* am going. The foreman says they only want one man.

OLD LEPA: (*to NANCY*) My heart races ... with regret, sorrow. I cannot see myself working alone without this mazur. This flat-faced fool in cracked boots ... crossing himself before he eats ... his fingers bleeding with callouses ... thanking God for the watery turnip soup we are about to swallow. Who gave away every second pay cheque to the church ... and sends the rest to his mother in Warzawa. Who does without tobacco or a new shirt so that the ones he loved will not forget him.

Music dies out. OLD LEPA turns to the FIGURE and shouts, for the FIGURE is slowly moving offstage.

Hey, mazur!

The FIGURE turns to face him.

Hey mazur! ... Write to me sometimes. Tell me where and how you are!

MAZUR: (*through tears*) Don't make fun of me now, Ivan! You know I can't write.

They wave farewell to each other. OLD LEPA wipes tears on the sleeve of his shirt and he stumbles blindly to his table, to sit wearily, his head in his hands.

OLD LEPA: (*to himself*) Mazur, my mazur ... how *did* you live? And where are you now? In some old man's home, or under the earth? You are on my mind, as is she ... the wife I lost so long ago. The mother of my Stefan, of whom I am not worthy. Had you and I remained in the old country, mazur, we would have been enemies ... soldiers in two different armies, and that's for sure. We might have shot each other dead for the honour of homelands that had no use for us. Yet thrown upon each other as we were for a few short seasons in this country of wind and ice, we became closer than brothers ... more loving than we were to our wives ... sisters ... children ...

NANCY has been busy writing notes in her papers during his memory dialogue. She rustles fresh paper. He looks up, startled by her. She glances up at him.

NANCY: Do you want me to make us some coffee, Mister Lepa?

OLD LEPA: You here again, woman from government?

NANCY: (*laughing*) Yes ... I came in while you were dreaming.

OLD LEPA: (*gruffly*) What's that *dreaming* business? I was busy writing. You should learn to knock on doors!

NANCY: (*smiling*) I find it difficult to understand how you never heard news of your friend again. It would help so much if we knew where he was.

OLD LEPA: Leave my friends alone—stay out of my life!

NANCY: (*rising to prepare coffee*) You shouldn't stay indoors like this. It's a beautiful day outside ... birds singing, a soft wind from the south ...

OLD LEPA: I like it right here!

NANCY: You're being stubborn ...

OLD LEPA: When I was young, and stood on my own soil ... I saw beautiful things ... so beautiful they almost left me blind! No birds ... no soft winds ... that is the woman's thing. I saw fire and ice ... I heard a land begging to be helped give birth to so many good things—iron, trees as hard as stone ... food. You don't know the land, so go away. Get in your goddamned car and drive so I never see you again!

NANCY: Later. But first, let me get your coffee.

She brings coffee to him, takes her seat.

OLD LEPA: Sure ... I'm old. You will do what you are going to do.

He sighs in resignation and takes a long, noisy sip from his cup. NANCY watches him and laughs, then tosses her briefcase on the table, scattering his playing cards, sheets of the letter he is writing. He bends to collect the items, then reconsiders.

You pick that up, woman!

NANCY: (*sternly*) Later.

OLD LEPA: (*angrily*) I said—pick it up! That's my property. I want to play cards or write, that's my business!

NANCY: Nope.

OLD LEPA: You say … nope?

NANCY: That's right. Later I'll even clean your house for you. But first, I have other work to do, and we'll do it my way from now on. Back to the beginning, Mister Lepa—what happened to your landing card? Immigration documents? All the paper you needed to get into the country?

OLD LEPA: (*wearily, still staring at papers on floor*) My Canadian papers got burned. Hanya was burning old catalogues and letters long ago. She made a mistake. (*furious*) But I don't have to tell you, so you get the hell out!

NANCY: (*crisply, ignoring outburst*) Hanya … burned them then?

OLD LEPA: Yes. She made mistakes like that. (*to himself*) What the hell am I telling her that for? …

NANCY glances quickly at him, but he is troubled by his own futility in being pushed along by her. NANCY hides a smile behind her hand momentarily.

NANCY: When did you apply for reissues?

OLD LEPA: Huh?

NANCY: You *did* get the documents replaced, did you not?

OLD LEPA: (*exasperated*) Sure, I applied.

NANCY: What happened?

OLD LEPA: The government sent me all kinds of questions. Envelope this big full of questions I don't understand … so I throw them away.

NANCY: One date … that's all my supervisor needs, Mister Lepa. One recorded date on which you were alive after your presumed death in the Timmins mine.

OLD LEPA: (*angry*) A hundred times I tell you already that I am alive!

NANCY: (*firmly*) I need something more substantial than your word for that!

He fumbles in his pants pocket and takes out a closed pocket-knife, which he opens and swings under her nose. She is startled and freezes.

OLD LEPA: Alright … get a quart jar by the stove! (*points knife to other wrist*) I cut that vein there and fill the sonofabitch to the brim … you can take *that* to your boss—a present from Ivan Lepa! Come on—you bring the jar, I do the rest! Come on, I got to die sometime, anyway!

NANCY is shaken. He puts the knife away.

NANCY: (*quietly*) I don't think … that would be necessary. An old bill of sale might do as well, Mister Lepa.

OLD LEPA: I bought seventeen cows … eight horses, and all my farm machinery on my word and a handshake!

NANCY: I'm glad it went that well for you. However, I can't prepare a legal statement based on your feelings. Not even when you fortify them with horses, dogs … goats … or any other peasant ammunition!

OLD LEPA: (*rising to the challenge*) Ah, ha! … Now it comes out! I'm an *old peasant* now … you have to deal with an old peasant, and you don't like that! It's not very nice for a pretty city girl with such soft hands and new clothes! You couldn't say that … it had to slip out by mistake!

NANCY: (*also roaring*) That's right … that's exactly it, Mister Lepa—you *are* an old peasant! An obstinate peasant who has no need of a pension. There should be no pensions for people like you!

OLD LEPA: What's that? What did I hear you say?

NANCY: (*nose to nose with him*) I think the government should give you a few carrot and turnip seeds. You can plant them … watch them grow … harvest them and make yourself soup. And as you eat your soup, you can pontificate to your four walls as to how you did right, while the rest of the world is skidding down to hell!

They lean across the table, glaring at each other. The old man suddenly breaks into laughter. She immediately laughs with him and reaches out to pat his hand reassuringly. They each pick up their coffee cups and toast each other silently. A long moment passes, while they listen to distant sounds of a train whistle.

OLD LEPA: Ech! What's the world coming to now?

NANCY: When you were first married ... what was it like?

OLD LEPA: (*with mock outrage*) Shame on you asking like that! Go try it yourself, if you want to know.

NANCY is embarrassed.

NANCY: I ... didn't mean *that* ...

OLD LEPA: Then what did you mean if you didn't want to know *that*?

NANCY: I wondered ... how difficult was it to live? My life was one where I had all the food I wanted ... there was television, books, records ... a car. Then when I went to work, I found there were people who had none of those things ... ever!

OLD LEPA looks tenderly at her.

OLD LEPA: (*to himself*) Aye, it was difficult, child ... Everything is difficult for some of us. It is difficult not to have an education. I think sometimes if I had been born to a different mother, I might have been a doctor ... or a train conductor. It's difficult to live longer than my father lived.

NANCY: I am afraid sometimes I would not survive if one day ... if one day the office where I go to work vanished. Or I went to start my car and found all its wheels gone!

OLD LEPA: When I was born, men cut fields with scythes, and women beat grain on the threshing floor ... like they did a thousand years before. In this country, as a young man, I ploughed fields with two horses pulling a hand plow. Today, twice a day, morning and evening, I see a jet airplane fly high over my house carrying people who never see me or my house, because it's too small to see from up there!

NANCY: That's true. When I fly, I bury my face in a book.

OLD LEPA: (*overwhelmed*) Think of it! A small book ... smaller than my hand. And what it says is bigger than my house ... my life. It is always more interesting to an educated person in the sky than me on the ground below! And here I am, with time left over to stand and watch the sunset ... and dream that in that great fire I see something ... something men call God, and my heart is filled with excitement ... thirst ...

He rises and hobbles with his weak back restlessly around the room. He is excited and, turning to her, his face reveals a profound agitation.

OLD LEPA: And yet, it's too fast, I tell you!

NANCY: What's too fast?

OLD LEPA: Life! ... The feeling ... the seeing ... the suffering!

Faint sound of robust folk music. His step lightens as he paces in time to the music.

OLD LEPA: I should live two hundred years to make sense of everything I have seen! But what have I learned? From one hurry-up day to another ... long winter and short summer ... then another, and another. Time ... she's like a hurricane over my head, and I am bent to the ground, tearing up roots and stones to make food to eat. Or cutting trees standing this deep in snow. Or repairing track to keep trains running in a straight line. I see so much that I don't know what I see! And to think—an educated person says—that's not enough—give me more!

NANCY: Are you religious, Mister Lepa?

OLD LEPA: (*vehemently*) No! Never!

He begins to pace angrily to sound of music.

OLD LEPA: (*to himself*) I have been called many things in my time, but never a religious man. I have no time for religious men! It might be different for a woman ... I think my Hanya did some praying when I was gone. I came to Canada so I would never bend my knee to another man. For me the road to God was always blocked by a priest.

NANCY: I don't believe you.

OLD LEPA: Believe what you want. When I was a small boy, I said to myself—if I'm that important to God ... if he really worries about me, then he must show me another road. So, one day I stood in a meadow and yelled to the clouds, "Show me! Show me another way with no churches ... no fat, sleepy priests in the pay of police and feudal landlords from some other country!"

NANCY: Did God reply?

OLD LEPA grins at her.

OLD LEPA: Naw. I think the God I was calling to was satisfied with what he had down there in that small village. I waited until night for him to speak to me. I lay on the grass ... tired and afraid. The sky got black, but there was silence. Either God had nothing to say, or there was no room in his temple for a man like me. I walked home in the dark to my father's house, thinking ... that's alright—if God has no time to speak with me, then I'm gonna find freedom for myself!

Music dies out. OLD LEPA returns to table and sits down heavily. He is depressed.

NANCY: Did you?

OLD LEPA: No. There is no freedom for the living. And right now there is a pain in my head from all this talking, child. You eat what I say without chewing. If I was to give you my whole life on a plate, you would eat it in ten forkfuls and then bang on the plate for more! What kind of person are you?

NANCY laughs.

NANCY: You're right. You're absolutely right!

NANCY begins to bang her teaspoon against the lip of her coffee cup. The banging subsides to a slow, rhythmical beat over OLD LEPA'S words.

OLD LEPA: I go to visit my son at Marina and Dmitro's house. I carry presents, for he is only a boy, and what little I send to support him is not enough. Not the money ... I always found money. It was not seeing him except on holidays, and always in *their* house ...

MARINA and DMITRO enter memory stage and mime preparation of food at a sink and stove which is not there.

OLD LEPA: Always in *their* house with its embroidered cloth over and under which costs more than fifty dollars ... *their* house with Ukrainian calendars printed in New York and all the saints' days in red. Paper flowers in vases. And on the wall the plaster crucifix of a tormented Christ with the face of a dim-witted time-keeper I once knew in a Winnipeg hat factory.

NANCY begins to laugh, still beating time on her cup.

I laugh through tears when I come into their house. Sometimes I have to have a few drinks before I find the courage to come through their door. After the first big laugh, I have to be quiet.

OLD LEPA turns to MARINA and DMITRO and laughs heartily. MARINA lifts her finger reproachfully to her lips and shushes him to be silent.

OLD LEPA: They learned to speak softly ... so softly I have to put my hand to my ear and holler.

Raises his hand to cup back of his ear. Loudly.

Eh? What'd you say?

MARINA: (*finger to her lips*) Shh!

OLD LEPA: (*still loudly*) Ah—shush yourself, woman! How are you both?

DMITRO: Keep it down! Keep it down, Ivan!

OLD LEPA: Dmitro, the merchant, is now wearing a small Englishman's moustache. A white shirt and dark tie. His shoulders hunch ... not with the cares of the world, but with the humiliation at the goodness of his life. He joins every club that will have him as a member ... but he is restless and driven by things he will not speak of ...

DMITRO: Keep it down, brother. The boy is sleeping.

MARINA: (*coldly*) Leave him be, Dmitro. Can't you see he's been drinking again! Phew! The smell of his breath would sicken a dog.

OLD LEPA: (*to NANCY*) My sister ... thin, sad ... polishes and cleans as if the stains of sin were smudged on everything she owns. She is leader of the local nationalist language group, determined to bring back the Dark Ages to the Ukraine.

Begins a slow, measured advance into the stage area of memory.

She is consumed with hatred and distrust of her homeland, now a socialist state for longer than she has lived. At the sink, she cleans. I come to her and put my hands on her shoulders. She stands like she was made of ice.

OLD LEPA has gone to MARINA and placed his hands on her shoulders. She becomes motionless at his touch.

MARINA: (*nervously*) What do you want, Ivan?

OLD LEPA: Go sit, Marina. Let Dmitro and me wash up the dishes.

MARINA: I'll do it. That is not a man's work.

OLD LEPA: To hell it is! In Soviet Ukraine, the communists made a law that says men and women who work in factories should cook, wash dishes and raise families together when they come home. Otherwise—divorce! On the spot!

OLD LEPA laughs. MARINA shudders.

MARINA: (*tensely*) Ivan, godlessness is no joke. Neither is the slavery of our people! I would not laugh in this house if I was you!

OLD LEPA attempts to kiss her cheek, but turns away and goes back to his seat at the table. He drops his head into his hands.

OLD LEPA: I will try ... not to laugh ...

DMITRO: (*tries to establish pleasantries*) It is good to see you again. You look good. You working men are sure lucky to have all that fresh air and exercise.

MARINA: (*concerned*) What's wrong, Ivan? Have I upset you?

OLD LEPA: (*mournfully*) Ask your husband ... ask yourself, Marina. Do you still remember words spoke by dying men to the living? Learn from others, but remember who you are, they said—for we were slaves tasting the freedom of escape.

DMITRO: I don't remember anyone saying that. But I'll ask my business associates to enlighten me if they can.

OLD LEPA: Your business associates, Dmitro, wouldn't know if their assholes came with their bodies, or were stitched on later!

MARINA: (*sharply*) Ivan!

OLD LEPA: I came to see my son. And to taste black bread, which has vanished from the earth ...

MARINA: Stefanko is asleep. I will wake him soon. (*pause*) I've ... enrolled him in language school this winter.

OLD LEPA lifts his head. He is startled.

OLD LEPA: No one asked ... or told me. But I'm glad. He will soon be able to read the old stories and poetry. Ah, but that will be something!

DMITRO and MARINA exchange glances. DMITRO is nervous.

DMITRO: (*with forced cheeriness*) Shall we talk about the old days, brother?

OLD LEPA: Shit on the old days! (*to MARINA*) What is going on?

MARINA: Perhaps ... in time ...

OLD LEPA: Is there something wrong with his eyes? Or his hearing? You can tell me!

DMITRO: When we went to school in the old country ... such books ... if they indeed existed ... were forbidden to us. I think ... *we* think ... for Stefan to learn to read and write in the language ... is enough.

OLD LEPA: (*stormy*) Prayer book language—is that it? *I* don't want my son crippled by ignorance, the way we were! To learn the dialect of a language ... which is all we learned ... is *not* enough! Some way, I'll move heaven and earth to pay, but he must have nothing less than the best education!

MARINA stiffens and glares at him accusingly.

MARINA: Listen to him—this father! Setting the world to rights again without benefit of God or people of some wisdom! Look at him, Dmitro ... look at him, will you? Homeless, calloused—a muzhik with nothing but a useless homestead to his name ... and he's demanding that his son become nothing less than a hetman himself!

She laughs scornfully. OLD LEPA spits to side of his table.

DMITRO: (*placating*) Enough, Marushka! That's enough! You hear what I say?

OLD LEPA: (*provocative*) Don't argue with her— hit her! Across the nose!

MARINA: (to *DMITRO*) Don't Marushka me! (*to OLD LEPA*) And you ... I'll forget I heard that!

OLD LEPA grins. MARINA sees and is furious.

Why are you smiling, eh? And who do you think you are to come here roaring like some wild animal? It was peaceful before you came ...

OLD LEPA turns away from her and shakes his head in dejection.

OLD LEPA: What sort of school have you put him in to learn the language? Why do I think I already know the answer to that question?

MARINA is on verge of tears. She wipes her eyes. She becomes quiet, conciliatory.

MARINA: My church runs language classes, Ivan. I take them there, and save on fees by helping the priest keep the children under control. You should watch your pennies. So should we ...

OLD LEPA grabs for his scribbler and begins writing his letter furiously. NANCY rises and, taking her briefcase, lingers.

NANCY: Mister Lepa ... I have to leave now ...

He is oblivious to her. DMITRO and MARINA exit. NANCY reaches with her hand to OLD LEPA, but reconsiders and leaves him. Frog sounds from outside of house. STEFAN enters into memory stage and looks down at his father expectantly.

OLD LEPA: (*as he writes*) My dear son—do you remember that Christmas when I came to see you at your aunt and uncle's house? "Look at what I brought you," I said to you, and together we opened the parcels ... a shawl for your aunt Marina ... a bottle of the good stuff for your uncle. And at the bottom of the bag—a wooden train—for you.

STEFAN: I'll come and help you with farm work in the summers, Father. But I can't live with you.

OLD LEPA: (*to himself*) Push it—pull it. Do anything you wish, nothing will break, even if you throw it, I remember telling you. And then I said ...

OLD LEPA: (*softly, gently, the old man*) Who knows? One day you may be a train engineer, and your old man working on the section to keep your train running through all kinds of weather.

STEFAN: Did you hear me, Father?

Music faintly in background—a plaintive warrior's lament.

OLD LEPA: That's it ... that's it—I shout to you ... as soon as you grow up, I will talk to my section foreman about getting you on with me. He's a Swede, but a good man. We'll make a team, you and I! They'll put our names in a book for what we did ... who we were ...

STEFAN: (*boyish, uncomfortable*) I'll help you with the farm this summer, like I promised I would do ...

OLD LEPA: He was a good worker, but he had weak lungs, like his mother. In the dust, he coughed, so I took it easy on him, like I would have with a girl. In the evening, we walked across the field to the house ... the field and stubble red with the setting sun. So beautiful, it took your breath away. He was seventeen ... a silky beard glowing on his cheeks, as if his face had also caught fire. "Do you like it here, Stefan?" I ask him ...

STEFAN: It's hard to make a living ... but I feel good ...

OLD LEPA turns to STEFAN in memory, brushing away tears from his cheek. Music rises slightly over his words.

OLD LEPA: It's hard to make a living, that's true. But in the morning, the air is sweet and clean. The soil has stones, but with good cultivation, crops will always grow. And on an evening such as this, the world wrapped in cold flame, and the land beneath your feet singing ...

STEFAN: (*tormented*) You need more land, Father!

OLD LEPA: What the hell for? There will be enough to eat for the two of us!

STEFAN: (*in a near shout*) You need more land!

Music dies. OLD LEPA looks down at his hands. He is a failure in his own estimation, and deeply distressed. His words lack conviction. The joviality is forced, strained.

OLD LEPA: No problem. We can clear another twenty acres of bush ... who needs that bush, anyway? Right after harvest we can start. You and I together ... oh, will we make our axes fly! Cut up and sell the bigger trees for cordwood and burn the rest. Next spring, we break the ground and every bit of land there is gets sown into wheat ...

STEFAN: That's not what I want, Father!

OLD LEPA straightens, but cannot face his son in memory.

OLD LEPA: In this house ... I'll build a room for you so you can have your own place to sleep. Nothing fancy like your uncle Dmitro's place, but clean, with lots of windows for the sun ...

STEFAN: I'll come to help you in the summers—I promise! But I can't live with you.

OLD LEPA turns to face STEFAN. His back is tormenting him and each motion is agony.

OLD LEPA: Why not? Are you ashamed of me because of who I am? ... That I never had a house like others ... or a car? What's wrong with this house? (*strikes table hard with his fist*) It's built to last, like the furniture! This isn't a mud hut I'm living in, you know! I placed the logs and she plastered with clay and straw so it would last a long time—show me a city house built today that's as strong!

STEFAN: (*upset*) Please, Father ...

OLD LEPA: (*with agitation and fury*) I did not give you up. I would, if I could, have cared for you myself. But who would hire a man in the mines or on the wheatlands when he comes to work with a child? ... What life would that be for you?

STEFAN: You don't have to tell me that ... I know!

OLD LEPA: So now you are a man ... Dmitro and Marina were *not* your parents—*I* am!

STEFAN: (*turning away*) I know ...

OLD LEPA: I love them for what they did, but I do not admire them, Stefan. They are timid, and they asked for, and received—the worst of things this land gives. I would have wished for stronger people to have helped raise you to manhood.

STEFAN stiffens.

STEFAN: Don't say that. They are good people!

OLD LEPA throws up his hands. But he is determined in his condemnation. Warrior music begins and builds softly.

OLD LEPA: If that were enough ... to be *good* people ... I would kiss their feet for joy! For me, poor as I am ... that is not enough. They have settled for a tray of coloured eggs at Easter, and promises of something else they will never taste or touch. Nothing is given to those who sit quietly ... trusting in the kindnesses of others. Nothing!

STEFAN: I don't know what you're saying!

OLD LEPA: This is a place where tenderness has no meaning ... no one weeps except the immigrants! We are not people, I have heard some angry men say ... we are not people until we learn to fight. Others say—do what the strong ones ask—even if it costs you pride. Who is right in this?

STEFAN: I have never heard such talk.

OLD LEPA stumbles up to memory stage and reaches to touch his son.

OLD LEPA: I don't know how the world is put together. It's enough to learn how to be a good worker and maybe if you're lucky, have a family. But I am afraid for you, Stefan.

STEFAN: Why? I'm alright. Really, I am.

OLD LEPA: Alright is nothing. I want you to understand this country and be ready for it. I want you to move away from the shadows of a priest's skirts ... there is no place for that here. The old men and women can talk about that if they wish ... but for you, it is an old darkness from which you must run if you are to be a man for this country. (*STEFAN shudders and sobs in his father's embrace*) That I know ...

STEFAN: I can't do that. I'm sorry, Father. But I am a Christian and I must go to church as I have been trained to do.

Music dies abruptly.

OLD LEPA: (*drily*) Yes ... yes ... I understand ...

OLD LEPA: (*to himself*) How wretched that moment was! I felt myself aging, turning grey in his presence ... the taste of ashes in my mouth and a coldness creeping through my flesh into my bones.

STEFAN: I don't want to farm. I'll help you, but I can't come here to live. I want to finish school and go to university. I want to become a school teacher.

They slowly begin to pace back and forth, side by side.

OLD LEPA: Good. (*begins to be excited*) There *had* been a teacher before in my family—did you know?

STEFAN: No one told me.

OLD LEPA: Uncle Mikita ... lived two doors down the street in our village in the old country. He walked with a stoop, but his eyes were those of an eagle. When they clouded with anger, heaven itself darkened ... there was a man! I can still see him like it was yesterday, coming down the road, his books on his arm ...

UNCLE MIKITA enters in shadows of memory stage. He has books on his arm. He raises his arm to OLD LEPA, who stops.

UNCLE MIKITA: (*declaiming*) Don't read Shevchenko like nuns murmuring vespers at sundown! Children! Read him with fists clenched ... blood racing in your ears ... your eyes turned to the uplands of the spirit!

OLD LEPA: (*to STEFAN, resuming walk*) I still hear his words ringing in my ears. As children, we were afraid for him, because the country was overrun by occupation troops of yet another foreign country.

STEFAN: Why? What would happen?

OLD LEPA stops and stares at STEFAN. UNCLE MIKITA remains frozen, one arm poised, the other holding books.

OLD LEPA: Dmitro and Marina never told you?

STEFAN: No.

OLD LEPA: Let me tell you then. Uncle Mikita, the teacher, was returning one evening from the library. Two soldiers, blind with drink, staggered out of the tavern, dragging their rifles with fixed bayonets, the stocks clattering on the cobbles. The soldiers saw my uncle. One of them raised his rifle and stabbed at the books my uncle was carrying. The books fell to the street.

UNCLE MIKITA mimes the incident, dropping the books.

SOLDIER: (*recorded voice*) (*slurring*) Stop! ... Are you a horse ... or a goat?

OLD LEPA: Uncle Mikita bent down to pick up his books ...

UNCLE MIKITA mimes action.

SOLDIER: (*recorded voice*) Yantik—look! He is not a goat or horse! He ... is a dog ... a field dog. See how he falls on all fours before his masters? Bark for us, dog!

OLD LEPA: They laughed, and my uncle reached for a loose cobble. But one of the soldiers saw the move and brought the butt of his rifle down on my uncle's hand ... smashing it with a crunching sound. My uncle said nothing, but I saw blood

trickling from his lips as he chewed his tongue with pain ...

SOLDIER: (*recorded voice*) (*in drunken anger*) I said bark for us!

Sound of people's angry voices in background—recorded. Music—melody of a traditional lament.

OLD LEPA: As a crowd gathered, the soldiers became wild with fear and rage. My uncle looked at the soldier who had hurt him. "You wretched fool," I heard him say ... the last words he said. For the soldier who had hurt him lunged at my uncle with his rifle, burying the bayonet to the hilt in his back.

In mime, UNCLE MIKITA plays out details of his mortal injury in shadowy stage.

The teacher coughed and slowly ... his head drooping first, died on the street where he taught children to read poetry and be proud ...

Music fades and dies out. Light on UNCLE MIKITA goes to darkness. Horrified, STEFAN stands frozen momentarily. Then he and OLD LEPA separate. STEFAN exits. OLD LEPA returns to his table and resumes writing his letter.

OLD LEPA: (*writing*) My dear son ... I remembered today when you were a young man. I almost forgot I wanted to write to you to scold you. It is a difficult thing to do. I remembered good things from the hours we spent together then ...

He lifts the scribbler and squints at what he has written.

OLD LEPA: (*impatiently*) Goddammit! Why am I afraid to speak directly to a son who is a grown man? This will not do! I have made up my mind to say it, and say it I will ... (*writes again*) Stefan ... your father is disappointed in you. There—that's better! (*ponders*) But he will read this far and wonder what I am saying ... why I say it. He knows ... sure he knows! And yet—is it his fault? Or was she to blame?

NANCY enters and sits across the table from OLD LEPA. She waves to him in greeting. He nods indifferently. She opens her briefcase and removes some papers.

NANCY: (*cheerfully*) I saw my grandfather this morning.

OLD LEPA: That's good. (*writing*) I start to write to you, and she comes to visit. She came yesterday morning—she came last week, and the week before that, with more forms to fill and news of her goddamn grandfather, who I think she put into an old man's home over his objections ...

NANCY: Are you ignoring me, Mister Lepa?

OLD LEPA: Yes.

NANCY: My grandfather is like you. You should visit him.

OLD LEPA: What for?

NANCY: He could use the company. So can you.

OLD LEPA: I don't need company.

She watches him for a moment as he struggles with his letter.

NANCY: If you wish, I could drive you over to the retirement home where he lives.

OLD LEPA: I don't wish.

NANCY: Well—excuse me for suggesting ...

OLD LEPA: Retirement homes are like ice in my heart. All these old men sitting around with blankets on their knees, listening for their hearts to stop.

NANCY grins.

NANCY: Not all the time. Sometimes they play bingo ...

OLD LEPA: (*gruffly*) How happy they must be. Now go away. I'm busy!

NANCY: Or get visited by unemployed youth on government grants, who instruct them in how to knit a pair of socks.

OLD LEPA: Shit!

NANCY: Or make a pot out of mud!

OLD LEPA glares in disbelief at her.

OLD LEPA: You shut up your mouth, okay? I'm not in a mood for funning.

NANCY: I don't think you've had breakfast, or you'd be in a better mood. Can I make you some food?

OLD LEPA: There's nothing to eat. My pension didn't come this month ... same's last month ...

He glares at her provocatively, to see if his barb has drawn blood. She does not respond. Instead, she rises and pours him and herself a cup of coffee.

NANCY: You don't look as if you slept much last night. Have you seen a doctor about that back of yours? You should, you know, or your pension—when it comes—will be going to a man in a wheelchair.

OLD LEPA: Yah? ... I went to a doctor for my eyes last summer. When I got there, the girl in front says to me—"Mister Leper—the doctor can't see you today. But he asked me to arrange your eyes four days apart next week, if that's convenient!" (*chokes on laughter*) I don't go to doctors no more.

NANCY also explodes into laughter. Neither of them can stop their amusement, and laugh like children.

OLD LEPA: (*to himself*) I must stop this laughing—what's wrong with me? Look at me—tears leaking out of my eyes—nose running—and all because I'm laughing so much! She may be a pretty girl, but she is the government ... who's starting to pour me coffee as if I was some thirsty paralytic. I know now I have let her visit too much and stay too long. I will throw her out of my house! ... But she stops laughing just like that and grabs her goddamned papers again. And I am staring at her through running eyes, my mouth wide open! ...

He stops laughing and warily takes out his handkerchief and blows his nose noisily, playing for time. She is over-confident.

NANCY: Well, that felt good, Mister Lepa. A few more questions to clean things up. Have you any bank records?

OLD LEPA: No.

NANCY: And, of course, no social insurance number?

OLD LEPA: If you know, why ask?

NANCY: (*grinning maliciously*) Thought I might trick you! What about hospitalization?

OLD LEPA: (*uneasily*) What about it?

NANCY: Have you been in a hospital since the mine accident?

OLD LEPA: I take good care of myself … jump out of the way fast.

NANCY: My superiors or bosses, as you might call them, have agreed to a statutory declaration you can sign after I've prepared it. Supported by declarations from your sister … your brother-in-law … your son.

OLD LEPA: Hold it! Hold it! You don't do that … no damn way!

NANCY: Why not?

OLD LEPA: I would die sooner than have my family swear I am old and need money to live! You think I have no pride?

NANCY: (taunting) Pride is cheap. Groceries cost money.

OLD LEPA: (angry) Hey … you watch what you say! I don't want to hear that kind of talk in my house!

She studies him. He turns his chair and back to her, then turns to pick up his coffee before turning away from her again.

NANCY: It would be so simple.

OLD LEPA: I'm not listening to you!

NANCY: If you'd been bad and done something to get yourself arrested years ago.

OLD LEPA: (visibly shaken) Shit! …

NANCY: That hasn't happened, has it, Mister Lepa?

OLD LEPA: (to himself) I'm not telling! No pension is worth that … I would rather starve, beg … steal. I know she's looking at me … I can feel that government smile, right in the middle of my back, like a needle …

NANCY: It's your pension, Mister Lepa …

OLD LEPA: I cancel! Get in your car and go to hell!

NANCY: (laughing) You cancel?

OLD LEPA: Yah. I cancel!

NANCY: I'm not a subscription to a newspaper. You can't just cancel me, Mister Lepa. (grins) After all, I represent the government of Canada … I'm a servant of the crown! Cancel that!

OLD LEPA turns his chair roughly toward her.

OLD LEPA: There's no king in Canada—so take your goddamn crown and …

NANCY: Now, now …

OLD LEPA: (inflamed) With these hands I make this country … I make the pensions! I make your job! So don't bring me no crown.

NANCY roars with laughter and slaps the table, as if goading him in her amusement. OLD LEPA settles down and holds his temper in check with difficulty.

NANCY: If I have to, I'll talk to your sister … your son …

OLD LEPA: (glowering) You keep my Stefan out of this! And you stop that hitting, right now!

NANCY: If he can help, so much the better.

OLD LEPA: He's a busy man … principal of a school and not to be bothered.

NANCY: (firmly) Then you tell me!

OLD LEPA: (to himself) Jesus, but her eyes are like steel. Whoever trained her trained a policeman, and that's for sure …

NANCY: If you were in trouble with the law, and the incident is recorded sometime after 1934, then it's all the verification I need. And by the way—I don't have the slightest interest in what you did to get in trouble!

OLD LEPA: (defiant) I bet you don't. To hell with you—you'll never find out!

NANCY: Oh yes I will—I'll find out!

OLD LEPA: Besides, I was never in that kind of trouble!

NANCY: I already know—the question remaining is the exact date.

OLD LEPA: (wary) Who told you?

NANCY: You did. I can see it written all over you—Ivan Lepa, the gangster!

OLD LEPA: I'm not gonna speak! My lips are shut! You sit and wait until tomorrow … but you don't hear me say a thing!

Sounds of happy country dance music rise in background. NANCY stares at OLD LEPA, who elaborately arranges contents of his table, sips his *coffee, goes to a cupboard and pours himself a drink of brandy. He carries the bottle to the table, but does not offer her a drink.*

OLD LEPA: (*to himself*) Three years after Vladek died, I go to Vancouver, I'm walking by the post office, and there is a big meeting on the street. Unemployed men are demanding work. All my life I give money to the labour movement, but I don't go to meetings. There's no work, and a meeting don't change that. But this time I stop to listen. I don't see the police—nobody does. They attack from behind where I'm standing—clubbing and pulling men away. Two of them knock me to the pavement. I'm big and strong in them days, so I jump to my feet and kick one bastard down and throw the other against the building so hard his hat falls off. Then I run as fast as I can. Behind me, they're chasing. "Get that big sonofabitch!" I hear one of them shout. I'm in an alley when they jump me a second time. I fall down and they hold me by the pantlegs. I get to my hands and knees and kick to get free. But my suspenders rip and I'm out of my pants. Now they got me around the neck …

At the table, OLD LEPA throws his hands up in resignation and enters into an animated, mimed discussion of the incident with NANCY. She laughs and makes rapid additional notes to an affidavit she has already prepared. She silently reads excerpts from it. He cheerfully corrects it, gets another glass and pours her a brandy. They have become friends again, and OLD LEPA pushes back his cloth cap as he tells her of additional facts related to the incident. Country music continues in background.

OLD LEPA: They take me in my shirt and underwear to the police station. They say they are going to charge me with unlawful assembly and resisting arrest. They use so many big words I don't know what they're saying.

NANCY: But that's not what you were charged with?

OLD LEPA: Naw … When I come to court the next morning, a judge with whiskers so big they cover his mouth asks me if I committed something called indecent exposure. (*laughs*) "Sure," I tell him, and I'm laughing, because I wonder how the sound came out so clear from his mouth with so much hair covering the hole.

NANCY: So he sentenced you …

OLD LEPA: He gives me seven days in jail. But I never see jail … because after he said that, I am taken to the room where there are a lot of other men … some from the meeting … others drunks … thieves … maybe murderers—I don't know. I can't tell what a man did by the look on his face. They divide us up after the morning court, and I get mixed up with someone else who is in the toilet and I walk out the door with the innocent ones and nobody calls me back or tries to stop me.

Music fades out over their laughter. NANCY completes her notation and hands the papers to OLD LEPA to sign. He hesitates, then shrugs and signs with a flourish. They share another brandy as she packs away her papers.

OLD LEPA: You … knew all about that business when you come here today?

NANCY: Yes.

OLD LEPA: Who told you?

NANCY: Come on … Mister Lepa … you know I can't tell you.

OLD LEPA: Stefan! You saw Stefan and he told you!

NANCY: Now what makes you think that?

OLD LEPA: If Marina and Dmitro told on me, they would come to me right away to say they betrayed me. That's what good people with no education do—they betray you and then ask forgiveness!

NANCY is amused and sips on her brandy.

NANCY: But your son is an educated man, so …

OLD LEPA: An educated man does what he thinks is right and forgets he did it. I don't like that forgetting. I will tell him that. I am going to write him a long letter to give him hell for saying what is none of his business. And for you … I thank you for doing your job. But I don't thank you for putting your nose into my personal …

NANCY: Your … *personal?*

OLD LEPA: That's right. And if you don't know what that means, then you got some learning to do yet.

OLD LEPA returns to his letter.

NANCY: My grandfather … you and he might have a lot in common. You and he should meet … someday.

OLD LEPA: Sure, sure, sometime when I got nothing to do. Maybe Monday, eh?

NANCY thoughtfully gathers her papers and exits. Country music comes up in background.

OLD LEPA: (*writing*) My dear Stefan … I am going to write him. My son—outside my kitchen window, the fields seem on fire in a red glow from the setting sun … (*stops writing briefly*) … That's a good letter—that's the way a man writes a letter to his son! (*resumes writing*) But even though the light of god—if there is a god—washes over everything I see, I feel stiff and drained this evening. She has been here … and we have both drunk brandy, like two men, from a bottle I saved for the difficult nights. Never mind—I can buy another. She wrote in her papers for over an hour today, and then she left. Meadowlarks were singing as she wrote … but I don't think she heard them. Now she is gone, and I feel like a dying man who has closed the big book on his life. I sit in a wooden chair … the light dying … and wait for the last forms to be filled before the gathering darkness shuts out all remaining light. (*he pauses and stares at the paper*) Stefan—a man wants to feel he can trust his children.

Writes quickly, furiously. Breaks his pencil and throws the pieces across the room.

No, that is not the way to say it …

He ponders. Music rises in volume slightly. Suddenly he slaps the table with his hands, his expression elated. He dictates the letter to himself.

OLD LEPA: Ah! it should go like this—Stefan … a man wants to be remembered for the good things he made possible … not the stupid things, but the good things. I once knew a man who always carried spare tobacco in his pockets. He was a blockhead with nothing to say, but men talking allowed him to stand with them, because when tobacco ran out, we could always turn to Ignace for a smoke! … For this, he is remembered … you see how easily he comes to mind, even now …

Light begins to die down. OLD LEPA chuckles and then laughs over remainder of his monologue.

I once worked for a widow who used the ashes of her husband to glaze a serving dish on which she put turkey meat. That was in Saskatchewan, where all things are possible, just before the war started. Another time, in Mundare, I saw …

Light goes to darkness quickly on OLD LEPA'S sardonic laughter. His laughter and background country dance music continue into darkness, the music rising to drown out his monologue.

End

ONE MORE FOR THE ROAD

It was at an Easter meal in Summerland in 1985 that *One More for the Road* began. Dick Clements, a good friend and guest of the Rygas, amused his hosts with recitations from one of his favourite shows, Hal Holbrook's perennial *Mark Twain Tonight*. To Clements's surprise, Ryga, who was cleaning up the remains of dinner, suddenly announced from behind a counter that he would write a similar one-man show, a series of personal reminiscences utilizing especially Clements's background in folk singing and storytelling—he had been a major performer at Chautauqua 333, the coffee house that he, Ryga, and several others operated in Penticton during the summer of 1968. There wasn't much more said about the project that evening, but two months later ten pages of typed script arrived at Clements's home in Vancouver. With these in hand, he approached Donna Spencer, managing director of Vancouver's Firehall Theatre. She liked the work, agreed to direct its première production, and scheduled it for an opening that coming October.

One More for the Road was Ryga's last new play to be successfully staged. Earlier in 1985 he had written a first draft of *The Children of Moses* for the Native Education Centre in Vancouver, but this work, although commissioned, was finally cancelled because of disagreements over the script. *Glaciers in the Sun*, another one-person show, written a year later for actor Cheryl Cashman, also never went into production.

Indeed, Ryga, in the last years of his life, wrote prolifically: he completed a number of short stories, four of which were published by Talonbooks, along with his final piece of writing, the poem "Resurrection," in their posthumous collection of George Ryga's work titled *Summerland* (1992). He also wrote two radio plays, both of which were broadcast on the CBC. These latter, like much of the writing of his final years (he died in 1987), concern older men reflecting on their life and purpose. In *The Legend of Old Charlie*, broadcast in May 1985, a retired miner recollects working at Frank, BC, where his faithful pit-horse, Charlie, became trapped and eventually died along with hundreds of miners and others (the incredible death-toll has never been quantified) in the wake of a tremendous rock slide caused by irresponsible mining practices, creating disastrously unsafe working conditions at the site. *The Legend of Old Charlie* was also published by Talonbooks under the title "The Frank Slide," in their *Summerland* collection of Ryga's previously unpublished work. In *Brandon Willie and the Great Event*, broadcast in January 1987, a feisty resident in a run-down Vancouver hotel stands on a ledge over the street to protest his eviction—the hotel planning renovations for upscale tourists attending the "big event," Expo '86, Vancouver's international transportation and communications exposition.

One More for the Road consists of the ruminations of two elderly men: in this case based on two real-life characters: Dick Clements, the narrator-performer; and, strangely enough for someone as seriously sober as George Ryga, Chester C. Sharpe, a re-invented persona of the author himself as a giddy, beer-guzzling, life-affirming, salt-of-the-earth playwright ("Hey—being alive, that is something!") who nevertheless remains a cranky social activist and self-deprecating senior approaching death and contemplating his legacy. The play even contains a hint at apotheosis as Chester, in a dream, sprouts angelic wings. Finally though, it should be remembered that the differences between the two characters are considerably and intentionally blurred: according to Clements, "it's a mix … of our personalities." As the play developed over several years, there was an increasing amount of input from Clements. While Ryga wrote many new verses for "Too Ree Ama," it was Clements who selected various songs and verses from other folk standards for the performances. It is also crucial to remember that *One More for the Road* was conceived and written with the intent of creating an open-ended performance piece, an adaptable dramatic critique of outrageous political events as they continued to unfold through time. There is a point to Ryga's darkly humourous hint at his own impending demise—the continuing evolution of the play was intended to outlast him.

This monodrama represents yet another return by Ryga, this time to the essentials of performance as a public vehicle for social change: he always preferred the personal, presentational style of the folk singer where, rather than acting out a fictional construct, the performer entertained with material drawn directly from his or her own experiences as these were shared with the audience. "It's the Homeric thing where a man goes with a lute and sings fragments of songs and makes commentaries, like a newspaper," he told a *Calgary Herald* interviewer (Dec. 14, 1985). The dedication in the première program is quite explicit about Ryga's understanding of the oral tradition and the way it has always been transmitted as a "gift" to succeeding generations and storytellers. It reads:

> This work is given to Dick and his friend, and the long, long generations of singers, minstrels, raconteurs, disbelievers and folk custodians of memory—who bring light and common sense into dark, ridiculous times. (George Ryga, 1985)

The original political context of *One More for the Road* was the British Columbia of the early and mid-1980s, a time of economic recession and the provincial government's severe "restraint" program of spending cuts, layoffs, and sweeping legislative changes to collective bargaining practices. As a result, under the "Solidarity" banner, tens of thousands of people from labour and community groups held noisy demonstrations and planned a general strike. It was one of the most rancorous periods of political dispute in the province's history. The protests abated somewhat when the Solidarity Coalition itself split between the labour wing and the more radical community factions—especially when Jack Munro, "representing" (some said "appropriating") the unions, met personally with Premier Bill Bennett at his home in Kelowna and agreed to call off the strike—a move many such as Ryga regarded as a betrayal. This incident is referred to in an earlier version of the play. In the revised text presented here (1986), we hear of figures such as the newly elected premier of BC, Bill Vander Zalm ("the fantasy salesman of tulip bulbs"), a federal Tory cabinet minister, Sinclair Stevens, then under investigation on charges of conflict of interest, and allusions to the building of the Coquihalla Highway through south-central British Columbia—a "tropical highway" because, with its concrete dividers, vehicles running into "unexpected" snow could not turn around. There are also autobiographical references—to Ryga's youth, battling nettles and dogs, and later, in early manhood, to his affair with a Persian poet (the "Arab" woman).

One More for the Road opened on October 10, 1985, at the Firehall Theatre in Vancouver, featuring Dick Clements and directed by Donna Spencer. It was generally well-received, Max Wyman of *The Province* calling it a "wonderfully ingratiating little show" (Oct. 11, 1985). It subsequently was reworked by Ryga and Clements in 1986, and toured the Okanagan and Kootenay areas of British Columbia, directed by John Taylor of Kelowna.

ONE MORE FOR THE ROAD

ACT 1

So ... Now is the winter of our discontent: the time of evening snow ... of labour lockouts ... and the poor chasing imagined jobs and money ... where neither is to be had. The chase becomes the game. And we elect stewards-of-our-discontent to care for our well-being. Wretched men who never studied economics, and who do not read or write ... who struggle painfully in understanding human thought. They do not make money. They take money paid in taxes and with it build tropical highways into an Arctic climate ... highways leading nowhere ... with concrete dividers copied from the freeways of San Diego ... racing to fifty feet of snow and no possibility of turning back!

The chase becomes the game, and little men fired with hopeless enthusiasm of the lost ... and damned ... argue the arguments of privilege which they will never know. They argue for unbridled free enterprise ... for infliction of injury and pain on their fellow-workers ... for feudalism on developing nations ... for war against any country where the workers took control ... more or less ...

I've been cold an' I've been hungry,
Seen my share of wealth an' pain,
Run my race against the weather,
Come in laughin' from the rain!

"The polyester days," my friend said in his last letter to me. "These are the polyester days. I seen our Prime Minister in sunlight at nine-thirty in the morning. Pancake makeup on his face an' a polyester blue suit on the rest of him. Smile of a polyester clothes model for one of them mail-order catalogues. An' a young woman standing next to me cooing, 'There he is! I seen him, an' he looks just like God! Oh, sweet Jesus, what a day this is!'"

Seen my share of fear an' hardship,
Rocked my baby through the night,
Never bent to another man's fancy,
An' never lost without a fight!

"Next day, I watch our glad-handing steward of the west," my friend went on to say, "the fantasy salesman of tulip bulbs an' South African fascism all mixed together, an' him not seein' the difference. And always that goddamned photo-album grin which sold the bundle an' now pays the bills for drug manufacturers ... and liquidators of publicly owned banks and transportation facilities ... who invested in, and got, a government to serve them ... from the White House to the cat house."

Seen my share of fear an' hardship,
Been pushed an' hustled here an' there,
Never took another man's money,
Never praised what wasn't there.

Out the door and onto the street to meet the fresh day with a shout an' a good laugh! My street—of fruit vendors who speak Italian with a Chinese accent ... of rounders and wasters ... actresses who worked the late shift in the all-night restaurants, feeding sailors from the sea and grey-eyed men who cannot sleep ... walkers and motorcyclists who sleep an' rise at roughly the same time, but whose daytime speeds of locomotion bear no resemblance to each other whatsoever ... the lovers and the killers brushing shoulders with good feeling on the way to feed ... a madman glowing with revelation from a dream he had of giving AIDS to everyone! ... two city fathers deep in thought look with unseeing eyes and return my wave, their minds so deep in deficit finance they have lost it as husbands, fathers, neighbours, or even as pedestrians on the way to somewhere ... an angry seagull cries and doubles in its flight path, returning to the sea and the long, sea sounding day ... a young woman on an early morning picket-line walks slowly with the rhythm of a dancer still, and the fear of failure in her eyes ...

On the hundredth day the summer ended,
Packed my bags to move along,
But Jenny stopped me on the corner,
With a chorus to my song ...

And still I cry—let those who must, do! Let the singers sing, an' men of forests work among the trees! It is not right a man who is at home on water should be a sailor for a season only—the ship beneath his feet burned or sold for salvage or for profit. It is not right a farmer lose his fields, or a merchant fail in his shop on the judgment of a money-lender. It is not right that truth and freedom can likewise fail in this way. So I cry, morning, noon, and night—let the singers sing, and men of forests work among the trees … and sailors face the rolling seas as front-yards of their spirit! And still I cry that no song falter, no field or river fail … no woman, child, or man pass this way in broken health for having dreamed of gaining on the gods! And still I cry that no song falter in the leading thrust of darkness, or a winter storm. That work providing pleasure be forever that … that failure be a lesson earned through labour, and never punishment for courage in the search for truth and freedom …

On the hundredth day the summer ended,
Turned once more to say goodbye,
Closed the doors an' locked the windows,
An' felt a tear come to my eye …

A man must have a friend. In normal times … but more so in times of revolutionary upheaval of the spirit. I had an' have such a friend … he played an old banjo like mine all his life. His name was Chester Sharpe … C. Sharpe they called him. An' he only had one tooth …

I've known fun an' I've felt sorrow,
A bit of anger now an' then …

Chester worries lots about what our election practices dredge up from time to time … A Sinclair Stevens an' his faithful wife with her dreams of Jesus medals for the two thousandth year of our Lord! Before that, long before, a Prime Minister who confided his misgivings about history to his dog … and now, a west coast novice enamoured of the racist gangsters of South Africa!

I demand the right to proper choices, my friend used to holler through his open window—if I vote for responsible men or women, I want at least two of them on the ballot, so I can choose! An' if I got no choice but to vote for a social disease, then I'll go with a clean dose of clap rather than waste time on these bastards. The clap I can cure. The other thing is with me for as long as I live, an' I

got to contribute to their pension plans, which I resent …

I've known fun an' I've felt sorrow,
A bit of anger now an' then,
But there'll always be tomorrow,
To get things straightened out again …

Banjo interlude.

I've known fun an' I've felt sorrow,
In places had no need of me,
But I stored up songs an' stories
To share with friends who shared with me …

Winthrop, Washington … with boardwalks and saloons … barnyard timbers the mainstay of architecture from a time long gone now. Ice-cream cone in hand, I meet a man with studied meanness in his eyes … him spitting to the left of him, spitting to the right of him … a six-shooter hanging from the belt of his ass-hanging pants. And a young girl following at a safe distance waves to me an' calls, "Welcome to Winthrop, stranger, an' stay a while! Next gun-fight starts in forty-five minutes …"

I'm a democrat an' human
With a strong dislike of pain …

In a great amusement park in southern California, a small church in a plastic wildwood waits for the unsuspecting, its white doors open … inside, a life-size plastic Jesus hangs from a plastic cross, his garish wounds oozing plastic blood. The church fills … the doors close … and Jesus wakes, opening his eyes, tears running down his cheeks. In John Kennedy's voice an' accent, he blesses everyone … the lights dim and he returns to his plastic sleep until the next time the church fills with people trying to get away from hamburgers an' hawkers … in the land of Walt Whitman … Thoreau … Emerson … Tom Paine … and Mark Twain … as well as Jesse James and Ronald Reagan …

I'm a democrat an' human
With a strong dislike of pain,
A lot of love for Dawson Jenny,
So I'll be coming' back again!

They are building another museum outside of Ottawa to house the history of man, and already there are charges of graft an' corruption—not over the history, but over construction of the building!

Banjo interlude.

"I believe there's got to be reincarnation," old Chester hooted in my ear one sunny morning ... us leaning on the rail of a dude ranch corral watching a city matron riding round an' round on a spirited gelding.

"Whoa," she kept saying in a low, pleading voice. "Whoa ... slow down, please ... Whoa!"

"There's got to be another life after this one!" Chester tells me, biting on his lip. "It's not right for it to end this way. They both got to come back again—in reverse order. She, an aging mare, an' him wantin' to ride her hard and fast. He pays his mare rent—the gate's thrown open an' he puts the spurs to her—hit it, old lady—let's go! Let's go! With the young fella wanting action, the old mare begins to prance ... out the gate an' heading that way—towards the Pacific Ocean at somethin' like a half gallop!"

Chester couldn't go on. He was laughing so hard the tears filled his eyes. And in the corral, the city matron on the spirited gelding kept moaning, "Whoa, boy ... slow down ... Whoa!" ... as she went round ... and round ... and round ... and round ...

> Riders of the evening desert
> Will find me waiting when they come,
> On golden horses swift as sunset
> Racing time, and wind an' sun ...

Old Chester only had one tooth, and a head not encumbered by too much learning. He used to write me letters ... when he got lonely. Wrote them like this, on scribbler paper with red crayon ...

Dear Dick—A young sonofabitch come by yesterday looking for money. Young man—maybe thirty years old, wearin' a nice jacket and clean shoes. He didn't ask for a contribution to his self-betterment. He just hinted around that whatever bothered me ... bothered him. Right there, I was on my guard! Nobody worried about what I worry about without some benefit for himself. So I said nothin' bothered me. Never did, never will. I don't grow a garden, so I don't need rain. I rent, so if a window breaks an' don't get fixed quick, I move to another place with windows that work.

Well, this young fella puts a foot into my doorway, which is kind of like putting a foot into what I think, and feel, and sing about. He tells me the problem with the world today is that the government's got too big. Got to cut down the size of government he says, so it don't interfere with our lives ... get rid of all them regulations ... as well as the unions, so that business gets a chance to make us all better off than we were yesterday! I wanted to pick up my banjo an' let rip with a bit of defiance that's never done me harm, but he held up his hand, like a benediction. An' he asked me what church I belonged to. I said nothing ... just stared at him. He took this for an invitation to continue. He then tells me as a Christian businessman he was willing to sacrifice his time an' career to work with me.

I don't know the guy. Never seen him before, and he's offering to work with me! What in hell can he do? I doubt he can sing, or play a fiddle with me. An' whatever other business he's in is of no interest to me. So when he stops talking long enough to suck in a spare breath, I tell him I am not a church-going man ... that I don't know how big the government's become because it's not something you can see, like an elephant ... or an oil tanker. But that I sure would feel better knowing the pork chop I buy has been inspected by someone whose job it is to do that ... that I got nothin' against unions ... except that sometimes they're hard to tell apart from the industries they're supposed to protect the workers against!

But that's alright—people who've lost their way will still keep having children to straighten things out in the future! I tell him that, an' he moves his foot out of my life ... into the hallway. He tells me now he's planning to run for government—the same government he wants to take apart because it's too big for him ... and that he hopes I change my mind an' help him when the time comes. Why does a young fella like that run for government when he doesn't believe in it? Is the pay better than what he earns now? Or is this some subversive little bastard out to destroy what belongs to us all? What stands between us and the dark night of the jungle? Do you know? ... does anyone?

> I've known fun an' I've felt sorrow,
> A bit of anger now an' then,
> But there'll always be tomorrow
> To get things straightened out again ...

I have a very wise dog. He will not chase cars or follow street parades. When I sing a sad song, he'll join in an' howl sympathy for all the miseries of man. He barks once to announce a friend coming to the door ... and three times if it's a stranger. In his sleep he chases things he dreams of—his legs twitching in a galloping sequence and lip curled back in excitement. But he does not understand high technology, even though he knows where my cigars have been left ... and forgotten. I recently played my short wave radio ... and listened to an Italian drama I did not understand. In the play, a dog in Milan barked, and my Lucifer was in the room like a shot ... and barking back at that other dog halfway around the world. Then he tried to find him ... in the clothes closet ... under the bed ... behind my bookcase ...

"Lovin' You"—verse and chorus.

"Stay away from the ladies," Chester Sharpe used to say to me. "Stay away from the ladies or you'll be coming to work without sleep an' an hour late for your shift! Bright-eyed and full of funnin', but an hour late ..."

If only life was that accommodating to good advice! But a man and woman aren't like that. Sundown and the heavens burning with the dying light, and he steps out ... his shirt open and tight pants caressing his ass ... looking for trouble! And she's hurrying toward him, her bouncing hair gleaming like flame ... on her way to the library. Nobody knows them but God ... and he set this game into motion to relieve the boredom of heaven. The boy bumps the girl, his mind racing among the stars. Her books spill ... this way, that way. He bends down to help her pick them up, his tight pants taut as a drumhead. The apologies that are mumbled over and over ... and the forgivenesses given ... would fill a book this thick! Nothing is planned, nothing anticipated ... as they walk away together ... in one direction now ... laughing. There will be tears—a river of tears. But who thinks of that now? When the sky burns on the summer evening, and a man wears tight pants and a woman's breasts ride high— who thinks of toothache, or the cost of rent?

"Lovin' You—Winter Street."

Looking for trouble, I went into a bar. A rock combo was tuning, its performers talking in whis- pers ... three young men and a woman with sad eyes. The bartender slapped a jug of draft before me and held out his hand: "That's seven-fifty." And then he said, "Good band playin' tonight. We can't afford 'em, but what the hell, eh?"

I paid him. At the next table, a big man with whiskers holding up his eyes blew the foam off his jug in my direction. It flew in my face, on my shirt, over my hands. A blind man with a white cane and a holy smile shuffled between us on his way to the john. "That guy's a sieve," growled the big man with the whiskers. "Pisses every five minutes an' gropes for the women in his way." Then he looked at me and politely asked, "You wanna fight?" I said no, and he lost interest in conversing with me further.

The performers on the plywood stage formed a straight line and threw back their heads. Lights began to blink. The first note of sound hit me in the eye like a fist. The second moved my chair back seven inches. The third note lifted me to my feet in the way a black plastic bag filled with garbage is lifted ... by its neck. And I was in the arms of the big man with whiskers holding up his eyes. "Come on, honey, let's dance," I heard him say before the band on the platform came into full life and I went temporarily deaf!

Oh, give me a home, where the buffalo roam,
Where the deer an' the antelope play,
Where seldom is heard a discouraging word,
And the skies are not cloudy all day ...

"Dad," my oldest daughter said. "Now that you are a grandfather, we must have rituals in the family so my baby will have good memories of all of us ... "

That kind of took me by surprise. I'm not one for cocktail parties, or hanging around people who bore me. I am, what some might call, a ritualistic savage! I enjoy a drink of tea or beer when I'm thirsty. I enjoy a good song. I enjoy a conversation with friends, and a good fight sometimes with them who aren't friends. Well, my grandson grew a bit, and as he grew, my daughter got more insistent ... So last Christmas when I was over visiting her, I couldn't escape. There was a get- together planned at the community hall, with carol singing and a lot of goodwill saved up over the year. Everyone got dressed up, including my grandson, young Percival. We all drove down through the snow. When we got to the hall, there were about twenty people outside, admiring the green an' red an' blue lights flickering on and off in the windows. Some were taking photographs with flash bulbs of the hall ... of each other ... of the nearby trees crowding the clearing like the memory of an old hymn whose opening verse you somehow forgot ...

I went back to the car to get a shovel to clear the snow from the steps of the hall, for the fresh fall was a foot deep. But a young woman with a thin oval face gave me shit. "Don't do that! It's just too beautiful to disturb!" she said. When everyone got thoroughly chilled by all this beauty, they went inside ... slipping and falling on the steps! In the hall, there was a huge cedar tree dressed out in bunting, lights, plastic birds. On the very top was a two-foot high angel holding a candle and looking down into the tree the way I've seen blue jays look, head cocked to one side.

Young Percival found a friend, and each of them found a wrapped gift under the tree before they were noticed and told to shush and leave things alone. There was an older man, a retired minister, in the crowd. After the food and coffee were brought in and everyone got rid of hats, mittens, and coats, this older man clapped his hands together for attention. "Before we begin celebrating, I think we should consider all those in the world less fortunate than we. But even more important, we should first give our hearts and thoughts to peace in these trying times ... "
There was a murmur of approval in the hall, and, encouraged, he continued, "If we, and others like us around the world, think of peace ... pray for peace ... we can will peace to prevail, for the soul of man is the mightiest force on earth, mightier than a hundred hydrogen bombs. It is the sign of our emerging civilization that we can now at least understand this. So I ask that we bow our heads for three minutes, during which we concentrate with all our hearts and minds for peace ... peace for ourselves, and peace for all humanity ... "

Well ... I think we made it through the first minute and a half. For you see, young Percival, my grandson, was a boy. And his friend was a boy. And what they'd each opened as gifts were two boxes of these put-together stick toys. Percival made a pistol out of his, and the other boy a machine-gun. They came out the kitchen,

through the crowd, and out the front door with all the speed and sound of two lads having a helluva good time ... rat-tat-tatting and pow-powing ... firing and pushing at each other on the run.

"It wasn't Percival ... It was that other little bastard set him up to it!" said my daughter, a long time after, when rituals and public display of private goodness seemed to matter less ...

Song: "Strangest Dream."

Two old men in a city lane, in rising disagreement over which year the Second World War ended ...
"Nineteen forty-five!" shouts one.
"Ya'll always argue over what you forgot! It was nineteen forty-six!" shouts the other.
One shoves the other—the other pushes back. Both are breathless and quivering now, with great principles of truth tilting on the outcome of this struggle. One throws a punch ... and misses ... shouts in a voice piping with youthful outrage and indignation, "Stand still, goddamn ya, so I can hit ya!"

Song: "Reuben James."

I drink too much. My old friend Chester drinks too much. Not the drinking of gentle women and their round-faced escorts ... sipping expensively from cut glass to the tinkling of ice cubes and muted Montavani waltzes. I drink to fill my belly and my head at the dripping table ... in the company of farters and pissers, who belch their stories into a hazy room of smoke, wild laughter ... and heart-rending sorrow ...

The backhoe driver at the next table holds up a wet finger to his nose ... inhales deeply and exclaims in rapture, "Ah, Louise ... Louise!" He has thick lips and a bristle of beard. And his friends laugh as he sticks all the wet fingers of both hands into the pizza in front of him—an anchovy pizza, whose odour reminds him of Louise ... or a bad joke to pass the sad time ...

Across the room, a woman with a bitter smile sits alone. She sits alone and stares at me. And I stare back ... I know I have been drinking too much. For I see ghosts pass between us—ghosts of laughter and remembered love ... chasing each other over fields of fresh snow ... entering a new apartment ... phantom children that might have been, carrying souvenirs of love and togetherness in their tiny hands ...

New ghosts now take their place ... rising from the wet, stinking floor. Loud, foul-mouthed visitors of violence ... shirts open to their navels ... thick lips spitting abuse at parked cars, children on bicycles, women who work, Pakistanis, and Jews. With heavy boots they violate floors they never laid nor polished. Nothing separating man from beast escapes their notice: poetry in schools ... the right to a political opinion ... the withholding of corporal and capital punishment ... An open-handed blow to the face ends all discussion, puts children into silence and women on their backs. Fed, fooled, and fucked, they growl out the open door ... prowling and staggering into other doorways, other lives, beating on tables with their fists and braying, "Gimme! ... Gimme!"

I drink too much, and stumble into spaces between tables in places of sadness and despair. But tonight ... tonight, it turned out for the best. I rise on my elbow, in a strange room, staring at the street below. She sleeps beside me—this Madonna with the bitter smile and dark mysteries I will never understand. This pied piper of ghosts and endless nights. This humanizer of men's souls ...

Song: "Belle Starr."

It is nothing compared to other things I have seen in other places. Old Chester knows them things, too ... and we talk about them sometimes ... The sea at the end of a sea sounding day ...

On a boulevard in Amsterdam, a child-whore gets time off to eat an ice-cream cone. She sits under a mulberry tree ... in the shade. What is she dreaming of? Does she know of summer camps for girls her age on Vancouver Island? Or of canoeing down the mountain rivers of Russia with the Young Pioneers? Of playing at keeping house and learning to hate, and then forgive, Mother ... who did everything wrong? I never asked her ...

A short distance from her, in the shelter of a stone wall, her pimp was negotiating the remainder of her day with three middle-aged men from Tangiers, who had bought everything with their wealth except this ...

The pimp had knife scars on his face, and a voice like gravel falling down a metal chute ...

Song: "In Amsterdam There Lived a Maid."

The sea at the end of a sea sounding day ... the wild gulls lifted by capricious winds, thrown this way and that, their white bellies catching the pink-bellied sunset. A solitary kite hanging ... holding up a golden haired boy from falling on the sand ... and a woman with a ragamuffin dog bundled in her coat, her head low, braced against the flying, foaming breakers dying on the sad, sighing seawall of grey granite ... pine trees on the promontory bend and groan ... a panting runner hurries with the wind, her bronze legs rippling like the living sea ...

The sea at the end of a sea sounding day ... and I climb down to the edge of the pounding surf, to be drenched in wind-torn mist, to be wakened fully to the whooping, tumbling eddies, to shout and be silenced by the thundering roll, to be part for a short moment in the play of wind and water and falling sun in a magic game of joy and frenzy which will remain like this long, long after I have gone ...

Song: "The Doryman."

My friend, Chester, got himself a hearing aid. He wore it the last time I saw him.
"How's it work?" I asked him.
"I can hear you clear as a bell. Haven't heard things so good in twenty years!"
"That thing cost you much?" I ask him.
"Four hundred and seventy-two dollars ..."
"That's a lot of money to spend on hearing ... What kind is it?"
"Twenty after three," he said, looking at his watch ...

Short banjo interlude.

Our summers seem to grow colder and shorter as I age, and it worries me ... I bought a new pair of shoes, and they pinch my feet. They will pinch my feet for as long as I wear them. They are made in Canada of Canadian leather grown on a Canadian cow ... I bought a pair of jeans, and the fly zipper broke the second time I used it ... The post office delivered my mail faster and more reliably thirty years ago than it does today ...

Bridges fall and stucco on new building splits, and the roofs leaked at Expo '86 ... I was in a new car two months ago, and the car changed lanes by itself ... twice... once on a bridge. Oh, the owner complained, and was told it was "a peculiarity of the model ... "

Our summers seem to grow colder as I age ...
We were proud once—the shoe repairman, the farmer, bricklayer, doctor, the builder of sky-scrapers—all of us were proud of our competence and skills. Today ... zippers break an' shoes pinch ... money for replanting forests vanishes ... mismanagement is rewarded as a national virtue.

Our summers seem to grow colder as I age and I watch our Prime Minister announce with boyish exuberance that he will outwit Yankee traders at their own game of free-wheeling trade and con-quest! While I ... and you ... watch our slide into a Third World economy without the benefits of a Third World culture with its promise of resurrec-tion and redemption ... Our summers grow colder as I age, and it worries me ...

Song: "If I Were A Carpenter."

A couple of doors down the street where I live, two Swiss carpenters are rebuilding a porch.
"Do you remember—have you seen the stone lion in Lucerne?" one asked the other. "It is ten meters long and as tall as a house. From the lake it looks small, but when you see it close, with the great lance in its body ... that is something to see! It is said it was made after the French Revolution, when the Swiss went to help save the King of France. It is said we fought more than once to save someone else's king ... but it could be, how you say in this country, bullshit?"
"I've heard that, too," the other carpenter agreed and lit a cigarette.
"Still, that lion is something to see! If I ever go back to Lucerne, I want to see it again. It is carved right into the mountain, they say. And they say the artist who made that lion killed himself when he finished ..."
"Oh? I didn't know that ..."
"Yah ... they say he got very unhappy. He made the tail on the lion too short, or something like that. He couldn't be happy again with something like that, so he killed himself. That's what they all say. Even my mother's sister, Marietta, she told me that, too ... "

Song: "I Went Up in a Balloon So Big."

The afternoon streets of Dawson Creek in the warm days of early spring. The snow banks melt-ing, resurrecting the cats killed by traffic during winter, and then buried in snow ... scraped and uplifted by snowplows into two cat grave mounds, one to the right of the street, the other to the left. Late afternoon in the warming days of Spring, and the cats emerging now from their graves—preserved as they were in their final moments through the wonders of chilling and highway salt ... black cats and grey cats ... tabby cats and ginger cats. Some serene, lying on their backs with four paws pointing upwards. Others agonized and contorted. And one ... with claws out ... paw upraised ... teeth bared and eyes open. Frozen in rage at some passing motorist who may himself have died since ... or left town ... or gone to work in the mines at Tumbler Ridge ...

I've been cold an' had things stole,
But minin' is the life for me,
Eating bacon, beans an' bannock,
I will live 'til I'm ninety-three!

In the courtroom, the day I had to appear to pay eleven overdue parking tickets, I found no one ... no one at all with the faintest glimmer of human compassion in their eyes! There were two murderers there ... one car thief, and a young man with a sallow complexion who had beaten his mother with a tire iron.
"Feeling better?" I asked the mother-beater by way of passing time while we waited our turn to be called into court. He kind of warmed to me.

"What are you in for?" he asked.
"Parking tickets," I said, and I saw the slight enthusiasm he'd revealed die in his face. The murderers and their heavy escort of police and lawyers had no interest in me, either. An' the car thief was on the phone to his shop, doing business ... and snapping at his lawyer over his shoulder to get him out in half an hour or he'd send him packing ...

Inside the courtroom ... the clerks and stenogra-phers ... police and witnesses stared straight ahead ... and they stared at nothing. Then the judge came in ... and his eyes looked like they'd been transplanted and hadn't taken root in his head. He called my name, then sneezed so powerfully the papers in front of him flew all over his desk. He gathered them together ... looked down at them, then lifted his head to look at me. He was a man my age ... and looking back at him, I suddenly saw fear ... and something like admi-ration in his eyes. Just briefly, but it was there ...

"Would you tell the court," he said, "what led you to … to take a tire iron to your mother …"

> I've sung songs an' told some stories,
> Lost my temper now an' then,
> Damn the banks an' the courts an' dealers,
> Dudes who rob with a fountain pen.
>
> When you see me bent an' lonely
> And bow-legged at the knee,
> Lock your jeans an' your banks of marble
> For I'll take what belongs to me.
>
> To them that hath it shall be given,
> God help poor men such as me,
> Until I die I shall be watched by
> The sheriff an' his deputy …
>
> Too-ree-ama …

I'm going to see old Chester Sharpe for the summer solstice, that's what I'll do! We will climb a mountain together to drink from a bottle of Jamaican rum an' watch the sun of the longest day rise … bursting like an electric arc over the dark ridge of mountains to the northeast … igniting with orange flames the trunks of pine trees around us … turning the blue grey sky into a rainbow of greens, reds, and purples!

What an hour to be alive! How many cold, short winter days have we suffered for this? How many times have we struggled against fevers … and the dark spirits of the night … because we knew such a morning as this was coming! I will take old Chester's hand … raise him to his feet … and together we shall dance on the dewy grass, under a heaven of indigo and red licks of flame … two snowy-haired men with banjos on their backs and something forever young laughing … laughing … laughing … laughing in their eyes!

(*on exit*)

> To them that hath it shall be given,
> God help poor men such as me,
> Until I die I shall be watched by
> The sheriff an' his deputy …
>
> Too-ree-ama …

ACT 2

Chester Sharpe's days are numbered.

"All my juices have dried out," he said when I saw him.

"All my juices are gone an' I sit by the window seein' the deed without feeling the pleasure. Yesterday, a healthy woman walked by, raking the street with her eyes, searching for anything to relieve boredom … an' you know, before she got to the tobacco store down on the corner there, I was dozin' off!"

Rising on his elbows he laughed, but his eyes were crying …

The sea at the end of a sea sounding day, and the wild gulls lifted by the winds …

The rundown room where he lives, half on memories and half on welfare, rings with a thousand songs. Each one pegged in his mind like an old shirt, or a souvenir … some carried from faraway places … some brought by women he loved once … and others picked up like stray paper in the alleys and the footpaths of this world. Love songs echoing among mockeries of people forming ideas from the crudest tools of language …

"Throw dat bull over the fence … some hay!"

"Twice time already, I say—no!"

"Big house, eh? Two storage wide garage even!"

"Ay-yay—dat minister of finance one greedy baster!"

"So I says to the fuckin' mechanic, eh—this fuckin' lawnmower doesn't work worth a fuck, eh … "

> So far art thou my bonnie lass,
> So deep in love am I,
> And I will love thee still, my dear,
> 'Til all the seas gang dry …

And all the sweet nonsense of the late afternoon people milling in village squares from here to forever were the domain of my friend, Chester! He missed nothing of mischief, pain, arrogance … all the things which take men and women from darkness to darkness. And when they sang, or mocked … or laughed at themselves, Chester stole these moments and carried them away with him. He brought them to where I live … and where you live … and we are all the better for it …

Song: "I'm A Rover."

I took a fancy to an Arab woman who wore a coat of wolf skins. She wore it that cold January night when I sang in a bar in Brandon, and she came to hear me ... and stayed long after closing time. A teacher who drove a red Porsche sports car with the roof down, even at twenty degrees below zero. An Arab woman, with dusky skin and dark eyes that laughed ... and teased! Even with wolf pelts on her back, her eyes still mirrored the pale sands of hot deserts ... minarets and bazaars scented with cloves and warmed by the hot winds of Africa. She was Islam-on-the-Arctic border, listening in a smoky bar while I sang,

> So fair art thou my bonnie lass,
> So deep in love am I,
> And I will love thee still, my dear,
> 'Til all the seas gang dry ...

With the skins of five timber wolves on her back, she hung around the borderlands of respectability, sipping orange juice ... and waiting for trouble. And I ... was willing to oblige! For I took a fancy to her ... and the worries of tomorrow, and tomorrow after that, meant nothing then. I was alive—in robust health, and budding as a man must to the end of his days. For what is life if we fear to leave others to follow through the sad and boisterous centuries to come?

She reaches for her coat and we are on the street, hurrying to her car. It is cold, and she is bareheaded. The wolf fur rises on her back to meet the chill ...
We drive toward the morning sun ... a tired ring of fire on the frozen plain. To the right of us, a hundred sheep are munching hay from broken bales. I touch her hand. It is cold. Hoar frost has frozen on her eyelashes, and the wolf fur has risen to her ears.
She stops the car to drop the roof against the wind. The sheep sense ... or smell her. There is a bleat, and then another, and they flee from the woman with five wolf pelts on her back. They strike the rail fence on the far side of the pen as one body. It buckles and falls to the snow ... and a hundred sheep gallop bleating for safety into the rising sun ...

Song: "Baa, Baa Black Sheep."

So we take food together, the Arab woman and I, and waste the time in conversations about Palestinians, comparative religions, and the annual snowfall in the Rocky Mountains! She is a sweet and gentle person ... with a mind running easy circles around this snow-clogged brain of mine. Yet ... it is all good fun—teasing and loving in the way it has always been when philosophers meet barbarians on the edge of the forest and try to engage them in conversation! I try to dispute something she has said, and knock the bread plate off the table with a wide sweep of my hand, intended to impress her with the force and size of the point I was about to make. She laughs ... and tiny devils dance in her eyes ... with their pale memories of deserts far, far away ... The wolf fur rises on her back in the winter night, and I cry out to her!

A man needs a drink ... a woman friend ... light music and summer stories to lighten the pain. For death will come in darkness, grazing my eyes with the feathers of its iron wings ... scarring them with after-images of failure ... of being chased through fields and forests ... of falling into chasms ... of loneliness so great it dries my throat and leaves me breathless and trembling in fear! The wolf fur rises in memory of the woman that I loved ... and in January ... every January ... I hunger for the flavour of fresh figs I have never tasted ...

Song: "The Summertime Is Comin'."

When I was a boy ... and the world I moved through was a boy's world with sweet sticky things to eat, handed to me by elder women with sweet sticky fingers and aprons that seemed to be made of cinnamon and burned sugar ... and in the sky, a sun moving through bandages of clouds so slowly ... so very slowly ... as to make each day feel like forever.

When I was a boy, there were things God put in my way to torment me. Nettles in the meadow stopped me as I ran from here to there. Like a policeman, dark and tall they stood, with one, sometimes two, upraised arms. "Pass by in peril," they said in silence I could hear. And I stopped, knowing even as a boy that I faced a weed with no intelligence, but an ability to hurt, much the way real policemen can ... so I walked around them, my mouth dry and eyes not blinking so as not to be surprised by anything I could not see. Many summer times I walked around the nettles. But a boy hurrying into manhood changes. So ... one summer afternoon, I took along a two-foot length of fallen fence rail and I beat that nettle bush down. But then ... still a boy ... walked around it, fearing the possibility of resurrection and revenge from that dark green mess of broken vegetation.

When I was a boy, even dogs held sway with me. The butcher's dog at the bottom of the lane waited for me ... waited for me in the mornings as I ran late for school. Chained to a stone gatepost, he would wait in ambush ... knowing I had only the morning school bell on my mind. He would lunge ... to the full extent of his rusty collar chain ... his fangs bared ... yellow eyes glaring ... flecks of hate spittle flying from his open mouth... his paws tearing at the cobbles as he tried to reach me with his teeth ... the collar chain ringing and a wet bark exploding from his throat. I would run to the end of the lane before I stopped and turned—to see him sitting, watching me ... panting with laughter, his tail wagging and the rusty chain hanging down his back ... still fastened to the stone gatepost ...

Song: "I've Got a Dog and His Name is Fido."

"Whose dog are you?" I once wrote for the hell of it on a piece of paper and stuck the paper in the neck chain of a big St. Bernard who took a liking to me in the park. Next afternoon, he saw me in the park again, an' came loping over, barking happy to see me. In his chain was a fresh piece of paper, folded in two. It read: "I am Abe McPherson's dog. And whose dog are you?"

Song: "I've Got A Dog And His Name Is Rover."

A happy drunk on a windy street waves to me an' shouts, "I am a buffalo an' I'm leavin' this place! Ya know?"
"Why do that?" I shout back.
"Because I'm certain I heard a discouraging word!"
And he points to a bar behind him an' calls over the wind, "In there!"

Short, lively banjo interlude.

You know, every man with a big belly fancies himself an athlete! That's why men go to hockey games, football, boxing matches, especially the ones carryin' another half man under their skins. They go to see if the fellows on the ice or in the boxing ring are doin' it right! No other reason ...

hear them in a bar or restaurant after the event, and listen to the great debates over who choked the puck ... which breakaway was missed ... or how the contender failed seven times in the first round and a half to flatten the title holder! Then ... they take to water—divers thirty-five years out of pools, throwing themselves off the diving-board in pursuit of lost graces—to land in a wide-buttocked splash ... inundating other swimmers, making children shriek in fear. The diving champ ... or chump ... sinks in the deep water ... then emerges in an unexpected place, water deafened, eye goggles filled ... and hoots with manly pride, "Hot damn, but I can still do it! Did you see me do that, Charlie? Did you see me? ... Eh?"
And an upset child dog-paddles to the safety of mother and shallow water, while a lithe twenty-year old woman, interrupted in her graceful laps, treads water, glares at the boisterous intruder and silently forms a word with her lips—asshole!

On the golf course, this old guy goes nuts! He's trying to put the ball in the hole. He's movin' like this ... his putter out ... an' he's talking out loud to the ball: "Get in there, you sonofabitch! Get in there, you syphilitic whore! ... Get ... Ay! She's in! Whoo-ee! ... Anyone see me do that, eh?"
There was no one. Nobody to tell the world, for this was not an organ transplant ... or a car bombing ... or even a conflict of interest in government scandal. This triumph of the spirit was nothing—just one fat man making a small, white rubber ball roll into a hole in the ground ... scooped out just for that purpose!

An' they all play
On the golf course,
An' they all drink
Their martinis dry ... (*etc.*)

"Watch out, Billy!" cries the grandmother to her disabled boy, for the helpless don't pay their way, and Billy is the loser in the growing new order of more for those who have, an' a little less for those who haven't.
"Watch out, Billy!" I echo granny, for Billy hasn't got a full deck to play with, and free trade negotiations with the Yanks are gibberish to him.
"Watch out, Billy!" I cry out with her ... for there is talk in the bars and rougher places of letting the sick and helpless migrate to Manitoba, or Ontario, where an auto industry can afford them! We're into trees an' mining here ... markets

fluctuate too much to burden ourselves with infirmities, old age, even education. As for the mentally handicapped, well, there's always privatized goodwill—no?

"Watch out, Billy!" I cry with his granny, for in this charity he is taught not to complain of toothache, hunger, or resentment. Not to complain of the training centres where he will work ... and get paid sixty cents a day. And the cruel joke roams the hallways of these places— why pay them more? What would they spend their money on—Smarties?

"Watch out, Billy!" I cry at the distance which separates his mind from mine. "Watch out, boy!" If someone pushes, you push back. An' if some- one hits, you holler loud enough so me an' him an' her can hear and come running to help you. For we all got to stick together ... old and young ... the sick an' healthy ... men an' women ... labourer an' teacher. We all got to help each other through the long winter coming our way!

> I've been cold an' I've been hungry,
> Seen my share of wealth an' pain,
> Run my race against the weather,
> Come in laughin' from the rain!

Hey—being alive, that is something! Even on the street ... with a cold wind cutting into the face at seven in the morning, and all hope dying, as a man gathers with other men in front of the food bank building. An' the stench of poverty and fail- ure like stagnant cabbage soup hanging in the air. Knowing deep inside that it was not economics or political philosophy which has brought us to this wet, cold morning of despair ... but that it is greed and stupidity. Greed in the pig-eyed faces of boy-politicians playing at men's games—and reducing each human life, like a sheet of plywood, to a bargain price. So much for an able- bodied man with a trade certificate, so much for a blinded child, and this much for a pregnant woman. For whom the good times were the days of twelve-year old boys working in the mines for fifty cents a day! Of women sewing shirts in unheated, dusty rooms at eight cents an hour. Of the aged and the ill reduced to survival through charity of children or parish. Of tuberculosis and other diseases of poverty moving from door to door like an unwelcome guest. Of slow death through surrender ...

But being alive—is something! They will not take this away now! To be alive is to fight back ... to turn our skills into weapons ... to make paper an' pen ... the artist's brush ... the camera thirsting after truth ... the singing and speaking voice ... the banjo ... into tools of resistance to darkness!

Song: "We Shall Not Be Moved."

My friend Chester used to call times like these "the season of the scoundrels" ... with big money moving against organized labour ... against family farms ... against the poor who seem to consume more than they produce. No mercy is shown, an' an independent mind is marked and tracked with the exuberance of a big game hunt. At the peak of hungry rage, entire countries are ticked for submission or death—Guatemala, Nicaragua, the Philippines, Syria ...

The sea at the end of a sea sounding day ...

And from the shorelines of Manila to Haiti, shoeshine boys with tired eyes splat and pop the dying moments of the long day over pointy-toed brogues encasing black, brown, and white feet of gangsters, land dealers, retired professors, rice merchants, bankers, and street thieves— the makers, shakers, and withholders of this world ...

> On the hundredth day the summer ended
> Packed my bags to move along,
> But Jenny stopped me on the corner
> With a chorus to my song ...

The sea ... at the end of a sea sounding day ... And on the shoreline of Managua, Alberta farmers wait for inbound spare parts for Massey- Harris tractors for the campesinos. Juan gets to know John, and a new brotherhood between peoples takes root ... built on trust, understand- ing ... love and concern of ordinary folk for one another ... nothing else ... just this. But what a difference it has made!

> I've known fun an' I've felt sorrow,
> A bit of anger now an' then,
> But there'll always be tomorrow
> To get things straightened out again ...

A gun-barrel highway into the setting sun, and the sky a great worn mat of orange and indigo of atmospheric dusts and wastes sky-borne to let the Almighty know we are a busy place here with debts to pay off, an' no time for play ... A gun-barrel highway spun with ramps entering and leaving this miracle of speed and indifference. And yet ... the fiery fingers of a wounded, shrouded sun reach for my eyes, my lips, my skin faded by twenty thousand nights and days ...

"Man remembers, and so man is holy," Chester Sharpe told me once, but his words were wasted on me then.

But now ... I roll down the window of the speeding car with feverish fingers ... gulp the air and light and shout to the driver, "Slow down! ... This ... is what I've been waiting for! The light of heaven itself!"

And somewhere beyond ... maybe ... perhaps ... just a chance ... the face of the Almighty Himself! Searching for me beyond a shrouded sun and a gun-barrel highway ... "Over there! I think ... I saw Him! I saw Him!" I shout. But my cry is the cry of the spirit, and no one hears me. Ahead, the road becomes night in a muddy shroud of debts to pay an' no time to play ...

Song: "I've Been Doing Some Hard Travelling."

"One more for the road!" Chester Sharpe would say at the end of a night in a bar ... or among friends, when all the songs were sung, an' he still remembered one he'd forgot ...
"One more for the road!" he said one night long ago in a whorehouse, unbuckling his belt, and the ladies not believing him, then breaking up in laughter when they saw he was funning!

He used to lead marches of strikers ... peace walks ... protests of minorities ... his banjo ringing and his funny feet plopping like those of a fat duck. He sang of romance, my good friend, Chester. He sang of men gone to war ... an' he sang of maidens left behind to mourn. But he was not a romantic. "I am a lover. I love women, life, and intelligence," he would say even when no one asked.
"But I have no sympathy or love for those who grovel in the presence of a foreman or a minister of state. I fear an unquestioning man as I fear winter."
"Where ... is hope in all this?" I asked.
And old Chester, he looked puzzled, like he'd lost his place in a book ...

Short banjo interlude.

In a windy town with bare linden trees and old country roofs with dry wood shingles moaning in the gale, Chester took sick an' I nursed him. We shared canned soup and talked of where John Diefenbaker had gone wrong ... at least, I did most of the talking an' Chester listened, his face shiny with pain sweat. On the fifth day, he sat up in bed, and looking down said, "You know, Dick, my legs should've growed another three inches when I was a boy." An' then he laughed over the wind sounds, and started putting clothes over his little body, his hands so thin I could almost see through them ...

I've known fun an' I've felt sorrow ...

Last night, I had a dream in which Chester had grown wings from the hunch in his back. He cut his shirt open to let them out. Because, he told me, now that his legs didn't work, he needed new means of transportation to get to his gigs! To get to his place in the front lines of marches.
"You are an angel ... those wings confirm it!" I said to him in my dream. But he laughed an' shook his head.
"You can't be an angel after fifty. You know too much, and the sins of not having done enough for the world cannot be washed away ... I'm no angel. Angels are babes sleeping in their cribs ... angels are student revolutionaries dreaming the impossible dream ... angels are whores against wars—who kept for themselves the one virtue that matters ... angels are men and women who have created more than they consumed, an' given the rest to others. I'm no angel. I ate most everything I made. And what's more ... I'd do it again!"

> I'm a rover, seldom sober,
> I'm a rover of high degree,
> An' when I'm drinkin' I gets to thinkin'
> How to gain my love's company! ...

End

PARACELSUS

Paracelsus is Ryga's grandest and most difficult work. Researched as he roamed the dusky, medieval streets of an utterly foreign town, written during the dark hours in another country, it wrung from Ryga some of his most towering poetry as well as his most unwieldy dramaturgy. As a stage play, it attempts the near impossible: to stage the "pageant of human suffering," to portray one of history's most clamorous rebels, and to create a strident cultural critique through the juxtaposition of ancient and modern medical practices. The work, when first published, was introduced by Peter Hay as "a challenge, an outright provocation" to Canadian theatre—would or could his own country stage him? For years it remained unproduced. Sprawling, combative, a wrenching piece torn from the depths, it remains Ryga's single monumental work, comparable to Ibsen's *Brand* or O'Neill's *Long Day's Journey into Night*.

Not surprisingly, the work loomed early in the playwright's imagination, probably as early as the mid-1950s when he spent a year in Europe attending highly politicized left-wing youth rallies and meeting a number of activist writers. Having personally befriended some of the major international figures instrumental in initiating many of the cultural changes of the twentieth century, such as Rewi Alley, the visionary who helped rebuild China during the 1930s, he was determined to develop his own critique of society—in this instance through evoking one of the giants of the medical arts. Glancing through *A History of Medicine in Pictures* (1957), which featured the oil paintings of Robert Thom—widely popular in the 1950s, reproductions of which were prominently displayed in many a doctor's waiting room—he was struck by the illustration of Paracelsus, the sixteenth-century physician-reformer, sitting alone, troubled, brooding over his medical papers in his laboratory, all the while staring harshly at the viewer. Ryga felt immediate resonance, "strange quiverings" as he later reported, between that early period of struggle for humanist medical reform and his own. In Canada at that time Medicare was a contentious topic: with only half of all citizens on a medical plan, there was growing debate over the need for nation-wide health protection—with the medical establishment, including many doctors, and of course, pharmaceutical companies, often in vociferous opposition.

It was not to be until the fall of 1972, however, after the *Captives of the Faceless Drummer* controversy, that Ryga was finally able to travel to Switzerland and conduct his personal journey in search of Paracelsus. For once there was no commission for him to fulfill: at his disposal were simply some available funds from a Canada Council grant, so he could chart his own course. He studied in the medical archives at the University of Zurich, then made field trips to Paracelsus's place of birth, the tiny medieval town of Einsiedeln in the heart of Switzerland, site of the enormous Abbey Church and home of one of the famous Black Madonnas. Indeed, the town is Switzerland's most important city of pilgrimage, founded by a revered ninth-century hermit (*Einsiedler* means "hermit"). Ryga immersed himself in the town's atmosphere, walking the same narrow streets, listening to the same mournful Abbey bells as had Paracelsus centuries earlier. He believed he came to know in his bones something of the town and a lot about the man. He wrote early drafts of his eponymous play in Mexico, where he had gone to live after this pilgrimage, once again writing late into the night and reflecting deeply on his home country. In *A Portrait of Angelica*, which he was also writing at the same time, his protagonist, Danny Baker, is made to say that he is "saddened that my country has so few heroic men." Clearly the awesome figure of

Paracelsus could be used as a touchstone for a critique of the ongoing public debate over the contemporary Canadian medical establishment and practice—as personified in the script by Doctors Guza and Webb.

The play was first completed in the early 1970s, and published in the fourth issue of the journal *Canadian Theatre Review* (Fall 1974), with an introduction by Peter Hay, then subsequently in book form by Turnstone Press in 1982, paired with *Prometheus Bound*. It remained unstaged until 1986 when, surprisingly, the Vancouver Playhouse Theatre, the company that had refused to stage his *Captives of the Faceless Drummer*, suddenly wanted to mount a full production of *Paracelsus* as part of the "World Festival" Expo '86 cultural series. It seemed like a dream of the prodigal son come true: here was the Company where Ryga had made his reputation with successful stagings of *The Ecstasy of Rita Joe*, *Grass and Wild Strawberries*, and his play for young people, *Compressions*, now planning to mount his most imposing work, and there appeared to be the necessary level of support in the budget, venue, and personnel—August Schellenberg, the original Jaimie Paul in *Rita Joe*, would play the lead role, John Juliani, of the Savage God production company, would direct, and Ryga's close associates, Cheryl Cashman and Dick Clements, would assist with workshopping the script.

The Vancouver Playhouse production of *Paracelsus* opened on September 26, 1986, a spectacular failure, brought down by almost everyone who could have and should have assured its potentially spectacular success: funding turned out to be significantly less than anticipated; there was a lack of firm direction; and the workshop process degenerated into a myriad of rewrites that left everyone, especially Ryga himself, confused, frustrated and deeply embittered. Reviewers were uniformly critical—with one of them, Ray Conlogue, of the *Globe and Mail* (Oct. 18, 1986) wondering "Where were the co-pilots that could have transformed Ryga into a major name?" It is a question that remained both unanswered and unaddressed at the time of George Ryga's death in 1987, ironically of stomach cancer (the medical establishment had been treating him throughout the *Paracelsus* production fiasco and its aftermath for misdiagnosed stomach ulcers until it was far too late), and it remains unanswered to this day.

PARACELSUS

CHARACTERS

A cast of 24 players, from which are drawn the secondary characters in the play. Human bodies must be used to texture the play with a sense of humanity relentlessly moving out of one epoch into another. This may be specifically medieval, or it may not.

The four principal players are:

PARACELSUS
FRANZ, *his student*
DR. PATRICK WEBB, *a young medical doctor*
DR. BETTY GUZA, *his colleague in a contemporary hospital*

ACT 1

Curtain up.

Three level stage. Lowest front level is sterile and tidy. This setting has a table that contains a coffee urn at one time—lab equipment at another. Two or three chairs.

Second and third levels are progressively darker and more medieval. The more distant and higher the set becomes, the more brooding and aged its atmosphere. There must be tension and violence in the set, but at all times it is only the canvas against which the pageant of human suffering is played out.

SOUND: Bells of Einsiedeln.

Faint silhouette light over highest level.

Barking of dogs. People fleeing in silhouette in rags, with their possessions over their shoulders. Movement of people is continuous. Soon, some are armed with staves, and turn to fight hack imaginary animals and attackers, as others flee past them. This gives way to defenders with swords. Now the injured are being helped as they flee for refuge.

Sounds of gunfire, and crude muskets replace the swords. Men carrying hammers and scythes pass

these to fleeing women, and picking up guns, turn to their unseen attackers, fighting as they retreat. Puffs of red light over sound of distant cannon fire.

Action and sound accelerate now. Distant sound of the "Marseilles" and fragments of songs from the German peasant rebellions, Russian revolution and the Chinese "Chilai." Rattle of machine guns, roar of aircraft, sound and flash of bombings.

Sudden end to panorama of flight and battle. PARACELSUS rises from back of set in silhouette, dressed in homespun robe. The people rise around him, bringing their wounded and sick. He heals them. They offer him goods and money. He dismisses the gestures with an abrupt, angry motion.

An insane woman is brought to him in manacles. He releases her, then holds her head until her wild movements subside. Similar actions of healing and compassion are played out during scene on lower level of set.

Light on lower level of set. Sound of bells abruptly out.

Two interns, DR. BETTY GUZA and DR. PATRICK WEBB, both dressed in medical attire, approach each other from opposite sides of stage.

DR. WEBB: How is she?

DR. GUZA: She's dead ... there was nothing we could do for her.

DR. WEBB: I'm sorry. Will you join me for coffee in the canteen?

DR. GUZA: Not just yet.

DR. WEBB shrugs and turns to leave.

DR. GUZA: There was nothing more we could do for her, Patrick ... You understand what that means?

DR. WEBB: *(nodding)* I was here four days when my first patient died.

DR. GUZA: *(becoming agitated)* That's not what I want to say ... We did everything according to procedures, yet ...

Loud laughter of PARACELSUS from darkened levels of stage. DR. GUZA is startled.

DR. GUZA: What was that?

DR. WEBB: Is something wrong?

DR. GUZA: I heard someone laughing.

DR. WEBB: You've been on call too long, honey ... let me buy you that coffee.

DR. GUZA: (*insistent*) I heard someone laugh!

DR. WEBB: We've both had twelve hours of surgical duty today. I'd be happier if we could leave after six hours, but we're low people on the totem pole at this hospital, so maybe we'd both better get used to the idea of suffering ... come on ...

Another laugh from PARACELSUS. DR. GUZA listens intently. DR. WEBB moves away, but seeing the expression on her face, returns to her.

DR. WEBB: Why are you staring at me like that?

DR. GUZA: You ... heard nothing?

DR. WEBB: Are you feeling alright, Betty?

DR. GUZA: Yes ... yes, I'm fine ... (*stares into distance*) I ... I sometimes wonder what a dying person in the ward thinks of us!

Another laugh from PARACELSUS. But DR. GUZA responds to it with only a slight movement of her head.

DR. WEBB: (*smiling professionally*) If you wish, I'll go through my lecture notes from med school and bring you a detailed report on the psychological responses to death in a metropolitan hospital. But not tonight ... not tonight ...

DR. GUZA: I'm sorry ... it's the first patient I've lost. And the experience is frightening. When I ... looked into her eyes for the last time ... I was scared. I wondered what I was doing here ... or if I was fit to be a doctor.

DR. WEBB: Hey—come on! We're doing the best we can with the finest support systems in the world, Betty.

DR. GUZA: But it's not enough!

DR. WEBB: You and I know it's not enough ... but to the sick and helpless world out there we're magicians ... we're like gods in the things we do with the human mind and body!

DR.GUZA: Are we treating illness, or only the symptoms?

DR. WEBB: (*grinning*) That kind of question is one sure way of flunking med school ... remember Black Mac and his pep talks? (*mimics a military-like medical instructor in a gruff voice*) Disease is the enemy, an' you're the army at war, an' the first stage of a good army is discipline! I want discipline an' I want order ... in this school an' in your goddamned heads. Is that understood? An' I don't want any questions when I'm talking! A good army doesn't vote!

DR. GUZA: If you still remember all that crap, then you're as sick as he was!

DR. WEBB: Alright! ... Who in hell knows the difference, Betty? People go to a doctor like they go to a shoe store—they pay for what they came to buy.

DR. GUZA: I lost a patient this evening!

DR. WEBB: And if you don't smarten up, you'll lose another! (*gently now*) Okay—it isn't what it might be, I know. But if a man comes to me asking for a week of illusion, am I to jeopardize my professional career by offering him ten years of difficult life instead? Besides, I wouldn't know how to do it—that's *my* illness as well as his ...

DR. GUZA: (*irritated*) What in hell kind of attitude is that? A girl who should have lived ... *had* to live according to my charts and test results ... died on me this afternoon!

DR. WEBB: What do you want me to do—sorrow for her? For you? The name of this game is efficiency and indifference, honey!

DR. GUZA stares at him, bewildered.

DR. GUZA: I'm sorry for jumping you, Patrick. That wasn't very professional of me.

DR. WEBB: You're a woman—you have that right. I'm not tough, either, Betty. So when I get through this, I'm going to specialize. The less I know about the patient as an entire person, the happier I'll be. I'm not a missionary. I'm not even very bright ...

DR. GUZA: Am I?

DR. WEBB: You don't have to eat yourself up in general practice, Betty ... there's not a helluva lot of money in research, but that's where you can still make a name for yourself. I can't belong in that league, but you do ...

DR. GUZA: That's a silly thing to say.

DR. WEBB: Then are you prepared to see people die in front of you? Baby, you an' I have enough problems just getting by in this world without that. I need more distance between myself and my work. So do you. Come on—I need a coffee.

Both of them move to leave.

DR. GUZA: I wonder what it would be like ... to be a real healer?

DR. WEBB: A living hell, I'd imagine ...

Light out on their exit.

Light up on centre level of stage. An ancient, disintegrating, dusty casket is being closed by hooded diggers, who pick up their shovels and leave. The casket remains in background.

PARACELSUS, old and pained, stands beside the casket, watching. As the diggers leave, he examines the stains on his smock and clumsily rubs dust from his face and clothing.

PARACELSUS: Once more
My bones have been disturbed ...
Pried from the earth ...
Examined in the sun ... pondered over ...
Wise pronouncements made
Over shape of skull—
Cause of death ...
All the nonsense of the learned
Whom I had to battle while I lived ...
Seven times have my bones been moved
To please some vanity or curiosity
Of those I could not bear in life ...
Other curses has my death endured—
The legend of a Doctor Faustus
Branded on my face;
There is no price in hell or paradise
To buy my name and reputation!

In anguish.

Leave me alone! Let me rest!
Let what is left of me endure
Among the poor I healed in Europe,
Asia, and primordial swamps of Africa!

Sounds of wind and storm.

A candlelight procession of people enter and stop before his casket.

CHANT: Paracelsus—save us! Paracelsus!

A MAN: *(frantic)* Cholera surrounds Salzburg!
We will die as they die
Beyond the city ...
We have no money!
They treat the wealthy
They will not help us
Who are poor ...
Paracelsus—we pray to you
Rise from your grave
And save us!

A low murmur as of prayer, from the crowd. PARACELSUS, unseen by them, looks at them and sadly shakes his head.

PARACELSUS: Good people ...
I was dead three hundred years
When you last came to me in this way—
Begging as the helpless begged
Since they first saw light and reason
On this poor and ravaged earth ...

CHANT: *(soft and reverent)* Paracelsus ...
Paracelsus ...

PARACELSUS: Those of you who knew me
Through your great grandfathers—
Peasants by the roadside ...
Beggars, thieves and merchants ...
Men paid to war ...
And after war—wounded,
Maimed, starved ...
Waving the black stubble,
Lost and nameless on the endless plains
Of death
You knew I would claw and chew
The centuries of earth above my bones
To reach you—to touch you—
For we are all first cousins
To the poor.

WOMAN IN CROWD: Paracelsus! Prince of healers—alchemist!
Our death is only hours away!

PARACELSUS: The dust of centuries around my skull
Could not mute your plea ...
The very earth moaned and twisted

With the outcry of ten thousand persons
Kneeling at my grave …
Like Lazarus,
You resurrected me—
A vapour rising from the soil …
The odour of my breath more foul
Than the ravages of cholera …
The touch of these hands,
Cut a thousand times by scalpels …
Burned by acids and essences of metal
So fierce that even gold would flow like wine
Before their gasp …
Unable now to clasp a vial of medication
Or turn the pages of a book …
Still called upon to save a city
Of forgotten, fearful people—
Threatened by an illness
For which I knew and taught
The cure.

WOMAN: Wagoners are falling at the gate,
Twisted with pain! …
Rats tear at their still living flesh!

PARACELSUS: Soundless I shriek
From within the earth—
Destroy the rats!
Light fires with cornhusks and oil
In every lane and passage!
Fast your bodies! …
Isolate the living from the dead
And dying! …
Feed the children only grain
And water from the deepest wells! …
And avoid the doctors who examine
First your purse and then your bodies
For they are murderers
Now and always!

WOMAN: We cannot wait! … Paracelsus!
Your spirit is alive—save us!

PARACELSUS: God, in your alchemy of blood and
spirit—
Help me who has neither now,
To reach them!

*Pealing of the bells. The people huddle and move
offstage. PARACELSUS sits wearily beside his casket,
his head in his hands.*

Bell sounds die.

*DR. WEBB and DR. GUZA enter on lower area of
stage and approach the table, which has a coffee*

*urn and cups on it. They pour themselves coffee and
sit at the table.*

DR. WEBB: Tired?

DR. GUZA: I'll say. I called my sister to put my son
to bed. A year of nights here and he won't know
me.

DR. WEBB: How many children have you got?

DR. GUZA: Just the one. Jerry is studying for the
ministry, so the next is about five years away …

DR. WEBB: Janis and I couldn't make it … It was
a med school marriage …

DR. GUZA: (*smiling*) She worked while you studied—and then the doctor graduated, looked
around and felt he was cut out for bigger things!

DR. WEBB: (*irritated*) You've no right to make
such assumptions! You don't know the story …

She laughs.

*Enter a TRADESMAN and a MASON on highest
level of set.*

TRADESMAN: With you, it was the same?

MASON: (*nods*) He came to me … in a dream!
He assured me
That all the minerals and essences
Of life … were now in harmony
With those of death!
That I was not to worry for myself
Or for my children …
That I was to stay home
And amuse myself and them with laughter
And with songs …
And not dwell on pain or fear …
For the body excites that which it dreads …
As a fearful man excites an angry dog!

DR. GUZA: If you were to marry again, what sort
of woman would you look for?

DR. WEBB: I would want obedience and beauty!

DR. GUZA: As in a house-dog?

DR. WEBB: (*grinning*) As in a sailboat … or a
European sports car!

They both laugh.

TRADESMAN: It was the same with me! I drank
Red wine and tea of ancient herbs
My mother left within the attic

Of my house!
Did you see him in your dreams?

MASON: I recognized him, but no,
I didn't see him …
His presence was like balm …
And I drifted into deepest sleep.

DR. GUZA: You have the makings of a first-rate
bastard!

TRADESMAN: We should show our gratitude
With candles and with flowers
At his grave.

MASON: No. Sebastian—let what is, be …
The authorities and church …
Have not forgiven him for what he was …

TRADESMAN: Will they ever?

*MASON and TRADESMAN exit. PARACELSUS looks
up, his face lit with excitement.*

PARACELSUS: The event is not recorded
In the history of medicine
That is respectable and well to do …
But I was there!
Three hundred years after they
Had laid me well to rest …
Through metamorphosis of spirit, earth and
Fire …
I was resurrected for a time …
Emerging through the pores of earth …
Congealing once again like beads of water
On an icy glass—
United with my God,
For whom I gave my talents
And my life …
But mindless now,
And without legs that once
Crossed the scorching plains of Asia …
Without these hands,
The uncomplaining servants of my skull
Who ached beyond endurance
With the pain of rickets …
And giving all, absorbed
The deadly essences of mercury
And lead that early were
To rack each moving portion of my body …
Age my face …
Thin my hair …
Discard my teeth with bursts of blood and pus—
Reduce my body to a twisted, wizened prune
Of age and agony …

With claws for hands,
Deformed legs,
Toes curled around each other
Like stubs of dying vines …
All this before my fortieth year …
Brothers of the sleepless night!
Sisters who have sat with death
Beside the cradle—
My return to you was both the privilege
Of victory and hell!
For I healed quickly,
Free of the encumbrance of flesh—
Roving like a flash of light
Through alleys, hovels, the marketplace,
Factories and caverns of the city
Touching with my medic
The fearful and the ill—
Reviving them to face the holocaust of pain
Like seasoned soldiers …
For though I found that honest brothers
Of my calling
Had devised new instruments
And perfected knowledge of the human body
Their healing was still blinded
By the ancient ignorance that fails to see
The harmony of God, stars,
Earth and man!
Pain is not the illness,
But a symptom of cosmic discontent
Whose qualities and cure
Are witnessed by a withered leaf …
A grain of troubled granite—
The tides and furies of the oceans,
Moon and stars!

*Through this speech, DR. WEBB and DR. GUZA are
in animated, silent conversation, laughing and
jesting with each other.*

Tolling of the bells of the Black Madonna begins.

*PARACELSUS rises to his feet and limps forward,
away from the casket. He winces with pain.*

*A YOUTH in turtle-neck sweater, jeans, enters on
PARACELSUS' level. He carries a notebook and
camera. Near the casket he stops and looks around
with unseeing eyes. PARACELSUS watches him.*

PARACELSUS: (*bitterly*) Yet another stranger
Comes to visit me …
A poet on the much travelled road to Einsiedeln.
The last one made a devil out of me,
Which pleased the charlatans

As apples please the swine!
You poets, scholars, mystics,
I linger as a chill presence
In the windy hollows of your minds.

Sound of bells dies out.

PARACELSUS: Some wise and gentle men along
with many fools
Have rummaged on the edges of my works ...
Translating that which fortifies their arguments—
Quoting passages to prove me nothing
But a raving lunatic ...
Fortifying a misbegotten faith
That I was prince of wizards,
Capable of darkest, fearful magic
For my ends ...

*The YOUTH has opened his books, scribbled a note,
and now exits.*

*DR. GUZA has become pensive as she rises to refill
her coffee cup.*

DR. GUZA: My grandmother was a Polish peasant
woman ...

DR. WEBB: Mine was an Empire Loyalist—true
red, white and blue she was ...

*On upper level, enter the hooded figure of a
WOMAN, who moves very slowly, watching
PARACELSUS.*

PARACELSUS: (*harshly*) She hangs above me still,
Her eyes inflamed with lust—
Her stomach and her breasts
The scented torso of a whore—
Her hands like silken shawls
In a southern wind ...
Enticing me with sleep and wealth
And all the soft indulgences
Of a gifted healer to bishops,
Kings and all the high-born harlots
Of three continents!

*On PARACELSUS' level, enter a gentle, THOUGHT-
FUL MAN.*

PARACELSUS: I possessed and still possess
The secret of a thousand years of life
For anyone I cared to damn this way ...
Once, when I offered my beloved friend,
Erasmus of Rotterdam, the choice
Of longer life and better health,
He blanched, and then replied ...

THOUGHTFUL MAN: Dear Paracelsus, do not
offend a friend,
Who loves you in this way!
Already I have lived to see the pain
My words create for other living men—
Do not let me live so long that I might see
All I thought noble, brave and righteous
Becoming poisoned conflicts
Drenched in blood and hatred ...
Let me live my allotted days with no more pain
Than is my rightful due ...

THOUGHTFUL MAN exits. PARACELSUS laughs.

PARACELSUS: So I blessed the syphilitic, inbred
Bodies of our kings
With Erasmus' wisdom
And no more ...

*The hooded WOMAN gestures offstage in a stylized
movement which gives her the significance of being
an angel of evil in the life of PARACELSUS.*

*Her action slowly brings out a straggling of rustic
medieval people who gather as amused observers to
some scene about to be played out.*

DR. GUZA: My granny was a religious woman,
who had a working relationship with her God.
Had God lived in the town where I was raised,
she would've baked buns for him and mended his
socks. To her, He was just like any other Pole on
hard times ...

DR. WEBB: Mine would've photographed Him,
sold copies of the photo, and kept all the profits
for herself!

They laugh and huddle together in amusement.

*PARACELSUS turns angrily on his angel, who
moves away a slight distance from him. He shrugs
with defeat and turns away from her.*

PARACELSUS: I was born of flesh that could be
and was tempted ...
Let no lies besmirch the truth of who I was!
From infancy I was prone to laziness, pride;
The coarse thickness of a peasant mouth and
reasoning—
The dazzlement of costly clothes—
The arrogance of a mind superior to those about
me ...
As a youth, I was portly and insolent,
Eating often for two men ...
Inviting brawls with my foul wit—

Doing battle at ten metres
With words more calloused
Than a peasant's fist;
More cutting than the rapier
Of a guardsman to the duke ...

Enter two peasant THUGS at a run, responding to the more urgent beckoning of the hooded WOMAN. They stop and peer about them, outraged.

FIRST THUG: Where is he?
He'll wish tonight his mother had miscarried him
Upon the dung-heaps of the river Sihl!

PARACELSUS: (*taunting coarsely*)
Have you business here?
You three-legged cocks
Hatched by scurvied rats of Basel!

Laughter from the people.

SECOND THUG: There he is! I'll thrash him into silence!

PARACELSUS: Wait, you buglers of the barn-yard—wait!

The THUGS pause uncertainly in face of more laughter.

PARACELSUS: How fortunate I happened on you at this time—
There is a well a thousand metres deep before you!
One step more, and both of you would vanish
In the bowels of the earth!

More laughter. The THUGS kneel and peer before them. Then rise with rage.

FIRST THUG: He lies! There is no well.
The street is cobbled to the public square!

SECOND THUG: I'll kill him for this!

PARACELSUS: Go home—you are not fit to raise a hand to!
If I must fight
Let it be with men of wisdom
And the icy nerve of marshals
In the fields of war ...
And not with braying asses
Whose tails drag like whips
Through piss-stenched alleys
Of inconsequential towns.
I am a countryman with long vision!
I cannot even see you
For the squatness of your stature!

(*with mock anger*) Be gone!
Before my rages,
Trapped like tigers in a cage of iron,
Break free and devour you
Like starving hounds devour two frogs!

More laughter. The THUGS hesitate. PARACELSUS moves to them and stops them with a gesture.

PARACELSUS: Wait, idiots! Can you read?

FIRST THUG: (*blurting*) No!

PARACELSUS: (*to SECOND THUG*)
Can you translate
The Latin mumbo-jumbo of the priest
Behind whose ass you crouch at sermons?

SECOND THUG nods that he cannot.

PARACELSUS: Pshaw then—be gone!

More laughter. The THUGS are defeated. The hooded WOMAN-ANGEL applauds with slow, measured claps of her hands, at which the crowd exits. She hovers over PARACELSUS, her face now exposed and radiant.

WOMAN-ANGEL: Oh, the swagger of the dandy—
Sent to study medicine
With a ready tongue and empty head!
What pain it gives him then and now
To comprehend that lifetimes can be spent
In weeds that grow no taller than this folly!
How trapped the humble-born can be
From realizing that the moment of their births
Were touched by God through His machinery
Of stars and chemistry of earth and fire!

PARACELSUS: (*anguished*)
Begone! I was a simple man,
Born among the pines!

WOMAN-ANGEL: You were never trained to be a healer!
A healer, like a saint,
Is born from time to time
To remind the human race
It must aspire to God,
To rise above the murk of slavery and war ...
Above the stature of a beast to other beasts—
Men, or the implements of men!
The upright man shrinks only to damnation
In the face of God—
To no other judgement
Is he answerable!

PARACELSUS turns and points an accusing, angry finger at the WOMAN-ANGEL.

PARACELSUS: That is *my* credo, devil!

WOMAN-ANGEL: Paracelsus—love me!

People, broken in body and spirit, move in opposite directions around him. PARACELSUS reaches out to them urgently.

PARACELSUS: From the moment of awareness
I never slept again! ...
I devoured twenty centuries of medic wisdom
In a few scant months ...
And then discarded it as false
And unworthy of my skills ...
Side by side with men
Who scarce resembled men
I crawled on my hands and knees
Through damp and dusty mines
Of Germany and England ...
Examining the lungs and skin of miners,
And searching for the cures
I knew were near at hand ...
If only I might have openness of mind
To find and rearrange them.
Above the mines, I probed
The earth for gold, zinc, arsenic
And other minerals I needed
For the formulas of ointments, salves,
Purgatives and vapours to blend
With crucible and flame
For the healing needs of patients
Numerous and distant ...
Ragged, endless as the groping
Soul of man ...

He continues attending to the animal-like progression of people around him. He touches and detains a person here and there, gently examining their eyes, mouths, lungs. He vanishes among the people and exits with them.

On lowest level of set, DR. GUZA and DR. WEBB remove surgical masks from their faces. DR. WEBB lights a cigarette. Both of them are weary.

DR. WEBB: That wasn't difficult, was it? From now on our biker's at the mercy of antibiotics and the ability to regenerate bone tissue.

DR. GUZA: He'll be a sick fella in the morning.

DR. WEBB: That's fine ... it might teach him a lesson in road manners!

DR. GUZA: You sound like a competent police-man.

DR. WEBB: I don't like punks—in hospital or out! I'm sorry if that irritates you, but it's the way I feel.

Three STUDENTS (two of them the thugs from earlier scene) enter on middle level of set. The WOMAN-ANGEL exits as they enter, orchestrating their arrival with movements of her hands.

The students' clothes are lavish, their manners haughty.

FIRST STUDENT: Who is this fool assigned to teach medicine at Basel?

SECOND STUDENT: More than a fool, I hear ...
He neither knows Latin
Nor the civil graces ...
Some rustic from Einsiedeln
Who has had quick cures
For simple ailments, no more.

THIRD STUDENT: A Luther of medicine
Our more excitable and simple-minded
Colleagues call him!

SECOND STUDENT: A Luther indeed!
He will roast upon the spit with Luther,
And dogs of Germany will lick their chops
As the tallow of their insolence
Drips into the street!

FIRST STUDENT: A cunning peasant, though ...
Those sent by the church to watch and listen
Have heard little to condemn him with,
Save his invitation to the barbers,
Midwives and other false practitioners
Of the medic arts
To attend his lectures.

THIRD STUDENT: Why tolerate this smelly, unwashed scum
Amongst us—who have paid in gulden
For our education?

SECOND STUDENT: True—a little knowledge is a dangerous thing
For the surly beggars of the town!
How can they comprehend that
Which they can neither cook nor eat?

Laughter from the three of them.

THIRD STUDENT: It is well he has not loaned them
Books on surgery
For they hold their hymnals in church;
Upside down—and back to front!

More laughter.

SECOND STUDENT: I could not bear today's lecture—I could not!
Listening to the forest boar grunt and squeal
About the filth and corruption of our apothecaries—
I *had* to leave—my sensibilities
Were outraged by such crudity …

THIRD STUDENT: He is out to maim the Christian practice
Of good medicine—but let him squeal.
Should his pimple-healing cause one death
Then beware Paracelsus, with the pompous name—
For we will war with the bandit
Who threatens what is our due
As doctors!

Like true gentlemen, they somberly shake hands on this commitment. Flickering of flame light over highest levels of set. Distant shouts and cheering.

FIRST STUDENT: How true—for we're not cobblers
Or sweepers of the streets;
Our profession is a noble one,
Built on the sacred rock of Avicenna's teachings.
And for this, we shall be paid with lodgings,
Clothes and stature beyond the view
Of cobblers or draymen!

SECOND STUDENT: Brothers, we worry needlessly—
Small rains will fall,
Leaving puddles in the street
Which the sun of the everlasting Faith
Dries in an hour and is forgotten!

Flame lights rise higher. Shouting and cheering increases and comes nearer.

THIRD STUDENT: But should our faith overlook this nuisance
We must petition our protest
To the university!

SECOND STUDENT: Aye—one must defend oneself
Against the squat and ugly toad!

Putting their arms around each other's shoulders, they turn to leave jubilantly.

But a small crowd of other STUDENTS, poorer and more determined, enter with FRANZ at the lead. They are drinking and unruly. At the sight of the three wealthy STUDENTS, they stop, embarrassed.

The three wealthy STUDENTS realize their momentary advantage, and to goad the poor STUDENTS, they fan the air before their faces, as if trying to drive away a bad odour.

SECOND STUDENT: Ah, but what have we here—
A procession of goatherds
On their way to dinner?

The poor STUDENTS' abashment begins to turn to anger.

FRANZ: Delinquents from the class
Who conspire how to purchase jewellery,
Whores, and positions of influence in medicine!
How dare you be absent
When the great Paracelsus teaches?

FIRST STUDENT: (*flicking his shawl at FRANZ*)
Begone … begone …
The smell of your unwashed arse offends me!

FRANZ: I'll have my arse upon your face if you
Play the whore with me!

FIRST STUDENT: (*mimicking FRANZ*)
I'll have my arse
upon your face …

But he is cut off in mid-sentence with a fist-blow to the shoulder from FRANZ. The rich STUDENT is shocked, but immediately responds by a courtly, formal stance for fisticuffs. FRANZ laughs, and removing his hat, pelts the rich STUDENT from side to side across the head with the coarse hat.

FIRST STUDENT: Let's have none of that!
Fight like a gentleman, you swine!

Laughter from the poor STUDENTS, who form a circle containing the two combatants.

FRANZ: Take that! … And that! … And that!
Ah, your eyes smart—yet there is no bruise
Upon your cheek!
Now you know—that not all wounds are visible!

FIRST STUDENT: You are a coarse villain,
Unfit for the study
Of Avicenna's teachings!

FRANZ seizes the FIRST STUDENT, turns him around and leaps on his back, riding him gleefully.

FRANZ: Gallop now, my wealthy gelding!
For Avicenna is no more!
This day, Paracelsus had the books
Of Avicenna burned in the college square!

Dismounts from back of the FIRST STUDENT, who stares with disbelief at FRANZ.

FRANZ: When Paracelsus spoke above the flames,
The blood began to boil—
And a great burden lifted
From our temples and our eyes—
The very vines upon the walls
Detached themselves and waved huzzanahs
To the liberation which we felt!

SECOND STUDENT: They lie! These filthy vermin lie!

Laughing, the surrounding STUDENTS pummel the three wealthy STUDENTS with their hats, notebooks and mittens. The three wealthy STUDENTS flee and exit.

FRANZ: Ah, what a day we've seen, brothers!
Today was the morning of a great new age in medicine,
And as true apostles we were blessed
With living through it!

PARACELSUS enters on topmost level of set, performing his lecture over FRANZ'S lines.

FRANZ: He is confident, cheerful, the teacher.

PARACELSUS: As town physician and teacher
At this university—I welcome you,
Students of medicine …
Students of the art of healing …
Those of you blessed with intelligence
But cursed with poverty, I take into my house,
Where, so long as I am able,
I will shelter, feed and clothe you
While you learn …
I have led you all outside the city
Through the hills and fields,
Seeking herbs where God had placed them—
For there medicines do grow by choice,
Drawing from the soil, air and the forge of heaven
The potent virtues in the great apothecaries
Of the mountains, valleys, meadows and the forests …

Everything I teach you
In the simple German language
Of my birth and yours …
Everything I teach you
I have learned from experience
And observation …
For nothing must be left to chance
And one published error may cost
Ten thousand lives of patients
In our care …
It is a lofty and a serious thing we do—
Healing is a gift of God to Man …
There is no oracle we dare not question!

POOR STUDENTS: (*chanting*)
Down with charlatans in medicine!
Down with rogues and murderers!

PARACELSUS holds aloft two huge books.

PARACELSUS: You have built a flame within the square
Against the chilling northern wind.
I would assist the progress of the fire
By disposing from this ancient school
The spirit of the antique cadavers of medicine—
Avicenna and Galen—who bedevil all enquiry
And have made of healing a priesthood
Of wealth, arrogance and power
Built on teachings which do not bear
The simplest tests of reason or effectiveness!

He hurls the books down.

PARACELSUS: Into St. John's fire now
So all misfortunes of the past
May at last vanish into air with smoke!

A cheer from the STUDENTS. PARACELSUS laughs with them, then grows stern and silences them with a gesture.

PARACELSUS: Let God ordain, and you apply yourselves
In such a manner that our effort to advance
Once more the art of healing may succeed!
One other matter
In which I require your awareness
And sympathetic understanding;
I have this day, as town physician,
Examined apothecary stocks within the city
And found them stale and worthless—
Priced to bring good wealth
To the charlatans who sell them …
I have also found

When I pressed these vandals to the wall
That they share a secret understanding
With the doctors—
To split the profits of their carelessness
And murderous neglect!

On lowest level of set, a patient enters and is examined by DR. WEBB, while DR. GUZA watches and assists.

FRANZ: Tell us who these people are, Paracelsus—
And we shall deal with them in ways
They understand—
Or put their filthy practice to the torch!

Three wealthy STUDENTS return, but remain in background, listening and taking notes.

A cheer from the poor STUDENTS greets the suggestion from FRANZ. PARACELSUS shakes his head and smiles.

PARACELSUS: Nay … nay … there are other ways
To deal with villainy.
I have written to the city magistrates,
(*winks mischievously*)
Who dispense all law!

A wave of laughter.

PARACELSUS: As well as make appointments to the university!

Another, longer wave of laughter.

PARACELSUS: (*sardonically*) I have written to the city magistrates of Basel …
Those grave …
Pious …
Strong …
Foreseeing …
Wise …
Gracious …
Favourable gentlemen!

More laughter on each adjective about the magistrates.

PARACELSUS: I have written to request …
In my capacity as town physician …
That proceedings of apothecaries
Be rigorously controlled;
Their recipes submitted to me
For opinion of worth—
That appointments of apothecaries
Be examined for approval—
That all medicines be priced

According to their worth …
The same rates prevailing
In each apothecary in the city;
That profiteering in the tools of healing
Be forever banished from the commerce
And affairs of Basel!
On this I take my stand
As healer, teacher, chemist—
And let those who profit from corruption
Rage until the pit of hell consumes their furies
And their worthless souls!

A sober murmur of approval. One of the three wealthy STUDENTS raises a fist to PARACELSUS.

WEALTHY STUDENT: Yours will be the first soul to roast!
Make no error of the heresy you've committed
Here this day!

FRANZ: Put down your fist, you ninny,
Who stands before this man
But for the graces of your father's purse!

WEALTHY STUDENT: The fool who screams revolt
In shelter of forgiving night
Will have a different morning to endure!
All the world's physicians are not wrong!

The STUDENTS become turbulent, surrounding the three wealthy STUDENTS. PARACELSUS comes down among them.

PARACELSUS: Hold your noises!
Remember why we stand before each other
As students and their teacher!
You are here to learn
That nothing which benefits the sick
Should be denied—
Not your services,
Nor medication,
Nor wisdom—
Nor the charity of pity!
The squeak of fear you heard
Has an element of truth;
A true healer fights for those he serves.
He must likewise be prepared
For the consequences of his mind and deeds—
In this way does God make great healers
On the anvil of his howling forge!
Let us leave now friends—
We have work to do.

The STUDENTS disperse, except for FRANZ, who remains, donning a leather apron, as does PARACELSUS. Patients enter and are treated with examinations, salves, lances and oral medication, with FRANZ assisting the doctor.

This action continues over dialogue.

FRANZ: You have turned both my flesh and brain
Upon that sacred anvil,
And struck sparks of comprehension
Like golden arrows through a mired beast ...

PARACELSUS: There is no one from whom greater love is sought
Than from a doctor—beware you understand
The meaning of this, Franz ...
Or flee now from my presence
As a doe flees the huntsman's spear!

FRANZ: No—let me stay beside you ...
I come from Meissen, and have wasted all my money
In the schools of Heidelberg ...
I will demonstrate your lectures ...
Run errands in the market for your house and surgery;
Keep your clothes and notes in order ...

PARACELSUS: Poor studious Franz ...
There is no fatigue within these bones
Or skull of mine—
You will be roused in the deadest
Hours of night
When my brain fevers
Like a newborn star;
You will enscribe notes
I dictate to you ...
You will suffer
So that others might be free
Of suffering ...
I will make a distinguished doctor
Out of you,
But it will not be
A key to riches and success;
It will be a scar of pain and wisdom
Etched upon your gentle, trusting face.
Your answer at this age
Will be immediate and sure,
But the burden of your life
Rests like a boulder on my neck—
For what if I should fail?

FRANZ: Never! I shall work and study
With what life is in me!

PARACELSUS: But if I should madden?
Or bring you to the scaffold
For your trust in me?

FRANZ averts his eyes from the withering gaze of PARACELSUS. They continue their work with their patients.

DR. WEBB and DR. GUZA complete their medical examination of their patient. As patient exits, she tidies up.

DR. GUZA: You have good hands for surgery, Patrick.

DR. WEBB: (*mocking*) If I can ever be of service ...

DR. GUZA: I could never work as quickly or cleanly.

DR. WEBB: Most surgery is routine—if the diagnosis is accurate, the treatment is nothing. I sometimes feel it's as predictable as mailing a parcel.

DR. GUZA: Then why did I lose a patient?

He shrugs and turns away from her.

On uppermost level of stage, PARACELSUS and FRANZ continue their work with patients.

Enter three wealthy, bejewelled, sophisticated DOCTORS on middle level of set.

FIRST DOCTOR: Paracelsus? ... Does this imply greater than Celsus?

SECOND DOCTOR: He certainly has pretensions to Celsus,
Physician to the emperor Augustus!

FIRST DOCTOR: What pomposity is this
For an unknown peasant on whom
The degree of Doctor was never given
By a university of reputation?

SECOND DOCTOR: Bare-assed-celsus is more in keeping
For the braggart!

THIRD DOCTOR: His ass is well protected, never fear!
Despite his lamentations
The hypocrite lives well.
The clothes he wears—
The swagger of his walk—
All reveal strong pretensions
To the title "doctor"!

FIRST DOCTOR: Who of us confronts him in his surgery?
I do not choose to sully my good reputation
In challenges with quacks and thieves!

THIRD DOCTOR: (*to SECOND DOCTOR*)
There is no danger—you insult him,
For you alone have read the insolence
Of what he writes on healing!

Brandishes his cane.

THIRD DOCTOR: Go to it—we'll protect you!
And if he tends to violence
We'll have him arrested
And trundled out of town!

The three DOCTORS move to upper level of set and approach FRANZ and PARACELSUS.

The SECOND DOCTOR throws back his shoulders and clears his throat.

SECOND DOCTOR: Are you called Paracelsus?

PARACELSUS: I am. What need have you of me?

SECOND DOCTOR: We are doctors of this city— tell us,
Has any physician of repute
Addressed you as "doctor"
To your face?

PARACELSUS: I have met no worthy doctors in this city,
So the question does not merit a reply!

SECOND DOCTOR: (*to his companions*)
He has not met a worthy
Doctor in this city … methinks that would be
As near as he would come to the healing arts!
(*to PARACELSUS*) Do my colleagues then
Not meet with your approval?

PARACELSUS: Good manners and the dignity of healer-teacher
Compel me to reply with silence!

THIRD DOCTOR: Ah, ah—be careful now!
These are learned men you speak to …
Where is your learning from, we ask?
Or are you a self-appointed peddler of rubbish
Whose concoctions of forest droppings
Might neither help nor hinder
The passing of some minor ailments
Had they been administered by the village idiot?

PARACELSUS: My teachers were the finest in the world—
Ancient and modern masters of their skills …

SECOND DOCTOR: Who were they, then?
Nowhere in your writings do you …

PARACELSUS: (*impassioned now*)
My father was the first …
From him came the title Paracelsus;
At ten years of age
I performed surgery at his side …
Surgeon and physician to the town of Einsiedeln—
I dressed wounds …
Helped him blend the salves and potions
He dispensed. Later in my life
I entered many universities—
Gleaning what I could from this learned
Scholar and from that …
Discarding all which defied experience or reason—
Many of the masters in whose steps you follow
I forsook as useless baggage for a healer
Ere I was twenty years of age!

FIRST DOCTOR: Then you are not a graduate doctor
From any school of medicine?

PARACELSUS: Test me on my practices
And not on superficial dressings
For a healer's pride!

FIRST DOCTOR: You are not a doctor, then!

PARACELSUS tosses a bloodied bandage in direction of the FIRST DOCTOR, who strikes defensively at it with his cane, missing it. PARACELSUS laughs and turns to help FRANZ blending chemicals.

SECOND DOCTOR: How many people have you killed?

PARACELSUS: How many have you cured,
You perfumed dandies
Overstuffed with capons
And the wines of France?

SECOND DOCTOR: I ask again—how many patients have you killed
In your departures from the proven remedies?

PARACELSUS: Thousands have I treated in the mines of Germany,
France and England against diseases of the lungs
And heart …
In every city of this continent,

Into Africa, and east, through the massive
Lands of Russia—
Through the Tartar lands and beyond
Samarakand
Where I was held a prisoner of war a time—
I healed diseases of the skin, digestion …
Gout … the injuries of men and women
At their work …
The ailments of children …
The ravages of madness in its many forms …

FRANZ: (*afraid for PARACELSUS*)
No! … Tell them no more!

PARACELSUS: The imbalances of acid on the
body …
Diseases caused by food …
The peculiarities and treatment
Of the wounds of war …
The affects of poisons
In the rocks and foliage …
Diseases of promiscuity …

*A stream of human bodies passes by, bent, hurt,
beseeching help.*

FRANZ: These are small men, Paracelsus—
Let them not draw you into danger!

PARACELSUS: There is no danger, Franz—these
vultures
Know me well, as I know them!

Points to THIRD DOCTOR.

PARACELSUS: This one treated Markgrave Philip
of Baden
To the edge of death when I was summonsed—
He knows me!
When I cured that wealthy wretch
This … doctor …
Interfered with payment of my fee.

THIRD DOCTOR: It was higher than the fee
I asked for treatment of the Markgrave!

PARACELSUS: The many thousand poor I heal
Without a fee—
For it is my credo
And the will of God in Heaven
That no human be denied relief
From pain and suffering
Because he lacks the wherewithal
To pay a healer.
Is it not just
The rich pay for the poor,

When they starve and bind
Entire kingdoms to such poverty?

THIRD DOCTOR: (*enraged*)
Oh, how fortunate I spoke
To the nobleman Markgrave
And persuaded him not to pay a gulden
To the devil for his guile
And false medicines!

PARACELSUS speaks to FRANZ now.

PARACELSUS: When he awoke, when human
gratitude
At absence of all pain still blessed
That chiselled face of wealthy breeding,
Markgrave Philip gave me this!

*PARACELSUS holds up a jewel which he wears
around his neck.*

PARACELSUS: A useless piece of decorative
stone …
I cursed it and have worn it since
As a burden of humility around my throat
Lest I forget the baser parts of man!

Turns on the three DOCTORS.

PARACELSUS: Not one person yet has perished in
my care,
Though I have been physician to more people
Than would populate a nation in these realms
There are great healers on this earth—
I know them all, and count them
On the fingers of this hand …
But there is one Paracelsus only,
And he has better work to do
Than fence with chimney-sweeps
In the temple of the healing arts!

*He turns his back on the DOCTORS, who pull up the
collars of their cloaks in the manner of assassins
and crouch to rush him with their canes.*

*The WOMAN-ANGEL appears, her hand in terror to
her mouth. FRANZ is afraid, and grasping a bottle
of clear liquid, uncorks it. He faces the three
DOCTORS, as PARACELSUS watches a mad
WOMAN being led to him, weeping.*

FRANZ: I hold acid here more deadly than the
hottest flame—
I will not hesitate to throw it at you
In defence of my teacher from attack!

The three DOCTORS turn away and exit, hooding their heads totally as they leave.

The WOMAN is brought to PARACELSUS by a MAN, her husband.

MAN: My wife is mad, Paracelsus, help her!
All day long she sits before the house
And weeps.

PARACELSUS: (*comforting her*) Why do you weep, woman?
The world was sad enough
Before we came—
So we must cheer it in the time
We live!

WOMAN: It is the soldiers passing on the road
To war—such lovely men …
I had a son their age …
It is … as if men …
Were born to die—
I can't endure it, doctor!

PARACELSUS: Have you a cow?

WOMAN: Yes.

PARACELSUS: Does she milk well?

WOMAN: A bucketful at sunrise
And as much at night …

PARACELSUS: And have you extra bread
Now that your children all have grown
And gone?

WOMAN: Yes … he and I eat little …
We feed ourselves and half the village dogs …

PARACELSUS: Rise early in the morning, then …
Milk your cow and bake your bread …
Make butter …
And when the men who march to war go by,
Invite them in for food,
For they are all your sons …

The WOMAN wipes the tears from her eyes and stares at PARACELSUS a long moment.

DR. WEBB sits at a table reading a magazine. DR. GUZA enters with a tray of sandwiches. She offers him one.

DR. WEBB: If medical care was introduced by the government for the first time, would you support it, Betty?

DR. GUZA: Yes … the same way I'd support old age pensions.

DR. WEBB: I sure as hell wouldn't!

DR. GUZA: Why not? At least you're sure of payment for your services.

DR. WEBB: I resent losing any more control over my affairs!

DR. GUZA: But medicine is not a personal affair— no more than aging or education is!

DR. WEBB: It bothers you that I can think the way I do, and still be a good surgeon, doesn't it?

DR. GUZA: Yes …yes, it does …

WOMAN staring at PARACELSUS smiles.

WOMAN: The men who march are always hungry?

PARACELSUS nods.

PARACELSUS: Gods and murderers alike have stomachs
Needing food …
Let the helpless sorrow—
Good women such as you
Have work to do!

WOMAN: Then … I am not insane!

PARACELSUS laughs and draws her to him with his arm.

PARACELSUS: Help feed the world
And you will have
No further need of me!

The WOMAN and her husband leave. The three hooded THUGS enter, staves in hands. They stand and peer at PARACELSUS, who tends to other patients needing reassurance and medication.

Enter hooded WOMAN-ANGEL, who moves between the THUGS and PARACELSUS. The THUGS retreat at sight of her and exit.

PARACELSUS: Are you condemned to follow me
Through all eternity?

WOMAN-ANGEL: How long will you deny me?

PARACELSUS: Until the earth disintegrates
And takes its place again
As dust within the cosmos!

WOMAN-ANGEL: They will crucify you
As they crucified the bloodless master

Whom you chose in passion
To dedicate your thoughts and actions to!

PARACELSUS: It was a choice from which I do not flinch—
I have endless things to do ...

WOMAN-ANGEL: With hands that centuries ago corrupted
Into soil to feed the roots of graveyard cyprus trees?
And will you spend eternity exchanging curses
With decaying scum
Of medieval Europe?

PARACELSUS: Nothing is in vain—
My life and work will be remembered!

WOMAN-ANGEL: By whom, Paracelsus? My dear child, by whom?
A few romantics—who will rejuvenate your memory
From time to time for some murky truth
Which irritates them in your work and life
As blisters irritate a distant traveller?

PARACELSUS: My time is short—begone!

He lights a chemist's distillery which FRANZ has prepared for him. Bending over his work, PARACELSUS trembles. FRANZ now takes over care of patients who pass in procession.

WOMAN-ANGEL: Already, cultists are intrigued
By the magician in your deeds—
The darker fears of man
Make my presence equal to your God, Paracelsus!

PARACELSUS: A lie!
My courtship with the darker arts of alchemy
And commerce with the dead was of short duration!
I sought truth—all that relieves suffering
Is sacred!

WOMAN-ANGEL: Why lock the deeper secrets
In your tortured mind?

PARACELSUS: Only the best of what I do matters!

WOMAN-ANGEL: You are dead, Paracelsus—
Your voice is silent now within the tomb ...

PARACELSUS: The chore of turning magic into alchemy
And then to science shall live
Beyond me!

WOMAN-ANGEL: Yes—it lives ... and delights me!

PARACELSUS looks up at her with anguish.

PARACELSUS: Why ... does it delight you, devil?

WOMAN-ANGEL: Did you dream your works would change
The nature of man's lust for power
Over human life, over mountains,
Oceans and the stars?
No great nobility emerged because
You freed mankind of pain—
And for this revelation,
I do thank you!

PARACELSUS picks up a clod of earth and throws it at the WOMAN-ANGEL, but it falls short. She laughs scornfully.

WOMAN-ANGEL: I would make a bargain with you—
Not for your soul—that means nothing
While I hold the souls of generals
And heads of states, so powerful
That the very mountains quake before them;
I hold the souls of healers in my hand
Whose avarice would make you blanch with fear
At the history of medicine beyond your day—
They make fortunes and great reputations
Over men in prison
On whose bodies and helpless minds
They conduct the most bizarre and dreadful surgery—
They create disease for which there is no cure;
They create medicines for which there is no illness!

PARACELSUS cringes. Turns to FRANZ, who is oblivious of the conversation.

PARACELSUS then faces the WOMAN-ANGEL, his face tortured.

PARACELSUS: (*shouting*) You lie! ... You lie!
Or if what you say is true,
Then some catastrophic changes overcame
The earth ...
'Tis true ... a disorder in the cosmos
Can affect death and madness on the earth ...
My observations of the great comet
Bore this out ...

WOMAN-ANGEL laughs at him. He becomes confused and searches the darkness and the faces around him.

WOMAN-ANGEL: For helping me to see
The full depth of human decadence
I could help you to return
To rectify the damage to your name!

PARACELSUS: I made no bargains with corruption in my life,
Nor will I sacrifice the peacefulness of death
By entertaining darker spirits in my grave!
Go away! ... Go away! ...
My great sword—hollowed through the clasp
And well into the blade as a dry compartment
For my most valued drugs ...
Is lost somewhere in the dust and waters
Of this world ...
My books, crucibles, most elementary tools
Of alchemy and surgery ... have mouldered back
Into the elements of which I made them ...
Nothing remains ...
Except the spare reminders of my life and time;
Fashioned out of paper,
Stone and bronze, by loving hands ...
Yet this restlessness beyond the grave persists—
I have work to do! ...
God did not accept me to His bosom
As I thought He would ...
I have work to do! ...
There has been neither peace nor wisdom for me
In my passing through the veil of wind and stars
Into the icy silence of eternity ...

WOMAN-ANGEL laughs again and exits.

A TRIBUNAL of city fathers enters. The three men seat themselves in a formal line in silhouette on uppermost level of set.

The movement of patients visiting FRANZ and PARACELSUS ends. PARACELSUS puts a soiled robe over his shoulders and moves slowly towards the TRIBUNAL.

On the lowest level of the set, DR. WEBB and DR. GUZA are playing chess. She makes a move and leans back in her chair.

DR. GUZA: Checkmate!

DR. WEBB: (*irritably*) I find it difficult to play with a woman.

DR. GUZA: That's your tough luck, baby ... what other hangups have you got?

He peers stonily at her for a brief moment. She smiles.

DR. GUZA: Suppose I wasn't a doctor ... I was a woman you'd never met, and I came to you asking for an abortion because I had no husband, and it would be difficult for me to ...

DR. WEBB: That's enough, Betty! (*glances at his watch*) It's time for my rounds ...

DR. GUZA: I'm serious, Patrick.

DR. WEBB: I know you are ... an' my reply is, I'm in the business of saving life, not destroying it!

He rises abruptly to his feet and leaves. She stares after him thoughtfully.

PARACELSUS comes to a stop slightly below and in front of the TRIBUNAL. The HEAD OF TRIBUNAL reads a paper before him.

HEAD OF TRIBUNAL: These charges are serious, indeed ...
The doctors of Basel speak with one voice,
Condemning your outrage at the university
And demands you make on healers and apothecaries.
We have much to ponder here ...

PARACELSUS: The outcries are from those who do not *know*!
A good doctor knows the sick and all pertaining to them
As a worthy carpenter must know his wood!

SECOND MEMBER OF TRIBUNAL: He is headstrong and proud,
With pretensions to knowing skills
Of his profession
Better than all others ...

HEAD OF TRIBUNAL: He does ... he does ...
The record of his cures is known far and wide,
Although it would be pertinent for him
Not to advertise his great success ...
All of us must not forget
It was the history of his healing
Which moved us to invite him to our city
In the capacity he now enjoys.

THIRD MEMBER OF TRIBUNAL: But his arrogance is now a matter for this office.

HEAD OF TRIBUNAL: True.

THIRD MEMBER OF TRIBUNAL: We risk the loss
and hostility of city doctors—
Even though Paracelsus is a legend in his arts …
The truth is this—we cannot lose the service
Of our men of medicine, be they good or bad!

PARACELSUS: The battle is not of my choosing!
They must conquer in their natures
All which darkens them
And betrays the causes they must serve!

*HEAD OF TRIBUNAL opens another letter and
reads.*

HEAD OF TRIBUNAL: This, Paracelsus has
addressed to us
In flattering and gentlemanly terms …

THIRD MEMBER OF TRIBUNAL: It's so unlike
him.
Perchance the man is ill himself!

Laughter from the three of them.

HEAD OF TRIBUNAL: Nay, he is not ill. (*reads*)
He requests authority to cleanse
The apothecaries of the city
And reduce the profits which they earn.
In truth, the claim has merit,
For we all have seen dispensaries about
Unfit in their condition to be hovels
For the swine!

SECOND MEMBER OF TRIBUNAL: That is not the
issue in dispute …
A filthy keeper of a shop, like a filthy beggar,
Invites contempt equal to his station …
Yet Paracelsus seeks authority to interfere
With earnings of natural commerce
And God-given trust between healers,
Apothecaries and the ill and stricken!
Let a headstrong rebel legislate
The qualities of healing and the healed …
And we will then be asked to legislate
Friendship between people in the streets!

HEAD OF TRIBUNAL: What is our decision then?

PARACELSUS: Let your philosophies concern
themselves
Only with the problems which I pose!

SECOND MEMBER OF TRIBUNAL: Though he be
a pioneer as doctor,
Beholding all things in a newer and truer light,

I am not made of his spirit …
And therefore vote against him …

*HEAD OF TRIBUNAL turns to THIRD MEMBER OF
TRIBUNAL. PARACELSUS paces nervously, hud-
dling within his garments.*

THIRD MEMBER OF TRIBUNAL: What I say is not
influenced by fear—
I dislike the man, but what is that to me?
Let him have his day;
Yet this issue now defies a simple judgement
Such as—let him live and work—
For in truth he does more good than harm.
I am torn in my verdict,
For although he enjoys the respect and love
Of the greatest body of his students;
Tends well to his practice in this town,
And criticizes with good cause
The parasitic doctors and their servants
Who besmirch the healing arts wherever
One might travel and observe them at their
craft—
Yet he inspires in dispute an element of danger
To us all—and that is most unfortunate.

HEAD OF TRIBUNAL: What is it that moves you to
this gloomy turn of mind?

THIRD MEMBER OF TRIBUNAL: Unlike you,
gentlemen, I have moved nearer to him
And his work than I was willing to admit.
I was there observing in the shadows
When defiance split the university,
And he threw the ancient books into the flames.
I noticed many cheer and applaud him in his act.
But I noticed, too, a wave of fear
Overcome the less hearty of his students
And his fellow teachers …
They responded within hours as fearful men
Will do—with hatred of him,
For he had moved beyond their comprehension,
And for this they could no longer tolerate
Or forgive him …
The world admires saints departed
From the thoroughfares of living—
But a saint still capable of voice;
Who shares the same food and sunlight
As your mother or the neighbouring cobbler,
Is a fearsome peer.
By his very being, he has savaged
The gentle life of the university
And for this we bear responsibility.
He surrounds himself with good devotees,

All admirable in their scholarship and dedication,
Yet the cries against his presence also mount
And can be heard if we but listen …

Voices in angry shouts from various sources.

FIRST VOICE: Luther of medicine!

SECOND VOICE: Vagabond!

THIRD VOICE: Fool! … I know as much as you and more,
Even though I cannot read or write my name!

FOURTH VOICE: Ox-head! … Forest ass of Einsiedeln!

PARACELSUS shouts back at his detractors.

PARACELSUS: You! … Doctors and hirelings of doctors!
You misbegotten crew of approved asses
In the skin and garb of men!
And you apothecaries … who cheat the people
With demands of gold for foul broths
From your filthy shops, less worthy
Than the dish they are presented on!

A rush of bodies come at PARACELSUS in attack, but he wards them off and sidesteps injury. The attack ends as quickly as it began.

THIRD MEMBER OF TRIBUNAL: Of course, he rises to the challenge—
Who would blame him?
But is the nature of his replies to his tormentors
Any worthier than theirs?
The man is flawed by a raging temper—
He creates enemies too readily …
I therefore vote against his further service
As town physician or a teacher,
But knowing the quality and distinction of the man,
I do so with a reservation rare for me—
That he be made familiar with our deliberations,
And that time be given to him to correct
The discordancy his presence has excited!

HEAD OF TRIBUNAL: That generous and wise decision do I share.
A letter with our thoughts shall go to him at once.
As for the authority he requests as town physician,
That must be denied—are we agreed?

SECOND AND THIRD MEMBERS OF TRIBUNAL: Agreed!

The TRIBUNAL rise and exit. PARACELSUS goes thoughtfully to where they sat and picks up paper they left, glances at it.

PARACELSUS: Two letters reached me on that day—
One from the cowards who regulate the affairs of Basel;
The other from former students who had met in Zurich
And awaited me …

Laughter. FRANZ and a group of ragged but animated STUDENTS enter on lower level of set. They carry wine bottles, books and musical instruments. One begins to play the lute.

FRANZ: Good news, brothers—our teacher arrives this night
To join us for wine and feasting,
For the gloomy days and illnesses of the German winter
Is heavy at this time upon us!

ANOTHER STUDENT: Red wine will warm his tired body
As a lusty, honest woman does with mine!

FRANZ: *(laughing)* You're drunk before we're gathered, Frederick!
Your words follow one another
With a sideways motion!

ANOTHER STUDENT: So did she, Franz … so did she!

PARACELSUS moves happily towards the STUDENTS, but doesn't reach them.

Above him, a thrashing body of a MAN is lowered into silhouette on topmost level of set. The man is dying.

Three DOCTORS enter, led by an anxious YOUTH, who points to the dying man. One of the doctors goes up to the patient, watches him, then turns away to join his companions, who are comparing their finery in pantomime.

PARACELSUS: *(facing his students)* For one week, I was blessed with such companions
As to more than compensate for all the hungers
Of my life!
We drank, ate, sang village songs
In the language and dialect of the countryside …
Often, our food and drink would scarce be touched

In the heat of argument on the future courses
Of our skills as men of medicine ...
Or the turmoil of the country,
Where peasants were wakening
From their sleep of centuries
And demanding land and bread,
Which was their right, as toilers of the earth ...
Of Luther, and the reformation
Of the wily, fatted church which long had strayed
From communion with any God ...
Of inventors and men of vision—
Painters and skilled tellers of tales ...
Of books and music they had heard ...
All the joy of life, confined into one week
Free from the daily drudgery and cares
Which occupy the minds of honest men!

He moves nearer to the STUDENTS and sits down to watch them.

The DOCTOR who observed the dying MAN on top level of stage approaches the other two DOCTORS and shakes their hands happily.

FIRST DOCTOR: Good news, my learned friends—
We have the ox of Einsiedeln corralled at last!

SECOND DOCTOR: How so?

FIRST DOCTOR: While his friend, Frobenius, lies ill
Paracelsus is carousing with hooligans in Zurich!

THIRD DOCTOR: Did he ask for another healer to attend him?

FIRST DOCTOR: He did. A messenger came
To request my services at his bedside.
But I said to myself—nay, better let
Some hours pass before I make my way
To the bookman's house ...
For suppose Paracelsus gave him medication
Out of spite—too strong for that gentle body
To endure?
Should I, then, be blamed
For what transpires? So I made excuses
To attend him later ...

With a groan, the ill MAN dies above them.

FIRST DOCTOR: When I did arrive, Frobenius was dead—
And whose responsibility was that?

SECOND DOCTOR: Not yours—you did wisely to delay your services.

FIRST DOCTOR: The city magistrates must hear the news at once—
They may view their wild charge in a different light
When word is out how he betrayed poor Frobenius
In carousal unbecoming a healer of the lowest order!

THIRD DOCTOR: Aye—it is time to act
Before the ass returns
From the cattle troughs of Zurich!

FIRST DOCTOR: And lest the claims against him don't suffice,
We would be wise to taunt him—
To raise such anger in the fool
That his own coarse mouth will crucify him
With the torrent of his untamed words!

SECOND DOCTOR: But how can we excite him to such fury?

FIRST DOCTOR: He burned the books of Galen—
Let us now say Galen, through some author,
Of which we have no knowledge,
Were to write a reply against Theophrastus Paracelsus ...
And again, through means of which we have no knowledge,
The letter were copied a hundred times over,
And posted on the walls of Basel
As a welcome notice for him!

SECOND DOCTOR: How this happened and through whom,
We have no knowledge!

FIRST DOCTOR: Oh, certainly—we are above such mischief!

THIRD DOCTOR: It is an anonymous attack that will raise
The blackest furies in that ill-bred bastard!
Away now—we have things to do—
Of which we have no knowledge!

Laughing, they exit.

The MESSENGER enters and approaches PARACEL-SUS to give him a sheet of paper. PARACELSUS reads it, and rises angrily to his feet.

Laughter in the darkness. The STUDENTS leave, still miming a heated conversation.

Three TRIBUNAL members enter and take their place in level above him.

PARACELSUS: Oh, God—first Frobenius! And now this infamy!
What hell on earth must man endure!
They are out to slander the very basis
Of my medicine—to destroy me
Both as doctor and a man!

More laughter. Hostile DOCTORS and STUDENTS now pass him, nipping at him with their words as dogs nipping at a wounded animal. Throughout their taunts, PARACELSUS staggers towards the tribunal.

HOSTILE STUDENT: Have you read Galen's reply to the fool
Who dares insult true genius—Theophrastus Paracelsus?

FIRST DOCTOR: No need to address him now with the dignity of a name
Call him what he is—a cacophrastus!

ANOTHER HOSTILE STUDENT: Cacophrastus—
Galen writes to you.
(*reads*)
I doubt thou art worthy
To carry the piss-pot of Hippocrates …
Or give food to my swine or herd them!

SECOND DOCTOR: Hey, Cacophrastus—you look unwell,
Methinks you need a doctor!

More laughter and taunting cries of "Cacophrastus." PARACELSUS reaches the TRIBUNAL. His speech is racing now, frantic.

PARACELSUS: I petition you … to counsel and protect me!
The author of this sad lampoon
Is a daily listener at my lectures—a student!
I demand the body of my students be examined
For authorship of this libel!
I will suffer no more insolence
In my pursuit of further learning …

HEAD OF TRIBUNAL: (*wearily*)
Theophrastus Paracelsus—another suit
From you awaits our verdict!

SECOND MEMBER OF TRIBUNAL: You charge here the canon of Cathedral Liechtenfels …
Had offered a hundred gulden to whoever cured him

Of a lingering illness …
You were summonsed, and did cure him
For which he handed you six gulden …

THIRD MEMBER OF TRIBUNAL: And you petition for recovery of the hundred gulden
You felt is owing you.

PARACELSUS: That wealthy priest will pay his due!

SECOND MEMBER OF TRIBUNAL: What is the customary fee for treatment of this nature?
Is there another medical opinion
To enlighten us?

A DOCTOR enters, bowing and scraping.

DOCTOR: Honoured and gracious gentlemen …
Far be it for me to question the learned wisdom
Of a peer in my profession—
But methinks the fee provided Paracelsus
For this treatment overpayment …
I would have done as much
For four …

HEAD OF TRIBUNAL: (*irritated*)
Theophrastus Paracelsus—
A petition of this nature absorbs our time
From matters of a worthier
And more urgent character …
Perhaps you would think again
Before you next trouble us
With trivia of this or like importance!

PARACELSUS glowers at them furiously.

PARACELSUS: So you would vilify the healer,
You pompous simpletons!

HEAD OF TRIBUNAL: Enough! I order you to silence!

PARACELSUS: Order your dogs to silence—
This is Paracelsus you address, idiot!
The wealthy and the law judge healing
As if it were a matter of repairing shoes!
Look about you, fools!
The canon you protect was never ill …
I knew as much from the moment that I saw him
In his silken bed … it was a ruse
To trick and humiliate the principles
On which I stand! By whom?
Those you protect in your foolishness—
The healers you allow to practise in this city …
Murderers who burn, cut and tear human flesh
Without understanding of why or what they do!

And their servants, the apothecaries
With their compounds of rubbish ...
You collude to destroy the brightest moment
Medicine has known yet—and for your ignorance
Neither history nor I will forgive you!

HEAD OF TRIBUNAL: I have heard enough!
Have him seized and imprisoned at once!

SECOND MEMBER OF TRIBUNAL: (*rising to his feet*) Guard! Seize this man!
We will deal with this impertinence
Tomorrow morning!

Two GUARDSMEN rush in and pin the arms of PARACELSUS behind his back. They try to lead him away, but he struggles, shouting after the departing TRIBUNAL.

PARACELSUS: (*raging*) Follow after me, Avicenna, Galen, Rhasis!
Follow you me, and not I you ... ye from Paris.
From Montpellier ...
From Wirtemberg ...
From Meissen ...
From Cologne ...
From Vienna ...
From the Danube, Rhine ...
The islands of the seas ...
Italy, Dalmatia ... Athens ...
Greek, Arab, Israelite ...
Follow you me, and not I you ...
I shall be monarch, and mine the monarchy
Which shall bind all your countries!
How will you shouters endure it
When your Cacophrastus from the dark hills
Of Einsiedeln becomes prince of the monarchy
And you remain the chimney-sweeps?
O, poor soul of Galen, had he but lived
In immortal medicine and not been flung
Into hell's abyss by such as me!
Follow him who dare—until your footsteps
Take you also to the devil's fortress!

He is now pushed violently away into the wings. Over his outcry, the chant "Cacophrastus" had been building from a gathering crowd until it begins to drown out his final words.

A sudden silence as all action freezes on upper levels of set.

On lowest level, DR. WEBB and DR. GUZA are seated at a table. She is reading. He is trying to stay awake.

DR. WEBB: What's the book?

DR. GUZA: A biography of Doctor Norman Bethune.

DR. WEBB: He was the guy who went to China ... died there, didn't he?

DR. GUZA: Yes.

DR. WEBB: People like that leave me cold.

DR. GUZA: You've no interest in remarkable men?

DR. WEBB: None whatsoever. (*smiles*) You find that strange?

DR. GUZA: No, I don't. I find it sad ...

She closes the book and follows him offstage.

Curtain

ACT 2

Curtain up.

FRANZ, gaunt and poorly dressed, stands on the topmost level of the stage, looking off to one side where the sound of barking dogs draws nearer and recedes.

DR. WEBB and DR. GUZA are bent over a table, examining a medical reference book.

DR. WEBB: This is a careless diagnosis, Betty, I wouldn't chance it if I was you ...

DR. GUZA: What do I do?

DR. WEBB: Do nothing ... As you say, there's no apparent discomfort. In the morning, one of the high-priced doctors can have a look at the kid!

DR. GUZA: Yes—you're right.

DR. WEBB: Why don't you sneak away and catch an hour or two of sleep? I'll wake you.

DR. GUZA: I don't dare close my eyes ... there are strange vibes playing in my head tonight!

DR. WEBB: What're you talking about?

DR. GUZA: I ... just feel trapped ... by my own cowardice! Marriage, children, responsibility ... are they real, or are they things we hide behind for anonymity?

DR. WEBB stares at her.

DR. WEBB: You're tired ... and I don't know what you're talking about.

DR. GUZA: I'm not sure I believe that, Patrick! A person like you can't exist and still be sane.

DR. WEBB: Has it occurred to you that I could be the only sane one around? *(grins)* Be a doll and get us some coffee!

FRANZ: Forewarned of imprisonment,
He and I fled Basel like two thieves
In the dead of night.
We carried little—some manuscripts
And books he had written ...
A few tinctures, his sword,
And what few clothes we wore.
It was one of many flights we were to make
For once the wolves were roused
They tasted death and pursued him
No matter where we stopped to rest ...

Dog barking suddenly comes nearer and louder. FRANZ turns as if to flee, but a PRIEST and an armed GUARD enter. The PRIEST points at FRANZ.

PRIEST: Stand, I say!
Are you the one called Franz—
Assistant to that heretic, Paracelsus?

FRANZ: *(aside)* He had taught me what to say at such a time.
(to PRIEST) Nay, I am an apprentice to the village weaver.
I know nothing of the man you seek ...

PRIEST: *(suspicious)* On your word?

FRANZ: On my word!

PRIEST: If you lie, an eternity of flame
Awaits your soul in hell—
For his heresy equals that of Luther.
Of the two of them,
I would choose that Luther live ...
It's the other one's more deadly to the faith!
(to GUARD) Proceed! We must find
And drive him from this town!

They exit.

FRANZ picks up a small bundle and jumps to lower level of stage, where he stirs a sleeping PARACELSUS.

FRANZ: We should leave, Theophrastus, before the morning light.
Men at arms accompany the priest ...

PARACELSUS: At last, the true face of the holy faith!
The cudgel and the cross!

FRANZ: They speak of you as the Luther of medicine ...

PARACELSUS: Luther, indeed! ... I've never met the man ...
(puts on his boots) But I distrust his sobriety ...
He has the qualities that tyranny embodies
In her icy portrait; We Germans
Make poor champions in the cause of truth—
Humourless and over-dedicated,
We sack old systems of philosophy and order
And in their place, erect the new—
More fearsome and less human than the old!

FRANZ: Hurry!

PARACELSUS: Perhaps, with such captors, it would be
A worthy end, for Luther and myself
To die within their flames!

FRANZ stares at him with alarm. PARACELSUS laughs and dismisses the remark as a bad joke.

PARACELSUS: Nay, nay ... do not blanch
As a widow in the presence of a stallion!
I do not yet contemplate my death—
But should I do so, it would be
At the hands of worthier foes
Than an idiotic village priest
And his illiterate cousin doctor!

FRANZ: Your arguments mean nothing
In this place!

PARACELSUS: *(contemplates his shoe)*
The down upon my chin
Knows more than all their writers;
My shoebuckles are more learned doctors
Than their Galen and Avicenna,
And all their syphilitic priests
That spy and pry throughout their universities—
And for this we are fugitives,
Hounded by common dogs
And brutish men with clubs!

FRANZ: Hurry, Theophrastus!

PARACELSUS: *(rising)* God will make other doctors
Who will understand—even all the wisdom
Of the magic arts—the very mention of which now
Is as vinegar to their throats,
Or cataracts upon their eyes!
And when that happens, lad—
Who will then redden the thin lips
Of their wives, and wipe their sharp little noses,
Unaccustomed as they are, to the smell of human toil?
The devil with a hunger napkin, that's who!
Gather my books and what is left of all my life and work—
We move onwards once again as shadows into night ...

FRANZ quickly collects PARACELSUS' belongings and leaves, but PARACELSUS hesitates.

The WOMAN-ANGEL enters on top level of set. She is dressed in a costume that is oddly contemporary.

Sound of the bells of Einsiedeln in far background.

PARACELSUS: Yet again ... and for eternity,
The bones and dust of me recall
The living and the dying ...

WOMAN-ANGEL: You may yet relive it all as it once was;
The warmth and cold ...
The touching of a desperate hand ...
The fumes and scalding acids of your chemistry ...
The odours and the silent plea
Of a dying woman begging through her eyes
To save her life, and spare her children
The agony of living orphans ...

PARACELSUS shudders visibly.

PARACELSUS: They still die in such a way?

WOMAN-ANGEL: They do ... and to the last gasp,
Hoping for a healer with miracles
In his enchanted hands and brain!

PARACELSUS: You taunt me, devil!
Inhuman suffering cries out
For super-human healing—
The impossible curatives
Must be applied, even when death
Has stepped between the healer
And the stricken!

Patients are being led and carried past him. He moves among them, administering and comforting.

PARACELSUS: My skills ... my very will to live,
Must transmute my spirit and my tissue
Into health and life within the patient.
Then I rejoice, for the harmony of life
And change has moved another mountain
From the sacred human skull!

A distressed COUPLE lead two MEN carrying a young GIRL on a pallet towards PARACELSUS. At sight of the doctor, the MOTHER turns away.

MOTHER: The priest did say he was a wizard
And in truth, he is ...
The girl will die, I tell you,
Spare her from dying
In the devil's hands!

FATHER: I cannot! Be he God or devil,
It is the same to me—the child must live!
(to PARACELSUS) Help me!
My only daughter ... has never taken step
From birth!

PARACELSUS deftly uncovers the legs of the GIRL and examines them. As he does so, he turns to the MOTHER.

PARACELSUS: Why the darkness in your face, woman?

MOTHER: Don't speak to me as an equal— I am a simple woman. If God chooses I should suffer—I am content With such attention!

PARACELSUS: This child is the work of God, as well …

MOTHER: Speak not His name to me! The flames of Hell Burn within your eyes!

FATHER: Hush, woman! He is our final hope!

PARACELSUS covers the girl's legs.

PARACELSUS: Her legs are healthy, as your own!

MOTHER: They are withered! Daily she dies! What sort of fool are you?

PARACELSUS: (*sharply*) Speak no more of dying In her presence! Methinks the cradle of your love Is damp and dismal as a pauper's grave! Has song and laughter ever cheered The hours of her sleep?

MOTHER: We pray, as Christians must! It is a sacrilege to sing When illness, like a hungry dog, Never leaves our door!

PARACELSUS speaks to the CHILD.

PARACELSUS: There is a river nearby—can you hear The murmur of the waters?

GIRL: Yes—it is like a wind Blowing through the garden!

PARACELSUS takes a piece of paper and fashions a boat out of it.

PARACELSUS: This river flows into other rivers, Which in turn, empty into stormy oceans Where giant fish and reptiles Pit their strength against the raging winds And lashing tides …

GIRL: Even as you speak, I can see high waves Such as would wash these hills Clean of homes, churches, markets;

And all people who work, worship, And inhabit them! Have you seen all of which you speak?

PARACELSUS: Yes—and a great yearning overtakes me For communion once more with strength That is greater than my own. But I need help …

The GIRL lifts her head from the pallet and stares quizzically at him.

GIRL: What help is it that you need?

PARACELSUS: I want you to rise and walk with me Towards the river, so that together, Good friends can bid farewell To this frail toy—a gentle sacrifice In memory of a summer evening When lindens whispered, and the river did invite A young girl and a tired man To think beyond themselves— Of meadows, storms and the mighty muscled sea!

PARACELSUS steps back. The GIRL rises, trembling, to a sitting position. PARACELSUS beckons her to her feet. She takes a painful step forward and into his arms.

The FATHER leaps forward, overjoyed, and takes the girl into his embrace.

FATHER: She walks—oh, God! My child walks! What is your fee for this miracle, doctor?

PARACELSUS: There is no fee—you are as poor as I. But if you have some bread, I would share it With you … Franz and I Have not eaten for two days.

The MOTHER reluctantly takes a small loaf from her satchel, breaks part of it off, and drops it at the feet of PARACELSUS. Then she crosses herself, and supporting her child, hurries the father and girl away.

PARACELSUS stares at the bread before him, then bending down, picks it up.

The WOMAN-ANGEL laughs bitterly. There are tears in his eyes as PARACELSUS looks up at her.

PARACELSUS: Why do you laugh? At human frailty?
It is a dream ... nothing more ...
I am vapour now ... four hundred years of age.
Still I tremble at the thought ...
Of finding God beyond forbidden doors!

WOMAN-ANGEL: Fool! You are as lonely as a speck of dust
Frozen in the cosmos!
Where now, is the king,
Whom you served with such distinction?

She exits. PARACELSUS thoughtfully chews on the crust of bread.

PARACELSUS: Christ made the healing of sick minds and bodies
His paramount preoccupation—
I cannot do less than follow
His example ... (*smiles*)
I praise the Spanish doctor,
For he does not go about like an idle fellow,
Finely dressed in velvet ...
He wears clothes of leather
And an apron on which to wipe his hands ...

A BEGGAR comes past, holding out his hand. PARACELSUS gives him the remainder of the bread. Then PARACELSUS examines his smock, which is stained.

PARACELSUS: The stains upon this smock
Are a badge of my profession ...
I was proud of every stain and burn
Upon my clothes, for these were
A diary of my treatments ...

FRANZ appears in a separate playing area. He is carrying paper, a quill and inkwell. Sitting down, he writes.

FRANZ: They were pygmies as compared to him—
These men who drove him from the city
And hunted him like some deranged animal
Through the villages and towns ...

PARACELSUS: I do not fear them, but I do fear
The discredit they may do my works ...
For there are always scholars
Who will defend the braying of an ass
When it issues from a soft, well-shaven mouth!

FRANZ: We fled from town to town ...
In Ensisheim we stopped,

For he desired to see a meteor
Which fell to earth a year before his birth ...

PARACELSUS turns and touches a stone in the set behind him. A PRIEST enters.

FRANZ: He examined it—touched it, and exclaimed ...

PARACELSUS: It is made of stone and iron, Franz!
And it weighs a hundred and ten pounds!

PRIEST: You are wrong, stranger ...
The components of the meteor
Are known only to the Lord!
And its weight is equal to the weight
Of the three sturdiest men
In this principality!

The PRIEST makes the sign of the cross over the meteor. PARACELSUS laughs.

PARACELSUS: My studies lead me to believe
The universe is one creation!
There is nothing in the cosmos
That is foreign to this earth!

PRIEST: What nonsense you prattle at your age!
Have you grown carrots on the moon—eh?
This is a virtuous town you visit,
With short temper for your insolence!

PARACELSUS laughs again, nudges the severe PRIEST in the ribs in the fashion of a countryman. The PRIEST recoils, and rubs the place clean where PARACELSUS touched his robes.

PARACELSUS: Tell me then, cowherd of the soul,
What is this stone?

PRIEST: It is a stone of heaven
Possessing secrets no man should understand!
It fell to earth on such a night
As still throws fear into the aged of this town ...
A night of wild lightning and deafening thunder—
And then the stone, like a flaming arrow,
Fell beside the city gates ...

PARACELSUS: And then it stood up, and asked directions
To the church!

PRIEST: Nay, Nay! ... When it had cooled
We rolled it on a pallet,
And eight virtuous men carried it
With the dignity becoming such a miracle,
To the church!

By now, the storm had passed,
And people of the town, even to the infants,
Gathered in the square to sing psalms
To this miracle the eight men brought
Amongst them!
Bow with me now, stranger,
And let us pray before it!

PARACELSUS: Go christen you some children,
fool—
Who, still not possessed of language,
Are lulled by the cadence of your voice.
You bore me, as a nightingale in time,
Bores a drowsy man ...

He yawns. The PRIEST angers.

PRIEST: We did not invite you here
To scoff at what our Lord,
In the bounty of His wisdom,
Left us as reminder of His awesome grace!
Begone! For you appear in your dress and swagger
As a ruffian, or a thief of horses!

PARACELSUS gestures derisively at the PRIEST and both men part. The PRIEST exits.

PARACELSUS moves towards FRANZ, who hands him a page of notes.

FRANZ: These are the ailments I treated
In the town last night—
And an inventory of our medications.

PARACELSUS studies the notes briefly, then smiles.

PARACELSUS: You have a habit, Franz,
For using Latin names for ailments
In a German body!
I knew a poet in Bavaria,
Who wrote his thoughts in Greek,
Believing this gave them dignity
And elevation!

FRANZ: I do feel that in medicine and in gentler arts,
German is a minor tongue ...

PARACELSUS: What a strange judgement you place
On the German word ... and on yourself!

FRANZ: How so, Theophrastus?

PARACELSUS: A man who trades his language
Might in time trade his home and motherland
For valueless refinements ...

Do not let the edicts of some mighty, distant empire
Rule your thoughts, *or how you speak them!*
That is the first threshold you must cross
On the rugged road to freedom ...
Be a Greek or Lithuanian, Magyar or a Turk ...
Whatever womb your mother bore you from—
Be that first!

FRANZ: But in medicine ...

PARACELSUS: Is mystery?

FRANZ: To the common people—yes!

PARACELSUS: Medicine, above all else—must nevermore
Be closeted in secrecy,
Either in language or its truths
From the common man and woman—
For as healing rises from the people
So must it be given back to people!
The healer understanding this
Has reached the first plateau
Of nobility among the human species!

They are interrupted by a noise of jangling chains. A demented MAN is led onstage, chained at the ankles, wrists and throat. He is naked to the waist, gleaming with perspiration. As he is brought to PARACELSUS, he is dancing insanely.

ESCORT: Can you do something for him, doctor, before he maddens our village?

PARACELSUS rushes to the man, inspects his eyes and mouth.

FRANZ retreats and continues writing.

PARACELSUS: How long has he been thus?

ESCORT: One week the spell has been upon him—
He has neither slept nor eaten,
But has broken dishes, trampled his garden
Into dust—alarmed his wife and children ...

PARACELSUS: Enough! Bring me a musician
Who knows the lively airs of country dancing!
Unchain him—he is not a beast!

The ESCORT unchains the demented MAN and runs offstage. PARACELSUS soothes the MAN with cooing sounds, stroking his chest and cheeks with gentle motions of his hands.

The bells of Einsiedeln begin to peal in far background.

A moment later, a FIDDLER is brought onstage by the ESCORT, who moves back from the jerking man.

PARACELSUS turns to the MUSICIAN.

PARACELSUS: Watch my hands—and play in time
To my gestures!

The MUSICIAN lifts the fiddle and begins playing his instrument to the conducting of PARACELSUS, who never takes his eyes off the demented MAN. The tune is in time to the rhythms of the possessed man.

Slowly, PARACELSUS slows the rhythm of the music. The spasms of the PATIENT also slow with the change in tempo of the music. The pacing becomes slower and slower, until at last it stops.

The PATIENT stands wearily, swaying from side to side, the spasms now ended, his head drooping. He falls forward and is caught by PARACELSUS.

PARACELSUS: (*to ESCORT and MUSICIAN*)
Take him home— the man is wasted with fatigue.
He will sleep a day or two,
And when he wakes, give him food and this—

Hands ESCORT a small satchel of medication.

It will prolong his sleep,
And when he wakes the second time,
He will not recall
This painful interlude.

ESCORT: The devils that possessed him—where are they?

PARACELSUS: (*gently*) There are no devils, brother—only pain.

ESCORT: No—there are devils in a man possessed!

PARACELSUS: Then I have freed the devils
And they have gone in pursuit
Of better things to do—go now!
The man needs rest from his ordeal ...

The ESCORT and MUSICIAN carry the sleeping PATIENT out.

Bells of Einsiedeln continue tolling.

PARACELSUS packs his manuscripts and laboratory supplies and fastens his cloak around himself.

DR. WEBB and DR. GUZA check out some surgical supplies on lowest level of set.

DR. WEBB: ... And then this sonofabitch pulls out in front of me in one of those one-man European cars. So ecology or not, I'm one of those fellows, Betty, who wants plenty of steel around me when I join my fellow humans on the freeway!

DR. GUZA: You're afraid of dying?

DR. WEBB: What sort of question is that? Sure I'm afraid of getting killed stupidly ... aren't you?

DR. GUZA: I don't know ... I suppose it depends on whether one dies stupidly ... or just ... dies.

DR. WEBB: Alright, then ... *any* death is stupid in this business. And until I hear otherwise, I'm gonna live with that and not worry about deeper meanings to things. Let's pack this stuff up!

FRANZ: Where do we travel now?

PARACELSUS: To Esslingen ... where my family of Hohenheim
Still have the relics of a family home.
There is a cellar in the garden ...
Where I have much to do ...
You may leave once you have moved me there ...

FRANZ: Am I no longer useful to you?

The WOMAN-ANGEL appears on top of highest stage elevation. A few peasants wander past her, cowering in her presence, but she watches PARACELSUS.

The bells stop.

PARACELSUS: I have now reached the limits of my scrutiny
Of illness in its myriad forms ...
And explorations of the cures of tinctures, salves,
Purgatives and essences which abound
In earth, rock and atmosphere ...
I must now search for the secrets of Christ Himself;
In the cures he wrought, even through the soil
Of the grave ...
There is something which defies me ...
Dazzling my eyes as lightning—
Lashing at my back as an autumn rain—
I feel, what wisdom I have gained is but a flicker
Of a candle in the centre of a vast,
Enshrouded sea ...

The WOMAN-ANGEL laughs.

FRANZ: I beg to stay with you.

PARACELSUS: If I loved you less, the answer would be—yes!
But it is a dark and dangerous thing I do—
For I must move into the realms of magic—
Of necromancy—the unspoken horrors
Of the opening grave ... Incantations, if need be ...
And the influence of tides, moon and stars
On human health and destiny.
In short—someone must sift the soil
Of the devil's garden, for perchance
Some unknown healing truth is buried there!

The WOMAN-ANGEL laughs again. FRANZ shudders.

FRANZ: (*bitterly*) So I am now unfit to work in any
But the safest surgery!

PARACELSUS: I am an aging man—I have no fear
...
The path I take may lead me to the gallows,
Or death upon the flaming stake as heretic ...
As a disciple of the devil ...
Against that, Franz, even my great name
Is no defence—I fear for you!

PARACELSUS scowls at FRANZ, who meets his gaze steadily. PARACELSUS turns suddenly and exits. The WOMAN-ANGEL also vanishes in the direction he has taken.

Over FRANZ'S lines, PARACELSUS reappears in another, lower elevation of the stage. He now wears a doublet, a furred cap, and a gold chain with a jewel around his neck. In a recessed area of set, he installs a small furnace and a crucible. A PEASANT HELPER of limited intelligence brings him a wooden table, on which PARACELSUS takes out paper and writing pens from his satchel.

FRANZ: Our destination was a damp, abandoned cellar,
Scarce larger than a prison cell ...
We arrived by night, for Theophrastus
Was now a furtive man ... setting out his laboratory
In a strange and innovative way ... some underground,
Some above ... Seldom did we eat, and never rested ...
Working like a man possessed—his eyes glowed
And sank within his skull ... The habit of his dress

More that of magician than a doctor ...
This man bore less and less resemblance
To the healer of a year ago
Than a raven to a frightened dog!

FRANZ moves to PARACELSUS, igniting the light below the crucible.

PARACELSUS: How often will this scene replay itself—
To terrorize and fascinate the Christian soul?
(*to FRANZ*) Melt me lead within that crucible
Then turn your face towards the wall—
And I'll transmute the lead into the purest gold for you!

FRANZ is startled and turns quickly to face PARACELSUS, who is chuckling.

FRANZ: You jest with me ... do you not?

PARACELSUS: Ah, so even you believe such foolishness—
What chance then has my reputation
To survive what flacks will say about these nights?

FRANZ: There is no harm in what I see you do!

PARACELSUS: You see nothing ...
Where we are settled now is foreign ground
To men of studied grace and learning.
Astrology is still the art of demons,
But its courses are too frequently exact
To be dismissed.

FRANZ: I feel no fear, why should you th—

PARACELSUS: You are a braver man than I, lad ...
For I confess I am afraid.
Did you decipher the cabalistic characters
I left with you last night?

FRANZ: No.

PARACELSUS: We will examine them again. Go to the roof ...
Compare this chart to the position of the stars—
And take you careful note of moon to Mars.

Taking paper and quill, FRANZ exits.

WOMAN-ANGEL enters on a higher level and hovers over PARACELSUS at his work.

WOMAN-ANGEL: As once before, I have informed them
Of your works!

PARACELSUS stares hard at her.

PARACELSUS: Who?

WOMAN-ANGEL: My primitives, who fly to fear,
As moths to flame!

PARACELSUS shrugs angrily.

PARACELSUS: Keep them from me, or I
Will end this exercise!

WOMAN-ANGEL *looks lovingly at him.*

WOMAN-ANGEL: You will end nothing, doctor.
The course of your enquiry …
As well as time of your birth and death,
Is as set as the pattern and movement
Of the stars you scan each night!
I promised you surprises
In a different age and time …
You choose instead, the folly
Of a noble and a misspent life …
I cannot save you now … Your doom
Is sealed by fools and hooligans.
Farewell, sweet healer—I will return
To celebrate your death!

She moves back from him and disappears into gloom. Three hooded THUGS pass on highest elevation, armed with cudgels, their empty faces turned to PARACELSUS as they pass.

PARACELSUS stares blankly at his notes, and a shudder passes through his body.

PARACELSUS: It is strange, how fear
As ancient as a suffocating dream
Still grips me with an icy claw …
I still might have withdrawn …
Returned to some obscure practice
Of my healing skills within a drowsy town;
Bathed in a glow of gratitude and fame—
And yet penniless and hungry—I
Entertain the devil for one purpose—
I must *know*!
God—please help and guide me!
For I do not understand your ways
With man!

FRANZ enters at a run.

FRANZ: Theophrastus—they are at the door!
Asking to see you now!

PARACELSUS: Who?

FRANZ: The devil's own servants, it would seem

From their dress and the strange mutterings
They make!

PARACELSUS: Then send them home to the devil—I have no time
To entertain the idiocy of fools and pranksters!

FRANZ turns to leave, but his path is blocked by the entry of THREE HOODED FIGURES with strange mystic designs on their long robes. FRANZ is alarmed.

FRANZ: My God—they have forced the door!

LEADER OF GROUP: Welcome to our town, great healer
And Philosopher!
We had an omen during secret meetings
Informing us of your arrival!

PARACELSUS: (*surprised by their costuming*)
Who in hell's name are you?
State your business and be gone!

LEADER OF GROUP: (*fawning now*)
It was wise of me to place a portion
Of my robe into the door when this callow youth
Tried to shut us out! Never fear, Paracelsus,
We are real, influential and of the true conversion.

PARACELSUS: What?

LEADER OF GROUP: But you have doubtless had a different story
From … this boy.
I would dismiss him now
And send him on his way …
We can provide you with a trusting servant,
Sworn to secrecy and such obedience
Your every wish, no matter how strange
Or possibly repugnant to him,
Would he as the wishes guiding his own spirit!

PARACELSUS: (*laughs*)
Oft-times I feel my lack of rest
Plays wonder with my eyes and ears …
Is it the same with you, Franz?

FRANZ: Aye … last night I dreamed of flying turtles.

LEADER of the group is miffed now.

LEADER OF GROUP: I am a forerunner of the militia crucifera Angelica,
As well as magistrate in town—
So you are well protected here!

SECOND MEMBER OF GROUP: And I am of the
brotherhood of mystic
Numerology—
Keeper of the largest inn—where food and lodging
Are available to you at moment's notice.

THIRD MEMBER OF GROUP: I am a magician of
the darker arts,
Well versed in exorcism;
Curses, which inflect great harm
On enemies and …

PARACELSUS glares at them.

PARACELSUS: What are you to me, or I to you?

LEADER OF GROUP: (*to GROUP*)
It is the boy—I like him not …
I see he will cause dissension …
(*to PARACELSUS*) Our brotherhoods are strong
And influential—we will protect you,
But in return, we ask—only as a gesture
Of our mutual understanding—that you share
Your secrets of the mystic arts with us.

PARACELSUS: Secrets?—What secrets?
Did you think that God has placed
Eternal blinders on the eyes of men?

*They glance uncertainly at one another. Something
is not as they had expected.*

PARACELSUS: (*curious*) What secrets do you
wish
Me to bestow on you?

LEADER OF GROUP: The secret of power—how
to alter minds
Of prince or duke, to influence appointments
Either from our ranks, or favourable
To our cause.

PARACELSUS: I see … (*to SECOND MEMBER*) …
And you?

SECOND MEMBER OF GROUP: The same …
For our brothers crave respect,
Since ours is the one and final truth of prophecy
And dominion over human frailty!

*PARACELSUS turns to THIRD MEMBER. THIRD
MEMBER hesitates and is nervous.*

PARACELSUS: Well?

THIRD MEMBER OF GROUP: It is said by many …
You possess the secret
Of transmuting lead to gold …

I would give the fingers of my hands
For the secret of that trick!

*PARACELSUS unbuckles the belt around his waist
and holds it threateningly.*

PARACELSUS: (*roaring*) Aye … I possess that
secret!
And others so fearsome, the very heart of a
witness
To my dark and magic arts would break with
terror!
With a gesture of my hand heavenwards, as thus,
I can cause deafening thunder and such deluge
Of rain and hail as would sweep your town
Into the river!

*Loud crack of thunder from outside. FRANZ and
three members of GROUP jump with surprise and
alarm.*

PARACELSUS: With a glance of eye, I can cause a
man
Of splendid health to clutch his throat and
scream
With pain so agonizing, the veins within his head
Would swell and burst, and all who saw his
suffering
Would be struck dumb for eternity!
I can summon devils, angels …

*Misshapen forms of people enter and pass on either
side of them. Members of the GROUP cringe away.
FRANZ is bewildered.*

PARACELSUS: The earth to rise and break within
The graveyard, releasing groaning skulls—
Still gnawed by dripping worms … to shriek
In a hollow wind of voice …

Passing misshapen people give life to his words.

PARACELSUS: Paracelsus …

PASSING MAN: King of magic!

PASSING WOMAN: Let us be, for you are stronger
…

PASSING MAN: Than the strongest devil …

PASSING CROWD: (*in unison*) We succumb!

In grotesque postures of torment, they flee the stage.

*PARACELSUS lays about him with his belt, over the
backs and buttocks of the three members of mystic
GROUP.*

PARACELSUS: Furthermore, as you will witness
now,
I can, with well placed strokes
Of my belt across the arses of the scum
Of basest greed, ignorance and infamy ...
Cause its disciples to scatter,
Mrahwing like a pack of alley cats!

Covering their heads, the three scatter in confusion.

*LEADER OF THE GROUP turns, angered and
humiliated.*

LEADER OF GROUP: You cannot bear more ene-
mies, Paracelsus!
It's unwise of you to handle us this way—
Our anger will bring you to account for this!
We will not announce the hour or location
Of our vengeance, but look you to your safety
now
Each moment of the night and day!

*PARACELSUS glowers at him in a terrifying way.
Raising his arms like an attacking hawk, he rushes at them, causing them to retreat, stumbling and
tripping over one another.*

PARACELSUS: Threaten me, would you ... Harrh!

*After the group has fled, PARACELSUS breaks into
jubilant laughter. FRANZ also laughs with relief.*

PARACELSUS: What strange bedfellows have our
studies brought us!
Grown men, with painted bedspreads
Wrapped around their bodies, like some
Weathercocks of China! Hoods upon
Their heads, like the beaks of drowsy magpies ...
Even witchcraft has lost what dignity it had!
(*mimics*) ... I am a magistrate, oh noble healer!
And I the keeper of an inn ... But me—
I am the lowest devil of the trio—
I am just a common thief ... Help me make gold
Out of common shit—and for this I'll give you
All the fingers of my hands! (*laughs*)
What could I do with his fingers?
Thread them on a string and wear them
'Round my neck?

Sounds of the bells of Einsiedeln.

FRANZ: I am now afraid, Theophrastus!

PARACELSUS: A man is known for his works, his
friends ...
The good he does—but a man is also known
For the stature of his enemies!

FRANZ: They will be back ... you know they will
be back!
With violence more cruel and stealthy
Than that of pompous doctors and of priests!

PARACELSUS goes to his burning forge.

PARACELSUS: Then I will fight them with their
weapons, Franz.

*Making a rapid gesture over the forge with his
hand, the furnace flares with white, phosphorescent
flame, then dies down. PARACELSUS takes the crucible in tongs and turns swiftly, holding it out to
FRANZ.*

PARACELSUS: (*frowning, urgent*)
Remember well, Franz,
What I did ask you to prepare
Within this crucible!

FRANZ: A balm of zinc and heavy oils for the
treatment
Of skin ailments peculiar to milkmaids ...

PARACELSUS: And what is it I hold before you
now?

*FRANZ stares into the crucible. Rubs his eyes with
disbelief.*

FRANZ: No! ... It is not possible.

PARACELSUS: What is it you see?

FRANZ: A crucible of the purest gold!

*PARACELSUS laughs and replaces the crucible over
the flames.*

PARACELSUS: It might do to trick some greedy
landlord
When next we lack money for our rent!

FRANZ: That *was* gold! I know the properties of
gold
For I have often worked with it!
That was no trick, Theophrastus—or was it?

PARACELSUS looks at him enigmatically.

PARACELSUS: Certainly, it was gold—what other
answer do you seek?
It dazzles fools—bewilders scholars—
Confounds kings—if such be the influence of
gold
Then it was gold!

*PARACELSUS laughs bitterly and turns his back on
FRANZ.*

Bells stop.

PARACELSUS returns to his observations at the forge and to his writing.

FRANZ is pained, looks at PARACELSUS a long moment, then turns to the audience.

PARACELSUS: (*harshly*) There is nothing in the stars!
It is in the human wisdom that the secrets lie!

FRANZ: The signs of his later torment
Were already there … in his twisted fingers
And his swollen hands …
The stoop of back …
The loss of hair and teeth …
He now treated patients often without surgery
Or drugs—and I rejoiced and shuddered
At the miracles he worked …

PARACELSUS: Don't look pained or startled,
Franz …
The patient's will to live is a potent medicine—
Despair and gloom are hand-maidens
To the monarchy of death …
Recognize the pain created of the heart and mind,
And prescribe from your own spirit
An antidote of joy and love so dazzling
It radiates like flame from your hands and eyes!
This, and the words you choose to speak
Are miracles of healing created
In a true physician's presence.
If you are incapable of such sacrifice
Of wisdom, spirit and yourself,
Go then into commerce or the priesthood,
For of a doctor you will only be a hollow sham!

FRANZ lowers his head in pain.

FRANZ: Why do I merit such anger and contempt?

PARACELSUS turns to him, his expression pained.

PARACELSUS: Don't whimper like a lowlands maiden!
I speak my mind openly to you, as to a son …

FRANZ: A son can be hurt by a thoughtless father!

PARACELSUS: *Hurt?* Look at me, wretch!
There is nothing theoretic in my teaching of you;
Everything I say I *know*, because I've *lived* it!
Listen to the hearts of things
Not the spoken or the written word alone!

FRANZ: Although I love you much, Theophrastus,
I am a man of reason—I weigh
Your arguments against the lesser ones
Of your opponents.

PARACELSUS: (*angry now*) Words devoid of passion
Are nothing—mere ashes in the wind
Of distant fires …
I was a lad on my way to school …
My mother led me to the bridge
On the river Sihl, which flowed
Beside our home …
The water in the river boiled and roared …
I heard not her words, but in her eyes
I saw her love and last farewell …
As if shrieked from the very edge of hell!
And then … in her madness, she dove
Into the river, her body breaking open
On the rocks below the bridge like some
Fragile vessel of the darkest, sacred wine …
In seconds, the plumes of churning water
Reddened with her blood as far as I could see …

FRANZ covers his face in his hands.

FRANZ: No!

PARACELSUS: I howled my love for her …
She was my mother, who had but an hour before
Wakened me from sleep, prepared for me a bowl
Of barley gruel with oil …
Dusted my satchel …
Combed my hair …

FRANZ: No Theophrastus—I have heard enough!

PARACELSUS begins to talk rapidly, as if deranged momentarily with the memory.

PARACELSUS: I watched the river wash her foaming blood
Towards the sea—
And remembered, as a dying man remembers birth …
She left me as an infant by the road
Which passed our house …
My father gone to tend to patients
In the town;
I was alone, when some soldiers,
Dark and snarling with diseases of the mind
Came by and saw me.
They removed the cloth around my loins,
And baring swords and daggers,
Amused themselves by cutting at my penis

As they had seen in Palestine
Done to Jewish lads in circumcision ...
Tiring of the sport and my shrieks of pain,
They left me there, unwrapped and bleeding ...
I tried to draw myself into the house,
But before I reached the door ... a wild boar,
Maddened by the scent of blood, came charging
From the woods.
He closed his steaming jaws around my wound,
And with jerking actions of his head,
Tore away my manhood and ran grunting
Down the road—masticating penis,
Testicles and strings of pale fibre
Torn from out my body ...

FRANZ: (*weeping*) Merciful God!

PARACELSUS: (*softly now*) Look gently when you
look on pain,
My student—it is not the duty of humanity to
suffer.
But only if you understand all suffering
Can you comprehend the meaning
Of a healer's obligation.

FRANZ: Then let me suffer as you suffered—
I am not afraid!

PARACELSUS: You will suffer, have no fear.
So do not whimper when you hunger,
Or the colour leaves your cheeks
For lack of sleep—
That is the pain of pampered dandies,
So break it in your nature now.
We have more lofty undertakings.
This is but an interlude.

The bells go silent.

PARACELSUS: Go tend your observations—
We have lost two hours of this night ...

*DR. GUZA and DR. WEBB are seated at the table on
the lowest level of set, poring through medical
journals.*

DR. WEBB: Look at this—ads and more ads from
the drug industry. I feel that when I grow up an'
become a big boy, ninety percent of my medical
practice will consist of dispensing chemicals
which I've never seen and know nothing about!

DR. GUZA: (*laughing*) Doctor Patrick Webb,
P.F.P.I. ... pusher for the pharmaceutics industry!

DR. WEBB: I only hope somebody up there
knows what the hell's going on. I don't.

DR. GUZA: And think of what happens when a
breakthrough is made in cancer and heart
diseases! The ranks of the unemployed will swell
by thousands!

DR. WEBB: How come?

DR. GUZA: What will happen to all the careers
dedicated to worrying about cancer and heart
sufferers?

DR. WEBB: They'll promote some new disease!
How about promoting mental illness to the
hungry? Or nuclear weapons to the starving of
the Orient?

DR. GUZA stops laughing.

DR. GUZA: That's not funny, Patrick!

DR. WEBB: Then so much for your faith in human
goodness—theirs or ours! I think the world
stinks, honey—and I want no part of it!

DR. GUZA: But you're a doctor!

DR. WEBB: What the hell does that mean? Words
like love, freedom, pity—have all been turned to
shit by this! (*angrily points to an advertisement in
the journal*) So if I want to live, I've got to play the
game—I'm a businessman, and screw your
Schwietzers and Bethunes! In the operating
theatre, I'll be as good as any of them. Outside
the hospital—who gives a damn anyway?

*They glower at each other, then return to their
reading.*

*PARACELSUS is at his laboratory, setting up exper-
iments and making hurried notes. FRANZ moves
away from him, speaks to the audience.*

FRANZ: The world needed a new birth, he told
me once ...
I did not understand his statement.

PARACELSUS: All created things are by their
nature
Hostile to men, and men to them ...
Why, I cannot answer—for that is the nature
And tragedy of human destiny
Beneath this canopy of heaven
And its mysteries!

FRANZ: At times he frightened me
With his suspended logic ...

PARACELSUS: If God works a miracle, He does it
through people!

In healing illness, He does it through the doctor …
And in this, there are two doctors;
Those who heal with medicine,
And those who heal as if by miracle.
I have done both, and do observe
That God accomplishes through a physician
A transmutation in the patient,
Should he will to live …
Yet medicine itself does not belong to faith
But to the sight of questioning and agnostic eyes.

FRANZ: He spoke to me of Asia,
And theories he had heard
From healers there …

PARACELSUS: A man is his own doctor,
Helping nature to provide the needs
Of his body and his mind …
All things are in the inner
As they are in the outer world—
Our wounds heal from within outwards
As nature heals itself and levels out the hollows
Of scars and injury—
Heaven and earth, air and water
Are a man … And a man is a world
With heaven and earth, air and water—
When we administer medicine,
We administer this entire world
To him …

A sound of tramping feet. Six hooded FIGURES appear over top level of set. The LEADING FIGURE carries a silver cross, the others carry staves and torches.

The LEADING FIGURE sees PARACELSUS and points.

LEADING FIGURE: There he is—Lucifer himself!

On signal, they rush down and surround PARACELSUS and FRANZ. FRANZ is fearful, but PARACELSUS slowly puts away his manuscripts into a satchel, buckles on his sword.

LEADING FIGURE: Are you the one they call Paracelsus, the healer?

PARACELSUS ignores him.

LEADING FIGURE: For if you are, then do you confess
With consorting with witches and the dead?
Evoking devils and creating magic
Through evil stars? … Answer me!

PARACELSUS continues to ignore him.

LEADING FIGURE is becoming disconcerted. Points to the laboratory equipment.

LEADING FIGURE: Are these the tools of your evil arts?

ANOTHER MAN: He is struck dumb
By the cross you carry!
Wave it in his face
To cause him blindness, too!

The LEADING FIGURE waves the cross before the face of PARACELSUS, who stares at him a moment, as if contemplating some reply, then thinks better of it, and with a derisive shrug moves away with FRANZ. They take a circuitous route to the top level of the set, returning to where the hooded figures have shunned hoods to become townspeople—INN KEEPER, TAILOR, MERCHANT, PRIEST.

As PARACELSUS and FRANZ leave, the hooded FIGURES smash the laboratory, and, in mime, exorcise the rubble with the cross.

FRANZ: The church is in uproar—their terror
Now precedes us.

PARACELSUS: Their church can go to hell for all I care!
Their hypocrisy and cant has stripped them
Of all claims to dignity …
Their buildings and cathedrals
Are nothing more than barns now
Occupied by fat and lazy herders …
Their sermons and manners are but imitations
Of posturing magicians …
Speak no more of Church and God
In the same breath—
For it demeans and humiliates
The God I know and love!

They approach the townspeople, who watch them sternly.

FRANZ: Gentlemen—we have been on foot since sunrise,
With neither food nor drink …
My master and I are weary,
And desire food and lodging,
At reasonable cost,
For we have little more than travel money.

INN KEEPER glances at the PRIEST, who nods, and turns away.

INN KEEPER: Is this man Paracelsus, the famed healer?

FRANZ: That he is, and I am Franz,
His servant and apprentice.

The INN KEEPER shakes his head.

INN KEEPER: I would it were different or another
evening.
But peddlers, merchants and soldiers
Now fully occupy my lodgings.

FRANZ: Is there a porch then … a barn,
Or some abandoned shop where we might …

PARACELSUS: Do not beg, lad … observe the
priest—
His face shrieks in its silence
As the page of a forbidden book!

PRIEST: (*stammering*) Ho … how dare you,
heathen?

INN KEEPER: (*nervously*) I do not lie to you,
Paracelsus!
Had I the wherewithal, I would be most happy
To have your famed person as guest
Within my inn!

PARACELSUS: (*angry now*) You do lie, and may
God spare you
The punishment you deserve for your unmanli-
ness!
What has become of our German race of men
Who now cower like slavish dogs
Before the cowled hooligans of Rome?

*The PRIEST spins on his heel and strikes PARACEL-
SUS across the face with his hand. PARACELSUS
staggers back, then regains his balance. He stares
at the PRIEST.*

PARACELSUS: (*coldly*) Weary with hunger and
fatigue, for I have travelled
Many miles this day, doctoring the stricken
I come by night upon this town …
To be struck across the face by you—
Wanton scum unfit to dust my shoes …
What is your proper German name?
So if I should chance to meet your mother
In my wanderings, I may share with her
The grief she bears at giving birth to you!

*More out of panic than anger now, the PRIEST
strikes PARACELSUS again. FRANZ tries to defend
him, but is pushed aside by another TOWNSMAN.
PARACELSUS is knocked down.*

INN KEEPER: If you've hurt him,

God in Heaven will not forgive us!

The PRIEST, in his own fear, becomes excitable.

PRIEST: No! God rejoices in this act—believe me!
Feel free to fall upon him now!
The doctor you respected is no more …
He has sold his talents to the devil—
So fall upon him! God will forgive you!

*But the PRIEST cannot entice the others to attack.
They are awed by the prostrate body before them,
and retreat, followed by the PRIEST.*

*DR. WEBB and DR. GUZA stroll back and forth on
lowest level of set, as if pacing up and down a
hospital hallway.*

DR. GUZA: (*shaking her head*) You're a gentle
person, and yet if I didn't know you …

DR. WEBB: Lay off me, will you! … That's your
husband's bag, if he's studying for the ministry!

DR. GUZA: You should meet him—how about dinner at our house next week?

DR. WEBB: Betty, I like women, but I don't get
along with men worth a damn! (*smiles*) Especially
the ones committed to save the world.

DR. GUZA: Keep talking like that an' you'll end up
believing what you say.

DR. WEBB: I want to be left alone, Betty.

He is tense, no longer smiling.

DR. GUZA: Why?

DR. WEBB: Because I can *pretend* to be human,
and not have to live the part. Can you understand
that?

DR. GUZA: No.

DR. WEBB laughs.

Curtain

ACT 3

Curtain up.

PARACELSUS, ragged and dirty, and followed by FRANZ, crosses top elevation of set. FRANZ is breathless, and pauses for rest.

Sound of dogs in background, yelping angrily in pursuit.

A peasant MAN and WOMAN enter. The MAN is limping badly, and leaning on the WOMAN. PARACELSUS sees them, and wordlessly goes to them. Kneeling before the MAN and lifting his pant-leg, PARACELSUS exposes a badly cut and dis-coloured leg. Unscrewing the hasp of his sword, he withdraws tinctures and salves, which he applies to the wound. Then from his satchel he takes dress-ings, with which he covers the wound. The peasant MAN and WOMAN bow to him and leave, their heads low.

Still on his knees, he receives a procession of other people who enter, all ragged, all silent, averting his gaze. He treats, examines and comforts them.

FRANZ: We slept in fields ... For food I stole
Vegetables from gardens and the marketplace ...
I lay awake at night, listening to his frail body
Rasp for breath ... and always, the pursuing dogs
Barking and yowling near at hand, on command
Of the henchmen of the church—the mystic brotherhoods,
And community of doctors throughout Germany
and Switzerland.

The last patient is treated and leaves. PARACELSUS stares for a long moment at FRANZ, who sits with his head in his hands, ashamed of his weariness and despair.

DR. WEBB and DR. GUZA enter on lowest level of stage. They are dressed in tennis clothes, and carry racquets. They watch an invisible game offstage they await their turn on the courts.

DR. GUZA: It's a good farm ... a place where children can ride horses on holidays ...

DR. WEBB: How much did it cost?

DR. GUZA: Thirty thousand ...

DR. WEBB: You're wasting your money. Thirty thousand in industrial stock is better investment than some rundown old farm!

DR. GUZA: It's worth forty now!

DR. WEBB: Which is no more than inflationary loss on the money you've invested. I can tell you of ways to beat the system, if you're interested.

DR. GUZA: (*annoyed*) Why is it that everything is an absolute value with you? When we invest, it's not because we plan to make more money ... we don't need it!

DR. WEBB: On this continent, honey, commerce is like sex—essential and guilt-ridden!

DR. GUZA: You're a fascist!

DR. WEBB: You know why I dislike small "L" liberals?

DR. GUZA: (*sarcastically*) Do tell me, so I, too, may see the light!

DR. WEBB: They're all self-righteous bastards, trying to keep a foot in each world! You can't have it both ways—either you oppress, or you're oppressed! Either you manipulate food, or you'll end up being the hungry one! ... There's not enough to go around ... that's the short and long of it, Betty! Something has to die for other things to live!

DR. GUZA stares angrily at him.

DR. GUZA: What sort of doctor are you?

DR. WEBB: I'm not smug and outside this world, if that's what you mean. (*with anguish*) Look, honey ... I'm lookin' for the answers too! I'm reaching out of self-preservation ... if someone has the answer, I wish they'd tell me! There's got to be room for those of us who've become hard-eyed conservatives ... I'm a good doctor ... you said so yourself.

DR. GUZA walks quickly past him.

DR. GUZA: Come on ... There's a couple leaving!

He follows her. They exit.

PARACELSUS: I can endure for entirety ...
But it is wrong of me to torture
Your young body and your mind
In pursuit of things known only to my enemies,
For my friends have left me now.

FRANZ rises hurriedly to his feet and joins PARACELSUS. They continue walking, making their way to another elevation, where a fat, haughty

BURGOMASTER is carefully packing a clay pipe for smoking.

FRANZ: It is nothing … sleep will help me.

PARACELSUS: (*to BURGOMASTER, in a pleading tone*) Is this Innsbruck, brother?

BURGOMASTER: It is, and your brother I am not!
Who are you? What is the nature
Of your business at this hour of evening?

PARACELSUS: I am Paracelsus, the healer,
And I request permission to practice
In this town!

The BURGOMASTER lights his pipe slowly, blows smoke into the face of PARACELSUS, then smiles coldly.

BURGOMASTER: You—are   Paracelsus? …
Begone!
I know the great Paracelsus as I know this hand!
I'll set my dogs upon you for your impertinence, beggar!
Take you and this ruffian lad, and be gone!
Paracelsus, indeed …

PARACELSUS chokes back his anger.

PARACELSUS: I will not beg … I cannot beg.
I am a doctor and request permission
To pursue my skills …
If I am not Paracelsus whom you know
Better, it appears, than I know him—
Then let me practice as a doctor—
Any doctor … nameless, if you wish!

BURGOMASTER: (*sarcastically*) Might I ask to examine
Your degree … *Doctor*?

PARACELSUS: I have no degrees, but leave me an hour
With ten of your most ill citizens
And my competence will not be questioned.

BURGOMASTER: Don't play the fool with me, you impertinent bastard!
A man in rags is not a doctor …
You are a swineherd, perhaps,
Or at worst, a beggar! Stand aside!
I have an evening meal waiting for me.

PARACELSUS: Damn you and all those like you,
Who created only doctors clad in silk,
And not in shabby rags grilled by the sun …

What a mockery you've made
Of practitioners of healing!

The BURGOMASTER spits at the feet of PARACELSUS and walks past him to exit. PARACELSUS unscrews hilt of his sword and gives FRANZ a leather pouch.

PARACELSUS: Take this laudanum, Franz …
Be sparing with the scalpel,
But when you must cut flesh or bone
Be merciful and generous in turning
Deepest pain to sleep …

FRANZ takes the drug pouch and watches PARACELSUS uncertainly.

FRANZ: Are we to go … in separate directions now?

PARACELSUS: From here on, I know not where
My destiny will take me.
I have premonitions of an early death …
You must go your way and fulfill
Work destined for a younger man.

FRANZ: (*shocked*) I wish to stay—to share
Whatever fate befalls you!

PARACELSUS: It is the fate of man to struggle
Against nature and his baser self.
His ultimate salvation is in loneliness.
I no longer ask—I command you leave!
You are a good lad and a competent physician.
May God be gentler to you
Than I have been …

He turns abruptly. Distant sound of barking dogs. PARACELSUS points and snarls.

PARACELSUS: Hear that? We, who make sport for the gods,
Are hunted to the end!

PARACELSUS exits. FRANZ moves slowly to highest levels of set.

FRANZ: The miles separating us
Became years …

Procession of people begin to pass below FRANZ.

FRANZ: (*calling to procession*) What news?

WOMAN: The plague is nearing Stertzing!

FRANZ: Are there doctors in the town?

WOMAN: No—they've left. But Paracelsus
Is arriving!

FRANZ: How fares the old man?

ANOTHER WOMAN: He is bookish and ill-tempered,
Never sleeping—harsh as frost;
But as a healer—
God Himself could not do more!

FRANZ laughs.

FRANZ: Affliction and misery has met its match
In the homeopathy of his being!

WOMAN: Nothing is eternal—particularly
The wisdom of a noble man …
Paracelsus will in time die
And we shall once again be tortured
With illness … and its cures!

FRANZ waves cheerfully to the procession. They wave back, laughing, and exit.

FRANZ: For the longest time, I heard nothing
From him—and then one night,
I was awaked from my sleep,
As if shaken by a nurse …
And when I woke, I heard
Within my brain his voice …

PARACELSUS: (*offstage*) Franz—do you hear me?
Have I communion with you?

FRANZ: Yes, Theophrastus!
But you are not with me!

PARACELSUS: (*offstage*) I am well and occupied
productively …
I have lately studied the transfer of thoughts
Over distances so vast that no phenomena
Of voice or presence can equate this feat!

FRANZ: Your thoughts reach me as if
You were present in this very room!

PARACELSUS: (*entering on a level below FRANZ, books in his hands*)
I cannot write you as I know not
Where you are. But I have
Some observations to provide you …
Diseases of the mind are not the work
Of forces emanating from the devil—
They are natural diseases as all others;
Treat them accordingly … I have found
Conclusive evidence of an unseen astral body
Within man—as in plants, capable of instant
Flight to distant places. Also,
I have found much that is curious and useful

In the arts of clairvoyance and levitation—
Do not neglect further studies of these things.
I have much to tell you of amulets,
To counter influences of forces electric
Which affect the human spirit and the body …

FRANZ, turned away from PARACELSUS, is writing furiously.

FRANZ: I make note of your instructions!

PARACELSUS: Believe in God and love,
But not the God or love which bears
Official approval, lad—
For every fool praises his own club!
He who stands on the Pope
Stands on a cushion! …
He who stands on Zwingli
Stands on emptiness! …
He who stands on Luther,
Stands on a waterpipe! (*laughs*)
Remain true to your inner wisdom,
The finest mind is an empty vessel
At the time of birth—fill it!

FRANZ also laughs, nods, and puts away his notes.

PARACELSUS seats himself on a small wooden bench and opens his books. He takes out a small piece of cheese from his pocket and munches thoughtfully on it.

FRANZ: … Nine months later, I did hear from him—
A messenger brought me news and a summons
To leave at once for Salzburg,
For Paracelsus feared that he was dying.
I turned my practice over to a trusted colleague
And filled with apprehension, journeyed to that city …

FRANZ exits quickly.

PARACELSUS: I have this day learned of the death
Of my father, whom I had wished to visit,
But my travels now are slow and tortured …

His hands tremble and the lump of cheese falls to his feet. He suddenly becomes very old and frail.

PARACELSUS: Farewell, gentle parent—may your deserved rest
Not be marred by pain and holocaust
The living share … I have lately dreamed
In short moments of my sleep, of my infancy …
Of my mother, poor demented soul—holding me to her …

He holds his arms in a crook before him, as a mother comforting an infant.

PARACELSUS: Her fearful eyes, dark as the forests
Of the Edsel ... her lips mute
On her suffering ... Oh, God!
Had I the time left to repay her love
For me with further studies
On congenital insanity!

Sound of the bells of Einsiedeln.

On topmost level of set, WOMAN-ANGEL appears, hooded and dressed in black.

On the level of PARACELSUS, three hooded, mystic FIGURES armed with cudgels enter silently. PARACELSUS looks at each of them, an expression of profound sadness on his face.

LEADER OF GROUP: It took us many years to find the place
And the moment for this meeting, Paracelsus!
Your screams will not be heard—
The streets are empty now ...
The stairway and the entrance to this house
Has been deserted of your patients
And ragged students and admirers!

PARACELSUS peers at the leader of the group.

PARACELSUS: Is it you, Oporinus?

On his words, a youthful STUDENT enters, hat in hand. He is well-dressed, bedecked with jewellery. Throughout following conversation, PARACELSUS peers into hooded face of leader of the group.

The student in memory is OPORINUS.

OPORINUS: My good wishes for your health,
Dear teacher, and master
Of all physicians!

PARACELSUS: What is it, Oporinus? Your wishes
For my health heralds a request for money
Or approaching fear of death ...
You seem hearty!

OPORINUS: (*grinning*) You jest, do you not, sir?

PARACELSUS: I know you better than our Lord
Knew Judas—what is it now?

OPORINUS: I was a dedicated student of yours,
Was I not?

PARACELSUS: No, you were not!

The smile fades from the STUDENT'S face.

OPORINUS: Why do you punish me with rudeness—
Yet keep as confidant and friend
That pale peasant, Franz?

PARACELSUS: (*sighs*)
You bore me with your treachery.
You know well why I dismissed you, Oporinus—
Consider it your fortune I had much to do,
Which spared you the thrashing you deserved—
You knave that dogs my heels as a gaunt crow
A gasping sheep!

OPORINUS: I was paid ... you know by whom ...
To write that public letter as a student,
Denouncing you as drunkard
On your journey to your friends
In Zurich ... It was my wife;
You know that wife of mine,
Who desires finery and a house
Beyond the limit of my earnings ...
Forgive my weakness—
But I am a driven man,
Having married foolishly ...

PARACELSUS: She deserves you, Oporinus—and you, her!
Never grieve—you are a knave and fool,
But still you are no worse than others
I have trained through apprenticeship and lectures
Doctors in the hundreds—yet other than Franz
Whom you resent, of true healers
I have trained so few ...
Two from Pannonia—three from Poland;
One from Bohemia, and one from Holland.
So much energy, for such a scant reward!
What is it you have come to beg this time?

OPORINUS: I ... do sorely need ... some precious laudanum.
I have three patients of great wealth
Who would see me through the darkest times
Of my debts if I but had a small container
Of the drug ... Paracelsus, please!
I am otherwise a ruined man!

With pained fingers, PARACELSUS fumbles in his pockets, and taking out a small package, throws it over his shoulder. OPORINUS falls to the floor to eagerly collect it.

PARACELSUS: Here, you worthless bastard!

May this give your wealthy patients
Needed sleep from the ravages
Of alcohol and whoring!

OPORINUS: Thank you, good friend and teacher!
I will repay you when I can,
I promise you!

PARACELSUS: Yes, you will repay me …
When might I expect to read another
Infamy above your signature?
Accusing me of what this time?
Black magic? Monsters?
A servant of the devil?

OPORINUS flees and exits.

PARACELSUS: (*to LEADER OF GROUP*)
Are you in the pay of priests and doctors?
… Or is your hatred such
That a century of waiting
Would not have cooled it
One degree?

LEADER OF GROUP: That is a question you may
ponder for eternity.
May your master, the devil, take pity
On your revolutionary soul!
There will be none on earth …
So long as earth endures!

The WOMAN-ANGEL signals. The three hooded MEN attack PARACELSUS in slow motion, in a scene of cruel medieval assassination.

PARACELSUS gives a low, moaning outcry as he lifts his arthritic, twisted hands to defend himself. But he is helpless over the blows of the clubs against the back of his head. He falls.

DR. WEBB and DR. GUZA enter, still in tennis wear. They have just concluded their game. They are in animated argument.

DR. WEBB: Alright—then forget it! I don't worry about me … but you do!

DR. GUZA: You're totally out of it, you know that?

DR. WEBB: Do I steal? Break up homes? Abuse my patients? … What is it?

DR. GUZA: No … no! What you represent is far worse than that! You would, in the last crunch, stand in the way of progress!

DR. WEBB: Sure I would, so would you. So would your preacher-husband … only I admit I would!

But what is progress? Giving every fool the right to vote himself a car for a faster ride to hell? Providing antibiotics to populations who will die of hunger?

DR. GUZA: There is always hope for new ideas … That's the value of mistakes … that's what great men are all about!

DR. WEBB: You can take your great men and put them down the tube, for all I care. They generally don't live long enough to see the harm they've done. The most this world can take with a minimum of damage is *competent* people. Great people scare me … they scare all of us.

DR. GUZA: What sort of damned nonsense is that?

DR. WEBB: We all voted for stringing Christ up on the cross—that's why we survived to make children, study medicine, create hybrid corn and fan-jet engines! And we'll do it again, and again … and again. There's nothing wrong with that—it's even democratic, because there are always more of us than you! Relax, honey—the kid you lost on the ward yesterday was just an average human being!

DR. GUZA turns away from him and begins to sob.

DR. WEBB: (*soberly*) What choices have we got? … What choices has anybody? I don't believe in God or people … I believe in myself being capable of doing good things sometimes—and even that seems difficult to accomplish.

DR. GUZA leaves him. He watches her exit. Bunting a tennis ball thoughtfully with his racquet, he exits in the opposite direction.

The slow motion assassination of PARACELSUS goes on. He is caked with blood, but still rises to his knees to escape, protecting the back of his head with his hands.

ANOTHER MEMBER OF GROUP: (*turning away, making a retching sound*) He won't die! … His skull is smashed and he
Won't die!

The WOMAN-ANGEL makes a frantic signal. The KILLERS lower their clubs. The LEADER of the group props PARACELSUS up against the bench. The KILLERS hurry away. WOMAN-ANGEL remains motionless on top level of set, looking down on PARACELSUS.

Bells of Einsiedeln peal loudly, then recede into background.

PARACELSUS shudders. His speech is halting and painful.

PARACELSUS: Though I have lived through the agony
Of this moment once before,
I have forgotten the excruciating pain ...
The hellions of light that dance
Before my eyes ... the growing chill
That deepens through my flesh ...
All feeling now has left my arms and legs ...

... Left for dead, I did not die ...
But raised by face from the acid,
Thickening blood to cry for help ...
A drunken mason, passing by, did hear me ...
Helped raise me to my bed and took my message
To what friends I still possessed ...
The rest is but a matter of an hour
Or a day, before the vital organs
Surrender in despair to the skull,
Shattered in a hundred pieces ...

He raises his hand past his open eyes.

PARACELSUS: ... Now the hallucinations come ...
Like visions of a prior life ...
How melancholy I do feel ... Father?
Is that you? ... Some nights I saw you
In my inner eye, hunched alone—
Your mouth drawn with age and sadness ...
Sitting at a solitary table to a meal
You could not eat—your wife dead ...
Your son a frightening legend ...
And you, old man, dreaming of a life
Of companions, children and domestic love ...
Until the spittle in your throat dried
To bitter ashes of regret ...

A distraught young WOMAN enters, carrying a dead child. PARACELSUS blinks and half rises, reaching out to her.

WOMAN: Paracelsus—healer from the gods!
My child is dead!
And so is his father—
Killed in their wretched wars!

PARACELSUS: God, oh God! ... Why do people suffer so?

WOMAN: (*handing dead child to PARACELSUS*)
Make him live! Please make him live!

PARACELSUS: I cannot help you—I, too, am dead!
Let sorrow for us both well from your heart
Like some gigantic storm, threatening screams
To wake Him who created us for grief ...
Rend your clothes and skin ... plunge headlong
Into flames of suicide or depravity ...
Cry to the heavens if it helps ...
Cry for both of us!

WOMAN: (*screaming*) Help us all, doctor!
You cannot die now!

PARACELSUS: The love I bore for you surpassed children ...
Parents ... husbands ... lovers ...
All, except the love of God Himself
For man and woman ...

He cradles the dead child with great tenderness and compassion. The WOMAN weeps quietly now, and removing her shawl, covers PARACELSUS with it. Then tearing off a strip of cloth from her skirt, she wipes his face.

PARACELSUS: He suffered much ... it is written in the purple flashes
In his face ... frightened, too young to understand
The philosophy of punishments for which
There was no crime ... (*looks up at WOMAN*)
You are mother to twenty children yet unborn ...
Builders of houses and roads as yet unplanned ...
Nurses ... caretakers of the fields ...
Rowdies and lovers ... Some in splendid health ...
Some maimed—but your own!
Bury what is dead, and turn to life again ...
Healers will attend you, and God,
Through His meadowlarks and nightingales
Will sing His celebration for your homecoming
From the deep, dark abyss that confronts us all ...

The WOMAN nods, takes the dead child, and pressing the hand of PARACELSUS to her cheek, leaves.

PARACELSUS: (*shouting*) Men of strong heart!
Who swore to walk erect into the raging storms ...
Where are you now? ... What jest of gods
Hobbles you—Women? Luxury? Fear?
Paracelsus calls you for the final time!

The bells of Einsiedeln go silent.

Sound of crickets. Distant barking of dogs.

FRANZ, well-dressed and prosperous, enters. He is followed by six WITNESSES.

On entering, FRANZ stops some distance from PARACELSUS, and motions to others to do likewise.

FRANZ: When your message reached me, I came
As quickly as I could … travelling
By night and day … stopping only
To change horses ridden at full gallop …

PARACELSUS: I care not if you flew or galloped …
Only that you've arrived in time, Franz.
(*smiles at him*) You've fleshed out …
Your hair has paled … I asked you
To bring six witnesses to hear
My testament …

FRANZ: They are here.

He turns his face away from PARACELSUS.

FRANZ: You are in hemorrhage, Theophrastus!
The years of work with antimony, mercury,
Opium, nightshade, monkshood and other poisons
In distillation near your body now rise in revenge!
… I cannot bear the pain within your eyes …
The hollow cheeks and thin lips of an ancient
man …
Theophrastus—you are only ten years older than
myself!

PARACELSUS: Your diagnosis is a hasty one,
Franz …
Whatever ravages the skills of my profession
Wreak within my flesh and bones is nothing
To what men have done with clubs to the
hindmost
Portions of my head …

Leans forward painfully.

PARACELSUS: I tried to live until I saw you …

FRANZ hurries to him, bends down to examine the back of PARACELSUS' head, then turns away, his face registering horror.

FRANZ: Who has done this to him—why? …
The entire skull in back is crushed
And hanging by some strips of scalp …
The brain, white and swollen,
Is exposed and drying …

FRANZ: (*to PARACELSUS*) I will gather the finest
doctors in this city
And we will tend you to good health!

PARACELSUS: No, Franz … Let God and I agree
Upon the moment of my death—
Each man has that right, and neither

Doctor, priest, magician or the king himself
Should interfere when the injuries are hopeless!

FRANZ paces with fury.

FRANZ: What villain did this to you?
I will revenge your death!

PARACELSUS: (*weary*) Only old enemies avenge
old slights …
Say it was some doctors, magicians and the
priests …
I know their names, but will not reveal them …
What hour is it, Franz?

FRANZ: It is evening now.

PARACELSUS: By night … thieves steal when
they cannot be seen …
So creeps in death when medicine is at its darkest
And steals away the life of man—
His greatest treasure.

FRANZ motions for the WITNESSES to come forward. They are nervous and respectful. One of them takes out paper and sits. The moment PARACELSUS speaks, he begins to write.

PARACELSUS: Write this then …

Bells of Einsiedeln begin to ring.

The three ASSASSINS enter. The WOMAN-ANGEL comes down to hover near PARACELSUS. The three ASSASSINS again mime the killing of PARACELSUS in slow motion. They are invisible to witnesses and FRANZ. Each time he is struck, PARACELSUS lurches and struggles with the agony. But he no longer lifts his hands to defend himself against the blows.

PARACELSUS: … I, Theophrastus von Hohenheim
… clear in mind
… And of upright heart … commit my life,
Death and soul to the care and protection
Of Almighty God … In the steadfast hope
That the Merciful God will not allow
The bitter suffering, martyrdom and death
Of His only Son … our saviour Jesus Christ …
To be fruitless and of no avail to him,
A miserable man …

PARACELSUS lurches from a blow. One of the witnesses presses a flask of water to his lips, but the liquid runs helplessly down his chin. He gazes at the man with gratitude, and shrugs to indicate it cannot be helped.

FRANZ: What barbaric villainy drives men
To inflict such injury on men among us,
Who in their deeds, wisdom and compassion
Surpass the God we claim to love above all else?
I am not a violent man, but I could sack a city
For this act!

PARACELSUS: I died … once … long ago …
But interpreters through passing ages …
Do this to me … for their own discoveries …
Of hope … futility … and perchance some glimmer
Of eternal reason … why man is cursed
With choices in the way he lives and dies …

FRANZ: I beg you—condemn them all by name!

PARACELSUS: Death is not fearsome, my beloved
Franz …
Nor angry … be not afraid for me …
It is my days' work ended …
And God's harvest time …
Man's power over us—ends with death.
Only God deals with us then,
And God is love!

*Another blow, which throws him forward. An
uncertainty flashes over his face.*

PARACELSUS: God *must* be love!
Else why this turbulent intelligence
And rage to serve the species
To exclusion of all else? Why?

*FRANZ cautions him to rest. But another blow rocks
him.*

FRANZ: I beg you—rest a moment!
The cavern in your skull
Has begun to bleed afresh
With your efforts!

*PARACELSUS, with a mighty effort, flings his covers
to the floor and staggers to his feet to confront his
KILLERS, who move back in slow motion.*

PARACELSUS: I am aflame! No glaciers nor
oceans
Can quell my fevers now! … Bury you my body
… Among the poor beyond the bridge …
At the church of St. Sebastian …
Between the singing of the psalms,
Give you a penny each to every poor man and
woman
Assembled for my funeral
… My father haunts me like a winter's night! …
I did not know … the day he died …

So many years ago … Had he called for me,
His son? … And I, deaf to his pleas …

FRANZ: (*desperately lying*) Be assured he died in
peace … my sister
Was a servant in his house …
He died in peace, she told me!

PARACELSUS: Thank God for that!

*He continues standing, gazing on his circling
KILLERS and the WOMAN-ANGEL who directs
them.*

PARACELSUS: Pay my debts, Franz … Assemble
all my books …
From wherever I have left them …
My complements of drugs and tinctures
And have Doctor Wendle in this city
… Care for them … so long as life
Is with him—he is a scholar and a careful man.
Pay yourselves twelve gulden each …
For your troubles here this night …
Disperse the rest to all my heirs …
The poor, miserable, needy people …
Without favour or disfavour …
Poverty and want are the only qualifications …
To you, beloved Franz … I bequeath my sword
And this amulet about my throat …

Hands it to FRANZ.

PARACELSUS: … And the most fearful legacy of
all …
The curse of continual enquiry …
Plus my eternal love to lift you to the lip
Of heaven, while still you pace and prod
This earth for what truth and honesty
Still unknown lies buried in the herbs,
Stones and essences like a mantel of the gods …
Waiting to redress human pain and want …

*With a groan, PARACELSUS topples and falls. The
stage darkens as a procession of people with candles
in their hands enter and weave their way through
the upper two elevations. WOMAN-ANGEL,
ASSASSINS and PARACELSUS disappear into and
become part of, the moving bodies. A flame flickers
back of set and continues burning, throwing entire
set outline into silhouette. Candles multiply.
Darkened set becomes gloomier with more moving
bodies.*

*FRANZ moves forward for final address to
audience.*

FRANZ: Paracelsus ... healer, philosopher, teacher
And stormy petrel of medical renaissance ...
Died and was buried on the twenty-fourth day
Of September, 1541 ... St. Rupert's festival day.
Through the next day and into the night,
The poor thronged the city,
As if knowing through some revelation
Of his passing ...

Momentary burst of human voices.

FRANZ: Thousands came ... thousands unto thousands ...
Filled the streets, and still they came ...
Not knowing where or how he died ...
Only that he had come to rest in Salzburg ...
Thousands and still more thousands ...
Moving slowly through the streets,
Carrying tapers which they lit at twilight ...
As if in honour of the greatest saint ...
Thousands upon thousands ... The tapers lit
Until at midnight the city was a slowly
Moving sheet of living flame ...
Orders were dispatched to silence
All the city bells, lest they excite
Some violence against the murderers
And those of wealth and privilege
Who could scarce disguise their pleasure
At his death ...

Babble of voices ends suddenly.

FRANZ: But at midnight, as if on signal,
The moving river of the country's people stopped ...

Candlelight procession of people stop.

FRANZ: And a great silence settled over them ...
More frightening than a howl of pain ...
And then ... With a sigh as soft as summer wind ...
The candles which they held were all blown out ...

Candles in procession are blown out in unison. Outline light of flame continues.

FRANZ: And in the darkness ... the tallow-incense
Burned like acid in the nose ...

Bells of Einsiedeln begin to peal loudly.

Slow curtain.

End

ACKNOWLEDGEMENTS

Special thanks to George, Norma, Anne, and other members of the Ryga family, and their many friends and associates, all of whom so generously provided information for my earlier book, *The Ecstasy of Resistance: A Biography of George Ryga*. I know they will hear their voices again, in large ways and small, in this present anthology and in *George Ryga: The Prairie Novels*, published simultaneously. My hope is that they, along with many other readers, will continue to discover more and more the awesome variety and power of Ryga's dramatic writing. I wish, too, to warmly acknowledge the contribution of Karl and Christy Siegler, Talonbooks editors, for their generous and extremely helpful editorial suggestions. Their long and fervent commitment to publishing Canadian drama, including many of Ryga's plays, is surely exemplary, and I know many of us are deeply grateful to them. Similarly, many thanks to Evelyn Hoffman, who is always my best critic, for ongoing encouragement and occasional proofreading duties. Finally, a very special thanks to Ken Smedley, an actor, playwright, and, lately, promoter, who first worked with Ryga in the 1970s and, even long after the playwright's death in 1987, continues to uphold not only the work but also *the spirit* of Ryga—such as directing the operations of the former Ryga house in Summerland as an Arts Centre, and, lately, instituting the annual George Ryga award, given for a socially conscious book publication. To him this book is gratefully dedicated.